CHAMBERS STUDENT

Guide to the legal profession

2001

Published by Chambers and Partners Publishing
(a division of Orbach & Chambers Ltd)
Saville House, 23 Long Lane, London EC1A 9HL
Tel: (020) 7606 1300 Fax: (020) 7600 3191
email: info@ChambersandPartners.co.uk
web: www.ChambersandPartners.com

Our thanks to the many students, trainees, pupils, solicitors, barristers, graduate recruitment personnel and careers officers who assisted us in our research. Also to Chambers and Partners recruitment team for their knowledge and assistance and to the researchers of the Chambers Guide to the Legal Profession 2000-20001 and Chambers Global 2000-2001 from which all firm rankings are drawn.

Publisher: Michael Chambers
Managing Editor: Nigel Ambrose
Editor: Caroline Walker
Writers: Anna Williams, Ed Freeman
Additional Research: David Lewis, Angela Woodruff
Database Manager: Derek Wright
Business Development Manager: Brad Sirott
Sales: Neil Murphy, Sam Nicholls, Richard Ramsey
A-Z Co-ordinators: Mark Lomeli, Al Baker, Richard Pettet
Proofreader: Neal Hooper
Production: John Buck, Paul Cummings, Laurie Griggs

Printed by: Polestar Wheatons Limited

CONTENTS

starting out

how to choose what you want to do –
where you want to do it and how to get it

choices

studying

getting your training contract

paralegals

the Bar

the true picture

the top 75 law firms

the true picture –

still want to go through with it but not sure which firms to apply for? Put down that firm brochure and get the true

picture here. We interviewed hundreds of trainees and qualified solicitors at the top 75 firms and asked them to tell us about their training contracts in their own words... And they did! They were remarkably frank with us.   **71-200**

salaries and prospects

NQ prospects –

it seems a long time away, but you should be thinking about it now – where are the best job prospects in private practice, in-house and elsewhere?   **220**

insider's guide to practice areas

what you should know about the main areas of law and a guide to who does them best. Information about the top firms hot off the press from the *Chambers Guide to the Legal Profession 2000-2001* banking, corporate finance crime, employment, environmental, EU, family, intellectual property, IT, litigation, media, personal injury, private client, projects, property, public interest law, shipping, sports, tax   **225**

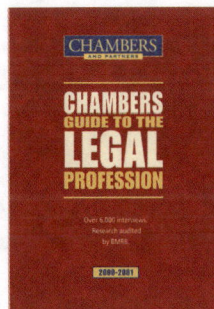

A-Zs

every phone number, address and e-mail you need to make your applications. In simple easy to

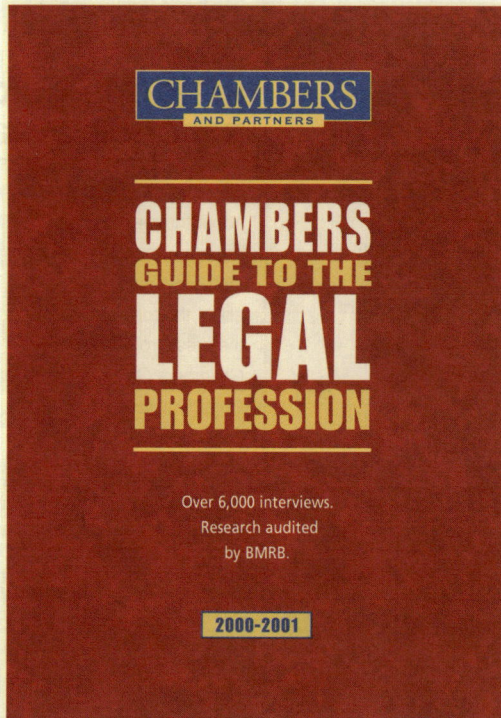

PRE-QUALIFICATION

barrister or solicitor? we help you decide...

Going to the Bar offers greater hardship than just buying the next round. Is it worth it?

The choice between going to the Bar and becoming a solicitor is one that most lawyers consider at some point, if only fleetingly. These days it is almost always assumed that you want to be a solicitor. Most find training as a solicitor to be the easiest route to legal practice. Get over the hurdle of finding a training contract and it is a long jog through the LPC followed by the certainty of reaching the finishing line of the two year training contract. Many will be sponsored during their LPC and well-paid during training.

So who would want to reject all this and go to the Bar? Only a complete masochist or the filthy rich, it seems. Or someone with immense self-belief, drive and commitment. You have to be really serious about this course of action. If you're not, give up now.

financial considerations

WARNING: A CAREER AT THE BAR MAY SERIOUSLY DAMAGE YOUR FINANCES

There's a huge divide between the haves and the have-nots. It begins at student level. Some may receive no funding for their BVC, then may have to take an unfunded pupillage. If they then fail to win a tenancy at the end of that period, they may find themselves up the proverbial creek. The lucky, or brilliant, few will win scholarships at every stage, get a pupillage at a salary-paying commercial set, pick up lots of devilling and some of their own briefs on the way and get a tenancy at the end.

A limited number of scholarships are available from the Inns of Court. Most students will have to fund the BVC year themselves. With fees reaching £8,000 for the year it can be twice as expensive as the LPC. Even for those with a scholarship, there are still living expenses to be taken into account. Then there

is the battle for pupillage. There are far fewer places available than applicants; in 1999-2000 only around 750 pupillages were offered by chambers.

During your year of pupillage, unlike your friends enjoying salaried training contracts, you may receive no funding and earnings only dribble in during the second six months. Even if you are earning, being self-employed means that you may not see the money for several months – until the client gets round to paying it! To compound this nightmare, the Inland Revenue promptly demands its share of all monies earned, regardless of when the cash is received by the impoverished pupil.

It is estimated that by the end of pupillage, barristers can be in at least £25,000 of debt. As for the hardy fools who take the CPE, the figure is even higher.

post qualification chances

Later on, differences between the two sides of the profession remain stark. The chance of being taken on as an assistant is not a hurdle in the current economic boom. Those who don't get taken on after qualification may find themselves sought after by other firms.

For pupil-barristers there is another battle ahead to secure tenancy. Even fewer places are available at this stage than the number of pupils. Some are forced to take a third or even a fourth six or to 'squat' in chambers. That's if they don't decide to call it a day. Many will. Meanwhile newly-qualified solicitors are just beginning to enjoy 'This Life' with mega-salaries, 25 days holiday and luxurious gyms. Junior barristers are struggling to make a living.

And what of the future? The bar is shrinking. Rights of audience for solicitors and the Woolf reforms mean less work for the junior bar, although at the very top specialist silks continue to command huge fees.

So, you are now asking, why even think about such a high-risk career?

employee or self-employed?

The bar offers two key advantages over the solicitors' side of the profession. As a barrister, you reap the benefits of the self-employed. Some negative effects of this have been indicated above. Income is erratic and variable and there is no such thing as sick pay or holiday pay. But on the positive side you are responsible only to yourself and your clients. You have no boss.

If the idea of responsibility appeals, the Bar can offer this from the very earliest moments. Not all the work is great, but it is rare for a pupil to get stuck with filing and bundling for months on end. After all, your instructing solicitor has a trainee to do that! A barrister can at least take his work home on a nightmare day and do it in comfort.

Certainly in those hard first years you will have to put the hours in, firstly to make ends meet, secondly to build up and then secure a reputation. But many senior barristers have greater flexibility than their instructing solicitors. Many have time to diversify or develop their outside interests as second careers.

client relationships

The Bar offers the opportunity to practise the law in a truly academic fashion. For those still studying at university this may not seem attractive. But as a practising barrister you will really have the chance to grapple with the law. You will be working at the heart of a growing, dynamic discipline. Many solicitors find that for much of their day they are working in a business advisory role. Barristers hone the law. They are at the cutting edge of the legal process. They are not administrators or paper-pushers.

but what's the difference?

Traditionally, it's the big personalities who want to go to the Bar. Supremely self-confident, they rather enjoy showing off and being the centre of attention. You'll spot them easily. They can always be found in the thick of arguments about absolutely anything. They are attracted by the prospect of a diet of advocacy for breakfast, lunch and dinner.

However, not all barristers are to be found in court on a regular basis. Tax counsel will rarely if ever end up in court. Criminal barristers, on the other hand, may be involved in a case only at trial stage. The last five years or so have seen the rise of the solicitor-advocate. But the Bar provides opportunities to sharpen your wits in legal debate which are second to none.

It would be a mistake to characterise solicitors as working with clients and involving barristers at one remove. But the solicitor will certainly have the initial contact with a client in most cases. It is only with certain professional clients that barristers have 'direct access.' That said, more and more in-house lawyers will go direct to their favourite counsel, side-stepping the solicitor.

As the two branches become increasingly similar, and as succeeding at the Bar becomes increasingly difficult, the decision of which path to take may make itself. The Bar may not disappear completely but the position of junior barristers is becoming more difficult.

Where do you see yourself in five years time? Perhaps in a large City firm earning £55,000 pa working on major deals or in chambers earning an irregular £30,000 pa, paying off at least the same amount in bank loans? The Bar is not an easy road to ready riches. But membership to the Million-a-Year Club increases every year. For the successful few – and it is a few – the Bar has much to offer.

alternatives

Even in a 'bull' market where there are plenty of jobs available, not all those who want to become solicitors will be able to do so. And not all those who take a law degree want to continue. Not all potential lawyers or barristers are able to obtain training contracts or pupillages and not all want to. But the skills acquired from a legal training provide a head start in a wide range of graduate jobs. Many employers favour law students even for positions with no legal dimension. They value a proven intellectual ability, an eye for detail and the ability to identify salient points within complex issues. Below we outline a selection of the possible alternative careers available to someone with a legal training.

accountancy

Accountancy is a profession with many similarities to the law. Some students struggle to make a decision between the two. A professional qualification will always stand you in good stead, guaranteeing a healthy income and career for life (or as long as you want it).

The large accountancy and consulting firms offer many similar advantages to the big City law firms and represent an increasingly popular option. All offer structured graduate training in a wide choice of disciplines (including auditing, tax, actuarial, corporate finance, IT and management consultancy). In addition they offer the chance of overseas placements, respectable remuneration and plenty of opportunities for career development. They also offer varied high-quality work with blue chip clients, and often have a strong legal dimension, with a growing international trend towards affiliation with law firms. The 'Big Five' firms offer many more places than even the largest law firms, and have numerous regional offices.

Susan Pankhurst is a trainee chartererd accountant at Deloitte & Touche. She earned her degree from Leeds University. After a spell working in Parliament and as an intern in Washington DC, she developed an interest in finance and applied to the accountants. She started with 60 other trainees, most of them working from the London office. Susan chose the 'Audit' route. Within Audit, the work is split further into Corporate Finance, Treasury, Regulatory and e-business. Trainees choose one area. Some are more popular, others more available. Within a group you work for whichever manager has a task to assign to you.

Susan has been happy with her decision. *"It's a good three years and you walk away with a qualification which can open a lot of doors. You get good, practical business experience."* She thinks the training is best suited to someone who's *"quite capable of working on their own, not needing supervision. There's a lot of studying."* She also thinks that you have to have the confidence to work unaided sometimes. *"Often at clients you won't have a senior member of staff with you."*

The downside is that audit can be quite monotonous. *"It's pot luck"* Susan told us. *"Good clients can be great but you can get into a rut with certain types of client."* Yes it can be long, tiring hours at times, just like in the law firms, but – and it's a big but – there's overtime pay!

Patrick Firebrace completed a law degree at Bristol then decided bar school wasn't for him. He changed tack, and is now about to qualify as an accountant with Ernst & Young. The training contract is similar to that in a law firm, though it takes three years. It consists of practical experience as well as exams. Salaries are probably £1–3,000 below salaries in law firms when you start. On qualification a lawyer might be earning £3–5,000 more than the qualified accountant.

He certainly feels he made the right career choice. *"Accountancy offered an opportunity to get a good qualification* [the ACA], *work on a wide variety of clients and meet a wide variety of people. You do need a lot of personal skills"* he says, *"you're attending a lot of client meetings."* It's not enough just to be numerate. Legal research didn't appeal and accountancy is certainly more practical. *"You also do very high level work early on in your career at Ernst & Young"* he says. *"You are drafting documents which will eventually be seen by clients, and you're meeting the people who are going to be reading those documents as well."* He appreciates the chance to work with and for people of all levels. *"Within Ernst & Young there's a lot of cross-departmental teamwork, regardless of whether the client is large or small."* It means working with your peers but also more senior people such as managers and partners, from whom you have an opportunity to learn.

At the moment he is seconded to Ernst & Young's graduate recruitment department for a year. This is included as part of his training, though he still does client audit work alongside. He wanted to gain some new skills and at the moment he is meeting students, advising them how to apply to accountancy firms, and doing a lot of presentations and some teaching work at universities. Asked to describe Ernst & Young he says they have *"a wide range of departments and career choices. A lot of people second to different departments and Ernst & Young are very receptive to it."* He sums the company up as *"flexible, very team-based with a flat team structure, and very friendly."*

Laurence Youngman graduated from UCL with a degree in law. He realised that a legal career was not what he wanted and that he'd *"reached the limit for full time study"* yet he still wanted to work in a career which would tap into his nascent legal skills. On the recommendation of a friend, he looked into tax consultancy at an accountancy firm and liked what he saw. He is now working in tax investigation at Arthur Andersen. He confirms that the work is a challenge, both intellectually and adversarially. There are opportunities to draw on what he learned as a law student. *"Everything in tax derives from statute and case law, so there is a lot of legal interpretation."*

Trainees study for exams leading to professional qualifications in one of the main disciplines (usually in tax or auditing). This opportunity to combine work and study straight after graduation was another factor in Laurence Youngman's decision to switch from law. *"I just wanted to be out there, training on the job."* Accountancy qualifications (ACA or ATII) are highly regarded in the business world, giving trainees a wide variety of options on qualification. It's worth noting that passing the LPC will qualify you for a Certificate of Eligibility to sit the Association of Taxation Technicians ATII exam.

We asked other accountants if all accountancy firms were the same. Like the law firms, each has its own reputation. Deloittes are seen as quite laid back and they deal with trainee applications quite promptly. Andersens are fiercely independent and a little more flashy than the others. They are high payers too. PWC was viewed as the most Oxbridge-oriented. Take these perceptions and test them for yourself. If you can, talk to those who should know – the trainees themselves. There's always a few kicking about at graduate recruitment fairs.

banking

transaction management: Most large international banks employ teams of legal workers, usually in capital markets and derivatives. They will often be legally qualified; typically working alongside other lawyers as part of documentation teams, assisting and supporting the completion of the deals. This is a competitive but potentially very lucrative career option. There are few structured entry routes into this specialisation. The LPC and/or an LLM in international finance might be a relevant starting point, although recruitment would always be based on individual-led non specific criteria.

compliance: Most major banks and financial institutions contain legal departments that have a compliance section. The head of legal services may also be head of compliance, for example. Such in-house legal departments offer a structured career path for those with a keen interest and superior abilities in banking. A career could start as an assistant monitoring internal banking rules and checking that external regulations are complied with. This may be fairly routine initially, but experience and career development provides greater scope for involvement in strategic issues. Senior managers at compliance departments in major international banks are highly paid.

general – graduate: Numerous other opportunities are available to law graduates in the training programmes run by the majority of domestic and international banks. NatWest Bank runs two annual graduate schemes, for regular management and IT/analysts. Both receive large numbers of applicants from law graduates and qualified solicitors. The head of IT graduate recruitment at NatWest recently took on a qualified solicitor as an analyst. Amongst other skills she had 'superb attention to detail.' No specific IT degree is required.

company secretary

If you're looking for an alternative to training as a solicitor or barrister, the ICSA qualification is well worth considering. A career as a company secretary is ideally suited to those with a background in legal studies and can lead to a broad and fulfilling commercial role in industry, private practice, charities or the public sector.

The Companies Act requires every UK registered company to appoint a Company Secretary. The post holder for a public company has to be suitably qualified, usually as an ICSA qualified chartered secretary, or as a lawyer or accountant. The board of directors of any company is responsible for appointing a company secretary, will look to that person for advice and guidance, and will rely upon that person's expertise to ensure that various statutory duties and obligations are fulfilled.

The defined role of the company secretary will vary depending on the size, structure and status of the employing company, but areas of work may involve any or all of the following: corporate, compliance, company administration, reports and accounts, legal, insurance, employee benefits and marketing

The Institute of Chartered Secretaries and Administrators offers a professional qualification. It comprises three programmes in total and 17 exams – the Foundation Programme, the Pre-Professional Programme and the Professional Programme. If you hold a degree in any discipline you are exempt from the first two stages of the ICSA exams and will be required only to sit eight exams on the final, Professional stage of the course.

It is very much a vocational qualification. It is usual to find a role as a trainee company secretary first and commence working in your chosen field before qualifying. Usually your employer will fund the ICSA course/exam fees and provide you with study leave. You may study full or part-time.

Once all exams have been passed, you are known as a Graduate of the ICSA. On completion of three years relevant work experience you can apply to become an Associate of the ICSA and then progress to Fellow of the ICSA.

The company secretary holds a key role in today's business world at a time when public and political concern about corporate governance, ethics, accountability and good practice is at an all time high. To succeed in this role it is essential to be able to keep up to date with current legislation, regulation and best practice. A good company secretary will be authoritative, able to identify potential problems, understand the issues and have the expertise to provide the right solutions: he or she will help to keep their organisation on track in order for it to prosper and develop.

Contact: company secretarial team at Chambers Recruitment.

Tel: 020 7606 8844

email: cosec@chambersrecruitment.co.uk.

corporate finance

Corporate finance is an attractive industry option for law graduates seeking a high-powered corporate career. A highly commercial outlook is essential to counter any preconceptions by employers about the pedantic nature of lawyers.

There are two stages at which a career change is most easily instigated. The first is immediately after graduation. Most large investment and merchant banks run structured graduate recruitment programmes. Completion of the CPE and/or LPC is not necessarily limiting, although some organisations express a concern that the commencement of legal training may raise questions over commitment to a corporate career.

Elizabeth Fisher, training and recruitment consultant at Dutch merchant bank ABN-AMRO received 900 applications for 24 graduate jobs last year. She welcomes applicants from any discipline. Numeracy is a prerequisite: *"Law students are desirable, especially those with corporate finance skills and commercial documentation skills,"* says Fisher

The other option is to qualify as a lawyer and obtain a couple of years PQE. Recruitment to banks and financial institutions at this stage occurs on an ad hoc basis. Related commercial experience in a City firm is highly sought after.

Corporate financiers require high levels of numeracy. Law students will be competing with graduates from conventional maths and science backgrounds, a point underlined by the recruitment manager at top investment bank, Schroders. *"We receive many applications from graduates with straight law degrees. They tend to have very strong analytical skills, good communication skills and a thorough knowledge of legal documentation in a 'deal-driven' environment."*

european patent attorneys

European Patent Attorneys (EPAs) act for clients in an international arena. They obtain, protect and deal with patents for their clients' inventions. Advocacy opportunities include tribunals of the European Patent Office and, domestically, the UK Patents Office and Patents County Courts.

Richard Williams of Hepworth Lawrence Bryer & Bizley confirmed that firms like his recruit legally trained individuals as trainee EPAs. This career path would particularly suit someone with a CPE and LPC who started off as a scientist. *"Candidates need a good 2.1 degree in a science or engineering subject and the ability to understand a broad range of technical matters."* It's not for the faint-hearted as it takes on average up to five years to become fully qualified. The rewards are likely to more than compensate though.

Contact: The Chartered Institute of Patent Attorneys
Tel: 020 7405 9450
Web: www.cipa.org.uk

information management

Most law firms contain information and library departments where personnel are employed as information managers/officers, database managers and librarians. It is a growing professional area as information and communication technology continues to expand its role in business.

Michael Martin, careers advisor at the Library Association's information section, describes an increasingly common career option: *"someone with a first law degree could do a one year postgraduate degree or diploma in information management and then has the opportunity to be employed by a law firm as an information officer."*

Several educational and academic institutions run full time or part-time (one and two years respectively) courses in librarianship/information management.

IT/contracts management

Many large software and hardware companies, such as Compaq, Dell and IBM negotiate huge commercial contracts for sales and distribution deals. These organisations usually contain dedicated contracts departments and/or in-house legal teams. They may take on law graduates, LPC- trained but not necessarily qualified, to work in tandem with the sales force drawing up contracts within certain parameters. The work can be 'glamorous' and international involving travel to high-tech areas of the globe such as the United States and the Asia Pacific region. Contracts professionals are highly sought after and well-paid. The positions may have the potential to lead into a formal offer of sponsorship through a training contract or an in-house position. It goes without saying that commercial acumen and an interest and understanding of IT are essential.

Work in this big growth area is advertised in the usual legal press, such as *The Lawyer* and *Legal Week* and *The Times* on Tuesdays.

law commission

The Law Commission is the statutory body advising on law reform. Several legal research positions are available each year to law graduates or to those with a CPE who have also passed the LPC/BVC.

The Commission offers fixed term contracts of 12 months, with the possibility of another years' extension. Researchers assist in the process of the Commission's work to make recommendations for changes in the law. You may get the chance to work with eminent judges, practising lawyers and university professors.

Louise Collet at the Commission explains that it is a useful option for those who have a gap year to fill but want to stay in a legal environment, either between university and academic vocational training, or between law school and a training contract. The salary offered at present is £15,900 with a small increment if the second year is taken. Legal research is likely to be in such areas as common law, public law and crime, using primary sources rather than a text book. It's ideal for someone with an academic bent who wants to get hands-on work experience in those fields.

Paralegals at law firms will be paid more but will not get the same quality of work. *"This looks better on a CV"* says Collet. *"We've never had anybody leave here without a pupillage or a training contract even if they arrived here without one."*

trade mark attorneys

Fully or partially trained barristers and solicitors are very attractive propositions for firms of Trade Mark Attorneys. The work involves instructions from a client typically with a new product, the name or emblem of which is likely to need protection worldwide. The vocational training takes at least two years. It requires great attention to detail and an ability to deal with large amounts of information quickly and efficiently.

Contact: Institute of Trade Mark Attorneys
Tel: 020 8686 2052

deloitte & touche

Hill House 1 Little New Street London EC4A 3TR
Tel: 0800 323333
Email: gradrec.uk@deloitte.co.uk
Website: graduates.deloitte.co.uk

firm profile

Deloitte & Touche is one of the world's largest professional services firms, and the fastest growing in the UK over each of the past 3 years. The firm has 21 offices in the UK and has offices in over 130 countries worldwide. Opportunities for graduates to work with its superb client list including Merrill Lynch, Morgan Stanley and Abbey National offer all who join an excellent start to their career.

opportunities for graduates

Deloitte & Touche will recruit over 500 graduates this year into the UK firm, across 20 different service lines. You may choose to train for the Chartered Accountancy qualification in areas such as Assurance & Advisory or Corporate Tax; join the firm's non-corporate tax areas and train for the Institute of Taxation qualifications; train to be an IT consultant or choose one of the other routes through the firm available for graduates.

The firm looks for candidates with a 2:2 in any discipline and 24 UCAS points from 3 A-levels (or equivalent) for most of the firm's positions.

After the initial 3 year training contract you would join the management group, either within your original service line or another if you wish to change. You may choose to go on an international secondment to any of the firm's offices worldwide, benefiting from the globalisation of the firm. Partnership is available, normally about 10 years after joining.

contact details

Deborah Black
Tel: 0800 323333
Email:
gradrec.uk@deloitte.co.uk

For an application form and brochure please contact your careers service, look at the firm's website or contact Deborah Black as above

Deloitte & Touche

ALTERNATIVE CAREERS

ernst & young

Becket House 1 Lambeth Palace Rd
London SE1 7EU
Tel: 0800 289208

firm profile

Ernst & Young is an international firm with worldwide revenues of $10.9bn. The firm has 675 offices in over 130 countries. Globally it has 6,100 partners and 75,000 members of staff. Within the UK there are over 6,500 members of staff with 451 partners in its 22 offices. The firm offers you an outstanding opportunity to develop your career. As one of the world's leading professional services organisations, Ernst & Young is dedicated to helping its clients identify and capitalise on business opportunities throughout the world.

opportunities available

The firm has opportunities in the following areas: Actuarial Group, Audit & Assurance, Business Risk Consulting, Company Secretarial, Corporate Finance, Corporate Tax, Economic Analysts, Entrepeneurial Services, Global Employment Solutions, Indirect Tax Consulting, Information Systems Assurance & Advisory Services and Management Consulting (Cap Gemini Ernst & Young).

training

Ernst & Young offers high quality training and development and has an intensive induction process which will develop the key skills and knowledge required to work in their client service teams. This offers the opportunity to learn more about the firm's culture and the way they work. Following on from the induction course, a wide range of in-house training courses will be on offer as part of Ernst & Young's commitment to ongoing learning and development.

disciplines required

Ernst & Young is looking for individuals who have demonstrated academic success. The firm asks for a minimum of 22 UCAS points (excluding General Studies) and a 2.2 honours degree (any discipline). Some business units require more.

contact details

Vanessa van den Bergh
Recruitment Manager
Tel: 0800 289208
Email:
gradrec@cc.ernsty.co.uk

address for applications

National Graduate
Recruitment,
Ernst & Young,
Becket House,
1 Lambeth Palace Road,
London SE1 7EU

Alternatively, you can apply online via the firm's website at:
www.ey.com/uk

ΞIJ ERNST & YOUNG

ALTERNATIVE CAREERS

funding

The law is not a cheap business, for clients or for lawyers-to-be. There are choices to be made at an early stage. A trainee solicitor who applies at the appropriate time for a contract at a large commercial firm will get sponsorship throughout law school and a generous salary during training. No problem. Even then many trainees find that their new-found riches do not adequately cover the expense of City alcohol prices, eating out all week and decent suits. If you burn to practise immigration law for asylum seekers then you will get no funding for law school. You will need to find up to £7,025 to cover your LPC and up to £4,950 for a CPE as well. As a trainee you may well be on the Law Society minimum recommended salary - currently a pitiful £14,600 in London and £13,000 outside London. Some firms cannot even afford to pay this. Laden with debt, you are unlikely to pay it off for years. As for the Bar, having paid your way through CPE and/or BVC, you must apply for pupillage with very little hope of being accepted.

trainee solicitors

Both the CPE and LPC are deemed to be full time courses of higher education. You will not be entitled to claim social security benefits. Many firms however pay not only for course fees but also provide a moderate living allowance which keeps the wolf from the door if not allowing for much luxury. For details of the sponsorship and awards available from individual firms see A-Zs and firms' own literature. Working in the college vacations or picking up evening work will help financially, although both courses require a degree of commitment which might mean that extra-curricular work could damage your academic prospects. The question of whether to work or not is one that you will have to consider carefully.

Leaning on the generosity of parents, and getting into debt with banks, are the most common approaches to that element of the cost of the academic training which cannot be resourced from scholarships or grants. A majority of LPC students are in debt and the average amount owed is over £7,000.

The major banks are willing to advance up to £10,000 per year to those on CPE and LPC courses. It is the security of a guaranteed income from the training contract which makes the student such an attractive lending proposition. At the time of going to press, typical interest rates were set at 1% over base rate and repayments were commonly delayed until part way through the training contract.

Once you have actually started your training contract you may also find that a number of the major banks will lend to you on quite favourable terms. Loan terms may include low interest rates, no arrangement fees and repayments deferred until after qualification. You may wish to consider whether you should transfer your existing loan debt to such a new arrangement.

trainee barristers

The issue of funding for Bar students and pupils has long been of concern to most individuals considering a career as a barrister. Not only do they have to deal with the idea that embarking on this route by no means ensures qualification, they also have to consider the financial implications of the decision. Many law firms offer trainee solicitors financial support and course fees whilst they are completing their LPC and even the CPE. At the end of the academic stage a reasonably healthy salary awaits them. For trainee solicitors, it is possible to guarantee solvency at a fairly early stage in their careers; not so for the majority of aspiring barristers. The average cost of completing the CPE and/or BVC is estimated at over £20,000, including living expenses.

the inns of court

Between them, the four Inns of Court distribute over £2 million a year in funding to those studying for BVC and/or CPE and in pupillage. Some awards are merit based, others take into account financial hardship. Students can only apply to their own Inn for an award and our interviews with pupils and junior tenants confirmed that the volume and size of awards is a key factor in choosing an Inn whilst a student. Some Inns opt for fewer larger awards whilst others offer a greater number of more modest ones. An outline of the awards available from each Inn are set out in the table on page 17. Contact the Inns for further information on how and when to apply.

chambers

Very few sets provide any financial assistance for the CPE or the BVC. It is not unusual for chambers to provide some sort of funding during pupillage and in the second six you can earn some sort of income from fee paying work. The practice of 'devilling' – earning money by carrying out work for more senior members of chambers – is a feature at some sets. However, in the Autumn of 1999, a pupil barrister, Rebecca Edmonds, won a High Court victory over her employer to establish that the Minimum Wage Act 1998, which had taken effect in April 1999 applied to pupillages. This decision was subsequently overturned in the Court of Appeal. The current situation is that a minimum salary of £5,000 is recommended. In the academic year 1997/98, up to a third of pupillages were unpaid. It is only a matter of time however before public pressure and falling pupillage applications force the Bar Council to make a clearer ruling.

work

The Education and Training Department of the Bar Council discourages students from taking a job whilst studying for the BVC full time. The reality, however, is that some students find it necessary to undertake some limited part time work in this period. The Bar Council's regulations do allow for pupillage to be broken down into smaller chunks of time, but in the second six, no break in the time spent with the pupil master may be more than one month in duration and the second six should not be more than nine months in duration. A second six must be commenced within 12 months of the completion of the first six.

benefits

The CPE and BVC are now both classed as full time courses of higher education. It is not possible to state that you are actively seeking work and are immediately available for work during your BVC. Therefore you may not receive state benefits.

loans

Banks provide loan packages for trainee barristers with repayments delayed until between six and 12 months following the completion of pupillage. Enquire in branches of the major banks located close to the law courts. Up to £10,000 is commonly on offer for each of the BVC year and the pupillage year. It is more difficult to come by loans for the CPE year however. Career Development Loans are another option.

the bar council

The Bar Scholarship Trust provides a small number of loans of up to £4,000 for pupillage.

stages in brussels

Six-month secondments with the European Commission count towards pupillage. Each candidate receives £5,000. Apply to either the EC or the Bar Council.

TABLE OF AWARDS AND SCHOLARSHIPS

NAME OF INN	TOTAL FUNDS AVAILABLE	CPE/BVC AWARDS	PUPILLAGE AWARDS	CONTACT DETAILS
Inner Temple	£616,950	£15,000 x 3 £12,500 x 4 £10,000 x 20 £272,000 split into awards of up to £10,000 £13,000 Benefactors Scholarships £160 x 50 admissions/ call fees £15,000 disability grants		Rachel Jenkins Tel: 020 7797 8210 Fax: 020 7797 8212 rjenkins@innertemple.org.uk
Middle Temple	£520,000	£1,000 - £15,000 x 80 - 100 (20 of which are allocated to CPE)	Pupillage awards under review	Students Department Tel: 020 7427 4800 student_enquiries@middletemple.org.uk
Gray's Inn	c. £600,000+	For CPE: £46,500 split into separate awards For BVC: £15,000 x 3 £12,500 x 12 £10,000 x 6 £5,000 x 22 £3,000 x 19 £85 admission fees x 25 Up to £10,000	£59,800 split between various awards £15,500 split between various awards for the 1st year of practice	Margaret Chadderton – Deputy Under Treasurer (Students) Tel: 020 7458 7900
Lincoln's Inn	£654,000	For CPE: admission/call/ dining charges x 100 Up to £8,000 x up to 8 For BVC: £8 - £15,000 x up to 32, £7,000 x up to 25 £8,000 x 2 15 rooms in self contained flats (7 at £5,500, 8 at £4,350) £2,000 sundry exam prizes	£46,000 split between various awards	Judith Fox Tel: 020 7405 0138 judith.fox@lincolnsinn.org.uk

NatWest

"Aiming to build long term relationships from postgraduate course through to qualification and retirement."

NatWest offers a wide range of products and services to meet the needs of students. Specifically it has a dedicated team of Managers working in the Strand who look after the changing needs of Legal Students. Building on over 100 years of experience of dealing with the Legal Profession, you can be assured that we offer a highly personalised, flexible, quality service which is tailored to meet individual needs. As the Legal Centre only deals with Legal Profession, we do understand how your business works.

We can offer the following:

- A dedicated Manager and Assistant to look after your long term financial needs, with a direct line to your Manager.
- Funding via the Professional Trainee loan scheme.
- A choice of fixed or variable rates.

To apply or to find out more please contact Ash Khan, Relationship Manager, on **020 7664 9166**, or alternatively write to him at the following address:

Law Courts Temple Bar Legal Centre
PO Box 11052
217 Strand
London
WC2R 1AR

LAW FAIRS 2000/2001

DATES	VENUE	CONTACT NAME	ACCESS	CONTACT NO
07/11/00	University of Leicester	John Harshorne	Not known	0116 252 5023
09/11/00	Manchester University	Alison Metcalfe	Open to students outside university	0161 275 2845
13/11/00	Queen Mary & Westfield College	Anne Glendon	University of London students only	020 7882 5065
14/11/00 & 15/11/00	Bristol University	Rose Conway	Bristol students and others by invitation	0117 928 8221
16/11/00	Southampton University	Jill Elliot	Southampton students only	023 8059 3501
20/11/00	Leeds University	Lynn Pattison	In theory open to all Most people are from region	0113 233 5300
21/11/00	Reading University	Roger Brown	Open to all students	0118 931 8351
22/11/00	Queen's, Belfast	David Foster	Open to all students	028 9027 4208
22/11/00 & 23/11/00	Cambridge University	David Ainscough	Cambridge students only	01223 338288
25/11/00	Oxford University	Dick Lidwell	Open to all students	01865 274646
27/11/00	Newcastle University	Judith Mason	Open to all students	0191 222 7765
28/11/00	Warwick University	Lynda Mitchell	Warwick students only	024 765 23766
28/11/00	Durham University	Margaret Stoyle	Durham students only	0191 374 2342
29/11/00	Birmingham University	Roger Hardiman	Birmingham students only	0121 414 6130
04/12/00 & 05/12/00	University College, London	Phil Howe	UCL students only	020 7679 7229
06/12/00	University of East Anglia	Maryanne Bhavsar	Open to all students	01603 592 483
22/01/01 & 23/01/01	King's College London	Stephen Hill	Kings students and other university of London Careers Services Colleges	020 7848 2616
30/01/01	Exeter University	Shirley Lovegrove	Exeter students only	01392 264418
07/02/01	Nottingham University	Pauline Armstrong	Open to all students	0115 951 3673
07/02/01	Sheffield University	Brian Read	Open to all students	0114 2220955
12/02/01	Hull University	Pat Broderick	Open to all students	01482 465 986

preferred universities

We conducted a survey amongst the largest 250 firms in the UK offering training contracts. We asked them to identify the universities from which they preferred to recruit trainees. 132 firms of all sizes and types and from all parts of England and Wales responded.

Notwithstanding widespread coverage of elitism in the legal profession, just over 60%, of the respondent firms confirmed that they have no preference for the universities from which they recruit. Some expressed their strong opinion that a recruitment policy which targets certain institutions only serves to reinforce old prejudices and discrimination. Others confirmed an unabashed attempt to recruit as many of their trainees as possible from a small number of universities.

survey results

The results of our 'preferred universities survey' show that for the second year running Bristol University (just) eclipses Oxford and Cambridge as the university producing the graduates most widely sought by law firms.

Regional bias is evident in the results. In particular firms in the south west, where there are several strong universities which run LLBs, had local preferences. Bristol, Exeter, Cardiff and University of the West of England scored highly and it is these extra votes from firms not aspiring to Oxbridge candidates that put Bristol on top. In firms from the north, Durham, Newcastle, Manchester, Leeds and Sheffield Universities perform well.

Larger London firms are more likely to indicate a preference than regional firms and the smaller City and West End firms. The larger firms expressing a preference were more likely to prefer Cambridge and Oxford graduates. There appeared to be some self-censorship amongst the smaller firms, particularly in the regions, who could not expect to attract the most popular candidates and therefore did not prefer Oxbridge or the top redbricks.

PREFERRED UNIVERSITIES

Bristol	32
Cambridge	30
Oxford	30
Nottingham	25
Durham	23
Exeter	22
Birmingham	21
Warwick	15
Manchester	14
Southampton	13
London (any college)	10
London UCL	10
London Kings	9
Sheffield	9
Leeds	8
London LSE	5
Edinburgh	5
Newcastle	5
Liverpool	3
Cardiff	3
Nottingham Trent	3
UWE	2
Leicester	2
Kent	1
Reading	1
Glamorgan	1
UEA	1
UCE	1
St Andrews	1
No preference	84

preferred lpc providers

law schools

We conducted a survey amongst the largest 250 firms in the UK offering training contracts. We asked them to identify which institutions were their preferred providers of the LPC courses. 132 firms of all sizes and types and from all parts of England and Wales responded. Overall only 28% of firms expressed a preference. This rose to 50% of the larger London firms (i.e.: over 200 solicitors).

The legal press has previously highlighted the trend for some firms to recommend, if not mandate, the law schools which their trainees attend for the LPC. This trend has now reached its apogee in the announcement that the City 'Gang of eight' firms were to set up a 'City LPC' and the tender for the course had been won by Nottingham, BPP and Oxford.

This big news has already had its effect. Nottingham Law School is now the overall choice of law firms nationwide. For the first time The College of Law is not the favourite. Still well-respected as an LPC provider when all responses nationwide are considered, it is not favoured by City firms of any size. Amongst the large City firms, both Nottingham Law School and the Oxford Institute of Legal Practice were the majority choice. Nottingham Law School is the favourite amongst City firms of over 50 partners. BPP performs well although not as well as other City LPC providers.

lpc annual inspection

The LPC unit of the Law Society conducts an annual inspection of all LPC providers nationwide. The following providers are ranked 'excellent': Cardiff, Exeter, Nottingham Law School and the University of the West of England. The Oxford Institute this year lost its 'excellent' rating. This has caused the course provider no little embarrassment, and is thought by some to have prejudiced the reputation of the City LPC. The Law Society will not currently release their criteria for these gradings. However, they will be available on the Law Society website in or after January 2001.

Our table shows the institutions ranked according to the number of mentions each one received from the largest 250 law firms in the UK.

PREFERRED LPC PROVIDERS	
Nottingham Trent	38
The College of Law (any)	29
Oxford Institute	20
BPP Law School	16
UWE	12
Exeter	5
Cardiff	3
Sheffield	3
Guildford (College of Law)	2
Birmingham	2
London (any)	2
Any approved	2
City University	2
UEA	2
Northumbria	1
Glamorgan	1
Bournemouth	1
No preference	94

LPC providers – the inside story

This year we interviewed hundreds of law school graduates. We asked them what they thought of their LPC year. Some had graduated from law school in Summer 2000, others were in their first or second year of training contracts. We have only focused on the institutions about which we received sufficient comment to be representative. Coincidentally, these include the top five in our preferred institutions survey. So these are the choices of the top law firms....

Nottingham Law School

facts

Number of LPC students pa: 504
Preferred LPC Providers Survey position: 1
Law Society Rating: Excellent
City LPC: Yes
Electives: Corporate Programme (mergers, acquisitions and takeovers; corporate finance, banking and security; corporate commercial) or any three of Commercial Law, Commercial Property, Employment Law, Family Law and Private Client.

Top of the pops with the law firms this year for the first time. Has consistently received an 'excellent' rating from the Law Society. Instructed by the City 'Group of Eight' to set up the City LPC in September 2001. All in all it's been a good year for NLS Ltd. And our student sources love the place.

Comments such as *"wonderful time," "really enjoyed it," "it was brilliant"* were typical. Recommended for the whole experience; work, environment and social life. Facilities are *"excellent"* if a little overcrowded. Because the popularity of the course has led them to squeeze a few extras in? The good news is that work is in progress to increase library/computer access. Teaching is in general *"very*

good, especially the business team," and *"everyone knew what they talking about."* But there are extremes. Some teaching is not considered *"very good"* whereas some is *"phenomenally impressive."* The school, even pre-City LPC, *"favours the corporate and commercial elements"* and the corporate module received particularly good reviews. When comparing their experiences to those of friends at the College of Law Nottingham people felt they *"worked harder."* The most critical comment we received was that the school is *"a bit 'fur coat no knickers."* It's shiny on the outside, with some problems on the inside (such as *"its fair share of bad teachers"*).

The *"social life was excellent."* It's a *"great city;"* student-friendly and socially fun, if *"aesthetically...dire."* Everyone mixes well and is keen to attend social events. And *"even when things weren't officially organised everyone went to the same place."* Course leader Bob White received special mention.

By the way, *"any rumour about 5:1 girls to blokes is wrong"* said a male source ruefully.

The College of Law

facts

Number of LPC students pa: see individual branches
Preferred LPC Providers Survey position: 2
Law Society Rating: Good
City LPC: No. But in talks with Wragge & Co etc re possible Birmingham City LPC
Electives: Any three of Acquisitions and Group Structures, Commercial Law, Corporate Finance, Commercial litigation, Personal injury litigation, Commercial property, Family Law and Practice, Welfare Benefits and Immigration Law, Private Client, Employment Law and Practice and Media and Entertainment Law.

For years literally the only law school. The College of Law has had an eventful time this year so far. Overlooked by the 'Group of Eight' Law firms for the City LPC, it has responded assertively. It is making an effort to attract the support of the remaining firms, attempting to deal with the issues raised by the City LPC project, establish its own City LPC and open a new school in Birmingham. Only time will tell whether the College of Law can mend its dented ego. With strong support for its new Birmingham office and the new initiatives the omens don't look bad. Support from smaller and non-commercial law firms is still widespread. But in our survey of the top 250 firms the College of Law has been overtaken by Nottingham Law School for the first time.

london – store street

Number of LPC students pa: 1,248

The Store Street branch was set up as the London replacement for the Chancery Lane and Lancaster Gate branches. After only 10 years or so the site could have become a victim of its own popularity as numbers grew too big for the premises. It takes almost twice as many full-time LPC students as the next biggest provider (Guildford). However, current rebuilding work should remedy that.

The majority of comments we received focused on the overcrowding on the course. Because of the number of students the college was described as a *"treadmill that churns them in and out"* and a *"production line."* The crowding made teaching *"impersonal"* (*"getting essays back through a hatch in the wall"*) and *"the schedule was run so that you didn't develop a relationship with your tutors."* Tutors themselves weren't the problem. *"It wasn't that they didn't want to help – their schedules were too hectic."* Although many criticised the teaching, there were positive notes. Some teachers were *"superb".*

The building itself comes in for some flak. *"It's a*

'70s ugly building" which is *"dark, dingy and overcrowded"* – *"the canteen was leaking water and the rooms were grotty."* Comments on facilities varied, with some being perfectly satisfied and some finding them insufficient. The College of Law has this year responded to criticism by investing £2.5m in improving the facilities, including improved library and IT facilities. Still, not much can be done about the sheer numbers of people.

"You suffer from being in central London." With so many students and many of them living at home there was felt to be *"less of a community"* than at other branches. As such the social life *"depends on your class."* Some found it *"great fun,"* the people were *"brilliant"* and everyone *"went out drinking after classes."* Others found the social life *"pretty much non-existent."* Perhaps one of the most positive aspects of the course was the *"broad spectrum of people"* with all different kinds of law firms represented by their future trainees.

chester

Number of LPC students pa: 864

Chester received far more favourable reviews. Facilities are *"pretty good"* although comments about the course itself were mixed. We were told that there has been *"a complete revamp of the course and teaching"* which has caused the pass rate to go up. Students received *"a lot of support"* and we received no complaints about the teaching.

An advantage of Chester is the *"mix of students – nice to meet people from different parts of the country."*

Everyone seems to have a great social life in Chester. It's a *"brill city"* although so small that it *"was a bit claustrophic"* and a year there is thought to be enough. But the size does have its advantages. *"You walk or bike everywhere. You all go to the same parties and venues."* There are only about two clubs, and you *"bump into people"* wherever you go.

guildford

Number of LPC students pa: 744

Comments about Guildford were something of a mixed bag. There was a general consensus that the course is *"well-managed."* Teaching varies. There are *"a couple of inspirational people"* and the *"business tutors are excellent."*

Several interviewees criticised the system of setting the same assignments for all groups as homework. This system was seen to favour students with a pre-existing clique, with whom they would study. *"All very conducive to knowing the right people."* In fact one ex-student claimed that the result of this was a running joke: *"Same paper – different marks."*

Socially Guildford is not everyone's cup of earl grey. The school is in a manor house in its own grounds. The atmosphere and social life don't suit everyone. It probably all depends on who you know. Seen to be *"cliquey"* and *"very Cambridge/Oxford"*, in fact the school has groups from a number of the top universities, including a *"Durham set and an Exeter set."* Some Durham students live together in a 'Frat house,' *"with tennis courts and everything."* There is little or no organised social life, which can be *"alienating"* to students from other universities. But it's a *"nice middle-class environment to be in."* There was *"a dinner party posse"*, *"a lot of sailing and croquet people"* and *"lots of convertible golf GTIs in the car-park."* Some interviewees see the place as *"pretentious."*

york

Number of LPC students pa: 696

Those we spoke to at York generally loved the environment and the socialising, so had a good year. Just *"like being back at school."* Funny that, because the college is actually in an old junior school and its playgrounds.

Students didn't necessarily appreciate the course so much but then, how many people really enjoy the LPC? Teaching is variable *"with some excellent but some not so good."* However, most found it *"very good."* Lecturers are *"like friends"* and even the *"librarian is on first name terms with people."* No complaints about facilities. Several students mentioned however that the course could have been better weighted. Some months were extremely hard work and *"very stressful,"* in others there was lots of free time. It's thought that this has now been sorted out.

York itself gets the thumbs up all round. As one person put it (presumably a southerner), there's *"a Coronation Street communal atmosphere."* *"I thought York was a perfect place. It's such a nice city."* It's a *"lovely place to be with a really good quality of life."*

The social life is *"great."* Students are thought to be mainly from the north or graduates of northern universities. It's small enough that people at least recognise each other. There's *"plenty going on if you wanted to put yourself about."* *"Everyone lived in the same area and went to the same pubs, there was inter-class football and netball"* and *"you got to meet lots of people."* There are plenty of organised social events in addition to sports, including visits to Tetleys Brewery and the racing on the next-door race-course.

With accommodation available from only £35 per week students can afford a *"good standard of living."*

Oxford Institute of Legal Practice

facts
Number of LPC students pa: 168
Preferred LPC Providers Survey position: 3
Law Society Rating: Good (recently downgraded from excellent)
City LPC: Yes
Electives: Any three of Banking, Commercial Law, Commercial Property, Corporate Finance, Law and Family Breakdown, Medical Negligence Litigation, Planning and Environmental Law and Private Client.

The Institute has recently been downgraded by the Law Society from 'excellent' to 'good,' to the potential embarrassment of the 'Group of Eight' law firms taking part in the City LPC. It is a popular choice for law firms around the country.

"Some subjects were partly taught by outside teachers." The full-time tutors *"knew what they were talking about"* and *"part-time practitioners were very good,"* but *"some were academics and didn't know much useful stuff."* Furthermore, some of the outside teachers *"sometimes contradicted things said by permanent staff, leading to the course not feeling coherent at times."*

As for Oxford itself, it is unsurprising that people *"loved the place."* After all it's made for students. There's a social committee on the LPC course but *"most of the organising and money was expended on the Law School Ball."* Apart from that *"everyone got to know each other well because it was quite a small place and everyone socialised together."* And there were always the social events organised by the rowing club!

It's not cheap to live there. Accommodation costs £60-65 a week.

BPP

facts
Number of LPC students pa: 288
Preferred LPC Providers Survey position: 4
Law Society Rating: Good
City LPC: Yes
Electives: Any three of Acquisitions and Group structures, Commercial Law, Coporate Finance, Commercial Litigation, Personal Injury Litigation, Commercial Property, Family Law, Welfare Benefits and Immigration, Employment Law and Practice, Media and Entertainment Law.

The course at BPP Law School came out well from our research. *"The majority of lecturers were really enthusiastic and wanted the students to learn. The tutors were second to none and we e-mailed them non-stop at exam times."* Having said that the course was such that they had *"pulled too much into the first bit. When doing the foundations stuff we didn't know whether we were coming or going."*

A new school, it is set in an attractive square in Lincoln's Inn. The building has been modernised and has all mod cons. Facilities are good but the library and common room can get a *"bit cramped."*

Socially the place is a good bet. Despite the fact that *"most people lived at home to save money,"* there is still a community feeling. *"I belonged there and made four or five good friends for life."* Students go out on Wednesday and Friday nights and a committee organises quiz nights and a summer ball.

University of the West of England

facts
Number of LPC students pa: 220-240
Preferred LPC Providers Survey position: 5
Law Society Rating: Excellent
City LPC: No
Electives: Any three of advanced Criminal Litigation, Banking and Capital Markets, Civil Legal Aid Practice, Commercial Law, Commercial Property, Corporate Finance, Employment Law(corporate client), Employment Law(private client), Estate Planning, Family Breakdown, Local Government Law, Media and Entertainment Law, Mergers and Acquisitions.

We received overwhelmingly positive comments about the LPC at UWE. Trainees couldn't praise it enough. The words *"brilliant"* and *"excellent"* were bandied about freely. *"The level of teaching is brilliant."* *"People who taught were very 'up for it;' inspirational and practical"* and *"not like a sausage machine." "The tutors really helped you with your problems."* The facilities and organisation were good. *"At the end of the day the facilities were there for you, class sizes weren't a problem,"* and lectures were not overcrowded.

Outside of lectures, *"the social life was excellent and everyone was very keen to arrange things."* You socialise with your group, but it's *"not at all cliquey,"* and even *"the lecturers will pitch up in the pub."* The course director came in for particular praise. *"He hosts parties every year for students and lecturers."*

University of Sheffield

facts
Number of LPC students pa: 120
Preferred Preferred LPC Providers Survey position: 8
Law Society Rating: Good
City LPC: No
Electives: Any three of Commercial Litigation, Commercial Property, Matrimonial Practice, Tax and Estate Planning, individual Employment Law, Personal Injury Litigation, Law and the Elderly Client/Wills and Probate, Corporate Administration, Corporate Finance, Commercial Law and Practice.

All our interviewees who attended the LPC in Sheffield were positive about the experience. *"Very well run and very friendly."* *"Facilities were good,"* and the standard of teaching was praised. Teaching is in small groups, classes of about 15 people. This makes it more *"personal."* It also allows for more inter-group socialising than is the norm: *"I socialised an enormous amount."* Many people on the course are from firms in the north such as Dibbs, Nabarros etc.

city lpc explained

Bridging the limbo between academic legal study and the practical realities of working life, the Legal Practice Course ('LPC') was introduced in 1993 to replace the rote learning of the Law Society Finals course. The LPC was designed to focus more on the 'hands on' skills of being a lawyer. But it has not had an easy ride. It has always been subject to accusations that it is not relevant to commercial firms. Its core modules include criminal procedure, wills & probate and family law. But the large commercial firms have tried to get over this by their considerable input into the courses of their favoured providers, such as Nottingham. Many reserve places on certain courses, resulting in a tendency to concentrate, as far as the Law Society will allow, on the commercial aspects.

Even so, large City commercial firms increasingly felt that their trainees weren't arriving with the necessary skills or commerciality. In particular they felt that trainees did not have a good enough grasp of the fundamentals of the law, especially those relevant for commercial practice. Comments that we received would tend to bear out the view that the LPC in its present form is not rigorous or relevant enough: *"Sometimes it was embarrassing having to answer questions because they were so easy. I didn't feel that the material was at all very challenging, in fact a lot of it was dull and monotonous."*

city LPC is born

On 14th February 2000 Allen & Overy, Clifford Chance, Freshfields, Herbert Smith, Linklaters, Lovells, Norton Rose and Slaughter and May (the 'Group of Eight') announced that they were to produce a revised course, catering more closely to their needs. The course will begin in September 2001, subject to accreditation by the Law Society. It will be available at Nottingham Law School, The Oxford Institute of Legal Practice and BPP Law School in London. The College of Law, which had traditionally trained many lawyers in the big law firms, was the significant omission from the firms chosen.

how is it different?

Peter Jones, Dean and Chief Executive of Nottingham Law School, explained that someone starting the new course would notice that it is *"mostly oriented towards the commercial"* and that they *"were concentrating a lot more on the law contained in the transactions."* There will be more preparation for students to do and a greater reliance on original sources. Significantly, students will no longer be able to take their manuals into exams. Regardless of the subjects that you elect to do in the second part of the course if you go to Nottingham, Oxford or BPP you'll notice more of a 'City' slant in the first, compulsory part of the course. There will be less emphasis on oral skills. Peter Jones admitted that the course will be more intense. *"Students will no longer be able to tread water for a year."*

why the controversy?

The decision of the Group of Eight hasn't been well-received by everyone. The main criticism is of élitism. Will it lead to the creation of a two-level system for legal training? The City LPC has even received an ear-bashing from Lord Woolf himself. He feels it could be damaging to the profession as a whole. Nigel Savage, Chief Executive of the College of Law, has attacked the course. *"I am not prepared to preside over a law college that is devoted to serving the needs of an exclusive few at the expense of the many."* A cynic might regard this as sour grapes. After all the College of Law unsuccessfully tendered for the City LPC. But these fears can't be ignored, especially by the Group of Eight.

where should I go?

There will be places on the course for people without a training contract at the Group of Eight. At Nottingham over half of the 650 places will be available to others. Peter Jones assured us that the decision on entrance will be based solely on the basis of *"academic ability"* and not on the relative size or merit of your law firm. Though the City LPC course will continue to offer non-City electives, the course will obviously be commercially biased. But what if you haven't got your training contract organised when you apply?

Two key issues emerge from this year's developments. First, the introduction of a two-tier system. The Group of Eight consists of the magic circle and the aspirationals, who can only benefit by association. This is clearly sending a message to firms and students that there is a first tier. It also results in a first tier of law schools.

Secondly the City LPC controversy has acted as the impetus for other schools to 'up their game.' But the College of Law is already fighting back. It's talking about setting up its own City course. The new Birmingham branch has already been the focus of interest from Wragge & Co and other commercial firms in Birmingham to tailor a City LPC for them. Some of the smaller providers have joined together. It is commercial pressure and not the Law Society influencing events now. After many years of maintaining secrecy, The Law Society has agreed to publish the criteria on which it bases its LPC gradings. *"We want openness so institutions can compete with each other."* It's hard not to draw conclusions as to the timing of this decision.

The Law Society has yet to accredit the City LPC. Lord Woolf's opposition may prove crucial in influencing the Group of Eight. Firms are bound to develop new allegiances as the process develops. We'll certainly be amongst the first to speak to students when they start the new course next autumn. Watch this space!

vacation schemes

Do you want a head start when you apply for your training contract? If you're serious about your career you should get on a vacation scheme. They've become a big part of the recruitment process. But many students don't make applications until it's too late, as one of our 'True Picture' trainees found to her cost. "*I was very disorganised when I was applying for them. I applied for a small number and did them all on deadline day, by which time they'd all gone.*" So – get your applications in early!

But what's all the fuss about? Why bother? A vacation scheme is the best way of improving your chances of getting a training contract. A trainee told us: "*The summer vacation schemes are the main source of recruitment here.*" Many others agreed. One reported that eight out of nine summer 2000 students were offered jobs.

Law Society guidelines state that no interviews may take place or offers of training contracts be made until 1st September in the final year of undergraduate study. Undoubtedly a fair few offers are made on 1st September. Sometimes a formal interview is just that; a mere formality.

the experience

"*It was fairly stressful*" one successful student told us. She said, "*everyone was watching you, taking notes.*" So is it a legal Big Brother? Less so than you might think. To have secured the place, students will already have beaten most of the competition and impressed the firm on paper. In many cases they will have been successful in an interview equally as tough as a training contract interview. The time spent with the firm ought to be an enjoyable few weeks, learning about what the firm does, whether or not you like the people – whether or not the chemistry is right. Think of it as a very long interview. Try to impress, don' t make a fool of yourself. Frankly, as

long as you're sensible, keen and likeable you can't go wrong. You are likely to get an offer. There's only so much you can get out of one interview, "*whereas if you're working for two weeks you get a much better idea in terms of internal structure and friendliness.*"

Many students will be checking out a number of different firms. So it's a hard sell. "*They made a fuss of us all, emphasising that we had done so well to get so far and how much training, how much care and attention were going to be lavished on you and that your training would be of the highest quality.*" A summer spent hopping from one scheme to another could also leave you loaded. Firms pay up to £300 per week.

Some firms take vacation schemes much more seriously than others. "*At Garretts they'd arranged lots of things, like taking us on City tours including the London Exchange and they arranged social things.*" Our 'True Picture' interviewees often speak of how the trainee social scene at their firms picks up during the vac student 'season' and the party budget goes through the roof. But remember, the aim is to impress. It's not always an accurate measure of the training contract. But you'll have ample opportunity to get to know people at the firm and find out how they work and what they work on. It may be a chance for you to find out whether the law suits you. That should be of greater concern to you than how many trips or nights out are laid on. In fact some firms, such as Freshfields, have stopped putting on the 'glamour' trips round the London financial institutions and try to give their summer students more 'real' work.

Keep your eyes and ears open and sharpen your wits. As one trainee told us, from a day's visit you may not get the full story. "*Everyone can put a brave face on things, if things are bad...It's a very different kettle of fish if you're there for three weeks because, although people may be on their guard, you actually get to experience* them in the working environment." Now who's Big Brother? *"At one [firm] a young assistant was talking about how it was wonderful to watch the sun rise over St Pauls, blah-de-blah-de-blah...trying to scare the summer students."* Which firm? *"Clifford Chance. They must have thought it was really funny and I just thought – no it's not."*

What appeals to one student may be anathema to another. We had dramatically different feedback about SJ Berwin. One trainee said *"The group of vacation students all bonded really well....It wasn't stuffy at all....I really enjoyed it. I was definite that I wanted to come here"* Another said: *"I found SJ Berwin a bit arrogant and for some reason I just didn't meet anyone who had much charisma. I was stuck in the banking department for the whole three weeks and they had nothing for me to do...when it came down to work. And I don't remember really meeting any trainees. The vac students tended to stick to themselves."* But a third student became about as involved in the firm's work as anyone could be. He helped on a busy deal, twice working all night in the run up to its completion.

Some firms really make the effort to keep students occupied. *"At Eversheds we were supporting or shadowing for 60% of the time and the other 40% was either talks given by people from the firm or group discussions and exercises. There were a couple of social events as well."* Others score E for effort. *"The firm that I was at I didn't like at all, so I didn't apply to them. I was put in a room on my own and just given the odd file to read. It was terrible. People didn't even come and talk to you. I had a miserable time. I went to complain to the personnel officer and she wasn't prepared to listen."* Another trainee at a reasonably-sized and well known law firm had a miserable time. *"I absolutely hated my vacation scheme*

placement with a passion. I just thought they were a small firm trying to act big. The training was based on a trainee room, so you didn't get to sit with a fee-earner. The trainee room was hideous. I couldn't see how I would learn anything that way."*

making the most of it

If you're not getting much out of a vacation scheme feel free to talk to personnel. Maybe the department you're in is too busy or particularly quiet. If there's a particular type of work you want to experience, ask the firm if you can spend time in that department. *"If it's well organised, it will give you a good chance not only to take in the environment but also to meet people.... Speak to people, that is the most important thing."*

It's not just the lawyers you'll get to talk to. Plenty of students pool information. One shared an experience of a visit to a magic circle firm, where a trainee showed her round. *"She burst into tears and said don't come here, it's horrible."* Sure, you should take such reports with a pinch of salt. Perhaps she hated being a lawyer. Perhaps she would have been happier at a small firm. Perhaps she was having a bad day. Use your own judgement; it's going to be your career.

Finally, an encouraging word from a trainee who really doubted whether she wanted to be a solicitor or not. *"I didn't enjoy studying law but thought I'd give it try. I really enjoyed it and so my vacation scheme inspired me."*

A warning from a head of graduate recruitment, though; *"We want to see that you've done more with your holidays than one summer scheme after another."* All work and no play....

VACATION SCHEMES TABLE

FIRM NAME	NUMBER OF SUMMER PLACES*	DURATION	REMUN-ERATION	2001 SUMMER CLOSING
Addleshaw Booth & Co	40	2 weeks	£150 p.w.	28 February 2001
Allen & Overy	60-70	3 weeks	£200 p.w.	31 January 2001
Ashurst Morris Crisp	60	3 weeks	£200 p.w.	16 February 2001
Baker & McKenzie	30	3 weeks	£250 p.w.	31 January 2001
Berwin Leighton	Available	1 week	not known	28 February 2001
Bird & Bird	12	3 weeks	£180 p.w.	March 2001
Bristows	36	Summer – 2 weeks, Christmas/Easter – 1 week	£200 p.w.	Christmas – 17/11/2000 Easter/Sum – 28/2/2001
Burges Salmon	30	2 weeks	£125 p.w.	23 February 2001
Cadwalader, Wickersham & Taft	Available	4 wks (3 in London and 1 in New York)	£225 p.w.	31 January 2001
Capsticks	yes	2 weeks	not known	28 February 2001
Clifford Chance	Available	2 weeks	£240 p.w.	9 February 2001
CMS Cameron McKenna	55	2 weeks	£200 p.w.	28 February 2001
D J Freeman	16	3 weeks	£150 p.w.	14 March 2001
Dechert	8	9 July to 20 July 2001	£190 p.w.+	Applications considered between: 1 November 2000 and 28 February 2001
Denton Wilde Sapte	120	On information week/ open day	not known	Applications accepted January to March 2001
Dickinson Dees	24	1 week	£100 p.w.	28 February 2001
DLA	180	1 week	£185 p.w. (London), £140 p.w. (regions)	28 February 2001
DMH	Available	1-2 weeks	£100 p.w.	31 March 2001
Eversheds	120	2 weeks	regional variations	31 January 2001
Farrer & Co	18	2 weeks at Easter, 3 weeks in summer	£200 p.w.	31 January 2001
Fenners	10	2 weeks	competitive	30 April 2001
Field Fisher Waterhouse	Available	July 2001	not known	31 March 2001
Freshfields Bruckhaus Deringer	100	2 weeks	£450 (total)	14 February 2001 apply ASAP after I December 2000
Garretts	60 throughout the UK	3 weeks	£225 p.w.	5 February 2001
Gouldens	Law: 35 Non-Law: 7 Non-Law: 14 Xmas	Summer: 2 weeks Easter: 2 weeks Xmas: 2 weeks	£225 p.w.	28 February 2001 28 February 2001 30 October 2001
Halliwell Landau	30	2 weeks	£100 p.w.	31 March 2001

*Schemes taking place in summer unless otherwise stated

VACATION SCHEMES TABLE *continued*

FIRM NAME	NUMBER OF SUMMER PLACES*	DURATION	REMUN- ERATION	2001 SUMMER CLOSING
Hammond Suddards Edge	48	3 weeks	£220 p.w. (London) £170 p.w. (regions)	28 February 2001
Herbert Smith	95	Christmas – 1 week (non-law) Easter – 2 weeks Summer – 3 weeks	£200 p.w.	24 Nov 2000 for Christmas 16 Feb 2001 for Easter/summer
Hill Dickinson	Available	1 week	none	1 April 2001
Holman Fenwick & Willan	12	2 weeks.	£250 p.w.	Applications accepted 1 Jan – 14 Feb 2001
Holmes Hardingham	Available	1-2 weeks	£250 p.w.	May 2001
Ince & Co	16	2 weeks	£200 p.w.	16 February 2001
Irwin Mitchell	30	2 weeks	£75 p.w.	1 March 2001
KLegal	12	4 weeks	£220 p.w.	31 April 2001
Knight & Sons	Available	During Christmas, Easter & Summer	not known	31 October 2000 28 February 2001 30 April 2001
Lawrence Graham	20-24	2 weeks Easter 3x2 weeks summer	£200 p.w.	28 February 2001
Laytons	6	1 week	n/a	31 March 2001
Lester Aldridge	8	2 weeks	£60 p.w.	31 March 2001
Linklaters	Available	Christmas – 2 weeks Easter – 2 weeks Summer – 4 weeks	£225 p.w.	n/a
Lovells	Available	Christmas – 2 weeks Easter – 2 weeks Summer – 3 weeks	not known	10 November 2000 12 February 2001
Macfarlanes	40	2 weeks	£200 p.w.	28 February 2001
Manches	24	2 weeks	£150 p.w.	31 January 2001
Masons	36 (London), 5 (Manchester)	2 weeks	not known	12 February 2001
McCormicks	Available	Summer	not known	1 January 2001
Mills & Reeve	25	2 weeks	£110 p.w.	1 March 2001
Mishcon de Reya	12	3 weeks	£150 p.w.	30 March 2001
Nabarro Nathanson	Available	3 weeks	not known	28 February 2001
Nicholson Graham & Jones	8	2 weeks	TBA	n/a
Norton Rose	45 summer, 15 Christmas	Summer – 3 weeks Christmas – 2 weeks	£225 p.w.	2 February 2001 3 November 2000
Olswang	10 (July), 10 (August)	3 weeks	£190 p.w.	28 July 2001
Osborne Clarke OWA	20	1 week	£130-150 p.w.	28 February 2001
Paisner & Co	20	4 weeks	£200 p.w.	15 February 2001

*Schemes taking place in summer unless otherwise stated

FIRM NAME	NUMBER OF SUMMER PLACES*	DURATION	REMUN-ERATION	2001 SUMMER CLOSING
Pannone & Partners	50	1 week	none	9 March 2001
Penningtons	Outside London only	During summer	expenses	30 April 2001
Pinsent Curtis	140	1 week	not known	28 February 2000
Radcliffes	10	2 weeks	£130 p.w.	31 March 2001
Reynolds Porter Chamberlain	12	2 weeks	£175 p.w.	28 February 2001
Richards Butler	45 + 4 overseas scholarships	2 weeks	£200 p.w.	28 February 2001
Rowe & Maw	25	2 weeks	£200 p.w.	28 February 2001
Shadbolt & Co	6	2 weeks	£150 p.w.	16 March 2001
Shoosmiths	25	2 weeks	£120 p.w.	29 February 2001
Simmons & Simmons	30	To be confirmed	£200 p.w.	24 February 2001
Sinclair Roche & Temperley	10-12	2 weeks	£160 p.w.	28 February 2001, subject to availability
SJ Berwin & Co	60	2 weeks	£200 p.w.	2 March 2001
Slaughter and May	60	2 weeks	£225 p.w.	9 February 2001
Speechly Bircham	8	3 weeks	£200 p.w.	14 February 2001
Stephenson Harwood	21	2 weeks	£200 p.w.	16 February 2001
Taylor Joynson Garrett	30	2 weeks	£200 p.w.	23 February 2001
Taylor Vinters	14	1 week	not known	n/a
Taylor Walton	2-3	up to 4 weeks	as agreed	30 April 2001
Theodore Goddard	20	2 weeks	£200 p.w.	End February 2001
TLT Solicitors	8+	To be confirmed	not known	n/a
Travers Smith Braithwaite	45	3 weeks	£200 p.w.	End March 2001
Trowers & Hamlins	15-20	3 weeks	£175 p.w.	1 March (Summer) Open Day (TBC)
Walker Morris	30-40	1 week	£100 p.w.	28 February 2001
Ward Hadaway	12	1 week	not known	not known
Warner Cranston	12	2 weeks	£400	31 March 2001
Watson, Farley & Williams	30	2 weeks	£200 p.w.	31 March 2001
Wedlake Bell	6	3 weeks in July	£150 p.w.	End of February
Weil, Gotshal & Manges	12	To be confirmed	not known	31 January 2001
White & Case	15-20	2 weeks	£250	End of February 2001
Withers	20	Easter – 3 weeks, Summer – 3 weeks	not known	23 February 2001
Wragge & Co	20 48	Easter – 1 week Summer – 2 weeks	£150 p.w. £125 p.w.	16 February 2001

*Schemes taking place in summer unless otherwise stated

PRE-QUALIFICATION

TABLE OF VACATION SCHEMES

selection

Ten years ago a third year student at Birmingham University did a summer placement with a top five City firm. She liked the firm and they liked her. Without a single interview or assessment they offered her a job. In 1990, this was not particularly unusual.

Now, however, it's a different story. Students applying for training contracts are likely to face an assault course of group exercises, written tests and day-long assessments before they secure a job.

assessment days

Getting a good night's sleep is an old interview cliché but has never been more important than now, with the new approach to graduate selection. An assessment day means just that. A whole day. You are continuously assessed from the moment you stutter your name at reception through spilling pasta down your front at the buffet lunch to the point where you wander out of the office at 5pm. The time when you could drink three cups of coffee, chat to a partner for half an hour and then fall asleep on the train home smug in the knowledge you had got the job are long gone. A typical assessment day consists of one or two written tests, at least one group exercise, one or two interviews and perhaps a group presentation. Firms place varying emphasis on the different elements. For some the interview is crucial while for others group exercises are of primary importance. If it is possible to find out in advance (from current trainees perhaps) then this might be advantageous.

group exercises

One student told us of her "nightmarish" experience at a large City firm. She and three others were given a group exercise where they had to imagine they were stranded in the desert. They were given fifteen items to rank in order of importance to their survival. The exercise lasted half an hour and a recruitment officer closely observed the whole process. What she found particularly difficult was the awkward behaviour of everyone in the group. Nobody seemed to know what was expected of them and the individuals ranged from being over-assertive to quiet and difficult.

A very different group exercise at another City firm involved a more business-like situation. Twelve candidates were divided into two groups and asked to advise on the purchase of two factories. One had union problems, but solid financial backing, the other had a different set of problems. Again the group was observed and again, our student found the experience quite "tense." She must have performed well though because she was offered a job. When asked why she thought she was successful at

> ## "be yourself and you'll find the right firm for you."

one firm and not at the other, she said it had a lot to do with the nature of the group. She felt more comfortable with the second set of people and also with the task. So, it was partly down to chance. However, she also felt more prepared second time round and realised it was better just to be herself. What can a candidate learn from this?

The most obvious answer is to be yourself and you'll find the right firm for you. Bob Llewellin, training director with Burges Salmon, says: "It's important not to be a pushover – say something, but it doesn't help to be bombastic." If your arguments aren't accepted by the group don't worry – you might have been asked to argue an unwinnable case. Firms are looking for how good a team player you are. Do you listen to other people's ideas, can you compromise, do you keep an eye on key factors such as time and budget?

Said one (successful) candidate, "I was told in the interview afterwards that the assessors had been impressed that I had noticed time was running out when the others were still arguing over who should be spokesperson."

You should also remember that firms are looking for all kinds of people – the more measured, thoughtful type as well as the outgoing team leader. Though these events always bring out the actor in people, it won't help to reinvent your personality.

written tests

These tend to fall into two types. Firstly there are the reasoning/personality tests, usually presented in multiple choice format. Though often a minimum standard is set, below which candidates must not fall, you will not get the job simply on the basis of your mental agility. In many assessment days the tests will be marked and returned to the assessors before you leave or even before your interview. As you cannot prepare for these tests the best advice is stay calm, work quickly but effectively and keep an eye on the clock.

There is often also a second, scenario-based written exercise. Candidates may be asked to note the issues and propose some solutions in a particular situation. You may be asked to put the answer in a particular form (i.e. letter, fax, report). Other things that you may be asked to do include advising on documents or rewriting something into 'plain English.'

Although spotting potential legal issues is sometimes an important part of the 'situation' exercises, the assessors will not want a detailed analysis of the caselaw, stuffed full of quotes by Lord Denning. Instead they want sensible, practical, often business-aware comments on the problem. So non-law students need not worry about their lack of legal knowledge. No-one will expect you to have learnt contract law before the assessment.

presentations

Two candidates at a City law firm were put together and asked to prepare a joint presentation to be given to a partner. To our source the task did not seem that difficult. After all the scenario was quite fun and the other candidate easy to get on with. It was only whilst doing the presentation that he realised that the other candidate would not let him get a word in. She even covered his areas in her speech. Yet halfway through her speech it became obvious from the partner's expression that the partner was not impressed by her attitude to him. Result: she did not get an offer and he did. She had failed to realise that a key point of assessment days is not just to assess your mental agility or oratory skills but how well you work with others.

a friendly chat?

If the day involves a session with trainees, be careful, particularly if it is one-to-one. They are not just there to answer your questions. They will be asked for feedback on you (do not believe them if they say otherwise) and will often be your harshest critics. So don't look at it as a chance to slag off your interviewer or confess that you don't really want to be a lawyer but your parents have forced you into it.

Lunch can also be a particularly stressful affair. Trying to eat tagliatelle with a fork, whilst simultaneously drinking a glass of wine and making small talk with a senior partner can be more taxing than any reasoning test. Remember: red wine on the carpet will not go down well.

The selection and recruitment process is in many firms a polished, highly professional procedure. City firms, in particular, waste no time in letting successful and unsuccessful applicants know. In many cases, candidates hear that day, especially if the firm wants them. With the benefit of hindsight, most of our interviewees said they enjoyed their assessments and "the day will almost certainly end with a drinks party." Don't relax too much – you're being assessed there too!

FIRM NAME	AF*/CV	SELECTION PROCESS	DEGREE GRADE	CONTRACTS	APPLICA-TIONS
Addleshaw Booth & Co	AF	Interview, assessment day	2:1	40	2,000
Allen & Overy	AF	Assessment centre	2:1	120	4,000
Ashurst Morris Crisp	CV	Interview with 2 partners	2:1	45-50	3,000
Baker & McKenzie	AF	Oral and written presentation, interview. Meeting with a trainee	2:1	30	2,000
Barlows	AF & CV	Interview	2:1	3-4	
Beale and Company	CV	2 interviews with partners	2:1	3	1,500
Berwin Leighton	AF	Assessment centre + partner interview	2:1	25	2,000
Bevan Ashford	AF	n/a	2:1	20	n/a
Biddle	CV	1 interview	2:1	4-6	1,500
Bird & Bird	AF	Assessment mornings	2:1	12	2,500
Blake Lapthorn	AF & CV	Interview with partners, presentation and group exercise	2.1	5	750
Bond Pearce	AF & CV	Interviews and vacation placement	n/a	10-15	500
Boyes Turner & Burrows	CV	2 interviews	2:2	3/4	2,200
Brachers	CV	Interview day with partners	2:1	6	n/a
Bristows	AF	2 individual interviews	2.1 preferred	10	2,000
Burges Salmon	AF	n/a	2:1	20	1,000
Cadwaladers	CV	2 interviews	2:1	4	500
Campbell Hooper	CV	n/a	2:1	2-3	n/a
Capsticks	AF & CV	Summer placement scheme. Final selection by interview	2.1 or above	6-8	1,000+
Charles Russell	AF	Assessment days	2:1	10-12	2,000
Clarks	AF	Open day/interview plus second interview (with limited written tests)	usually 2:1 or above	5-6	5-600
Cleary, Gottlieb, Steen & Hamilton	CV	2 interviews	2.1	up to 4	n/a
Clifford Chance	AF	Assessment day	2:1	130	2,000

* AF = application form

FIRM NAME	AF*/CV	SELECTION PROCESS	DEGREE GRADE	CONTRACTS	APPLICA-TIONS
Clyde & Co	AF	Individual interview with Georgia de Saram, followed by interview with 2 partners	2:1	20	2,000
CMS Cameron McKenna	AF	Initial interview followed by assessment centre	2:1	80	1,500
Cobbetts	AF	Half day assessments	2:1	8	700
Coudert Brothers	CV	2 interviews with partners	2:1	4	n/a
Cripps Harries Hall	AF	1 interview	2.1	8	Up to 1,000
Cumberland Ellis Peirs	CV	2 interviews with partners	2:1	1 or 2	600
D J Freeman	AF	Interview	2:1	12-15	600
Davies Arnold Cooper	AF	Open days and individual interviews	2:1	n/a	n/a
Davies Wallis Foyster	CV or AF	Two stage interview/selection process	2:1 preferred	at least 6	c.1,000
Dechert	AF	1 interview with at least 2 partners	2:1	up to 15	over 1,000
Denton Wilde Sapte	AF	2 interviews	2:1	50	3,000
Dickinson Dees	AF	Interview	2:1	14	700
DLA	AF	First interview and assessment afternoon	2:1	70	2,200
DMH	CV	n/a	2:1	4-5	350-450
Eversheds	AF	Selection days	2:1	100-110	3,000
Farrer & Co	AF	2 interviews	2:1	6	1,500
Fenners	CV	2 interviews with partners	2:1	3	400
Field Fisher Waterhouse	AF	Interview	2:1	10	2,500
Finers Stephens Innocent	CV	2 interviews	2:1	3-6	1,500
Forbes	CV	Interview with partners	2:1	3	350
Freshfields Bruckhaus Deringer	AF	1 interview with 2 partners	2:1	95	c.3,500
Garretts	AF or CV	2 Interviews (London & regional office of choice)	2:1	40	2,000
Goodman Derrick	CV	2 interviews	min. 2:1	3	1,200

* AF = application form

FIRM NAME	AF*/CV	SELECTION PROCESS	DEGREE GRADE	CONTRACTS	APPLICA-TIONS
Gouldens	CV	2 interviews with partners	2:1	20	2,500
Halliwell Landau	AF & CV	Open days or summer placements	2:1	8-10	1,000
Hammond Suddards Edge	AF	2 interviews	2:1	45	1,500
Harbottle & Lewis	CV	Interview	2:1	3	800
Henmans	CV	Interview	n/a	3	500
Herbert Smith	AF	Interview	2:1	90	2,000
Hewitson Becke + Shaw	AF	Interview	min. 2:1	15	1,400
Hill Dickinson	CV	Assessment day	n/a	n/a	n/a
Hill Taylor Dickinson	AF	Interview/Assessment Day	2:1	4	400-500
Hodge Jones & Allen	AF	Interview and selection tests	pref 2:1	n/a	n/a
Holman Fenwick & Willan	CV	2 interviews & written exercise	2:1	7	1,200
Holmes Hardingham	CV	2 interviews	min. 2:1	2	500
Howes Percival	AF	Assessment centres	2:1	6	300
Hugh James Ford Simey	CV	2 interviews	2:2	5	700
Ince & Co	CV	Interview and written test	2:1	10	1,200
Irwin Mitchell	AF	Assessment centres & 2 interviews	n/a	15	1,000
Jeffrey Green Russell	CV	n/a	n/a	4	n/a
Kennedys	AF & CV	Minimum of one interview with 2 partners and personnel director	2:1	6-8	1500
KLegal	AF	2 interviews + assessment exercises	2:1	30-40	c.750
Knight & Sons	CV	n/a	2:1	3-4	n/a
Lawrence Graham	AF	Interview and written exercise	2:1	15	1,500
Laytons	AF	2 interviews	1 or 2:1	8	2,000
Le Brasseur J Tickle	CV	2 interviews	n/a	4	1,500
Lee Bolton & Lee	CV	Panel interview	2:1	2	800
Lester Aldridge	AF & CV	Interview by a panel of partners	2:1	5	300
Lewis Silkin	CV	Assessment day	2:1	6	1,000

* AF = application form

FIRM NAME	AF*/CV	SELECTION PROCESS	DEGREE GRADE	CONTRACTS	APPLICA-TIONS
Linklaters	AF	2 interviews (same day)	2:1	150	2,500
Lovells	AF	Assessment day	min 2:1	80	1,500
Mace & Jones	CV	Interview with partners	2:1	12	1,500
Macfarlanes	AF	Assessment day	2:1	20	1,500
Manches	AF	Individual interview with 2 partners Possible 2nd interview	2:1	7-8	1,000
Martineau Johnson	AF	Assessment centre – half day	2:1	14	500
Masons	AF	Assessment day & interview	2:1	26	1,200
May, May & Merrimans	CV	Interview	2:1	1	200
Mayer, Brown & Platt	AF	2 interviews	high 2:1	2	600
McCormicks	AF	Selection day and interview	2:1	4	1,000
Mills & Reeve	AF	Interview and Assessment	2:1	20-30	500
Mishcon de Reya	AF	n/a	2:1	6	800+
Morgan Cole	AF	Assessment centre and interview	2:2 or above	n/a	n/a
Nabarro Nathanson	AF	Interview and assessment day	2:1	30	1,500
Nicholson Graham & Jones	AF	Interview and assessment	2:1	10	1,000
Norton Rose	AF	Interview and group exercise	2:1	65-75	2,500+
Olswang	AF	Interview; psychometric tests.	2:1	25	3,000+
Osborne Clarke OWA	AF	Individual interviews and group exercises.	2:1 preferred	20	1,000-1,200
Paisner & Co	AF	Application form and interview	2:1	10-12	2,000
Pannone & Partners	AF & CV	Individual interview. Second interview comprises a tour of the firm and informal lunch	2:2	8	500
Payne Hicks Beach	CV	Interview	2:1	2	1,000
Penningtons	AF & CV	Interview	2:1	10/11	2,000
Pinsent Curtis	AF	Assessment centre	2:1	25-30	4,000
Pritchard Englefield	AF	Interview in September	generally 2:1	4	300-400

* AF = application form

SELECTION TABLE *continued*

FIRM NAME	AF*/CV	SELECTION PROCESS	DEGREE GRADE	CONTRACTS	APPLICA-TIONS
Radcliffes	AF & CV	2 interviews with partners	2:1	4	1016
Reynolds Porter Chamberlain	AF	Assessment days held in September	2:1	10	600
Richards Butler	AF	1 interview	2:1	20	2,000
Rowe & Maw	AF	Selection workshops	2:1	25	1,250
Russell Jones & Walker	AF	n/a	2:1	8	1,000
Russell-Cooke	AF	First and second interviews	2:1	4	500
Salans Hertzfeld	CV	2 interviews with partners	2:1	3-4	500+
Shadbolt & Co	CV	Interview(s)	2:1	6	200
Sharpe Pritchard	CV	Interview with the Senior Partner	n/a	4	n/a
Sheridans	CV	2 interviews	2:1	2-3	700
Shoosmiths	AF	Assessment centre – half day	2:1	12	2,000
Sidley & Austin	AF	Interview(s)	2:1	6-8	500
Simmons & Simmons	AF & CV	Assessment day	2:1	50-60	2,700
Sinclair Roche & Temperley	CV	Interview	2:1	6-8	1,500
SJ Berwin & Co	CV	Interview (early September)	2:1	40	2,000
Slaughter and May	CV	Interview	good 2:1 ability	75+	3,000
Speechly Bircham	AF	Interview	2:1	5	1,000
Steele & Co	CV	Interview	2:1	6	300-400
Stephenson Harwood	AF	Interview with 2 partners	2:1	18	n/a
Tarlo Lyons	AF	2 Interviews with partners	2:1	3	400+
Taylor Joynson Garrett	AF	2 interviews, 1 with a partner.	2:1	25	1,600
Taylor Vinters	AF	Interview with 2 partners	2:2	5	300
Taylor Walton	CV	First and second interview	2:1+	n/a	n/a
Teacher Stern Selby	AF	2 interviews	2:1	3	500
Theodore Goddard	AF	First and second interview	2:1+	20	3,000
TLT Solicitors	AF	Assessment day	n/a	8	1,000
Travers Smith Braithwaite	CV	Interviews	2:1	20	1,600

* AF = application form

FIRM NAME	AF*/CV	SELECTION PROCESS	DEGREE GRADE	CONTRACTS	APPLICA- TIONS
Trowers & Hamlins	AF & CV	Interview, essay and practical test	2:1+	12-15	1,500
Walker Morris	AF	Telephone and face to face interviews	2:1	15	600
Ward Hadaway	AF	Interview	2:1	8	400
Warner Cranston	AF	Assessment day	2:1	4	1,000
Watson Burton	CV	Interview	2:1	2	1,800
Watson, Farley & Williams	AF	Interview and assessment	2:1 preferred	12	1,500
Wedlake Bell	CV	Interviews in September	2:1	6	800
Weightmans	AF	Interview with partners	n/a	8-10	n/a
Weil, Gotshal & Manges	AF	n/a	2:1	10	n/a
White & Case	CV	Interview	2:1	20	1,300
Whitehead Monckton	AF & CV	Interviews	n/a	2	n/a
Wiggin and Co	CV	2 interviews	2:1	2/3	1,700
Withers	AF	2 interviews	2:1	10	1,500
Wragge & Co	AF	Telephone interview and Assessment Day.	2:1 preferred	25	1,000

* AF = application form

what are law firms looking for?

The obvious – great academics, communication skills, a good sense of organisation and attention to detail. The confidence to carry yourself through an interview or assessment day. In addition, some firms look for more. Trainees highlighted a few things to us when we interviewed them for the 'True Picture' section of this book and the firms themselves often give clear indications.

languages

Will always stand you in good stead. A clear advantage where the firm has overseas offices and also where it has existing business with the particular countries which speak your second language. Hill Taylor Dickinson says: *"Good foreign languages are an advantage due to the international nature of the firm's work."* Pritchard Englefield is more specific. *"Normally only high academic achievers with a second European language (especially German and French) are considered."* Withers indicates *"...foreign languages, particularly Italian, would be an advantage."*

law or non-law degree?

As a rule, a non-law degree is no drawback. Most firms are very positive towards non-law graduates. Clyde & Co confirms: *"Non-law graduates are welcome, especially those with modern languages or science degrees."* Macfarlanes seeks candidates from *"Any degree discipline."* These firms are not alone. A few, however, indicate that a law degree is required. For example, Cleary Gottlieb Steen & Hamilton states that it wants *"at least a 2.1 law degree from a top UK university."* Paisner's website implies that it prefers law graduates.

class of degree

This is usually critical. A 2.1 or better will almost always be a requirement of the commercial firms.

There are one or two exceptions but firms such as Morgan Cole (*"Seeking applications... preferably with at least a 2.2 degree."*) receive many hundreds of applications from candidates with a 2.1 or better. Their policy is not an indication that they prefer to take those with a 2.2, just that they are prepared to be open minded about the result. Similarly, Pritchard Englefield confirms that *"exceptional subsequent education or experience"* can sometimes make up for a 2.2.

your university

It's the old school tie phenomenon. The better regarded your university, the greater your chances of securing the training contract that you want. It is as simple as that. The top City firms still have an overwhelming Oxbridge bias and there is then a pecking order of other unis. Check the 'Preferred Universities' section of this book. A majority of City trainees will have come from 10 or 15 institutions. Those with degrees from new universities (the old polytechnics) do have a harder time breaking into the City firms. Regional firms tend to have a greater affinity with universities in their region (whether new or old).

local connections

These definitely count for something at many regional firms. The reason why firms look for local ties (family or an education in the area) is that on qualification, they want to retain their young lawyers, not see them drawn to London or other big cities such as Bristol or Leeds. Forbes in Blackburn seeks *"high calibre recruits with strong local connections..."* Knight & Sons (Manchester and Newcastle-under-Lyme) requests *"trainees who will stay on once they have qualified."* Pannone & Partners looks for those with *"a connection with the North West."* The 'True Picture' highlights other firms looking to recruit locally.

previous careers

The 'True Picture' flags a number of firms that seem to have woken up to the fact that those with first careers often make great lawyers. They already know what work is all about. Many bring client contacts with them and a number find themselves on a fast track through to partnership. The following careers are particularly popular: shipping, insurance, pharmaceuticals, medical professionals, engineers, surveyors, accountants, IT, the armed forces. Here's what some of the law firms said on the matter. Addleshaw Booth & Co: *"Applications from mature applicants are welcome."* Beale and Company: *"... experience or an interest in construction, insurance and IT will assist."* Davies Arnold Cooper: *"Welcomes applications from all age groups and backgrounds."* Richards Butler say that *"Candidates from diverse backgrounds are welcome, including mature students with commercial experience and management skills"* and Holman Fenwick & Willan look for those with *"a scientific or marine background."*

personality

You should definitely have one. Each firm knows what it's after. Many firms ask for *"creative problem solvers,"* others request those with a sense of humour, others enthusiasm. Not every firm has a particular type in mind and there are firms that stress that they look for a range of different characters. For example, Biddle seeks to *"build a team of complementary personalities where, for example, the more bookish are balanced by the charismatic."*

commercial awareness

They all seem to be after it. Only Slaughters *"does not expect applicants to know much of commercial life."* The firm expects you to have been busy with academic work. Other firms expect more. Aspiring City lawyers must read the business papers. For those interested in employment law, keep abreast of changes in legislation. Not everyone has the opportunity to fill their CV with acres of relevant experience, but do your best. There are some clear messages from the firms in their own literature. Hodge Jones & Allen, for example state that candidates should have *"a proven commitment to and/or experience of working in legal aid/advice sectors."* Sometimes it's more vague. Farrer & Co says those who *"break the mould – as shown by their initiative for organisation, leadership, exploration, or enterprise – are far more likely to get an interview than the erudite, but otherwise unimpressive student."*

travel

At last! Travel is now seen as a positive advantage. It shows that you have a bit of spirit and the recruiters assume that you will have benefited from time abroad, especially if you had to organise things for yourself whilst you were out of the country. Baker & McKenzie says *"The firm encourages their trainees to take time out before commencing their training contract, whether just to travel or undertake further studies."* Hill Taylor Dickinson also confirms that previous travel experience is taken into account. Osborne Clarke OWA say that *"...time spent travelling [is] viewed positively."*

team spirit

Most firms like to see that applicants can demonstrate an ability to work with others. Some place a very high priority on team working and, for these firms, you must be able to demonstrate appropriate characteristics and experience. Insurance firms in particular value team working.

are you interesting?

To get a firm interested in you, it's of real importance that you demonstrate that there's a little bit more to you than the next candidate. The firm looks to how you spend your free time, whether you are a person who interacts or remains a loner. Eversheds tells us that it wants *"candidates that appear to mix well with others, take part in team events, get involved in projects that necessitate dealing with people at all levels. Interests don't have to run to the exotic or unusual; down-to-earth and unstuffy but not dull is what we are looking for."*

will i get a training contract?

People often phone us up with particular questions. *"Which firms do shipping?"* Easy. *"Which of my offers should I accept?"* We chat with the person and they usually answer their own question. Most enquiries are from people struggling with applications.

how many applications should I make? The aim behind the Chambers Student Guide is focus. Read the 'True Picture', the 'Practice Areas' and identify the firms that interest you. 10 focused applications are better than 30 CVs plus identikit letters. Unless your CV is stunning, in which case it may need no introduction.

Most firms now have application forms anyway. But it's remarkable how many people fill them in with nothing more than the firm's own brochure to help them. Using the information in our book you will buy yourself more time so that you can research each firm and make intelligent applications. If you concentrate on ten firms you may be able to make contacts at all those firms who may get you that all-important interview. Then it's down to your presentation skills.

Some candidates have the confidence to go for the under ten firms strategy. They can probably choose between the magic circle. Some candidates have applied to a couple of hundred firms. Most will be somewhere in between these numbers, at about 25 or so applications.

I've only got a 2:2 in my degree, does it matter?: Sadly, yes. You will need a superb CV to get the attention of a recruiter and it's not sufficient to explain away the poor result yourself. You should include an academic reference with the application form, sealed if necessary. The referee will need to give very convincing reasons why the result was poor. Recruiters tell us that it is useful to know if something went wrong – but only if the referee says it. *"It makes no difference if the marks were just short of a 2:1, candidates often labour that point but a 2:2 is a 2:2. When you are flooded with 2:1s and firsts you have to draw the line somewhere."*

Work experience may help. As one recruiter told us, *"off the record, someone with a 2:2 with no legal experience at all will be out the window straight away...they can't justify to me that they want to be a lawyer."* A personal contact at the firm who can ensure your CV is looked at may help. The primary message we have is don't leave it until the deadline to apply. Your application will arrive with the bulk and will be instantly discarded. Our advice? Get in there early.

I have a degree from one of the 'new universities.' Does that make a difference?: Again, yes. *"I try to be generous"* a City source said, *"but applications from the more established universities tend to be better."* A few of the best regarded law departments at former polytechnics (for example UWE, Nottingham Trent) turn out graduates who do well in the legal job market. Firms outside London are often better educated about the new universities in their region and may favour them.

I'm a mature applicant will that put firms off?: It depends what you've been doing and where you're applying. *"You expect candidates to be more mature and to have been in positions where they have had to communicate with and handle people. Experience in commercial or legal areas is important"* said one source. The law firm wants to see that you know how to handle client relationships. The perennial student represents a worry to recruiters.

As for those who have drifted from one thing into another since university *"Forget it! We're looking for commitment."*

how to get work as a paralegal

FAQs (frequently asked questions)

What is a paralegal?

Do I need experience?

Which firms take on paralegals?

Is paralegal work a route to a training contract?

what is a paralegal?

Paralegals are extra fee-earners. That means their services can be charged to the client by the hour. Their job is to cover cost-effectively the sorts of tasks that don't need to be done by someone with legal training. These are usually administrative. They are therefore not qualified UK lawyers. They may be lawyers qualified in other jurisdictions waiting to requalify into UK law. They may be LPC graduates who have not yet got a training contract. Or they may be career paralegals. Jobs are full or part-time, temporary or permanent, at all types of firms.

experience: Most law firms want applicants with at least six months experience already. At Chambers and Partners, paralegal consultant Jo Salt's clients consist of magic circle and other City firms, niche firms, quality regionals and US firms. She will not even put forward a CV to a law firm if there is less than six months' experience on it. Many also require a 2:1 at degree-level as well as completion of the LPC.

For many without that vital experience there may be no invitations to interviews. Competition is extremely fierce and firms can afford to pick and choose.

work type: Your daily routine will reflect the type of work the firm does. Large-scale litigation requires a considerable amount of document-copying, organising and scheduling. Ditto large-scale corporate and property transactions. You may be asked to sit and watch rooms full of documents (datarooms) and those who come to inspect them. In smaller firms there will be much less of this type of work. Firms sometimes take on a team of paralegals to deal with a particularly large and document-intensive piece of litigation. Some of those with most experience may be given management responsibility.

law firms who recruit

All types of firms employ paralegals, from the smallest high street practice to the largest magic circle firms. The larger firms will pay better and provide benefits. However, most larger firms like to use people who have studied law up to LPC level.

applying on spec: The easiest way to get work as a paralegal is through contacts. If you have previous experience then use a recruitment consultancy with a specialist in paralegal recruitment, such as Chambers and Partners. Keep an eye out for any vacancies that may be advertised in the legal press and regularly trawl through firm websites. A number of them advertise paralegal positions.

no route to a training contract: A paralegal will rarely be offered a training contract. It's more likely at some firms than others. Most have a policy of actively discouraging applications for training contracts. One of our graduate recruitment sources enlightened us: *"It's embarrassing if you have to effectively tell a paralegal that they can't cut it as a trainee. That's the main reason most firms try to discourage such applications – the embarrassment factor."* Reading 'The True Picture' may help you spot firms who don't follow this approach.

contact: Paralegal consultant Jo Salt at Chambers and Partners on 020 7606 8844 or jos@chambersandpartners.co.uk

paralegal salaries

london

We asked firms to provide basic salaries for paralegals with various levels of experience. We publish the average figure in bold for each sector and also the upper and lower quartile. The upper quartile means that 75% of all salaries are below that level and 25% of all salaries are above that level. The lower quartile shows that 75% of all salaries are above that figure and 25% are below it. Paid overtime was not taken into account, overtime is shown in a separate table.

LONDON PARALEGAL SALARIES TABLE

UP TO SIX MONTHS' EXPERIENCE

NUMBER OF PARTNERS	AVERAGE	LOWER QUARTILE	UPPER QUARTILE
150+	£16,900.00	£15,171.57	£18,040.18
75-149	£16,500.00	£15,451.19	£17,548.81
45-74	£16,833.33	£15,644.29	£18,002.38
20-44	£16,950.00	£15,720.16	£18,179.84
1-19	£16,250.00	£13,076.45	£19,423.55
US firms	£20,000.00	£19,375.00	£20,375.00

SIX MONTHS' TO TWO YEARS' EXPERIENCE

NUMBER OF PARTNERS	AVERAGE	LOWER QUARTILE	UPPER QUARTILE
150+	£18,050.00	£15,759.82	£20,290.89
75-149	£18,416.67	£16,919.45	£19,913.89
45-74	£17,700.00	£16,725.32	£18,674.68
20-44	£19,500.00	£16,716.12	£22,283.88
1-19	£16,875.00	£14,412.79	£19,337.21
US firms	£22,250.00	£21,375.00	£22,500.00

TWO OR MORE YEARS' EXPERIENCE

NUMBER OF PARTNERS	AVERAGE	LOWER QUARTILE	UPPER QUARTILE
150+	£18,750.00	£15,909.11	£20,828.43
75-149	£19,625.00	£17,489.00	£21,761.00
45-74	£20,200.00	£17,611.56	£22,788.44
20-44	£23,900.00	£19,710.73	£28,089.27
1-19	£21,375.00	£17,066.58	£25,683.42
US firms	£26,178.00	£24,125.00	£27,500.00

regions

The data for the regions has been divided into the following geographical areas: South East, South West/Wales, Midlands and North. We found from the data collected in the regions that the partner size of the firms had a much smaller impact on paralegal salaries than it did in London and therefore we have not subdivided the regions into partner sizes as in the previous table.

THE REGIONS PARALEGAL SALARIES TABLE

UP TO SIX MONTHS' EXPERIENCE

LOCATION	AVERAGE	LOWER QUARTILE	UPPER QUARTILE
South East	£12,714.29	£10,472.08	£14,956.49
South West/Wales	£11,800.00	£9,609.36	£13,990.64
Midlands	£10,935.00	£9,006.79	£12,863.21
North	£12,887.78	£10,106.32	£14,489.60

SIX MONTHS' TO TWO YEARS' EXPERIENCE

LOCATION	AVERAGE	LOWER QUARTILE	UPPER QUARTILE
South East	£15,390.67	£12,856.19	£17,925.15
South West/Wales	£13,468.75	£11,221.76	£15,715.74
Midlands	£13,812.00	£11,054.15	£16,569.85
North	£13,833.33	£11,285.95	£17,560.35

TWO OR MORE YEARS' EXPERIENCE

LOCATION	AVERAGE	LOWER QUARTILE	UPPER QUARTILE
South East	£19,960.71	£15,119.54	£24,801.89
South West/Wales	£15,736.11	£12,527.16	£18,945.10
Midlands	£15,730.00	£13,037.19	£18,422.81
North	£18,000.00	£16,000.00	£20,000.00

LONDON AND THE REGIONS ANNUAL BONUSES TABLE

LOCATION	AVERAGE	MINIMUM	MAXIMUM
London	0.63%	0.00%	5.00%
Regions	2.00%	0.00%	15.00%
US firms	2.43%	0.00%	10.00%

These figures show the average, minimum and maximum annual bonuses (shown as percentage of salary) paid to paralegals in London and the regions:

SOLICITORS TIMETABLE

LAW STUDENTS PENULTIMATE YEAR

October 2000 – February 2001:	Research directories and websites. Compile information about law firms. Obtain firm brochures. Attend presentations and law fairs.
January – March 2001*:	Apply for open days and vacation schemes.
Spring – Summer 2001**:	Attend vacation schemes. Apply to law firms for training contracts for 2002. Apply for a place on the LPC.

LAW STUDENTS FINAL YEAR

September – December 2001:	Attend interviews for training contracts for 2003.

LAW STUDENTS AFTER GRADUATION

September 2002:	Start LPC.
July 2003:	Finish LPC.
September 2003:	Start training contract (first intake).
March 2004:	Start training contract (second intake).
September 2005:	Qualify as a solicitor (first intake).
March 2006:	Qualify as a solicitor (second intake).

* It is important to check closing dates for each firm as these will vary. Many close in January or February. Some firms will only accept applications for vacation schemes from penultimate year students whether law or non-law. See pages 18-20 for further information.

** It is important to check closing dates for each firm. Many firms will not accept applications after the summer. A few firms accept applications into the autumn or even into the following year. Some firms require very early applications from non-law graduates. See pages 22-27 for further information.

*** Some firms may interview earlier or later than these dates.

SOLICITORS TIMETABLE

NON-LAW STUDENTS PENULTIMATE YEAR

October 2000 – February 2001:	Compile information about law firms. Obtain firm brochures. Attend presentations and law fairs on campus.
January – March 2001*:	Apply for open days and vacation schemes.
June – August 2001:	Attend vacation schemes.

NON-LAW STUDENTS FINAL YEAR

October 2001 – February 2002:	Compile information about law firms. Obtain firm brochures. Attend presentations and law fairs on campus. Apply for training contracts to those firms with unusually early closing dates.
November 2001:	Apply for a place on the CPE course.
January – March 2002*:	Apply for open days and vacation schemes.
January – Autumn 2002**:	Apply to law firms for training contracts for 2004.
September – December 2002***:	Attend interviews for training contracts for 2004.

NON-LAW STUDENTS AFTER GRADUATION

June – August 2002:	Attend vacation schemes and interviews for training contracts for 2004. Apply for a place on the LPC if your CPE institution does not guarantee you a place.
September 2002:	Start CPE.
July 2003:	Finish CPE.
September 2003:	Start LPC.
July 2004:	Finish LPC.
September 2004:	Start training contract (first intake).
March 2005:	Start training contract (second intake)
September 2006:	Qualify as a solicitor (first intake).
March 2007:	Qualify as a solicitor (second intake).

the bar system

definition of terms

Brief: document by which a solicitor instructs a barrister in court

Chambers: the offices occupied by a barrister or group of barristers; the collective name for the barristers practising from that set of chambers

Clerk: administrator/manager for barristers who organises diaries, payment of fees etc

Counsel: barrister, or barristers collectively

Junior: a barrister who is not a QC, however senior in age or experience (a 'senior junior')

PACH: Pupillage Applications Clearing House, through which pupillage applications are received

Pupil master/mistress: barrister who supervises the training of a pupil in chambers

Set: set of chambers

Silk: a Queen's Council(QC), so called because s/he is entitled to wear silk robes

Tenant: a barrister who is a member of Chambers

The majority of barristers in England and Wales are in independent practice as tenants of sets of chambers. Essentially, they are self-employed, running individual practices within a support network of other barristers, clerked by increasingly commercial and professional managers. The London Bar is the largest, but nationally the six court circuits are served by chambers throughout the country.

Members of the 'employed bar' work in industry and finance and for a range of government bodies from the Crown Prosecution Service to the armed forces. For further information on the employed bar refer to the 'Options' section.

Each set of chambers will have its own reputation and specialist practice areas. The following sections of the book expand on just some of these practice areas. When applying to chambers through PACH or to sets that take direct applications, it is essential to select those that specialise in the practice area to which you

are best suited. Consider carefully whether you have an interest and an aptitude for their practice area before applying to a niche set. The choice of pupillage is one of the most significant career decisions you will make – so get it right. Have you always pictured yourself in court defending the defenceless from a criminal charge or are you intent on making money and a name for yourself as a commercial counsel?

Mini pupillages are a great way of gauging which sort of practice you are most in tune with and the opportunity to work for one or more sets for a few weeks can really make a difference. It will ensure that you move forward to the next stage of training with your eyes wide open and a feeling of greater confidence in what can, at first, be an unfamiliar world. Per Laleng of 42 Castle Street in Liverpool told us that "the deep division between the theory and practice isn't emphasised enough at university or bar school. You're really ignorant in the early stages of training and you start to pick up the secret language and understand things during pupillage. Students could help themselves by going out and gaining experience doing mini-pupillages. Try to decide quite early which area to specialise in and make sure you really want to do it."

So what do barristers actually do? Their role is twofold; as advisor and advocate. Solicitors have always turned to barristers for second opinions on complex issues, such as whether or not a scheme or contract clause is lawful or valid or whether or not their client has a viable claim against another party. This advisory capacity seems set to continue unhindered by the changes that are now affecting the profession. The other role of the barrister is that of advocate. Solicitors enlist the services of proficient and practised court performers, who know the judges, know how to present a case and how to maximise the chances of victory in court.

Is there still a need for two branches of the profession and are solicitors really a threat to the Bar? The Bar is staring at two very significant issues at the moment, each posing at the least a challenge to the profession and at worst a threat to the livelihood of individual barristers. First, the increase in solicitor advocates who can take a case through from start to finish without recourse to the Bar. The Access to Justice Act 1999 contains the latest in a series of measures which have had the effect of removing the exclusivity of the Bar's rights of audience in most courts. Then consider the impact on court procedure and case management brought about by the Woolf reforms. The overriding theme of the changes to civil litigation procedures is the requirement to keep costs to a reasonable minimum and to use all means to avoid trial. Solicitors now think twice about instructing counsel for advice, and may completely avoid using them for advocacy.

Barristers remain specialists, however, and solicitors will continue to seek their assistance whilst the two branches of the profession remain distinct entities. It's a long, tough and winding road to make it through the first few years of practice. The journey is an expensive and often precarious one, but once there the financial and professional rewards have the potential to be huge. If you have strength of character and a tenacious, independent nature; if you can marshall your thoughts and present concise and clear advice with confidence; if you can hold the attention of all and be persuasive in your argument then this may be the career for you.

the inns of court

The bar of England and Wales is comprised of four Inns of Court: – Inner Temple, Middle Temple, Lincoln's Inn and Gray's Inn. Physically they are Oxbridge-like oases of gardens, squares, staircases and chapels around the Royal Courts of Justice in London. Historically all barristers would have lived and worked within one or other of these Inns. Only the Inns have the power to make new barristers. Students who successfully complete the Bar Vocational Course are 'called to the Bar' by them.

In order to qualify as a barrister you must join an Inn before the end of June in the year that you start your BVC. Choice of Inn is completely personal and does not dictate the subsequent choice of chambers. Most people choose their Inns for practical or social reasons. All provide broadly the same services: a library, lunching and dining facilities, a collegiate support network, common rooms, training and social activities. They also provide the opportunity to network with qualified barristers in your chosen area of practice. However, for many students the first role of the Inn is as a funding body for the BVC.

"At the time," one new tenant told us, " I based my decision as to the choice of Inn solely on the likelihood of getting an award. But now I wish I had taken other factors such as the quality of their advocacy training into account. Some Inns are definitely better than others for training."

dining

One of the peculiarities of qualifying as a barrister is the requirement to dine in hall at your Inn. Dining is divided between education dinners (includes lectures and talks), domus dinners (when students and seniors dine together) and social dinners (such as Grand Night or nights when students may bring guests). Most students are at best ambivalent about the whole question of dining, feeling it is an old-fashioned and daunting process. Daunting because part of the process is for barristers to pick on new faces and challenge them to make a speech or raise a toast for example. However, it does give students a chance to meet and talk with other prospective pupils and with the barristers and judges themselves. It is also a chance to become acquainted with a number of old traditions and customs of the Inn. One pupil who recently left Bar School advises against caution; "You have to do it, so make the most of it." You won't get very far in your quest to become a barrister if you are put off by a bit of tradition, embarrassment or laddism!

Many pupils and junior tenants feel that there is still an 'ivory tower' feel to the bar and that nepotism is still a factor. As with any profession, you will come across individuals of all types and views. Your choice of set will be the most crucial factor in determining the cultural environment in which you will find yourself. Some sets are more 'pc' than others; some more set in their ways. After speaking with black and Asian barristers we conclude there is no overt culture of racism in the profession. Some women barristers considered gender to be an issue. The most prominent cultural influence is that of educational background. Whilst an Oxbridge degree is not a passport to the Bar, it is of great assistance.

pupillage and tenancy

pupillage structure

This is an apprenticeship in chambers normally of two six month slots called 'sixes.' Adding a third six is increasingly more common, allowing for a second bite at the cherry of tenancy. First and second sixes can be served at two different chambers. Indeed, with the prior consent of the Master of the Bench of their Inn there are several options open to pupils during their second six, such as an EU 'stage' or marshalling with a judge of the High Court or a Circuit Judge for up to six weeks.

However, the harsh fact is that completing pupillage is absolutely no guarantee of tenancy.

Pupils are assigned to a pupilmaster/mistress who they shadow during the first six. Performance assessment is on-going and the pupil becomes introduced to 'real work' via the practice of the master or mistress. As time goes by other members of chambers will seek the pupil's assistance, thus adding to their workload. "You're being assessed the whole time," Claire Weir of Blackstone Chambers told us. "It's a fairly impressive year – you learn so much. However it can be stressful." As you progress through the second six, more opportunities arise to take on cases and earn fees for yourself although this is unlikely to be a significant amount.

applying for pupillage

There are two methods of getting pupillage and most students are likely to use both. Around 70% of chambers are members of PACH, a system which operates rather like UCAS and is monitored by the Bar Council. You will need to obtain a copy of the Chambers Pupillages & Awards Handbook, together with the application form which is on disk. The handbook covers both PACH and non-PACH chambers giving details of the types of work undertaken and very useful statistical information as to the numbers of pupils taken on and the numbers of tenancies granted in recent years. The book will also indicate whether or not an award is paid by the set to the pupil.

Students may apply for 12 PACH chambers plus three reserves. There is no limit to the number of separate applications that can be made to non-PACH chambers. Adhere closely to the handbook's timetables which in past years has been produced in April before the year to which it applies. Applications to PACH have, to date, had a July deadline.

tenancy

This is the final cut. The lucky will be offered a tenancy in chambers. Competition is fierce and performance over the previous year will be crucial. But do not despair if you find yourself without that elusive place. Try to get a third and even a fourth six or look elsewhere, to the employed bar for example or to the public sector. A training at the bar will never be time wasted. It is a highly respected training which will have equipped you with transferable skills, invaluable for other legal careers or careers outside the law.

a final word

Most of you reading this will not become barristers in independent practice. Competition is probably tougher than you imagine. It is a long, stressful and expensive process battling your way to the independent bar. Only the academically strong, the career-driven and the most organised will make it. If you intend to apply to bar school then you must prepare yourself for the struggle ahead. Be smart.

Plan your strategy and arm yourself with the best information that you can. Seek experience widely. Evaluate yourself and understand what it is that you have to offer. Try to strengthen weak areas. Be clear about where you want to go and be focused. Disregard factors over which you have no control, such as nepotism, and find your own strategy to compensate. Only you are responsible for maximising your own individual potential.

chancery

If you don't already know anything about Chancery work then you're missing out on a fascinating area. Take the time to investigate further. You may find that you uncover the place at the bar that is everything you fantasised the law to be. 'Equity' and 'justice' are coins in the everyday currency of the Chancery Division of the High Court, together with hard legal principles and a rigorous examination of facts.

Chancery barristers are a different breed to their common law and commercial peers. Facts are always crucial, but in chancery there is a definite emphasis on the application of the law and its principles. Chancery barristers are sometimes described as 'lawyers' lawyers'- the tools of their trade are legal principles and arguments. The skill in Chancery work is applying these tools to real situations.

Barristers at the premier end of the Chancery bar have a reputation for being quite expensive and maybe a 'cut above.' This is an area in which only the highest quality of advice is viable.

Chancery work comes in two flavours, most often referred to as 'traditional' (trusts, probate, real property, charities, mortgages, partnerships) and 'commercial'(company cases, shareholdings, banking, pensions, financial services, insolvency, media and IP, professional negligence). The division between traditional and commercial Chancery is vanishing in that most sets will now do both types of work.

There are some fine brains at the Chancery bar and it has a reputation for producing highly respected QCs and judges. But don't labour under the illusion that it's all paperwork and lofty academia. Rupert Reed, a tenant at Wilberforce Chambers, told us how real and relevant Chancery work felt. "After six months at the commercial bar, focused largely on dry reinsurance matters, I switched to the Chancery bar to complete my pupillage. There is enormous human interest in contentious probate work and even corporate work, involving shareholder disputes in small companies for example."

You'll have plenty of opportunity to spend time in court developing your advocacy style. You should be aware that the volume of court work tends to be higher in other practice areas. As a junior led by seniors you'll be introduced to the specialist work of your set. You'll probably cut your teeth on County Court landlord and tenant actions, winding up applications and insolvency cases allowing you to hone those courtroom skills. After a few years you may find that you have ended up with a fascinating overseas practice. The offshore tax havens provide plenty of high value work for Chancery barristers.

skills needed

You need to be pretty bright to succeed within the Chancery Bar. More importantly, you must be an excellent communicator. Solicitors will sometimes come to you with extremely complex and puzzling cases. These must be pulled apart and analysed. You must adore research and get a buzz from getting to the crux of often very interesting and intellectual questions. You then need to be able to interpret and communicate these conceptual ideas to your client and feel confident in your findings.

You can tell pretty quickly when someone's right for the Chancery bar, says Brian Green QC at Wilberforce Chambers "it's a spark of inventiveness and imagination" that singles someone out. "It takes more than being persuasive on paper, you need to have life in the way you communicate."

the sets and the big names

Wilberforce Chambers (Edward Nugee QC) is the chancery name to conjure with. Top ranked in both traditional and commercial work, the set has truly crossed the boundary between the two types of work. The result is huge cases dealing with staggering amounts of money, such as the Thyssen-Bornemisza case in Bermuda – the opening argument alone took six months! The set is also top-ranked for pensions and highly ranked for property work, mak-

ing it the overall überset for chancery work.

Other strong traditional chancery sets are **5 Stone Buildings (Henry Harrod**) also strong for pensions, **3 New Square (William Goodhart QC)** and **11 New Square (Sonia Proudman QC)**.

The leading commercial chancery sets are **13 Old Square (Michael Lyndon-Stanford QC**; **Serle Court (Patrick Neill QC)** and **4 Stone Buildings (Philip Heslop QC)**.

Many members of the chancery bar can command such high fees that they are in the million a year club, for example Jules Sher QC who handles both commercial and traditional chancery work.

Gray's Inn Tax Chambers (Milton Grundy) is a *"prestigious set"* with *"top quality and interesting work."* It shares top slot with **Pump Court Tax Chambers (Andrew Thornhill QC)** who lead on *"day-to-day tax work"* The top property set is still **Falcon Chambers (Gaunt Lewison)** – the best keeps on getting better. **9 Old Square (Michael Driscoll QC)** follows behind with a number of top silks and juniors. **Wilberforce** pops up again for property work, has very strong individuals and is both *"relaxed"* and *"efficient."*

commercial

The work handled by the commercial bar will cover a broad range of business disputes and problems, for a variety of industry sectors. A barrister may be asked to advise on the breakdown of a contract between a supplier and its customer or on a dispute between a record company and its artist. There are as many different types of case as there are different types of business relationship. There are more opportunities to get a variety of work at the commercial bar than you might think.

Barristers and whole sets may develop a niche area in work such as shipping, banking or construc-

tion, for example. Increasingly, specialisation is seen as the way forward by some, whilst for others, a more general practice can be maintained in one of the top league of commercial sets. There is certainly an overlap of work between the Chancery bar and the common law bar, but that merely reflects the fact that commercial work is an umbrella term and not a rigidly defined practice area.

Commercial work, in its purest sense, is dealt with by the Commercial Court or one of the County Court Business Courts. However, a large amount of work is also heard by the High Court (both Queen's

Bench and Chancery Divisions) or dealt with by way of arbitration. ADR is an increasingly common way to conclude business disputes and at the same time allow for the possibility of the commercial relationship continuing without full blown litigation.

type of work

Instructions are generally paper – and fact – intensive. They may involve huge sums of money. There may be multiple parties. In a construction case any number of contractors, subcontractors, suppliers or professionals could have contributed to a defect in a building or a delay in its completion. With the increase in globalisation commercial barristers are advising increasingly on cross-border issues. This includes EU/competition, international public and trade law and conflicts of laws.

Do you have business acumen? You'll certainly need it to feel comfortable advising lay clients in conference, such as the reinsurance head of department who comes to you with a highly complex point, or the shipping company that wants your opinion on how an international trade treaty impacts on its liability on a certain dispute.

Prepare yourself for a career which is mainly advisory. You won't be on your feet in court every day like a criminal advocate, for example. However, there is likely to be a steady flow of arbitrations and County Court hearings during the first few years. As one pupil in a leading construction set notes, even drafting pleadings in the early stages of your career can be exciting "when you have a case looming and, as a pupil, it's one of the few times when you are on the cusp of litigation. Although you don't have the fear of having to stand up in court, you know that the stuff you're drafting is going to be used."

skills needed

"It's a fiercely practical area of the law," states Deepak Nambisan, tenant at Fountain Court. "Often it's less about black letter law and more about being a business adviser. You're always trying to gear towards the business solution. You need an eye for detail and to be fully on top of the facts."

As so much of the contact with your clients will be by way of written advice, you need to be a skilled paper advocate. You need to absorb yourself in the world of commerce and have a genuine interest in it. If you become specialised (and many believe that this is essential) the requirement to be steeped in your particular niche is paramount. Some previous industry experience could be the thing that marks you out from the rest of the pack. You will need to prove you have what it takes.

big sets, big names

The leading general commercial sets are **Brick Court Chambers (Christopher Clarke QC)**, **Essex Court Chambers(Gordon Pollock QC)**, **One Essex Court (Anthony Grabiner QC)** and **Fountain Court QC)**. These are the 'magic circle' of the bar, well-established in pole position, unthreatened by other sets and at the head of the game in size and number of areas of recognised expertise.

All the silks at the very top of the list can earn fees sufficient to put them in the Million-a-Year Club. Peter Goldsmith(**Fountain Court**), Anthony Grabiner (**One Essex Court**), Gordon Pollock (**Essex Court**) and Jonathan Sumption (**Brick Court**) are all stellar performers, in great demand and able to command the best work and the most generous fees.

The 'magic circle' sets appear over and over again in the more specialist areas of the commercial bar, such as aviation, banking, insurance etc.

Erskine Chambers dominates overall on the more financial side; banking, company and financial services. **Atkin Chambers** is the one to use for the related areas of construction, IT, arbitration and energy advice.

For media work, there are quite different celebrity sets. Popular superset, **Blackstone Chambers(Baxendale/Flint)** is the one to look out for. It also scores for its sports work.

5 New Square (Rayner James QC)and **8 New Square(Fysh QC)** are other star players in media. The latter is perhaps better known for its leading IP and IT work.

Monckton Chambers (Swift QC) is ahead of the game for EU/Competition work.

You would go to **7 King's Bench Walk (Tomlinson QC)** for cutting edge insurance work and **3-4 South Square (Crystal QC)** for insolvency work.

common law

The body of common law has developed through precedents set in previous cases rather than from statutes. The majority of these cases are dealt with in the Queen's Bench Division (QBD) of the High Court and the County Courts. Most cases turn on tort and contract claims. However the work handled by the common law bar is very broadly based and its edges blur into both chancery and commercial law.

Certain factors have reduced the volume of instructions currently available to junior barristers. Solicitor advocates are definitely on the increase. Coupled with legal aid cutbacks and the growth in ADR and mediation this has cut down the number of available cases. The Woolf reforms have certainly changed the adversarial nature of claims and many preliminary hearings simply no longer take place. One set told us "We're waiting to see the real impact of Woolf but 50% of the smaller end diary work is no longer there." Competition for the sort of work that juniors cut their teeth on is fierce and rumours circulate about brief fees tumbling to uneconomic levels.

type of work

The variety of work at the common law bar is huge. Many sets offer a mix of other types of work such as crime, family or personal injury. This mix forms a significant part of the junior's common law caseload. In the early years, much of the work will involve drafting pleadings and attending hearings. These could be on anything ranging from RTA's and consumer credit debts to criminal hearings at the magistrates court and arbitrations, employment tri-bunals and family cases. The more general the profile of the set, the more general your experience. The opportunities for advocacy are fewer than at a specialist criminal set but greater than with a Chancery or commercial set. Your workload will be a blend of drafting, advice and court work.

skills needed

You'll need to be a quick learner and have a good short term memory for facts and the law. This is particularly true during the initial stages of your tenancy when your practice will probably leap-frog between many different types of case. Perseverance is essential if you are to get to the stage where routine matters become familiar and straightforward and you can begin to specialise in a chosen area. If work really is scarce in the early years you'll have to be impressive to justify your next instruction and part of that boils down to personality and how well you interact with your client. "Clearly we look for someone who's pretty bright," said Practice Director Joanna Poulton at 9 Gough Square, "but personability is the key. You've almost got to have a sixth sense about people. The common law bar needs people who can get on with clients, be prepared to listen but not get taken in."

You'll probably be doing a mixture of written advice and presentation in court. There will be less client contact than in criminal law, but probably more more than in commercial or chancery practice, so you'll need good people skills and an ability to adapt to a range of clients.

big sets, big names

The leading employment sets are **11 King's Bench Walk (Tabachnik/Goudie)**, also sprinting forward in personal injury, and **Blackstone Chambers (Baxendale/Flint).** David Pannick is their leading silk, best known by you no doubt as a columnist for *The Times* weekly law section.

For personal injury, **39 Essex Street (Nigel Plem-** ing QC) fields all the top silks and **3 Serjeants' Inn (Philip Naughton QC)** for clinical negligence.

Choose **1 Brick Court(Richard Rampton QC)** and **5 Raymond Buildings(Patrick Milmo QC)** if you are interested in defamation work. High-profile defamation work is carried out at **4-5 Grays Inn Chambers (Appleby/Ousely)**, the set of recently retired George Carman QC.

criminal

There's certainly plenty of courtroom drama in films and on TV and its pretty hard to avoid reading the odd John Grisham novel. Those fictional criminal advocates are portrayed in an exciting and dynamic environment, but is your perception of the reality anywhere near accurate? In terms of the buzz you can get from the work, the sense of being involved in something of key social importance and utility and the adrenaline levels, then yes, it probably is. When you speak to a criminal barrister, there's a genuine feeling that this is a really challenging and rewarding area of the law. We suspect that you probably already know if you want to be a criminal advocate – its almost a vocation, not a career choice.

On the whole, the criminal bar fears no shortage of work. Whilst that may be a sad indictment of our society, it is encouraging for those in the early stages of a career. Despite talk of an assault on traditional bar work from solicitor advocates and the Crown Prosecution Service there is still plenty of work keeping the junior bar busy. In fact, many juniors would say that, given direct access to clients, they could do without solicitors and their practices would be thriving.

type of work

The first year or so will be a continual round of magistrates' court appearances on minor matters like motoring offences, committals to the Crown Court, sentencing, pleas in mitigation and directions hearings. This, however, is where you'll learn to develop court skills, confidence and client handling techniques. With just a little time you'll progress to trials themselves, initially on smaller crimes such as common assault and the taking of motor vehicles, then graduating to ABH, robbery, indecent assault, and possession of drugs with intent to supply. You may get the opportunity to be a junior working with more senior members of chambers on white collar crime, kidnapping, rape or murder for example.

During your first six in pupillage you'll shadow your pupil master or mistress and see first hand how a criminal advocate operates. The seriousness of the crimes you'll be involved with will be a taste of what is to come in the long term future. It's a time to observe how an experienced barrister interacts with all the other participants in the case; the instructing solicitor, the defendant, the prosecution barrister, the witnesses, the judge and the jury. You'll be of assistance in researching points of law and helping to prepare skeleton arguments. But be prepared for mundane work too – photocopying and running around for other members of chambers. Many chambers will also send you out to court with juniors to give you a more immediate experience of the work you'll be handling following pupillage.

Almost immediately after pupillage you may apply to be included on the CPS List, which will enable you to receive instructions to prosecute as well as defend private clients. There will be opportunities to appear in the Crown Court on sentencing and pre-trial review and gradually you will move towards your own trials in that venue. Some juniors also advise on Criminal Injuries Compensation and do voluntary work for legal advice centres or organisations such as Victim Support, the Free Representation Unit and Justice.

The criminal bar is no different to any other area of the law in that the volume of work available to you (and potential earnings) in the early years depend on the reputation and fortunes of your chambers. Some barristers at less well known sets pointed out the unpredictability of criminal bar work. You may be kept busy for weeks and then suddenly have nothing for days on end. At the leading sets, however, it is not uncommon for you to be in court almost every day and in any set you must be prepared for action at any time and often on no notice.

skills needed

The work of a criminal barrister centres on people. Those who commit crimes, the victims and witnesses of those crimes, the juries that must reach verdicts and the professionals who administer justice. You need to be a good judge of character and to exercise good judgement yourself. You will be in the spotlight and it's important that you enjoy this. You will be responsible for your victories – and for your defeats. As an advocate, your audience includes lay members of the public and you must speak their language and not just that of the other lawyers.

As a junior you will be asked to do unappealing work. You will often be required to travel a great deal with papers you have had little or no time to prepare. You may find that when you get to the trial your witnesses are not there.

One junior tenant related the time her train ticket to a hearing cost more than the brief fee. "You just have to grin and bear it – you need the experience."

It's hard work, so stamina is essential. Instructions will often come to you on short notice so you'll need to be flexible and quick thinking. In court too, you need to think quickly on your feet; you can't just turn round to the judge and ask him for half an hour to figure out how to deal with a witness's response to a question in your cross-examination.

The job requires immense sensitivity at times, especially in cases of child sex abuse and rape. It is vital that you take great care with some witnesses. You also need to be thick skinned in order to deal with often very dislikeable clients or defendants who have committed serious crimes. You don't have to be a hard person but sometimes you have to be tough in court. Tough, yet appealing. Jury skills are vital. A winning smile, a cheeky turn of phrase, a sensitive approach with witnesses are all invaluable. If you're popular with juries and get a good success rate, you will never be short of good work.

Benjamin Squirrel of **2 Tudor Street (Richard Ferguson QC)** has some hard words for those thinking of going to the criminal bar. "The criminal bar is an insecure and fickle profession. Competition is intense. Success does not only depend on ability. It depends upon self-promotion, practical awareness and luck. If you can combine this with genuine skill as an advocate then you should succeed."

big sets, big names

Criminal sets tend to specialise purely in criminal law. There are many superb sets in London. General crime leaders are **2 Bedford Row (William Clegg QC), Doughty Street Chambers(Robertson), 6 King's Bench Walk (Michael Worsley QC), Queen Elizabeth Building(Bevan/Whiteman), 3 Raymond Buildings(Clive Nicholls QC), 18 Red Lion Court(Anthony Arlidge QC)**.

There are many top sets in the regions, but focus tends to be more on individuals.

family

The popular image of family law is of feuding couples and desperately bitter child custody battles. It is certainly a demanding practice area for a barrister, who will only be involved in the most complex or combative cases.

In truth, a large amount of court time in England & Wales is allotted to divorce, separation, adoption, child residence and contact orders, financial provision and domestic violence. Family barristers cut their teeth on simple County Court matters. They then progress over time to more complex matters which might be heard in the Family Division of the High Court. Some practitioners see this area of the law as a market for legal services that won't shrink. People will always end up in messy matrimonial and family situations that need sorting out in court. But in the last ten years or so, there has been an increase in the profile of mediation between parties to attempt to resolve disputes.

At one stage the family bar was worried. It seemed that a wave of mediation and a surge of new solicitor advocates would lead to a sharp downturn in the amount of work available. But work for the bar appears to have continued unabated. One senior barrister told us that "the family law bar definitely has a future because there will always be family disputes and people who want to go to court. There are surprisingly few specialist solicitors. Most don't have the time to take cases all the way to court."

type of work

Typically in pupillage and in the early period of tenancy your caseload will include a lot of private law children work. At first this will be minor appointments, directions hearings and time-tabling. Soon you'll begin to receive more substantive work, including final hearings. The ancillary relief work (financial arrangements between the parties) can be more complex and it takes a little longer to become proficient at it. To do well on the financial side it helps to have a flair for things like pensions and shares and to have a grounding in the basics of trusts and property. After a few years of experience, and having built up a reputation amongst instructing solicitors, a barrister will often specialise, whether in the field of work relating to children, their custody, access and adoption or in matrimonial finance following marriage breakdown. The two specialisms draw on very different skills, but some barristers build up excellent reputations in both.

Whilst conflict is often deeply embedded in a case, the law requires an attempt at resolution through mediation. A tough adversarial approach is generally not appropriate and practitioners need to focus on client contact and genuine discussion. They must bear in mind that at the heart of child cases is the paramount consideration of the child's best interests.

skills needed

Sometimes it can feel as if everyone concerned is in a no win situation, particularly where children are concerned. The talented barrister will sift through the facts of a case and find something worthwhile rather than merely assuming that there is little prospect of any sensible solution. The ability to maintain an even keel when dealing with distressing matters and to remain positive towards clients is essential. A genuine empathy for your lay client and his or her position is a must; no solicitor would wish to instruct a barrister who seems aloof or disinterested in the specifics of the client's case. At the same time, it is not the barrister's role to issue handkerchiefs.

Omar Yaqub, a tenant at specialist family law set One Garden Court Family Law Chambers, feels that you must really know yourself before embarking on a career at the family bar. "Inevitably you'll be affected by the work sometimes, especially on difficult cases such as child abuse. But because you do it every day and the issues are often the same you don't have the time to become over-involved. It's not your job to get emotional; it's to help your client. You're the one who knows the system and it doesn't serve a purpose to get emotional. Sometimes you have to be forceful because clients in the midst of a crisis often lose sight of things, including the welfare of the child."

Perhaps the thing to remember is that in family cases the ruling made or the settlement reached can have a massive impact on each of the human lives touched by it. As a consequence, it is vital that the barrister recognise the appropriate course of action in each case and work with the solicitor in managing the case from an early stage.

big sets, big names

One Kings Bench Walk (Anthony Hacking QC) is known for its children's work but with a significant and growing reputation in matrimonial work it moves to share top ranking in family work with **1 Mitre Court Buildings (Blair)** and **Queen Elizabeth Building (Paul Coleridge QC)**. 1 Mitre Court Buildings remains a leading set which *"delivers across the board service,"* with matrimonial and children expertise and *"good all round ability at all levels."*

Queen Elizabeth Building continues to share top billing in the field owing to its prominence in matrimonial work.

public law

A decision made by a publicly accountable body is subject to question by an affected party. For example, the decision of the Home Office to deny a non-national the right to remain in the country, or the decision of a Local Planning Authority to refuse permission for an out of town supermarket. One of the most recent public law cases concerned the extradition proceedings of General Pinochet to Spain.

The new Human Rights Act is expected to have a marked affect on numerous areas of law. Practitioners predict a increasing amount of work over the next few years dealing with issues thrown up by the act.

Public bodies operate within statutory constraints. Their decisions may be challenged. Have they considered the relevant facts in reaching decisions? Have the officers acted strictly in accordance with the correct procedure? Did the body or officer have the authority to make the decision in the first place? If these questions interest you and you are passionate about principles of justice and the advancement of the law, then read on.

type of work

A public law barrister will receive instructions to act on a case by case basis. Those building up a Local Authority clientele, for example, may find themselves acting for a number of different departments on a range of work, often leaning heavily towards decisions concerning planning, housing or environmental matters and education, health and children.

By far the most common public law matters is the judicial review of an immigration decision. About half of the Crown Office List is comprised of immigration cases. This work is likely to feature prominently in a junior barrister's practice.

Not all public law sets limit themselves to this practice area. Many combine the work with general common law, competition or employment. Others which do not hold themselves out as specialist public law sets carry out judicial review work.

Public Inquiries are raised where an event or series of events is deemed to be of great significance to society as a whole. The Bloody Sunday Inquiry, the BSE Inquiry and the inquiry following the death of Stephen Lawrence are examples of the very different types of issues under scrutiny.

Alex MacQueen, a pupil at local government and planning set 4 Breams Buildings, particularly enjoys the developing nature of public law. With new grounds for judicial review emerging through case law, "there's a lot of room for creative thought." He is also enthusiastic about the variety of clients; "your contact could range from dealings with Customs Officers to Secretaries of State, from Police Constables to the Football Association, from the local City Council to the new National Assemblies."

Pupillage at a public law set will often consist of drafting opinions and shadowing your pupilmaster, with some advocacy in the second six such as applying for urgent injunctions. As applications for judicial review are heard in the High Court, it is not usual for the most junior barristers to provide advocacy in this area, but after a few years you should have a highly interesting practice with a good balance of advice and advocacy.

skills needed

Its all about understanding red tape and wanting to battle through it for your client. You have to really care about the development of the fundamental laws by which we live. But remember that the work doesn't necessarily involve close contact with your lay client. In many cases the client does not attend the hearing in person at all.

You must develop a comprehensive knowledge of administrative and constitutional law and be familiar with the inner workings of central and local government generally. Familiarity with EU and international law is increasingly important.

The courts deal with such a high volume of cases that you need to develop an efficient style of advocacy. This is not an area in which long and dramatic performances are well received. You'll have to learn how to cut to the chase and deliver the pertinent information, draw on the relevant case law or statutory regulations and present your arguments promptly. An inquiring and analytical mind is essential.

big sets, big names

The biggest thing to happen at the public law bar has been the birth of **Matrix Chambers (Blake).** This all-new, famous name human rights set came into being to coincide with the Human Rights Act 1998. The set has already moved almost to the top in human rights issues and is surging ahead for admin and public work, crime and immigration.

We can hardly get away with mentioning **Matrix** and fail to mention the ubiquitous Cherie Booth QC. She has become a strong figurehead for the set.

Doughty Street Chambers(Geoffrey Robertson QC) is still expected to get the top cases in human rights work, combining this with a strong admin and public law and immigration practice. **Blackstone Chambers(P Baxendale QC)** leads in admin and public law as well as commercial. Head of Chambers Presiley Baxendale gained profile from the Scott report into the Matrix-Churchill 'Supergun' affair. David Pannick QC also has a high-profile name. **4-5 Grays Inn Square** remains top for admin and for planning. Distinguished elder statesman Michael Beloff QC is leaving for **Matrix Chambers** in 2001. **4 Breams Buildings (Lockhart-Mummery QC)** leads in planning with further strengths in admin and parliamentary. **Cloisters (Laura Cox QC)** is a niche discrimination set which inevitably holds an advantage in human rights law, having had many dealings with the European Court of Human Rights while fighting race, sex and disability discrimination cases.

Ranked by number of recommended practice areas in Chambers UK 2000 – 2001

NUMBER OF TENANTS	NAME OF SET	HEAD OF CHAMBERS	RANKED SPECIALIST AREAS
57	Brick Court Chambers	Christopher Clarke QC	Admin & Public, Aviation, Banking, Civil Fraud, Commercial, Competition, Environment, Insurance, Media, Sport (10)
65	Essex Court Chambers	Gordon Pollock QC	Arbitration, Aviation, Banking, Commercial, Employment, Energy, Insurance, Media, Shipping (9)
56	Blackstone Chambers	P Baxendale QC/C Flint QC	Admin & Public, Fraud, Commercial, Employment, Financial Services, Human Rights, Immigration, Media, Sport (9)
58	One Essex Court	Lord Grabiner QC	Arbitration, Banking, Fraud, Commercial, Company, Energy, IP, Tax (8)
51	Fountain Court	Anthony Boswood QC	Arbitration, Aviation, Banking, Civil Fraud, Commercial, Energy, Insurance, Professional Negligence (8)
59	Doughty Street Chambers	Geoffrey Robertson QC	Admin & Public, Clinical Negligence, Crime, Human Rights Immigration, Personal Injury, Product Liability (7)
45	Serle Court	Lord Neill of Bladen QC	Civil Fraud, Commercial Chancery, Company, Financial Services, Insolvency, Partnership (6)
30	Matrix Chambers	Nicholas Blake QC	Admin & Public, Crime, Employment, Environment, Human Rights, Immigration (6)
70	Crown Office Chambers	M Spencer QC/C Purchas QC	Clinical Negligence, Construction, Personal Injury, Product Liability, Professional Negligence (5)
35	4 Breams Buildings	Christopher Lockhart-Mummery QC	Admin & Public, Environment, Parliamentary & Public Affairs, Planning, Property Litigation (5)
34	7 King's Bench Walk	Jeremy Cooke QC	Arbitration, Commercial, Energy, Insurance, Shipping (5)
25	2 Harcourt Buildings	Mr Gerard Ryan QC	Admin & Public, Church, Environment, Parliamentary & Public Affairs, Planning (5)
61	Two Garden Court	I. Macdonald QC/ & O.Davies QC	Admin & Public, Crime, Human Rights, Immigration (4)
51	4-5 Gray's Inn Square	E Appleby QC/D Ouseley QC	Admin & Public, Environment, Planning, Sport (4)

NUMBER OF TENANTS	NAME OF SET	HEAD OF CHAMBERS	RANKED SPECIALIST AREAS
45	2 Temple Gardens	Dermod O'Brien QC	Construction, Personal Injury, Product Liability, Professional Negligence (4)
44	39 Essex Street	Nigel Pleming QC	Admin & Public, Construction, Immigration, Personal Injury (4)
39	20 Essex Street	Iain Milligan QC	Arbitration, Banking, Commercial, Shipping (4)
38	3-4 South Square	Michael Crystal QC	Banking, Comm Chancery, Company, Insolvency (4)
37	Wilberforce Chambers	Edward Nugee QC	Comm Chancery, Pensions, Property Lit, Trad Chancery (4)
32	Cloisters	Laura Cox QC	Clinical Negligence, Crime, Employment, Human Rights (4)
24	4 Stone Buildings	Philip Heslop QC	Comm Chancery, Company, Financial Services, Insolvency (4)
24	Erskine Chambers	Robin Potts QC	Banking, Company, Financial Services, Insolvency (4)
17	7 Stone Buildings	Charles Aldous QC	Comm Chancery, Company, Media, Pensions (4)
48	3 Verulam Buildings	C Symons QC/J Jarvis QC	Banking, Civil Fraud, Commercial (3)
43	Old Square Chambers	John Hendy QC	Employment, Environment, Personal Injury (3)
41	2-3 Gray's Inn Square	Anthony Scrivener QC	Admin & Public, Consumer, Planning (3)
40	4 Pump Court	Bruce Mauleverer QC	Construction, Insurance, Professional Negligence (3)
38	3 Raymond Buildings	Clive Nicholls QC	Crime, Fraud, Licensing (3)
37	14 Tooks Court	Michael Mansfield QC	Crime, Human Rights, Immigration (3)
37	4 Essex Court	Nigel Teare QC	Arbitration, Aviation, Shipping (3)
32	11 King's Bench Walk	ETabachnik QC/J Goudie QC	Admin & Public, Employment, Planning (3)
25	13 Old Square	Michael Lyndon-Stanford QC	Comm Chancery, Company Trad Chancery (3)
21	9 Old Square	Michael Driscoll QC	Comm Chancery, Professional Negligence, Property Litigation (3)
20	8 New Square	Michael Fysh QC SC	IT/IP, Media, Fraud (3)

TIMETABLE FOR TRAINING AS A BARRISTER

SECOND YEAR LAW STUDENTS /THIRD YEAR NON-LAW STUDENTS

Autumn Term: Compile information about sets of chambers. Obtain chambers' literature. Attend law fairs on campus. Look into funding possibilities for the conversion course and/or BVC.

Spring Term: Apply for mini-pupillages and other work experience. Apply for the conversion course before February closing date if necessary. Attend law fairs on campus.

Summer Term: Obtain application details for BVC from CACH (Centralised Applications Clearing House). Find out about pupillage application. Attend pupillage fairs.

FINAL YEAR LAW STUDENTS /CPE STUDENTS

Autumn Term: Apply for BVC. Sort out funding if possible. Research the Inns of Court and join one. Make further pupillage enquiries.

Spring and Summer Terms: Attend pupillage fair in London and pick up copy of Chambers Pupillages and Awards Handbook, complete with application disk. Make PACH (Pupillage Applications Clearing House) and non-PACH pupillage applications. Closing date for PACH is in July. Non-PACH chambers all have their own application methods and closing dates.

BVC STUDENTS

Autumn Term: Attend pupillage interviews. In mid-November offers of pupillage are made through PACH. Applicants must accept or reject offers within seven days. The PACH pool system begins in December. Candidates will be informed of any remaining pupillage places.

THE TRUE PICTURE

SALARIES AND PROSPECTS

the true picture – a guide to training with the top 75 firms

methodology

In preparing this section we interviewed trainees at the top 75 firms (the largest by number of partners and assistants) about their training contracts. We asked their firms to provide us with a list of trainees and newly-qualified solicitors. We then chose names at random from these lists. We also used our own sources. Some firms declined to give us lists of their trainees, for reasons which are set out in the relevant firm review. All interviewees were promised complete confidentiality, and no quotes used have been attributed to named individuals.

our findings

There are some points made every year by interviewees at firms of all kinds. Client contact and responsibility vary depending upon where the trainee is working. In property everyone appreciates the experience of handling 40 or so small files single-handed. Many trainees choose to do the seat for this reason alone. Litigation may vary hugely from firm to firm or within the same firm depending on the caseload. You may experience many small cases and progress them through pleadings, disclosure, witness statements and court procedure. Or you may be stuck on documentation for months in a big case.

Long hours are generally a feature of corporate, where they will increase as a transaction comes to closure and climax with the dreaded all-nighters. The bigger the firm, the more likely this is. Outside London deals tend to be smaller and the pace less frenetic. However hours are intense at the nationals and the largest regional firms. In the current busy climate everyone is finding the hours longer.

Most firms surveyed provide the traditional training structure of four six-month seats. The trainee will physically move from department to department. They share a room with a partner or senior assistant for whom they mostly work. Some firms vary the number and length of seats. A number of firms provide radically different training contracts. At Gouldens trainees don't move. They take on work from all areas of the firm and continue to progress that work throughout their training contract rather than handing it over at the end of six months. This is more like the experience of young US lawyers, who have no training contract as such, but are qualified from day one in the office.

Your choice of firms that interest you will be based partly on location, partly on size, partly on practice areas available. Then it's a matter of chemistry. Do you like the place, the people, the atmosphere? We can't do this bit for you. It's down to you to attend law fairs, open days and vacation schemes. Talk to any contacts you have at law firms. Beg to visit, shadow someone, meet a trainee. Go into reception and try to get a feel for things. Phone graduate recruitment and get chatting to them. This is a decision that will affect you for a long time. Make it an educated one.

During our interviews we noticed that different issues affect trainees at different types of firms.

what's new at magic circle firms?

- Salary rises. Newly-qualified salaries have soared this year – and trainees are benefitting.
- An increase in the numbers of paralegals taken on since 1999 means less dross work for trainees. But the mega-value of deals/cases means you won't be on the front line.
- No one stays late just to be seen to be keen. They stay late because there's so much work.

- The chances of getting an overseas seat are high. Start campaigning for the most popular ones as soon as you can.
- A shocking number of trainees do not intend to remain in their magic circle firm for more than a couple of years after qualification. Trainees know their value and may predict that their quality of life after qualification will be abysmal.

what's new at mid-size firms?
- A surge in corporate/private equity work has meant higher salaries, longer hours.
- A wide spread of types of work on offer within the mid-range of firms. If finance doesn't get you excited, you can find a commercial firm which will allow you to skirt around the whole 'City' thing.
- You are much less likely to get an overseas placement.
- Less of a herd mentality than at the biggest firms. Partners know who you are and you're likely to know a majority, if not everyone at the firm. At some firms the trainees can all fit around one table in the pub.
- Technology and media clients are catapulting some understudy firms up the leader board.
- On qualification, some trainees are finding that their firm cannot yet offer jobs in the areas of work that have set pulses racing e.g. IP/IT/ e-commerce, corporate, tax.

what's new at national firms?
- Some firms require trainees to move around the country, some offer opportunities to work in more than one office, at others movement is almost impossible in practice.
- Although the money is improving, salary differentials between the different offices may cause a bit of trainee pouting.
- You don't always get the same menu at each office. Make sure the one you choose to work at does the kind of work you think it does and does it as well as the other branch offices.
- The firm may be as big as the magic circle firms, but (with a few exceptions) deals and clients are not likely to be as blue chip.
- You get the advantages of a more intimate atmosphere in a smaller office with the benefits of a larger network of lawyers across the country. You'll always be able to communicate with someone at the firm who knows the answer to your question – even if they are 150 miles away.

what's new at regional firms?
- At the top regional firms you will find great quality work. They compete with the finest in the City. They often win. Look at the success of Burges Salmon, Wragge & Co, Dickinson Dees etc.
- Many firms prefer to recruit trainees with strong local connections. They suffer badly from the pull of London on qualification.
- Older trainees often appeal to the regional players. Not only do they have deeper roots locally but they sometimes bring first career skills and contacts that help the firm build its niche areas of work.
- Pay is good in Leeds, Birmingham etc. You'll work hard for less money but the cost of living is lower.
- There's a strong general trend towards commercial/corporate work. Many firms have shed private clients/crime/family/PI or are in the process of doing so. The hybrid commercial/ private client training is becoming rarer.

what's new in niche firms?
- If you join a niche practice, experience in other areas of work may be minimal. You may not be able to qualify into another practice area. So be sure this is what you want to do.
- Niche practices are subject to fluctuations in the market. This has become marked at insurance

firms. The consolidation of the insurance market has left some firms feeling the cold as they fall off the companies' panels of solicitors. Some firms have shrunk in size, others merged.

- There are boom salaries and big hours for booming sectors, such as IT/new media.
- These firms are attracted to applicants who can bring something with them – industry experience, good contacts.
- Competition for trainee places can be the fiercest in this part of the profession. For example Wiggin & Co (media and technology), Townleys (sports), Sheridans (music and entertainment).

and finally...

As an applicant you are motivated by two concerns. Finding a firm you want to work for and finding a firm that wants you. We hope the True Picture will help you to find a firm that will meet both criteria. You may be wasting your time applying to firms which are very unlikely to accept you. Look at the statistics in our selection table on page 38.

Look at the number of applications received by each firm and the numbers of contracts available. There are some eyebrow-raising revelations there. Wiggin & Co is a niche media/IT firm acting for leading TV and telecoms companies. It's in Cheltenham, pays London salaries and is anything but traditional, with a full-time dress down policy. A job in a million. Well, almost – it's actually a job in several hundred. At the other end of the scale, on statistics alone, the easiest firm to get a contract with is the biggest magic circle firm Clifford Chance. The odds are just over one in 15.

The statistics reveal an interesting picture – small general practice firms such as Lee Bolton & Lee (1:400) and Boyes Turner (1:550) receive many more applications per place than large City firms Lovells, Klegal and CMS Cameron McKenna (all at 1:19) or Herbert Smith (1:22). This goes to prove that candidates are self-selecting. Most modest students would think they had more of a chance of getting into Boyes Turner than Lovells, but look at the competition!

TOP 75 FIRMS by number of partners and assistant solicitors

RANK	FIRM NAME	CITY	TOTAL TRAINEES	TRUE PICTURE	PAGE REFS A-Z
1	Eversheds	London ‡	224	113	422
2	Clifford Chance	London	327*	97	403
3	Freshfields Bruckhaus Deringer	London	155	118	428
4	Linklaters	London	257	143	456
5	Allen & Overy	London	321*	73	380
6	DLA	London ‡	100	111	419
7	Hammond Suddards Edge	London ‡	94	125	433
8	Slaughter and May	London	142	182	496
9	CMS Cameron McKenna	London ‡	90	101	405
10	Lovells	London	125	147	457
11	Herbert Smith	London	150*	129	436
12	Denton Wilde Sapte	London ‡	127	105	415
13	Beachcroft Wansbroughs	London ‡	66	81	n/a
14	Norton Rose	London	103	160	473
15	Simmons & Simmons	London	148	178	494
16	Ashurst Morris Crisp	London	109	75	381
17	Wragge & Co	Birmingham ‡	42	199	521
18	Pinsent Curtis	Birmingham ‡	66	167	480
19	Addleshaw Booth & Co	Leeds ‡	60	71	379
20	Nabarro Nathanson	London ‡	56	156	471
21	SJ Berwin & Co	London	70	180	387
22	Morgan Cole	Cardiff ‡	36	155	470
23	Masons	London ‡	45	152	463
24	Baker & McKenzie	London	55	77	382
25	Berrymans Lace Mawer	London ‡	31	82	n/a
26	Barlow Lyde & Gilbert	London	34	79	n/a
27	Osborne Clarke OWA	Bristol ‡	45	164	475
28	Berwin Leighton	London	38	84	386
29	Irwin Mitchell	Sheffield ‡	30	138	445
30	Bird & Bird	London	21*	87	390
31	Rowe & Maw	London	42	172	485
32	Taylor Joynson Garrett	London	43	187	501
33	Bevan Ashford	Bristol ‡	40	85	388
34	Clyde & Co	London ‡	37	99	404
35	Mills & Reeve	Cambridge ‡	25	154	468
36	Shoosmiths	Northampton ‡	26	177	492
37	Theodore Goddard	London	33	189	505
38	Garretts	London ‡	52	121	429

* Denotes worldwide figures   ‡ Indicates branches elsewhere in England and Wales. Only head office location listed.

RANK	FIRM NAME	CITY	TOTAL TRAINEES	TRUE PICTURE	A-Z
39	Lawrence Graham	London	30	142	450
40	Burges Salmon	Bristol	31	93	396
41	Macfarlanes	London	37	149	460
42	Stephenson Harwood	London	40	186	499
43	Richards Butler	London	56*	170	484
44	Bond Pearce	Plymouth ‡	31	90	392
45	Field Fisher Waterhouse	London	20	115	425
46	Charles Russell	London ‡	22	95	400
47	Thompsons	London ‡	†	190	n/a
48	Olswang	London	22	162	474
49	Gouldens	London	26	122	431
50	Halliwell Landau	Manchester	16	124	432
51	Dechert	London	24	104	413
52	Blake Lapthorn	Portsmouth ‡	21	89	391
53	Travers Smith Braithwaite	London	36	190	507
54	Davies Arnold Cooper	London ‡	28	103	411
55	Hill Dickinson	Liverpool ‡	17	131	438
56	Weightmans	Liverpool ‡	17	195	515
57	Russell Jones & Walker	London ‡	15	174	487
58	Ince & Co	London	23	136	444
59	Walker Morris	Leeds	20	194	509
60	Browne Jacobson	Nottingham ‡	20	92	n/a
61	Dickinson Dees	Newcastle	22	107	416
62	Reynolds Porter Chamberlain	London	17	168	483
63	D J Freeman	London	25	109	418
64	Holman Fenwick & Willan	London	18	133	441
65	Hugh James Ford Simey	Cardiff ‡	14	134	443
66	Paisner & Co	London	19	165	476
67	Manches	London ‡	20	151	461
68	Argles Stoneham Burstows	Brighton ‡	8	75	n/a
69	Hempsons	London ‡	†	129	n/a
70	Trowers & Hamlins	London ‡	26	192	508
71	Withers	London	21	197	520
72	Shearman & Sterling	London	7	175	n/a
73	Nicholson Graham & Jones	London	20	158	472
74	Kennedys	London ‡	14	140	447
75	Freethcartwright	Nottingham ‡	8-10	116	n/a

* Denotes worldwide figures   † Not currently recruiting

the true picture – top 75 firms

Addleshaw, Booth & Co.

the facts
Location: Birmingham, Bristol, Leeds, London, Manchester, Sheffield, Winchester
UK ranking by size: 19
Total number of trainees: 60
Seats: 6 x 4 months
Alternative seats: Secondments available

Addleshaws don't like people calling them a northern firm. Created in 1997 out of a merger between Addleshaw Sons & Latham of Manchester and Booth & Co of Leeds, the firm has developed a grandeur beyond its northern roots. A couple of years ago it tried to rebrand itself as a City firm. Established City firms may have scoffed, but Addleshaws is now viewed as a heavyweight serving clients nationally with high-quality advice. And its London office is growing in leaps and bounds, garnering respect and causing some concern from competitors.

northern nights
"You could literally lift up the building and plonk it down in the City and you would call it a City firm." This is the message we get from clients too. So how does it resemble a City firm?

City firm means City quality work. And trainees can benefit from this "Once you've shown you can get your head around the work you are given responsibility." City firm also means City hours. It is the corporate department which offers trainees the greatest opportunity to bond with their office furniture. They can expect to work "at extreme capacity" which includes "working very late and at weekends." This was the low point of training for many, but they take a resigned view. "You have to learn to cope with that sort of pressure." Part of the reason for the unsociable hours could well be the working practices of the corporate team. "The culture in corporate is that they don't actually get cranked up until lunchtime." This can prove frustrating for the trainee, "especially if you're there late at night, clearing up the pizza and photocopying."

There is a particularly sad story of a trainee who spent New Years Eve in the London office completing a deal. He then faced the prospect of taking the train all the way back to Leeds before he could celebrate with his friends. As midnight struck he was sitting on the train, alone. On the plus side "people enjoy working hard because they get on together." Which is just as well really. Furthermore, whilst there "is the potential to do London hours" you "might only do this three or four times in a seat."

out of the frying pan
Once out of corporate or when things are not so pressured hours may vary between 9-5:30pm and 9-7pm. Trainees feel that there is a "good quality of work and better responsibility than in London." This feeling stems from being treated "like an employee not a lowly trainee" meaning that "partners throw you in at the deep end." In areas such as insurance litigation, employment and property trainees were given their own files to get on with. "I had my own files for debt collection, harassing people who hadn't paid." Trainees were very happy with this. "In fact you are just about as exposed [to clients] as you can get."

not waving but drowning
But "some of the partners forget what it is like to be a trainee." They may throw you in at the deep end but they won't be understanding when you start to flounder. "Partners are generally very easy-going but a few are irascible." The important point to note here is that these partners "are in the minority." Indeed many

trainees spoke of their ability to go out for drinks and generally socialise with partners. *"There is no doubt that trainees have had problems with supervisors but they have been dealt with subtly."*

only human

"The firm really stressed that it was looking for human beings." A comforting thought. It specifically takes into account non-academic interests and achievements, and is one of the few firms specifically to invite applications from mature students. The firm character is summed up as *"down to earth, realistic with their feet on the ground; not prima donnas."* The thing that made the atmosphere good was the *"variety of characters."* *"They seem to be going for people from other routes and with life experience."* As such they are quite prepared to give training contracts to paralegals. However, sources felt the need to point out that the jump from paralegal to trainee was not automatic. *"It happens sometimes but you need to have worked there for at least three years."*

There is *"quite a mixture of people who have done other things; everyone gels very well."* Though backgrounds vary there is a large number of people from the local area. Perhaps 70% of people in the Manchester office are from the north west.

pond life

"It rains 11 months of the year in Manchester but it has really taken off as a city." This means a busy social life if you want it. *"The place"* for meeting Addleshaws people on a rainy Friday night is the Pitcher and Piano. *"You are guaranteed to see people you know."* The place is *"packed with Addleshaws and Dibbs people."* But never the twain shall meet. Dibbs people think of Addleshaws as *"stuck-up"* (which they strenuously deny) and Addleshaws think the Dibbs people are *"aggressive."* But the rivalry is not too serious – *"it's all a bit tongue in cheek."*

The Leeds social life is *"very good because people get on and...make a big effort."* So many of the trainees live in the same area of Leeds that it is easy for them to meet up. The meeting places of choice are Revolution and Break for the Border.

trans-pennine express

So what is it like working at a post-merger firm? The *"impression is that it has integrated well"* – this view is shared by the whole of the legal marketplace. As well as the popular cross-site socials (*"we go there or they come here, everyone gets a meal, bottle of wine and entry to a club. It's carnage."*) people are encouraged to do a seat inter-office. The firm may not force you but *"they push it a bit more now"* and will *"strongly encour-*

> "You could literally lift up the building and plonk it down in the City and you would call it a City firm."

age you to go." When there is pressure on popular seats you may have to cross those Pennines to get the one you want.

Getting out of the office is a popular pastime at Addleshaws; perhaps five Manchester trainees are away at any one time. Manchester has the pick of the placements giving opportunities at, amongst others, BAE systems, Astra-Zeneca and Airtours. This has caused *"a bit of resentment"* amongst Leeds trainees.

london calling

"Leeds is possibly a little more laid back, Manchester a little more sociable" but *"both are full service offices and both have full service capability."* The still-infant London office does not yet offer a full range of practice areas but the office is *"building up area by area so that it will be fully operational like the other offices."* An interesting by-product of the London office is its positive effect on retention rates. Despite high levels of pay at the firm trainees wanting bigger salaries have tended to seek their fortunes in London. But now the London office is a carrot dangled in front of qualifiers. It pro-

vides an irresistible temptation that effectively *"stops people from leaving the firm."*

Whichever office you are in, you will find yourself immersed in Addleshaws branding. Just like Sainsbury's, the layout is always the same, whatever the location. Identical interiors. Identical atria. Identical furnishings. Identically stunning (click onto their interactive website to see)....

and the winner is...

It's every man and woman for themselves on qualification. Following the general trend, IP and employment are extremely oversubscribed. The competition divides people. *"It affects the atmosphere between trainees – makes it difficult." "You come up against your friends, that's a fact of life."* There is always pressure on commercial litigation where there are *"too few spaces"* on qualification. Corporate is *"generally popular but there are lots of seats since it needs more people."* Bear this in mind if you're interested in corporate work. *"If you want to qualify into corporate there would be no problem."* Do not think that your days of interviews are behind you. If you want to get into trade and regulatory *"it is very popular and you have to be interviewed for it."* In general the future looks rosy for trainees. There are *"invariably"* vacancies.

and finally...

Amongst competitors in Leeds and Manchester lawyers at Addleshaws are known as the *"gentlemen."* Somewhat reserved about their abilities – which are many. Perhaps a little backward in coming forward. Subject to a few niggles most trainees were very happy at Addleshaws and were very positive about its future. Despite the high quality work trainees felt that the firm *"may have City pretensions in how it likes to be perceived but in reality it is a step back from the intensity."*

top recommendations in Chambers UK 2000-2001:

Banking, Competition/Anti-trust, Construction, Employment Law, Family/Matrimonial, Financial Services, General Corporate Finance, Insolvency, Intellectual Property, Litigation (Commercial), Litigation (Property), Pensions, Projects/PFI, Property (Commercial), Tax (Corporate).

Allen & Overy

the facts

Location : London
UK ranking by size: 5
Total number of trainees: 321 (worldwide)
Seats: 4 x 6 months (can shorten to three months)
Alternative seats: 3 secondments, many overseas
Extras: Pro bono, language training

What do you know about A&O? They're in the magic circle, we all know that. But they have to be the most low-profile member. Not too slave-driving, not too brilliant, not too arrogant. One of the less élitist of the five. International, but without high profile mergers. That's all the negatives. What do they have going for them?

out with the old

Slap bang next to St Paul's Cathedral in a sweeping red brick building, Allen & Overy has been in the press recently over the appointment of its new senior partner. To everyone's surprise, including apparently his own, Bill Tudor John was voted out in November 1999. Said our source, *"Bill had been here a long time and was from the old boys club era."* It was time for new blood. Whilst the firm had been *"changing for a long time, this was a watershed."* Their unique (for the City) five day a week dress down policy is an example of this forward-looking approach. More changes are afoot. The A&O building is being redeveloped in a few years time. The firm will have to move out, losing its ultra-cheap rent and bomb-proof basement.

finance finance finance

You really ought to know by now, but if you don't we'll tell you. Allen & Overy is renowned for its banking work above everything else. *"Banking still really is the forte – you will spend a significant proportion of your time in finance."* But corporate is also a key part of its work and the firm fights to be known as something other than just a bunch of banking lawyers – *"Corporate now wants a bit of attention."* Maybe new senior partner Guy Beringer will be the harbinger of a new dawn – he's a top corporate partner himself.

You could spend up to 18 months in finance and/or corporate. What this means is that *"if you're going to be interested in the financial side of the legal profession then it would be a fantastic choice."* On the other hand, *"if you want to qualify into niches"* remember this is not the firm's main focus. Seats in private client are popular. *"Everyone I know goes there and loves it because you get a lot more hands-on experience. And there are opportunities to qualify into the area. A&O is the only magic circle firm, and one of very few City firms, to maintain its private client department.

what's up doc?

Don't expect all the work to be legally challenging. In insolvency and litigation the work is *"not Perry Mason but closer to it than corporate or banking."* Or at least the trainee's part in them is. *"It's not all LA Law and standing up in court."* Finance and banking are all about using precedents, not setting them. *"There are documents to be produced and you do have to check that those docs are correct."* But the real 'dogsbody' work is out of their hands. There's *"no late night photocopying because there is good support."* The work that trainees do is still responsible work. *"In a lot of deals I am the first port of call for the clients and am doing first drafts (of documents) and agreeing changes and stuff like that."*

seat magic

A&O has a couple of devices to ensure your happiness during training. The first trick up their sleeve is the 'priority seat.' This wildcard can be used once

to get the department and trainer you want. So *"you can practically ask as you go along"*? It doesn't always work. *"I got exactly the right department but exactly the wrong person."* Still, *"perhaps only one in 30 would be unhappy."* The other ace in your pack is the ability to cut seats short to three months. *"There's no point in spending another three months somewhere if you're not enjoying it."* When leaving a seat midway through, tact is in order. *"It can be difficult to explain but you get the seat planner to deal with it."*

the human face of the magic circle

One source's claim that *"people rarely have a bad thing to say about A & O"* held true in our interviews this year. Said one trainee apologetically, *"the old cliche that it is friendly does apply here."*

That doesn't mean it's a laugh a minute. *"There is a job to be done and people are going to work hard when they have deadlines to meet. At times when the deadline is further away...people tend to smile and chat more."* Allegedly some partners will lose their temper under pressure. *"They scream their head off when you make a mistake and then get over it. Sometimes you feel a bit hard done by."* At the same time *"partners will pop in and say hello and have a bit of a laugh."* It's not a cut-throat environment. *"They are not aggressive people."*

In a City firm you expect long hours. The truth is that the hours can be bad but are not consistently so. They have a *"fairly balanced attitude towards work."* Like many of the big firms the real issues arise post-qualification. In the transactional departments (e.g. finance and corporate) there was an element of *"disenchantment"* amongst assistants. *"You could regularly have your weekends and evenings shafted."* This engenders disenchantment with the lifestyle.

social whirl

If you relish opportunities to schmooze during your time as a lawyer, Allen & Overy may provide a particularly attractive training. Trainees spoke of the excellent courses they attended, especially 'How to Behave at a Client Do.' Involving role-playing with your colleagues, it teaches you *"body language," "how to look interested"* and *"how to make people feel happy and then move on."* Having honed your social skills you can then proceed to the A&O bar (no, really) to practise your skills on the unsuspecting secretaries who frequent the place. Like a *"hall of residence bar at university"* it's a good place to catch up with people and sells beer at £1.70 a pint. It is *"popular as a place to start off"* your evening. Despite regular theme nights and jazz evenings people don't stick around. An active social committee organises a pretty evenly spread *"mix of drinking nights and things such as go-karting."* For the loners there's a soundproof music room and even a gym.

and finally...

It's more relaxed than the others in the magic circle. But no less successful. For the first time this year its top partners earned over £1m each. But its fee-earners earned much less per head than the other magic circle firms. Perhaps here lies the key to its more relaxed image.

top recommendations in Chambers UK 2000-2001:

Banking, Capital Markets, Corporate Finance, Environmental Law, Fraud: Civil, Insolvency, Partnership, Projects/PFI.

Argles Stoneham & Burstows

the facts
Location: Brighton, Crawley, Croydon, Horsham, Maidstone.
UK ranking by size: 68
Total number of trainees: 8

A welcome entrance to the top 75 firms list for newly merged south east player ASB. This is the product of a tripartite union in November 1999 of mixed commercial/private client firms in the region. The merger is so fresh, and so few trainees have previously been taken on that any trainee interviews would be relatively meaningless. We already have our pencils sharpened and poised for next year.

The variety of work conducted by the firm (which includes corporate, planning, aviation, PI/med neg, employment, insolvency and property) ought to allow for a training that covers a fair few bases. The profile of the merged firm is set to rise. Could be a good bet for applicants looking for broad-based firm in the south east.

top recommendations in Chambers UK 2000-2001:

Insolvency

Ashurst Morris Crisp

the facts
Location: London
UK ranking by size: 16
Total number of trainees: 109 (worldwide)
Seats: 4x6 months
Alternative seats: Singapore, Tokyo, Paris, Brussels, Milan. Secondments e.g. IBM
Extras: Language classes, pro bono

A millennium merger is off the cards. Failed talks with Clifford Chance have been followed by failed merger talks with top five US firm Latham & Watkins. In the run-up to the talks, the powers that be at Ashursts were shifting in their leather seats, musing over how to pump up size and profitability. Despite the non-mergers, fees and profits have soared in the last couple of years. Phoenix-like, the firm opened its wings and caught the updraft of corporate and financial activity, carrying it into the '£100 million a year club.' What's all this got to do with students looking for training contracts, you might ask? It's to do with the ever so subtle changes going on....

size matters

The number of trainees at the firm has almost doubled in the last three years. *"It's definitely a lot larger...it's good in some ways, bad in others. As the intakes grow it's going to be less personal"* one interviewee said, adding *"when I joined there was just one building. We've now got an admin building next door."*

"We were the first big intake" a second year trainee told us.*"It's trying to grow with the market and compete with the big players. It's struggling with the balance of getting the best work and growing and losing personal attributes. There has been lots of dialogue between partners and trainees on an official level. We'll wait and see if they put it into practice... they want to be seen as a more approachable firm than the bigger ones."*

blue bloods

Of those starting their training contracts between Sept 1998 and March 2000, 50-60% graduated from just five universities: Oxford, Cambridge, Bristol, Durham and Exeter. This actually represents a broadening of the horizons. *"Ashursts has historically had a reputation for being a little blue-blooded and...pretty conservative."* One trainee confided, *"some partners at the top – without a doubt – wouldn't understand why you would take trainees from outside Oxbridge."*

But now? *"There's a mix of Oxbridge and some of the new universities."* Actually, looking at the firm's own graduate recruitment statistics, only around 2% come from new universities (as in ex-polys). But the demographic profile is definitely changing. *"A lot of younger partners don't fit entirely comfortably into the old image."* Here you have it.... with the growth of the firm, Ashursts has diluted its blue blood. The trainees of today are recruited by the partners of today.

losing your mind

Ashursts has long had a reputation for its staunchly independent nature. Trainees told us that the sort of applicants that the firm looked for were *"individuals who have their own mind."* What happens if you and the person who's training you don't have a

meeting of minds? We were told that Human Resources has sought and taken note of trainee feedback. *"You write about the good and bad aspects of a principal's performance. A couple of people will not have trainees in the future."*

A number of interviewees this year and last talked about personality clashes. It's more a case of big personalities. *"You can get situations where some of the juniors are trying to emulate the partners and if those partners tend not to be the sort of people you'd get along with it can make it difficult."* This is the exception to the rule. But don't come here for dull and unchallenging colleagues.

open house

Relationships with partners can be warm and not just based around work. They sometimes invite groups to their homes. *"One of the partners had a lunch at his house in the country and invited everyone down."* *"If you make an effort you can go out for a drink with a partner...I don't think hierarchy is a bar to the establishment of good personal relationships."*

> "A trainee getting into Ashursts and saying I don't want to do corporate would quite rightly be laughed out of the building."

Ashursts is *"not an overtly political firm. It allows you to get on with your job and not worry."* The opportunity to mix in the local pub beyond trainee and junior assistant level is definitely there, but it is not uniform. *"The partners in charge of trainees like to be seen to be there. You don't know them well though. You have more contact with the lower ranks. It depends on personality and character. Some are more open and easy."* One source concluded simply *"Most people have very strong characters."*

tax heaven

There are three popular bars *"very, very close."* The *"full and noisy"* Lime Bar has *"not quite worked."* The *"hip and trendy one"* is The Light on Broadgate – *"it's really popular."* On Broadgate Circle is a *"normal pub"* called The Exchange. It sounds as if you'll have time for a few drinks. *"Tax is extremely friendly. You'll always find them in the pub after work."* Yes you did read that right... the tax department is currently the most desirable place to be in Ashursts. It's *"a small, fun and sociable department. Employment used to be the sexy place. Now it's tax. There are seven trainees. There's a growing acceptance that wherever you go you will be a worse lawyer if you don't know the basics of tax."* You heard it here first. Tax lawyers rock!

home and away

Where there's competition for seats, such as overseas placements, there's *"only a little bit of fighting...At the moment we have only six or seven overseas offices and so places are obviously limited."* We were told that on one occasion two seats were created in Paris because two trainees were desperate to go. *"Some people are more swift on their feet and within a week they have trotted down to personnel... obviously someone who does that immediately puts himself in the frame."* The key is to sell yourself if there is competition.

The number of client secondments is increasing at trainee level. Pro bono work on Caribbean death row cases and a scheme with Clerkenwell Legal Advice Centre are popular. *"A lot of people start when they first join. They are quite bright-eyed and bushy-tailed and they think 'wow – that would be a really good thing to do', which it is. But then it's very hard to give it your full commitment when you are working flat out."* Don't let it interfere with fee-earning work because *"it's not encouraged but accepted."*

corporate identity

"Corporate is definitely compulsory." Property isn't. Is this because in the last year the firm has lost a number of property partners? The firm's reputation is for finance work: *"There's a very, very strong emphasis and* recruitment policy on corporate. The bread and butter of the firm is corporate.That's a strong message to take into account."* We were told; *"a trainee getting into Ashursts and saying I don't want to do corporate would quite rightly be laughed out of the building."*

and finally...

"They like to have someone from the right background and with the grades, but the trainees are all extremely down to earth." Will its growth change it? *"It's not a sausage factory, although how long we remain the Ashursts that everyone knows is quite an interesting question. Time will tell."* How can the firm keep up its pace? Its largest competitors are merging successfully at home, in the US and in Europe. *"If you say no to Clifford Chance, there's no one else in England you'll say yes to. Latham & Watkins made perfect business sense."* But where next?

top recommendations in Chambers UK 2000-2001:

Corporate Finance (Equity), Commercial litigation (fewer than 40 litigators)

Baker & McKenzie

the facts

Location: London
UK ranking by size: 24
Total number of trainees: 55
Seats: 4x6 months
Alternative seats: Secondments, overseas offices
Extras: Pro bono

A long time ago the concept of an international law firm was a mere twinkle in the eye of the legal profession. But one precocious law firm, Baker & McKenzie, had a global vision before the term 'global' was coined and a constellation of offices worldwide. Since its inception in Chicago in 1949, the firm has added on office after office around the world. Each is staffed with local lawyers.

In the BakerMac galaxy, the London office is a large and lustrous star. In the UK firm solar system, it shines less brightly than top planets such as Clifford Chance. Huge international firm. Medium UK firm. Its local reputation rests on its IT and telecoms work and contentious work in areas such as IP and employment. It's the firm of choice for applicants wanting an international training, but also wanting to be a fish in a goldfish bowl rather than a tiddler in a well-stocked tank.

once upon a time in a land far far away...

...there was a Baker & McKenzie office. And in another land, and another, and another. In fact 60 offices in 35 countries. Until recently those offices remained far far away. Almost unbelievably trainees didn't get to visit overseas offices. They had to wait until at least two years PQE to get onto the Associate Training Programme (ATP). This allows qualified lawyers to spend 6-18 months in an office in another part of the world. But for the last two years some trainees have had the opportunity to do a three-month secondment overseas. So far, these have been taken in Sydney, Canada, Hong Kong, San Francisco and Frankfurt.

Not everyone wants to go abroad. One contact told us of the relative ease of securing a seat overseas. "I found the selection was done on a meritocratic basis. You send them a memo saying where and why you want to go. Anyone who has wanted to go has gone." Once out there, wherever 'there' may be, "the office culture is not so different. It was relaxed."

mcfirm

Is Baker & McKenzie really the same in 60 different countries? Will the standards, the service, the flavour and the staff be the same world-over? That's the theory. Does it matter to a trainee in London? They certainly talk the talk. "We were on the global thing before anyone else. Never having merged makes us different. In other offices they know the background. They are not alien."

Says another: "You're constantly aware of the ease of getting information from all over the world just from your desktop. This is in the context of an environment which is not culturally different because it's Baker & McKenzie all over the world. You have the global experience from your desktop. It's a constant thing." The desktop global experience is BakerNet, the firm's international network through which lawyers and clients have access to all other offices.

get back to where you once belonged

French, Russian, American, Bajan (that's from Barbados), Tanzanian, Asian, German and trainees of other nationalities have all been employed by the London office. The cultural diversity extends upwards too. This is a truly cosmopolitan firm.

The pattern of retention of newly qualifieds is an interesting one. It is not 100% but they don't tend to leave for rival UK firms. Of the 10 who qualified in September 2000, two have moved to the US, one has gone to Paris and one to Brussels. Of the 10 who qualified in March 2000, one moved back to Germany and one left the law to become a fund manager. "Most of us were headhunted over the last six months" one trainee told us. But none had been tempted by any offers. Of those who stayed on in September, three are going into employment (regrouping after recent high level defections), one into Financial Services and the rest into Dispute Resolution. None has gone to corporate.

habitat

The office is a modern building on Farringdon Road, now looking pretty cool after a major refit. There is "an unwritten policy that partners try and buy art that inspires conversation. You end up with some bizarre pictures by local, and I suspect, struggling artists. It's a cross between Ikea and Habitat with a central atrium." There's no canteen but with Prêt à Manger virtually in the building and £30 a month luncheon vouchers, you won't starve.

what's on your mind?

A compulsory seat in corporate is the only must during the training contract. The contentious requirement can be fulfilled in one of many departments, including the perennially popular employment, IP or EC groups. *"In my intake, only one person didn't get a chosen seat"* one source reported, adding, *"It's easier to get known. You are an individual and not trainee fodder. There's not enough of you to be fodder."* That's not to say that every day is as rewarding as you'd like. Last year we heard that *"In corporate it's the luck of the draw. For the first few weeks I was forever indexing everyone else's due diligence and whilst it would have been useful to do it once, more than once was a waste of resources."* We asked the same question this year and were pleased to hear that the firm has taken on more paralegals in the last 12 months. *"There are four paralegals in corporate and four or five in dispute resolution. Financial services has one."*

> "Cultural diversity? – This is a truly cosmopolitan firm."

Every three months four trainee reps meet with members of the management committee. In the meetings the reps are asked to canvas the views of their peers on various issues. *"In the last one, topics ranged from dress-down to language classes to events out of the office."* The day we interviewed at B&M this year the qualifying trainees had (quite coincidentally) been asked by the powers that be what they would have done differently or wanted to happen differently if they had their time again. *"You are never deprived of an outlet"* our source said.

thank god it's friday

On the subject of dress down, consensus has not been reached, so for now its business dress every day other than Fridays. *"It makes Friday quite special."* On the second Friday of every month a conference room becomes a free staff bar. Other weeks there are more spontaneous gatherings, usually in Brodies, a wine bar almost within the building. *"All levels hang out reasonably informally. You are made to feel you are part of a team and that whatever you contribute is of value."* One trainee remarked that he had just received two joke emails from partners. Shouldn't they be working?

But it's not all fun. *"Corporate has its demands but I never felt this week after week after week....I'm not aware of having to be seen to be keen. I worked all night only once."* Others more or less confirmed this pattern; most leave times pivoted around the 7pm mark.

and finally....

A big firm with a medium sized office and a small trainee population. The trainees at B&M wouldn't trade their lot for anything and, best yet, they really don't seem to have any major grumbles. Baker & McKenzie is not regarded by the legal community as quite as high powered and dripping in status and glitz as the magic circle but (in spite of the fact that B&M's clients do actually include loads of high fashion names) not everyone wants to be seen out wearing the haute couture, do they?

top recommendations in Chambers UK 2000-2001:

Information Technology, Litigation (Commercial)

Barlow Lyde & Gilbert

the facts

Location: London, Hong Kong
UK ranking by size: 26
Total number of trainees: 33
Seats: 4x6 months
Alternative seats: Hong Kong, secondments
Extras: Pro bono

Insurance, reinsurance, personal injury, professional indemnity. Get the connection? Barlow Lyde &

Gilbert has a powerful reputation as one of the leading insurance litigation firms in the UK. It does it in large amounts and exceedingly well. It has now set its sights on enhancing its reputation in non-contentious areas of practice.

the aeroplane test

This year and last year, we noticed that the number of trainees who had either paralegalled or completed a vacation scheme at the firm was unusually high. It certainly appears wise to get work experience there if you are seriously interested. *"It is basically an extended interview…to see if you do fit in. Are you prepared to work? Are you prepared to do it to a high standard, even the sort of jobs which may be really boring? Are you sharing commitments with them?"*

Lawyers sometimes use the aeroplane test. No, that doesn't mean they want to see how far you fly when they launch you out of the fifth floor window. It means are you the sort of person they'd enjoy sitting with on a long flight. If the partners at BLG say yes, you're in.

So does your face fit, or not? It must be wonderful, of course, if it does. *"One particularly intellectual trainee was told 'your face doesn't fit'"* one source commented. Another confirmed *"mavericks don't do well here."* So somewhere between the maverick and the intellectual lies the perfect trainee. And, yes. They do aviation law as well.

team barlows

So your face doesn't offend. You are happy to conform to BLG norms and adopt its ethos. What does that mean in practice? *"It's pretty friendly here"* one trainee told us. *"There's not too much unhealthy competition."* And here we get to the crux of the matter. BLG operates on a team basis not on an individual level. The negative spin? *"You have to be someone who can put the team in front of themselves. It's all about not rocking boats."* And the positive spin? *"The team is at the heart of it. Every piece of work I do is part of a chain. If I do it well the chain won't break."*

So as a paralegal on a vacation scheme you will be observed. You know how so many law firm application firms cry out for answers relating to being a team player? Here's a firm where it seems to be of particular relevance. This ability to work, and interact well with your team mates extends to your dealings with clients too. At the end of the day, Barlows' insurance clients give a lot of repeat business to the firm and even as a trainee you will need to learn how to build up good working relationships with them. You won't be hidden away in the back room.

litigation

Let's address the main question now. Is this just a litigation firm? *"Automatically you think insurance litigation"* said one interviewee *"but that takes a whole range of different shades."* Most trainees will do three litigation seats. The fourth will be non-contentious. This could be corporate, property, employment or commercial. *"Some people can get two non-contentious seats but you'd have to lobby. And it's difficult."*

BLG literature now plugs its corporate work and certainly not all trainees have come to the firm to get wall-to-wall litigation experience. *"Corporate finance and banking are really expanding…I mean it's taking off very quickly and a lot of NQs come to this division. There's an even split now; people are coming to do the corporate finance and banking as well as the litigation."* But the overriding message is still *"if you do want to be a litigator there's plenty here for you."*

breakdown

Collaborative defence work defines the firm. It *"dictates the ethos"* and *"provides the softness of the firm. The camaraderie is its roots."* So it came as a big shock to this year's qualifiers when collaboration and camaraderie broke down early in 2000. This is a tale of the exception that proved the rule.

Essentially, when the 2nd year trainees were ready to talk post-qualification jobs, the firm evaded the issue. Upset and thinking there were no jobs, many looked outside the firm. Although the situation was ultimately resolved, it has left scars. We talked to second year trainees staying on as well as those who were leaving. Both groups felt equally bruised. *"They didn't look after my year well...in April people started talking to the partners and asking about jobs. The powers that be tried to avoid the issue...a meeting was arranged and the partner didn't show up. We all got a bit peeved."*

Another takes up the story. *"It was handled very badly and I was terribly hurt. I worked very hard over the two years and then there were rumours of no positions... people went out and found other jobs."*

And the outcome? 10 of the 16 are staying with the firm. Two are leaving involuntarily. Four chose not to apply for jobs when the debacle was resolved.

the all-important seat three

It's an environment in which *"most people get on with each other and if they don't they say nasty things in private not in public."* Again and again we were told there's no strong hierarchy. *"No matter what happens at work, as soon as you walk out of the door everybody sort of comes onto a level and everybody goes out for a drink and has a laugh."* The local pub, the Water Poet, is so close that people tend to congregate there quite regularly. Being sociable counts a lot. Never forget that aeroplane test.

A newly-qualified told us *"Whilst you have to make sacrifices, nobody loses sight of the fact that the reason you are working is so you can afford to go out and live your life. A very senior partner came to me in my first couple of days and said that I shouldn't ever, ever stay later than was absolutely necessary. Its not the type of place where you stay back late for appearances. If you can go then go and you will get more respect for it."* This rang true in interviews this year too. Only in crucial seat number three did trainees feel that display was important. There you have to be seen to be keen. There's a bit of jockeying for your preferred seat on the third rotation. When you get it you have to put in slightly longer hours. But this still won't mean burning the midnight oil. An average day in the second year might range between 8.30am and 7pm.

and finally...

"Get under the right partner and you'll get excellent training" said one trainee. We're almost certain he didn't mean anything improper. He added *" You'll have the opportunity to do a wide range of contentious work but it is heavily insurance based. There are some brilliant litigators and some of the best insurance gurus."* This firm wants characters who get into the thick of things with their team mates.

top recommendations in Chambers UK 2000-2001:

Insurance & Reinsurance, Personal Injury (Defendant), Professional Negligence.

Beachcroft Wansbroughs

the facts

Location: Birmingham, Bristol, Leeds London, Manchester, Sheffield, Winchester
UK ranking by size: 13
Total number of trainees: 64
Seats: 4x6 months
Alternative seats: Secondments

We were asked not to interview trainees at the firm this year. In fact, our attempts to give voice to trainees' ideas about their firm in the True Picture have been rebuffed for the last couple of years. This has been the story ever since London firm Beachcroft Stanley merged with the national offices of Wansbroughs Willey Hargrave and Manchester firm Vaudreys. The firm's recruitment page on its website gives relatively little to go on but an information pack is available from the firm.

in good health

Feedback on the firm from clients and other lawyers is good. The merger has 'bedded down' well. Strength in the health sector and insurance was a defining trait of the pre-merger firms, and these areas have gone from strength to strength. This year has seen an increased profile in corporate finance and property work. Traditionally strong areas of practice – professional negligence, PI, clinical negligence and insurance litigation – remain so. The PFI strengths of the firm took a knock with some high profile departures.

and finally...

Before the merger Wansbroughs Willey Hargrave was able to give its trainees excellent litigation work, providing advocacy training at an early stage in both High Court and County Court. There was always heavy interaction between all regional offices. Beachcroft Stanley was a more traditional medium-sized City firm catering to the insurance industry and covering a wide range of practice areas. We'd like to tell you more about Beachcroft Wansbroughs. Maybe next year.

top recommendations in Chambers UK 2000-2001:

Clinical Negligence(Defendant), Healthcare, Insurance & Reinsurance, Personal Injury(Defendant), Professional Negligence.

Berrymans Lace Mawer

the facts

Location: London, Manchester, Liverpool, Birmingham, Southampton
UK ranking by size: 25
Total number of trainees: 31
Seats: 6x4 months

One firm, one key practice area. Insurance, and personal injury acting for defendant insurers. The firm prides itself on being on the panel for 'all the major insurance companies.' As such it would be a bad move for someone to apply to the firm without any desire to be involved in the insurance law field. But from a trainee point of view each office is a separate

entity, to which you are recruited and between which you do not move. This made an holistic view of the firm hard to obtain. As one trainee put it: "*if you join at another office you will probably have a completely different experience.*"

personal injury followed by... personal injury

Be aware that you will probably spend the whole of your first year in the personal injury department in two separate seats. "*You need a strong interest in litigation here*" for obvious reasons. After PI, other options include the other PI (professional indemnity), insurance/reinsurance and construction (for that all-important non-contentious work), clinical negligence, recovery and commercial litigation. There is a small family department in Manchester and a small probate department in Leeds.

> "The firm prides itself on being on the panel for all the major insurance companies."

Will you get the seat you want? It very much depends on the office. In London the process had been "*really frustrating and very haphazard.*" In 2000 it was "*very efficient and everyone got what they wanted.*" This is down to new trainee manager Elizabeth Normand, who has impressed the trainees with her efficiency and organisation. (No, she hasn't paid us, every trainee we spoke to raved about the difference she's made.)

hands on

Expect to deal with a "*great level of responsibility*" right from the start. Trainees are largely positive about the level and quality of work they are given. "*You are given as much responsibility as you want – you* are always a fee earner." Those we spoke to feel "trusted to do things." They are certainly trusted to run case-management conferences by themselves, sometimes against partners on the other side. Certainly "not for the fainthearted" but it is "first class training."

There is "plenty of work to go around" at the firm. Work levels border "the 'just about able to do it' and the 'having too much'." Some partners at the firm "won't take no for an answer" (in the work context, we hasten to add) and "find it hard to accept that you have too much work." Nevertheless, with occasional exceptions, people "work hard all day but leaving at 6:30 is late." All things are relative.

more open than usual

In the Personal Injury department, where London trainees will spend half their time, the offices are open plan with groupings based around particular clients for which fee-earners work. For once no open-door policy. In these groups there are no doors. "I sat opposite the partner, there is no sense of them being locked away." However, despite the fact that the partners are only a desk away and to this extent approachable, "partner supervision is a little bit lacking, since partners tend to be quite busy." The new trainee manager is dealing with this issue. A plus point of open plan offices? "All of the group would go down the pub together" with the partner leading. A sort of 'pied piper'of Berrymans. The other departments in London and the Liverpool, Manchester and Leeds offices stick with the more traditional two person office. Trainees were very positive about Leeds (which has just been refurbished) and Manchester (being refurbished, next to the stylish Kendalls department store). The Liverpool office is described as "messy, full of filing cabinets and with files strewn over the floor."

staying put

'Get used to your location, you are going to stay there' would be the best advice for a prospective trainee. Things are "getting better, more things are being done nationally" but there is still "no movement between offices." In fact the biggest move any trainee in London had heard of was from EC2 to EC3. So unless tube rides set your pulse racing, don't get too excited at the prospect of long distance travel. We get the same feeling up north, with "very few trainees" moving between offices and then only if you "really push for it." In other words you have "very little chance."

The north-south divide is alive and well within Berrymans. The London crew "only saw the northern trainees on one training day" and there are separate summer parties for northern offices (Liverpool and Manchester)and southern offices(Birmingham, Southampton and London). Our sources assumed that "partners are very protective of their trainees" and "don't want to lose them to other offices."

out of hours

We end with the social life, just as every good day in the office should. Like many places, the office in London has a typical "Friday night in the pub round the corner" scene. What really comes across from our interviews is that the social scene knows no hierarchy."There is no solicitor/trainee divide" nor is there a "paralegal/trainee" divide. "Everyone socialises together." In the Leeds and Manchester offices the social life is good with the usual Friday night extravaganza. Not so in the Liverpool office: "there doesn't seem to be one, if any. Every now and again the trainees may go out together for an evening, though this is very rare."

and finally...

You had better make sure of a couple of things before starting. Firstly, that you like the idea of personal injury work. Secondly, that you are happy with the city and office you are working in. Because once there, you are there to stay.

top recommendations in Chambers UK 2000-2001:

Insurance & Reinsurance, Personal Injury (Defendant).

Berwin Leighton

the facts

Location: London
UK ranking by size: 28
Seats: 4x6 months
Total number of trainees: 38
Alternative seats: Brussels, secondments
Extras: Language training

Once upon a time, 30 years ago, a brand new firm was born. Its name was Berwin Leighton. It had two godfathers and their names were Berwin and Leighton. Two years later Berwin and Leighton had a disagreement. Berwin left to start his own new firm, SJ Berwin. This firm was young and energetic and grew and grew until pretty soon it was bigger than the first firm. And more profitable.

choices choices

Berwin Leighton set about quietly bedding down into the property market. Its name has become synonymous with big property deals, planning, property finance and just about every other related activity. This is what it's known for. It's led to some internal tension. Corporate partners are thought to be fed up with the tag that they merely support the firm's property practice. Another industry of significance to Berwin Leighton is media. It doesn't have a 'meejah' image in the same way that Olswang does, but it's known for its great film finance work.

Though there is *"an element of input from you"* when it comes to choosing seats, *"at the same time they'll look at what will enrich you."* That's a generous way of saying that the firm knows best and you'll get what you get. To be fair, when you start you will be asked to identify your ideal and second preference seats. These will most likely be allotted to you during the two years...at some point... probably. There's *"not much say"* in the rest. You *"have to do property."* Obviously. A corporate seat is *"more likely than not."* Even if the general seats are reasonably fixed, the fact that

you can do a finance seat as your corporate seat and a variety of niche areas such as IP/IT and film finance does compensate. There's no seat for which competition is overly robust. We're told that the firm has an excellent retention rate. This year 100%. Slightly less last year. 100% the year before.

grown up attitudes

In some departments you are offered a laptop. Once you've got it there's no need to hand it back again. This sounds like a great bonus, we thought. Spend the morning at home drafting, rather than battling the northern line to the office. So what's the catch? Well, for starters, bunking off from the office and working at home is a non-starter. The earnest young trainees take their jobs so seriously that the laptops have begun to allow the office to intrude into personal time. *"Sometimes your conscience makes you think that it would be good to do some extra work at home."* It starts early....

Last year the firm shook a few things up, including senior management. Changes have been received positively and our sources told us of new initiatives including *"a new client suite, a dining suite and dress down days."* Trainees spoke of an 'optimistic feel' and implied that the image you get from the website (check out the photograph of a trainee clutching a leather-bound law book – apparently the poor lad was really embarrassed) is becoming fast outdated.

the fun house

If you look at the firm's website (always a good idea if you're going to apply) you'll notice the quote *"Just ask yourself – are you having as much fun as you could at Berwin Leighton?"* The Lawyer, 3 April 2000.

We looked up the article to see the results. Oh no, what's this? The line was a sarcastic barb from the columnist Tulkinghorn, king of the legal banana skin. The article referred to the firm's *"happy hour and three quarters"* on Friday nights in local bar, F.O.B. or on The Regalian, a boat moored near the firm's London Bridge offices. *"Free beer... every Friday is a very good idea"* said one philosophical trainee. Apparently *"everyone is there,"* *"there is quite a natural atmosphere"* and *"everyone talks to everyone else."* *"It's good for inter-firm gossip and gives you the chance to talk to the nice looking women who have recently arrived in personnel"* another mused.

Unlike some 'party hard' firms, fun is optional. *"There's not a rigid social life, not all the people would go out too regularly."* Many of Berwin Leighton's young lawyers have more pressing concerns than a few pints on a boat bobbing up and down on the north bank of the Thames. In each year there are a couple of trainees who were *"married with children before they arrived."*

night of the living dead

It's not all dress down days and happy hours. Berwin Leighton is a hard graft environment with *"quite a work ethic."* *"You need to be able to put the hours in"* just as you do at any firm with a corporate client base. One trainee spoke of an experience in the corporate department; *"people were walking round like zombies. They had only had three hours sleep all night each week, including the trainees."* Thankfully our sources perceived no element of compulsion to work late just for the sake of it. *"By 7pm there has to be a reason for you to stay any longer."* Naturally, hours vary from one department to another. Trainees need to be *"flexible"* about their hours.

Those we interviewed noted a leaning towards the privately educated, but not the *"academically snobbish."* Some of the firm's paralegals have been given the opportunity to take up training contracts.

monaco or tescos?

Our sources spoke of *"a collegiate atmosphere"* making the firm feel *"close-knit."* *"The firm is paternal; it looks after its people."* Remember 105 minutes of free booze on a Friday? Some trainees felt valued by partners and treated *"as if they were friends."* But before you get the idea that this is just one big luvved up

firm, others told us that some departments are not given as much respect as others. Property and corporate rule the roost.

The firm intends to enhance its international position. As yet the trainees are still waiting for new opportunities to go overseas. One lucky individual at a time gets to spend six months in the firm's Brussels office. Another way to get time out of the office is to get one of the three-month secondments to a client in Monaco or one to Tescos, two or three days per week. We are assured that shelf stacking is not part of the job.

and finally...

Berwin Leighton is trying to shrug off its very traditional image. As adviser to First Tuesday, it has obtained a fair number of new dot.com clients and leapt into the 21st century. Could be a good idea to climb on board now...

top recommendations in Chambers UK 2000-2001:

Planning

Bevan Ashford

the facts

Location: Bristol, Cardiff, London/Plymouth, Exeter, Tiverton, Taunton
UK ranking by size: 33
Total number of trainees: 40
Seats: 4x6 months
Alternative seats: Secondments
Extras: Pro bono

Bevan Ashford has experienced massive growth, doubling in size in the last five years. For the most part, it's a young-feeling firm with *"energy,"* self belief and ambition. Changes in the NHS (a major client and a major focus of the firm's work) in the 90s saw Bevan Ashford's activities expand and multiply with the NHS as it developed on a commercial as well as a medical level: *"The amount floating round an NHS trust is easily comparable to an average plc"* one trainee pointed out.

the seven pillars of wisdom

The firm has offices in seven different locations. If you think that makes it impossible to get to know everyone in the firm then you'd be absolutely right. Two distinct profit centres operate, the West Country four (Plymouth, Exeter, Taunton and Tiverton) and the golden triangle of Bristol, Cardiff and London. We asked trainees whether staff at the two profit centres interacted on any real level. The answer was a categoric no. From the eastern offices *"there's no connection with the West Country offices apart from a trainee weekend away in Exeter early on in the two years."* From the West Country offices *"you don't feel as a group with Bristol/London/Cardiff."*

"break open the bubbly!"

This doesn't have a negative impact on either grouping, but it is an important thing to bear in mind if you are choosing the firm with the idea that you want a 'Bristol and west' training. That won't happen. The most useful thing to do is to check out the 'true picture' at each office and decide which half of the firm appeals.

shipshape and bristol fashion

The Bristol office is home to the largest trainee population and offers a wide variety of seats from company/commercial, PFI, litigation and employment through to clinical negligence. All trainees will do a clinical negligence seat (acting for the NHS Litigation Authority) and up to a quarter find themselves *"one of the unlucky few who is made to do two."* This is all well and good if it's the sort of work you want to spend a year on but not everyone feels it's the best use of their time.

You will *"rarely work past 6.15pm"* and the sporting and social scene is relatively active. Bristol is big enough and so well-positioned that, whatever your interests, you can build a good lifestyle for yourself. If, on the other hand, you are into Friday night boozing and schmoozing with the legal community, walk right up to the ubiquitous ivy-decked doors of All Bar One. *"You do see partners there and trainees are all there en masse."* Expect plenty of shoptalk. *"It's all lawyers down there. It's outside the barristers chambers and by the court so barristers and other firms go too."*

Break open the bubbly! The loathesome post opening rota, so disliked by trainees, has finally been kicked into touch. *"You can start work at 9am now,"* said one source. We'd like to think the *Chambers Student Guide* was instrumental in lighting the touchpaper of revolution. After all, we brought the plight of these trainees to the attention of the world outside. But apparently the trainees' own collective action secured their liberation from the mountain of manila envelopes. *"We have bi-monthly meetings for which we set the agenda and have a discussion. The post issue was sorted out that way...if you want to ask a question it does get answered."* And about time too, we say.

the welsh and london connections

Three trainees a year are recruited into the Cardiff office. At any one time, at least two out of the total of six will be on transfer either to Bristol or London, with a pair of Bristol's seconded to Cardiff. Work in Cardiff is similar to that in Bristol. *"We do insurance litigation; largely defendant work, RTAs, industrial accidents etc. Company and commercial, commercial property and medical negligence."*

The link with Bristol is pretty tight. Trainees are certainly encouraged to spend a seat there and the two offices' social committees interact well. *"We had a beach BBQ two weeks ago and tomorrow there's a trip to Chepstow Races."* All this socialising helps with Welsh/English relations *"...there was an English trainee a couple of years ago."*

At the time of writing, the London office does not yet recruit its own trainees. It is still too small an operation to take more than one at a time on a six month placement from either Bristol or Cardiff. It is a popular option and the work varies between med neg and employment/commercial. Trainees do feel that it is hard being the only one there sometimes and that there was more admin work to handle, such as closing files, than in the bigger offices.

plymouth ho!

Another office with a tiny trainee population (one per year) is the Plymouth office. This office was the first in the Bevan Ashford empire. It is a commercial office where the partners muck in ("*they're friendly and ready to pitch in…its not just the trainees – everyone opens the post in the morning.*") The sort of person who'd be suited to the office is "*someone with a strong personality because you are here by yourself and you've got to get on with people.*" You also have to have an interest in the West Country as you won't get the chance to move to the big city offices. If your request for another seat is met, it will be in Tiverton, Taunton or Exeter. You get to leave at "*5.30pm on the dot!*"

on your best behaviour

"*Some of the partners are a little traditional*" in the Exeter office. We were told that an Exeter trainee was once sacked for being drunk in public. We were pretty concerned about this. After all, if every trainee in the UK lost their job for abusing alcohol then you could kiss the legal profession goodbye. Obviously there was more to the tale than meets the eye. Whatever the rights or wrongs of the case, the Exeter trainees feel that there are definite expectations as to how they ought to behave and the image they ought to present, even in their own time. "*We have been told that outside work we are still BA lawyers …they expect a certain high standard…one person has been told that he should tone down his [Essex] accent. There's definitely an Exeter office type – someone respectable with a good background from a good uni. Basically an Exeter Uni type.*"

There's a good connection with trainees at other Exeter firms. The local Trainee Solicitors Group is a strong and well supported organisation. They often all meet up in the local bar, nicknamed simply The Braz. There isn't really any informal socialising with the partners although trainees see some of them at the firm's annual West Country Summer Ball.

and finally...

As with any multi-office firm, experiences can differ depending on the office. The West Country offices are probably more traditional, but the firm as a whole is becoming more dynamic. One insightful young lawyer put it in a nutshell. "*There is a difference between the established partners and those who have joined in the last five years. The younger partners are very energetic and want to do a lot more than we are doing now. There still is some baggage. You will see in the profits that some areas don't perform perhaps as well as they should and there are reasons for that, which some of the newer partners are beginning to address. I think the next few years will be quite interesting. In terms of junior partners that trainees work for, they tend to be the forward thinking ones with the get-up-and-go.*"

top recommendations in Chambers UK 2001-2002

Admin & Public Law, Clinical Negligence (Defendant), Employment Law, Healthcare, Local Government, Projects/PFI

Bird & Bird

the facts

Location: London
UK ranking by size: 30
Total number of trainees: 21 (worldwide)
Seats: 4x6 months
Alternative seats: Secondments (e.g. BT), Brussels
Extras: Language training

www.twobirds.com is the address of this firm's website. And two birds is about the number of female trainees at the firm, moaned the boys. Otherwise, complaints are few. Bird & Bird is a 'niche' IT firm. It acts for Amazon, Lastminute.com and many others.

Highly aspirational, it has recently pledged to build a pan-European technology practice.

a bird in the hand...

A training contract here *"gives you a real chance to get involved in the technology industries."* Hardly surprising in the current dot.com frenzy that the firm is extremely popular. Last year it received 2,500 applications for 12 training contracts. The firm has been splashed over the front pages of the legal press after a planned merger with US firm Orrick Herrington & Sutcliffe fell through. How did this affect morale? Interviewees *"couldn't possibly comment."*

big birds

The firm is expanding massively, and has gone up 15 places in our size table since last year. This can create problems. *"There simply aren't enough trainees"* sighed one interviewee. *"They are looking to double the number of trainees this year and then increase the number further next year"* and are also *"looking to recruit more at the recently qualified level."*

"Very busy? – Oh God Yes!" Levels of work vary from department to department, with company the toughest. *"We were working hours equivalent to big firms on and on for weeks."* At the time of our research there was only one trainee in this department, who was working *"a lot harder than others, 8am-9pm every day."* Salaries at the firm have gone up but not to the same extent as those at the biggest City firms. There are advantages to the high workload within the firm. It was having great positive effects on seat availability and standard of work available to trainees.

where to perch

Expansion means more jobs on qualification – the firm has a 100% retention rate. Nevertheless there's a pecking order for seats. As the firm's reputation is mainly in IP and IT *"that is what people apply for."* In IP they are *"very, very keen that trainees have a science background."* You could get there without one but not without a struggle. In sports there's also pressure for jobs. *"Sometimes you get it, sometimes you don't."* Officially you must do a seat in company, litigation and property. However, the view from trainees is that *"property is not always a requirement."* A further thing fledglings noticed was that on the 'company' floor for corporate finance, telecoms and sport there is flexibility in the type of work given to you. *"It's so busy you could get nabbed for anything."*

earning your wings

Trainees are impressed by the standard of work. Partners *"give you files, are very keen to get you involved in things and keen to give you credit for the work you do."* Sources spoke of taking the initiative themselves. *"I had huge responsibility and had a real opportunity to rise to the challenge."* They are not asked to work late *"just to watch over the photocopier. You'd stay if there was something important to do."*

Client contact is equally praised. *"I couldn't have had more, they were always on the phone."* Client care involves fun and games – literally. The banking department took clients to a Varsity match, the IP department has a sports day with clients, there is an annual B&B golf day in which lawyers (including trainees) play clients.

birds of a feather

The massive expansion has not had an adverse affect on the atmosphere. *"The partners don't want it to spiral out of control."* In terms of personalities, they want *"people with their feet on the ground, they don't want anybody off the wall."* Having said that, the sources we spoke to felt that trainees *"all have a little spark, are a little odd."* Not your average flock. *"They all have interests other than just being efficient lawyers."*

At present the flock is not so big that it's impossible to organise a spontaneous night out in the pub, but the trainee brood is increasing in size. There's plenty of organised sports events (usually with booze and food afterwards) and every three months there's 'partners drinks'.

and finally...

Applicants with a scientific or technical background are always going to be of interest to Bird & Bird. There are few opportunities to fly the nest yet. But the overseas offices are becoming increasingly important and a new Brussels seat has been created so watch this space. And you may get the chance of a secondment to BT for three months. *"You get to go home at 5:30pm." "Great experience,"* said one. *"They put you on the spot and it teaches you to blag."* It's good to talk....

top recommendations in Chambers UK 2000-2001:

IT, IP(General and Patent), Internet/e-commerce, Telecommunications.

Blake Lapthorn

the facts

Location: Fareham, Portsmouth(2), Southampton, London
UK ranking by size: 52
Total number of trainees: 21
Seats: 4x6 months (but see below)*
Alternative seats: Brussels, secondments (e.g. ICI)
"This is not a frilly firm. I can't think of anyone pretentious here...nor is the advice we give to clients." This is Blake Lapthorn, the south coast firm which is enhancing its reputation as it grows in size and consolidates into a leading commercial firm outside London and south of the Watford Gap.

a varied diet

If you are looking for a firm that can give you a real variety of work during your training contract, if you want a pleasant work environment on the south coast, then this firm is your biggest and arguably best bet. It hits the legal press on a frequent basis and almost always in a positive way, through references to commercial deals and client wins. The legal world knows and respects Blake Lapthorn. As evidence you need only look at the firms recruiting its newly qualifieds.

The seats on offer range from commercial litigation, matrimonial and child care work, through to white collar crime, environmental and company & commercial (including IP). There's a very popular option to do six months in the commercial property department in London. The partners who run the London office have a good reputation amongst the trainees. The Brussels option is popular too. The firm has an association with a Belgian firm and every so often a trainee gets the chance to work there for three months. There's also hot competition for the secondments to client ICI, in Slough.

*Seats are anything between three and six months long. When you first start you get allotted a seat timetable but it's not hard to change that as you go through your training contract. Usually it is the less popular seats like domestic conveyancing and probate that get shortened to three months.

access all areas

It's *"incredibly friendly"* say sources at the firm. It is easy to *"strike up a conversation with most partners." "The majority of people will have a laugh and a chat"* and you can always ask for advice and help without *"the partner constantly looking at his watch."*

"No one here is spoddy; there's no boffins" and, for a while at least, they're *"not fussed about chasing the limelight in London."* As a trainee you'll see the inside of the County Court and see and speak to a variety of clients from day one. This is a training that has the quality of work offered by a commercial client base and the advantages of client contact and high levels of responsibility often only found in smaller firms.

motorway madness

If you're seriously into motorways, Blake Lapthorn has to be top of your list. Its two main offices at Segensworth and near Port Solent each sit adjacent to the M27. *"It has its advantages"* we were told. *"It's easy to get to work and parking is OK."* Well there's always a silver lining...How many people really yearn to work in an out of town business park? The words 'easy parking' surely translate into 'must drive to work', don't they?' Yes we thought so..."*You have to get in the car to go anywhere though, even at lunchtime. After work people don't tend to go for a beer as everyone is driving and there's nowhere to go.*"

living together, working together, paying back the loan together

A bit like in the TV series 'This Life', most of the trainees live together. It's not mandatory but they tend to do it. The firm has three trainee houses in Portsmouth, which it rents out. "*Most people live in them. In your first year you are allocated. It's a good basis for getting to know people.*"

There is interaction between the firm's different offices. Sporting events are organised, such as football, cricket and softball. As for the Friday night pub thing, a vital part of most trainees' lives, it doesn't seem to happen. There's not one pub or bar that the firm associates itself with. Maybe they just drive home, watch 'This Life' together and compare lifestyles....

Blake Lapthorn offers no sponsorship to future trainees. What it does offer is a loan, as if it was in the same league as small non-commercial firms. Maybe it's time to look at the issue again?

thanks, but no thanks

But Blake Lapthorn has a problem. A big problem. The irresistible gravitational pull of London causes large numbers of its trainees to kiss the firm goodbye when they qualify. The issues are clear. London is bigger and buzzier than Portsmouth (not to mention Fareham). London is where their old mates are and London is where the money is. The trainees who go are those who are younger and have no long-lasting ties to Hampshire. The trainees who stay tend to be older, perhaps with family locally. This year only three out of ten stayed (six were offered jobs in total). "*The firm is scared of the London*

pull and they will address it. They are looking for people who won't run off to London." Another trainee agreed with her colleague's sentiments, adding "*At the moment, the pull to London is extreme. People our age are making career decisions not lifestyle decisions.*" Maybe if you can prove you'd be likely to stay locally after qualification you'd increase your chances of appealing to Blake Lapthorn's recruiters.

and finally...

Nice firm. Nice part of the world. Good work, client contact, responsibility. Training here will set you up for your entire career. It will appeal to many, but may put some off by its lack of benefits. You've got to pay back those loans sometime. And you'll do it faster in a firm that pays more. Or gives you a scholarship for law school. So our advice to Blake Lapthorn...show us the money!

top recommendations in Chambers UK 2000-2001:

Charities, Clinical Negligence, Environmental Law, General Corporate Finance, Insolvency, Licensing & Leisure, Litigation (Commercial), Professional Negligence, Property (Commercial).

Bond Pearce

the facts

Location: Plymouth, Exeter, Bristol, Southampton
UK ranking by size: 44
Total number of trainees: 31
Seats: 6x4 months
Alternative seats: Occasional client secondments (e.g. B&Q)

This is a four office firm breaking out of its traditional stronghold in the West Country as part of a move to become more of a national player than a regional player. It is known for the quality of its work and the quality of its clients. It acts for a number of household names, including Virgin Group, The Post Office and B&Q. In contrast to some other multi-centre practices, "*You feel like you are employed by the firm as a whole and not just the one office.*"

plymouth: bracing sea air

Plymouth takes on large number of trainees each year and whilst some of those will want experience in Bristol or Exeter, others will want to stay put in Plymouth. It offers plenty of choice in terms of seats. From the commercial stalwarts of corporate and property through a range of litigation, including claimant PI, defendant insurance and professional negligence. There's also family and taxation, employment and planning.

The office is right on the sea front so you need plenty of paperweights on your desk if you want the windows open. The office operates the Plymouth way – nobody in town works beyond 6pm. The social committee organises a number of events for the staff, including sports and boat trips, but informal socialising is not a major feature of the normal week. "*The bar people sometimes go to is called Sippers, but it's a bit slack in Plymouth.*"

This office would suit someone who's set on making a career in the area and maybe offers more of a spread of activities than the other Bond Pearce offices, which are primarily commercially driven. "*If you're not fussed on staying in Plymouth you are not going to stay here*" one trainee commented, adding: "*At the end of the day, if you are looking for major commercial stuff then the West Country is not the place. Bristol has been opened up for a reason.*"

exeter

In terms of seats, there's a pecking order at the somewhat "*smaller and claustrophobic*" Exeter office. Claimant personal injury is the least popular; invariably two first years are ascribed to it. More popular is the defendant personal injury work and the professional negligence seat. Commercial property is also disliked. "*We do a lot of Highways Agency bulk compul-*

sory purchase work," which is regarded as less than stimulating. Corporate and financial services are popular as is commercial litigation ("*which includes a bit of employment if you are lucky – in other offices we have pure employment seats.*")

The social scene is fairly active. "*It's definitely a young people Friday scene; a standing arrangement at Chumleys.*" There's also a wine bar in Southernhay, which is where a lot of the law firms are located. "*A couple of partners come along but the more senior partners don't want to get lagered up on a Friday!*" As trainees have pointed out before, "*it's fine if you stay at Bond Pearce but what is there down here?*" The quality of life is fantastic but opportunities in Exeter are limited and on qualification this is brought home to you. If you have a partner who also needs to be employed in the region, there can be limitations. Sometimes the pull of Bristol is too great.

> "The office is right on the sea front so you need plenty of paperweights on your desk if you want the windows open."

bristol: centre of the universe

The Bristol office has only been open for two years and already it has grown considerably. Like the youngest child in a family it receives a lot of attention, both from the big wigs at the firm and from the legal press. It started out as a newly-formed insurance-led outfit and now, having had to take on new space, it has grown in all sorts of areas of commercial practice. The office, which is open plan, is described rather enviously by trainees from other locations as "*like Habitat it's so trendy.*"

Bristol is clearly a core part of Bond Pearce's strategy for growth. No West Country operation could thrive without a Bristol base and its significance to the firm ought to keep increasing. More trainee opportunities will arise in the coming years. The opening of a small Leeds office is in response to the needs of one particular client, Sumitomo, and it is too early to asses whether or not it will have any impact on trainees.

southampton: odd man out?

A prized jewel in the Bond Pearce crown. Two years ago a strong and well-established Southampton practice merged with the firm and instantly gave Bond Pearce a significant south coast presence. Trainees recognised that there were differences between the Southampton office and the others, and that the firm was trying to "*iron those out.*" The office has more of a national client base than those further west and it boasts some big name clients, particularly in retailing. Trainees have had the opportunity to go on secondment to clients like B&Q. In short, it's a purely commercial office which handles work at the larger end of the Bond Pearce scale. On the litigation side, for example, the smaller scale work has been moved west to Plymouth.

The Southampton office is presently split between two sites, although we are told that the firm is looking for a single location. We were also told by one trainee that they had noticed a definite preference for graduates of Southampton University. The overriding Bond Pearce trait of 'quality' is no less prevalent in Southampton than it is in the West Country and added to the quality of service is quality of clients and quality of deals.

and finally...

"*They are looking for people who are very sociable, prepared to build a career in one of their centres*." Trainees in all offices feel that at Bond Pearce "*you are encouraged to progress*." The sense of being drawn into the firm and belonging to it (as a united firm, not four separate operations) was felt strongly by everyone we spoke to. "*There's a culture of involvement ... a culture of 'we're going places'*." When trainees sat down together once, trying to analyse what it was they had in common, (aside from the usual "*outgoing, friendly*" etc, etc) they noted an interest "*in the whole team succeeding*." Of course it's impossible to tell if Bond Pearce only recruits team players or whether its training produces them.

top recommendations in Chambers UK 2000-2001:

Debt Recovery, Education, Employment Law, Energy & Utilities, Environmental Law, Family/Matrimonial, General Corporate Finance, Personal Injury (Claimant), Personal Injury(Defendant), Planning, Professional Negligence.

Browne Jacobson

the facts

Location: Nottingham, London, Birmingham
UK ranking by size: 60
Total number of trainees: 20
Seats: 4x6 months
Alternative seats: Occasional secondments

Midlands based Browne Jacobson is a respected insurance practice. Its main office is in Nottingham and there's a pair of smaller offices in Birmingham and London. It is of the increasingly rare breed that offers trainees the chance to work on both commercial and private client work. It has a strong focus on clinical negligence/PI and health-related claims.

a word in your shell-like

Trainees feel it's advantageous for applicants to have a strong connection to the area. "*It's a definite plus – they want people to stay on after qualification*." The region's universities (Nottingham, Derby) provide good hunting ground for the firm's recruiters. Trainee demographics confirm that the firm has no qualms about recruiting older trainees. It's certainly not all fresh-faced graduates.

One of the first things that occurs to you when you chat with a Browne Jacobson employee is that they like to socialise. Graduate recruitment called the pub next door "*the second office.*" It is actually called The Royal Children but we suspect there's nothing precious about its customers. "*Most people go over for at least one drink to catch up with everyone.*" And 'everyone' is likely to mean everyone, including trainee supervisors. It's where decisions get made, where words are spoken into ears. "*We have a trainees' committee*" one source said. "*They do move issues along bit by bit, but a lot can be gained informally in the pub over a drink. You can have good relationships with the partners.*"

in corporate

The firm no longer has family or crime departments and the PI/clinical negligence work is for defendants only, ie insurance companies. This represents the shift towards commercial work. The táx seat still represents the hybrid nature of the firm's practice. "*It's three months of corporate tax and three months of tax planning and wills for some of our wealthy clients.*" The Public Authority department is another unconventional and popular seat.

There are no compulsory seats but you will probably cover six months in each of company/commercial, litigation and property. It comes as no surprise that corporate work offers the longest hours. These are sometimes much longer than the 8.30am–6pm average day in other seats. In corporate "*you sometimes work at weekends although it's rare.*" There will also be the odd few occasions when you might find yourself in the office at 10pm and very, very rarely far later. That's the nature of corporate work, yet in spite of the hours, it's become the most popular area of practice for trainees. The fact that only two company/commercial jobs were offered to qualifiers in September 2000 meant that Browne Jacobson's normally high retention rate slumped to just three out of eight. Those that left found jobs at good firms in both Nottingham and London.

getting out and about

Historically, however, the firm had its strongest reputation in the contentious sphere, not just in insurance-based work but in other areas of litigation too.

The clinical negligence department is felt by some to show the most cross-office cohesion. So, do trainees get the chance to spend time out of the main Nottingham office? Absolutely. In fact we heard of one trainee who spent three of her four seats in the London office. "*Quite a few people*" sample the different offices. London is certainly not felt to have as strong a social scene as is experienced in Nottingham, but it's still early days. Client secondments have cropped up in the past, but there's no established scheme. One lucky trainee had a placement as an assistant to the judges in the Royal Courts of Justice in Fleet Street.

and finally...

Browne Jacobson is definitely making a play for supremacy in the east Midlands. It has recently established itself in Birmingham and has put down roots in London. For those who want an intimate feel to their work place and want to experience a cross section of work for a varied client base then BJ should be on their shortlist. But the firm does need to address the question of how many of its newly qualifieds can be given their job of choice.

top recommendations in Chambers UK 2000-2001:

Personal Injury(Defendant), Professional Negligence

Burges Salmon

the facts

Location: Bristol
UK ranking by size: 40
Total number of trainees: 31
Seats: 6 x 4 months
Alternative seats: Secondments.
Extras: Pro bono, language training

in the pink

One of the élite Bristol firms. By a shade the largest, it is certainly the longest established. If you want a City-style training but don't want the London experience, then you can hardly do better. As a commercial practice it has been very successful in the last five years. Last year turnover increased by 23%.

on the waterfront

The office (as usual "*client facilities are excellent and the rest is a mixed bag*") occupies a building which is slap bang on Bristol's trendy waterfront, surrounded by bars, art galleries and cinemas. How enticing is that? The city itself is cited as a real draw by interviewees. It enables those who shy away from the engulfing metropolis of London to participate in mainstream commercial activities of London quality, whilst maintaining a more relaxed lifestyle. Sports and socialising are a big thing at the firm. The quality of life of its lawyers comes not only from the fact that they have adequate time for home and extra-firm lives but also because they have fun together. Examples being the 'Wrong Trousers Day,' a 'Blind Date' spoof and, our favourite, 'Twanging Lawyer Philip Davey's Braces'. These fund-raisers illustrate a healthy heartiness present at Burges Salmon (although apparently it's OK to be a bit 'bah-humbug' about them if they aren't your thing). With a working day that's pretty much 9am to 6pm, Burges Salmon trainees are clearly all getting the right amount of sleep and not breathing in too much lead on the way home.

well-oiled

Jolly japes aside, "*it is extremely efficiently run and sometimes comes across as, not exactly machine-like, but efficient and business-like.*" The firm has doubled in size over the last five years. It is changing in other ways too. In the past it had a more conservative and stuffy image than major rival Osborne Clarke. We were told that "*the emphasis was previously on organic growth – not over-reaching ourselves – slightly cautious.*" But the growth "*is bringing a lot of new people to the firm…. younger people, so that is changing the atmosphere and making it more outward-looking and possibly more aggressive.*" Possibly more fun too….

grown ups

Younger in outlook it may be, but the firm also likes applicants who have already proved their worth in some way. An unusually high number of trainees are on their second careers – university lecturers, biochemists, engineers to give examples. The firm shows no desire to take only those who are wet behind the ears and pliable enough to be moulded into a certain fit. From the trainees' point of view it creates a varied atmosphere rather than "*us all being 24 and straight out of law school.*" Some trainees are as old as the partners. An ingenious strategy on the part of the partnership. Older trainees are more useful from earlier on and often come with good contacts. They don't have to learn how to work.

keep talking

Given that many of the trainees bring a strong skills base with them, its good to hear that the firm "*bends over backwards to build the experience around our wishes. There is an intense interaction between ourselves and management in terms of where we are going.*" The 'Between Seats' meetings seemed to fit in with the firm's pink and fluffy self-image. These are opportunities for a good old fashioned "*whinge.*" It means that the firm knows which partners the trainees really do and don't want to sit with. One trainee was keen to tell us "*we had the support of the firm to set up a trainee forum as a kind of formal body to get together to talk about anything. The firm does a lunch and makes rooms available.*"

a cocktail of clients and work

The training contract is taken 'straight up' without a mixer. There are no overseas seats and only occasional ad hoc secondments to clients. A training at Burges Salmon will cover mainstream commercial work, but also includes private client ("*a mix of old money and new money*") and agricultural seats. The firm is very well-known for this work, (hence the stuffy image) and the interesting cases in the department may come as a pleasant surprise to trainees. Certainly on the agricultural side, the work is high profile and you will be doing some cutting edge stuff. They're "*a bit mad*" though.

In terms of responsibility, we got good feedback from those we interviewed. One just laughed at our question. She'd got so much responsibility she probably couldn't have handled more. Client contact varies between departments. "*Certain departments have certain types of clients, which makes it inappropriate for trainees to have contact. For example in Property Litigation with Nationwide...or in some cases it's inappropriate, because of either the wealth or standing of the individual client, for them to be talking to a trainee.*"

and finally...

The retention rate on qualification is usually very high. This year it is total. Need we say more?

top recommendations in Chambers UK 2000-2001:

Agriculture & Bloodstock, Banking, Competition/Anti-trust, Debt Recovery, Employment Law, Environmental Law, Family/Matrimonial, Financial Services, Investment Funds, Litigation (Commercial), Litigation (Property), Partnership, Pensions, Property (Commercial), Tax (Corporate), Trusts & Personal Tax.

Charles Russell

the facts

Location: London, Guildford, Cheltenham.
UK ranking by size: 46
Total number of trainees: 22
Seats: 4x6 months
Alternative seats: Secondments
Extras: Language training

The very name sounds old-fashioned in an era when law firms are abbreviating their names to single words or acronyms. And the firm asks for "balanced, rounded" individuals with "solid" academic results.

Nothing to set the world on fire. But there's more to the firm than its gentlemanly credentials suggest.

changing rooms

Think about that show in which Carol Smillie takes in a bunch of DIY-crazed neighbours and does a makeover on the house next door. Now think Charles Russell. Don't get the connection? The changes have not been quite as dramatic, and we're not sure if there's any MDF in amongst the wood panelling, but the firm is not what it was. If you were a longstanding client using Charles Russell after five years or so, would you recognise the place? Yes and no. Read on...

Charles Russell has a new image. Two centuries (yes, centuries!) of soldiering on as a trad private client firm with a jolly good reputation for charities, family and trusts. But now it's branching out. The 70:30 private client to commercial workload has been turned on its head. The firm is now acting for pop stars, dot.coms and hi-techy clients. What's going on?

split personality

In the last two years or so the firm has built up a healthy appetite for new partners in three areas; private client/family, employment/pensions and media/telecoms. Most City firms ditched their private client practice in the '80s. Private client work just didn't pay. A move which some are already rueing as they watch the likes of Charles Russell growing this work at such a rapid rate. It acquired a 16-strong team from Norton Rose. Last year it pillaged whole family teams from two smaller practices. Charles Russell obviously believes it can succeed where others have chosen not to. It wants to be a modern commercial advisor to the sexiest of industries but it won't let go of its old private client base and "*two hundred years of diligent client service*" and "*traditional values*" (quote – Charles Russell website). Is it possible for both aspects of the work and both parts of the client base to co-exist? It's early days but so far so good.

The appeal of a combined commercial/private client training is a very strong one for many trainees.

They told us that *"there isn't an implication that you should go for commercial or private, they encourage you to take the mix."*

its more difficult than I want it to be

It's OK to be *"a bit shy"* and *"low key."* Insiders say progress comes from being *"personally motivated"* because *"nobody is going to crack the whip."* We interviewed some trainees who felt worried by the amount of responsibility they were given in some departments. Others relished *"not being smothered"* and deciding for themselves whether they wanted to take the next step on a file. We got the impression that you could exist satisfactorily for two years without sticking your head above the parapet. But to be really successful you need to be *"gregarious and able to stand up for yourself."* No surprises there! The brash, competitive hearties who thrive in some firms are probably not quite Charles Russell. There's an absence of the 'work until you drop' culture, but both this year and last we were told that levels of responsibility could be a touch scary.

getting bigger

In the face of merger-mania and world domination, Charles Russell maintains its position as one of the largest 50 firms partly through organic growth and lateral hires and partly because a few of the bigger firms have fused together and left some vacant space in the table. The firm is bucking a lot of trends. The changes it is undergoing are major for the firm, and it has been dubbed *"booming Charles Russell"* in the legal press. At the end of the day it is still relatively old-style and low key in comparison to many firms.

It keeps its provincial (with a capital 'P') offices and has none overseas. It is getting bigger in part off the back of work that many firms have not deigned to touch for years. Yet in spite of all of this, it is attracting some major clients in its target areas. For example it has been advising Cable & Wireless on its purchase of ISPs in Europe.

The metamorphosis of the firm is apparent to the trainees. It is now well past the stage when current trainees would have applied whilst it was still the old family firm, with a member of the Russell dynasty at its head. Does the firm retain its old appeal? It prides itself on the value it places on personal relationships with clients and staff. Trainees still notice the 'people thing' though and sometimes it's just *"small things that make you think that you are more than just on a conveyor belt."*

in the country

Training contracts are available in the main London office, the newly consolidated Guildford office and a long-established Cheltenham location. The latter two are much smaller operations, but at the same time large for the size of firms in those towns. The trainees at the branch offices feel the benefit of links with London in terms of back-up but the work undertaken is not of the same scale. We were told that London back-up is vital to the Guildford office. Without it *"we'd have to burrow around"* for know-how. Indeed Guildford has *"more in common with high street firms."* The Cheltenham and Guildford experiences are clearly not comparable to working in the City. But does everybody want the City experience?

An insurance litigation seat is located in the firm's satellite office in the Lloyd's Building. Arguably the word satellite should be used to describe all three of the smaller offices. There is not, as yet, a great deal of movement between offices in terms of trainee seats. On the subject of satellites, did we say that Charles Russell was highly-rated for telecoms work?

and finally...

It takes on a low number of trainees per partner. In other words there is one trainee for every 3.5 partners. This should mean plenty of quality work to go around. In some cases it means rather more responsibility than individuals feel comfortable with. A recent leap in fees per fee-earner shows that they are working harder than ever, and the firm's early recognition of the IT/communications boom distances them from their old-fashioned image. But conventional wisdom about law firm strategies says that medium London firms should focus on a few key strengths. This is a firm with a truly broadbased practice. We watch with interest to see where it goes next.

top recommendations in Chambers UK 2000-2001:

Family, Trusts [Band 2]

Clifford Chance

the facts

Location: London
UK ranking by size: 2
Total number of trainees: 327
Seats: 4x6 months (can divide into 2x3 months)
Alternative seats: Secondments, many overseas offices
Extras: Pro bono, language training

So it's the biggest law-firm in the world. We all know that. In the magic circle but perhaps near the bottom of the élitism pecking order. More egalitarian. Not as hard to get into. Not as snobby. A big brash show-off, it sits at or near the top in practically all the commercial practice areas. Not yet top-ranked in the all-important corporate finance work, it leads on banking and finance. It is the most expansionist, the boldest, the biggest long-term strategist. It has invested vast amounts in its recent mergers with US firm Rogers & Wells and the German Pünder.

"the needs of the firm come first"

There can be no denying the sheer scale of Clifford Chance. Its building towers over our offices here at Chambers, dark and menacing, absorbing light. We call it Gotham City. Its size seems to overpower individuality. The result? *"You can feel like a small part of a big legal machine."* Insiders *"do joke about it."* So do we. The sense that you are *"a small cog in a big wheel"* can only be augmented by the mantra frequently quoted at trainees from the moment they join 'The Firm': *"the needs of the firm come first!"* So leave your ego at the door.

size matters

But maybe we're getting carried away here. Trainees don't actually feel oppressed by the firm. Its size brings them numerous advantages. The 'corporate personality' of the firm overrides any need to attract a particular type of person. *"There aren't the big egos or stereotypes that you get at other firms."* By now, you will have an idea of which 'other firms' are meant. There is a degree of *"open-mindedness"* about the people taken on. *"There is a lot of Oxbridge but I don't think that is a conscious thing because there are also lots from the usual top end of the red bricks."* So a broader cross-section of life. *"Good students from good unis."* Given the worldwide reach of the firm *"people are very international."* Many are from other jurisdictions. Lots have language skills. *"It adds to the atmosphere making it a very interesting place."* Indeed, with *"people from all different jurisdictions, you have to be open-minded."* This applies even more to clients. Ascend the escalator to the Aldersgate Street reception and you'll instantly hear a babel of languages.

Trainees agreed with our analogy of the employees of Clifford Chance with the population of London. Operating in groups, the firm is *"like a collection of small firms"* in the same way that London is a collection of small villages. Since your *"immediate work environment is your group, all that matters is that your working relations with the people in your department are good."* Everybody needs good neighbours. All in all it is *"unpretentious but serious. People work hard."* After all 'The needs of the firm come first.'

variety pack

One of the great advantages of Clifford Chance has to be the range of areas and quality of deals that the firm can offer. You *"do get to work on very cutting edge transactions"* and *"the reputation and broad variety of work"* is a real draw. But remember that finance is *"a really big part of what the firm does."* Apparently you can escape a finance seat but *"they really like you to do one."* *"Anybody that has accepted a training contract with CC who says they have no intention of being a finance lawyer or at least doing a finance seat in their training contract is probably under some sort of misapprehension."* And since *"the vast majority of jobs on qualification are going to be in the finance practice"* you should look elsewhere if *The Financial Times* leaves you weeping with ennui. As so many seats are finance-oriented, *"many trainees do three seats for six months and then two seats for three months"* in order to broaden their choice. This is because *"for the very small groups there is huge demand that can't be fulfilled"* and there *"are not enough spaces available for litigation."* But *"by and large you will get something approximating the training contract that you want."*

spice up your life

In terms of work and hours, the key word is variety. *"I don't think that you escape admin work but…it's a myth that admin is what you do to the exclusion of everything else."* As at all firms carrying on high profile corporate and finance transactions, *"there are times when there are jobs to be done which means relatively mundane work."* As such the low point for many trainees *"was the sheer drudgery and utter crap work for days on end."* This makes you feel a real *"lack of appreciation of where you are and what you are doing."* At the other end of the scale trainees felt they can be *"given an enormous amount of responsibility"* (especially in the niche areas) which balances out the dross. Perhaps for *"every one hour that you spend proof-reading, you will spend two to three hours at meetings, calling people, doing drafting…."* But this balance may depend on whether your department has paralegals to do the 'dogsbody' work.

"You'll work quite late into the night quite frequently" and *"I would imagine that in some departments it's possibly considered slacking to be the first to leave."* The feeling is that working long hours is random. Some worked hours that were *"really nasty"* whilst others got away with only one all-nighter in two years. And it's not that trainees don't feel appreciated for working hard. *"They'll put in the hours and get the job done and there's a very great sense of teamwork here."*

school's out

With 130 trainees in each year, trying to arrange a night out with everyone is like inviting your entire school year out to the pub. You just don't do it. But the advantages of size are obvious. You are bound to find some people you get on with. *"It's nice being in such a big firm; nice to know so many people. When I worked in a smaller overseas office it was great but it gets boring going to lunch with the same people every day."* Trainees *"fragment"* into little groups of like-minded friends, then head down to the Lord Raglan across the road or to Poets Corner, the pubs of choice. A trainee social committee with *"a pretty large social budget"* takes care of big nights out. Drinking tends to be departmentalised. Some departments are more sociable than others. Some even have their own drinks trolley.

If you get really hot under the collar and you can spare the time, cool off in the firm swimming pool. It is, unsurprisingly, very popular.

hobson's choice

For many trainees one of the key factors is the ability to go on an overseas placement. With 28 offices all over the world the opportunities are certainly there. Of those who want to go abroad trainees *"don't know anyone who hasn't been able to go."* At the same time, be warned they tend to *"put people where their language skills apply."* Obviously they would rather people went of their own accord but if trainees speak a language, especially German, they might find that they are *"placed more on their abilities and the usefulness to the firm than they are on where they want to go."*

all change

By the time you join the firm, it will have uprooted from Aldersgate Street and plonked itself down in

Canary Wharf. The move out of the City is certainly controversial. But for many we spoke to, it seems far into the future. For those of you applying now you might consider aligning yourself along the Jubilee Line. Whilst trainees will not miss waiting ages for a lift to get around the firm and all agree that *"more space is a necessity,"* others are more concerned. *"I hope that we don't feel stuck out there,"* said one. *"I hope they have a big fish tank so that people can look at it and calm themselves down."* Oh dear....

Meanwhile the litigation department is squatting in Simmons & Simmons' new offices, City Point at Moorgate. Let's hope the empire-builders don't take over.

Another 'interesting' development is news of an 'e-meal' system enabling you to order lunch from your desk by email. Our interviewees thought the idea *"very disturbing."* It didn't work at Eversheds because people want to have a quick chat and a change of scene even if only to fetch a takeaway. *"It's an incredibly sad situation if you don't have 10 minutes to get a sandwich."*

and finally....

"It is certainly not a firm that I recommend you work for by accident; it isn't the easiest work. Go in with your eyes wide open and don't be under any illusions. But at the same time get out of it everything that it has to offer." And the firm has a lot to offer trainees. You don't have to have been to the right school or speak with the right accent to work there. But as one of 130 you are unlikely to stand out either.

The firm is *"serious and business-like and also friendly and unpretentious."* Those in charge *"make it clear that they are running a business and that business comes first."* Only the 'co-operative' nature of a partnership prepared to sacrifice this year's profits for the gains of the next 10 years has allowed the firm to become the international trailblazer that it now is. As a Clifford Chance lawyer you won't be a big brightly coloured fish. You'll be part of a shoal. Grey and unimpressive alone, maybe, but unbeatable en masse.

top recommendations in Chambers UK 2000-2001:

Banking, Capital Markets (Derivatives, Securitisation & Repackaging). Commodities (Futures). Corporate Finance (Debt and Equity) Financial Services. Fraud, Information Technology, International Arbitration, Investment Funds. Parliamentary & Public Affairs, Social Housing, Telecommunications, Travel (Hotels & Leisure).

Clyde & Co

the facts

Location: London, Guildford, Cardiff
UK ranking by size: 34
Total number of trainees: 37
Seats: 4x6 months
Alternative seats: Dubai
Extras: Pro bono, language training

Clyde & Co has key strengths in shipping and insurance. The corporate department has been growing in line with its aim to be a medium-sized multi-centre commercial firm. The larger office is in the City and a second is in Guildford. A third office is located in Cardiff, but is not of any real significance at trainee level. Trainees can choose to 'belong' to either of the London or Guildford offices. The work will be the same at each, so it's more of a lifestyle decision. City or leafy – it's up to you. Around two thirds choose lead fumes and the London Underground.

in too deep?

This is a firm with a very particular angle on training. *"Clydes is not afraid of pushing their trainees forward."* *"If you can deal with a difficult client, you can deal with anything – it's a skill which I learned early as a trainee."* You don't share an office with your supervisors but sit on their own in offices variously described as *"beige"* and... well, *"beige."* *"They bust a gut to get as many people into their own offices as possible."* Overall, most trainees preferred being king of their own small castle. In fact it heightens the sense of being *"thrown in at the deep end."*

Trainees are not totally home alone. Each one is assigned a mentor on joining, someone two to three years qualified who can give advice and reassurance for as long as needed. A nice touch from a firm that doesn't appear to treat its trainees like executive stress toys. There's a *"good attitude here"* one source said. *"No slave drivers."* The atmosphere is far from frosty. One source warmed to the firm the first time she stepped through the doors. *"More or less the moment I got in the lift, people said hello and chatted to me. They weren't anything to do with the interview process."*

social scene

Nights out include trips to the dogs and regular Monday night football matches against clients. Throw into the mix a game or two of golf and softball. On Thursday evenings, free drinks in the canteen get people socialising. Drinks in the real world are in The Ship (appropriately enough) in London and RSVP in Guildford.

It's refreshing to come across firms where the subject of hours doesn't cause trainees to pull a face like a bulldog chewing a wasp. *"We usually work from 9am to 6pm or 7pm. Beyond this time it's unnecessary."* *"Sometimes you have to work to a strict timetable, so everyone helps. But it's a rare occasion that you have to work late and hard and in a rush."*

shipping: the mainstay of the firm?

The firm recently acquired a fisherman (with his own boat). Was it the boat that got him the job, we wondered? What about the trainee who used to work in insurance as a placing broker or the medical professional? Skills from a previous life are valued. Not everyone is fresh-faced from university. An application to Clyde & Co from someone on their second career might go down well, especially if that first career has a nautical or insurance flavour to it.

So to what extent is this a firm that's all about shipping and insurance and why is it that shipping seats are unpopular? Our lady with the lift story told us: *"They have no pretensions about what they do and who they are."* She's spot on. Look at the Clyde & Co recruitment pages on the website. The message is clear – be aware of the firm's specialisms and orientation. Look at the page headed 'Our Reputation' and the examples of work that it has handled. Look at the 'Core Areas' page and note the *"distinct flavour"* of the different teams. Note that some teams offer one year seats because the work is so specialised. It's not pure shipping and it's not all insurance but there's a lot of that. *"If you want a particular type of work you should lobby for it"* one trainee said. *"They are keen to stress that there are some trainees that never do shipping or insurance but I don't think that's very strictly true. You are probably going to end up doing one of those two."*

multilingual

As part of your training contract you could have a chance of going to Dubai. Every six months there's two seats available there. This is your only real opportunity as a trainee to work abroad, but what an opportunity. The anecdotal evidence is impressive. One trainee found himself out in the Gulf for a short while in his first seat. *"I was four to five months into the job and they sent me abroad. I was lucky enough to be sent to visit the client and explain the deal to them. They didn't send me with another solicitor, they sent me on my own. The client was based in Kuwait, Bahrain and Oman so I went on a tour of the Middle East."*

Back home in London language skills are seen as a bonus. Translation work might come your way and the firm keeps a logbook detailing which members of staff are fluent in useful languages. But the reality of a Clyde & Co training is that whilst it offers you a ticket to the Gulf (and an apartment and car whilst you're out there), there's not much else, as yet, on the departure board. However, the firm has offices in Caracas, Hong Kong, Paris, Piraeus and Singapore, which are pouring in up to 20% of the firm's turnover, so further openings may appear.

something funny happened on the way to qualification

You have just spent two years training with Clyde & Co. The big day finally arrives. You qualify. You've had great responsibility from the firm and the quality of work has been excellent. So what's the problem? This year around half of September's 13 London qualifiers stayed at the firm. Some found it necessary to leave in order to work in their chosen areas of practice and not everyone was offered a job.

and finally...

The niche shipping firms are all taking different approaches. Clyde & Co is following its Lloyd's clients into corporate deals and is doing very nicely thank you. You must be confident to take up a training contract at the firm. In the main the recruitment process is successful, but some don't take to the proactive, 'in-at-the-deep-end' approach. If you're the type who wants to prove yourself and take early responsibility, and you like the international flavour to the work, sign up now.

top recommendations in Chambers UK 2000-2001:

IT, Insurance, Litigation (Commercial, fewer than 40 litigators) Shipping, Transport [Band 2]

CMS Cameron McKenna

the facts

Location: London, Bristol, Aberdeen
UK ranking by size: 9
Total number of trainees: 90
Seats: 4x6 months
Alternative seats: Secondments, Hong Kong, Brussels, Prague, Warsaw, Budapest, Frankfurt.
Extras: Pro bono, language training

CMS Cameron McKenna has put a girdle of offices around the earth, with a particular emphasis on eastern Europe and the central Asian republics. With firms in Germany, Austria, the Netherlands and Belgium, it is a part of the CMS Alliance, a first step to creation of a pan-European law firm. It orbits the magic circle, while not necessarily aspiring to the same goals. Its reputation is strongest for the sort of work that the magic circle firms see as secondary to their City and financial focus.

since we've been together

Born in 1997 out of a merger between two medium-sized firms, Camerons has excellent projects and energy practices and all-round strength. The merger was a success.

The trainee assessment of the merger: "*It was two firms completely reassessing what they wanted to be. It's now motivated and forward-looking.*" This enthusiastic attitude amongst our interviewees was marked, and impressive. "*We are young and hungry – wanting to be successful and to prove to people that the merger was a good idea, not wanting to sit back on our laurels.*" The atmosphere is not as driven as this may sound. It's "*open and contented.*"

third time lucky

It's not an environment where you can sit back and relax. It's important to be assertive to get the experience you want. "*You can either fill in your form and send it in to personnel and if you don't get [what you want] complain like hell, or you can give the guy a ring and explain why you want to do to a particular seat. Just communicate with somebody.*" Some of the trainees do complain about not getting the seats that they want. You only have yourself to blame if you suffer in silence. "*The fact is that it is a bit of a lottery. When you ask 'Well, what did you do to make sure you got the seats you wanted?' and they haven't done anything, then they really can't complain.*"

"*From my experience, partners here will react to people who show a bit of initiative*" said one source of the race to get the right seat. A number of our interviewees told us that "*your third seat is the most important one in terms of where you are going to qualify,*" and that *"because generally a third seater will qualify into the department that they do their third seat in, a lot of departments want to attract third seaters."* Second or fourth seats are the most common time for an overseas placement of either three or six months. Hong Kong is particularly competitive and Prague also pretty well sought after. Warsaw has its takers, as does Brussels. *"They have remarkable difficulty in getting people to go to all but the most glamorous overseas offices."* One source said *"I don't think they'd send someone to Kazakstan if they don't want to go!"*

popularity contest: london one – aberdeen nil

One of the firm's major clients, Lloyds TSB, set up its HQ out of Bristol about 10 years ago and the Bristol office was opened as a result. It's not full-service but revolves mainly around banking and insurance litigation. There are always two trainees in Bristol, one in banking and one in insurance. There may also be a corporate seat in future. *"Usually people don't want to go"* we were told. However, those that do go will enjoy the benefits of a smaller office and living in a more manageable city. *"In Bristol everyone will go out socialising together. In London that generally doesn't happen."* The office is located close to plenty of bars around the waterside.

The Bristol seats are only marginally more popular than the seats that *"require you to clear off to Aberdeen"* for three months of oil and gas work. Another less popular department is immigration. *"It's obscure. A lot of people come to a law firm to do City work and it's a bit of a standstill seat."* Never mind that the firm's business immigration expertise is second to none, and it's a very high-profile team in the outside world.

show a bit of initiative

We are told that trainees are expected to take the initiative in asking for work. The right attitude will be rewarded. *"If you show a willingness on a one-to-one basis it is acknowledged very quickly."*

The emphasis on secondments is evident.

Trainees will find themselves at clients such as Lloyds TSB, SmithKline Beecham and Airbus. One told us of his time at the BAA Terminal 5 Inquiry. *"I was permanently installed down there as part of the project team. I mean it was bizarre. Going into my training contract, the last thing I would have expected to do would be to sit in the control tower with a headset listening to a controller bringing in aircraft."*

second time arounders

This firm has a real interest in those who can bring skills, contacts and industry knowledge from a previous career into different market sector-oriented practice groups. For example, the projects and construction teams include a number of former engineers. The Healthcare group includes toxicologists, doctors and those who have spent time in pharmaceuticals companies. The tax department includes lawyers who previously trained as accountants. Real world experience doesn't go unnoticed although it is fair to say that most trainees have come straight through from academia.

What type of person is the firm after? Those who are *"normal, healthily ambitious and fairly level headed"* one source observed. Another felt more moved to say *"I do notice that trainees here are very, very driven. They like to make things happen rather than being prompted to do things. You can just tell that by some of the emails that go around...There are trainees who have looked for marketing opportunities themselves and have been successful in bringing in work for the firm."* Does this sound like you?

could it be magic?

There are ups and downs with the hours, but it won't be constantly tough. *"I do know of some firms that don't have an up and down, they are very consistent in that people are there from around 8.30 until late in the evening, and I think that is tied into a macho culture."* CMS trainees are keen to draw a line between their own experiences and their perception of the experiences of friends in magic circle firms.

"When I came here for interview I heard somebody laughing and I had not heard that in any of the other places at all" one trainee told us. "It's a youngish firm in that their attitudes are quite young." The place to wind down on a Friday after work is the (tiny and slightly tatty) pub round the corner called The Hand and Shears. As a trainee you are quite close to your intake but "it fades a little as you qualify" and the focus goes more to your team or department. Some teams manage a high degree of social interaction. In Corporate Recovery, ten people from all levels (including partners) went on a walking weekend recently, staying in a B&B. This is the "friendly and unstuffy" Cameron McKenna that we've been told about year after year.

sexual harassment and discrimination

Some of you may have read reports in the legal press about claims made by six of the firm's employees from the CIS Group. We asked trainees how such news had affected them. "It's fairly far removed – half way round the world. I don't think there was a feeling that because it happened in Moscow it could happen here. The press articles reflected badly on the firm." Apparently a staff review took place not too long afterwards (we don't know if it was connected or just coincidental) and staff were asked if there were instances of harassment in London. The reports we had were that this was not a problem affecting the London office.

and finally...

A firm that doesn't want to stay still, that wants to expand into new areas. It will suit "those with an interest in corporate style work" although the breadth of the practice will allow for more people to slip into noncorporate careers, especially if they bring skills and experience with them. A high proportion of trainees stay on qualification and this may well be because the firm still has a feeling of "we are all in this together rather than orders being barked down." This is a young firm in the sense that it has only been merged for three years. It still feels a need to prove itself.

top recommendations in Chambers UK 2000-2001:

Energy, Health & Safety, Immigration, Product Liability (Defendant), Professional Negligence.

Davies Arnold Cooper

the facts

Location: London, Manchester
UK ranking by size: 54
Total number of trainees: 28
Seats: 4x6 months
Alternative seats: n/a

It must feel for some at DAC as though the firm has gone ten rounds with Mike Tyson. In the mid-90s it was a much broader based firm, which had just opened an office in Manchester. As 1999 approached, it began to examine its activities and strategy. This came at a time when many of the firms that serviced the insurance industry were having to take tough decisions. Many were merging, others tightening their belts. Woolf was biting.

In February the exodus started. A mass of support staff, 19 lawyers from London and another 19 from Manchester were told that they were no longer required. These lawyers included a number of partners, one of whom had been made up just one month before. DAC decided that it would focus on just five areas of business and that it would centre its activities around litigation, insurance and a few other target industries. Drastic surgery. A spate of resignations followed. Competitors and critics had a field day.

bad smells

A year and a half on and the firm has proved itself to be a survivor. Many a firm would have folded. The new 'five pillar' plan was slimmed down to just two pillars of strength: dispute resolution and property/banking. There's a very small corporate department to provide support to the firm's main areas. Trainees applying to the firm should be aware of what the firm does, for which industry sectors it works and what it can offer by way of experience and training. The managing partner at the time of the first partner fallout said: "*We smelled too much like a full service firm.*" It smells nothing like one now.

and finally...

After all of this, it didn't come as a huge surprise to us that DAC weren't keen on participating in the research for The True Picture. Who knows what trainees might have said to us. But that's just the point isn't it? This is the firm that won a 'Britain's Best Employers' award before its surgery. Trainees may well have given us something to counterbalance the horror story. The recruitment pages of the firm's website hint at a softness and flexibility that might still pervade, even after such hard times. Maybe next year we'll be able to find out. For now, it's up to you to ask the tough questions – and do ask them.

top recommendations in Chambers UK 2000-2001:

Personal Injury (Defendant), Product Liability (Defendant) [Band 2]

Dechert

the facts

Location: London
UK ranking by size: 51
Total number of trainees: 24
Seats: 6x4 months
Alternative seats: Secondments, Brussels

Dechert is not your standard run of the mill City outfit. It exudes a calmness that others in its size range don't. It is obviously trying to move up a gear in terms of clients and profits. At a time when many larger law firms are caught up in merger mania, Dechert (né Titmuss Sainer Dechert) has taken its time arranging its formal marriage with US firm Dechert Price and Rhoads, after a six-year engagement. The newly-weds now have ten locations on both sides of the Atlantic and there is a clear policy to lavish attention on their European offspring.

separated at birth

Dechert's funky award-winning website shows a photo of Steven Fogel, senior partner of the firm. He looks spookily like 'Notorious Scientist and Inventor' Professor Heinz Wolff. You may remember him from TV shows such as Young Scientist of the Year and The Great Egg Race. Well, maybe not. He (Fogel not Wolff) is apparently the brain behind the snakes and ladders game on the website. This is aimed at giving prospective lawyers a tongue in cheek view of the ups and downs of becoming a solicitor. During our research we hit upon a number of endearing things about the people and culture of Dechert. It comes across as a place you can be comfortable in. We're not talking cardie and slippers, but if it's true that Fogel's desk contains his prize collection of shells and pebbles, we have a feeling he'd probably let you play with them. Trainees like him. "*He's dynamic – he leads in a refreshing way.*"

Before we got too carried away with hip and happening Dechert, we checked with trainees whether the website gives an accurate image of the firm. The truth? "*We are not amazingly unconventional. It's a nice, light atmosphere though. The website looks like we might be a funky media company but....*" We thought not.

retail therapy

Property is a big department. A fistful of national retailers such as Currys, Sears, Dixons, Tesco, Etam and WH Smith are on Dechert's books. Not the most glamorous but amongst the most well-known. You'll be reminded of work every time you go shopping but you'll also feel a surge of pride every time you go to...well, any high street in the country. Property may be a hefty chunk of its work but the firm covers plenty more besides. Trainees get the chance to sample a range of very different departments. "*Litigation, business law and property there's not a lot of fighting over* because everyone gets to go" but "the niche seats, such as tax and financial services and investigations (white collar crime) are very popular." There's a "new push in finance" at the moment and IP and employment seats are ever-popular. In a six seat rotational system the chances of sampling work that appeals are good.

st bernard

Not every head of training gets the kind of praise lavished on Dechert's ex-College of Law Head of Training, Bernard George. "He's a fantastic guy who has made a world of difference" said trainees. "He sits you down early and asks what you want to do." Nice one Bernard. Maybe his job is made easier by the fact that there's not a single 'type' of trainee at the firm. Not everyone wants to do the same thing at each seat rotation. "There's a real mix" one trainee explained. "We have a serious corporate department. If you are interested in that, then you can do well there – similarly in Financial Services. But not everyone is of that type. The firm has no agenda in looking for trainees."

close to home

For a 10 office firm, the overseas opportunities are limited. There's only one four month seat in Brussels at any one time. It is very popular. "Normally a couple of people want it each time so it's pot luck really." The sort of work on offer there is EC/competition and financial services. "There's talk of a Paris seat and hopefully they will think about a US seat!" Wishful thinking? Sometimes secondments happen for newly qualifieds but there's no formal programme for trainees.

The "tired" offices may be "in need of renovation" but they are in a "fantastic location on Fleet Street near to Leicester Square and Covent Garden." But from what we hear, trainees often don't get further than their local, The Clachan. It could not be more conveniently located, as it's in the same building as the office. "The partners often turn up for one or two in the pub on Friday. They work very hard but after hours they are great" and all "treat you like an equal." Point of order for any partners reading this – you "don't all buy a round!"

choices choices

This last year eight out of ten qualifiers got offered their job of choice and another turned down a job that wasn't quite what they wanted. It's a pretty good retention rate. Apparently "almost everyone wants to stay" at the firm. Now that the formal merger with Dechert Price and Rhoads has been cemented, there's every reason to look at Dechert's London office as a place that will continue to do well at what it already does well (retail, regulatory, tax) and a place where resources will be injected into developing areas (finance, European clients). "All departments are looking for trainees now" we were told.

and finally...

If you want to sample a range of work and you don't want to be backed into any corners on qualification then Dechert is a smart choice. This firm has a past and a bright future since two became one.

top recommendations in Chambers UK 2000-2001:

Customs and Excise

Denton Wilde Sapte

the facts

Location: London, Milton Keynes
UK ranking by size: 12
Total number of trainees: 129
Seats: 4x6 months
Alternative seats: Secondments, many overseas seats
Extras: Language training, pro bono

Leaving behind their history of failed romances, Denton Hall and Wilde Sapte tied the knot last October. Denton Hall had previously been linked with Theodore Goddard and Richards Butler but the firms were not happy with the proposed threesome. Wilde Sapte was practically at the altar when it was jilted by Andersons.

Now the Denton Wilde Sapte honeymoon is over, how's the relationship going?

young love

"I had only been there two weeks when the firm merged. All of the partners were very positive. They said 'it will be good for you.' It was like your parents were moving house." Trainees were also very positive about the effects of the move. "We now have a new bunch of friends to play with" and "a lot more opportunity."

Despite the 'new blood' former Wilde Sapte trainees are a bit disappointed by the standard of Denton Hall "totty." In some parts of the firm the potential for mixing with the new neighbours has been less than in others and much depends on the location and degree of overlap between departments. One former Wilde Sapte trainee admitted that they "haven't met all of the Dentons trainees because they are in the other building." Property, litigation and media are based in the former Denton Hall offices in Chancery Lane. Banking, corporate and energy are in the former Wilde Sapte offices in Fleet Place. In departments which were pretty much exclusive to either firm not much has changed. Since the two firms seem to be "complementing each other really well" the potential for overlap hasn't been huge. Where there has been a true merger of people, such as property, there has been "more scope for friction" and a "few teething troubles." Apart from minor niggles, for example the document exchange systems are not compatible, they "have just got on with it." They have "even merged the football teams."

spot the difference

Did Denton Hall and Wilde Sapte each take on a particular type of person? Certain similarities and differences emerge from our interrogations. Trainees on both sides are "people you can have a laugh and a joke with." "Both groups of people have a pretty warped sense of humour." "We were looking for laid back people and Wilde Sapte had the same approach." Differences may stem from the interviewing styles of each firm. Whereas Wilde Sapte followed the usual City firm procedure

involving a high degree of input by the personnel department, Denton Hall had more of an old school approach. "When I applied to Denton Hall I just chucked a CV in the post." Having got an interview "we talked about everything except the law." Partners appeared to be picking people in their likeness. "Some of the partners at Dentons are quite maverick" and they "picked people that had done other things." "The people I met were mostly partners and they just wanted to know 'do I like you?'" Ex-Wilde Sapte people think there's probably more diversity of background amongst former Denton Hall-ites. Perhaps "50% of people had done other things" before they started. The merged firm is doing the conventional thing and moving towards the Wilde Sapte form of recruitment. Will we see a change?

opportunity knocks

The word on the lips of trainees at Denton Wilde Sapte, whether spontaneously or because of very gentle brainwashing, is 'opportunity.' Wilde Sapte's dowry was its reputation in banking and finance. Denton Hall brought its highly respected media and energy groups to the party as well as a large property practice. The result is a "broad training."

Some ex-Denton Hall trainees feel that Wilde Sapte trainees have done better out of the merger. "We did everything they did and more" said one, not quite accurately. Now that the barriers have come down, it appears likely that there will be scrums for the 'cool stuff.' The media department, in particular, is "really popular," as is the corporate group that's doing a lot of dot.com work.

never-neverland

Located in the "ivory tower" that is the 5th floor of the Chancery Lane office, you will find the media department. There are movie posters on the walls, lawyers playing with plastic bricks and "a few bow tie wearers up there." It is a floor with its own rules and in something of a time warp. "The merger hasn't really affected it." Given the perceived 'coolness' of the area, "most trainees will want to do at least one seat" in media.

The department lives up to its reputation. *"It's exciting and can be glamorous, but it is just contract."* Those we spoke to said they had been to awards ceremonies but corporate tickets to football matches didn't stretch to trainee level. Apart from wearing bow ties to work people in the media department are felt to be *"more socially skilled, have more charisma"* although they *"are slightly batty."* Given the department's popularity, competition for seats on qualification exists. To get that seat, you *"really need to get on with the people and have that extra something."* A bow tie perhaps. However, for all those aspiring legal Peter Pans, a word of warning: *"I must say that it is a sober law firm and we don't just play with toys."*

worlds apart(I)

The firm now has two offices. The finance departments are based in the new, more glamorous City offices in Fleet Place. The litigation/media departments are conveniently located nearer the courts, chambers and the West End. The latter positioning might seem more ideal but *"the consensus is that Fleet Place is the nicer (building), but it is more informal at the Chancery Lane office."* Certainly the *"beige walls"* of Chancery Lane came in for some flak when compared with the more modern Fleet Place offices. Trainees think it *"would be nice"* to have a restaurant in the Chancery Lane office. Fleet Place has a subsidised restaurant with great cheap food and fabulous capaccino and muffins. The real issue though, was whether having two offices that distance apart affected the atmosphere. Many pointed out that the distance is walkable but *"socially it would be better if there was one office"* since you can *"lose touch with former colleagues."* That would be a shame because trainees were positive about the social side of the firm. *"They are people you would like to drink with after work – and you do." "It's easy to get people to go down the pub. Too easy."*

worlds apart (II)

Should you feel the need to travel further than Chancery Lane and Fleet Place, trainees are happy that there are *"quite a lot of overseas seats. The choices are quite endless."* The locations of offices range from romantic (Paris), through the exotic (Cairo) and the oriental (Singapore, Hong Kong, Tokyo). It's planning to integrate its overseas network – Denton International – financially by the end of 2002. To the relief of trainees, there is no seat in Milton Keynes.

and finally...

It's still early days for the fledgling Denton Wilde Sapte. Teething problems, such as the two sites, may well be settled by the time your training contract begins. The two firms were complementary. Denton Hall had its strong energy, property and media/sports practices. Wilde Sapte was the finance and property finance firm. The two had quite different cultures; Denton Hall perhaps more old-fashioned (even if it had the 'sexier' work), Wilde Sapte much more 'City' (although relatively relaxed with it). Interestingly, there were marked differences between the people we spoke to from each of the different firms. Ex Denton Hall trainees are lively, friendly and generally happy with their lot. Those from Wilde Sapte are more circumspect, more guarded.

top recommendations in Chambers UK 2000-2001:

Aviation, Energy, Media, Property, Sport

Dickinson Dees

the facts

Location: Newcastle
UK ranking by size: 61
Total number of trainees: 22
Seats: 4x6 months
Alternative seats: Brussels, secondments

Fancy heading into border bandit country, home of Sid the Sexist, Newkie Brown, the Toon army and Alan Shearer? We took our lives into our hands (we're soft southerners at Chambers), put our Geordie dictionary in our pockets and set off from King's Cross.

if it's legal, we'll do it

That's what Dickie Dees says about itself on the website. It's a site jam packed full of useful trainee info and, so far as we can tell, seems to be 99% accurate. The only line we have a problem with is *"Fact: we can provide a better service than most major City of London law firms but without the airs and graces and we don't charge anywhere near as much."*

What we can and will say, hand on heart, is that this is the Rolls Royce of commercial law firms in the north east of England with a reputation nationally. What its trainees say is that *"Everyone is very aware that this is the best firm in Newcastle – there's a sense of quiet pride. There's not a feeling that you have to get aggressive about it."* And further: *"it considers itself to be thoroughly modern but has an element of tradition still; a sense of moving on but still a sense of old responsibility in attitudes to clients. It's modern but there's a sense of stability."*

club 22 – 38

Three seats are taken in compulsory areas; property (commercial, residential or agriculture), litigation (employment, construction, property lit, commercial disputes, personal injury) and commercial (banking, IP, M&A). A fourth 'choice seat' can be taken back in one of the compulsory areas or in private client, insolvency, pensions, tax, family or planning. There's really no shortage of choice and the fact that trainees don't all come from the same blueprint means that competition for any one seat in particular is minimal.

"Everyone comes from different backgrounds. A couple were policemen, one was in marketing in Australia for ten years, one worked in Africa, one was a teacher for five years." The majority aren't straight from law school. The firm values the experience and the age range is from 22 – 38. This report shouldn't discourage youngsters who are going straight through from uni – the firm takes them on too.

lukewarm brussels

"You can shop around when you're in a particular department. If you're in litigation, and if you're interested in environmental law, you can take work from another person who's not your supervisor. They're quite flexible like that."

Everything points to the fact that the firm has a 'champion' attitude towards its trainees. *"I've been invited along to meetings all over the country where it wasn't really necessary for me to be there, but they paid for me to go along just to get some experience"* one source said.

Each year, two trainees are encouraged to go to Brussels for a *"mainly research-based seat"* which, surprisingly, seems only *"reasonably popular."* From time to time there are secondments to clients. The firm is opening up a small new office in Gateshead. At this stage it's not known if this will provide any new opportunities for trainees.

hada way wi' ye ti the yelhoose

Or 'get on down the pub'. There's plenty of social activity, with each department organising nights out and *"meetings with clients; you go out with them a lot."* In recent years, the trainees have mixed well. *"We all go out together every week and see a lot of each other outside of work as well."* The regular hang out is the Pitcher and Piano. Reports indicate that trainees sometimes spend weekends together (no, not like that ... as a group. Well, maybe like that as well.)

should I stay or should I go?

Maybe one thing that adds to the *"collegiate"* feel amongst trainees is the well-stated intention of the firm to keep up a 100 % retention rate on qualification. It means that *"you're not fighting with each other to stay on."* So proud are Dickie Dees of their retention rates that the lovely Jamie Pass (check him out on the website: corporate partner, in charge of trainee recruitment and the work experience programme; mid-thirties, fresh-faced, cheeky grin) faxed us some stats (thanks Jamie). Of the 38 who qualified since 1994, 35 were offered jobs and, of those, 28 accepted. 21 still work at the firm.

All this begs two questions, 'why do some stay?' and 'why do some go?' Old 'Canny Toon' itself (Newcastle) may be the answer to both. The trainees we spoke to estimated that around half of them were local to the area. If you are a Geordie born and bred, or a Geordie by adoption, and this is the only place you ever want to work, then you probably can't do better than linger with Dickie Dees for the rest of your legal career. It does have national clients on its books and it is outward looking not gazing at its corporate navel. But, and there is a but...if you want consistently blue chip work or you feel hemmed in by the invisible yet perceptible ring fence around the far north east then you may itch to move.

Money considerations will crop up at some point. Even between Leeds and Newcastle there has traditionally been a £3,000 pay differential. Think what a financial chasm there is between Canny Toon and London. There are reasons why Dickie Dees is able to claim "we don't charge anywhere near as much." We say, go figure the maths.

> "The firm has a champion attitude towards its trainees."

and finally....

Talk is cheap, so is office space (DD are renting more and more of it by the minute to keep up with booming business). In the north east, lawyers are relatively cheap but Dickie Dees trainees feel valued (they have their opinions sought) and know that no expense is spared on bringing them on as the newest generation of the firm's lawyers.

top recommendations in Chambers UK 2000-2001:

Agriculture & Bloodstock, Banking, Employment Law, Family/Matrimonial, Financial Services, General Corporate Finance, Insolvency, Planning, Property (Commercial), Social Housing, Trusts & Personal Tax.

DJ Freeman

the facts

Location: London
UK ranking by size: 63
Total number of trainees: 25
Seats: 4x6 months
Alternative seats: Secondments
Extras: Pro bono

DJ Freeman promotes equal opportunities, and claims to have more female partners than any other City firm. It reorganised itself in the early '90s into a number of multi-disciplinary teams. It has a quill-pen and four snooker balls as its motif.

you must concentrate

The firm's outlook is 'things we can't do well we won't do at all.' In 1992 it changed from a medium-sized general commercial firm. It is now divided into four core client-based areas: property, insurance, media/communications and commercial litigation. This approach is very popular with most sources we spoke to. It seems to be true externally as well: *"the client is confident that the department can deal with it."* However, potential trainees must be aware of what this means. Our sources were blunt to say the least. *"People should do their research"* and *"be aware of our market focus." "It's not for a trainee who wants to do competition law."* Don't even think about the firm if you are primarily interested in corporate work. One moan received from sources was that, *"it's quite difficult to get good experience, since the client focus limits the sort of work you can do." "You can't get much experience in particular areas such as MBOs and flotations and there are few big corporate deals."* You have been warned.

multiple personalities

With three different offices and four distinct client-focused areas, it is hardly surprising to hear trainees admit *"some people say that it feels... like four firms."* Sources emphasised that cross-department events take place regularly and trainees have training sessions together. However, because of the separate offices and distinct client focuses it is possible to *"keep yourself quite insular."* DJ Freeman is reputed to be looking for a building under which to unite the whole firm. The sooner the better.

swings and roundabouts

The training contract brochure contains so much pink it's hardly surprising that trainees feel there is *"no macho attitude"* at DJ Freeman. *"It isn't a hardcore place, it isn't for ambitious cut-throat City lawyers."* People work hard but *"don't stay if you have nothing to do."* Interviewees spoke of a *"small firm atmosphere."* The firm has an active social committee and the trainee social programme for the first six months was particularly praised. The flip side of all of this small town friendliness? *"Our wages have gone up but not as much as other law firms. The firm has gone for quality of life."*

life's a beach

Pretty much every one of our interviewees had done a placement at Shell with (generally) positive responses. The usual in-house comments applied. *"It was more relaxed."* *"Everyone goes home at 5:30 on the dot."* *"Everyone is really old."* On the other hand there was a view that *"people felt dropped in at the deep end to start with"* because there is *"a lot of specialist knowledge you don't know."* The real bonus as far as DJ Freeman is concerned is that almost all have the opportunity to do an in-house placement. The secondment to Harrods makes trainee shopaholics green.

It's just as well that people have the opportunity to go on secondment, since there is *"no great ability to travel."* Apparently one person had been on a trip to Bermuda, but this is unusual.

media frenzy

The media section was singled out for particular mention. Everyone we spoke to said how popular it is as a seat. *"Everybody wants to go there."* Though *"generally everybody gets a fair crack at the whip,"* you could certainly help yourself by *"making early suggestions"*

that you wanted to do that seat. We feel obliged at this point to say that the seat will not be to everybody's taste. Many trainees were attracted to the firm to do media and ended up preferring something else. Whilst *"there is a definite good feeling in the department"* with *"so much going on,"* *"you are not going to be on the Big Breakfast"* and *"some people find it completely boring."* The firm acted for Al Fayed in his successful defence of Neil Hamilton's libel action, instructing 'Gorgeous George' Carman QC.

girl power

With its claim to be the City law firm with the most female partners, and with the predominance of pink in its training contract brochure, we could sense that this is a firm in touch with its feminine side. Indeed one source told us that the media department *"feels predominantly female"* and that this year's trainee intake was *"about 75% female."* People we spoke to could see many women progressing up to equity partner. This is no doubt helped by the firm's policy of allowing homeworking for things that can reasonably be done there. *"It's very good for women who have children."* The firm is also said to have a relaxed approach to people's sexuality.

are you free?

The firm is still relatively young and the original DJ Freeman, David, is still on the scene. At Chambers we amused ourselves with delightful images of a frail old man being wheeled in on high days and holidays by a busty young nurse in a skimpy uniform. "You've all done very well" he would announce like 'young' Mr Grace on 'Are you Being Served.' To our disappointment, we hear that he is a hale and hearty 70-something. And there's not a nurse in sight, busty or otherwise.

and finally...

Four snooker balls. Four client sectors. This is not a general commercial firm. It is not the place to go for huge corporate work. It's not the place to go thinking that it does media so it will be desperately trendy. It is simply a firm that knows what it is good at and does it well. And knows how to treat clients and staff.

top recommendations in Chambers UK 2000-2001:

Defamation, Litigation (Commercial, fewer than 40 litigators) [Band 2]

DLA

the facts

Location: London, Birmingham, Manchester, Leeds, Liverpool
UK ranking by size: 6
Total number of trainees: 100
Seats: 4x6 months
Alternative seats: Secondments, Brussels
Extras: Pro bono, language training, cakes in reception (London only)

DLA is going through a period of 'newness.' New offices(London, Birmingham and Leeds), a new name (was Dibb Lupton Alsop) and a new outlook (it wants to be top 10 in the City and eventually an integrated European law firm). That name. Said one trainee: *"the clients used to call us DLA so we changed the name but now everyone asks us what it stands for."* They'll always be Dibbs to us.

rottpoodle

Plans to break into the top ten in London. Plans to become an integrated european law firm. You'd hardly describe DLA as modest. *"It doesn't see why it shouldn't be a top City firm."* Trainees' reasons for joining reflect this. *"I applied because DLA stood out from all the others as a businesslike, go-ahead firm."* The firm has a reputation for being aggressive. But the image of DLA as a rottweiler was dismissed by our internal sources. *"Five years ago we had to be more pushy"* but they've calmed down since the merger between Dibb Lupton and Alsop Wilkinson. They're now

"half poodle, half rottweiler."

"Aggressive" is a word that still crops up, though trainees prefer to use terms like *"expansionist"* and *"go-getting."* The firm's ambition is a key attraction to trainees, and *"in the last year it has been hard work for people here."* So do the figures reflect this? A trainee admitted last year that *"there are certain departments where things have been choppy,"* with losses on a few fronts. The firm has not made huge gains in a year when other firms have made vast increases in profitability, well into double figures. In terms of its regional rivals, Hammonds and Eversheds, its figures for profitability were very good. But if the firm wants to be up there in the City, it must boost its profits considerably.

eager beavers

Perhaps it will come as no surprise that trainees here are not shy or retiring. Many had lives before law. Previous careers are as diverse as working at Lloyd's and flying fast jets. The firm *"welcomed people who had done things before."* *"They really wanted people who could bring things in."* It's a bit different in London where *"people are predominantly straight from university, younger, from the better-known and highly regarded universities."* Elsewhere the statement that *"two people had done a gap year and that was the least previous experience that anyone had,"* seemed more appropriate. In the regional offices, the firm likes to recruit locally. That there is, in general, a *"real cross-section,"* is difficult to dispute. The result is that they want *"very outgoing people, not wallflowers, people who are very proactive and keen."* This also means that they want people who are *"willing to do their bit in terms of marketing."* We are *"positively encouraged to get involved in marketing – nice meals out."* At the end of the day you must ask yourself, are you keen enough to be a Dibbs person?

extra hands

In Manchester we were told *"there's no sitting in the office for no reason."* Indeed, *"we are very busy at the moment"* and *"we need our trainees as an extra pair of* hands." There's a definite hierarchy of 'keenness,' when it comes to the various offices. Liverpool is *"very laid back."* It is *"not as stressed and high-pressured as Manchester."* Trainees in Manchester, Birmingham and Leeds have a similar working experience. But *"the hours are worse in the City than elsewhere."*

> "'Aggressive' is a word that crops up. Trainees prefer 'expansionist' and 'go-getting'."

In general, trainees appreciate the responsibility they're given. One trainee proudly proclaimed *"trainees at Dibbs tend to be more involved in proper work as opposed to making coffee and photocopying which is what most trainees experience in bigger firms."* Said another *"there is lots and lots of responsibility and sometimes seat of your pants stuff."* However, there are some important qualifications to this. Firstly a number of the people we spoke to had previous relevant experience and felt they got better work because of this. Especially in London, the low point was often the corporate work, *"the long nights and data room verification."* With the firm's ambition to become a top 10 firm and its drive to get more corporate work this is likely to become a more common tale.

get outta my seat!

You should do your research carefully. Different practice areas are available in different offices. Most notably there's marine insurance in the Manchester/Liverpool offices and nowhere else. Opportunities exist in niche seats but you have to be lucky. Or dogged. *"The seat was made for me. There was no seat in existence and there wasn't afterwards. If I hadn't been in the right place at the right time I would never have found it."* Finally, in Leeds expect a scrap for that treasured seat. *"People were scrabbling over litigation. It will always happen, the falling out."*

office politics

Though it's not easy to move offices it is possible. Everyone we spoke to is chuffed with their offices, except in Manchester, where the open plan experiment of a while back is *"not universally popular."* Read that as you will, it's not a model that has been copied in the newer offices. When designing the new offices the firm has tried to be hip and trendy. There are *"TV screens everywhere"* and *"funky cafés."*

Will you get to see people in other offices? Apart from the Liverpool and Manchester offices, which to some extent are *"treated as one,"* the firm *"would prefer you to stay at the office you were at throughout your training contract rather than swapping around."* A request to move will be accommodated, if possible. In London the social situation has been helped by the fact that four offices have now become one. The best social life seems to be in Birmingham. *"There is always something going on. You are constantly getting e-mail."* In Leeds there's *"always someone you know in the new [Wetherspoons] pub."* Devotees of chain pubs will be pleased to know that Manchester trainees frequent the Pitcher and Piano and Henry's. Finally what about the much-hyped overseas connections known as D&P? Will you go abroad? Possibly, but probably not. Only seats in Brussels and Hong Kong are available at the moment. Something for the future perhaps...

and finally...

A firm with big ambitions both collectively and individually. Trainees want the firm to get what it wants. And they want to get what they want. They've been working hard to get there and no doubt will continue to do so.

top recommendations in Chambers UK 2000-2001:

Banking, Employment Law, Environmental Law, Food, Insolvency, Intellectual Property, Licensing & Leisure, Litigation (Commercial), Parliamentary & Public Affairs, Pensions, Projects/PFI, Property (commercial).

Eversheds

the facts

Location: London, Birmingham, Bristol, Cambridge, Cardiff, Derby, Ipswich, Leeds, Manchester, Newcastle, Norwich, Nottingham, Teesside
UK ranking by size: 1
Total number of trainees: 224
Seats: 4x6months (except Leeds/Manchester – 6x4 months)
Alternative seats: Secondments, Brussels, Monaco, Paris

Look at the size of Eversheds relative to other UK firms. It's the biggest. It would be easy to compare it to the magic circle, who follow closely behind in size. But this would be a mistake. Eversheds is a collection of offices nationwide and increasingly in Europe. *"The thing is"* said one source, *"in the regions we are big fish in small ponds, whilst in London we are a medium-sized fish in a big pond."* But they have some stunningly successful niches. The intellectual property and employment departments are top nationwide.

variations on a theme

When we told a trainee that we were going to write an editorial piece on Eversheds the response was *"I don't think that you can do one piece on Eversheds because everywhere is completely different."* Researching and writing has certainly proven difficult; there is so much variation between offices. The spread of manpower throughout the country and the diversity of the offices is reflected in the fact that branches have only just become truly profit-sharing. Like a chain of pubs the firm has used local firms as franchisees and branded them as Eversheds. But each retains its original atmosphere and individuality. Recruitment in the regions is biased towards those from the local area. We *"try and recruit people...with a local bias or a lot more local knowledge or a strong connection"* (Norwich) and *"we try and recruit locally"* (Brum) to get people *"who are going to stay."*

Some offices are close geographically and historically. Leeds and Manchester are closely linked (they do 6x4 month seats rather than the usual 4x6 months) and anyone at the Norwich office should expect to travel to Ipswich. Apart from this, the potential for travel nationally during the training contract is limited. For some trainees the *"high point was the training"* as *"you get to meet people from other places."* At the end of your contract movement does occur. *"If you want to go to another office on qualification you can. It's good for people with relationships."*

Trainees are increasingly using other offices as a resource. *"Quite often partners will tell you to call up someone from the Birmingham office or Leeds and they'll be able to help you."* The branch network means there is always someone somewhere who will know the answer to your problem." The breadth of knowledge and potential experiences at the firm is something that really appeals.

choose life

With the offices different in culture, size and work, it is very difficult to make any definitive statements about the work and the hours. Trainees across the board were keen to point out that you should not expect to be out of the office at 5:30pm`. At the same time they did not feel they suffered as much as at some of the big London firms. *"I want to work and need money to live and enjoy life, not necessarily because I want to climb the greasy pole and then die prematurely."* But in some offices there are *"some partners who think you should stay until 7/8 at night."* London is more hardworking (till 5.00 in the morning, three days in a row was one trainee's low point) but if you want to be in London, *"choose it if you're not too keen to work all of the hours God sends because you won't have to work as hard here as at some of the big fellas – but don't come here if you want to get out of the door at 5.30."*

There are great variations within the type of work you will see. The *"mind-numbingly dull stuff"* is there, most notably in London, where 'paralegal quality' work falls to trainees. *"Some of the stuff they do here is* big cases and there is lots of document management. In the big cases the trainee is always going to get [that] role." A whole Saturday at the photocopier is not unheard of in regional offices either. The real message that came across was the satisfaction the trainees had with the quality of their training."I got the impression that they invested a lot of time, money and effort, and were very particular about training." Trainees appreciate the responsibility and client contact they receive. "What really struck me was how little client contact other people got compared to here. You have got to be prepared to be in the thick of it from day one."

club together

A few general themes emerge. Several sources mention that "quite a few people have done other things before starting," especially from a business background. But one of the more mature students still feels that "the composition of trainees is all very young. For them it's almost like an extension of student life."

Trainees at all the offices are a tight-knit bunch. Especially where they are working in a new area. "The trainees are one bunch of people who do a lot of socialising together. Nearly everyone I know is through the firm"(Leeds). "We go out clubbing together at the weekend" (London).

Whilst regional offices accept applicants from the local new universities, (Liverpool John Moores and Manchester Metropolitan for the Manchester office for example) there are "more redbrick" people than anything else in the regions. In London, as the firm grows in size and becomes more cohesive, there are felt to be "more and more Oxbridge" recruits.

european cup

The firm's expansion into Europe is currently getting trainees really excited. Last year's reality was "If you want to go abroad you have to go to London." Ominously this is because "they need the break." But they're no longer the only ones to get the chance now. All trainees are eligible to apply for overseas seats. But the only places with vacancies for trainees are Brussels, Monaco and Paris. In Paris there are two trainee seats, one French-speaking, the other in the Public International Law department (unique to Paris), open to non French-speakers. The Monaco office, whilst "very popular in the summer months," is not so in winter when it gets "quite lonely."

Due to pressure on overseas spaces the seats are for three months. This can be frustrating when you've just started making friends with people from other firms abroad. But perhaps a good idea when you're stuck in Monaco in January all alone.

As to the future in Europe? The firm moved aggressively into the Netherlands, and intends to expand further into Germany and Italy.

and finally...

It's always been easy for City firms and the élite non-London firms to be terribly snobby about Eversheds.They were labelled the MacDonalds of the legal profession, and that has stuck. But they have gone from strength to strength since 1988 when the original group of firms formed the Eversheds law group. They are known as "creative and practical" rather than over-legalistic. The 'blue-chip' firms may turn up their noses, but this is what many clients prefer. And who knows, they may be just up your street.

top recommendations in Chambers UK 2000-2001:

Admin & Public Law, Banking, Clinical Negligence(Defendant), Competition/Anti-trust, Construction & Civil Engineering, Debt Recovery, Education, Employment Law, Environmental Law, Food, Franchising, General Corporate Finance, Health & Safety, Immigration, Information Technology, Insolvency, Intellectual Property, Licensing & Leisure, Litigation (Commercial), Litigation (Property), Local Government, Pensions, Pensions Litigation, Personal Injury (Defendant), Planning, Projects/PFI, Property (Commercial), Shipping & Maritime Law, Social Housing.

Field Fisher Waterhouse

the facts

Location: London
UK ranking by size: 45
Total number of trainees: 20
Seats: 4x5 months and 1x3 months
Alternative seats: Secondments to BBC, Mitsubishi Bank, Colt Telecom, London Underground.

Until the last couple of years FFW has not had a strong image. But, since the time when e-commerce was first a glint in most lawyers' eyes, the firm has really come into its own. Its IP/IT/Media & Communications practice is moving forwards at a pace. It has placed a renewed emphasis on other areas such as banking, German and French desks and professional regulatory work, taking on new partners and winning some top clients.

spreading the net

The internet is a key tool in the revamping of its strategy and image. It has been a part of an on-line one-stop advice shop called MatchCo. It also has its own in-house on-line legal advice site called Incubator, designed to help dot.com start-ups start up and survive. The type of client now attracted to the firm is, according to e-whizz Michael Chissick (arguably the main man behind FFW: The Next Generation) *"much faster and much younger."*

Trainees are not oblivious to this and we noticed a quiet buzz from our interviews that wasn't audible last year. *"At law school very few people had heard of FFW. Now because of IP/IT the firm has a much higher profile and it has spread into other areas."*

hidden agenda

Claimant-based medical negligence and personal injury work. What's that doing in the heart of the City? Current trainees and newly qualified lawyers chose the firm for its varied appeal. They wanted to sample a wide variety of work during their contract and Field Fisher has it on offer. Many shuddered at the idea of a hard-core corporate training. Some went as far as to say *"you get the High Street experience here too – a taste of different things."* If this sounds nothing at all like the training brochure, that may be because the firm wants to gloss up its image, taking on recruits keen to get into banking and corporate seats, areas of work which are actually *"unpopular"* amongst today's trainees. Inside sources tell us that the 'unCity City firm' angle isn't being pushed any more in the literature. Recent and current trainee populations aren't corporate enough.

no stamina

Last year we reported that a trainee social committee organises regular evenings out and sports events, including a monthly Happy Evening, bringing together members of the firm from partner level down to trainees. Recent interviews have cast doubt on the wisdom of plugging that aspect of the firm's life. It has a habit of periodically running out of steam. *"They had to abandon the Happy Evenings due to poor attendance!"* Still none of those we interviewed had any doubts that Field Fisher are a thoroughly nice lot.

close encounters

The training offers plenty of real contact with clients (*"we are not hidden away"*). Aside from banking and corporate work, levels of responsibility are rewardingly high. This sometimes brings on a feeling of *"absolute terror."* It is up to trainees to seek help. In some contentious seats you can run your own cases. *"I did a lot of things on my own at court"* one NQ told us, *"such as Master's appointments at the High Court."* This is refreshing, given how frequently we hear criticisms about lack of real involvement in the work in litigation seats.

The firm has a strong tradition of top quality client secondments for trainees, allowing an insight into *"life on the other side."* How to get the one you want? *"Jump up and down a lot."* The same is true of seats in the office. *"Talking to the partners and* [the trainee administrator] *is important. You have to look after yourself so that you don't miss out on the seats you want."*

dressing down... and dressing up

When they happen, social events can be a giggle. One trainee got rather excited about the time she dressed up as a cowgirl for a theme night(!) Yee Ha! Apparently the young gun slingers in the IP/IT group have gone renegade on the partnership, which recently voted down a proposal for 'dress down' Fridays, and are doing it anyway.

Trainees would love the firm to dress up the office a bit and there may be moves afoot. Aside from the plush first floor conference suites *"the decor is a negative thing. It's grey, drab and out of date."*

staying power

Unless you're in banking or corporate, you'll probably leave the office between 6pm and 7pm. *"People here would hate the magic circle experience. They are here because they knew they would hate it."* It happens, but rarely. *"I've had to work all through the night a couple of times"* one trainee admitted.

Last year, out of 12 qualifiers, 10 stayed. It's the sort of place *"you can spend a lot of time wandering around smiling at people."* As one of our interviewees put it: *"I didn't fancy the big firm mentality and basically I didn't fancy the little firm pay. When it comes to law firms, it's remarkably nice, relaxed and friendly."*

and finally...

Field Fisher Waterhouse is attractive to people who want a large firm without big finance work and the hours that go with it. The firm now wants those seeking corporate experience. Will both parties get what they want?

top recommendations in Chambers UK 2000-2001:

Franchising, Licensing & Leisure, Travel, Tourism & Package Holidays.

Freethcartwright

the facts

Location: Nottingham, Derby, Leicester.
UK ranking by size: 75
Total number of trainees: 10
Seats: 4x6 months

At Freethcartwright (no, that's not a typo, just a trendy new branding) according to their website, 'less is more.' Maybe the new mantra refers to the fact that the firm recently underwent a rebranding exercise by dropping the Hunt Dickins from its name and simultaneously losing all sense of capitals and spacing. But what's in a name?

you can't always get what you want

In the last year, the firm has axed two of its departments – housing and crime. The family department, although not looking over its shoulder the whole time, is, according to insider reports, unlikely to grow in the new commercial climate at the firm. Private client work is tucked away in its own building.

The clinical negligence and personal injury departments are a real draw for trainees. High profile actions, such as the 'Measles, Mumps and Rubella' multi-party claim and soya breast implant claims have given the firm a nationwide profile in product liability work. But, as the trainees pointed out to us, *"PI and med neg are too popular"* and there's a bit of fighting to get in. Those teams tend to be well staffed at junior level already and there's not always enough room for all the trainees who want a seat there. This is not a difficulty unique to this firm. In the current climate of shrinking public funding, claimant PI/med neg firms are less commonly encountered than they once were. Freethcartwright has a deservedly good reputation in this field and, naturally, competition for slots is stiff.

The commercial seats are being pushed. *"If you want to get ahead, you have to do corporate or commercial property as those are the areas that are expanding."* Whilst the firm is *"trying to enhance the commercial,"* there is a confidence that as *"PI and med neg are so huge, we'll never be a truly commercial firm."* That's good news as far as trainees are concerned. They chose the place because of its diversity of activities.

dot to dot

Look at a map of the east Midlands and you could do a dot to dot picture connecting the firm's six separate locations. Four in Nottingham and one each in Leicester and Derby. 'How does that impact on the trainee experience?' we wondered. The good news is that trainees, more than most, will get to know the different locations, and the staff at each, as they circulate between offices from seat to seat. *"You go where the department is. All of property is in a posh modern building, commercial, corporate and litigation are in the main central office"* and *"private client is in an old building." "The Derby office is a bit like an aircraft hangar"* one trainee told us *"and the Leicester office has moved out of an oldy worldly building into a newer, cleaner, fresher open plan office building."* Isn't it a bit fragmented? *"Of course, but they are all now more or less networked"* and there are inter-office newsletters.

sticky situations

"Trainees stick together" as almost all work out of Nottingham. *"You don't run into all the others on a day to day basis"* but the local pub is next door to the main office and *"everyone piles in on a Friday."* The firm sponsors trainee nights out every couple of months. There were a few comments about fragmentation and the two firm-wide annual bashes, a summer BBQ and the Christmas party, do not always turn out to be the catalyst for inter-office interaction. At the last Christmas party the aim was to seat staff so that they got to know new people because *"someone in private client may never have met the corporate department."* Sadly, *"people didn't like it. They wanted to sit with their friends."*

The firm tries in other ways to ensure that the different offices hang together. *"It's definitely part of the firm's motto to have a social life." "We have all sorts of sports – netball, rounders, dragon boat racing..."* Sadly the dragon boat racing is in Leicester not Hong Kong, but it's a fun event.

hatching and growing pains

There's a perceived link between the presence of newly qualified and junior lawyer numbers in a department and the volume and quality of work you'll get as a trainee. *"On the whole you do get enough responsibility"* we were told. *"You're never undervalued but sometimes you're underemployed and bored, scratching around for work."* This is not linked to any particular department but seems more the result of the flow of work and staffing levels at any particular time. Trainees were occasionally frustrated by levels of responsibility, partner contact and client contact.

The message from interviewees is clear. Commercial work is the future. *"It's suddenly becoming more corporate, more trendy."* We were told that six out of eight 1999 qualifiers stayed with the firm, but that already three of those have left. The reasons behind this indicate no great dissatisfaction. It just happened that a number of the NQs realised that Nottingham was not the centre of their universe. Of this year's eight qualifiers only three accepted jobs, two turned them down and three others were not offered anything. London, personal relationships and families can all exert a stronger pull than the prospect of a career in Nottingham.

and finally...

Perhaps a key thing to bear in mind is that Freethcartwright now is not Freeth Cartwright Hunt Dickins as was. This is a time of flux for the firm. Maybe it is appropriate for us to throw in one of those dreadful clichés. You can't make an omelette without breaking eggs.

top recommendations in Chambers UK 2000-2001:

Clinical Negligence (Claimant).

Freshfields Bruckhaus Deringer

the facts

Location: London
UK ranking by size: 3
Total number of trainees: 155
Seats: 4x6 months (but see below)*
Alternative seats: Many overseas offices, second-ments.
Extras: Language training, pro bono.

As a member of the 'magic circle' it sits at the top of the pile, usually found in the top five firms in the commercial sphere, always at or near the top in corporate finance and asset finance. In the last two years, Freshfields has broadened its horizons and on 1st August 2000 it successfully completed the second of two mergers with German firms. The international nature of the firm and its work will hit home in your first weeks as a trainee, when the new recruits from all its offices worldwide come to the London office for induction into the ways of the firm.

blues and blondes

"You're so Freshfields!" one of our sources was told by her Director of Studies at Oxford. She didn't know whether to be flattered or not. What does it mean to be 'so Freshfields'? Ask any lawyer what a Freshfields type is. A ready response will spring to their lips. They'll tell you they are *"all blonde, blue-eyed, tall and athletic"* or *"all Oxbridge"* or *"sporty, sloaney. All seem to have a self image of being beautiful – even if they are not! They can really get up your nose."* Ouch! But it could be worse. No-one's trying to make blonde jokes about Freshfields lawyers – they're all extremely bright. They just have other things going for them too. So is there any truth in the myth? One said: *"It's only true if you're ultra sensitive to that sort of thing – given the reputation, I was surprised that it wasn't worse!"* In other words, don't panic if you're not a Jennifer or Brad look-alike.

The hallmark of a Freshfields trainee is an innate self-confidence and a natural identification with group activities. Many are sporty and most are outgo-ing. *"You don't generally find shy and retiring types here."* Freshfields best suits those who are *"very confident and very personable"* as *"if you're not confident, then this is not a good place for you."* Of the magic circle, this is the 'coolest' firm. *"Freshfields certainly has a more trendy image. They are interested in you having at least a 2:1, with a bit of sport and a couple of clubs, a decent outlook on life, a bit of confidence...being a happy person."*

Freshfields still assumes that it's most likely to find its high-achieving, bright all-rounders at Oxford and Cambridge. At least half of the trainees and (according to our sources) a huge proportion of vacation students come from these universities.

choose life. choose a job. choose a career...

We asked Freshfields trainees and newly-qualifieds why a student should choose the firm over others in the magic circle. Most said *"I don't think there is a great deal of difference between them."* Answers like that make for a quick analysis of the firm. We expected more from the golden boys and girls. Come on, why did they choose Freshfields? Here we got more variety in the responses, illustrating the different characters recruited by the firm. But still their responses could apply to any of the magic circle firms. Some find that they don't love big corporate culture: *"If I had had more of an idea, then I would probably have chosen to go somewhere smaller. That's why I've ended up in a small specialist department,"* said the non-conformist. From the majority: *"It had international offices and big commercial deals." "They were in the magic circle and they were so slick and impressive."* From the already cynical: *"I ended up going to Freshfields basically because I had resigned myself to going to a big place."* From the ambitious high achiever: *"You've got to think of your career and how it's going to look.*

Choosing the firm over a near doppelganger, like Linklaters, often depends on individuals you meet at university events or vacation schemes. Or perhaps the chemistry was right when you went for an interview. Most choose the firm because of its genre and because it offers the potential of working overseas.

21st century colonialism

The pull of the international offices is *"absolutely huge"* sources confirmed. Hong Kong is the most popular overseas seat with NY, Paris and Madrid all in hot second. But if trainees want to boldly go where few trainees have gone before, say Bangkok, Ho Chi Minh City or Hanoi, then they probably need to *"make a specific beeline for it earlier on and have a reason why they should go there."* You'll certainly go abroad if you're not choosy about where you go. *"I said I want to go to Paris and if I can't go there I am not going anywhere, so, of course, if you do that you expect not to get it ... and I didn't!"*

Most trainees go overseas, usually in the final seat. The firm has offices across Europe and Asia and two in the US. Some require languages. You might want to play down your Russian if you don't fancy six months in Moscow. *"At the beginning there's a bit of sucking up"* one source said of seat allocation, *"but it doesn't really make a difference... they discourage it."*

corporate identity

*Freshfields trainees have a reasonable degree of flexibility in terms of being able to move on after three months of a six month seat if it's not to their liking. *"Generally you get to choose or at least have a say in whether you have to move on after three or six months."* There's a compulsory three months of contentious work (to satisfy Law Society requirements). *"The firm doesn't absolutely insist on that being a litigation seat in London."* There's also nine months of compulsory time in corporate and finance. *"As a general rule you do that first or near the beginning. They want you to have done a fair chunk of corporate and finance first."*

What if you're not cut out for corporate or finance work? One of our interviewees advised: *"When you are looking at coming to any of the top five then you give due consideration to what they are looking for, because if you are going to be going home late each night full of resentment you will be pretty pissed off in month one."* Another suggested that we remind students that *"Corporate work is the mainstay and so you will definitely be doing six months in corporate and at least three months*

in finance, probably six." Take note. That said, if you are truly determined enough, very skillful and make yourself indispensible early on in a particular seat you could avoid some time in corporate and finance by doing extra time there.

hard labour

Freshfields has had a certain reputation in the City. One aspect of that reputation is that its young lawyers work harder than their counterparts at other firms. Naturally we were eager to get to the truth. *"I heard it after I accepted the contract... and I have got no interest in denying it"* one source told us. However, the message from the market is that corporate lawyers across the City are busier than ever and that maybe they are now all working Freshfields hours. *"It is a shock if you have been a student and then you come and work here. You hear all the horror stories of people working until all hours of the morning, and you don't really think that it will happen – but it does."*

What trainees actually meant by *"long hours"* was pretty consistent throughout our interviews and they also agreed that they had no control over this aspect. *"You really don't have much control over how bad your hours are and certainly there is a lot of luck involved. I do think some people arrive at big firms and dive in and work very hard from the outset and so that becomes normal."* This is an interesting topic – the self-imposed stay-late-whatever culture, which requires trainees to be seen to be putting in as much if not more effort (and hours) than others. Last year Freshfields' trainees were among the few that admitted that this culture had pervaded the firm. This year we got the impression that 'stay-late-whatever' had been overtaken by 'stay-late – we're-bloody-busy'.

wake up and smell the coffee

One source spoke of a corporate seat in which he did *"probably 40-50 nights after 9pm out of six months plus twice all night and two or three weekends."* Another confirmed *"you can be in every night until three for an entire week and the weekend just proof-reading."* *"You go in blind and you know the hours are awful but it is one of* those things that does not really strike home." You have to have physical stamina for this and you have to be prepared to put your social life on hold. *"It does intrude into your personal life. You have to be prepared to cancel evening plans and work weekends... It's a shock to the system. I lost my own life for periods."*

The good news? If you need caffeine to keep you awake, the coffee machine serves up free lattes and if you work all night you can nip off to M&S and the firm will reimburse you for a fresh shirt. Apparently the ladies prefer to take up the offer of new undies.

fear of commitment

If you go on one of the few client secondments *"it tends to be a bit of an eye-opener."* *"Less hours in total; loads of responsibility... relaxed atmosphere, more regulated hours."* One thing that Freshfields trainees have no illusions about is that the training contract is a tough two years and not for the faint-hearted. Not all trainees make it through to the end of their contract. Sometimes, one or two drop by the wayside. Those that do complete the training are very likely to stay at Freshfields... at least for a little while.

The magic circle increasingly finds it's a challenge to hang on to young assistants. Trainees and qualifieds know full well that *"if you go to one of the top five magic circle firms, you've got a golden CV. And then, if you want to, you can go on from there."*

Many going into this type of firm are open-minded as to where they end up. Often they aspire to become the client and be the one calling the shots rather than wondering how high (or more pertinently for how long) they'll have to jump when the client says so. Are the ambitious youngsters looking ahead to partnership now in the minority? *"People who would get the most out of a place like this would have to be pretty driven and quite discerning because otherwise with the kind of hours we do you can get sucked in."*

a supportive environment

"I didn't know it was unusual to be given a laptop." Well it is. Particularly when you're still at law school.

Lawyers at Freshfields have it made when it comes to IT, professional know-how and support services, 24 hour secretaries, on-site gym, yoga classes, canteen, taxis home after 9pm, dinner when you work late etc. On all fronts the back-up is *"second to none, amazing."* If you're the sort of person who won't settle for second best then make sure Freshfields is on your shortlist.

The battalion of paralegals is useful, although *"to get paralegals onto a job, it depends on how enlightened the person giving you work is and if a deal has a dedicated paralegal."* Paralegals are a godsend but don't relieve trainees of the mundane *"document-jockeying "* that is intrinsic to high value deals and cases. *"Someone has to do the grunt work and, a lot of the time, they don't want to give it to a paralegal."*

When you do get out of the office you may not want to spend your valuable free time with your work-mates. The social scene is not especially frenetic. There's a few pubs on Fleet Street that small clusters of trainees frequent – The Cheshire Cheese and The Old Bank of England. But as one source put it, if you're a junior manager and you're working 100 hours a week, you probably want to get home to see your wife.

and finally...

The firm's buildings are, surprisingly, on Fleet Street in the shadow of the Royal Courts of Justice rather than in the City. However much trainees may demur, the glamorous stereotype sticks. Freshfields lawyers are outgoing types who were captain of sports at school or uni; these were the people you used to hero-worship. People with something more to them than the fact that they are bright.

top recommendations in Chambers UK 2000-2001:

Asset Finance & Leasing, Competition/Antitrust, Corporate Finance (60+ solicitors in Corporate Team), Environmental Law, Pensions, Tax (Corporate), Transport.

Garretts

the facts

Location: London, Reading, Birmingham, Leeds, Manchester
UK ranking by size: 38
Total number of trainees: 50
Seats: 4x6 months
Alternative seats: Secondments, Sydney, Singapore, Paris, Milan

Garretts is the legal arm of 'Big Five' accountants Arthur Andersen. It is the product of the first real attempt at Multi Disciplinary Practice (MDP) in the UK. The Law Society presently bans Garretts from full integration with the accountants. But in location, marketing, clients and day to day work, 'Andersen Legal – Garretts' is definitely *"married and in bed with Arthur."*

resistance is futile...

For the last few years Garretts trainees have explained to us why they were attracted to the firm. Already they are fluent in Andersenspeak, the official language of AA. They speak of *"global reach"* and the merits of MDPs. One stated her decision was made *"because it was really new and obviously the chances of doing really well and progressing to partnership are really good here."* Of which more later.

The firm sends most lawyers *"at least once to the Andersen Worldwide Centre for Professional Education – a private university style campus near Chicago"* for 'training' or reprogramming or whatever it is they do to you. The idea of MDP is viewed by Garretts trainees as *"new and inviting"* and they value *"doing stuff with AA graduates."* *"Everything's pushing towards greater integration with AA"* we were reminded. This is the firm for you if you want to be a part of an extremely large organisation. Otherwise the corporate 'theme tunes' and slogans might get a bit too much....

(it's been grim) up north

Giving Garretts a good kicking has become a popular sport in the legal press. In 1999 the Leeds office was hit by defections. A handful of partners left with their teams, including a couple of trainees, and set up shop at Leeds giant, Addleshaw Booth & Co. *"When all these lawyers leave in one morning, it feels pretty unstable for the rest of the day."* However, one year down the line *"the 'one firm' ethic has been instilled into us now; it's a lot more integrated. It has made us make more effort with AA...I am happier now"* a trainee confided. Trainees were given assurances that, in spite of corporate and property partner losses, there would be enough work and that their training contracts would be honoured. Leeds has now replaced the property partners that left and we assume that seats for trainees in the property department will resume once more.

brum deal

In many ways, Birmingham is the middle ground. It's neither the largest nor the smallest office and has a representative workload: *"Corporate is the main thrust of the firm and the others are built on that."* Secondments to clients are possible in theory but in practice have not been seen so far in Birmingham. Overseas seats may be on the cards. The office is going open plan (the way forward for the firm we are told) and the social scene is there if you want it. *"On the last Friday of every month we all have AA drinks in the office. You get in as many freebies as you can and then go to Henry's afterwards."* Monthly drinks with AA take place in each of Garretts offices. *"When you get to know AA people you get invited* [to their events] *too."*

bustin' a gut

The Reading office benefits from its M4 corridor location, acting for a host of technology clients. All departments are maniacally busy – *"we are flat out."* This is reassuring for trainees. *"When the Leeds partners left we thought it was bad* [for Leeds trainees] *but we didn't worry at all."* Closer to home though, the managing partner of the Reading office left. Trainees felt anxious but ultimately received *"a morale boost. The second in command got on really well with everyone, he's an easy going, good person."* However there has been a knock-on effect from the loss of this work-winning partner. *"The problem was that the managing partner left and that put a spanner in the works. They didn't know if clients were staying or going and it messed up the figures."* This caused a delay in the identification of potential jobs for NQs. *"Accountancy firms are figures-oriented. They look at them month to month. Traditional law firms take a longer term view."* This initial wavering caused September 2000 qualifiers to secure positions elsewhere. When two jobs did come up in corporate there were no takers.

The open plan approach is not to everyone's liking in Reading. One observer likened visiting the office to going to a call centre. But it's a young action-filled office, if you can cope with the noise, and is a real IP/IT hotspot. Sometimes London trainees will ask to spend six months there.

first among equals

The chances of going abroad are good – if you are in London. *"When we were recruited they dangled the carrot of secondment overseas in front of us. I joined because of the reach of the offices."* Many have reached Sydney, Paris, Singapore and Italy. In this respect, one disgruntled regional trainee pointed out: *"It feels like a two-tier firm. London trainees get what they want. Regional ones don't."*

Something else makes London different. This, the largest branch of Garretts, is considerably more stand-alone than the others. *"In many ways, our two floors at the front of the building feels like a whole building in itself. You don't actually feel part of the Andersens thing."* Not until manager (assistant) level do they *"push the wider picture."* This contrasts to the regional offices where trainees work with AA graduates every day. *"You're two desks away from an accountant and three away from a consultant."* For them, that proximity was *"the main draw – by osmosis you look at problems more commercially and less legalistically."*

and finally....

Excellent client contact. No shortage of responsibility. A pioneering mentality from a firm aiming to train business advisers. The bad press *"creates a siege mentality which is a coping mechanism."* To some trainees this is *"almost a plus, as it indicates that the marketplace is worried."* Whether or not the firm's internal propaganda reflects the true picture, we certainly noted a strong survival instinct at Garretts. None of our interviewees felt that the AA tie-up was anything other than a massive benefit to the firm. Just as well really, since that is its whole raison d'être.

top recommendations in Chambers UK 2000-2001:

Corporate finance, IT, Litigation (Commercial) [Band 2]

Gouldens

the facts
Location: London
UK ranking by size: 49
Total number of trainees: 26
Seats: Non-rotational

Prospective applicants usually know just two things about Gouldens. First, it pays. You practically have to wheel it home in a barrow it pays so much. Second, it has a unique non-rotational seat system for the two years of the training contract. You get your own office from the outset complete with your first piece of work waiting on the desk. You then juggle work for all three main departments for your two-year contract or longer, if you stay post-qualification.

read on...

...if you are confident...if you are ambitious...if you crave control over your career...

This system will not appeal to everyone and neither will our description of the training experience at the firm. But that's the whole point isn't it? Shrinking violets need not apply.

nice threads

Trainees tell us that they tailor-make the experience to their own requirements. *"You can make yourself seen and heard in the particular area where you want to qualify."* We're told that this versatility allows trainees to avoid personality clashes and develop working relationships with their favoured seniors. *"I'm not particularly interested in property,"* said one *"so I don't want to do more than I need to."* Another described her impression of other firms: *"I have heard of people at other offices sitting with partners they don't get on with and they sit there thinking 'I've got three months to go before I can leave!'"* If one of the guiding principles of the Gouldens system is that you see a case through from start to finish, we wonder what happens when a trainee takes on a piece of work which turns out to be something in which they have no real interest or which turns out to be for a partner with whom they don't enjoy working. Surely they have an obligation to the partner and his client until the case concludes?

> "Your own office from the outset with your first piece of work waiting on the desk."

the chosen few

Gouldens trainees are adamant that their firm provides a better training. They believe that they were chosen because of their excellent academics, strong personalities and interesting hobbies. This seems to be pretty accurate. It is more than apparent that Gouldens trainees have more self-confidence than most of their counterparts. They carry the air of successful, well-paid, well-dressed fearless young professionals. They are convinced that Gouldens is the best place to train. Maybe these are people who need to believe that this is the case. *"I wanted my real job to start straight away. I didn't need to be told how to do basic stuff."* Really?

in the driving seat

The Gouldens system has a beautiful logic to it. More like a junior associate at a US firm than a trainee at other UK firms, you start as a fully-fledged fee-earner on day one. You take responsibility. If you want full control over your working life, then arguably you shouldn't even contemplate the long-winded process of training as a solicitor. But at Gouldens you have a good chance of taking a high level of control. This is not to say that you do not get a training at the firm. You just get less spoon-feeding.

Trainees decide what work to take on and whether they will have the capacity to handle it. If you are snowed under, then you soon learn that you may have bitten off more than you can chew. It's very much the case that you only kill what you can eat. As one of the trainees we spoke to said: *"It has been quite hard work at times because of the responsibility we're given...or rather that I have taken. You take on as much as you can handle."*

So, in theory the trainees decide how busy they are going to be. They are not likely to have a wasted six months in a quiet or dull department. *"It's always testing and you won't get bored."* In terms of the manic busy times, which you can predict for corporate seats in other City firms, *"I think it fluctuates more than a traditional seat system, we have intense periods at times."* A weekly workload sheet is completed by all trainees and yes, the training partner does look at it. In theory things shouldn't get out of control but trainees have to learn how to prioritise and how and when to say no.

put it on the tab

There's a no holds barred social life, with *"a lot of drinking,"* much of it at the partners' expense. The Gouldens' card is accepted in a few of the local bars and sometimes trainees are sent off with it burning a hole in their pockets. *"Obviously I don't phone up the senior partner and ask him if he fancies coming to the pub"* said one. *"But he does go to the pub and if I am standing next to him we will talk."*

grub's up

At least once a week, trainees have *"a fantastic cooked lunch"* combined with a formal training session. There are no complaints about either the food or the quality of the sessions. *"They want to develop the areas of strength that you have"* and will send trainees on external courses whenever appropriate.

and finally...

This is a firm making substantial profits. No expense is spared in ensuring that funds are applied to trainees. Gouldens is a firm for high achievers, who want to make their mark from a very early stage in their careers. It won't suit everyone but it will suit some very well indeed. The quality of work of the largest of firms is combined with the intimacy of a smaller firm. Stirred into the mix is a level of self-belief rarely found outside the magic circle.

top recommendations in Chambers UK 2000-2001:

Litigation (commercial, fewer than 40 litigators) [Band 2]

Halliwell Landau

the facts

Location: Manchester
UK ranking by size: 50
Total number of trainees: 16
Seats: 4x6 months
Alternative seats: secondment to pharmaceuticals company

And so on it grows...In Manchester the firm has been growing for the last few years. It is expanding in its new London office. The firm's expansion is *"incredible."* 'Ambitious' is a word that we used to describe Halliwells last year and we'll be damned if every single trainee didn't mention it this year. For those at the firm these must be exciting times. But Halliwells is not for all-comers.

show me the money

Let's face it, lurking behind the civilised facade of every commercial law firm is the crude desire to earn large sums of money. Halliwell Landau does not try to cover up its consciousness of the amount passing into its coffers. The *"entrepreneurial awareness"* spoken of by the firm on its website was translated by one insider as *"money-minded and very profit-driven."* For trainees this can mean *"you are aware of your billing from very early on. Some people can find it a strain – you know what the department earns, you know what the department budget is, and you know how much you're earning for the department from very early on. Even as a trainee. Qualification is a simple commercial decision."* 'Start them young' may be the secret to the firm's success.

> "Everyone is ambitious for themselves and the firm and trainees are forward-thinking and entrepreneurial."

go sell yourself.

All of this expansion has to come from somewhere. The ambitions of the firm are exemplified by the way in which even trainees are expected to grab new clients. *"Everybody is encouraged to get involved in marketing from trainees upwards. Marketing is at the forefront of the firm's strategy."* Not for the timid.

"It's quite an aggressive firm" one trainee remarked; *"– not internally"* she added. Competitors in the north west attest that its lawyers are tough negotiators, risk-takers, *"sometimes over the top"* but slick and professional. This is a firm that does things its own way. Our favourite example of this was the pair who allegedly bypassed the usual long application procedure by selling themselves successfully to the firm after deciding its 'go-for-it' approach was for them.

it's my seat!

Don't expect to get a seat in the firm's newest areas without a struggle. Trainees felt that *"there was quite a lot of competition between trainees to get into some departments,"* with the IP and employment singled out for particular mention. A more typical training contract might involve stints in PI, commercial litigation and corporate – *"the biggies."* On the other hand it may be possible to combine more than one department in a six month seat, giving you more of a chance to sit in the department of your dreams.

Trainees also get the chance to get out of the office. Many spoke of the secondment to a pharmaceuticals company. This has proved popular, with one trainee stating that he was still invited to social events there.

trainee errol flynns

The 'swashbuckler' image of trainees we used last year has only been confirmed by this year's interviews. *"Everyone is ambitious for themselves and the firm"* and trainees are *"forward-thinking and entrepreneurial."* Whilst trainees did not seem to work particularly long hours (9am till 6pm or 8am to 7pm in corporate) there did seem to be a real emphasis on being *"the sort of person who puts their head down and gets on with it."* This could well be the flip side of all that ambition and fast expansion. It does not suit everyone. *"I have got to be seen to be working hard"* stated one trainee, who commented that many stayed at their desks emailing friends until 6pm just for the sake of being seen.

It's not all serious though...it is a *"very young firm"* with a relaxed atmosphere in the office. As a trainee you need a sense of humour and something *"a little bit extra about you."* Bright, but less of the academic 'Oxbridge' type, more of the *'entrepreneurial and forward-thinking'* type.

and finally....

Aggressive, ambitious, entrepreneurial, money-minded, maverick. Northern upstarts advising northern start-ups. This firm will continue to go far.

top recommendations in Chambers UK 2000-2001:

Banking, Intellectual Property, Planning, Property (commercial), Trusts & Personal Tax

Hammond Suddards Edge

the facts

Location: Birmingham, London, Leeds, Manchester
UK ranking by size: 7
Total number of trainees: 94
Seats: 6x4 months
Alternative seats: Brussels, secondments to clients.
Extras: Language training, pro bono

Hammond Suddards Edge has emerged as the 7th biggest firm nationally, following the sudden merger in August 2000 of Birmingham/Leicester/London firm Edge Ellison and Leeds/Manchester/London firm Hammond Suddards. Called a shotgun wedding by some, from a trainee's perspective this is an irrelevance. The marriage could provide a lively and nurturing environment for young lawyers.

ying and yang?

"Everyone's really happy with the merger" Hammonds' trainees told us *"...It gives us a better image in the market place."* During interviews we were told: *"We all know it's a takeover; they have adopted our ways – changed to four month seats."* Edges' trainees were reluctant to agree but the Hammonds muscle is evident already. At the top level, a number of Edges' partners have left the firm, mainly from the Midlands. At junior level it is the Hammonds training method which is being adopted by the merged entity. The main casualty has been Edge's former Leicester office, which has shut up shop altogether. *"The main people who are disgruntled are the Leicester office. They thought that there was a link between Leicester closing and the merger."* In truth, Leicester had already been seen as marginal to the future success of Edge Ellison.

The story so far is…short. Any analysis of Hammond Suddards Edge would, out of necessity, be speculative. What we can do is let you know what trainees and NQs at each firm think about their training. Each firm is well liked by its trainees. Each has engendered a high degree of loyalty in them. But this is not a match of two equals nor two identicals.

up north

"*Home base*" Leeds is the archetypal and the original Hammonds' office. It's one of the big six in the city and known to slug it out with its competitors for the best work. "*To be fair, that's been the firm's traditional route in getting where it has done in the past, certainly in the 1990's anyway. It's always been one of the players in Leeds.*" Ask any lawyer about Hammond Suddards lawyers and you will get a strong reaction. They are known for being the rottweilers of the legal profession. "*They have been aggressive in the sense that they go out and actively try to win new clients. It's a very small business community in Leeds, you know who's out there, you know who the competition is.*"

> "Hammonds trainees are bright, sparky individuals who have always struck us as more up front and vocal about their lot in life than trainees at the majority of large commercial practices."

Trainees confirm that an aggressive approach to winning work and conducting work does not manifest itself into an aggressive working environment. It's just work-focused. "*People start between 8 and 8.30am*" in Leeds. "*I hated it*" one source said of the hours. "*I'd walk in at 8.45am and feel as if I was late – there were very few deadlines that had to be met by 9am – that was just the way it was.*" Early birds and worms spring to mind.

In comparison Manchester is frontier land. "*Manchester was built up from nowhere.*" The Mancunians are "*young, ambitious go-getters*" and more "*relaxed*" in comparison to Leeds lawyers. It's less establishment, more "*energetic*" and staffed by "*young people.*" These perceptions don't appear to have arisen from any differences in the work carried out. Each practice has a similar work profile.

the back way into the city

But the northern raiders have continued their incursions. "*We see there is more and more of a London emphasis*" our trainee sources said. People coming in now want to be in the London office. "*That's the sort they are recruiting at the moment.*" There is a new attitude. "*We'll do our time, but ultimately we want to be in London.*" This represents a change from the staunchly northern Hammonds' orientation of years gone by. There's recognition "*in terms of quality of work and client base,*" that London is "*more exciting.*" Hammonds has changed its game. "*Even before the Edge merger was announced, we got rid of PI in Leeds. We were going to be very corporate-led.*" The writing was on the wall: London will be top dog. "*Traditionally we have relied on our brothers in the north to give us our clout. If you took the office on its own as a City presence, traditionally it hasn't been anywhere.*" But the London office has been making headway in the mid-tier corporate market, despite some partner losses this year. The firm knows "*that they won't be a magic circle firm and there's an acceptance of that. We are in a totally different league. We want to be amongst the best of the next strata.*"

Some applicants turned down by London firms have viewed Hammonds as a "*back way into the City.*" But it shouldn't be seen as a consolation prize. Hammonds trainees are bright, sparky individuals who have always struck our researchers as more up front and vocal about their lot in life than trainees at the majority of large commercial practices. It's been part of their gritty northern charm. They have always struck us as high on realism and commitment to the firm, low on élitism and old boy networks. These people certainly wouldn't come across as typical 'City types'.

young free and single?

"*At the moment there is a leaning towards London recruiting*" one source told us. All agreed that the policy has changed. Since the firm first took on a graduate recruitment officer it has been targeting the younger, less local, more establishment type. "*It's changing. When I started everyone had a Yorkshire accent. It's not staying like that. There are more 'external' people in the firm now.*" As well as the swing away from the old 'Leeds type' fewer paralegals are getting opportunities. "*Before, a lot of paralegals came from our insurance department and commercial dispute resolution too. It doesn't seem to happen nowadays.*" But this hard-line establishment approach has been slightly softened. "*Previously, the firm wanted Oxbridge candidates. Now we just want the best we can get. The firm wouldn't turn its nose up at those who are not from the top universities.*"

There's a danger that Hammonds will lose the wise heads on (relatively) young shoulders that we have come across in trainee interviews in the last few years. Maybe their boldness and rational analysis comes from their greater experience of life, work and social interaction. If Hammonds can find these qualities in fresh graduates it will have succeeded. Trainees we spoke to assume the firm wants 22 year olds because they are better suited to dealing with Hammonds 'round Britain' policy.

just love those motorways

Last year we were told that to really be suited to Hammond Suddards you have to have a reliable car and a love of the motorways of England. All trainees (except, we are asked to point out, those with children) are required to move around the firm's offices. There's no problem with accommodation; the firm takes out leases on "*absolutely gorgeous*" city-centre flats, such as Salford Quays in Manchester and the Barbican in London. So long as you don't mind shar-

ing with fellow trainees, you could get the chance to live in locations well beyond the price range of all but the wealthiest young lawyers. "*It can be a fun four months*" we were told. Sometimes "*close friends move round together.*" Just like being students again.

Good for the blissfully unattached. Good if you're flexible about where you want to be. Otherwise, bad. "*Your personal life is a disaster,*" and moving around is "*a major pain.*" In previous years, trainees have been bitterly critical of the policy. But these days everyone joining the firm knows what they are in for. And if trainees are now younger, the policy is more suited to them. Their advice is to "*plan it well*" and combine a seat you are least interested in with a location where you have no intention of qualifying. From the firm's perspective, the policy ensures that "*the new blood will know people from different offices.*"

the come back kids

One of the big four in Birmingham, Edges were seen as the 'wideboys' of the marketplace. They performed consistently well until a number of defections to rival practices a couple of years ago. Since then they have been struggling against accusations that they are a spent force, although they have remained profitable. Certainly ground has been lost in Birmingham. One source said candidly: "*There was a point when I was slightly worried about all that, I have to admit. I thought 'what am I coming to?' For the trainees who joined the year before us it was all a bit difficult.*"

guinea pigs

Against the odds perhaps, Edges turned things around. They rebranded. The old Edge & Ellison became 'edge ellison'. "*The new direction brought back people's enthusiasm. It was a whole new concept that worked with the kind of people that are here at Edges.*" Much of the new direction seemed to centre around developing a sense of belonging at the firm and making it into the sort of working environment that couldn't be found in too many other places. Drawing lawyers closer into the workings and strategy of the firm, by defining and strengthening its ethos, fostered loyalty. "*Over the last two years the firm has definitely rejuvenated and management is different now.*" And senior management is different again following merger.

Part of the refocus rested on various self-development programmes, which were introduced for the whole firm, from admin staff right up to the senior partner. The Coaching Pioneer Scheme included optional skills training, such as self-motivation and assertiveness and there were compulsory self-management sessions for all employees and partners. "*Even the partners you would think would be stuck in their ways generally aren't. They are very up for going along to these workshops and learning all these skills.*"

Courses have included speed-reading, mind-mapping and recharging your batteries. Whilst "*you wouldn't imagine a trainee going on a recharge your batteries course, things like mind-mapping, brain-storming and speed-reading courses are encouraged.*" Obviously this American corporate approach is not for everyone. "*It either works for you or it doesn't*" But you don't have to buy into it. "*It isn't a case of 'you will mind-map/speed-read, etc.' It's very much a voluntary thing.*"

meet the family

Edges' Birmingham office was particularly attractive to the roving eye of Hammonds. It could never have built up a stake in the city's legal market of the size that belonged to Edge Ellison. But Edges' real pulling power was its London office. The combined strength of the two has now given a position of strength beyond the grasp of either firm independently. Like Hammond Suddards, Edges was injecting resources into the growth in size and importance of the London office to the practice as a whole. Together their potential is big.

Edge's trainees are not so different from Hammonds trainees. There's nothing self-congratulatory about any of them and they're all set on long term legal careers. Edges' trainees also feel the pull of Lon-

don. They enjoy an easy interaction with partners and they're bright and engaging individuals. One advantage they've had up until now is the opportunity to develop good working relationships and friendships without having to constantly move around the country. "*It isn't someone standing in the lift looking at somebody else, thinking 'I have no idea who you are'.*"

Socially, it is "*any excuse for a celebration and most of the time the partners buy at least the first round of drinks.*" Some see the firm as a family – the champagne comes out regularly for engagements, babies etc. Sports, bowling and lots of weekend hiking add to the sense of being drawn into the Edges 'community.' If you fancy treading the boards rather than putting on your walking boots then there's always the annual pantomime. We're not surprised that some of Hammonds' second year trainees have already volunteered their services for the Birmingham office.

and finally...

Who knows how Edges and Hammonds will fare together. Who knows whether the training experience will be to everyone's liking. But there's been an overwhelming level of satisfaction amongst trainees at both of the old firms. Maybe the "*scrap for the Brussels seat*" will get messier. Maybe the Hammonds domination will lead to more Edge departures. Maybe the gritty northerners won't like the psycho-babble of mind-mapping and battery recharging. Interesting times lie ahead. If Hammonds' trainees are right and it's the way of the firm to "*focus in on the result quickly and take a realistic view straight from the start*" then there should be plenty for us to discuss next year.

top recommendations in Chambers UK 2000-2001:

Corporate Finance(under 30 Solicitors in Corporate Team), Debt Recovery, Employment Law, Health & Safety, Litigation (Commercial), Media & Entertainment, Partnership, Pensions, Sports Law.

Hempsons

the facts

Location: London, Harrogate, Manchester
UK ranking by size: 69
Total number of trainees: not recruiting for the time being

It obviously has its own reasons but sadly, very sadly, Hempsons has decided to take a break from trainee recruitment. Its client base is dominated by health and it provides a range of appropriate services to that sector. It always used to encourage applicants with relevant work experience, was happy to take older trainees, and encouraged those wishing to become dual qualified medically and legally. The firm may not thank us for suggesting this, but any candidates who are already medically qualified could do worse than to drop the firm a line anyway.

top recommendations in Chambers UK 2000-2001:

Clinical Negligence (Defendant), Healthcare, Partnership

Herbert Smith

the facts

Location: London
UK ranking by size: 11
Total number of trainees: 151 (worldwide)
Seats: 4x6months
Alternative seats: Several overseas seats, secondments
Extras: Pro bono, language training

Herbert Smith is a firm with a larger than life character. Couldn't exactly say why. Maybe it's their stunning offices astride Liverpool Street Station. Maybe it's because litigators are such characters. Maybe it's just that they have a fabulous head of marketing who does a great job for the firm. Part of the 'other three' who have cleverly allied themselves with the magic circle in the 'Gang of Eight' firms setting up the new City LPC, they are clearly aspirational. Stereotyped as *the* litigation firm, they are trying to slough off that old skin and re-emerge as corporate bigwigs (yawn). With what success? We asked their trainees and young solicitors.

so it's all about litigation then?

"We are the most balanced of the major law firms in the City of London. Of all the firms, we offer the broadest and most varied environment in which to begin a legal career." Or so says the Herbert Smith recruitment site. But we don't necessarily buy into that. Renowned as the premier litigation firm, it needs to redress the balance amongst its lawyers of the future. People train here because they want to be litigators. Herbert Smith wants people who want to do corporate work and has even engaged in advertising campaigns in order to emphasise this desire.

Actually, take a look at the contribution to fee income provided by different areas. Company, litigation and property contribute 53%, 38% and 9% respectively to the firm's total fee income. The firm still tops the litigation tables. With Clifford Chance, it has more solicitor advocates than any other firm. It has even established an office by the law courts for them at 5 Bell Yard, previously occupied by specialist aviation barristers. So it's hardly surprising that most trainees over the years have cited this as a major reason for applying. *"I was very keen on litigation and they are very big litigators"* was a common cry. But did you know that 'Herbies' is also creeping up on the magic circle in corporate finance, sharing second place with A&O and CC.

jobs for the boys and girls

Those of you with a keen eye for detail (and that should be all of you, would-be lawyers) might sense a tension between the aspirations of trainees on applying to Herbert Smith and the reality of what they do. The problem is simple but crucial: the firm needs to attract corporate keenies. *"Every time it comes to qualification there are people who want to qualify into litigation and who don't get to qualify there."* In one intake the *"retention rate was 75%, possibly lower because of the number of people wanting to do litigation."* Our interviewees told us that the firm has moved *"towards promoting the corporate side; there are more vacancies there, perhaps more than 50% of the jobs are in the company departments."*

During your training contract *"you are expected to do a seat in corporate and a seat in litigation."* They are also 'keen' for you to do property although whether this will be true in the future is a different matter. Apart from the seats that you can't get out of, the hot options are the usual IP and employment, together with tax and planning/environmental.

the ego has landed

With its reputation for breeding 'barracudas' one might expect the firm to have an aggressive atmosphere internally. Said one trainee *"There's no point in being soft if your client goes away unsatisfied. It's a question of litigation being a dirty business."* But whereas the firm *"does not pull any punches on behalf of its clients"* junior staff do not feel that it is *"over- aggressive internally."* But there's no doubting the strong personalities of a significant minority of Herbert Smith partners. *"There are a few big egos,"* and for some trainees the low point was *"being stuck with a difficult supervisor."* *"A lot of partners don't have trainees for that reason"* but some that do can be *"irritated by their incessant questioning."* The big problem is feeling appreciated. *"You can shine like a supernova and not get noticed because the partner you are sitting with has no time for anybody."* said one. Other firms have their problem partners. But last year and this, we were told that this is a significant issue at Herbert Smith. *"Even if you are really good it does not mean that you will be listened to,"* and you *"should never assume that your work will speak for itself."* The best advice we can give is that since the partners are extremely busy, if you

want to be noticed you have to be *"confident in talking to them."*

work

In the light of above what is the work like? Trainees at Herbert Smith have very mixed experiences and opinions as to the work they carried out. Some trainees could not be more positive *"I've been to court, I've made applications to judges sitting in the technologies and construction court,"* and *"I went before a master when I was doing the litigation seat which was terrifying and nerve-wracking but good."* At the same time *"You are a very small cog in an enormous wheel."* The real point is that what happens to you is very much out of your hands. What work you get *"depends whether there's a big case on at any one time. If you need to be doing bundles for trial for three months then the person incumbent at the time will end up doing it. But I think you have to take a long-sighted view and say that it was circumstances that meant you ended up doing that. They weren't being vindictive. It's just that it needed doing and you were the person in line at the time."* A significant factor in the life of a trainee is luck.

We were told that the firm simply does not *"employ enough paralegals to do the work that paralegals could do."* Perhaps *"a third"* of trainee work fits into that category. There are real issues about responsibility here. *"The worst thing is the lack of responsibility and ability to use your initiative."* There was also a feeling that at times trainees could be given too much work to do. *"You have been given a fair amount by the partner and then the assistant gives you more. You can feel dumped on heavily."* The trick is you need to learn to say 'no' but make it sound like 'yes'."*

the lost world

Several of our informants think that Herbert Smith *"has a reputation for being traditional and stuffy."* Most agree that to some extent the firm is *"quite conservative in its ways; less forward thinking, more reactionary, more cautious, not Linklaters, not Clifford Chance."*

Certainly there are *"some old dinosaurs still around."* At the same time the whole firm is felt to be changing. The corporate department is *"quite progressive"* and *"always trying to introduce new things."* Maybe if this was to become the dominant ethos, Herbert Smith could begin to show that it is *"not just a litigation firm."*

Egos aside, trainees at Herbert Smith liked the atmosphere there. *"Support and collegiality"* were terms that cropped up. The types at the firm *"are those you feel happy to socialise with."* Both *"sociable and hardworking"* lawyers at the firm are characterised as *"confident and chatty."* In other words *"not for you if you are too shy or introverted."* You have to be able to fend off those dinosaurs after all. *"To be honest most of us are quite loud and outgoing."*

Our impression is that if there is a type, it's pretty close to the type who would have been happy at the Bar. In fact we were told that for those thinking of joining the Bar going to Herbert Smith is a *"natural progression."*

Trainees honestly believe *"one of the key recruiting techniques is to try and recruit as broad a range of people as possible. It just targets quality individuals."* The result? There is *"a real mixture between the people here – a wide range of backgrounds."*

a right bunch of herberts

If you're shy or easily embarrassed you almost certainly wouldn't survive the Herbert Smith initiation. Rookies are sent around the offices and surrounding area on a treasure hunt, sporting a trendy Herbert Smith baseball cap. Just 'Herbert' might be more appropriate. *"Feeling like a bit of a plonker"* is probably pretty close to defining this seminal experience. But after this rite of passage, you will find *"a big social side."* September intakes are *"quite chummy"* with March of the following year but *"when we socialise it's not a question of trainees on their own."* *"A lot of the social life is in the groups."*

herbie rides again

"I know that a lot of people were disappointed," said one trainee about the overseas seats.*"The seats are hotly contested."* And there aren't that many of them.*"If you wanted to go abroad I'd say join Clifford Chance, Allen & Overy or Freshfields. Don't join Herbert Smith."* Always popular, they are *"by no means guaranteed"* for all who want them. Hong Kong is particularly competitive. If you do decide to go for it then you will need to have a good appraisal from the seat relevant to the one abroad. Though the decision is *"totally merit-based"* the law of the jungle applies. *"Certain partners have more sway"* and *"lobbying does go on."* US presidential hopefuls only need apply...

and finally...

Without serious competition for its litigation practice, this is a firm worth considering for strong corporate work too. It's not quite making the international bigtime yet, but it's trying hard. It's the nearest to the magic circle that you'll find outside the magic circle.

top recommendations in Chambers UK 2000-2001:

Admin & Public Law, Competition/Anti-trust, Energy & Utilities, Fraud, Litigation (Commercial: 40+ Litigators), Partnership

Hill Dickinson

the facts

Location: Liverpool, Manchester, Chester, Stockport, London
UK ranking by size: 55
Total number of trainees: 17
Seats: 4x6months
Alternative seats: secondments to insurance clients

A top reputation in the insurance field shores up this north west firm allowing it to practise a wide spread of work. At the time of writing, merger talks are ongoing with Weightmans, another north west firm known for insurance litigation work. Management at the two firms are not being liberal with information, either internally or externally. Anything could happen. Well, almost anything. One thing we definitely can't confirm is that any new firm would be called 'Weighty Dicks,' as one source suggested.

big spread in areas

The firm markets itself as 'offering a full portfolio of specialist legal skills to a wide spectrum of businesses and private individuals.' It originally started off as a shipping firm in 1810. But *"the tide has turned"*(groan). General insurance work was a natural child of their shipping expertise. Medical negligence and transport specialisms followed swiftly behind. In fact perhaps 50% of the firm's workload is litigation, mainly insurance litigation.*"Most people would do a seat"* there, possibly even two. At the same time the firm continues to carry out a wide range of work including private client. The internal marketing is that Hill Dickinson is *"keen to expand into new areas,"* since it *"wants to be able to offer clients full service."* IP is a recent key area of expansion although trainees are not yet being taken on in the specialist IP office in Stockport.

courting success

"Trainees do get the rubbish, as they do anywhere, but they also get quite a lot of responsibility." This is because the firm is *"still very litigation-based and you get lots of 'hands on' stuff."* Trainees get the opportunity to work for the firm's dedicated court section, with advocacy opportunities after a short while. They also get their own files. *"Trainees will get to do quite a few applications. You need to make sure that you know the law before you get to the application or you will get shouted at by the judge."* A baptism of fire that all trainees should go through! Certainly *"if you show that you can stand on your own two feet you will get lots of responsibility."* This also applies to working for the health department.

"You get offered quite good stuff in health; proper fee-earning stuff."

keep that suitcase packed

Hill Dickinson is firmly based in the north west of England. Offices are in Liverpool, Manchester, Stockport and Chester and there is also an office stranded down in the City of London. Whereas the offices in the north west (and hence the trainees) are fairly close the *"London office is a long way, you can't just pop down there for the weekend."* There are trainees down in that office and those from the north *"could probably ask to go down there"* but the London office was thought to recruit its own trainees. Do London trainees ever go to the north?

For trainees the Liverpool office is still very much the hub of the firm. So close together are the north west offices that *"trainees do get shunted around...at fairly short notice."* So be prepared to do a seat out of Liverpool.

lively scouse banter

From a social point of view also the *"heart definitely remains in Liverpool."* Most trainees are there after all. *"There is a nice little social group"* and a good social committee at the firm. Everyone tends to start out at the same pub in the evening. *"Whoever is at the pub will then move on"* usually with a mix of trainees and assistants. But the social life extends beyond the weekday pub outing. *"We arrange to meet up at the weekends and do stuff."*

The working day runs from 9.00 till 5.30. You may have to work longer, *"but it doesn't happen often."* Therefore work should not significantly interfere with your social life. One thing that people should be aware of is that a trainee at the firm needs *"to have good banter"* to get along with the people there. So get working on that witty repartee.

be a good loser....

In the competitive insurance world staying on the panel of the big insurance firms is key. Corporate entertainment is intrinsic to the work. *"If you can show initiative and the partners know you"* you can join in while still a trainee. Maybe you'll get to play cricket and golf with clients. This will give you an opportunity to perfect the art of losing graciously and convincingly. Or perhaps you'll be sent on secondment to an insurance client for a couple of months. Buttering up NHS clients in the health department is not allowed, so don't expect any lavish events while you're there.

and finally...

So what would be the effect on future trainees of a Hill Dickinson-Weightmans merger? The insurance departments would undergo a major shake-up, but the new firm would have by far the largest insurance capability in the region, making it a choice for those who see their future as tied to the insurance industry. After all, the trend for insurance firms to broaden their practices is a trend that follows the clients' own business needs. So watch the legal press or contact the firms to find out what happens next....

top recommendations in Chambers UK 2000-2001:

Shipping & Maritime Law, Transport

Holman Fenwick & Willan

the facts

Location: London
UK ranking by size: 64
Total number of trainees: 18
Seats: 4x6 months
Alternative seats: Occasional secondments, overseas seats

Ahoy there, land-lubbers. Shiver me timbers and hoist the mainsail. All aboard the good ship Holman Fenwick. Shipping firm? Whatever made you think that?

chart your course carefully

Sources we spoke to at HFW agreed that the firm would be a *"bad place to turn up on your first day if you didn't know that the firm was about shipping."* Founded towards the end of the last century as a shipping firm, *"it is still anchored to its traditional base"* said one. Exactly how much shipping you'll do in your training contract varies from person to person. However, you will do one non-contentious and three contentious seats out of which *"quite a lot"* of the work will be shipping. Interviewees were keen to point out that the firm does areas such as IT, energy, insolvency and reinsurance. However one source we spoke to felt that the expansion into these areas followed the ship-owning clients. *"If they take on a new business we follow them."*

it's all greek to me

"Recent trainees...following graduation, have worked in areas as varied as the Lloyd's market, the shipping industry and the Royal Navy," states the HFW website. Variations on a theme, then. Indeed they *"like people who have worked at sea or who speak other languages."* Some intakes consist almost entirely of people such as this, some are said to be 50:50 and some of the more recent intakes are apparently younger with *"more people straight from uni."*

You should not be put off applying if you haven't spent the last two years at sea or are not fluent in five languages. But of the five or six people they recruit each year they will be *"all different,"* with a *"mix of different nationalities."* Greeks, in particular, take to shipping law. *"Very intellectually stimulating"* is the general view of this discipline. It is a very complex area, with one source pointing out that many of the top English judges of all time had started out doing admiralty work. Certainly you need to be *"very intelligent"* and have a *"good understanding of contract law."*

shipmates

One of the best things for trainees is that *"you feel that you know all the people at the firm."* *"It is no longer a* small firm but it has one central staircase where you see everybody." Trainees feel that they knew "everyone by sight, if not by name." The senior partner seems to know who people are straight away. Even Lord Byron, who is a partner at the firm, is known as 'Robin.' But the firm's growing and there is "a danger that it'll get too big" for this to be true any more. On the social front views are mixed. It's "affected slightly by maturity." On the other hand there are "a lot of sports" for people to get to know each other at. Most significantly, with the "trainees getting younger the social scene has definitely picked up recently."

Like most firms the amount of responsibility you get will vary from department to department. Unfortunately, photocopying was something that trainees seemed to encounter and clients something they didn't feel they encountered enough. Shipping was the area in which trainees said the "firm taught you the importance of clients." This was felt to be because the ship owners tended to be rich individuals. They are "demanding clients."

staying aboard

"With the firm only taking on half the normal amount of trainees (for its size) you know that it is quite keen to keep you on." This was the prevailing view of the people we spoke to. This certainty stemmed from the type of work that the firm did. "Shipping is not as sexy as it used to be, it is not expanding like mad, but it is a stable business." In contrast to shipping, newer areas were expanding said trainees. All this meant that NQs all had places. Not only did the firm want to keep people on but NQs wanted to stay. The view "in my year all stayed on," was pretty typical. "People carry on here for years," said one trainee, and one got the feeling that he meant for ever... .

and finally...

Stability is the key message we get from Holman Fenwick. It's a cosy, intimate environment with high quality work. It is sticking to what it does best, which is shipping and insurance. It's a profitable firm which doesn't need to think about expanding into big corporate work. Unless, of course, that's what the shipping clients want.

top recommendations in Chambers UK 2000-2001:

Shipping & Maritime Law.

Hugh James Ford Simey

the facts

Location: Cardiff, Merthyr, Blackwood and nine offices in Wales and the south west
UK ranking by size: 65
Total number of trainees: 14
Seats: 4x6 months

In May 1999, Welsh practice Hugh James merged with Exeter firm Ford Simey Daw Roberts. Both were insurance-oriented litigation practices. Law firm mergers like this have been a result of the shrinking of the insurance industry and, therefore, its panel lawfirms. What is now known as Hugh James Ford Simey is an interesting hybrid of a practice. Part commercial, part private client. Part defendant PI and part claimant. Much of the claimant work is very high profile. The firm has a solid reputation in the south Wales mining community and handles claims against the Government for respiratory disease and Vibration White Finger.

valley girls (and boys)

"The Cardiff office does have a strong Welsh theme and it helps if you've been to Aberystwyth University." But there's less of a Welsh bias than we expected. Trainees suggested that some sort of logical reason for coming to train in Wales would be needed to persuade recruiters. "If you were from London and applied out of the blue, they would question why." HJFS is remarkably open in its recruitment choices. Two new qualifiers had started out as paralegals and mature trainees (and we don't just mean two years on a Thai beach) are thick on the ground.

This is a very Welsh training and you'll need to go native. You'll be expected to visit at least two different offices, so don't expect to sit in Cardiff dealing with commercial clients for the whole period. It won't happen. *"Merthyr and Cardiff are mainly commercial clients but in the regional offices it's individuals."* *"The clients you deal with are truly from all walks of life."*

trains and robberies

The numbers of non-solicitor fee earners in the firm are high. This indicates a large volume of lower value work, such as residential conveyancing and smaller PI claims/defence. This isn't the kind of work trainees do for two years though. We came across what is possibly the broadest training contract in the UK top 75. Seats can be taken in family, crime (white collar and common or garden), PI, commercial litigation, construction, employment, corporate, commercial property and residential conveyancing. There's probably more.

In your first year you'll have no choice about location or work. If crime isn't what you're after and you're allocated the crime seat in Talbot, well… tough. *"The established etiquette is that you don't complain."* *"You really must be prepared to try everything."* There's no point in turning your nose up at a posting to one of the 'regional offices'. If you've based yourself in Cardiff you won't need a car to reach them. All are within 25 miles of the city and there's a railway station very near almost every one. So far, the trainees have only ever spent time in the Welsh offices. Exeter and the West Country wasn't a part of the consciousness of those we spoke to.

village people

The Merthyr office has a wild reputation, born of the antics of certain partners at Christmas parties. *"I was shocked"* one trainee told us. *"It's one of the freakiest things I've seen – four partners dressed up and on stage as Village People. One of them has just completed the biggest claim against the Government (miners' respiratory disease claim) and he was up there dressed as the Red Indian doing YMCA."*

The whole of the Blackwood office (*"I mean everyone but everyone"*) goes to the local pub for lunch once a week. There's a similar lunchtime scene in the Merthyr office and those who don't need to rush back to families will also congregate after work in the local brasserie for a few drinks. In Cardiff there's a fair few laughs in the local HaHa Bar. Trainees don't see each other as a group much but this doesn't stop them from having a decent social life. There's a culture of sharing the good times with everyone, from support staff up to partners.

sink or swim

Trainees don't have to bite down their fingernails waiting to find out if there's a job for them on qualification. In January of the second year the firm announces which jobs are available for the following September's qualifiers. The fourth seat in the training contract will always be in the department that the trainee is going to qualify into. Almost everyone stays at the firm. They like it there.

Only one grumble – but a significant one. The firm could make more of an effort to help you to swim rather than let you sink. Levels of responsibility are high from early on, as is the pressure. Trainees step out of the comfort zone into areas of decision-making that they are not always happy with. One trainee suggested that the firm ought to set up a weekly meeting between trainee and supervisor to discuss current work, case strategy and anything else that needed to be addressed. *"Sometimes you feel desperate, but the next day the partner gives you advice"* one source said. Another said that it felt like a choice between *"hassling people"* or *"making a foul-up of it."* We wondered how some City trainees would fare if asked to spend a day as a HJFS trainee. *"You have your own files and meet clients on your own although sometimes a partner sits in. It's more like the partner shadowing you rather than you shadowing the partner."*

and finally...

Hugh James Ford Simey is a top choice if you're confident enough to deal with people from all walks of life and you're certain that you want a career in south Wales. This is a real 'Heinz Beans' training. 57 varieties of work. Don't apply to the firm with fixed ideas about how you want to spend your two years. You could end up trying anything. Do apply if you have a particular interest in serious class action work, such as miners industrial disease cases. Or it may be that you want to train at one of the best regarded commercial firms in Wales. Either way, you must be committed long-term to a life in Wales.

top recommendations in Chambers UK 2000-2001:

Family/Matrimonial, Litigation (commercial), Litigation (property), Personal Injury (Claimant, Defendant), Social Housing

Ince & Co

the facts

Location: London
UK ranking by size: 58
Total number of trainees: 23
Seats: 4x6 months
Alternative seats: None

For shipping and insurance work it doesn't get any better than Ince & Co. The firm's work is 40% shipping and international trade, 40% insurance and reinsurance, 10% professional indemnity and just 10% split between company, commercial and property. It offers a rare brand of training, almost non-rotational in approach (along the same lines as Gouldens). It develops good lawyering skills from very early on.

F-A-B

One look at the firm's website and you'd think that Ince & Co is not a law firm at all. That big red but-ton on the home page ('Emergency Response Team – Click Here') is a dead give-away. So the Tower Hill office is in fact a smokescreen for Thunderbirds heroes Incernational Rescue waiting to spring into action as soon as anything larger than a model aeroplane drops out of the sky or disaster occurs on the high seas. Oil spills, rig explosions, sinkings, crashes. Disaster in any shape or form – that's Ince's business.

Sounds exciting. But will you be manipulated like a puppet or will you get to strap yourself in, pump up the adrenaline and fly the training contract equivalent of Thunderbird Two? Trainees tell us that you need to be a 'have a go hero' to make it at Ince & Co. It's not just the nature of the work that differentiates this firm from others in the City. After all piracy, disasters and emergency rescues at sea are not usual City fodder. But the way in which trainees acquire experience also sets the firm apart.

every (black) cloud has a silver lining

Ince & Co doesn't split itself into departments, but into three loose groupings of partners, roughly representing different client sectors. Pretty much everyone is a litigator. *"About 98% of what we do is contentious"* one trainee estimated. And that's probably not far off the mark. As a trainee you'll sit with four different partners for six months and get first hand experience of their style of working, but you won't belong to them. It's up to you to acquire work from other partners and assistants, irrespective of whether or not they are in the same grouping. *"There's definitely pros and cons to the system. You get exposure to different partners and their work but you are at the beck and call of everyone.* "It's great for case handling skills as you don't have to leave a case behind just because you move into a different office." *But that also means that some cases follow you around like black clouds!"* Everyone who's been in practice knows that you always have a 'lemon.' That's a case you hate, that you're desperate to pass on to the next trainee. At Ince & Co you have to deal with it.

"*The learning curve is much steeper here.*" This is what we are told by Ince's trainees every year. No messing around – you sink or swim. You are more responsible for your work from earlier on because "*you don't down tools and hand over cases every six months. You feel like it's your work.*" The biggest plus is that you can get onto a case early and see it through to a conclusion. "*You are really thrown in the deep end. It might be scary but you'll really learn.*"

on the rocks

There's not a great deal of corporate work to go around but you will find some. You can get non-contentious experience by approaching partners doing aircraft or other finance deals. As with any type of work, "*Once a partner has used you a couple of times, you end up building up a relationship with them. They'll probably then give you more work.*" Trainees take the view that when you've got a training contract "*you can treat it as a long term job offer.*" Almost everyone is offered a job and most stay. There's been a blip on the radar this year, with five out of 11 qualifiers jumping ship. One left over money (salaries have not soared as they have at other firms), one to become a barrister (he got a great grounding in litigation), one for IT/e-commerce work ("*our practice is developing, but it's not there yet*"), one to do corporate work (remember, this is a litigation firm) and one was not offered a job. 2000 is an unusual year in this respect.

"Oil spills, rig explosions, sinkings, crashes. Disaster in any shape or form – that's Ince's business."

Ince & Co comes across as a harmonious place. Some older partners may be traditional and "*a little bit set in their ways,*" ("*they refuse to have voicemail*" and trainees have to use one of two computers in the library for full internet access) but it's not the type of firm where partners don't interact with the staff and trainees are seen and not heard. "*Teams working on cases often go out for lunch or after work drinks.*" The local All Bar One is the "*alternative office.*" Other favourite drinking establishments are the Crutched Friar and Foxtrot Oscar, the usual venue for Ince's happy hour(s).

midnight oil; a rare commodity

There's one distinct advantage to working for a litigation practice. The hours are not stupid. "*After 6.30pm is classed as working late here!*" It would be unusual for even a partner to stay after 8pm. Occasionally there might be a team burning the midnight oil: "*the sale and purchase lot might do that for a couple of days when completing a deal,*" but that's rare.

Decent hours are a compensation for "*scruffy late 70s/early 80s*" offices that are definitely "*not five star!*" "*We are of the philosophy that money doesn't get spent on the interior... they are not decked out in the best quality materials.*" Trainees said that the firm's clients were "*not the kind of people to spend money on frills.*" Don't expect modern art on the office walls. Do expect "*pictures of oil rigs and ships.*"

stand up for yourself

The firm has overseas offices in the shipping centres of the world but as a trainee you won't be seconded to any of them for a seat. As and when a case requires your presence, you'll fly out to visit a foreign office or a client. In the last few years, trainees have found themselves on planes bound for Singapore, Bahrain, the Yemen, Newfoundland and... Sheerness (to interview a captain aboard ship). Overseas secondments (for up to two or three years at a time) are reserved for qualified solicitors.

One of the messages trainees wanted to send to students reading this book is that you need to be confident and able to handle pressure when things get tough. "*You work for a lot of people and you have got to learn to stand up for yourself. It can be a harsh environment.*" So would they choose another firm if they had their time again? Never. Despite the fact that its work is so specialised? *"At first you think 'I know nothing about ships' but you pick it up as you go along"* one trainee said. Another agreed: *"It's one of those fields that people don't know that they want to do before starting – unless you have family connections."* But we detected no nepotism. The few who had experience of shipping or insurance before starting their training had as often as not had it arranged by the firm.

and finally...

You have to be a bright cookie and a tough cookie to be chosen for this training contract. There are only 11 or 12 trainees per year, each of whom takes on as much responsibility as he or she can bear. So you can certainly make your mark. You must be able to handle stress, because it won't all be plain sailing. And the physical environment isn't all ship-shape. But what a great training you'll get. And even those who move on have their pick of the top firms.

top recommendations in Chambers UK 2000-2001:

Shipping & Maritime Law

Irwin Mitchell

the facts

Location: Sheffield, Leeds, Birmingham, London
UK ranking by size: 29
Total number of trainees: 30
Seats: 4x6 months
Alternative seats: None

For over 80 years Irwin Mitchell has been a name to be reckoned with in Sheffield. With a blinding reputation for personal injury and clinical negligence work, it is also known for its claimant work on high profile group actions. Of more interest for aspiring trainees and newly qualifieds is its position as a business adviser. Now in four different cities, high profile PI firm Irwin

Mitchell has been rebranding, painting itself as a commercial firm. How accurate is this self portrait?

location location location

The number one reason for applying is location. Many trainees are originally from Sheffield or Leeds, some from the Midlands. Where are the offices? Sheffield, Leeds, the Midlands. Oh and a trainee satellite in London. Second most popular reason for applying? *"I wanted the benefits of a corporate firm with the benefits of a wider range of practice areas"* and *"It gives you the opportunity to do everything really."* Which translates as *'I wanted to keep my options open.'* Fair play, we say.

In each of the three main trainee locations, the spread of work is similar. Seats can be taken in company and commercial, commercial property, litigation, PI, employment and family. The well-known and popular business crime unit is only available in Sheffield. Other areas of law such as IP, insurance and private client, including family, wills and crime, are also available. This gives a very wide and flexible spread of work.

So don't people apply to the firm because of its top notch PI/med neg/disaster work any more? CJD and disease claims for miners; Lockerbie and Piper Alpha; Marchioness and Herald of Free Enterprise? Don't these cases motivate young lawyers in the same way that they used to? Apparently not. Or at least not to the extent that we were expecting. The buzz word amongst today's trainees and qualifiers is 'corporate.'

hanging together

The relationships between different offices of a multi-site firm are not always as harmonious as they could be. Sometimes people don't know those who work in other offices, sometimes the movement of trainees is non-existent and sometimes it is enforced and unpopular. Irwin Mitchell trainees are perfectly comfortable with the idea of the firm as a multi-office organisation. Somehow it all works. Leeds and

Sheffield are viewed as a single profit centre. *"A certain amount of flexibility is necessary, but as the distance between Sheffield and Leeds is small you tend to be fine. If you start off at one office you tend to stay there."* Moving between Birmingham and another office is by choice.

The social scene in Birmingham works well. There's not a huge number of trainees in the office at any one time (between four and six) so the winding down happens in teams. *"Trainees go out together a couple of times a month for moral support or a moan or whatever. I go out with the team two or three times a week. Sometimes it turns into a session."* On Fridays at 5.15pm the venue is Bennetts – by the firm's old office. The new office is *"Near the cathedral and it's funky and swanky and new. The one before was horrible and depressing. They are making an effort so we are too."*

lawyers in wellingtons

"We here in Leeds try and avoid All Bar One." These people have discerning taste and plenty of style. *"We go to Wellingtons, the pub at the end of the road. Friday night on the Headrow, there's loads of lawyers out." "You socialise more as an office here in Leeds as it's smaller."* In Sheffield, with the greater numbers, there is more scope for trainees-only nights out but mingling takes place on a firm-wide basis too....in All Bar One and The Shenanigans. To be sure, *"You have to make the effort to mingle with the partners. The ones offered jobs were the ones who went out and socialised a bit."*

What's this? A hint that not everyone gets offered jobs? Reality bites. This year, Irwins has kept around half of its trainees post qualification. That's not a particularly high proportion, but not out of keeping with previous years. Birmingham came up trumps in 2000 – it kept on all three of its qualifiers. One each in PI, employment and corporate/commercial. In Sheffield and Leeds, trainees were *"not so lucky"* and *"more people are moving on than staying because there's no jobs in the areas they wanted to qualify into."* Now that the firm is becoming more corporate, many trainees want to qualify there. But the firm has not caught up with its own zeitgeist. The corporate ele-

ments of the practice are developing, not yet fully developed. By the time you qualify, it may be that there are enough jobs in corporate for all who want them....

the good stuff

Where do we start? There's no shortage of positive feedback on the IM training experience. The hours are perfect for those who don't crave *"a lifestyle of hard grind."* Hours tend to range between 8am and 6pm, with a 5pm leave not viewed as abnormal. There's *"a get in early ethos rather than a stay late one."* In fact *"it's seen as bad time management if you are here much longer."*

"It's an easy place to come and enjoy being a trainee – informal and sociable" one source said, adding *"You are not made to feel as if you are supposed to sit here and work away at the grindstone... What you put in and how questioning you are determines what you get out."* We were told that *"You can have an easy time and they won't push you"* but *"the people who have made a real effort are the ones that are staying."*

A source in Sheffield told us how to differentiate between an Irwin Mitchell trainee and one from rival firm DLA. *"When we see each other in bars, they look more business-like!"* At Irwin Mitchell there is less homogeneity. *"PI lawyers are different to corporate lawyers who are different to family and crime. People are different entirely; it comes out in the dress sense."* We really got the impression that you can go to Irwin Mitchell and come out the other end of your training contract intact. You will not be processed and shaped into an identikit solicitor.

We must not let graduate recruitment/trainee supervisor, *"ab fab"* Sue Lenkowski, off the hook. She's definitely up there as one of the most admired trainee guardian angels in the country. Keep up the good work, Sue.

and finally...

The firm is changing. Irwin Mitchell's national profile is growing and its reputation for matters commercial is increasing. Its London office takes at least one trainee at each seat rotation. Niche commercial practice areas, such as IP are developing well. Its Birmingham office continues to establish itself. The 'northern PI specialists' are way more than that these days. Don't let this firm pass you by if you're not from up north and you want a commercial training. Trainees were especially keen we get that message across. In the final analysis, according to Irwin Mitchell trainees, variety is the spice of life.

top recommendations in Chambers UK 2000-2001:

Clinical Negligence (Claimant), Personal Injury: (Claimant), Product Liability

Kennedys

the facts

Location: London, Brentwood
UK ranking by size: 74
Total number of trainees: 14
Seats: 4x6 months
Alternative seats: None

More than 80% of this firm's work is insurance litigation. It is a niche firm. It will offer you the requisite non-contentious experience, perhaps in the small company/commercial department, perhaps in the small property department. But it is not a corporate firm. You have to want to be a litigator. The firm's raison d'être is the insurance market. So this is not just a litigation firm, this is an insurance litigation firm. Now we've made that clear, read on...

vertigo

Kennedys is smart. On its website it doesn't pretend to be anything other than what it is; a firm serving the litigation needs of the insurance market. It doesn't try and attract anyone other than applicants who would assimilate easily into its own unique world

order. We take our hats off to it. Don't be put off by the rather oppressive nature of the website. The black and white graphics may give you the impression that you'll be working on the set of a Hitchcock thriller for two years. *"That website is sinister – the firm is far from it."*

the 'burbs

Poor old, dull old Brentwood. You'd never choose to live or work there would you? Kennedys trainees have an initial resistance to the idea too. The firm has an office in this particular east London suburb (so much of a 'burb that it's in Essex and outside the M25). Each rotation, two trainees get allocated to the office, which handles mainly motor insurance claims. *"You'll get over the fact that you have to travel"* said one trainee *"because the experience is worthwhile. You gain confidence – it gets pretty hands on."* Another agreed. *"Initially you think 'Oh no!' but then you love the work. You can get to see a case almost from start to finish."*

If, as the trainees acknowledge, the Brentwood experience *"prepares them so well,"* does that mean that time spent in one of the two London offices is less productive? No such thing. *"You get much better quality work in the City offices, from trips and slips at one end to big construction related claims, employers liability and public liability."* Trainees are more than happy with the levels of responsibility they get. *"When you are in court you usually have a barrister or solicitor on the other side, not a trainee"* one told us. *"You get used to going to court – at least twice a month here. At Brentwood it's about three times a week."*

intercity

The two City offices are separated by about a 15 minute walk. The Mark Lane office is right by Lloyd's in the heart of the underwriting sector of the City. The office is *"extremely smart and modern"* and is *"geared around clients."* It houses about 60 lawyers from the firm. *"At least once or twice a week, events are organised for clients there."* The Chiswell Street office is the main one and it *"deals with everything."* There seems to be no desire at this stage to move everyone under one roof.

The firm has a staff drinks party on the last Friday of every month. *"It's the main social and quite a few partners go to it."* There are also *"not so well attended"* drinks every Friday for fee earners and trainees. Some people hang around at those weekly bashes – *"the usual suspects."* Additionally there is socialising in work groups of around eight to ten lawyers. As well as having the most interesting work, the 'BR unit' (so called because of the origins of the unit's lawyers) has the best social scene. The combination of interesting work and a good team spirit makes this the most popular and oversubscribed of the trainee seats. One other reason that seat is so popular is that the incumbent often gets work from the employment team as well.

philosophy

Kennedys states that all of its lawyers operate with the *"product"* in mind; the *"economic resolution of the claim, not merely the legal services necessary along the way."* Implying that Kennedys is not a firm to place the highest value on pure academics. The basic skills needed to resolve claims are those sought out by graduate recruitment. *"A wide variety of people work here"* one trainee said to us. *"I have got quite a few friends here at Kennedys so we must have something in common."* The work is very team-based and so too is the ethos of the firm. As contact with clients tends to be frequent and long term, the teamworking ethos is prominent.

something for the ladies

Client events and marketing to the industry play a big part in day to day life at the firm. Trainees are certainly expected to want to be a part of this. *"We are very closely tied to them. It's social – lots of meeting up with clients, lots of events, quiz nights etc."* Indeed the etc. stretches to Premier league football matches, the firm's sponsorship of motorsport and – for the ladies – Ascot. We wondered if the insurance world was male dominated, by any chance. The trainees responded variously to that question. *"It is a laddy industry"* one thought. *"There are so many types – in claims, barrow boys"* and in underwriting *"cigar smoking"* men who *"have been in the profession for about a hundred years."* But, despite this ethos, another felt that there was a perfectly healthy gender balance and that about half of his clients were women.

uninsured losses

The good news is that, almost without exception, everyone is offered a job on qualification. But of those who stay *"everyone is going to become a litigator and work in insurance."* One trainee who wanted to practise in a different area of law felt that *"my chances have been harmed"* and that he/she would have been better off at a less specialist firm. Whilst there is no criticism of the quality of experience at Kennedys, it is not always the best choice for those who are undecided as to the type of lawyer they want to become. *"There's two sorts of people who come here"* one source said. People fresh from uni and law school and people who spent time in the insurance industry beforehand. It suits the latter better. *"They have made a concerted effort to come here and sometimes others don't know an awful lot about the firm."*

At qualification, a good proportion of the trainees will *"jump ship,"* having decided that insurance is not for them. They are perhaps also attracted by higher salaries on offer elsewhere. Many will find that the decent hours at the firm (*"8.45am to 6pm generally"*) are not repeated elsewhere and it'll be pot luck as to whether they will find their new firms as easy to fit into. *"It's like a family here"* one told us, adding *"nearly anyone would fit in here."*

and finally...

So you want to be an insurance litigation lawyer? You've come to the right place.

top recommendations in Chambers UK 2000-2001:

Professional Negligence

Lawrence Graham

the facts
Location: London
UK ranking by size: 39
Total number of trainees: 30
Seats: 4x6 months
Alternative seats: Occasional overseas seats

One of the quieter ones. Outside the City, with offices on The Strand and a tiny enclave in St Mary Axe (heart of the City, in the shadow of the Lloyd's building) for insurance and shipping. Its low-key image belies its position as 24th largest in London, just behind Baker & McKenzie. It's enhancing its reputation in sexy new corporate work.

who?
The firm is best described through negatives. *"Not really aggressive,"* it avoids the limelight. Neither loud nor self-promoting, Lawrence Graham rarely hits the headlines in a spectacular way. The most recent big news was of merger talks with Stephenson Harwood. Somewhat disappointingly for journalists, but to no-one's great surprise, the talks came to nothing. Trainees feel that the firm is aspirational but wants to grow organically. Hardly the stuff of headlines.

the 'f' word
Despite our most valiant attempts it has proved impossible to avoid using the word 'friendly' in relation to Lawrence Graham. All our interviewees mentioned it at least three times per interview. *"Everyone gets on really well"* was another phrase which popped up with sickening regularity. Trainees seem genuinely happy with their lot, describing the firm as *"laid back"* (*"not a sausage machine"*) if *"traditional."* There is no huge pressure to stay late; *"if there's nothing needing doing you are told to go home."* If you want friendliness this could be the firm for you. If, on the other hand, you are the competitive type, looking for a thrusting City practice, you could feel a little frustrated by the laid back atmosphere.

"absolute carnage"
Being in the West End of London you would expect shopping and drinking to play a big part in the firm's social scene. You can always *"bomb off to Covent Garden"* said one trainee. Moreover, there seems to be enough to keep trainees busy in their social lives. Paragliding, curry nights and a separate trainee Christmas event are highlights. The atmosphere is helped by the comparatively small number of trainees. *"Trainees have lives outside work"* stated one trainee, only to confess that this meant everyone being *"down the road in the wine bar."* The firm-organised social events also seem to have gained a reputation for being lively. One trainee described the summer party as *"absolute carnage from the partners down."* The mind boggles. It certainly seems that the firm is not laid back when it comes to socialising. This attitude towards life may emanate from the senior partner. *"He is the first one to say he wants everyone to have another life other than work."*

melting pot
We hear that the firm used to have a reputation for enlightened employment practices. It was known to take on staff with disabilities as well as a higher than average number of minorities. Like liquorice allsorts Lawrence Graham trainees are still a *"mixed bag"* coming from *"many different backgrounds."* Resisting the temptation to be a part of the law degree to law school to training contract conveyor belt, the firm is *"very good at looking around for trainees."* Many have had other careers. Insiders applaud this. *"The life experience helps"* making people *"very open-minded"* and *"interesting."* Former lives have included the army and banking, as well as the insurance industry and accountancy. Not so much social awareness as shrewd client-savviness perhaps; all of the above represent key client groups of the firm. Former paralegals have been taken on as trainees. One

trainee thought that as many as half her intake had been to 'newer' as opposed to more traditional universities.

the muppet show

Though trainees admit that it varies from department to department, most feel they get a lot of client contact, *"dealing with them on a regular basis."* Frontline contact with big clients was common. One trainee spoke of dealing directly with Legal & General and several told of *"one-to-one* (sic) *contact with Cellnet."* Trainees are taken along to corporate client events, giving rookies the perfect opportunity to cut their teeth despite *"feeling like a bit of a muppet."* Lawrence Graham is not embarrassed by its trainees; it does not feel the need to keep them hidden from view.

getting away from it all

Apart from an office in the Ukraine, which did not seem the holiday destination of choice for LG trainees, the firm has no overseas offices. However, it does have foreign connections via the Associate Business Lawyers in Europe group. Some trainees do manage to get abroad to these European firms but their success in so doing depends on perseverance and language skills. If there was any substantive criticism from our interviewees, it was that trainees feel international opportunities are too hard to come by. There's an easy answer to that – they should have done their homework.

and finally...

It may be 100% commercial, but it's cuddly, good for shopping and drinking and supports new artists by displaying their work around the office. Does this sound like a law firm? No, we didn't think so either. Worth checking out then.

top recommendations in Chambers UK 2000-2001:

Corporate finance (fewer than 30 solicitors in corporate team), Trusts [Band 2]

Linklaters

the facts

Location: London
UK ranking by size: 4
Total number of trainees: 257
Seats: 4x6 months
Alternative seats: Several overseas offices, secondments
Extras: Language training, pro bono

"Not a terrific performance. It seems the thrill of doing the quiz has affected your judgement! There's a Circus School just down the road from our London office – perhaps you should try there."

With years of experience in practice to our names, we were rather upset to receive this response when we tested our mettle against the Linklaters quiz on the website.

So what does it take to make a good Linklaters person? It's a magic circle firm which excels in practically every commercial practice area so you clearly need a quality CV and strong ambitions. The firm has the second highest turnover of any UK firm (after Slaughter and May) on the back of its corporate work. So you need an interest in the corporate world. The firm is the dominant partner of a high-profile alliance of European firms. Language skills and an international outlook are 'advantageous.'

the future's so bright I gotta wear shades

Reasons for choosing Linklaters over other magic circle firms range from the random *"I chose them over Slaughters because their application form was a lot nicer to fill in!"* to the strategic *"International expansion was on the horizon then."* Almost everyone we spoke to only considered the magic circle firms, based either on advice from a director of studies or on a notion that it was the only training worth having. But how do you distinguish between those top-banded corporate firms?

There's definitely something there but it's a whisper of a difference, a hairsbreadth crack between the personality of Linklaters and say, Freshfields. The UK profile of the firms are so similar – which to go for? A recent law school graduate summed up the Linklaters trainees of the future as the head boys and head girls of this world. *"These people are diligent, confident, independent, hard-working and responsible."* In other words the bossy but nice types. Whereas Freshfields trainees were captains of sports at school and university – the type you had a childish crush on.

The firm's own trainees admit that there's a Linklaters type: *"focused and determined in terms of their career and how well they do here."* They are *"confident and outgoing people, prepared to appreciate that their career is in their own hands and that they have to go for it."* We expected that trainees in such a large firm would feel like pawns in someone else's chess game. In fact time and again they told us how in control they are. *"People make their own careers here. People take the initiative and carry things through."* They have usually been bred on success and achievement. *"They recruit the same type of people – I see that again and again. I have just come back from* [an overseas seat] *and there are two new rounds of trainees that have come in since I have been gone. They are the same type of people, really friendly, chatty and bright."* Yes. This is a recurrent theme over the years. *"Even the quieter types are pretty confident in their abilities,"* and *"the average person is really bright."* Here's the rub. Linklaters lawyers have an edge of intellectual arrogance. They marvel at how intelligent they all are. And no doubt it's true. But this is what the firm values above all else.

blue chip

This is a top ranked corporate firm with an astonishing reputation amongst blue chip clients. It's an obvious and undeniably clever decision to come to the firm if you want to forge a career as a corporate lawyer. The deals are high profile and often involve large teams of lawyers working on document intensive projects. As a trainee you are close to the bottom of the food chain, however bright you are. Your role in headline-hitting deals can be a chore. Junior solicitors must also learn the ropes on these deals, so tasks that trainees in smaller firms would do on lower value deals will be beyond the reach of Linklaters trainees. *"It is true of corporate, but long-term corporate offers some really good work."* Of the wait to get into the front line of a deal, *"the grim truth is that in the short term you will be given tasks such as staffing the data room."* This is the documents room on a deal. Trainees are sometimes put in charge of it, meaning sitting in the room for hours while the other side comes to inspect documents. *"I have heard of people who literally just sit there, which is crazy. Now they've set up a Legal Service Group of paralegals. Clients shouldn't be paying you to do this kind of work."*

But good news from another trainee lucky enough to get some interesting tasks in corporate. *"People must remember that all our clients are big clients but they are not all big deals. You do get more and more responsibility on the smaller deals."* Corporate is the epicentre of the firm and there's a sense of being required to show that you really do belong there. *"In corporate, I think it has a kind of atmosphere where you should be seen to be working quite hard and it's a kind of old boy network."*

fresh approach goes stale

On arrival, the firm conducts workshops for the new intake, in which each department does a presentation on the type of work that it does, indicating *"the kind of person you should be and the kind of things that you should be interested in. Some areas are more academic than others, some more transactional and document-intensive."* The firm needs to do this because within the first few weeks of training you will be asked to indicate where you want to qualify. *"It's quite daunting because you're doing it cold and having to choose where you want to qualify. But you can change."* Good job too! This notion of choosing what sort of lawyer you want to be up front (and without any experience of the work) is one of the main tenets of the 'Fresh

Approach', which was seen as the panacea for all training ills only two years ago.

Some of the current trainees were recruited into the Fresh Approach. Six four-month seats, with a double seat in your chosen field encouraged for the early part of your training. *"They use the word 'encouraged' a lot but there's an element of stick as well as carrot."* Now, trainees are started on a four by six-month seat rotation. So why did anything change in the first place? *"In the past there have been complaints that people don't get valued enough and their solution is to have you commit yourself to a practice area earlier so that you were more useful."* There had also been complaints that newly qualifieds weren't experienced enough in their chosen areas on qualification. Some had done less than five months in the relevant practice area. Hence the idea of getting trainees to do a double seat of eight months in their preferred department. Additionally, *"what they were trying to do was get everyone through the corporate department, because it's the big strength of the firm."* So it's important that everyone understands the nature of corporate transactions.

pre-judgement day

Last year we reported that the trainee jury was out on the Fresh Approach and that there were doubts about the practicality of deciding where to qualify before starting the training contract. *"It's naive to think that someone fresh-faced from university will know all about the work of a corporate firm"* said one. It certainly isn't universally popular. *"It's pigeonholing people much earlier than you did before, which from a business point of view is very, very good but from a trainee's point of view isn't."* *"It works well for some people but not for others."*

Even before starting the training contract, the firm keeps in contact with students in order to help them make the decision about where to qualify. *"Everyone is educated before they actually arrive and are encouraged to make a decision."* One source confirmed, *"it's almost like Freshers' Fair at uni. Each department is given carte blanche as to how to market themselves at law school."* Most of those we spoke to believed that *"trainees have to have some idea of what they want to do before coming here. I don't think anyone comes here with absolutely no idea."* Those who have not made a decision are apparently put into corporate for their first seat.

doing a ton

There is no end of opportunities to be involved in international work from London. But this often means long hours. *"We do lots of cross-Atlantic deals and the Americans don't work to our timetable. They call the shots. That's a symptom of business generally growing globally. Also the desire to do it with as few people as possible for the sake of continuity. One £30bn deal was just three people and a junior partner – 100 hours a week every week for three months."*

Secondments to UK-based clients, such as banks and BA tend to be taken up by those who don't want to go abroad. Litigation secondments include the opportunity to work at the Mary Ward Legal Centre.

intellectual giants

Getting shot of the drudgery has been an issue on trainees' minds in the last few years. Linklaters are in step with a change currently evident in City practices, taking on more paralegals and allocating more appropriate tasks to trainees. *"That is one thing the trainees campaigned for a bit."* So despite their feeling of being in control Linklaters trainees have been dissatisfied by work. *"You always think that you're more capable than people perceive you to be and I think that's difficult to deal with."* It can be frustrating, but trainees understand that *"there's a ceiling of responsibility because there are people above you who need their own responsibilities in order to gain experience."*

"When I enjoyed it most was when I had a discrete task to do myself and I was dealing directly with the client. Being the 16th person in the conference room can be interesting in that you can follow the proceedings, but it can be dull as well." Like many young City lawyers, they subscribe to the theory that *"joining a large firm is a*

longer-term strategy than joining a smaller one. You're most marketable at one or two years qualified when it's more hands-on." A degree of patience is an asset that isn't sufficiently emphasised in graduate recruitment literature. *"The transactions are worth lots and lots of money. You're not going to be let loose on something like that because the ramifications of messing up are frightening."* But juniors at Linklaters are pragmatic. Maybe *"you don't have as much hands-on experience as people at smaller firms,"* but the client experience you do get is probably going to be pretty memorable. Some partners are hero-worshipped as *"intellectual giants."*

after hours

"You have to be enthusiastic because you are going to have to work hard…. The flipside to that is, as a general rule, you are looked after." *"Often when people feel pressure to stay late it's largely self-induced, it's a guilt thing."* Average time to leave tends to be 6.30pm–7pm but, *"if I am here past 8pm then it'll be midnight."* With mobiles and laptops *"if anything goes wrong you can be contacted at home or on your mobile."* New technology means certain raised expectations – that you'll be contactable outside the office.

> "Once you've trained here you're pretty marketable."

Remember, there's no such thing as a free lunch. *"Linklaters will say you are free to go home at 5.30pm if you've got no work to do. If you're in litigation or employment or tax then no one will bat an eyelid."* But do it every day and people will start to wonder. *"In corporate…you shouldn't be seen to be going home too early, certainly on a regular basis. People would raise an eyebrow if you went at six."* Sounds a bit harsh. *"Other firms and other people at this firm will tell you that's not true and they are lying…It's just so not true it's ridiculous. Possibly if it's the end of the deal and it's 2am on Friday morning. But not in the middle of the deal – no way. That's*

something you have to accept. You do pay with hours."

Long hours there may be during the week but most trainees only worked the odd weekend. There's a lot of social stuff laid on for you if you want to take advantage of it. Not everyone does, especially when they've had a big week. *"I've found that I have a lot in common with the people here and it's quite nice to go out with them sometimes."* The two pubs local to the office are the St. Paul's Tavern and the King's Head, but Links trainees are trying to shift their scene over to trendy Smithfield Market, into cool bars like Smiths and Fluid (also the Chambers locals). The office is just across the road from the Barbican centre, so culture is on your doorstep.

self portrait

This is how Linklaters trainees see themselves in contrast to trainees at other magic circle firms: *"Outgoing. It's a sexy firm. Of all the leading firms it's quite sexy…..Linklaters have always been thought of as the friendly firm and people enjoy being here. That's the thing that's sold it to trainees."* Interesting self-image.

listen and learn

"Recently a committee took up some issues with personnel very effectively…pay, seat allocations, jobs on qualification, better use of paralegals. The firm generally listens." You can also go on a one to one basis to the group training partner, usually drawn from younger, more human partners at the firm. Those who are *"still relatively understanding – the fluffy partners."*

At some point, the firm is going to have to address a disease infecting trainee populations at large City firms. The idea is that with a bit of experience under your belt, you cut and run. *"Once you've trained here you're pretty marketable."* And applicants are surprisingly cynical about this. *"Every trainee has an idea of their own worth – what the quality of life would be if they worked elsewhere."* Linklaters, are you paying attention? Young lawyers are often worn down by their careers, yet have a high sense of self-worth. Trainees envy the client's role in transactions. *"Relief and satisfaction is what they have as a client – it's the lawyer who is staying late. As a client you know that they have to stay there and do it as you are paying them."*

and finally...

The minute you walk into the Silk Street reception you know you're dealing with a class act. Silent automatic doors. Glass. Leather. Clocks showing international timezones. Newspapers from across the world. Discreet staff offering drinks and biscuits. Almost overwhelming and very glamorous to the wide-eyed applicant. Behind the façade are busy, hard-working, stressed lawyers. There is hard graft before you can hope to get real responsibility. But when you do, you'll be working on top international deals, with the gods of their sectors. And Linklaters' name on your CV is a passport to anything.

top recommendations in Chambers UK 2000-2001:

Capital Markets (International debt/equity issues), Competition/Anti-trust, Corporate Finance: (60+ Solicitors in corporate team), Employee Share Schemes, Financial Services, Fraud, Investment Funds, Pensions, Property (Commercial)

Lovells

the facts

Location: London
UK ranking by size: 10
Total number of trainees: 125
Seats: 4x6 months
Alternative seats: Brussels, Hong Kong, Moscow, New York, Paris, Prague, Tokyo. Secondments (3i, BAA, John Lewis, BATCo)
Extras: Language training, pro bono

In days gone by Lovells was two firms. Lovell White & King and Durrant Piesse. One was known as Lovely White & Clean. The nice firm. After the merger the name changed to Lovell White Durrant. The image stuck. And now there's been another merger. The firm has gone truly international. It's got a streamlined name. It's moving into new purpose-built offices. With sleeping pods. And still it's known as the firm with the nice, clean image. The partnership is happy. There's a collegiate atmosphere. But the firm lacks the crucial elements of glamour, high-profile and runaway profits which characterise the magic circle. Nibbling at the toes of the upper echelons, it's now part of the 'Gang of Eight' sponsoring the new City LPC. It wants to sit with the glamorous firms, but seems destined to be always the .

guten tag deutschland

The year 2000 saw a high profile merger with leading German firm Boesebeck Droste. *"A lot of trainees apply as it's a big firm so the merger is a positive thing. We expect more "* we were told. The trainees expect to be offered the opportunity to go out to the German offices on secondment. *"German linguists will find that they are sought after."* Boesebecks didn't have a London office so there's *"no change in culture or atmosphere"* in London following the merger. *"It's just like having the number of overseas offices expanded."*

Plenty apply to Lovells because of its international offices. *"I think a lot of them come along with a sense of the travelling bug, because a lot of them are fresh out of school. Our generation is very international, multi-cultural and travelling is a big feature of lifestyle."*

As with all firms offering seats overseas, there's stiff competition for some (Brussels, NY and HK) and little competition for others (e.g. Moscow). *"Certain intakes get it into their heads that they all want to go abroad, and also Lovells does a lot of client secondments."* Up to three quarters of each intake will get the chance to spend time out of the office.

the corporate bridesmaid

Why Lovells? Why a firm that sits outside the magic circle? What is it that leads a number of trainees to reject the magic circle in favour of the firm that tries so hard but doesn't quite make it? The most common response goes like this: "*I wanted a large firm with a broad base so I would have the opportunity to try as many different areas as possible.*"

Pretty much all interviewees this year and last thought they benefited from the broad church approach. *What sets us aside is that its a truly broad-based practice. Our speciality areas are proper practices in their own right.*" If you are not especially corporate-oriented then Lovells may be an excellent choice. "*At other firms you can be expected to do two corporate seats, whereas at Lovells you wouldn't need to.*"

finding your niche

Of its work 45% is corporate, so be under no illusions. Most trainees will do a seat there. "*People appreciate that for certain types of corporate work Lovells isn't quite up there but overall we think we have a better deal because it's a nicer place*" one source put it quite simply. Lovells is right up there in a number of areas. "*Here you have a realistic chance of staying in a more niche department.*"

> "Pro bono is definitely encouraged ...it's award-winning"

If you do have a wish list for seats, it's very important to communicate this to personnel as early as possible as "*they can't read your mind.*" Do people get what they want? "*They encourage you to have a plan of sorts. It means, in personnel terms, that if they can't give you what you want this time they can see in what direction you are going and give it to you next time.*" You don't have to have a plan but it helps. "*You have to push yourself, nobody is going to shout for you.*" EU and IP are particularly popular. Of those who qualified this year, around a third left the firm, many because they weren't offered jobs in their preferred practice area. Two IP jobs were offered. Almost a dozen qualifiers wanted them. "*The jobs offered were across the*

board, but the two bottlenecks were EU/competition and IP.*" This September's departures were "*a bit of a haemorrhage....They need to recruit more corporate trainees.*"

the price you pay

"*To be honest I have been bloody lucky. I haven't really worked past 8 o'clock... I have never been involved with the high value corporate deals.*" You can get away with leave times between 6pm and 7pm if you steer clear of corporate. But in corporate or banking? "*It's disingenuous to say that you don't have to stay late, because you do. But it's only if there's an urgent issue, not because it's part of the culture.*" It really depends on what's going on in a department. "*In banking, hours were long. I did quite a few all-nighters, quite a lot of 2am or sometimes just 10pm-11pm. I was really involved so I didn't mind at all.*"

The flipside of all the frenetic activity is that there may well be times when a department is not busy or it is too busy to lavish attention on you. "*There's lots of photocopying in some groups. They sit the most junior trainees there. It's the price you pay for being here.*"

and the price they don't

There's a couple of solutions to feeling unfulfilled. "*You have to ask for more meaningful work. The ones that are unhappy are those that sit there and don't say anything.*" Another trainee referred us to the pro bono work the firm undertakes. "*I have got involved with the pro bono unit. I like doing it because there is a bit of a moral and a social kind of angle, also you get amazing experience because you get your own clients, you go to court etc.*"

There is a recognition amongst the partners in the firm that pro bono work is a valid way of spending time. It's actually put on your timesheet and nobody questions it. "*Pro bono work is definitely encouraged.*" At Lovells it's award-winning and very well-managed by a full-time lawyer.

going (not too) wild...

"*It's not a stuffy, leather-bound old boys club.*" But not particularly unconventional; "*it's sensible, middle of the* road." More than one trainee referred to the social scene being *"what you make it."* There are groups of trainees who hit it off and go out quite a lot. But this is in pockets. On Fridays there will always be a few people in Terry Neill's Sports Bar or The Bottle Scrue, both underneath the office. *"It's a relaxed Friday night scene – this isn't the sort of place where everyone goes out every Friday night."* *"We are not the party animals of the City!"*

Lunch in the staff canteen is *"not bad. People all moan about it, but the food is pretty good and cheap."* Once or twice a year all members of staff will have the opportunity of attending a 'partners lunch'.

all walks of life?

As one trainee put it, *"there's enough opportunity here that there are people from all walks of life. The pro bono unit is a great anchor as well, to make sure you don't get carried away with yourself."* A number of interviewees mentioned an increased emphasis on Oxbridge recruitment. *"We've just finished vacation schemes and virtually all were Oxbridge law undergrads. We invest so much money in the Bodleian Library that we want to get our money out of them."*

and finally...

Lovells the cuddly City firm, with barely a freckle, let alone a blemish, on its character, is still seen to be one of the most forgiving environments inside the square mile. Hard work but *"at the same time there's a common ethic that if you're happy where you are, we are going to get more out of you."* But it's a big firm. *"I feel a bit out of the loop. In the long term I'm not entirely sure if I have a personal stake in the firm. The trick will be keeping people loyal. People are not willing to take it for seven years just to get partnership. People are much more cynical nowadays."*

top recommendations at Chambers UK 2000-2001:

Fraud, Insurance & Reinsurance, Parliamentary & Public Affairs, Pensions Litigation

Macfarlanes

the facts

Location: London
UK ranking by size: 41
Total number of trainees: 22
Seats: 4x6 months
Alternative seats: occasional foreign seats

'Conservative with a small 'c'.'Traditional values. Intelligent hard-working lawyers. Getting the idea?

On its website the senior partner states that the firm values *"decency, responsibility and helping people in trouble."* As most clients are commercial or high net worth individuals trainees were unsure about 'helping people in trouble' – *"it makes us sound like Help the Aged!"* They admitted that *"some people have an image of the firm as being outdated and stuffy."* They themselves felt this was going too far, but their various comments about the firm were epitomised by one trainee's description of it as *"solidly dependable."* Overall Macfarlanes is a safe, stable and well-managed bet, with quality work and little of the scandal attracted by other firms. It practises a sort of *"good conservatism."*

border control

Macfarlanes does not pretend to have the empire-building international ambitions of larger City competitors. Internationally it may be *"a bit staid when compared to the thrusting, bigger firms."* A *"smaller Slaughter and May,"* it has 'best friends' relationships with top firms in other jurisdictions but eschews international mergers. The firm maintains that *"A more effective solution for our clients is provided by the close relationships we enjoy with first class lawyers in other jurisdictions.*

The important consequence for the prospective trainee is the lack of dedicated foreign seats at Macfarlanes. Trainees we spoke to said that a few people each year were able to go abroad. One had recently been to Abu Dhabi. However if you see yourself as wanting to 'chill out' in Moscow or take a bite out of the 'Big Apple' during your training contract then Macfarlanes is probably not the firm for you.

pick 'n' mix

There is a rare breadth of work available at the firm. Despite its strong corporate departments, Macfarlanes has never lost touch with its traditional legal roots. It not only continues to support its private client and agricultural practices but is a market leader in both. In this respect it resembles the law firm of old. A "real draw" for some trainees, others saw these departments as anomalous, although the work "has a feed both ways." In fact clients are by no means limited to rich landed gentry. "Most of the agricultural work is done for pension funds and other institutional investors." It begins to look less like a blast from the past and more like shrewd cross-selling.

If you get your kicks from the fast-moving world of advertising and marketing, the team is a sector leader. "The clients are fun but they can be difficult. They might send through an advert, saying that they're putting it on air that day and ask 'Is it OK?' on a hand-written fax. They operate to very close deadlines and expect a tremendous amount from you."

happy families

No partners have defected to other firms since the early 1980s. It does not have a partnership deed but an undocumented 'gentleman's agreement.' 65% of its partners joined the firm as trainees. Join Macfarlanes and it seems you could have a job for life. It must be doing something right in the trust and relationship department. The firm claims to emphasise internal communication and indeed the comment "all the partners know you" was heard from many we spoke to. Not only do partners know you but "they treat you like equals who just don't know as much yet." There is regular feedback of the official type (three monthly and six monthly reviews). However, it is mostly of the unofficial type (work comes back covered in red ink or they have your "guts for garters").

Good relationships with clients are equally emphasised. This has both positive and negative effects for trainees. One trainee spoke of meeting one of the Alchemy Partners and driving Jackie Stewart's racing cars. However "you don't get much in private client because the partners have built up long-term relationships with the clients. They don't want to let trainees talk to them."

get on with it!

The message we get from trainees each year at Macfarlanes is that they are encouraged to stand on their own two feet. You "need to be the sort of person who will thrive in an environment where you will be given a lot of responsibility early on. The partners want you to be able to stand alone as quickly as possible." Those of a more cautious disposition " could find this daunting."

There is backup for this responsibility. "You get all the supervision you want, they really do care." However, "what you're not thanked for is if you put your hand up and plead ignorance before you've even given it a shot."

Don't join the firm thinking you'll get an easy ride; Macfarlanes' trainees are kept on their toes. It is not uncommon to work 12 hour days in corporate and commercial departments. Even in property a 10 hour day is normal. As a result, people who fit in best are those who are prepared to "muck in" without complaint. Trainees admit that they work hard but they make time to be "quite social as a group as well."

will I fit in?

Second only to Linklaters, trainees emphasise intelligence as a key word. "Everybody is highly intelligent." When asked whether it is true that Macfarlanes has an academic environment one confirmed, "I think the approach...is to try and recruit people as bright as possible. They sort of pride themselves on having bright people working for them."

shall we dish the figures?

The Macfarlanes approach to giving information does not extend to making public its profits. Despite this, the medium-sized firm has a reputation for *"successfully competing with much larger firms for big ticket work."* On the strength of the unofficial figures published in the press, trainees are proud of *"the fact that it manages to be the eighth most profitable* [firm in the UK per partner] *whilst being 50th in size."* No wonder partners don't leave. No wonder trainees are kept working hard.

and finally...

So, hard work, long hours, early responsibility, high intelligence, big profits. It sounds like a serious, competitive place. Last year we quoted a trainee who said *"It's not Lord of the Flies. No one is going round chucking spears at each other."* We asked interviewees for their comments this year. *"No, it's not like that"* we heard repeatedly. An escapee told us otherwise. We think they protest too much.

top recommendations in Chambers UK 2000-2001:

Advertising & Marketing, Agriculture & Bloodstock, Corporate Finance, Trusts

Manches

the facts

Location: London and Oxford
UK ranking by size: 67
Total number of trainees: 20
Seats: 4x6months
Alternative seats: None

Medium-sized, in London and Oxford, this firm sends out mixed messages in terms of its culture and work-type. On the one hand it describes itself as a *"major commercial law firm."* At the same time it continues to stand by its renowned family department when many other medium-sized firms would long since have hived it off to concentrate on commercially-related work only. It describes itself as *"progressive"* yet its website defines the firm's culture in terms of male rugby players and female ballet dancers. What is the truth?

family values

Family and corporate finance work seem just about as far apart as areas of law could be. Yet Manches continues to be involved in both, which is interesting in a world where many larger firms have long since chosen to focus on specific areas. *"It's not Olswang, not focusing on this or that but it is not trying to do everything. A traditional multidisciplinary firm."* For those who apply to do corporate work, it may be surprising to hear that *"generally everybody ends up doing a family seat."* There can be no doubt that, amongst trainees, the family department is still popular. Sources that we spoke to said that in some years family is the department everybody wants to go into on qualification. Obviously the seat allows for a lot of client contact. However, according to insiders, it *"doesn't want to be known as a private client firm."* Like many a medium-sized firm *"family is not being used as so much of a seller"* for the firm. Its drive is currently into IT and IP. Indeed, the private client work has all been packed off to Oxford. A trainee described the situation well. *"Because it* (the family department) *is so prestigious....this is a commercial firm with a family department."*

stay where you are

We spoke to people in both London and Oxford offices. It appears that, for most trainee purposes, the offices are separate. *"You will stay with that office for all of your work."* With only one or two trainees at the Oxford office, *"there is more...cameraderie between trainees in London."* However, in Oxford *"the atmosphere is more relaxed and there is more fluid contact with assistants and partners."* The training in Oxford is fairly fluid as well, with trainees able to combine seats (eg. family with litigation). The pay is lower than in the London office but trainees feel that the salary compares well against other firms in Oxford.

Within the London office some feel that the firm could be better integrated. *"Within the departments there is a very good team spirit but you are pigeon-holed into departments and you don't get to know people that well."* These problems with cohesion may well be a direct or indirect result of the fact that *"it has had a lot of mergers."* For those who do know each other, *"everyone gets on really well."*

which ones are the rugby players?

In an attempt to find out more about the people and atmosphere at the firm we asked about the rugby players on the website. Sources disagreed with this apparent macho image. *"There are a lot of very powerful ladies in the family department who wouldn't put up with that."* Oops – scary! Not unusually, with the exception of employment and family, all departments have traditionally been male-dominated. But the firm is now *"changing quite a bit."* Corporate still feels a bit *"laddy"* but otherwise it no longer feels male-dominated.

mad as hatters

One thing coming through very clearly was eccentricity. *"There are quite a few eccentric characters here. After a while you forget that they are eccentric and probably become a bit eccentric yourself."* This is certainly *"better than having those with no personality."* Eccentric, yes. Stupid, no. Said one source; *"we don't suffer fools."*

building relationships

"People have to develop their own relationships within the firm. You need to make yourself feel like part of the club. There isn't a department that sorts everything out for you" was the view of one source. This seems to apply to the social life as much as the work. The social life *"depends a lot on the intake."* With sources describing the place as *"chummy,"* *"gossipy,"* and everybody being *"quite a good laugh"* it should not be a problem. You might even get to meet Lara Croft – *"the clay model not the human one"* – she's a client.

and finally...

A training at this firm will certainly suit someone who isn't ready to commit one way or another, but wants a top quality firm. The broad training you get here will set you up for your career – in whichever direction you want to take it.

top recommendations in Chambers UK 2000-2001:

Charities, Family/Matrimonial

Masons

the facts

Location: London, Bristol, Manchester, Leeds, Glasgow, Edinburgh
UK ranking by size: 23
Total number of trainees: 45
Seats: (London) 6 x 4 months (Leeds) 4 x 6 months
Alternative seats: Brussels
Extras: Pro bono

Masons – the construction firm. That's what people say and there's good reason for doing so. They may hate the label at times, but the trainees know that they're working for one of the world's best construction law firms. *"Most people are keen to get away from that construction juggernaut tag."* Why? If you've got it flaunt it – that's what we say.

what's it all about

Masons bills itself as a firm with four target sectors. Following its recent rebranding, its partners have now been asked to align themselves with one of the following four business divisions: IT, energy, infrastructure and construction/engineering. As one source pointed out, *"You've got to realise that it has two main areas; construction and IT, with the projects cutting across."*

The practical effects of this are that trainees will do two four-month seats in construction and will probably get another four in the popular IT department.

"Most people will do IT. It's a good opportunity. Your four months includes contentious, non-contentious and new media/e-commerce." The training contract divides up into thirds so you're told at each eight-month rotation where you will be going for your next two seats. Whilst there's plenty of opportunity to cover a range of practice areas, you should remember that one third of your time will be spent in the construction department. You should note though, that construction is broken down into specialisms such as oil/gas, power/water etc.

the new black

The most popular seats are IT, tax (this year's 'new black' according to trainees at most firms) and, until very recently, Financial Planning – a.k.a. private client. Sadly this last option (seen as a skills seat because it was very hands-on and its small matters were good learning tools) is no more. The firm shed this department in the spring of 2000. Other departments tend to work on large projects; ie property, corporate. Projects are *"the whole aim of the firm."*

Its work is increasingly international. World over, Masons projects and construction lawyers have a fantastic reputation. You are likely to find yourself working on major deals and disputes concerning places as far flung as Hong Kong and Brazil, India and the Middle East. There's a regular overseas seat in Brussels, covering EC/competition work and very occasionally a more exotic posting might crop up. But don't bank on it. Brussels is naturally very popular and oversubscribed.

never knowingly underlawyered

The Masons equivalent of the mega corporate deal is the huge piece of construction litigation. Paralegal support is adequate. There's roughly the same number of paralegals as there are trainees. Over the last few years, about one per year seems to have crossed over to a training contract. There's a vast amount of documentation, so you'll work in teams. One source said that there's sometimes a perceived

risk of 'over-lawyering' in meetings, so there may be a reluctance on the part of your supervisor to take you to everything. Certainly competitors and clients have noted that Masons is a firm which will never under-resource a matter. Every piece of work is taken very seriously. It's the Masons' way.

"They take you seriously" one trainee told us. *"There's a real desire to put you with people who will train you well."* With only 20 or so taken on per year throughout its offices, the firm can afford to keep trainees away from anyone too egotistical or bad tempered (and one or two partners do have a reputation for being well-endowed in the ego department).

macmasons

Life as a London trainee is felt to be *"fairly regimented"* in comparison to the regional offices where life is a bit more ad hoc. This is because there are many more trainees there. The Glasgow office of the firm is a relatively new venture and operates on an open plan, hot-desking basis. Much of the work there is IT/internet law, which *"has a nice informality about it – being a bit 'hippy' – and because of the nature of the industry."* Some desks in Manchester are also warm to the touch, but at this stage no one sees the whole firm opting for hot-desking.

You don't have to move around the offices. Some trainees ask to move and usually manage to. Manchester is the more established of the offices 'up north' and seen to be the stronger player by the market. Why might you want to work in the Leeds office? *"I can be in the Yorkshire Dales in 40 minutes."*

on the set of Ally McBeal

"Modern hi-tech offices with warehouse style windows" mean that your working environment in London will be *"not dissimilar to that office in Ally McBeal."* Better yet, it's located in trendy Clerkenwell, close to endless cool bars and restaurants. There's no excuses for a feeble social scene. As there's no separate partners' dining room, everyone sits down together in the staff canteen. This is not a pretentious

firm. Many of its clients are in construction. This is a down-to-earth industry sector.

The managing partner meets formally with trainees to allow them to raise any 'hot' issues they feel to be of relevance. Maybe he doesn't need to. *"Raising issues is not a formalised process. You'd usually meet socially and discuss problems with the person directly responsible. If they wanted to implement a change of some sort they would canvass our opinion."* You really do get the impression that the Masons lifestyle is not set in stone.

So is this the kind of firm that can hang onto its young lawyers? Pretty much. In London, nine out of the dozen newly qualifieds stayed with the firm in September 2000. We thought the following story was of interest. In September 1998 a surveyor started as a new trainee. Ideal material for one of the construction groups you'd think and, in reality, he probably was recruited as a future construction lawyer. Apparently he decided that he actually wanted to become an IT lawyer. In September 2000 that's just what he did. And the moral of the story? Well, it's obvious isn't it? *"Without towing the party line"* one source said *"it is genuinely happening."* The firm is broadening its base. IT, projects, employment, corporate, commercial litigation and tax all took on newly qualifieds this year. You don't have to end up as a construction lawyer. *"There's no rigid template"* one source stressed.

and finally...

"As a trainee you're never pushed towards qualifying into construction." It's not going to be a constant diet of hard hats and builders bums. But (yes there is a but after all) at the end of the day, do be aware of what the firm does.

top recommendations in Chambers UK 2000-2001:

Construction & Civil Engineering, Information Technology, Projects/PFI.

Mills & Reeve

the facts

Location: Cambridge, Norwich, Birmingham, Cardiff
UK ranking by size: 35
Total number of trainees: 25
Seats: 4 x 5 months + 1 x 4 months
Alternative seats: secondment to Norwich City FC

Last year Mills & Reeve was one of the fastest growing firms in the UK. Since the breakdown of merger talks between the firm and Martineau Johnson, the expansion has continued apace. It opened up an office in London (which one trainee described as *"booming"*) on 1st February 2000 and has been growing its other offices. A firm which is *"keen to expand and invest in people,"* it offered lots of jobs on qualification in 1999 – *"perhaps twice as many as trainees."*

out with the old

The expansion of the firm does not appear to be across the board. Based in East Anglia, it was traditionally known for its 'old money' agricultural private clients. In March of this year, however, a long-standing private client partner left saying that he wished to return to traditional private client work. Commenting on this, one source at Mills & Reeve observed that *"Mills &Reeve are moving towards being a more commercial firm – more business focused"* and that *"private client is losing out."* On the other hand the commercial departments are felt to be *"booming."* Adding weight to the idea that the firm is changing, another source felt that whilst there were some *"more traditional partners and fee-earners"* more recent recruits are far from the stereotypical East Anglian lawyer.

regional variations

Despite Cambridge and Norwich both being situated in East Anglian 'tractor country' the offices operate in different fields. Whilst the Norwich office handles a lot of the agricultural and employment work, Cambridge is doing a lot of the funky IT/IP work by reason of its situation in 'Silicon Fen.' We were told that there are significant differences in atmosphere between the two offices. The Cambridge office is felt to be more *"hard-working."* Clients are *"different and more demanding."* By contrast it is difficult to work very long hours in Norwich because *"they put the burglar alarm on and then you have to go home."*

pulling together

The general feeling from trainees was that Mills & Reeve was *"very much one firm"* and that *"everything is done that can be done to make it feel such."* Trainees from different offices do the Professional Skills Course together and there are cross-office social events. Trainees said, with only one dissenting voice, that they were not only allowed but *"encouraged"* to move between offices.

The only negative comment was about the Birmingham office. It was a 'bolt-on'; a highly-regarded clinical negligence firm with a top quality NHS client base. One source said that it was proving *"a bit of an uphill struggle"* trying to integrate this very different office.

the trainee experience

Trainees feel that working at Mills & Reeve was *"much less dog eat dog"* than working in London. They talked of working for good clients without doing London hours. Indeed none of the people we spoke to talked of working past 6:30 on a regular basis. *"It doesn't want to be a London firm"* said one source in relation to its work ethic. It will be interesting to see if this changes with the growth of the London office and its commercial work.

_and finally...

In the land of the Barbour the firm has made a valiant effort to escape the 'green welly brigade' and rebrand itself as a modern, young commercial firm. There have been a few casualties along the way but the firm now offers a quality commercial training in a pleasant environment (if you don't suffer from agoraphobia).

top recommendations in Chambers UK 2000-2001:

Agriculture & Bloodstock, Charities, Clinical Negligence (Defendant), Construction, Education, Employment Law, Environmental Law, Family/Matrimonial, General Corporate Finance, Healthcare, Litigation (Commercial), Litigation (Property), Local Government, Personal Injury (Defendant), Planning, Professional Negligence, Property (Commercial), Trusts & Personal Tax

Morgan Cole

the facts

Location: Cardiff, Swansea, Newport, London, Croydon, Reading, Oxford
UK ranking by size: 22
Total number of trainees: 36
Seats: 4 x 6 months
Alternative seats: secondments

Nearly two years ago a Welsh firm and a Thames Valley firm merged their various offices into one – Morgan Cole. Subsequently they were joined by a single office London insurance practice Fishburn Boxer. The firm is now one of the largest in the country and has a solid reputation in a number of different areas, including insurance and litigation. But nearly two years on it still seems to be getting used to itself. The firm was too nervous to let us speak to its trainees, but we hope that normal service will be resumed next year!

a moving experience

Trainees are taken on in London, Wales and the Thames Valley. Applicants are asked to state if they have a preference to treat one particular region as their home region. Trainees will be expected to move according to the business needs of the firm, although the HR department has traditionally exhibited a degree of flexibility on this matter. Graduate recruitment tell us that these days there are plenty of *"willing volunteers."* Trainees are quite keen to see the workings of more than one office. There's more movement between the Welsh offices and between the Thames Valley/London offices than between these two geographical areas. Moves may be for merely a week or up to a full six-month seat.

Salaries differ between the regions. That said, the cost of living in Wales is dramatically lower than in London. A move to a different office is reflected in a compensatory salary adjustment. The Thames Valley offices have the greatest concentration of trainees.

second chances

Secondments to clients include a couple of substantial blue chip names. These opportunities are a popular way of spending six months of the training contract. We understand that whilst it's quite common for trainees to arrive at the firm with preconceived ideas about the areas of work they want to cover (eg. private client or family), their experiential tour around the firm's wide range of practice areas leads many to change their minds about what type of lawyer they want to become. *"Corporate and IT/e-commerce have become very popular."*

the laws of physics

Morgan Cole is not the only firm to have felt the gravitational pull of the healthy London recruitment market for newly qualifieds. A number left on qualification from the Thames Valley and London offices. The Welsh offices' trainees showed themselves to be much more loyal to the firm. All stayed on qualification in September 2000.

It's another law of physics that one person can't be in seven places at the same time. When this was three firms, there were three heads of training. Now there's just one (in Oxford), the training principal has a much bigger remit and seven offices to cover. It's not always a case of popping down the corridor for a chat.

and finally...

The firm clearly has plenty to offer as a sizeable national firm. The implication is that in time it will feel more settled.

top recommendations in Chambers UK 2000-2001:

Agriculture & Bloodstock, Competition/Antitrust, Construction, Employment Law, Environmental Law, General Corporate Finance, Licensing & Leisure, Litigation (Commercial), Media & Entertainment, Personal Injury(Defendant),Professional Negligence, Property (Commercial)

Nabarro Nathanson

the facts

Location: London, Reading, Sheffield
UK ranking by size: 20
Total number of trainees: 56
Seats: 4 x 6 months
Alternative seats: secondments
Extras: Pro bono

Nabarro Nathanson's senior partner was quoted in the legal press in April 2000 as saying *"We have limited resources to invest and our main aim is servicing clients. Opening offices all over the world is an ego trip."* So this is one firm that won't be going global. It is presently considering selling its small Paris and Brussels offices, planning instead to have looser alliances with more firms in Europe. If you are seeking overseas placements and want to be a part of the race towards globalisation, turn the page. If all of that is of little consequence to you, then read on...especially if property work is your bag.

result

This 'archetypal property practice' really excels at property and planning. Property accounts for around a third of the firm's turnover and, until recently, was second only to Linklaters for property law expertise in the UK. This is great for those who want to become property lawyers but is a bit of a turn off to those not so inclined. Last year trainees had a bit of a moan about this. The property bias was becoming a worry, as none wanted to qualify into it but all wanted to stay with the firm after training. The good news is that of 22 qualifying in September 2000, just one went into property.

> "One of Nabarros' strong characteristics is that it is an incredibly relaxed firm."

It's still not all that popular a practice area for trainees. *"You have to do a property seat and that's a problem for a lot of people. I am pleased I did one. In corporate you work for property clients. A large element of the* [firm's] *established clients are property companies."* However, the message given out by this year's job offers is that Nabarros is not just for budding property lawyers. So don't be put off. If, on the other hand, you aspire to being involved in major property deals and where property lawyers, in essence, drive the firm, this may be your best bet.

new beginnings

Nabarros had developed a certain reputation amongst interviewees and vacation students. That reputation was for untidiness. Corridors were stacked high with old files. The firm's move from its old offices in Green Park to its new *"well designed, light and more organised"* location in Holborn enforced a general clear-out.

The move to Holborn also gave trainees a chance to address the issue of community involvement and Nabarros' pro bono scheme. *"They decided to get trainee members on the committee"* and *"as we were moving from a rich to a less rich community we wanted to have an effect on the local community. We are now involved in reading schemes with a number of local schools."* Sadly trainees *"are not all convinced that their input is valued as much as pure fee earning."*

One of Nabarros' strong characteristics is that it is an incredibly relaxed firm. It is not 'City' and the trainees talk of an environment in which it is easy to *"be yourself"* and where *"people genuinely feel supported."* 'Who would NN suit?' we asked. *"Able – strong willed. Not non-conformists, exactly but not conformists."* NN's people are conscious of having taken a non 'City' option, that there are differences of style, culture hours and work between their firm and the magic circle or firms that may be more conservative. *"It's a lifestyle choice"* one told us. One of the mature trainees said *"I am too old and grumpy for a stuffy firm."*

enterprising young things

There's a couple of pubs across the road from the office and although *"first years stick together,"* the pub *"doesn't tend to be just trainees."* If you want to have a natter with some of the partners over a drink, the most likely time will be at one of the organised events rather than in one of the locals, either *The Enterprise* or *The Queen's Head*. The Friday night scene often sees the youngsters in All Bar One (Oh no!) or The Pitcher & Piano.

Nabarros acknowledges that its trainees can have an effect on the firm's business and can help develop client relationships. Many trainees get involved in Contact NN, a long-standing scheme by which trainees get to know other young professionals, such as surveyors and accountants. Contact NN has a handsome budget from the firm to organise social and training events. It's *"an excellent way of learning to organise events and manage the contacts made. After Contact NN talks you get to practise mingling."*

upstairs downstairs

Three or four trainees at any one time will work in the small Reading office. Until last year, it did not recruit its own trainees but this has now changed. "*Whereas for most things Reading is the extension,*" for IP Reading is the firm's number one location. The IP seat is consequently popular but if you start your training in Reading and then move up to London it can take a while to become integrated with the rest of your cohort.

"*It's quite a young office in Reading*" on two floors of a very nice building. One source alluded to the two faces of the office. "*Upstairs you've got company, litigation and IP/IT, which attracts quite a lot of younger lawyers...the upstairs floor is probably a better laugh to be on. It's more relaxed and ...people will take longer lunches.*" Downstairs, on the other hand in private client and property, "*It's busier and it's harder work. The lawyers are slightly older and you perhaps don't get so much from the social side of things... but then the work is very good.*"

Working hours are more moderate in Reading. One source told us "*I did work hard in Reading and I did do a few late nights. I had days when I didn't stop for lunch or anything....but* [in London] *I've certainly done late work later here more regularly.*"

at the coalface

The Sheffield office receives most attention from northern applicants, wanting to be part of a large firm but not wanting to make the move to London. In fact sources indicated that the Sheffield office could even use a few more applications. For some reasons graduates seem to overlook it. Its origins lie with British Coal. Nabarros took over its legal department a few years back and the reality of the situation is that British Coal is still the office's biggest client.

It's easy enough to get yourself a transfer to London for six months but not that many trainees request this. Maybe they just don't feel the need. "*Everything is there for you and it is like a 24 hour a day building. You can get anything any time of the day. There is always someone there to help you, to produce a document or whatever. So it's incredible to have that.*" Particularly in Sheffield.

Socially, the hierarchy doesn't appear to be particularly strong but people do tend to socialise cross-hierarchically within their own departments rather than across the firm. "*It's nice walking around the office. It's difficult to tell the differences between staff.*" "*But there's not so much of a social scene in provincial firms as most people drive in and don't go to the pub so often.*" That said, maybe The Waterways, a new cafe bar which has opened up opposite the canalside office, will reinvigorate the scene. Sheffield's TSG organises things throughout the year for all breeds of young professionals in the city. The popular London group Contact NN is also run in the Sheffield office.

and finally...

Nabarro's trainees like being all that makes the firm what it is; unstuffy and 'unCity'. The property bias, whilst not quite leaving them cold, doesn't exactly cause ripples of delight. That said, it does not mean that qualifiers have to become commercial property lawyers just to stay at the firm.

top recommendations in Chambers UK 2000-2001:

Energy & Utilities, Environmental Law, Health & Safety, Information Technology, Litigation (Property), Local Government, Pensions Litigation

Nicholson, Graham & Jones

the facts

Location: London
UK ranking by size: 73
Total number of trainees: 20
Seats: 4x6 months
Alternative seats: secondments
Extras: Language training,

Medium-sized City firm Nicholson Graham & Jones has rebranded itself as a 'better partnership.' All staff (including trainees) received a degree of instruction as to what this meant. *"It's a tricky business working out which firm is the one for you without spending some time there,"* says their website. We'll do our best to help...

relax

"We're not trying to compete with the big City firms...instead we're finding our feet as a medium firm" said one source; *"we are more of a 'quality of life' firm."* The common view of trainees about the working environment was *"relaxed."* Ditto to to relationships between people working at the firm. Unfortunately it was also how some trainees felt the secretarial support for trainees was best described.

Partners take *"a real interest in the trainees."* They told us about a birthday party at which partners turned up and stayed until three. Whole departments organise regular social events; litigation goes to the races every three or four weeks. Trainees are also *"quite close"* and were all invited to one of their number's wedding recently. When asked whether they went out together every week they replied not just every week but sometimes *"five nights a week."* The day we spoke to most of the trainees they'd been out for a meal the night before and were *"absolutely ratted."* Hence the brevity of this entry, perhaps.

The 'bread and butter' work of the firm is still general commercial work, so expect to do seats in company, litigation and property. There is an IP/IT department which is thought of as 'trendy' within the firm, so there are battles for seats during the training contract and for jobs on qualification. Our sources really hoped that there would be more scope for getting seats there as the department grows.

"a better partnership"

"Some people don't know who we are," trainees told us, *"so we are raising our profile."* About time too. *"We haven't been as well known as we should have been for a firm our size."* Indeed. All members of the firm have had to attend meetings about the rebranding, and *"the whole firm had an input."* It's not simply a case of selling the firm to others but also of selling it to itself. It has lacked self-awareness in the past. Some lawyers *"didn't even know what other departments of the firm did."* We asked the trainees where they think the firm is going. *"It does what it does and is trying to improve its current areas"* and *"it's quite happy to be the size it is."* Whatever it's doing, however quietly, it appears to be doing it right. Profits are up by a healthy 14% and the firm punches above its weight in terms of profitability. It just doesn't shout about it, that's all.

sporting life

The firm has a strong reputation for sports work, acting for football clubs and cable companies buying TV rights. Before you apply to the firm on the basis of your burning desire to be a sports lawyer, bear in mind that it only constitutes a tiny percentage of the firm's workload. This is a small niche area. There isn't a separate sports department for you to go into and trainees don't know of anyone who has done a dedicated sports seat. *"The principal partners are in corporate"* and the main work of the firm is property and corporate. Since this is where most of the fees come from, and they are the most profitable departments, they are also likely to be the source of most jobs in future.

and finally...

It's unfortunate that this firm does not have a stronger identity in the marketplace. The offices are quite traditional and so is the firm. But that's not a bad thing. In this case small means friendly and intimate, with none of the glossiness and corporate hype of bigger, slicker firms. It means modest success, without fanfares.

top recommendations in Chambers UK 2000-2001:

Litigation (fewer than 40 litigators), Sport, Travel [Band 2]

Norton Rose

the facts

Location: London
UK ranking by size: 14
Total number of trainees: 103
Seats: 6 x 4 months
Alternative seats: Several overseas seats
Extras: Pro bono

Norton Rose has it made. It's growing at a pace commensurate with other top eight City players. It's expanding overseas, primarily in Europe. There have been plenty of mutterings about merger in the last year or so and perhaps merger is the only way it will leapfrog its way up the size leader board. It won the Chambers & Partners 'Law Firm of the Year Award 1999-2000' to reflect its improved standing in several areas of practice. Plenty will be watching to see where this 'Group of Eight' firm now goes.

an offer you can't refuse

The firm attracts international and UK applicants with an interest in spending time overseas. It offers seats in Asia and Europe. And though the list of locations may not be as long as your arm, there are usually plenty of overseas seats to go around. Certain locations are fought over fiercely, such as Paris and Singapore. Be prepared to prove why you should be the one. *"They won't send you to Singapore because your girlfriend is there"* joked one insider. But *"if you have European languages they try and encourage you to the relevant office."* Bear that in mind if you are a fluent Italian speaker with your heart set on Hong Kong. But hey, Milan's not that bad!

"Piraeus is popular as you get to go island hopping." Moscow and Bahrain are not exactly fought over. Recently *"someone had to be asked to go"* to Bahrain. And there's a problem with the Hong Kong seat – it no longer exists. A restrictive covenant still enforced by a former joint venture partner prevents the firm from practising there. *"A lot of people were disappointed*

by the HK office closing, but to compensate they have made more seats available in Singapore."*

booze and twiglets

The office is not the flashiest building in the City. It's *"adequate"* but in a good location. *"Liverpool Street Station is very useful. The area is fantastic with a good choice of restaurants for lunch and the East End for markets and curries."* Beneath the office is *"the Norton Rose pub"* The Old Monk. It's the venue for team drinks on a Friday night. At the top of the week there's a free bar for trainees in one of the conference rooms on Mondays with *"a whole array of booze. And Twiglets!"* It's not universally popular though. *"It's the worst night they could have it…maybe that's why they do it! It's well attended at first"* but after a while it's *"just for the diehards."*

There are two intakes a year and it's hit or miss as to whether you start with one that bonds like araldite (one intake all went away together for a weekend in the Lake District) or one in which trainees don't feel much of a connection to their cohort. The good news is you'll get a lot of your social contact with office people through work teams. *"The really sociable teams are in corporate finance and banking. People work longer hours there but it's work hard play hard."*

Lunching with your supervising partner is a good way of getting more than a work relationship going with those higher up the food chain. *"Free interaction of thought between lawyers of all levels"* was stressed by one of our sources. Another confirmed that in terms of confidence lunch with the big man (or sometimes woman) in your life is important. *"Instances are quite common. I can think of no better way of boosting confidence than having lunch with a partner and talking about partner stuff."*

thank your lucky stars

Norton Rose has this reputation as a friendly place and in this respect, of the top 10 firms size-wise, it is undoubtedly up there towards the top of the warm and cuddly rankings. *"It's a City firm without*

City attitudes. You can get a good training here without the posturing and hang-ups of other large firms" one source explained. *"It retains its friendly reputation but some say it's not as friendly as it was three years ago – based on the fact that it's growing at quite a rate."* This is a very important issue as Norton Rose has clearly stated its intention to grow further.

polyglots

So what type of person is Norton Rose recruiting? Trainees thought that there was a particular interest in Oxbridge and 'ivy league' –*"it's an increasing tendency unfortunately."* They also thought that a degree from an old polytechnic was not a bar to acceptance by the firm, but at the same time couldn't point to any such successful candidates. All in all those we spoke to were not especially privileged, had a variety of accents and came from a variety of places across the UK and Europe. The firm appears to have simply targeted successful individuals from the better regarded universities.

We were told that the two intakes are different. *"The September intake tends to be slightly older people or people who have already settled in London because they are the people who have turned down the opportunity to go traveling for a few months. The second intake in January is mainly people straight from university who are just taking a bit of time off before they start."* Or as one trainee put it *"The lazy lot turn up in January!"* The differences between the two intakes are apparent to all trainees *"We had a lot of Europeans: a Swede, 2 Dutch, a Dane, 2 Greeks, a French girl. But in the January intake it's more the traditional uni – law school – training contract route."*

Is there an active approach to recruitment for the overseas offices? Our sources thought so. *"The Greek office beckons to Greeks."* Nationality aside, NR could be said to be picking like-minded individuals. It is after people who are *"flexible and friendly – team working rather than individualist."* *"I thought it would be much more competitive than it was"* one trainee told us of the interaction between trainees. *"Norton Rose tries to employ people like this who will work in teams and will con-* sult others and are not going to be individualist." "They don't tolerate ambition to the point of crushing others."

nirvana: smells like team spirit

We're back again to this idea of the team being of greater value than the individual. *"The team notion is very important at Norton Rose. You can have a reasonably cosy atmosphere through the teams.* There are opportunities to be recognised for good work by partners and by other departments. As trainee, you will be the team's first port of call with other departments. *"There are certain informal groupings between departments. Trainees across the two years can get aligned to invisible networks. It's not a conscious process but if you have a gut feeling about where you want to qualify you begin to notice those who work on deals together and are a good source of info."*

You need to make sure you get into a team which matches not only your work interests but also your preferred working patterns. *"You will get a sense of which teams are harder working than others. Some are late and some are early starters. You can pick and choose. Some teams really value their weekends."* There is one particularly full on, hard-core team which has been dubbed *"the team of death."* Guess where? *"In corporate and banking you can work all night. In some teams that's what they thrive on. You give those teams a wide berth"* one of our interviewees said. Another talked animatedly about the hard-core times. *"On BMW we had our backs to the wall, working really hard. At the end they sent us to Greece for three days on holiday on a yacht – at the firm's expense. That's a cracking team."* Ahhh! If only island-hopping was a regular perk...

guns 'n' roses

Every interviewee spoke of the corporate finance and banking teams as if this was where the real action took place. As a trainee, two of your three compulsory seats will be in banking and corporate finance. The third will be in litigation. We asked if you could come to the firm without a real interest in corporate law and were told *"you would do so at your peril as it could become boring for you.*" The litigation seat is a popular third compulsory. "*The departments here differ widely and the sort of people that are in those departments are very different.*" Commonly, litigation seats come with many administrative tasks but, thankfully, not overly-long hours. "*You can fire a bullet down the litigation corridor at 6.30pm and you'd be lucky to hit anyone.*"

There's no doubt that in any department "*as a trainee you can do an awful lot of proof reading*" and, as with any firm, "*you can get bad seats*" but in general, trainers were seen to be "*keen to bring you on and develop you.*" "*You'll be given interesting work if you go looking for it.*" "*The banking department has given more responsibility because of the nature of the work.*" Apparently "*there are a million and one different courses that you can do from 'assertiveness' to 'how to behave at drinks parties'; from 'IT' to 'how to get out of tight corners'.*" We liked the sound of the course on voice control, which involved assuming yogic positions on the floor of the conference room.

Norton Rose trainees consistently stay at the firm after qualification. Only a tiny minority do not get offered a satisfactory job at the end of their two years of training. In September 2000 all but one of the qualifiers stayed – a high proportion in mainstream corporate departments. "*It's a banking/corporate finance intake*" a source said.

and finally...

"*You should be under no illusions about the hours. They can be long. Perhaps longer than you'd hope. Others should tell you the same or it's rubbish.*" Don't go to Norton Rose if you aren't prepared for it to continue its growth and focus on corporate finance and banking. It's unlikely to pull emphasis away from specialist areas such as shipping, IP, energy or EU. But remember where the big money is being made.

top recommendations in Chambers UK 2000-2001:

Aviation, Fraud, Shipping & Maritime Law

Olswang

the facts

Location: London
UK ranking by size: 48
Total number of trainees: 22
Seats: 4 x 6 months
Alternative seats: None

Chambers and Partners Law Firm of the Year 2000

Consistently rated at the top for media, entertainment and defamation, Olswang is renowned for its trendy image. It has also developed a strong reputation for information technology. The firm has expanded massively on the back of the media and communications developments which have changed our lives over the last 10 years. We set out to find out if there is more to the firm than that.

it's media darling!

The firm caters to its media clients at all levels. Its Covent Garden location fits in with its media firm image. Rather than a 'City' or business-oriented reception, the new arrival is greeted by "*cool seats and Sky TV on the wall.*" Indeed, apart from property, which has its own big clients, most of the firm's work is connected with media and telecommunications. For instance the corporate department "*complements the work that is done in the media/telecommunications department.*" People applying must understand "*what the firm does and what it does not*" and "*have an interest in the areas.*" For many the media work will appear extremely glamorous. Indeed some of our sources have had their names in the credits to films. However, don't get the impression that you will be dining daily with directors. "*The clients are exciting but you are just the boring lawyer they have to have.*" The film work is "*like property; the film is the property.*"

dull seat information (the info not the seats)

Everyone **has** to do corporate, litigation and an 'ents' seat at Olswang, we were told. We were then told that in reality there was an element of flexibility. Those who make their preferences well-known have sometimes been able to do an extra corporate seat instead of a media seat for example. For some seats there was *"a bit of competition between trainees,"* especially for telecoms. As for jobs on qualification, there seemed to be a form of telepathy going on. There was a *"meeting of the minds"* which resulted in *"everyone getting what they wanted on qualification."*

growing pains -

"Olswang is London's fastest growing law firm," states their publicity. Whilst the firm is obviously proud of its growth, for those at the firm the increase in size has had both positive and negative effects. It has impacted on just about every area of the firm. But *"corporate has really rocketed. There is a danger that it is becoming a City firm, though partners want to avoid this."* With the firm setting up an independent corporate finance house and fast *"running out of space"* in its current offices it will be interesting to see where the growth takes it.

"not a chimp bean-counter"

Trainees have been able to see Olswang changing in a short period of time. *"It has doubled in size in the past two years. I applied to a different sized firm."* It has affected their working environment. On the down side, *"before, in corporate everyone knew everyone. Now that isn't true."* Corporate departments everywhere are notorious for long hours. Nevertheless, the amount of hours here still seemed considerable, with some trainees *"working for at least 12 hours each day."* The work is still coming in faster than the expansion of the firm. The massive influx of work benefits trainees. There *"is better work because it is bigger."* In Property (which Olswang made a 'conscious decision to expand' last October), sources spoke of dealing with *"higher up"* people on the other side. *"You don't get mundane work, you're not treated like a chimp bean-counter."* Most telling is the retention rate on qualification. Trainees understand it to be 100%. *"People say the culture is changing, but I really like working here."*

west end girls (and boys)

The fact that there is a lot of work for trainees means a high level of responsibility. *"You need to be confident, to be able to get on and do things."* Trainees feel that there is no hierarchy at the firm. You *"couldn't be the shy and retiring type,"* *"building up personal relationships in the firm is quite important if you want to be noticed."* Despite their location in the heart of the West End, sources have mixed views on the social life. How much you socialise with your fellow workers seems to depend on your department. *"Some people think that there could be more of a social life at the firm."* This seems to stem from the fact that a couple of years ago the number of trainees was so small that no arrangements were needed. The firm has apparently taken notice of complaints and now *"people have been appointed to look after trainees."* Good for them.

and finally...

This is a firm which seems to be teetering on the brink of something. It is currently a lively entrepreneurial place, where trainees work hard but enthusiastically for a very particular brand of client. Will it stay the same but bigger? Or will corporate and property gradually overtake the 'sexy' areas and take this West End firm into the City both physically and metaphorically? We know what current trainees would prefer. And we tend to agree.

top recommendations in Chambers UK 2000-2001:

Defamation, Internet/e-commerce, Media & Entertainment (Broadcasting and Film & TV Production)

Osborne Clarke OWA

the facts

Location: Bristol, Reading and London
UK ranking by size: 27
Total number of trainees: 45
Seats: 4 x 6months, though flexible
Alternative seats: Secondments, some European opportunities

Do you want to train at a full-service commercial firm based in Bristol? Two firms instantly spring to mind. Burges Salmon and Osborne Clarke. But this is the beginning and the end of the similarity. As the trainees say *"I don't think that we are really competitors."* The real questions – is Osborne Clarke even a Bristol firm any more? And what does OWA mean?

the alliance – "making waves"

Whereas Burges Salmon remains firmly rooted in Bristol, it is fast becoming a fallacy to call Osborne Clarke a Bristol firm. It has thriving offices in the Thames Corridor (basically Reading) and London. The London office is *"getting so big it could be as big as Bristol one day"* and Reading *"has grown so much it has expanded on to another floor."*

OWA? Osborne-Westphalen Alliance of course. Sounds like a military pact. In fact, in a bid to develop itself into a truly international presence the firm has entered into an alliance with five other European firms. The axis of the alliance is clearly Anglo-German, but there are firms in France. A full merger seems some way off. There are implications for trainees. Some lucky individuals have been to Paris (ooh la la) and Frankfurt (well, win some, lose some). Before you go and pack your bags, you should realise that to get overseas your language abilities will need to be such that you are, as one trainee put it, *"fluent or bloody, bloody good."*

Some interviewees admitted that there is *"a danger that people might lose contact with each other because of the expansion,"* but feel that the firm is trying to avoid this. Nevertheless, there is certainly an *"upbeat"* atmosphere. Our sources feel *"part of an expanding forward-looking business."* You need *"a fair amount of drive"* to fit in with the firm. Said one; *"it's making waves."*

hard work- "the nature of the beast"

Hard work is *"the nature of the beast."* And the beast in question? The firm's logo after its rebranding is a prowling wildcat, ready to pounce. So the new look OC is streamlined, fast, ruthless, an efficient killing machine? If not, it's not for lack of trying. As with most firms, hours vary from department to department.

Along with an aspirational firm goes a particular work ethic. Perhaps you could call it a City work ethic. For the most part *"you are not just a photocopier"* but *"because of the size of the firm you do sometimes get dross work to do. You are a junior."* At the other end of the scale, you may find yourself struggling. *"Partners expect you to have psychic abilities. They don't explain things."* One interviewee felt *"thrown in at the deep end, with too much on his shoulders."* On the positive side, trainees were able to *"ask for more responsibility in some areas"* and say when they *"didn't feel quite confident in others."* So whilst the partners may expect you to be Mystic Meg, they certainly can't read your mind. It's very much up to trainees to be vocal and manage their own workload.

go west, young man

Bristol trainees say the firm *"feels like a London office outside of London."* *"A lot of the clients are in London and you may go there quite a lot."* Long hours (till one in the morning) and weekends are certainly not unknown. But partners *"recognise that we work hard"* and are happy for trainees to go home early when they can.

And going home has never been so easy! The office is in the traditional business and legal centre of the city and many who work at the firm live in Clifton or Redland, a pleasant walk up the hill past the University and up trendy Park Street. Or you can make a diversion via the two arts complexes down on the waterfront.

twenty-four/seven

Our sources could not be positive enough about the relaxed working environment at Osborne Clarke. Like many firms, it has adopted a dress-down policy (smart casual, if you can work out what that is). But, unlike many firms, theirs is every day, all year round. In fact, if you are the sort of person who insists on wearing a suit all the time people will think you *"very strange."* The social scene varies from office to office. Bristol is socially *"fantastic."* Sheer numbers allow you to arrange things on an *"ad hoc basis."* One trainee enthused that he *"never thought (he) would make so many friends at a law firm."*

In marked contrast is the social life in Reading, which is *"not good."* This is partly because there *"aren't so many trainees in Reading,"* making you *"feel a little cut off from the rest in Bristol."* Also *" a lot of people commute to Reading to work"* and therefore aren't around for long drinking sessions. Nothing to do with the place of course...

and finally...

Make no mistake. This is an ambitious firm which hates to be called a Bristol firm. Don't think you will get a 'regional' training, meaning going home at 5.30pm every day. They expect much more than that from you. OC means to compete with the City, it already attracts many ex-City lawyers, and it means to be seen as an international firm. You need to match the firm in drive and ambition. You will be rewarded for it. Salaries compete with the highest in the UK. Newly qualifieds now get £30,000 in Bristol, £38,000 in the Thames Valley (a new record for the highest sum paid by a UK firm outside London) and £40,000 in London. If all this appeals, you should think very seriously about this firm.

top recommendations in Chambers UK 2000-2001:

Advertising & Marketing, Banking, Corporate Finance (London, under 30 Solicitors in Corporate Team/ Bristol), Debt Recovery, Employment Law, Environmental Law, Health & Safety, Information Technology, Insolvency, Intellectual Property, Litigation, Pensions, Property, Sports Law, Tax (Corporate), Trusts & Personal Tax

Paisner & Co

the facts

Location: London
UK ranking by size: 66
Total number of trainees: 19
Seats: 4 x 6 months
Alternative seats: Paris, secondment
Extras: Pro bono

A fast growing mid-size Fleet Street firm. It covers mainstream commercial work as well as some quirky interesting areas to boot.

size matters

The best thing about working for Paisners? Unlike bigger firms with whom they'd done vacation schemes, where *"if you weren't top dog you were nothing,"* the firm acknowledges you. There's only a couple of handsful of trainees in each year so *"you're not trainee number 87."* *"If you've done something people will hear about it...you're not going to be anonymous."* More so than most firms, we got the impression that you won't be left to your own devices. You're likely to know almost everyone who works at the firm. If they don't know you they'll probably stop you in the corridor and ask who you are. *"You take interviewees round on tour and you spend all your time saying hello."* No point in applying to the firm if you want to blend into the background.

shiny happy people

Paisners trainees are the bouncy and enthusiastic sort. They all seem to be very content with their lot, which is rather encouraging. But it's not the flat contentment of the unambitious. Those we spoke to weren't Stepford trainees. OK, we interviewed at a time when trainees were just qualifying. Everyone was on a high. But just because something sounds too good to be true doesn't mean that it's not. Anecdotal evidence suggests that when trainees get together and ask for change, it does sometimes happen. First years asked for a pay rise. Second years got one too. Trainees asked for mentors – they got them. Seat rotation was put under the spotlight and *"we have more say now."*

> "Deals such as...Hammer Film Productions have grabbed the attention of the press and the imaginations of trainees."

Paisners knows its type. They have *"confidence from the start"* but it's *"boosted by virtue of the way you're treated – you're given independence."* This is a firm where your face needs to fit. If it does (and most of the time it does – Paisners seems to identify the right type at interview), then you'll be given interesting work, meet clients and integrate well into departments. *"If you prove yourself, things work out. You need to establish yourself and you'll be treated as an individual."* The flipside of this is that, even on the firm's own statistics, there's always going to be someone who's not offered a job at the end of the day. If their face is all wrong.

fleet street and beyond

Paisners sit in the shadow of Freshfields, just off Fleet Street. Our sources chose Paisners in preference to the magic circle. They mentioned interviews and vacation schemes at these firms and others in the City. Joining Paisners was a deliberate choice. But what it doesn't offer, which the big firms do, is a vast array of overseas opportunities. It has no foreign offices of its own but it does have a close link with a French firm. Those with good French ought to be able to persuade the firm of the benefits of time spent in Paris. It's also possible to spend a few weeks, maybe longer, with a client on secondment. At the time we interviewed, one trainee was working with insurance client Aon. It's an ad hoc system. The message is 'If you want six months in Hong Kong then join Clifford Chance!'

Seat allocation is far from ad hoc. Trainees will generally do a seat in corporate/commercial, property and something contentious, be it commercial litigation, construction or employment. One of the most popular seats is CMIP (Computers, Media and IP). Corporate has also become a popular area with three of the five NQs taken on by that department in September 2000. Deals such as the purchase of Hammer Film Productions have grabbed the attention of the press and the imaginations of trainees. Not quite so nail-biting is the Trusts and Estates Planning work. That produced a big yawn all round in our interviews.

not such a long way to Tipperary

As well as finding the library, the coffee machine and the stationery cupboard in your first few days, you'll want to start learning 'the knowledge' locally. The social scene is an important aspect of life at Paisners. There's not just one local pub, there's several. The Tipperary over the road used to be the favourite but, having almost doubled in size in just a few short years, the firm has outgrown it. Popular now are The Old Bank of England, The Hogshead in Fetter Lane, Hodgsons, Wheelers...and the list goes on. Every month there are departmental 'dos.' *"Everyone goes – from secretaries to partners."* *"Assistants' drinks once a month is quite a new thing. The firm is growing so rapidly that we said 'Let's have assistants' drinks'."*

We got the impression that Paisners would be in the Premier division if we were to rank firms on how many get togethers there were in local boozers. It might not win the Treble but it could give any firm a run for its money. One trainee thought that things were likely to get even better as the firm grew. Speaking of the fact that only seven trainees were taken on when she joined, she thought that *"There is room for a few more...15 would be a good number. They make a conscious decision to take fewer trainees and only very rarely employ paralegals."* Aside from the corporate department (where you'll do your fair share of late nights), 6.30pm-7pm is not an uncommon leave time for trainees.

the crystal maze

Everyone we spoke to had a healthy level of disdain for Bouverie House, Paisners' home. Even a corporate partner, keen to muscle in on our interview, yelled out *"Tell her the offices are ****!"* before stealing the trainee's cigarettes and nipping off for a fag. *"It's a maze"* we were told. *"It's difficult to find your way around and, as we've outgrown the building, we'll be moving in the next couple of years."* Good job too. *"You could lose people in here"* one source said. We wondered if there were a few starved new recruits festering in forgotten corners. Or maybe it's just a good place to hide out from your superviser? Whatever... *"At first you won't be able to find your way around the offices – you'll be lost for about three days. On the fourth day you'll be laughing."*

and finally...

Paisner & Co may not be as well known as some similarly sized firms, but it's been doing very well recently and there's every likelihood that its profile will continue to rise as it grows. Trainees exhibited a good deal of satisfaction with the tasks they were asked to perform and cited with enthusiasm the size of deals on which they worked. One to consider if you like standing out in a (small) crowd and you want a broad-based City training and a bit of a laugh. And a life.

top recommendations in Chambers UK 2000-2001:

Corporate Finance (under 30 Solicitors in Corporate Team), Food, Licensing & Leisure

Pinsent Curtis

the facts

Location: London, Leeds, Skipton, Birmingham
UK ranking by size: 18
Total number of trainees: 66
Seats: 4 x 6 months
Alternative seats: Brussels

A firm which once was two. In 1995 Birmingham firm Pinsent & Co hooked up with Leeds firm Simpson Curtis. Together, they've since opened up a London office. But the market has been left scratching its head a little. Why hasn't it grown its London office as have other regional firms. Why hasn't it broadened out into Europe? The answer is, it's continuing to build its strong Leeds and Birmingham offices. And it's putting all its resources into London.

sleeping with claudia schiffer

Early in summer 2000, one of Pinsent Curtis' regional managing partners told the press that the firm's decision not to try and enter into mergers with European firms was like deciding not to attempt to sleep with Claudia Schiffer. What's behind Pinsents decision to keep its hands off Europe? London?

The London office is likely to receive a good deal more attention now. The firm wants to double the size of the operation and focus on corporate finance and more City-oriented work. This is a rallying call to applicants with corporate leanings and a desire to work in London. Gone are the days when you applied to work for one of the most respected regional players out there. If the firm has its sights set on a City target then it's going to want trainees who are ready to chase that quarry too.

pinsent courteous

The Birmingham legal scene is a bit of a rodeo as partners switch between the leading commercial firms. First Edges lose out. Then Eversheds partner numbers change. Wragges hoover up a few more.

DLA spills a little. Pinsents trades. But there has actually been very little change in the Birmingham or Leeds offices. Why hasn't Pinsents surged forward? The competition in Leeds is tough – and we mean tough. The leading Yorkshire firms are like a pack of fighting dogs. Maybe Pinsent Curtis is unwilling to get bloody in a scrap. It's a firm with a lot of class and an almost aristocratic reputation. It's certainly not as aggressive as some others. Less daring maybe? If a lack of daring is a shortcoming, the firm makes up for it with polish, credibility and gentility. Plenty of clients like that. It inspires a good deal of confidence.

something for the weekend

Pinsents always performs well in key areas of business and attracts leading lawyers from London who *"have made a lifestyle decision to move up to Leeds."* You can be sure that you'll be trained by partners and senior assistants with plenty of top quality experience. Now under one roof in a new building in the city centre, the Leeds office has gone open-plan and the feeling is that *"it's more friendly, you know more people in the firm and see more of what's going on."* This is in sharp contrast to the cluster of gracious Georgian buildings it occupied around Park Square until recently. The new state of the art offices have that little something extra to help busy trainees through a hard night's work – machines in the toilets that dispense pain killers, tooth brushes and condoms. In corporate and banking or finance seats you may see the odd all-nighter. *"You have to mix the rough with the smooth. I have had late nights. Once a month maximum until 4am or more and a few until 9pm-10pm at night."*

shaken but not stirring

In July 1999 the firm started a shake up of management. It reviewed its strategy. When six partners defected from London last winter (including the London managing partner), things must have looked rather bleak. London is increasingly the focus of attention and money (London assistants' pay has been hiked up to equal that of leading City rivals). To achieve its national goals, Pinsents has to see its London office succeed and win big work. You can expect there to be increased opportunities in corporate and finance work for London trainees. A majority of trainees stay with the firm. In Leeds, of the ten offered jobs, seven accepted them. That's a moderately good retention rate.

The highest value City work is in the London office. Both Birmingham and Leeds offices have strong corporate and banking groups but trainees sense that on the finance side the two regional offices *"feed off London."* If you want to switch offices during your training contract, there's no bar. *"There are options to move"* but it rarely happens. Why not? London trainees do have to go to Birmingham or Leeds for a property seat as London has no property department.

and finally...

The trainees we spoke to confirmed that you will receive an excellent training at Pinsent Curtis. They're a sensible lot. They get to see great deals and work for blue chip clients in a variety of different areas. But Claudia Schiffer remains unattainable. So Europe looks a long way off.

top recommendations in Chambers UK 2000-2001:

Admin & Public Law, Banking, Competition/Anti-trust, Employee Share Schemes, Employment Law, Environmental Law, Financial Services, Intellectual Property, Litigation (Commercial), Litigation (Property), Partnership, Projects/PFI, Tax

Reynolds Porter Chamberlain

the facts

Location: London
UK ranking by size: 62
Total number of trainees: 17

Seats: 4 x 6 months
Alternative seats: Secondments, Boston
Extras: Pro bono

"Primarily an insurance firm." Clients are drawn heavily from insurance companies. The workload is oriented towards litigation. However, non-contentious work is being targeted as the firm makes efforts to broaden out the practice. Last year it increased its corporate team and acquired media lawyers from Davies Arnold Cooper. This is enhancing the range of seats available during the training contract.

in defence of negligence

RPC does a large amount of professional negligence work. If you're not sure exactly what this involves, it is litigation against solicitors, surveyors, accountants and other professionals for losses arising out of their negligence to clients. RPC has traditionally acted for the insurers of professional partnerships, defending such claims. In the first year of their contracts, trainees had, until recently, always spent their time in litigation (mostly professional negligence) seats. In the second year they could and would choose non-contentious seats, such as corporate and commercial property.

This has changed following a request by current trainees. Now only the first six months of the training contract is a compulsory litigation seat. It is possible for a first year to get a desired seat such as corporate, although second years still get first preference and are, in fact, likely to fill the few corporate seats on offer. *"Generally it is litigation for the first year and non-contentious for the second"* a trainee explained. *"I think this is made clear at open days."* If you want a primarily corporate training then RPC isn't necessarily the place where you can guarantee getting the most experience, as the department is smaller in comparison to others and places are limited. That said, with the rise of internet related business, *"the opportunities in corporate are increasing."* But still *"cor-*

porate and property are not keen on first years doing seats with them."

holding hands

In your first six months you get bags of supervision in litigation. You will take on more responsibility once you have learned the ropes. *"It absolutely fills you with horror when you hear at law school that you will be dealing with your own files, but they hold your hand."* *"In insurance"* one trainee told us *"I had my own files; solicitors' indemnity cases – one of mine settled for £250K. I had lots of little files for about £20K on which I did the negotiations on the phone."* The first year is definitely good experience; *"you learn a hell of a lot."*

Whilst one trainee said that there wasn't a huge amount of client contact initially, *"in corporate I was constantly on the phone to clients"* working on *"internet contracts and employment contracts."* *"The internet work is new and exciting"* they confirmed. Also on offer are family (including child abduction cases), commercial property and tax and trusts work. The only unpopular seat is the insurance seat in the second, smaller office near the Lloyd's building. The reluctance to go there is because it only takes one first year. *"It can be daunting and you can feel a bit left out."*

finding the perfect partner

Just as the recruitment Q&A section of the firm's website confirms, all trainees sit with an assistant solicitor. There seems to be no difficulty in gaining access to those with the experience needed to help out whenever required. *"On the whole doors are open"* and the tight pack of a half-dozen-plus trainees in each year are usually more than willing to help each other out. *"Not everyone is competitive and we've all swapped seats so we know the issues…. emails asking for help frequently go round."*

In property one trainee had a half hour set aside each day to chat about her work with her supervising partner. We sought confirmation of the website's statement that trainees got daily feedback on their work from supervising partners. This was not in fact always the case. In other departments it might only be two or three times per week. Recently trainees have campaigned (successfully we understand) for mini formal reviews mid seat, rather than just every six months.

first thursday

The building is *"lovely downstairs"* but *"upstairs it changes and it's quite dated."* The offices at the front of the building are definitely more attractive than those at the back, we are told, although all of them seem spacious enough and nobody is offended by the magnolia decor. Upstairs there's a *"drop out room"* which the trainees colonise at lunchtime. Every so often staff are invited to lunches with the partners on a group by group basis.

None of the trainees have a problem with the hours they are required to work. *"We stay until about 6pm or 7pm, there's no pressure to stay late."* As ever, *"corporate is more sporadic."*

After hours the trainees meet regularly for drinks in one of three local pubs The Three Cups, Penderels Oak or Courts. Once a month the partners foot the bill on 'First Thursday' night. It's mainly trainees, young assistants and support staff who go, but some of the partners let their hair down. In particular some of the younger partners in corporate are regarded as less conservative than others in litigation.

amazonian women

The RPC website gives potential applicants a number of strong messages. One trainee summed it up for us. *"People looking at the website have been pretty much fed a line – 'these are the things you have to do to get a job here.' Look at the focus on travel and sport."* Look indeed. Sport holds a prominent position on the CVs of most trainees. Pistol shooting, encounters with pirhana and snake charming. And that's just the women! Watch your back, Lara Croft. *"They want superwomen"* one said; *"they are looking to recruit bubbly girls."* The same trainee also felt the firm would

love to attract more similarly disposed *"thrusting blokes."* They're all off to the big corporate firms to earn big corporate money.

Does this tie in with the fact that the firm is trying to broaden out from its professional negligence base? One astute source told us that, in past years, assistants had no need to go out and *"fight for work."* Now *"the firm has seen the future ...and has taken an active decision to recruit more sociable and outgoing trainees, those who will go out and market the firm."* Sporting prowess is vital to this. *"Of two identical candidates, the one who has the best golf handicap will get the job."*

and finally...

Are you sporty enough? And do you want to do litigation? If you can answer yes to both of these questions, this could well be the firm for you. Small enough to be sociable, large enough to give quality work and a variety of seats. Three out of seven of those qualifying at the firm are staying on this year. Next year sees the arrival of what we believe to be the firm's first ever four-legged trainee – a golden labrador who will guide his owner around the building and to court. Should enhance the atmosphere considerably.

top recommendations in Chambers UK 2000-2001:

Professional Negligence

Richards Butler

the facts

Location: London
UK ranking by size: 43
Total number of trainees: 56 (worldwide)
Seats: 4 x 5 months, 1 x 4 months
Alternative seats: Secondments, Hong Kong, Paris, Abu Dhabi, São Paulo
Extras: Language training

As part of the tri-partite merger (with Denton Hall and Theodore Goddard) that never was, Richards Butler had a busy time in the legal press last year. Remaining a medium-sized firm for now it has continued to expand since the failure of merger talks. In May 2000 it pushed partnership numbers past 100 for the first time in its history. But the expansion doesn't seem to be across the board. Certain areas have been picked out for special treatment. Sources tell us the firm is concentrating on banking, insurance and media. It will certainly be interesting to see over the next year or two if it continues to expand on its own or seeks other potential brides with the right vital statistics.

chill out

"*Relaxed*" is the common description of the atmosphere at Richards Butler. One interviewee was at pains to point out that this "*did not mean sloppiness.*" What it did mean was that "*if you get your work done then there's no medals for sticking around.*" Overall the firm feels informal and trainee perception is that there is less of a hierarchy than in the 'magic circle.' There is "*an ethos of* (the partners) *not being condescending towards trainees because of their position.*" The people in charge "*wanted you to have a life and wouldn't want you to sit in an office until midnight.*"

Richards Butler describes itself as "*dynamic and modern*" on its website. Certainly sources we spoke to said that the firm was "*not old-fashioned, with a lot of partners being quite young.*" On the other hand "*some departments could be described as dynamic but the firm as a whole probably couldn't.*"

basically, it's all to do with shipping

Trainees disputed the common misconception that Richards Butler is all about shipping, emphasising the reputation of its other departments such as Media. It is a "*myth that the firm is keen to dispel.*" In fact shipping, commodities and insurance work combined account for only about 20% of the firm's workload. By far the biggest work type is corporate/commercial and finance-related work. On the other hand "*as they've got a big shipping department quite a few people go there.*" One interviewee said of the international trading commodities department; "*the people who worked there were a very elite group of people, super-intellectual and academically orientated.....I felt consistently stupid all the time.*" Another described the department as "*having quite a few oddbods in it.*" You have been warned!

getting away from it all

With offices all over place and big media clients there are good opportunities to get out of the office. This was an important factor in attracting many of our contacts to the firm. Trainees are interviewed for the posts and decisions are made on the basis of individual suitability. There are opportunities in Paris (French speakers only), Hong Kong, São Paulo and Abu Dhabi for one or two people at a time. The Abu Dhabi secondment is "*highly enjoyable.*" At the same time, it is "*harsh*" in terms of both climate and culture. By virtue of its media department, the firm is also able to send people on secondment to clients such as Rank and, most notably, MTV. One source described the latter secondment as "*great,*" involving lots of responsibility. However "*it wasn't as glamorous as people might think. Richard Blackwood walked past my office a couple of times, but that was it.*" More than enough for some...

will I get a job?

Past interviewees have been stressed about the lack of job offers at the end of their training contracts. In previous years, retention rates have sunk as low as 60%. This year, however, those we spoke to felt that there had been a bit of a turn round with the majority of trainees being kept on after qualification. Readers should note that retention rates can change from year to year depending on the fluctuations of the legal market.

not a number...

It is "*not a machine firm. They don't try to make you into an android.*" Each year we are told that there are no clones at Richards Butler. There is a great variety of people with many coming into the firm after previous lives (jobs or travelling). Indeed when it comes to trainees the firm is keen on *"life experience."* The only common factor one trainee could sense was that most people *"seemed to like drinking."* The social life is good *"with all of the intakes socialising together"* and many sporting opportunities.

and finally...

In previous years, the main downside to training at this firm has been concern that so few people might have the opportunity to stay on. With a relaxed atmosphere, a good social life and interesting secondments, people did not want to leave. There is now less chance that they'll have too.

top recommendations in Chambers UK 2000-2001:

Commodities, Licensing & Leisure

Rowe & Maw

the facts

Location: London, Manchester
UK ranking by size: 31
Total number of trainees: 42
Seats: 4 x 6 months
Alternative seats: Brussels, secondments (Unilever, ICI, GE)
Extras: Language training, Pro bono

Not too daring and a little safe. Not too corporate but aspiring to a bigger profile in the M&A stakes. Good on public law, matters litigious and always picking up interesting, quirky cases. This is Rowe & Maw. It won't blow you away with dynamism but you'll have a thoroughly pleasant time at this mid-tier MOR unCity firm. If you are a Rowe & Maw type you're probably not inspired by the law factories anyhow.....

whatever you do don't call them dull

What is Rowe & Maw all about? Click for their dot.com presentation and see what impressions you get. Does the home page look very conventional in comparison to many of its competitors? Yes. Are you filled with a surge of excitement? No. Do you think that they look harmless and that you probably want to apply to this law firm....yes.

Rowe & Maw has long pursued a dream of being a thrusting corporate player. *"We're certainly changing to a more corporate firm and a couple of the smaller departments have been sidelined or moved, so the ethos of this firm is turning....It's quite a drastic change for us."* It is cultivating overseas relationships (eg. with a Hong Kong law firm) and selling itself in the US (through a PR company). It is pushing to get more business from media and telecoms clients (currently including EMI and Cable & Wireless) and wants to be seen as a more serious, gutsy outfit.

Some departments, such as private client (axed last year), have lost out in the race to get all big and shiny. However, Rowe & Maw has a well-established and respected name for litigation and in areas such as projects, planning and environment. In both construction and public law it has a truly stunning reputation. In the past, the unCity attributes of the firm were what attracted trainees, very many of them of an Oxbridge background.

the demise of the oxbridge WASP?

Rowe & Maw now acknowledges that it needs to recruit a different type of trainee. Initially there was a knee jerk reaction against trainees showing a marked lack of interest in corporate work. Now it wants commercially minded individuals who will fit into the new-style Rowe & Maw. A series of tests on the assessment day is designed to weed out the bumbling academic types from the go-getting corporate partners of 2010. On the menu? *"Confident, gregarious, social interaction."* *"Quiet and diligent"* is off today, Sir. Some trainees are worried.....*"they are worried that they are not going to be kept on because perhaps they are not the type that* [the firm is] *looking for."*

In times of change there's always a little discomfort. But we've had no reports of unhappiness or walkouts. Contrast this with other firms in metamorphosis. The million-dollar question? Will it lose its conventional, unchallenging, middle class image? It has recruited heavily from Oxbridge, Durham, Bristol etc. in the past. Will we see more diversity at the firm in the future?

buddha and mr blobby

The firm comes across as such a wonderfully nice place that it's difficult to see how it could suddenly lose that benevolent air of care and concern. That determination to keep its corporate soul pure and worthy. This is what it still has over many of the firms it tries to emulate. *"It's a bit more relaxed and not quite so in your face."* said one trainee. *"They weren't quite so arrogant. Down to earth really"* another agreed. *"I didn't want to go where they just churn out trainees"* a third confirmed. *"If you're looking for swimming pools and gyms....it doesn't have any pretensions like that. I always come back to the people. It's hard-working but it does have a nice face to it and we don't have too many arrogant sods here."*

> "not the trendiest or the slickest of the mid-tier firms but it's a fairly balanced and unstressful place to be."

Maybe, just maybe, the firm has a different approach. An understanding that success is not all about profits (though these are not small) and long hours; a whiff of an ethical approach to being a law firm. If you want to get spiritual you need look no further than the firm's instructions on the project to build the world's largest Buddha, in India. It's not all so cool though. They recently worked on a matter relating to Mr Blobby and the Crinkly Bottom theme park based on Noel Edmonds' creation. Sad.

But the firm is instructed on plenty of interesting and high profile work. It acted for the District Auditor in the Westminster 'Homes for Votes' scandal and for a fertility clinic in its attempts to bring about the legal fertilisation of frozen human eggs.

less navel-gazing

Enough touchy feely stuff. Time for more facts. Two seats are available at any one time in the firm's Brussels office. There is a plethora of client secondments, both in the UK and elsewhere in Europe. About half the trainees are enthusiastic about going on secondment. Some felt that *"it's a sort of unwritten code that it's good to be seen to have done a secondment."* It is advantageous to have a link with one of the firm's main clients. If you've been with the firm throughout your training, *" I don't see that you've had much ability to network really."* *"In the first six months you don't do much networking and then you start to realise that it does matter."*

Mixing with the partners is neither difficult nor unpleasant. There is enough social interaction to enable bonds to be built up. The firm organises interesting social events on a regular, if ad hoc, basis. Trainees quite often get together for Friday nights in the local, The Booksellers.

and finally...

If you don't mind not having a business card to slide out of your wallet and swap with your mega-City firm friends, like the twenty-somethings' version of Pokemon; if you don't want to work *"killer hours;"* if you do want people to know your name; if you do want a diverse range of options, then Rowe & Maw is right up your street. It may not be the trendiest or the slickest of the mid-tier firms but it's a fairly balanced and unstressful place to be. Slow & Bore? We don't think so. Death Rowe? Now we haven't got to the bottom of that one...

top recommendations in Chambers UK 2000-2001:

Corporate Finance, Partnership, Pensions, Professional Negligence, Travel

Russell Jones & Walker

the facts

Location: London, Manchester, 8 other offices in UK.
UK ranking by size: 57
Total number of trainees: 15
Seats: 4 x 6 months
Alternative seats: None
Extras: Language training

Russell Jones & Walker is an unusual member of the Top 75 firms list. Not because it's one of the UK's national firms (with 10 offices, it's in expansionist mode); nor because it is a litigation oriented firm. But because it offers a combination of work that's not on the menu at most large firms. It is thriving in the areas of claimant personal injury and clinical negligence. It has a criminal division which owes much to its niche involvement in white collar fraud and Police Federation work. Its client list has a heavy trade union content – in other words it's on the side of the workers and not the bosses.

the rjw belief system

Browse the firm's website and you'll find statements not often found on other law firms' sites. You'll trip over the worthy sentiments on the RJW site if you're not careful, so heavily are they scattered across the pages. Here are some examples. *"Upholding the legal rights of individuals is at the heart of a civilised society."* *"We will not act for clients where this would be contrary to our mission, values or ethics."* *"We will not hide anything from you* [the client]."

Whilst the client base, language, approach and beliefs of the firm make it an ideal choice for someone who shares the firm's ethics, it's probably an inappropriate choice for those of the opposite political persuasion.

fight the good fight

The trainees we spoke to knew there were characteristics that they all shared. *"There is something there, but it's hard to put your finger on it."* Some are Oxbridge graduates, others are not. Academics don't seem to be of primary importance when it comes to recruitment. It's more of a personality thing. So what type of person do they want? Our sources summed up the required qualities: *"Individuals"* who can be a part of a collegiate environment, *"open-minded"* characters who display *"a sense of humour."* And at the end of the day, think about the work you'll be doing and who you'll be acting for. This firm acts for the Davids of this world, not the Goliaths. It holds itself out as a firm which fights the good fight. If you want blue chip clients and mega deals to boast about at dinner parties then back off now. If you feel passionate about being a lawyer, of the sort they make BBC TV drama series about, then RJW could be for you.

On the subject of the media, there are occasions when you might end up with a big hairy mike in your face and a camera homing in on your best/worst features. One trainee was thrilled to read in the press about cases she had worked on. *"Medical negligence involved a lot of high profile cases at the High Court, which attracted a lot of media attention."*

less glamorously...

Time for a quick reality check. The firm maps out a conventional rotation programme for trainees shortly after arrival. It is possible to vary it later, if necessary. You will do four of the following: personal injury, criminal, commercial litigation, employment, family/probate and property. The list reflects the relative descending order of size of the practice areas. So nearly all trainees do a stint in PI. The non-contentious requirements of the Law Society will be fulfilled in either family/probate or property. This, as you can see, is not a mainstream commercial firm. It pays accordingly, although certainly not badly. Salaries put the firm in line with medium-sized London firms.

The property seat provides the most client contact, much of it on the phone. A couple of our interviewees alluded to the fact that they looked forward to more after qualification. *"I haven't had a great deal of face to face client exposure,"* said one. *"It varies"* said another, *"in PI you talked to a client when you went to a conference or when you went to a meeting. In employment you actually had your own clients and dealt with them,"* although this was *"a lot more on the phone than face to face."*

The irregular hours of the criminal seat can be demanding. *"In criminal you have to hit the ground running"* one source said. *"I found criminal very emotional. If you're affected by things like that it can be quite difficult."* But this is not your typical High Street crime practice. Much of the work is white collar fraud and Police Federation instructions.

principal(ed) boys and girls

Three pounds a month buys trainees admission to the social club that organises events for the firm as a whole. The fun stuff includes sports, boat parties and a Christmas Panto (...Oh no it doesn't! Oh yes it does!) The social scene is good if not as frequent and large scale as some larger City practices. *"There's a pub across the road that we all go to on a Friday. Everyone's usually out."* Hours are radically different from City firms too. *"If you are not needed, then no one will bat an eyelid if you leave at 5.30pm."*

and finally...

Common ground between partners and staff makes for an egalitarian workplace. The high profile nature of certain aspects to the firm's work makes for a sense of real purpose and achievement. The continued growth of the firm makes for good prospects. No one pretends that a training contract anywhere is always going to be the stuff of fairy tales, but for a number of individuals out there reading this, the RJW glass slipper will definitely fit just right.

top recommendations in Chambers UK 2000-2001:

Personal Injury (Claimant)

Shearman & Sterling

the facts

Location: London
UK ranking by size: 72
Total number of trainees: 7
Seats: 4 x 6 months
Alternative seats: Paris

This US firm has had a London presence since 1972 and now operates from 14 offices worldwide. Continuing in its expansionist phase, it has been slugging it out with competitors in Germany and Italy in the last year or two and has been eager to plump up its London presence. This is the era of 'overpaid and over here' US firms in London. As it matures into the London market, expect to see a greater concentration of effort into graduate recruitment. The Shearmans' website, being US-oriented, is not much help in putting you on track to an application for a contract in the London office, and they don't have a dedicated graduate recruitment officer yet. But the firm is well worth checking out.

loadsamoney?

Mixed responses from our interviewees. *"I remember people saying to me at law school that I must be getting loads of money. It wasn't a huge consideration. The pay differential is not significant enough to be a factor"* one source said. But another cited money as a key motivator, pointing out that a huge salary never goes amiss. Trainees even get a firm credit card and more than generous expenses allowances.

Of great importance was the idea of working for

a small firm that handled high profile deals. One in particular knew that she wanted to practise in banking law and simply didn't see the point of a broader training.

Given that Shearman & Sterling is one of the world's largest law firms, is the London office the master of its own destiny or a part of a bigger machine? The New York office is reputed to be rather traditional and not exactly the funkiest in the Big Apple. The London office has its own independence and has cultivated its own style. *"It's young and relaxed – quite casual."* Size is obviously a factor, as is the fact that most lawyers have trained and built up their practices at other firms, rather than training and developing in the firm's mould. *"It's a casual dress policy full time and always has been"* one source said. Contrast this with the fact that New York has only recently introduced a dress down policy.

oh lord, won't you buy me a mercedes benz

The word on the street is that an assistant is expected to do a whopping 2,200 billable hours a year. Is life going to be all work and no play? Hours are deal dependent. No prizes for discovering this. When nothing special is happening, on a regular day a trainee might expect to be in the office 9.30am – 7pm. Obviously there will be ups and downs. *"I had a quiet summer. It was just a matter of months but it was quite frustrating."* Work centres on M&A, project finance and acquisition finance, which produces hard-core deals and hours. Expect long hours to take over at times. All-nighters and weekend working will be a normal part of life. If you work after 9pm, you'll have the opportunity to get home in a chauffeur driven black Mercedes. How cool is that?

Mixed responses again on the social scene. Perhaps this reflects the variety of characters that are taken on. Apparently *"not everyone is a Stephen Mostyn Williams."* (Mr MW is the charismatic banking partner who has earned himself the nickname 'Stephen Costin' Millions.') The firm moved recently to offices in Liverpool Street. There's a bit of a party/weekend get-together scene if you want it. Sometimes staff go on holiday together. If you're just up for a quicky then the local bar is the Lime Bar.

personal space

The new building is *"pleasant, not dingy"* and has a *"good cafeteria."* Whilst *"the offices could be bigger, you're not nose to nose with the assistants"* with whom you'll share a room as a trainee. You certainly won't feel like a number or part of the herd. *"You need a bit of your own initiative"* one source emphasised. *"You must be able to articulate yourself and have a reasonable idea of what you want."* Remember, the Shearman & Sterling London training contract is still in its infancy and only a handful of trainees have worked there. The numbers are going to increase (a bit) in the coming years, but you'll still need to drive much of your own training. A training liaison officer has recently been recruited from A&O.

It's not all pure corporate and finance work; the arbitration department offers variation in the diet. So far all trainees have worked to get some time in the Paris office doing arbitration work, although the clear message from our interviews that you should not consider an overseas placement as guaranteed.

and finally...

Not the biggest of trainee schemes but one which operates in the context of paralegals vastly outnumbering trainees. That means that there's none of the 'dross' that trainees have traditionally moaned about. It is likely that a new area of work – securitisation – will be available for trainees in the next year or so. If you know you want a finance-based training, why wouldn't you apply?

top recommendations in Chambers UK 2000-2001:

Corporate Finance(US firms acting from London)

Shoosmiths

the facts

Location: Northampton, Nottingham, Reading, Banbury, Southampton
UK ranking by size: 36
Total number of trainees: 26
Seats: 4 x 6 months
Alternative seats: Secondments

Shoosmiths is a national firm with six major locations. Its heart is in the Midlands with a firm presence in the M4 corridor and south to the coast. Unpretentious and unstuffy, its trainees report a well defined and well organised training. "*Striving for greater efficiencies*," last year it closed its Rugby office.

name-dropping

The firm formerly known as Shoosmith & Harrison may not be the most glamorous, big-bucks firm out there. As it's acutely aware, critics sometimes compare it to a factory. It has made a success out of lower value bulk work in the fields of conveyancing (Property Direct), financial recoveries for financial institutions and personal injury (Claims Compensation). A large part of the firm's fee income comes from these areas, with work typically handled by huge teams of unqualified staff in out of town locations. If this conjures up an image of two years in a warehouse by the side of the motorway, pressing the same key on your keyboard day after day, then fear not. Trainees spend their time almost exclusively in the Business Services division of the firm(the law firm bit), with a wide range of commercial options at their fingertips.

northampton: mission control

Most trainees join the Northampton office at 'The Lakes,' its out-of-town-by-the-motorway location. There's no problem with parking. In fact the spacious facilities for motorists help to keep the firm in shape. "*We have a football pitch in the back carpark!*" It seems to be a sporty office with plenty of fixtures against clients and local professional firms. Sadly, it doesn't

have a pub nearby and although there's a drinks do in the office every Friday, there's less than full attendance. "*Most trainees will go at some times throughout the year, but often you are doing your own thing on a Friday*."

"*Life is very well run for you.*" There's a canteen on site and, so far as skills training is concerned, more often than not the Northampton office is the centre to which trainees from all offices come for their professional edification. It provides the opportunity for the otherwise widely dispersed trainees to get to know each other and other parts of the firm.

Litigation and commercial property are compulsory seats in Northampton. You can try for a corporate seat or perhaps one of the secondments to clients such as Barclaycard or the Open University. The range of work on offer is good; "*everything under the sun*" and it's open for trainees at the other branches to request time at the Lakes.

nottingham; where small is beautiful

"*We do three different departments in Nottingham and then you have to repeat one of the departments.*" Trainees thought it was possible to go and do a seat in an office with a wider variety of work (ie. Northampton) "*but it doesn't usually happen.*" There was a real sense of enthusiasm from Nottingham. "*The work in corporate has been fantastic. Its a real team thing...it's never you just being the trainee. You are an extra pair of hands.*" The fact that no one seems to move to another office may be a ringing endorsement of the Nottingham experience.

"*Because there's so few trainees (only one or two per year), you do socialise with the partners – there's no one else to socialise with!*" our source joked. "*We all go out to the pub on a Friday evening and you know who everyone is.*"

solent; another great location for motorists

Historically this was a personal injury office before it took over a commercial practice a number of years ago. It was as if "*the volume litigation and the commercial were run as two businesses*" one contact said.

However, in the last year, all PI work has been moved to the firm's Basingstoke *"warehouse."* Solent is now one of the smaller offices and there's *"a less formal atmosphere"* than in Northampton. It covers the basic range of commercial seats. If you want PI then you can request a slot in Basingstoke.

If you're up for a bit of marine work then ready about and full sail to the Solent office. Anchored in a business park off the motorway near Fareham, the office has two local bars The Waterside, which has a late licence and The Parson's Collar. *"The problem is that we are not near town and it's an expensive taxi ride back to Southampton."* It's a young office and every so often a night out is organised. *"There's a healthy rivalry between the trainees"* one source confided, *"and it's not expected but it is hoped that as a trainee you'll stay and do the work for as long as necessary...in corporate that's normally 7pm."* One corporate trainee had apparently been clocking off at 2am but *"that's the exception rather than the rule."*

reading is it

"Just off the London road in a big building" you'll find the firm's Reading office. What is it with large buildings on the side of busy roads? The region has its own flavour and this translates through to the work of the office. *"There's quite a lot of IT in the Thames Valley area and so you get the feel that we are quite IT orientated. Shoosmiths has spent millions on its IT information system."*

We got the impression that the firm tried its best to accommodate trainees' desires in terms of seat allocation. As usual, second years do get first choice of seats but *"If you want to do something, all you have to do is ask. They jump at the chance of having an eager trainee."*

and finally...

The *"Shoosmiths way"* has changed in the last couple of years one source told us. Before, *"I was surprised to find the offices working separately, each office having its own budgets and targets; managing itself."* And the new way? It has come out of the major reorganisation of the firm's business. *"Divisions are now by practice area not by office."* There is no real bias towards recruiting trainees with a local connection; for many, like university, their training represents *"new people, new turf."*

top recommendations in Chambers UK 2000-2001:

Debt Recovery, Food, Personal Injury (Claimant)

Simmons & Simmons

the facts

Location: London
UK ranking by size: 15
Total number of trainees: 148
Seats: 6 x 4 months
Alternative seats: many seats abroad, secondments
Extras: Language training, pro bono

iceberg ahoy

Anyone reading the legal press over the past couple of years will know that Simmons has had a busy time. Not all for the right reasons. Banking, finance, financial services, capital markets and international securities areas have all seen high-profile departures. *"Quite a few senior people went to American firms"* said one source on the defections last year. *"They wanted more money. I can't blame some of them."* Possibly as a response to events, Simmons has restructured the groups into one financial markets department. But is it too little too late?

Inside the firm the mood amongst the younger lawyers does not seem to have been badly affected. *"It has had a bit of a battering in the press recently, but I think it's made a lot of large steps which are only now being seen."* Members of the firm feel *"hard done by."* Certainly those we spoke to had strong views. *"From the outside it always looks worse than it really is."* *"There was a period when it was down, now it is turning a corner."* Whatever past aims were, it is not aiming too high. *"It is concentrating on what it can do rather than what it aspires to.*" With profits per partner up by a healthy 21% this year it is set for a smoother ride.

isn't a lot of the trainees' work very boring?

A question posed by the Simmons website. We thought we'd find out for you. Trainees we spoke to were generally positive about the standard of work they were given. "*I have some of my own files incorporating small companies etc.*" *The work I was doing was great, I was off down to court, going to see the clients at their properties, negotiating with liquidators, it was brilliant.*" But inevitably this varies from case to case. In the big deals you will feel like a "*small cog in big machine.*" It was"*a good overview and the best introduction you could get*" but "*boring work can happen on a big case.*" The quality of supervision is "*excellent,*" though a lot depends on who you sit with. "*There are a lot of junior assistants who are getting the chance to do a hell of a lot of decent work, and this filters down to trainees.*" When things are not so rosy, action will be taken. "*One department had a bad reputation with trainees and they had to act on it, which they did to their credit.*" The firm is known for having a very human atmosphere internally. The fact that it contains the top employment lawyer and team in the country may go towards ensuring that employee relations are harmonious.

ships that pass in the night

When asked for a low point, one trainee sighed "*being tired in corporate.*" Obviously in any law firm handling 'City' transactional work you must expect to work well beyond 5:30pm from time to time. Nevertheless, trainees at Simmons work very hard, of that there is no doubt. "*At times, some have done at least 12 hours every day.*" Even "*Non-stop for three days with perhaps two hours sleep a night.*" Ouch!

If you don't work the occasional weekend you'll probably be the only one. You might expect trainees to be dismayed by this but they "*don't feel exploited.*" The partners "*do thank you for working hard.*" The

"*interest that people take in trainees is noticeably stronger than at other firms.*" In fact, the atmosphere and level of involvement mean that "*often it's the nights that you are in late that are the best.*"

in a blind taste test...

The place "*just seems nicer.*" Trainees constantly reiterated "*people are very happy.*" There's no partner trainees are scared of and people are approachable. "*If I have an idea I can go to them* [partners] *and I can go out drinking with all people.*" But one comment many of them made very loyally is that "*People need to be more positive about the work the firm does.*" Whilst partners might leave Simmons for more money they "*don't leave because they don't like the working atmosphere.*" During these interviews we specifically ask people not mention the word 'friendly' or the phrase 'open door policy,' largely because the graduate recruitment ordeal that trainees are forced to go through inevitably leaves these words permanently stamped on their brains. When told this one Simmons trainee stated "*I thought that was a peculiarly Simmons thing.*" 'Fraid not.

meet the gang

People "*have lives and don't do nothing but work*" (hang on – see the section on hours) and there's "*plenty of room for colourful characters.*" Sports are high on the agenda. Cricket is "*very well supported.*" The Rugby players say; "*we are the winner or runner up on a regular basis.*" And there is five-a-side football "*for girls only.*"

After hours, "*different intakes go to different pubs.*" The Red Lion and All Bar One are regular haunts for all. Socialising across the age ranges is common. "*It's quite normal to socialise with partners*" indeed, "*some partners will round people up.*"

Most trainees mentioned the 'Simmons soirees.' We had visions of candlelit dinners produced by Hyacinth Bucket. In reality she would be horrified to find just "*drinks and sausages.*" The name 'soiree' is just to keep up appearances."*We prefer to call it that *rather than a blatant piss-up."* If truth be told, the *"wine-tasting is an excuse to get drunk."*

happy together now

There is a real buzz in Simmons at the time of writing. The firm is to complete its move to the new offices by December 2000. Everyone is happy at the prospect of being together in one place. Maybe *"people will be more integrated."* All approve of the *"huge and very well thought- out design."* And they're looking forward to the new restaurant. The firm has a large collection of modern art, having accepted some in lieu of payment of fees. A selection, which includes works by Damien Hirst, will be decorating the new restaurant. One interviewee commented that *"half a cow could be a bit distracting."*

hitting the headlines

You *"have to do a corporate and a litigation seat."* However, litigation has a wide meaning, including IP and employment. *"Employment is the most popular seat because of the firm's reputation there,"* and also because of the work. *"My high point would have to be my employment seat. Because I got so much involvement and had day to day contact with clients and lots of responsibility and so many different things. Sex discrimination claims, very exciting headlining stuff."* What this means is that not everyone will get a seat in employment,or the chance to qualify there. *"I know that they do try hard to give them what they want, but there are just too many numbers to go around."* People are often offered a straight litigation seat when they start. Since employment counts as a litigation seat, *"quite a lot of people by accepting litigation blindly stop themselves from doing employment."* This is not a hard and fast rule and you would not necessarily be completely excluded. But it's worth considering. Put in an early word. *"If you indicate before your first seat, your intentions are taken on board."*

Trainees think the firm tries very hard to keep them on. If first choice jobs aren't available *"People are offered second or third choices. One guy was sent on secondment for a year so he could have a seat on his return."*

survival of the fittest

Some 20 people disappear overseas every 6 months. For once in this *"friendly"* firm *"competition is very fierce for some overseas seats."* The successful applicant must do well in a special mid-seat appraisal and an interview. Apparently *"a lot is on the appraisal."* For those who do not go abroad, there are many secondments with clients such as Reuters, Smithkline Beecham and Credit Suisse First Boston(it helps to have done a banking seat for this one).

and finally...

Simmons people are upbeat and confident about the future. The firm may have abandoned ambitions to expand into a firm of magic circle size. Trainees have plenty of work, enjoy the atmosphere and are proud of their cutting edge new building. And the only way is up.

top recommendations in Chambers UK 2000-2001:

Employment, Environmental Law

S J Berwin & Co

the facts

Location: London
UK ranking by size: 21
Total number of trainees: 70
Seats: 4x6 months
Alternative seats: Brussels, Frankfurt, Madrid, secondments.
Extras: Pro bono, language training

First some questions. Do you really know what private equity is? And venture capital? If not, then stop reading now. You probably don't read the right pages in the newspaper, in which case, your interest won't lie in this arena. If you do, and if you like the sound of it, then read on. Some 40% of this firm's work takes place in the corporate sector and a great part of it is done by the Private Equity Group (PEG). There are a number of practice areas which orbit the venture capital focus of SJB and this high achieving firm is doing characteristically well in a those areas.

sweated labour?

If you're considering SJ Berwin, you may have been scared off by its reputation as a sweatshop. A sweatshop implies long hours at low wages. In fact, the firm pays at the higher end of the scale for UK firms and triggered the recent wage war within top City firms, now paying £42,000 to newly-qualifieds. Hardly the classic case of sweatshop conditions. Will you work long hours though? Yes you will....and many choose to. *"I do work hard. I do long hours. I am very, very keen."*

> "This is a dynamic and fast-moving environment in which you have to be brave."

Why such an approach at trainee level? It's all down to motivation. This is a highly successful, extremely busy firm. In recent years it lost a number of assistant solicitors so there is no shortage of good work for trainees willing to take it. Many do, perhaps responding to their inner drive to succeed, perhaps dragged along by the groundswell of ambition. *"It's very easy to get swept along here with the long hours and the quality work. It becomes very important to succeed."*

But this hot-house environment does not nurture everyone. *"The firm is not always patient with those who are not brilliant."* However, the same source added that *"trainee development has come on – when I started it was incredibly tough."*

growing pains

18 years ago SJ Berwin was an embryonic firm. Now it's one of the biggest in the UK and ranked 10th for profitability. How has it done that? Blood sweat and tears, some would say. No doubt many ex-assistants would agree. But we are told that *"the senior assistants are happier* [now]" following a 'McKinsey style' review of their role and lifestyle at the firm. The money is even better, they have more holiday allocation and their request to be 'cared for' has been acknowledged. They were *"concerned about continuing development. Assistants said 'we want someone to take stock of where we are going and how we are doing'."*

exodus

An exodus of assistants may have been halted, but September 2000 qualifiers must have been saying something when they voted with their feet. Although 90% were offered jobs on qualification, our sources at SJ Berwin tell us that a significant number of these declined the offer. They're now either working for the Yankee Dollar or specialising in the type of finance or public company work which SJ Berwin cannot offer. Their work tends to be for an entrepreneurial client base.

The most interesting issue emerging from these statistics is that this year it was the more niche departments that attracted newly qualified solicitors. The busy PEG recruited less than a handful. In successive years this may determine what jobs are on offer to qualifiers.

if you can make it there...

This is a young firm; partners are not too crusty. It became obvious during the course of our interviewing that the trainee population is more multicultural than at most firms surveyed in this book.

SJ Berwin isn't after the classic public school swot. Although it takes *"lots from 'ivy league' universities,"* sources feel that *"people can penetrate"* from outside traditional recruiting grounds. They pointed to the fact that a number of trainees had proved their worth in paralegal positions. A high proportion of training contracts run off the back of the vacation schemes.

Under such conditions the firm can see whether or not the applicant has sufficient energy, drive and staying power. Being keen really counts."*They want to see real enthusiasm for what they do.*" The firm says it is looking for people who are 'ambitious..commercially-minded...bright and determined to succeed.' And they mean it.

square peg in a round hole

Always remember what it is that SJ Berwin does. Remember who it acts for and what it is trying to achieve. The PEG is key to this firm. "*When I started*" one trainee told us "*we had to do one corporate seat. It's now two compulsory corporate seats.*" Think very carefully about this before you even think of applying. If you don't have an interest in corporate you won't get in. "*They are looking for corporate, corporate, corporate. It's venture capital not public company stuff. Transactions tend to be very complex.*"

"*They come to us to do media but it's such a tiny department.*" For the majority of applicants, prospects at the firm lie with corporate work. Those we spoke to were keen to emphasise this. Competition for media, sports, employment and IP seats is tough. A small number of these jobs do exist. For those who access this work and qualify into it, SJ Berwin can appear like a dream come true.

Similarly, for those who are as go-getting as their corporate bosses and clients this is a top choice. You can be challenged here. You get out what you put in. "*I have put myself in a position whereby I get this* [demanding] *work*" one trainee explained to us. "*Other trainees at my level don't do this sort of work. It's about putting yourself forward. You can go anywhere. If you like them and they like you, you are made!*"

continental breakfast?

The number of seats in overseas offices is small but not massively oversubscribed. In September 2000, the Madrid office took its first London trainee for a six month placement. Brussels and Frankfurt always take trainees – one lucky devil spent six months in each. The focus of these European offices is private equity work. Unusually, the EU department is essentially London-based.

If you're not lucky enough to be grabbing a croissant somewhere across the Channel, you can break your fast in the well-attended staff dining room in London. You can get a free lunch and hang with your homies or mix freely with partners and assistants.

After hours (if you are still up for it – average hours are 8.30am–7pm or, in corporate, 8.30am–9pm) the two local drinking holes just across the road from the office are The Blue Lion and a tapas bar called Centros. "*There's definitely always people over there on a Friday*" but "*the social scene is really cool as there's no obligation. You're not expected to go out with your colleagues once a week.*"

and finally...

This is a "*dynamic and fast-moving environment*" in which "*you have to be brave.*" We felt energised after our SJ Berwin interviews. Training there is not for the faint-hearted, or the laid-back. And you must be interested in corporate finance, more specifically venture capital work for entrepreneurs, rather than plc work. But if this suits you (sir), you will have it made here...at least, those of you with the adrenalin levels to keep up the pace...

top recommendations in Chambers UK 2000-2001:

Litigation (Commercial under 40 Litigators), Media & Entertainment, Parliamentary & Public Affairs, Travel, Hotels & Leisure

Slaughter and May

the facts

Location: London
UK ranking by size: 8
Total number of trainees: 138
Seats: 4 x 6 months

Alternative seats: Several overseas offices, secondments

Extras: Pro bono

Slaughters. Even the name sounds sinister. But does the firm deserve the scary reputation that attaches to it at the junior end? Well certainly, of all the City firms, S&M (ouch!) shrouds itself in mystery to a degree. It never bothers with hard sell tactics. Why would it need to? Its reputation in the corporate arena is so good that the clients, and the deals with which it is associated, do all the marketing the firm could possibly want. So, no marketing department. You begin to scent the uniqueness of the firm already.

the embodiment of subtlety

With over 3000 applications for just over 75 training contracts, there's no shortage of eager applicants. Remarkable then that on more than one occasion trainees from across the City told us that their interviews had been conducted by partners who had some sort of link with them. One discussed obscure Russian literature with a knowledgeable interviewer, another remarked that the trainee showing them around the firm had attended the same college, another was interviewed by a fellow alumnus. There's some smart thinking and careful planning at work. It's all very subtle.

Subtlety, it's a hallmark of the firm. There's a cool refinement about the way it works. *"It's not one of the aggressive in-your-face law firms."* There's no special effort to look and sound fabulous; *"what you see is what you get."* Clients tell us that you'll always get an answer from the firm's lawyers, there's no sitting on the fence with their advice. We put this to trainees and asked them if there was anything about their training which might breed that type of lawyer. The answer was interesting. Whilst there's no shortage of training sessions and seminars given by lawyers from within and outside the firm, the general consensus is that Slaughters *"promotes individuality and there's a hugely diverse range of characters who are taken*

on." Some may be strong and overtly confident *"but you do not have to be. There is room for shyer types"* one source said. *"You make your mark in your own way. People here can be super bright. Some are simply extremely hard working. Some are witty. The hard working types are not trying to be super bright. The sharp and witty are not trying to be the most thorough."*

state of independence

If as a young qualified lawyer you shoulder a lot of responsibility and must be seen to be *"standing on your own two feet"* quite early on, it follows that as a trainee you need to develop these skills. As a trainee you share a room with your supervisor, but *"they do expect you to think independently."*

Slaughters assistants, ex-assistants and trainees we spoke to told us that their time as trainees was an excellent two years and that choosing the firm was a great decision. *"I listened when people said go for the best and then it's easier to move down to a smaller firm."* They appreciate the quality of work (*"Generally the work is quite interesting because of the client base"*) and the opportunity to build up good friendships at the firm (*"With around 70 starting in each intake you can't fail to find people you like"*). We have to admit we were a little surprised to hear this. We had expected major horror stories.

body parts

You and your crew will no doubt get to know the inside of a few of the local watering holes. Because they are *"two minutes away,"* Dr Butler's Head and Corney & Barrow in Mason's Avenue are the favourites. Also on the list is the Rack & Tenter in Moorgate. Would you be joined by the partners? Unlikely. Indeed one source asked *"Would you want to? They have a different lifestyle...these people are successful individuals earning more than a million a year."* The firm retains a strict hierarchy.

You'll do two compulsory seats in corporate (which include finance and commercial seats) and as long as you fulfil the Law Society requirements for contentious experience, you need not set foot in the litigation department. Property is optional as are many of the more niche areas, such as tax or employment. We were asked to make it very clear that *"niche departments, such as EC law, are very small. Even larger departments like litigation are a support function for corporate."* More than half of the firm's work is in the main body, which is the corporate practice, not in these supporting limbs.

> "There must be a reason why more Slaughters partners earn over a million a year than at any other firm."

Some interviewees thought these supporting areas were actually the really popular seats to do. *"Litigation and property are easier seats. You can get out early, say sixish, and after corporate that becomes the be all and end all. You're really glad to be there after a busy corporate seat. You're looking for time off."* There's no time off if you want to secure one of the overseas placements. There aren't many so you'd think there'd be a lot of *"scrumming"* for the seats. But not everyone thought this was true. *"It's entirely about getting in the good books of the right people"* we were told. A couple implied that they had been approached by personnel for an overseas seat. Curioser and curioser. The more general message, however, is that at this firm hard work is what *"will get you far – better than networking."*

breathing different air?

There's none of the self-imposed stay-late-for-show that has gone on at certain other firms. *"As a trainee you stay late because there's so much to do."* With a reputation of the size and calibre of Slaughters', the multi billion pound deals just keep rolling on in through the door. The volume of deals means that trainees need to be part of a well-oiled machine. They need to be willing and able to do the dull stuff as well as the tasks that require a bit of brain. *"As a trainee you can get responsibility"* one of our sources confirmed, *"but of course there's dross involved. There's photocopying and checking and all that kind of rubbish as well."* It seems that even working at an élite firm, you'll still be breathing the same air as the rank and file of trainees.

profits of doom?

So is Slaughters so very different to any other magic circle firm? Maybe. There's a distinctive culture to the firm. We'll begin with a few stats. At number one in any table of profits at UK law firms – Slaughter and May. It earns nearly twice as many fees per fee earner as its nearest rival in the table – Linklaters. An unsophisticated interpretation of the figures is that Slaughters squeezes a lot more out of its fee earners.

Our discussions with junior assistants past and present confirm this. *"This firm is all about hard graft. There's no way of getting around it."* *"After qualification it becomes nasty in terms of hours."* So this is *"a great training, but then you have to start questioning what happens."*

Certainly at trainee/NQ level the interviewees had a refreshing outlook. They don't think Slaughters differs from its magic circle counterparts in terms of hours and responsibility. They told us they were totally satisfied with their training. Those with a few years under their belts agree that as a trainee life is very rewarding.

But in comparison with other firms a lot more is expected of you when you qualify. *"Partners come in and say on the day after qualification 'I've got a deal, can you do it for me?"* Is the stress bearable? *"You are not equipped for it at first. There's standard forms and a good precedent library but at first you will not look good in front of clients. It's a baptism of fire and one that many can't stick through to partnership."* Strong words.

the headmaster

Dealings with some of the most high profile partners are *"very scary"*. That said, interaction with such individuals is rare and *"like going to see the headmaster on your first day at school."* Sitting with partners (as opposed to senior assistants) can be a double-edged sword. Assistants tend to be more hands on with the deals and as their trainee you may do longer hours. But *"you learn the most from the assistants in the corporate seats."* With partners *"Sometimes it's quite boring as it's too much of the complicated bits of the deal."* One source said that *"you don't always get as much attention as you'd like as there's a lot of people who are very busy. When they are working on major deals, you can't expect them to have time for you."*

The firm requires those that work there to absorb themselves completely in the client matters on which they are instructed. Niceties and chit-chat don't make for big profits. There clearly must be reasons why more Slaughters partners earn over a million a year than at any other firm. You'll have to be a truly remarkable individual to join them some day. *"Most people accept that they'll never be made a partner"* one lawyer told us.

getting your hand in the sweetie jar

Slaughters has been through its stage of going for *"straight down the line firsts from Oxford"* and although our interviewees still noted that *"a majority"* of successful applicants were Oxbridge, it is not an essential qualification. Sources felt the most important qualification was a love of the law and a real interest in corporate work. Most important of all, if you want to make a career at the firm *"you have to devote your life to it."* Some suggest an air of traditionalism at the firm (*"plenty of old-school types"*) No-one denied that Slaughters has a reputation for being old-fashioned. One said *"People take the mick out of you, saying 'you all work with quills' but it is quite modern. But it's subtle. People don't take account of that. It is a traditional firm but subtle."*

Slaughters offices are legendary. Pretty good in the client reception area; a selection of childhood favourite sweets keep the waiting visitor absorbed. (Jelly babies, liquorice allsorts and wine gums – sometimes chocolate eclairs.) The rest of the premises are a bit of a laughing stock amongst others in the City. Again and again we were told how parts are in a very sorry state. *"35 Basinghall Street is like an old science lab and it's boiling in the summer. All the non-corporate service departments and admin staff are there. It's an old 1960's building in an area that was rebuilt very quickly after the war."* Trainees who'd visited the firm in the course of their work had alerted us to this. One talked of going to *"a sweatbox... a fair country walk away from the public face of S&M."* As an insider put it *"it's tatty and it affects morale."* It must be hard maintaining that cool reserve when you have to put up with *"not having proper air conditioning."* In 2001, and much to the relief of its staff, Slaughters is moving to new offices.

and finally...

There's no back-biting between trainees coming up for qualification. Almost without exception everyone is offered a job. A majority accept. It would be wrong to assume that a S&M training is simply that; two years of sadism and masochism and tougher than a training at any other magic circle firm. Despite plenty of rumours to the contrary, there is no evidence to suggest this.

When thinking about training, bear in mind that corporate work is the firm's major focus and that areas of practice such as property and litigation are, in the main, seen to be supporting areas.

top recommendations in Chambers UK 2000-2001:

Competition/Anti-trust, Corporate Finance(60+ Solicitors in Corporate Team), Tax (Corporate)

Stephenson Harwood

the facts

Location: London
UK ranking by size: 42
Total number of trainees: 40
Seats: 4x6 months
Alternative seats: Madrid, Piraeus, Hong Kong, Singapore, secondments
Extras: Language training

There's all sorts of turbulence at 'shipping firm' SH. It seems that they don't want the shipping firm image anymore. They don't want their old 'Est.1828-serious-and-important' image either. Where's it all leading to? A large number of partners have walked the plank recently. A few senior assistant solicitors have also left to pursue their careers at other firms.

rock the boat

This warrants a bit of investigation, we thought. The firm's Chief Executive wrote an article in the legal press in June, discussing the *"tough test"* posed by partners *"whose individual professional ambitions do not fit in with the new common purpose."* The trainees know they have *"been fed the line"* and this is what they understand to be behind the sea change. *"Of late the partners have been concerned about profits and have been trying to boost them. This has meant changes in the partnership and some dead wood has gone."*

branded

It's impossible to say how the changes affect trainees, given that the 'new improved' Stephenson Harwood is still nascent. But what's this 'new common purpose' the firm now boasts? They have indicated a desire to achieve a more corporate-driven turnover. The shipping angle is being played down, though this flies in the face of alleged merger talks with shipping giants Clyde & Co. Their litigation and IP departments are well established (although the latter has recently sustained top-level losses) and the property department gets a lot of work from hotels and leisure related clients. This was the firm that put the planning and finance together for the London Eye.

no bumfluff

"Nasty 80's decor" in the London office is counterbalanced by the camaraderie between staff, making every day *"a buzz not a slog."* *"Most people would enjoy office banter"* a NQ told us, adding that *"people socialise in teams."*

There may not be a canteen in the building, but trainees *"often meet up for lunch at Ossies, the greasy spoon down the road."* One source admitted that *"we are all here because the pressure isn't as high as it is in many firms. I wanted somewhere that was small enough not to drown in and had no beds on the premises."* These people want a life.

Partners will ask you about your social life and there's an impression that *"they don't want to take on daunting intellects, they want friendly people who display openness."* Trainees hinted that the firm quite likes recruits to take time out after or between academic training. *"There's not too many bumfluff moustaches here"* one told us. Another said *"at interview they say 'take some time out, join us at a later stage.' It is reflected in the standard of trainees here... you are more able to deal with things, take things in your stride."* The firm itself says that it welcomes "candidates from diverse backgrounds...including mature students with commercial experience and management skills."

the long wait for responsibility

Not everyone we interviewed was happy with the level of responsibility given to trainees. *"If that's what you really want then don't go to a City firm, go to a High Street practice!"* they said. Interestingly, those who were disappointed about the lack of responsibility were also able to give examples of court appearances with more senior lawyers on the other side. They understood that it was the nature of the work, rather than any specific policy, that was behind the issue.

To the extent that there isn't an official forum for feedback on the training experience, it can be left up to individual partners to be the listening ear when problems arise. *"With mine I'd cough the lot and get advice on what to do. If it was sufficiently important the partner would take it further."* One interviewee told us *"actually nobody ever asked me for my feedback after I qualified. Older and more senior partners don't believe in criticism from trainees – maybe those partners still regard trainees as expendable."*

pack your bags and go

In the second or third seats, trainees have the option of spending time in Hong Kong (*"most attractive"*), Singapore (*"essentially shipping"*), Madrid or Greece. However,*"people don't want to go to Piraeus."* We bet they don't – not when you can go to one of the further flung locations and get onto the lively Asian trainee circuit. More often than not, the overseas seats are linked to the shipping practice. For most people shipping does play a part in the two years of training. *"I think it took me a bit of time to get into it. It is a lot of terminology, it is like a whole new world in itself."*

be reasonable

Here's some prophetic wisdom SH-trainee-style: *"Lawyers advise clients as to what is reasonable but often have no idea themselves about how to be reasonable. At Stephenson Harwood they are."*

and finally...

To be honest, we approached our research for this firm with a yawn. None of us knew anything interesting about them. But our eyes have been opened. Stephenson Harwood has sharpened its focus. More newsworthy but still a pleasant place to work. And you get to go abroad.

top recommendations in Chambers UK 2000-2001:

Litigation (fewer than 40 litigators)

Taylor Joynson Garrett

the facts

Location: London
UK ranking by size: 32
Total number of trainees: 43
Seats: 4 x 6 months
Alternative seats: Secondments, Brussel, Paris

TJG is experiencing a renaissance. The paradigm shift caused by the internet, other new technology and developments in life sciences has plucked the firm out of a batch of mid-tier edge-of-the-City firms and turned it into a swelling practice with surging profits. It has long been known for top quality IP work and a real involvement with technology and life sciences clients. This base has now enabled its other focus areas, such as corporate and telecoms, to gain increased profile.

wanted: scientists and 'techies'

The firm's strength in IP is obvious to all but the extremely myopic. Someone choosing a legal training after graduating in a science subject and also wishing to make use of their previous education could do worse than apply to TJG. One trainee confirmed that, in spite of a mutually beneficial bond between the firm and such graduates, *"not a huge number* [of trainees] *have science backgrounds even though the firm is desperate for science graduates....they are quite forthright about that being their intention."*

hard v soft

If you're thinking about doing an IP seat then the decision to do hard IP (patents) as opposed to soft (trade marks and copyright) is a touch more important a decision than, say, thin 'n' crispy or deep pan in Pizza Hut. To non-scientific trainees *"Hard IP is not that popular as it doesn't hold out any prospects of a job for most people. It's a bit of a wasted six months, if you are hard-nosed about it and view every seat as a potential job."* On the other hand, if you are up for a hard-core patent training then think how easy it will be to stamp your mark.

Soft seats are more popular than hard seats. That's a general rule in life anyway isn't it? It's seen as a more accessible area of law. The good news for anyone with a particular interest in a specialised area is that not everyone will compete with you for the same work. *"There's a good mix of personalities. People have a wide range of ideas about why they're here, where they're going and what they want to qualify into."*

picky picky

On the subject of getting the seats you want, several trainees reported difficulties in the seat allocation system. *"There have been one or two examples where things have gone badly wrong. There are other examples where people didn't get particular seats – mainly personality differences."* Successive interviewees told us that, in spite of the efforts of personnel to match trainees to the seats they wanted, they had been overridden by certain personalities at partner level. *"Not everybody has got what they wanted. I think that the graduate recruitment department try as much as they can but to a certain extent their hands are tied because there are partners who ask for certain people or not to have certain people... People then end up in seats and they don't understand why they have ended up there."* And again, perhaps rather worryingly, *"it's supposed to be straightforward and fair. We give our preferences on a form and have a chat with HR. Supposedly they allocate us. But you're never sure who's pulling what strings."*

A six month placement in the firm's Brussels office is a popular and busy alternative to London. We are pleased to report that selection takes place based on merit, with the Brussels partner considering CVs, appraisals and conducting phone interviews. In the past there have also been instances of trainees spending time with an affiliated firm in Hong Kong and on part-time secondment to clients.

bringing in the paras

TJG have made a number of smart business decisions in the last few years. Example: spotting that its future e-millionaire clients will need the services of a private client department. Example: having close links with firms across Europe (Interlex) and in the US. Example: Bringing in many more paralegals to relieve the burden of irksome tasks from trainees. *"When I started, there were only one or two paralegals. Now there's a couple for each department. They take away some of the dross, but it's still there for trainees."* There is a reward system going on though. *"I had to do all the bundling for a big trial but when the trial came round I got to see the whole thing"* one source said.

In terms of responsibility and client contact *"there's no firm culture either way."* Whether you feel frustrated or deeply fulfilled seems to be totally dependent on the trainer to whom you are allocated. *"Trainees all meet before seat moves and discuss who's not worth the time of day and who's worth sitting with. When graduate recruitment get five people all asking for the same seat and none asking for another, it must be fairly obvious."*

swan-song of the social scene

The office is an attractive place to be in a wonderful location on the north bank of the Thames at Carmelite, Victoria Embankment. The only downside is that the only really local pub, The Swan, was recently knocked down to make way for a redevelopment. It's now about a ten minute walk up to Fleet Street to the nearest watering hole and *"this reduces the numbers going to the pub."* The firm doesn't put on a regular drinks evening in the office and whilst first year trainees are quite a sociable bunch, meeting up regularly after work, it sounds as if by the second year *"it's easy to drop out of the loop as people get preoccupied."*

The hours are not as punishing as a few hundred metres further east in the heart of the City. Typically *"9.30am–7pm"* or a little earlier. In corporate this might be a little longer. *"There are weeks when I haven't left before 8pm or 9pm – a bit attritional."* There is no real sense of having to be seen to be there late at night. We did believe the trainees who told us that *"It's fine to go home."*

seeing red

That's something that strikes you about TJG trainees; you can believe everything they tell you! No one's trying to hype the firm by describing its successful corporate department as a red-braces-wearing, red-eyed, red-bull theatre of blood, guts and M&A deals. The only really red thing is the wallpaper in the corridors and whilst corporate does very nicely thank you, its just one aspect of the firm's persona. Interesting fact: this year out of 20 qualifying, and 18 staying with the firm, nine are choosing to go into corporate. It's really popular.

The firm sells itself as being friendlier than most. How can it judge? If the comments of trainees are to be believed (and remember, these are believable trainees) this is not a firm which parties hard ...or much. What we must measure then is the interaction along those red-walled, teal-carpeted corridors. *"They pride themselves on being relaxed and friendly – it's definitely not a stuffy environment. It has quite a young feel; a majority of people are under 45."* Another joked *"It's not Disneyland, but it's quite friendly."* Indeed.

and finally...

"Make it clear that as a trainee you'll be valued" trainees told us. *"You can have a corporate training without it being an IP training"* they added. We are also instructed to tell you that it does appear that the managing partner is trying to listen to trainees' comments. And *"the amount that they have felt able to say to the managing partners has increased."* Jolly good we say – but a word to the wise. Get the seat system sorted.

top recommendations in Chambers UK 2000-2001:

IP, Media [Band 2]

Theodore Goddard

the facts

Location: London
UK ranking by size: 37
Total number of trainees: 33
Seats: 4 x 6 months
Alternative seats: Brussels, Paris, secondments
Extras: Pro bono

Theodore Goddard offers 20 of the most oversubscribed training places in the UK. More than 3,000 hopefuls apply for only 20 or so contracts per year. They are eager to be a part of its success and eager to work for media, entertainment and hi-tech clients. It's a well rounded practice, with clients in a variety of sectors and it's looking to grow. With profits in 1999 rising by a virtually unbelievable 48%, this is a firm that's working hard. Very, very hard. That kind of environment usually makes for early responsibility and long hours. Sadly we can't confirm whether or not this is the case at Theodore Goddard.

hush hush

We're constantly amazed that Theodore Goddard won't let us speak to its trainees and newly qualifieds. Unless we give it editorial control it refuses to take part in the True Picture. Read into that what you will. We couldn't possibly comment...Good job we've got our own sources. They tell us that it's the sort of firm where staff and partners mix easily, and *"you get to know people from across the firm quickly."* This is partly helped by the very popular restaurant on the ground floor of the firm's Aldersgate Street offices. The building itself may not be inspiring to look at and isn't located on a particularly 'meejah' street (its next door neighbour is CMS Cameron McKenna and it sits in the shadow of Clifford Chance's Gotham City edifice) but it's functional. On qualification it's highly likely that you'll stay with the firm as it offers everyone a job, *"although not necessarily in what you want."*

matchmaker, make me a match

In 1998 Theodore Goddard was in merger talks with Denton Hall and Richards Butler, two firms with a not dissimilar profile in the legal market. When Dentons walked away from the talks (and subsequently went on to merge with Wilde Sapte) Theodore Goddard and Richards Butler were left staring at each other, wondering whether or not to go ahead. They didn't. But Theodore Goddard has made no bones about the fact that it's still willing to be courted by a suitable partner. A US merger has not been ruled out and the firm is likely to want to build up to critical mass in London. Anything could happen in the next couple of years, but Theodore Goddard has shown that it doesn't take rash decisions.

and finally...

The firm has never shown quite the same interest in overseas offices that many of its competitors have. Eight seats are available in Brussels or with an associate firm in Paris each year. Theodore Goddard is definitely going to be an interesting firm to watch. It's not a mega global player like its neighbour Clifford Chance, but it's a strong mid-sized outfit that will be looking to make inroads into some of its neighbours' domestic territory. What a shame we can't tell you what trainees really think about life at the firm.

top recommendations in Chambers UK 2000-2001:

Media [Band 2]

Thompsons

the facts

Location: Offices spread nationally
UK ranking by size: 47
Total number of trainees: Not recruiting at this time

A firm with an interesting profile, it has abandoned the recruitment of trainees for the time being.

Thompsons is a large practice which, like many of its competitors, has suffered somewhat from the biting effects of the Woolf Reforms. Its client base of trade unions and their members instruct on employment issues and personal injury work. It's handled claims concerning serious disasters, such as the Kings Cross fire, Piper Alpha and Hillsborough.

Earlier in 1999 a fifth of the partners were asked to resign. The firm may be taking time to catch its breath. For those applicants interested in this area of the law, we hope for a speedy return to the training arena on the part of Thompsons.

top recommendations in Chambers UK 2000-2001:

Employment Law, Personal Injury (Claimant)

Travers Smith Braithwaite

the facts

Location: London
UK ranking by size: 53
Total number of trainees: 36
Seats: Four x 6months
Alternative seats: Secondments, Paris
Extras: Language training, pro bono

"*A lot of good work to get involved in. Gives you a warm glowing feeling.*" Does it now? Travers does high-quality work in a medium-sized firm. Particularly in its "*excellent*" corporate finance department. Like many firms it's growing in size, unlike many it's not expanding maniacally. It has opened an office in Paris, but is not planning to take over the world. Instead the firm is "*doing what Slaughter and May does.*" It is cultivating 'best friends' in other countries. 'The club'(see below) is expanding its membership "*organically.*"

tsb – the firm that likes to say "yes"

"*Like a club*" we were told. What kind of club, exactly? "*It's quite incestuous, a lot of gossip and snog-*

ging," said one female source (giggling flirtatiously with our male researcher).

You need not worry about feeling stranded in a sea of strangers. It's *"not a huge firm, you do get to meet people"* and *"after 18 months you know everyone,"* said sources. With club membership growing, one newly-qualified thought that when he was a trainee *"it was more cohesive."* Another felt that *"the atmosphere is changing as the firm gets bigger."* Nevertheless, they still seem to love the place, with the word *"loyal"* being mentioned a fair bit.

Looking at its headed paper we were not surprised to hear that the firm is *"traditional." "Changes don't happen overnight here"* said one interviewee. *"You can only become a better version of what you are."* Expect *"evolution not revolution."*

jovial oxbridge types?

We could not help noticing when looking at the website that just under half of the people profiled were from Oxford and Cambridge. Is this representative or the impression the firm wants to give? When we put this to interviewees, without exception they said that they *"didn't really notice that lots of people are Oxbridge, it doesn't give that impression."* Maybe one third Oxbridge. More important is personality. Apart from being *"easy to get on with,"* common traits are that trainees are *"jovial"* as well as *"confident and relaxed about themselves." "If you take them down to the pub they are all entertaining."* And go to the pub they most certainly do...

social club

That *"alcohol plays a big part"* in the life of a trainee is not surprising. To hear a source say *"it did so more than when a student"* maybe. To hear a trainee say *"every Friday an e-mail would go round and every Friday*

we would end up at the same place" is not out of the ordinary. The TSB regular is The Bishop's Finger in Smithfield (...is it you that's always up there on the first floor?). Yet friendships at the firm go further than this. Trainees talk of meeting up and going out at weekends, *"girlie nights out"* and *"playing golf with buddies." "People at the firm are sporty"* was a general view, though *"you wouldn't think so by looking at them."* Certainly the opportunities are there, except five-a-side football, which is strangely only for women. In terms of organised social events, *"most of the stuff is departmental"* with, for example, the employment department having a barbeque where the *"partners do the cooking."* Apparently the new Travers building (currently going up) will have a restaurant (they don't currently have one). Sounds like the safer option.

life membership

"One of the best things about the firm is that they want to keep everyone on." Indeed since the firm's recruitment policy is *"we don't want many, just the best"* it would be silly if having got the best they got rid of them. But getting the right job is *"not a foregone conclusion: you have to put yourself in the driving seat."* This year *"two out of 15 or so left. Both could have stayed. One wanted to go to Birmingham, one went to a US firm."* In terms of seats some are very popular. Employment and commercial were felt to be heavily competitive. Unfortunately *"They won't deliberately create space."*

"frazzled" but appreciated

As TSB competes with the huge international firms for corporate finance work, it is hardly surprising that *"everyone is prepared to work hard."* Sources spoke of working *"until 9pm or 10pm at night for say three weeks and doing a couple of all-nighters." "You can get a bit frazzled."* However trainees rejected the suggestion that the partners would expect you to be in early the next morning. *"If you work an all-nighter they do give you time to recover." "Partners do thank you if you work hard"* and *"some take you out for a meal if you have worked late."* In fact trainees were generally very positive about the partners. *"They make you coffee rather than the other way round "* and *"are really good about being constantly interrupted with questions."*

three in a bed

Every trainee sits with both a partner and an assistant. Even so, one complaint was that the place *"was sometimes so busy that you are scrambling to find someone to answer your questions."* So much work, so little time.

and finally...

Not quite a gentleman's club, certainly not a nightclub. But somewhere in the middle lies Travers Smith Braithwaite. More like the Oxford and Cambridge Club maybe. They're all jolly friendly and very very nice indeed. They like nothing better than spending time together. They work hard but are always thanked for it. Everyone gets on well. Particularly after a few drinks on a Friday night in the Bishop's Finger. (Remember...sometimes we're watching!)

top recommendations in Chambers UK 2001-2001:

Corporate finance (30-60 solicitors in corporate team) [Band 2]

Trowers & Hamlins

the facts

Location: London, Exeter, Manchester
UK ranking by size: 70
Total number of trainees: 26
Seats: 4 x 6 months
Alternative seats: Dubai, Oman, secondments
Extras: Pro bono
This is a firm distinguished by its fantastic UK reputation in social housing and its top profile in the Middle East. Both will impact directly on the training experience. So what is the nexus between these two limbs? It's not immediately apparent so we'll discuss them quite independently of each other.

...and can I get a side order of property with that?

"I was fairly focused on property firms" one trainee gave us as his reason for applying to the firm. He'd done three property-related seats and was very happy about that. Trowers kicks sand in the face of every other firm in the country in relation to its key client base, the social housing sector. That said, *"an inherent interest in housing is not a pre-requisite for joining the firm."* The high profile housing theme touches most seats and generates related work such as PFI and commercial work for social landlords. Trowers has a healthy commercial property department and good construction strength. Public sector clients also instruct the firm, many on property related work. There's a defendant clinical negligence seat and a small private client unit.

Much of the litigation handled by the firm is property litigation. Not every applicant sees property in the same light as our property-loving interviewee, so those sworn off this area of law should think very carefully about why they are applying.

sun, sea, sand and...more sand

Each year, between a third and a half of the trainees will get the chance to spend six months out in one of the firm's overseas offices. Trainees into the Oman and Dubai offices, with time in the latter often taking in a spot in Abu Dhabi. You must make it clear from early on that you want an overseas posting. *"You put your case to the training partner. If you have been canny you have probably already lobbied."* The type of trainees taken on by the firm definitely reflects the rise of the Gulf offices. *"Quite a few are Arabic speakers, maybe had an ex-pat childhood in the Middle East."* You don't have to be an Arabic speaker to go abroad, *"but obviously if you're competing against those people..."* The work is high value commercial or corporate in Oman, and is likely to be for the energy industry or the government.

The overseas offices are busy and trainees speculate that this might soon mean more opportunities to experience the sand devil hyperactivity of Trowers'

Gulf outposts. "*Working in a small office is great. You get to do everything and anything*" one trainee told us. Another confirmed that the experience was really rewarding. "*It's about as front line as you can get, a big baptism of fire. You're running with files from the word go, case managing from the first day.*"

The small Manchester and Exeter offices are not so popular, usually taking one trainee at each rotation. Some people really don't want to go to either, but "*if they're adamant they won't get sent.*" However, they provide valuable experience of life without all the support.

> "between a third and a half of all trainees experience the sand devil hyperactivity of Trowers' Gulf outposts."

stay...just a little bit longer

"*The hours are less than the big City firms, I've never had to do all-nighters*" we were told. "*I've never been pushed to breaking point, it's always been nicely busy.*" This perception could be the result of the relatively low proportion of corporate work in the overall training experience. "*They try to cycle everyone through corporate*" (which includes construction and the overseas seats)so if you experience it in Oman you won't get a UK corporate seat.

If you want a personal life, Trowers is a good firm to look at. "*I've only had to cancel evening plans just the once in two years*" one trainee confirmed. It's almost a shame that trainees get to go home at such a civilised time (6.30pm, except at the time of their housing/public sector clients' year end). We say this because the office building got the thumbs up from our interviewees. Nice atrium, plenty of space and a canteen which everyone uses.

respect...

The close social interaction between trainees and partners in the Gulf seats is not matched drink for drink in London, but "*a mutual respect does exist.*" There's only a dozen or so trainees in each year – the right amount to "*get around a pub table*" so "*everyone knows who you are.*" "*They are never too busy to talk to you,*" one trainee remarked of the supervising partners, "*there's an interaction.*" Another confirmed the absence of ogres. "*They are prepared to listen to our choices*" and "*they are decent in the way they go about things; there's nothing sly.*"

...and loyalty

We looked for the downside. Assume for a moment that you click with property-related work and you don't necessarily want a hard core corporate training. Is there anything that might put you off the place? One trainee offered up her best effort at criticism. "*You don't get things organised on a big scale like at the big firms.*" She didn't sound too disappointed, though.

Almost everyone stays with the firm after qualifying. The pay may not be "*top whack,*" but generally speaking interviewees weren't worried about that. They are "*the sort of people who have loyalty,*" not necessarily the cut-throat competitive type.

and finally...

Slightly schizophrenic in its practice, the firm has a fantastic profile in social housing work and a great reputation and client-base in the Middle East. If you have similarly diverse interests and you're looking for an intimate environment with top quality work, look no further.

top recommendations in Chambers UK 2000-2001:

Social Housing

Walker Morris

the facts

Location: Leeds
UK ranking by size: 59
Total number of trainees: 20
Seats: 6 x 4 months
Alternative seats: Paris, secondments.

Leeds attracts trainees who want the experience of a commercial training but don't want to endure the stresses of London. Trainees who select Walker Morris from the Leeds Big Six cite the usual reasons for avoiding the 'Battlestar Galactica' firms of the magic circle. They prefer to get the most corporate training they can get in a smaller and more intimate firm in the provinces. Walker Morris, they believe, has the potential to give them that, albeit that it is the smallest of the Big Six.

The firm is looking to take on an increasing number of trainees in coming years. We were interested to note that two of the current trainees had transferred from other firms. This is rare.

a load of bankers

The Banking and Insolvency group has been growing and the focus of the firm is very much on consolidating its position as a leading corporate practice in Leeds. Whilst it is not the number one player, it's doing not half bad.

So far it has stuck like superglue to its one office strategy and those we interviewed liked that. They know that they will be able to train in the city for the whole two years without having to do some unwelcome tour of Britain, as at certain other Leeds Big Six firms. The trainees are under no illusions as to what's on offer at the firm, (a good, solid commercial training) and there seem to be no nasty surprises as to what can be achieved.

In the first year, you'll have no choice as to where you sit. Usually you'll pass through each of the three core areas of corporate, property and litigation. The six seat deal means that you can do a quick 'suck it and see' exercise on the three departments before taking matters into your own hands in the second year.

self help

The seats are allocated in a rather unorthodox fashion in the second year. The trainees all sit round together and *"thrash it out"* between them. This is either laziness on the part of the training partner (unlikely – he is openly admired and pro-active) or a smart move on the part of the firm. *"If there was a problem we were told not to flip any coins,"* said one trainee, *"if we couldn't sort it out ourselves, then we were told to go to the training partner."* Often the second years take the opportunity to do an eight month stint in a favoured area of practice. Secondments to a client and a four month stint in an affiliated Paris firm are on the cards for second years.

Certain aspects of the website give the impression that Walker Morris is a tree-hugging self-help therapy centre. The home pages are graced by slogans such as *"Free the imagination -Minds are like parachutes – they only function when open"* and *"Think tomorrow – you can't think clearly about the future if you're obsessed with the past."* Dotted around are some confusing pictures, including the one which could be either a temple of spiritual enlightenment or a piece of debris from Battlestar Gallactica. Hello? What has all of this got to do with Walker Morris? The trainees we spoke to didn't seem to know either.

the local boozer – "a home from home"

Round the back of the office is the local hangout, called Wharf Street. Socialising in departments is both ad hoc in the pub and organised, with outings to dinner and bowling. The *"everyone's in it together"* atmosphere means *"no barriers with partners."* Trainees also gather together every couple of weeks to wind down and compare notes.

The opportunity to socialise doesn't translate into pressure to do so. Those who prefer to hang out with mates from their other lives or with family, feel no pressure to participate in the firm's social scene or the Friday night 'conventions' of upwardly mobile young Leeds lawyers who populate bars like Parisa (the latest edition to the scene) and All Bar One (a bit *"too predictable"* now).

nine out of ten

Pretty much top marks on quality of work, hours, supervision and responsibility. There were no notice-able trends in complaints about any of these topics, implying that the success or otherwise of a seat came down purely to individuals. Trainees seemed gen-uinely happy with their lot and pleased that they had chosen the firm. And what sort are they? *"Ambitious"* but *"not stepping on toes"* was the assessment.

Ah yes, on the subject of assessments, this is where Walker Morris just fails to score top marks all round. It seems that the perennial problem of part-ners sometimes being too busy to give formal appraisals continues. An assessment way after the event is often of little use to either trainee or trainer.

About 90% of trainees are offered jobs on qualifi-cation. The fact that they always knew what was on offer at the firm and that there has been no radical overhaul of the practice has meant that trainees hap-pily take the jobs.

and finally...

Like Slaughters, like Macfarlanes, like Wragges before it, the firm has been very vocal about its refusal to expand into a multi-branch firm. It's quite happy to be rooted very firmly in Leeds as a broad church commercial firm working for both local and national clients. Time will tell whether this can remain the case in future.

top recommendations in Chambers UK 2000-2001:

Insolvency, Litigation (commercial and property) Pensions, Planning, Property, Sport [Band 2]

Weightmans

the facts

Location: Liverpool, Manchester, Birmingham
UK ranking by size: 56
Total number of trainees: 17
Seats: 4x6 months
Alternative seats: Occasional secondments.

Traditionally an insurance litigation firm, Weight-mans has had to ride the rollercoaster that is the modern insurance market. Certainly it has not had a quiet life. It merged with midlands firm William Hatton, has been in (as yet unresolved) merger talks with North-East rival Hill Dickinson and has had a change of top brass.

over the edge

In recent years Weightmans had been expanding, opening new offices in Manchester and Birming-ham. Senior partner Michael Edge was a key figure in these developments. But internally this expansion wasn't universally popular. *"It's lost its identity, you don't know half the people here. People miss how it was before. They used to just sit around drinking tea and eat-ing biscuits."* Not any more they don't. *"We have to go out to impress now."* The problem has largely been *"uncertainty in the insurance market."* Big insurers have been merging and cutting back on law firms.This was reflected in last year's retention rate on qualification. It dropped.

The big shock came in mid-July 2000 when Edge stepped down, shortly after his re-election as senior partner in April. However at the time of publishing *"things have picked up. The atmosphere has changed in the past month or so."* With new senior and managing partners, and a new strategy board being voted in, sources felt the firm now has *"good potential."* Cer-tainly the firm's reputation for defendant personal injury and professional negligence remains second to none in the region.

insurance litigation and nothing but

Last year we spoke of insurance litigation making up about 75% of the firm's work. Trainees told us of the *"need to do"* a non-contentious seat, quite the opposite of most commercial firms. *"If someone wants to come to Weightmans, (they must) make sure that it's personal injury or civil litigation they want to specialise in."* But with current difficulties in the insurance market and changes in management, sources agreed that the firm has been looking elsewhere for work. After a period of stagnation the firm is becoming more dynamic. *"Younger people are trying to push the new areas."* What does this mean for a trainee? By the time they start there may an emphasis on areas other than insurance. By September 2000 the figures were about 50:50 insurance litigation to other practice areas.

As for getting the seats you want; *"you can very much choose what you want to do…"* The addendum *"…as long as it is insurance litigation"* may no longer apply.

weighty work?

As a large proportion of the work done by the firm is insurance, a lot of client contact is over the phone with *"faceless insurance companies."* There is significant variation between seats with *"a lot"* in employment and an *"awful lot"* in commercial. *"You have to be on top of things. When the partner is not there managing directors will ring you up and want answers."* Trainees we spoke to were very happy with the levels of responsibility they got for litigation work. *"As long as it's not your first seat they will give you your own files and occasionally check up on you."* As a result of all this Weightmans trainees are *"self-confident and able to roll with the punches."* For those who want to get involved in advocacy there is *"a lot of time spent in court."* *"They certainly believe in trying to get you in front of a district judge as soon as possible."* Weighty hours do not appear to be the order of the day for now. Working until 6 was thought to be *"a bit late."* Hours on the corporate/commercial side are longer. The face of things to come?

mersey blues

"It was not a great year last year and we did not feel in a party mood." The firm's happiness is closely related to the state of the insurance industry. *"The social life dropped off with the insurance work."* Now that the insurance work has picked up *"immeasurably"* so too has the social life. The trainees at Weightmans certainly seem to bond well. They're all *"very close, all know each other."* One source spoke of *"going out 3 days out of 5 during the week with trainees"* and another of meeting up at weekends, though the Mersey does appear to get in the way of some social events. *"It can be a little difficult because people live all over the place."* Apart from things organised informally there are booze cruises on the Mersey and meals to which trainees from all offices are invited. Sport plays a big part in the life of a trainee at the firm. Football, cricket and rounders are on the menu although they're usually *"just an excuse to go to the pub afterwards."* As a sign of things getting better, the Christmas party has now been reinstated.

There may be offices in Manchester and Birmingham but Liverpool remains the place where most trainees will be based. They *"may have a preference for people from the area"* and *"most of the people had done the LPC at Chester."* But there is *"quite a bit of movement"* between the offices when people want to do work only found elsewhere. The employment section, for example, is largely in Manchester. A good reason for getting out of Liverpool would appear to be to leave behind the *"crap building with concrete cancer."* Whatever that is.

and finally...

From a trainee's perspective there is now sunshine after the rain. The firm has a positive feel to it. The possible merger with Hill Dickinson is on hold for the time being, but the firm may be very different in future. Those we spoke to thought that a London presence was next on the agenda since *"Hill Dickinson has a London office."* The firm's expansion has always followed the insurance companies. They have now become very big. So future moves will also follow the industry. Watch out for future editorials about the merged firm - Weighty Dicks.

top recommendations in Chambers UK 2000-2001:

Personal Injury(Defendant), Professional Negligence

Withers

the facts

Location: London
UK ranking by size: 71
Total number of trainees: 21
Seats: 4 x 6 months
Alternative seats: None

What do we think we know about Withers? A real quality establishment. Very traditional extremely highly rated private client and family law firm. Some very wealthy and very famous/posh clients. Just off Fleet Street, not quite City, not quite West End. Sounds a bit stuffy, what? Not any more, we hear....

the way it is

The firm is divided into five departments: family, private client, property, litigation and corporate. Private client is compulsory, but trainees may choose three out of the remaining four at will. The firm is still trying to fight off the stuffy image associated with its private client credentials. Let's face it, it is a traditional firm. But now that private clients mean e-trepreneurs, and millionaires are a dime a dozen in the UK, it is seen internally as *"incredibly progressive,"* moving away from old money to new money clients, many of whom are international (particularly Middle Eastern) or celebrities.

Less of a hothouse than a townhouse, Withers rarely requires trainees to work weekends or all-nighters. Plenty of scope for socialising so if you want to work hard but have a life outside, this is a firm to consider. Trainees are a fairly tight-knit bunch, particularly those new to London, who often meet at weekends and are all invited to each others' weddings. Those who are more mature, and there are several, or who have a full London social life anyway may not be quite so involved. That trendy modern establishment The Old Cheshire Cheese is a favourite haunt, as is Drakes, the firm ejector seat (ie everyone has their farewell drinks there). It's not just trainees out on the razzle – the whole firm may turn out for a popular departee.

the Italian job

What is this mysterious Italian connection at Withers? They have about 20 fluent speakers, aim to recruit an Italian-speaking trainee each year, and keep a 'representative office' in Milan, the legal centre as well as the fashion centre of Italy. Result – a massive culture clash between young Italian stallions in Armani suits and cool shades versus old English buffers in hairy plus fours? *"At the extremes, yes!"* we were told; there are some real characters of both sorts. However, most fall, disappointingly, somewhere in the middle. The niche work for Italian clients dates back to a merger with McKenzie & Mills and is spread across all departments. Any cultural divides within the firm tend to be departmental rather than national. In fact the Italian speakers are mainly British born. The firm acts across the board for Italian clients with domicile or businesses in this country, and for some mega household names such as Benetton and Max-Mara.

family fortunes

40% of the firm's work is for private clients or charities. Withers handles UK private client work for unimaginably wealthy individuals. Tantalisingly, it has strict rules of confidentiality about such clients, but do the names John Paul Getty and Richard Branson mean anything to you? Nice work if you can get it. Every trainee is expected to do a seat in private client, so be prepared. However, the department is so big that it's divided into several very different groups. Wills and probate is sedate and gentle. Partners are *"delightful"* but tend to be older with distinguished clients (perhaps a few hairy plus fours after all?). It's heads down from 8.30am to 6pm and the department is quiet with less interraction between fee-earners. This is as far as possible from the atmosphere in commercial, a tiny yet fast-growing department, *"very on the ball and doing cutting edge stuff"* for entrepreneurs.

it's a family affair

The family department is the best in the country. Because of this, and because it's what Withers is famous for, it has a *"pretty scary reputation"* and is *"not a relaxing place to be for six months."* This does not stop it from being a *"fantastic experience"* given the quality of the work and the lawyers. It is massively busy, provides loads of client contact and advocacy experience(mainly applications before the District Judge)and pitches you against more senior lawyers who are intimidated by the firm's reputation. But the partners are so busy they're *"not always the most friendly."* In fact the word 'temperamental' has been mentioned.(*"And that includes the men as well! They can be real prima donnas!"* Even the men? Who'd have thought it.) The seat therefore requires a robust approach. The most confident may have to steel themselves and be *"willing to take the flak."* Although most partners are male, the group is predominantly female in the ranks. They *"desperately need more men."* How's that for an invitation, boys?

all kinds of everything

The firm prides itself on having no 'type.'It is trying to move away from people keen to do family and litigation only, and from the traditional image. So those we spoke to thought it was recruiting people from different backgrounds. *"Such diversity suggests they know what they're looking for."* This means room for all sorts. There are always some *"absolute brainboxes; very nice but with no social skills,"* offset by others who are all-rounders. As a firm it is *"not madly sporty"* with more female than male trainees so *"it's hard to get a rugby team together."*

But there's no getting away from the fact that the firm is still attractive to the more establishment type. It just doesn't have a trendy image. Take a look at the website.

all change

The firm is currently housed in two offices. The main HQ is in Gough Square and provides *"superb"* facilities. Meeting rooms on the top floor have breathtaking views over the City, including peeka-boo at those beautiful Freshfields people. The other building on Fleet Street is less glamorous and inmates can *"feel cut off."* In November 2000 the firm is to move directly into the shadow of the scales and sword of Justice on top of the Old Bailey. Members of the firm have been invited to look round the new offices. Although support staff are allegedly none too happy at being downstairs with no windows, fee-earner offices look good. One astute source saw the design of the new building as symbolic of the firm. A professional, corporate office block further into the City, with a progressive modern interior behind a traditional, old frontage.

and finally...

So why choose this firm? *"The world's your oyster"* in terms of great diversity of seats. And you will have plenty of client contact and responsibility if you are willing to grasp the nettle with both hands. With only 12 trainees there is plenty of *"room to shine."* But look elsewhere for a decent game of rugby.

top recommendations in Chambers UK 2000-2001:

Agriculture & Bloodstock, Family/Matrimonial.

Wragge & Co

the facts

Location: Birmingham, London
UK ranking by size: 17
Total number of trainees: 42
Seats: Four x 6months
Alternative seats: Brussels, secondments

Last year's winner of our unofficial "Happiest Trainees in the UK" competition. Based in Birmingham, they dominate the local marketplace. Their work is of a quality commensurate with many City firms. The firm positions itself as the real alternative for big ticket clients. The past year has seen it grow further and acquire the local construction boutique Neil F. Jones and London IP firm Needham & Grant. This is slightly at odds with its long-stated policy of maintaining its single-office status and refusing to join the national firms in their game. So now it has a London office. In every other high-quality firm in the country a London office is an immediate bonus for trainees. What effect will it have on Wragges trainees? At this stage there's one seat at a time available with the London IP group.

message in a bottle

Last year we wrote about a client who said that if the firm could bottle its atmosphere it would make a fortune. Like a legal Disneyland, it is full of happy, smiley-faced people who are always having a nice day. As one trainee put it *"the firm is known for being happy and therefore somehow just is."* You *"just don't hear employees complaining"* (except about space-see below). This has led to 100% retention over the last two years. This is also due to the growth of the firm, meaning that there are more jobs available than qualifiers. As one trainee put it; *"if people weren't happy they wouldn't stay on would they?"*

Will the atmosphere stay the same as the firm grows and sets up other offices? Sources tell us the firm is making a lot of effort to keep the culture. So far so good.

open government

A key element contributing to the feel good factor is the 'inclusive' nature of the firm. Trainees feel visible, and looked after. *"You feel that you have a valuable place at the firm."* Senior management fosters this perception. *"When I arrived at the firm we were encouraged to pester Quentin* [Poole-managing partner] *with ideas. He told us that he was a paid servant of the firm and a very well-paid one at that."*

After suggestions to management, trainees have been involved with, for example, an exchange with the Bar and software development for the firm. Bad feedback is as welcome as good. *"Senior management come round, talk to groups and really find out what we think."* Strategy is always made known to all members of the firm. There's no culture of secrecy. More than this, though, trainees find people at the firm *"fun to work with and totally unpretentious."* Sometimes *"it's hard to tell who the partners are."*

> "On vacation schemes they are really looking for people who are willing to get involved in the karaoke."

fun with the characters

It's a two-way street. Disneyland Birmingham may be fun and unpretentious, but you must be prepared to 'get down' and throw yourself into things. *"They like you if you let your hair down."* This may be with other trainees or *"with a cross-section of the firm."* There's a very corporate/team-building/bonding trainee 'away day' with a training session followed by tank driving. It's popular. There are *"perhaps far too many"* karaoke nights.

There's a firm band Platinum Sponge consisting of a group of assistant solicitors. It has just taken on several 'bottle blonde' secretaries as backing singers.

"*The tickets are bought from the singers' secretaries and everyone goes.*" Performances are in local venues.

Wragges encourages membership of the Birmingham branch of the Trainee Solicitors' Group. It is one of the most active in the country. Indeed, "*you could socialise every day.*" All in all the firm is looking for people who will do more than just knuckle down to hard work. They want "*lively people who want to get involved.*" One trainee admitted that on vacation schemes they are really looking for people who are willing to get involved in the karaoke. All those applying for vacation schemes, be warned. You'd better polish up your Abba numbers.

space invaders

Wragges has become a victim of its own success. There is "*pressure on space.*" Insiders think the growth is good but the result is that some areas have become "*cramped.*" Hence the conversion of much of the office space into open plan. Another reason for trainees to feel "*very visible.*" Opinions about this are mixed. "*Some people prefer it, some hate it with a vengeance.*" But you can "*get an office to yourself if you put forward a good case.*" Getting an office is "*not based on hierarchy.*" "*Even the Managing Partner sits open plan.*" Trainees like sitting so close to the partners and being able to "*talk to people on the way to the drinks machine.*" But they're looking forward to the space problem being remedied.

no mickey mouse work

Trainees get their own files, "*even in corporate.*" Shirking responsibility is not an option. "*You are expected to stay if you are needed, it's the nature of the work.*" But only when you are needed. In corporate the atmosphere is "*work hard, play hard.*" One trainee spoke of a friend who was "*sick of champagne*" by the time he left the department. The firm successfully targets large plcs, so work is on large transactions for high-quality clients.

Three compulsory seats are taken in corporate, litigation and property, but within each you can generally request a particular specialism. A fourth optional seat can be taken at any rotation. "*Construction is a really popular team because it's a laugh...they are such lads,*" whilst "*Employment goes in peaks and troughs.*" There's a good variety of work on offer but a large proportion of it is corporate and that's where many of the trainees will qualify.

out and about

In addition to the IP seat in London, other trainees may travel down to the office, as much of the corporate work involves London-based clients. The second purpose of the office is to provide working space for those stranded in London on a deal. There are other opportunities to get out of the office on secondments to clients and to the Brussels office. Competition for Brussels is certain to be strong. But most people come to the firm accepting that "*they probably won't go abroad.*"

and finally...

The Magic Kingdom that is Wragges asks of its prospective trainees "*Are you the star that twinkles brightest at night*" (see their website). Perhaps a more appropriate question would be "*are you the person who can sing loudest at night?*" Certainly there is no shying away from the Wragges experience.

top recommendations in Chambers UK 2000-2001:

Banking, Charities, Competition/Anti-trust, Construction, Debt Recovery, Employment Law, Energy, Environmental Law, General Corporate Finance, Information Technology, Intellectual Property, Litigation (Commercial), Litigation (Property), Local Government, Pensions, Property (Commercial), Tax.

TRAINEE SALARIES TABLE

FIRM NAME	IST YEAR SALARY (2000)	2ND YEAR SALARY (2000)	SPONSORSHIP/ AWARDS	OTHER BENEFITS	QUALIF- ICATION SALARY
Addleshaw Booth & Co	£16,000-£16,500	£17,000-£17,500	CPE and LPC fees + maintenance award of £3,500	Corporate membership of gym, season ticket loan.	£29,000 (Manchester & Leeds) £40,000 (London)
Allen & Overy	£25,000	£28,000	CPE and LPC fees and £5,000 maintenance p.a. (£4,500 outside London, Oxford and Guilford).	PPP health scheme, season ticket loans, gym membership, subsidised restaurant, 6 weeks unpaid leave on qualification.	£42,000
Ashurst Morris Crisp	1st seat (first 6 months) £25,000 2nd seat (6-12 months) £26,000	3rd seat (12-18 months) £27,000 4th seat (after 18 months) £28,000	CPE and LPC funding and £4,500 maintenance allowance p.a. (£4,000 outside London and Guildford). LPC Distinction Award of £500.	Season ticket loan, medical cover, life cover, membership of a gym/ squash club.	£42,000
Baker & McKenzie	£25,000	£28,000	CPE Funding: fees paid + £5000 maintenance LPC Funding: Fees paid + £5000 maintenance	Health & life insurance, private medical insurance, group personal pension plan, gym membership, luncheon vouchers, interest-free season ticket loan.	£43-45,000
Beale and Company	Not less than £18,500	Discretionary review every six months	n/a	Season ticket loan (after 6 months), private health insurance (after 2 years)	£33,000
Berwin Leighton	£25,000	£28,000	CPE funding: Fees paid + £4,000 maintenance LPC funding: Fees paid + £4,000 maintenance	Private health insurance, subsidised gym membership, season ticket loan, life assurance.	£42,000
Biddle	£22,500	£24,000	CPE and LPC fees paid and maintenance grant offered	Bonus upto 25% of salary, BUPA, life assurance, season ticket loan.	£37,000
Bird & Bird	£22,500	£24,000	LPC and CPE fees paid Maintenance grant of £3,500	Season ticket loan, life insurance, medical insurance, PHI	£37,000
Blake Lapthorn	£14,000	£15,000	LPC: loan of £4,000 repayable from salary.	n/a	£23,500
Bond Pearce	up to £16,250	n/a	LPC financial assistance	n/a	up to £28,000
Boyes Turner & Burrows	£17,000	£18,000	£3,000 CPE & LPC loan – one per applicant. Interest free and re-paid over training contract	Free medical insurance	£26,000

TRAINEE SALARIES TABLE *continued*

FIRM NAME	IST YEAR SALARY (2000)	2ND YEAR SALARY (2000)	SPONSORSHIP/ AWARDS	OTHER BENEFITS	QUALIF-ICATION SALARY
Brachers	£13,500	£14,500	LPC/CPE £1,000 discretionary award.	n/a	£22,500
Bristows	£21,200	£23,200	CPE and LPC fees plus £4,000 maintenance grant for each.	A competitive package, firm pension scheme, life assurance and health insurance.	£36,000
Burges Salmon	£17,500	£18,500	CPE and LPC tuition fees at the institution of your choice, maintenance grants of £3,500 to LPC students and £4,000 to students studying for both CPE and LPC (£2,000 p.a.) are paid.	Rates of pay are substantially in excess of the Law Society recommendations and reviewed on 1 November each year.	£30,000
Cadwalader, Wickersham & Taft	£25,000	£28,000	CPE Funding: Fees paid + £4,500 maintenance LPC Funding: Fees paid + £4,500 maintenance	Permanent health insurance, season ticket loan, BUPA and life assurance.	£54,000
Capsticks	£22,000	£24,000	Scholarship contributions to CPE and LPC courses	Bonus scheme, PHI, death in service cover, interest-free season ticket loan.	£33,000 + bonus scheme
Charles Russell	£23,000	£24,500	CPE and LPC fees paid and annual maintenance of £4,000.	BUPA , PHI and life assurance after six months, 25 days holiday.	£39,000
Clarks	£15,500	£17,000	n/a	Pension, free conveyancing.	n/a
Cleary, Gottlieb, Steen & Hamilton	£33,000	£39,000	LPC funding; Fees paid plus £4,500 maintenance award.	Pension, health insurance, long-term disability insurance, health club, employee assistance programme.	Salary varies from office to office
Clifford Chance	£25,000 (2001)	£28,000 (2001)	CPE and LPC fees paid and £5,000 maintenance p.a. (£4,500 outside London, Guilford and Nottingham).	Prize for first class degrees and distinction in LPC, interest free loan, health insurance, subsidised restaurant, fitness centre, life assurance, occupational health service, and permanent health assurance.	£42,000
Clyde & Co	£22,000	£24,000	CPE and LPC fees paid if no local authority funding.	Subsidised sports club, interest free ticket loan, staff restaurant and weekly free bar (London); monthly staff lunch and monthly free bar (Guildford).	£36,000

FIRM NAME	IST YEAR SALARY (2000)	2ND YEAR SALARY (2000)	SPONSORSHIP/ AWARDS	OTHER BENEFITS	QUALIF-ICATION SALARY
CMS Cameron McKenna	£25,000	£28,000	CPE and LPC funding: fees paid and a maintenance grant of £4,500 (London and Guildford), £4,000 (elsewhere)	n/a	£42,000
Cobbetts	£16,250	Reviewed each year	CPE and LPC grant available.	Social Club and L.A. Fitness Pool and gym.	n/a
Coudert Brothers	£25,000	£28,000	CPE Funding: fees paid + £4,000 p.a. maintenance LPC Funding: fees paid + £4,000 p.a. maintenance	Pension, health insurance, subsidised gym membership, season ticket loan.	n/a
Cripps Harries Hall	£14,500	£16,000	Discretionary LPC Funding: fees – 50% interest free loan, 50% bursary.	PPP, DIS, PHI, Pension.	£25,000
D J Freeman	1st six months £25,000 2nd six months £26,000	3rd six months £27,000 4th six months £28,000	LPC Funding	Subsidised meals in staff restaurant; BUPA after three months; a variety of social and sporting events.	£37,000
Davies Wallis Foyster	£16,000		LPC funding.	Life Assurance. Pension scheme to be introduced.	n/a
Dechert	£25,000	£28,000 (to be reviewed in October 2001)	LPC fees paid and £4,000 maintenance p.a. for those living in London and £3,750 for those outside (where L.A. grants unavailable).	Free permanent health and life assurance, subsidised membership of local gym and interest-free season ticket loans.	£40,000 (to be reviewed in October 2001)
Denton Wilde Sapte	£25,000-£26,000	£27,000-£28,000	CPE and LPC funding: fees and a maintenance grant (less any local authority funding).	21 days holiday rising by one day for every full year served, meal away from home allowance, private health cover, season ticket loan, subsidised sports club membership, permanent health insurance, death in service cover	£42,000
Dickinson Dees	£16,000	£17,000	CPE/LPC fees paid and £2,000 interest free loan	n/a	Under review
DLA	£25,000 (London) £18,000 (regions)	£28,000 (London) £20,000 (regions)	CPE and LPC fees paid and a maintenance grant is offered for both years	Pension, health insurance, life assurance, 23 days holiday	£40,000 (London) £28,500 (regions)
DMH	£14,500	£17,000	n/a	n/a	£25,000
Eversheds	£15,500 to £24,000	£16,500 to £27,000	CPE/LPC fees and maintenance grants.	Regional variations	Regional variations

FIRM NAME	1ST YEAR SALARY (2000)	2ND YEAR SALARY (2000)	SPONSORSHIP/ AWARDS	OTHER BENEFITS	QUALIF- ICATION SALARY
Farrer & Co	£24,000	£26,000	CPE Funding: Fees paid + £4,000 maintenance; LPC Funding: Fees paid + £4,000 maintenance	Health and life insurance, subsidised gym membership, season ticket loan.	£36,000
Field Fisher Waterhouse	£23,000	£24,000	Tuition fees and maintenance grant paid for CPE and LPC.	25 days holiday, season ticket loans, health insurance, private healthcare.	£37,000
Finers Stephens Innocent	£20,000	£22,000	Contribution of £3,000 towards LPC course fees.	20 days holiday, private medical insurance, life insurance, long term disability insurance, subsidised gym membership, season ticket loan.	£33,000
Forbes	£12,000	n/a	n/a	n/a	highly competitive
Freshfields Bruckhaus Deringer	£25,000	£28,000	CPE and LPC fees paid and £5,000 maintenance p.a. for those studying in London and Oxford and £4,500 p.a. for those studying elswhere.	Life assurance; permanent health insurance; group personal pension; interest-free loan for a season travel ticket; free private medical insurance; subsidised staff restaurant; gym.	£42,000
Garretts	£25,000 (London)	n/a	CPE + LPC fees paid and £3,750-£4,000 grant p.a.	BUPA; subsidized gym membership; S.T.L.	n/a
Goodman Derrick	£19,000	£20,000	LPC fees plus maintenance grant.	Medical Health Insurance, season ticket loan.	£31,500
Gouldens	£27,000	£29,000	CPE and LPC fees paid and £4,500 maintenance p.a.	BUPA, season ticket loan, subsidised sports club membership, group life cover	£45,000
Halliwell Landau	£16,750	£17,750	Contribution to either CPE or LPC fees	A subsidised gym membership is available.	£26,000-£28,000
Hammond Suddards Edge	£19,500 + accommo-dation	£20,500 + accommo-dation	CPE and LPC fees paid and maintenance grant of £4,100 p.a.	Subsidised accommo-dation in all locations. Flexible benefits scheme which allows trainees to choose their own benefits from a range of options.	London £40,000 Other £28,000-£30,000
Harbottle & Lewis	£21,500	£23,000	LPC fees paid and interest free loans towards maintenance.	Lunch provided, season ticket loans	£37,000
Henmans	£13,500	£14,600	n/a	n/a	£24,000

FIRM NAME	IST YEAR SALARY (2000)	2ND YEAR SALARY (2000)	SPONSORSHIP/ AWARDS	OTHER BENEFITS	QUALIF- ICATION SALARY
Herbert Smith	£25,000	£28,000	CPE and LPC fees paid and £4,500 maintenance p.a. (£4,000 outside London)	Profit share, staff discount scheme, permanent health insurance, private medical insurance, season ticket loan, life assurance, gym, group personal accident insurance.	£42,000
Hewitson Becke + Shaw	£15,750	£16,750	n/a	The PSC is provided by the College of Law during the first year of the Training Contract. This is coupled with an extensive programme of Trainee Solicitor Seminars provided by specialist in-house lawyers.	Under review
Hill Dickinson	£15,000	£16,000	Discretionary LPC funding	n/a	n/a
Hill Taylor Dickinson	£21,000	£23,000	£5,000 scholarship for LPC plus a £2,500 interest free loan (repayable over training contract).	STL; Private Health Insurance; Gym loan	£36,000
Holman Fenwick & Willan	1st six months £23,000 2nd six months £23,750	3rd six months £24,500 4th six months £25,000	CPE Funding: fees paid + £4,500 maintenance LPC Funding: fees paid + £4,500 maintenance	Private medical insurance, permanent health and accident insurance, subsidised gym, season ticket loan.	£38,000
Howes Percival	£15,500	£16,750	Payment of LPC & PSC course fees.	n/a	n/a
Ince & Co	£23,000	£25,000	LPC fees £4,000 grant for study in London £3,500 grant for study elswhere	STL, corporate health cover, PHI, discretionary bonus	£36,500
Irwin Mitchell	£16,000	£18,000	CPE and LPC fees paid and £3,000 maintenance grant	n/a	n/a
Kennedys	£20,000	£22,000	£9,000 towards fees and assistance for LPC only.	Life assurance, PHI, private medical insurance, season ticket loan, subsidised gym	£33,000
KLegal	£25,000	n/a	CPE Funding: Fees paid + maintenance. LPC Funding: Fees paid + maintenance.	Non-contributory pension, life assurance, free lunch, Flextra, 25 days holiday.	n/a
Lawrence Graham	£25,000	£28,000	CPE Funding: Course Fees and £3,750 maintenance grant LPC Funding: Course Fees and £3,750 maintenance grant	Season ticket loan, on-site gym	£40,000

SALARIES AND PROSPECTS

TRAINEE SALARIES TABLE

FIRM NAME	IST YEAR SALARY (2000)	2ND YEAR SALARY (2000)	SPONSORSHIP/ AWARDS	OTHER BENEFITS	QUALIF- ICATION SALARY
Le Brasseur J Tickle	£18,000 (London) £14,250 (Leeds)	£20,000 (London) £15,000 (Leeds)	n/a	n/a	£30,000 (London) £22,500 (Leeds)
Lee Bolton & Lee	£18,500	£19,500	A contribution towards LPC funding but dependent upon being offered a training contract	Season ticket loan, non-guaranteed bonus	£29,000
Lester Aldridge	£15,000	£16,500	Discretionary	Life assurance scheme.	£24,500
Lewis Silkin	£22,000	£23,000	Full fees paid for LPC	Life assurance, critical illness cover, health insurance, season ticket loan, group pension plan.	£36,000
Linklaters (A member firm of Linklaters & Alliance)	£25,000	£28,000	CPE and LPC fees paid in full. A maintenance grant is also provided of £4,500 – £5,000 per annum. Language bursaries are also offered, upon completion of the LPC.	PPP medical insurance, life assurance, pension, season ticket loan, in-house gym, corporate membership to Holmes Place, in-house dentist, doctor and physio, 24 hour subsidised staff restaurant.	£42,000
Lovells	£25,000	£28,000	CPE and LPC course fees are paid, as well as a maintenance grant (in 2000/01) of £5,000 for London and Guildford and £4,500 elsewhere; £1,000 advance in salary on joining; £500 bonus; £250 for distinction for LPC; £250 for a 1st class degree result.	PPP, PHI, season ticket loan, corporate gym membership at Homes Place, staff restaurant, life assurance, in-house dentist and doctor.	£42,000
Mace & Jones	£13,000	£13,500	None offered	Health Insurance	negotiable
Macfarlanes	£25,000	£28,000	CPE and LPC fees paid in full and a £4,500 maintenance allowance for courses studied in London and Guilford and £4,000 for courses studied elsewhere. Prizes for those gaining distinction or commendation for the LPC.	21 working days holiday (rising to 26 days on qualification); interest free season ticket loan; free permanent health insurance after 12 months; free private medical insurance; subsidised; conveyancing; subsidised health club/gym; subsidised firm restaurant; subscription paid to the City of London Law Society or the London Trainee Solicitors' Group.	£42,000
Manches	£22,000 (London)	£24,600 (London)	CPE and LPC Funding: tuition fees and maintenance.	Season ticket loan, BUPA after 6 months, perma-nent health insurance, life insurance, pension after 6 months.	£36,180 (London)

FIRM NAME	1ST YEAR SALARY (2000)	2ND YEAR SALARY (2000)	SPONSORSHIP/ AWARDS	OTHER BENEFITS	QUALIF- ICATION SALARY
Martineau Johnson	£16,000	£17,500	CPE – discretionary loan; LPC – grant for fees and maintenance.	Pension; private health; life assurance; permanent health insurance; interest free travel loans; critical illness cover; Birmingham Hospital Saturday fund; domestic conveyancing; will drafting and sub-scription fees.	£30,000
Masons	£25,000 (London)	£28,000 (London)	All fees paid for CPE and LPC, plus a bursary of £4,000 for the year.	Life assurance, private health care, subsidised restaurant and season ticket loan (London)	£42,000 (London)
Mayer, Brown & Platt	£26,000+	£27,000+	100% funding for CPE and LPC plus maintenance grant	Private medical insurance, season ticket loan, life assurance (4x basic salary). Long term disability insurance.	£54,000
McDermott, Will & Emery	£29,000	n/a	CPE and LPC funding; tuition for relevant courses.	Private medical and dental Insurance, life assurance, permanent health insurance, non-contributory pension, interest-free season ticket loan, gym membership.	n/a
Mills & Reeve	£15,750	£16,750	The firm pays the full costs of the LPC fees and offers a maintenance grant for the LPC year. Funding for the CPE is also available.	Life assurance at two times pensionable salary and a contributory pension scheme.	£28,000
Mishcon de Reya	£22,000	£24,000	CPE and LPC funding with bursary.	Health cover, subsidised gym membership, season ticket loan, permanent health insurance, life assurance and pension.	n/a
Nabarro Nathanson	London & Reading £25,000; Sheffield £18,000	London & Reading £28,000; Sheffield £20,000	Full fees paid for CPE and LPC sponsorship and a maintenance grant. London and Guilford: £4,500 Elsewhere: £4,000	private medical insurance, a season ticket loan, subsidised restaurant and subsidised corporate gym membership. Trainee salaries are reviewed annually.	London £40,000
Nicholson Graham & Jones	£25,000	£28,000	CPE and LPC full fees and £3,000 maintenance for each.	Life assurance, season ticket loan, subsidised gym membership, BUPA, salaries reviewed every year	£40,000
Norton Rose	£25,000	£28,000	£1,000 travel scholarship, £800 loan on arrival, 4 weeks unpaid leave on qualification	Life assurance (25+), private health insurance (optional), season ticket loan, subsidised gym membership	£42,000

TRAINEE SALARIES TABLE *continued*

FIRM NAME	IST YEAR SALARY (2000)	2ND YEAR SALARY (2000)	SPONSORSHIP/ AWARDS	OTHER BENEFITS	QUALIF- ICATION SALARY
Olswang	£23,500	n/a	n/a	Upon qualification: pension, Medical cover, life cover, dental scheme, gym membership.	£40,000
Osborne Clarke OWA	£17,000-£22,000	£18,000-£23,000	LPC fees paid. CPE fees paid. Maintenance grant of £2,500 for each.	None until qualified	£30,000-£40,000
Paisner & Co	£22,000	£24,000	LPC Funding only	n/a	£40,000
Pannone & Partners	£16,000	£18,000		n/a	£25,000
Payne Hicks Beach	£21,000	£23,000	Fees for the CPE and LPC are paid.	Season travel ticket loan, life assurance 4 x salary, permanent health insurance	£34,000
Penningtons	£21,000 (London)	£23,000 (London)	LPC Funding is available. Awards are given for commendation or distinction in LPC.	Subsidised sports and social club, life assurance, season ticket loan.	£34,000 (London)
Pinsent Curtis	£23,000	£25,000	CPE and LPC fees are paid. In addition to this, maintenance grants of £2,500 for CPE and £4,500 for LPC are offered.	n/a	n/a
Pritchard Englefield	£19,000	£19,250	£2,000	Some subsidised training, luncheon vouchers.	Approx £30,000
Radcliffes	£20,000	£21,500	n/a	Health insurance, season ticket loan, life assurance, PHI.	£33,000
Reynolds Porter Chamberlain	£22,000	£24,000	CPE funding: fees paid + £4,000 maintenance LPC funding: fees paid + £4,000 maintenance	Bonus schemes, private medical insurance, income protection benefits, season ticket loan, subsidised gym membership, active social calender.	£36,000
Richards Butler	£25,000	£28,000	CPE and LPC fees and maintenance paid	Performance related bonus, life insurance, private patients' plan, interest free season ticket loan, subsidised staff restaurant, staff conveyancing allowance.	£38,000 plus bonus
Rowe & Maw	n/a	n/a	CPE and LPC fees paid and £4,000 (£4,500 for London/Guildford) maintenance p.a.	Interest free season ticket loan, subsidised member-ship of sport clubs, private health scheme	£40,000
Russell Jones & Walker	£19,500	£21,250	CPE/LPC Funding: interest free grant to assist with fees available (£1000).	Season ticket loan, pension, private health-care (optional), group life assurance.	£30,000

FIRM NAME	IST YEAR SALARY (2000)	2ND YEAR SALARY (2000)	SPONSORSHIP/ AWARDS	OTHER BENEFITS	QUALIF-ICATION SALARY
Russell-Cooke	£18,500	£20,000	n/a	n/a	Market
Salans Hertzfeld & Heilbronn HRK	£22,500	£23,500	n/a	n/a	Variable
Shadbolt & Co	£20,000	£24,000	LPC fees partly payable when trainee commences work	Permanent health insurance, pension (qualifying period).	£30,000
Sharpe Pritchard	c.£20,000	c.£21,000	Possible financial assistance with LPC	Season ticket loan.	n/a
Sheridans	£20,000	£22,000	LPC funding is variable for those who have accepted training contracts.	Life assurance.	£32,000
Shoosmiths	£16,000	£17,250	Funding £10,000 – split between fees and maintenance	Life assurance, contributory pension after 3 months.	£30,000
Sidley & Austin	£26,250	£29,500	CPE and LPC fees paid and maintenance p.a.	Healthcare, disability cover, life assurance, contribution to gym membership, interest free season ticket loan.	£44,100
Simmons & Simmons	£25,000	£28,000	In the absence of Local Authority funding we will pay LPC fees and, where necessary, CPE fees and offer a maintenance allowance of £4,500 for those at Law School in London or Guildford and £4,000 elsewhere.	Season ticket loan, fitness loan, PRP, group travel insurance, group accident insurance, group health insurance.	£42,000
Sinclair Roche & Temperley	£22,500	£23,500	CPE and LPC fees paid and £4,000 maintenance p.a.	Private health cover, discretionary bonus, PHI, accident insurance, subsidised sports club membership	£37-40,000
SJ Berwin & Co	£25,000	£28,000	CPE and LPC Fees paid and £4,000 maintenance p.a.	PRP, corporate sports membership, free lunch, health insurance	£42,000
Slaughter and May	£25,000	£28,000	CPE and LPC fees and maintenance grants are paid; some grants are available for post-graduate work.	BUPA, STL, pension scheme, membership of various sports clubs, 24 hour accident cover	£42,000
Speechly Bircham	£23,000-£24,000	£25,000-£26,000	CPE tuition and LPC tuition fees plus a maintenance grant of £4,000.	Season ticket loan, private medical insurance, life assurance.	£38,000

FIRM NAME	IST YEAR SALARY (2000)	2ND YEAR SALARY (2000)	SPONSORSHIP/ AWARDS	OTHER BENEFITS	QUALIF- ICATION SALARY
Stephenson Harwood	£23,000	£25,000	£6,900 fees paid for CPE and LPC and £4,500 maintenance p.a.	Subsidised membership of health clubs, season ticket loan and 25 days paid holiday per year.	£40,000
Tarlo Lyons	£20,000 on average	£22,000 on average	LPC fees paid	Contribution to private health insurance and season ticket loan.	£37,000+
Taylor Joynson Garrett	£24,000	£27,000	CPE and LPC fees paid and £4,000 maintenance p.a.	Private medical care, permanent health insurance, STL, subsi-dised staff restaurant, non-contributory pension scheme on qualification.	£41,000
Taylor Vinters	£15,000	£16,500	n/a	Pension, private medical insurance and life insurance. Many social activities are actively encouraged, from a theatre club to karaoke. Cambridge of course now has the largest pub in Europe.	£27,000 plus benefits
Teacher Stern Selby	£20,750		CPE Funding: none; LPC Funding: unlikely	n/a	£31,000
Theodore Goddard	£25,000	£28,000	CPE and LPC fees paid in full. £4,200 mainten-ance paid for London and South East, £3,750 elsewhere.	Pension, profit-related bonus, permanent health insurance, private medical insurance, subsidised health and fitnesss club membership and firm restaurant.	£40,000
Travers Smith Braithwaite	£25,000	£28,000	LPC and CPE fees paid and between £4,000 and £4,500 maintenance p.a.	Private health insurance, season ticket loans, luncheon vouchers, sub-sidised sports club membership	£42,000
Trowers & Hamlins	£23,000	£25,000	CPE and LPC fees paid and £4,000-£4,250 maintenance p.a.	Season ticket loan, private health care after six month's service, Employee Assistance Programme & discretionary bonus. Death in Service.	£37,500
Walker Morris	£17,250	£18,500	CPE Funding: Fees + £1,000; LPC Funding: Fees + £1,000	n/a	£27,500

FIRM NAME	IST YEAR SALARY (2000)	2ND YEAR SALARY (2000)	SPONSORSHIP/ AWARDS	OTHER BENEFITS	QUALIF- ICATION SALARY
Ward Hadaway	(1st six months) £15,500 (2nd six months) £16,000	(1st six months) £16,500 (2nd six months) £17,000	LPC fees paid and £2,000 interest free loan.	23 days holiday. Death in service insurance. Pension (post qualification).	£25,000
Warner Cranston	£22,500	£25,000	CPE/LPC fees and maintenance grant plus interest-free loan.	BUPA, IFSTL, life assurance, permanent health insurance, pension contributions (after qualifying period).	£39,000
Watson, Farley & Williams	£25,000	£28,000	CPE and LPC Fees paid £4,500 maintenance p.a. (£4,000 outside London)	Life assurance, PHI, BUPA, STL, pension, subsidised gym membership	£43,500
Weil, Gotshal & Manges	above market rate		The firm will pay tuition fees and a maintenance allowance for CPE/LPC	Pension, Permanent Health Insurance, Private Health Cover, Life Assurance, subsidised gym membership, season ticket loan.	
White & Case	£30,000		CPE and LPC fees paid and £4,500 maintenance p.a. Prizes for commendation and distinction in the LPC.	BUPA, gym membership contribution, life insurance, pension scheme, permanent health scheme, season ticket loan.	£55,000
Wiggin & Co	£22,000	£25,700	CPE and LPC fees and £3,000 maintenance p.a. Brochure available on request.	Life assurance, private health cover, pension scheme, permanent health insurance	£32,200
Withers	£23,000	£25,000	CPE and/or LPC fees are paid and £4,000 maintenance p.a. A cash prize is awarded for distinction or commendation in CPE and/or LPC.	Interest free season ticket loan, private medical insurance, life assurance, social events, cafe facilities	£33,500
Wragge & Co	£17,000	£18,500	CPE and LPC fees paid. Maintenance grant of £3,500 for LPC, and £3,000 per year for CPE students.	Life assurance, permanent health scheme, pension, interest free travel loans.	£30,000

international firms...international locations

This is a revolutionary age in the legal profession. The globalisation of the world economy has led to the creation of the global law firm. Several UK firms claim the title. Many were already international, with offices in several jurisdictions, mainly practising UK law and staffed by UK qualified lawyers. In the last couple of years international mergers have appeared on the menu. Clifford Chance was the first, with mergers in Germany and the US. Freshfields, Lovells and Linklaters soon followed suit, and now everyone's trying to be a player. Slaughter and May remains resolute. It has a few international offices and other firms with whom it has 'best friends' relationships.

You can go to a UK firm which is a top international player. Or you can go to a firm with foreign offices and apply for an overseas seat. Or you can choose to train at one of the US firms in London.

the top international players

We picked our Top 12 international firms, after consulting research from *Chambers Global 2000*. We counted the number of rankings each firm received. Each ranking represents recommendations from the market place in an individual practice area in a separate country or region. The number of rankings received is shown in brackets. All of these firms have multiple offices in other jurisdictions.

For more information refer to *Chambers Global* on **www.chambersandpartners.com**

trainees abroad

Favourite locations overseas for trainees are New York, Hong Kong, Singapore and Paris but, in these days of globalisation, the list of locations grows ever longer. In the Middle East, Dubai is a trainee hot spot. Seats in Eastern Europe are now more common and trainees from UK firms can work as far afield as China, Brazil, Venezuela and Russia. Closer to home, secondments to Brussels offices are the most plentiful.

Although the time abroad gives you experience of working in another jurisdiction, you are, with some exceptions, unlikely to practise foreign law. However, as international merger follows international merger, offices are increasingly staffed by lawyers who are dual qualified.

Repeatedly, trainees tell us that overseas seats are hard work. Offices abroad are much smaller than main offices in London and this requires trainees to shoulder more responsibility. Almost all trainees welcome this; for most the overseas seat is the highlight of their training contract.

How do you ensure that you get a preferred seat abroad? Generally, trainees feel that selection is based on merit and suitability for the job. Language

GLOBAL TOP 12

1	Clifford Chance (83)
2	Baker & McKenzie (80)
3	Freshfields (69)
4	Linklaters (57)
5	Allen & Overy (56)
6	White & Case (45)
7	Shearman & Sterling (34)
8	Norton Rose (26)
9	Denton Hall (24)
10	Slaughter and May (24)
11	Cleary Gottlieb (23)
12	Herbert Smith (22)

ability is essential for some seats like Paris, São Paulo or Milan, but unnecessary for most Asian or Middle Eastern seats. We're told of trainees 'dumbing down' their language skills in order to avoid being sent to an unpopular seat – Moscow, for example. The trick to securing certain of the most popular seats is still, to a degree, a case of waging an effective campaign of self promotion. At firms with less of an emphasis on overseas placements, at least half of the trainees usually decided against time abroad as a result of commitments in the UK, or simply a desire to spend all of their seats in the home office. Sometimes trainees have told us that they feared six months away from the action in London might mean that they were out of sight and out of mind. Invariably, the award of an overseas seat will be an endorsement of recognised ability.

Remember, an overseas seat is an opportunity for networking and will give you valuable work experience. In New York you'll get the opportunity to meet finance trainees as well as associates from the US firms. Brussels will give you proximity to the EU institutions and opportunities to meet stagiaires or other interns.

It may be hard work. It may be an eye-opener. It may even be lonely. But the overwhelming feedback from those we spoke to is that working as a trainee abroad is an unmissable experience.

brussels

the work: Many trainees had already spent some time in EU/Competition departments back in London. This improved their time in Brussels. Having said that, much of the work will be *"big ticket"* corporate.

the place: Much smaller than London, the general consensus is that Brussels is *"a pleasant place to live and work in."* Many trainees live in the old part of the city, which is *"very pretty"* and *"a nice place to spend the summer."* Belgians are found to be *"friendly and very courteous."* That is until French and Flemish speaking Belgians cross paths. *"Despite being bi-lingual, they end up speaking English as a compromise."* 80% of Brussels is francophone.

getting together: The Law Society organises a list of trainees in Belgium. Group e-mails follow inviting trainees to events *"a couple of times a week,"* though whether people went out *"depended on whether they had work on."* With *"no licensing restrictions"* and *"exceptional beer,"* the social life is good, though things don't really get going until 9 or 10 o'clock. If you know people doing 'stages' at the Commission, then you can get involved in the *"young scene"* and its *"country parties in weird and wonderful places."*

accommodation: There is no trainee 'ghetto' as such, but *"Brussels is much smaller than London and has good public transport. No place is too far away."*

advice from trainees:
- Buy the mini Rough Guide to Brussels
- Take advantage of the location. A return ticket to Amsterdam is just £20.
- In many offices you don't need to be 100% fluent in French, but it helps in the city at large.

the verdict: A 'nice' place to go, especially in the summer when you can sit outside in the cafés. The presence of the Commission is not only the raison d'être for UK firms, but also enhances your social life if you know someone doing a 'stage'.

hong kong

the work: Project finance, corporate and banking work are the most common practice areas. Some firms, such as Lovells, also offer litigation. Depending on the firm much, indeed possibly all, of your work will be based on Hong Kong law, *"which is different but familiar."* Hours can be long; 12 hour days are *"fairly regular."* Saturday mornings are a standard part of the working week (but are dress-down).

the place: *"There's no grass and nothing flat. Everything is built on"* so don't expect rolling green countryside. The weather is 'interesting'. From March to July it's *"really lovely,"* in July it becomes *"really sticky"* and in August it's typhoon season. Should there be a number nine or 10 strength typhoon, you'll be stuck wherever you are. This was particularly hard on one trainee we spoke to. She was marooned in a five star hotel. Hong Kong is *"very busy."* Expect the pace of life to be hectic.

getting together: An *"unofficially organised"* e-mail list gives phone numbers for UK trainees in Hong Kong. Freshfields' trainees are rumoured to be responsible for this. This list is the key to your social life, which will be busy to say the least. Trainees go out *"five times a week."* Towards the end of your seat it can become more cliquey. The social life seems to revolve around the 'junks' and the bars. No self-respecting firm in Hong Kong is without a 'junk,' a large 'Chinese style' motorboat you can book for trips. They vary in size (taking from around 18 to 32 people) and in facilities. Most have a speedboat for waterskiing and some sort of bar. The Linklaters junk is a favourite because of its air-conditioning and karaoke machine: *"It's the most like a gin palace."* The boats are staffed by 'boat-boys' who *"will take you everywhere"* and look after you attentively. On the boats *"you feel like you're in Miami Vice!"* Some advice on the bars. Prepare to spend a lot of money as *"beers are really expensive."* During happy hour, beer prices can be as 'low' as £3.50 a pint. At other times a pint could cost as much as £9/10. One way to save money on booze is to visit an unlicensed bar. In one, Chop-Chop, beer is cunningly disguised in coffee cups and is half the price of anywhere else.

accommodation: A significant number of firms have flats either in Mid-Levels on Victoria Peak or over in Happy Valley, which is convenient for the racecourse. You will usually share with one other.

advice from trainees:
- Don't expect to take work easy, you'll get into huge trouble
- Don't think you'll save any money
- Mind the sharks

the verdict: Definitely one for people who like to play hard and work hard. You need to have the energy for a busy social life *"even if you're working until three in the morning."* As one trainee put it, *"I was partly relieved to come back. I needed a rest from the drinking."*

new york

the work: Unsurprisingly finance work (such as securities) and general corporate feature highly. Trainees thought that hours in New York were similar to those in the London. However, the day can be *"very fast-paced,"* partly because hours are governed by *"the fact that you are working with Europe and you have to deal with everything before they go home."* New York offices are very much smaller than London offices of UK firms, so there's more responsibility. You may be the only trainee.

the place: *"There really is a lot going on."* *"Parades all the time,"* *"rollerblading in Central Park,"* *"horse riding in New Jersey."* The list of things to do goes on forever. It's fast paced; there's no time for hesitation. Happily, New York now feels *"very safe, a real difference from four or five years ago."* *"You can get the subway in the evening without any great problem."*

getting together: There's no comprehensive list of trainees in circulation. Instead, newcomers need to *"use the grapevine"* and *"contact the other trainees themselves."* The US summer associate social events provide a stream of new lawyers to meet and often there's English people sent out by US investment banks as part of their training. And, with a flat in New York, *"there are always friends from England wanting to visit you."* With bars open *"throughout the night,"* *"people tend to go out at 9 or10pm, eat at about 11pm and stay out until 2 or 3am."* *"You still have to be in work at the right time though,"* pointed out one trainee. Eating out gets pricey in New York as trainees have got into the habit of going to more expensive restaurants than they would in London. New York's 'lounge bars' with DJs prove popular, in place of the 'clubbing' back home. With so much to do, your experience depends entirely on *"how you decide to live your life."*

accommodation: Usually you'll get an apartment in Midtown Manhattan, near Central Park on either the Upper East or Upper West Side. Each lucky Linklaters trainee gets their own apartment. Those with a fear of heights be warned, some of the apartments in New York are 50 storeys up. To calm you down, many of the blocks come complete with gym and jacuzzi.

advice from trainees:

• Use the inter-firm grapevine to find other trainees
• You can get everything you need out there but take marmite and ribena as it's very expensive
• Get out of New York to New Jersey, Boston, Cape Cod...
• Do all you can, even though it can be very tiring

the verdict: New York has so much to offer, both work-wise and socially. Retail opportunities abound. It's really up to you.

paris

the work: Lots of corporate, international finance and M&A work, with a French language element. Some firms (e.g. Herbert Smith) do some domestic French work. Probably some translation work will be required of you. You'll only be sent out to Paris if your French is good. As for the hours, you shouldn't expect to get out of the office early. Nevertheless trainees admit that by 7:30/8pm *"everyone is heading out."* In some Paris offices the long continental lunchbreak dies hard, *"especially when taking out interviewees."* And in August…*"everyone is on holiday."*

the place: For many trainees this will be a return to Paris, having studied there at university. Being there as a worker can be a shock. The truth is that *"corporate law in France is a serious business. It's a lot more professional than people think."* So to those who think that Paris life means spending all day philosophising in cafés, think again. On the plus side the Metro is cleaner and cheaper than London's tube. And it works.

getting together: As a number have been to Paris before, it's inevitable that many trainees have *"large groups of French friends."* For those without such a network, an e-mail list is created *"pretty quickly"*

and things are organised such that you *"could go out every week."* The social network starts off *"quite big,"* but by the end *"only the hardcore is left."* Parisian life is altogether more civilised. *"You don't just pile out of the office into the nearest pub."* You tend to go to cafés for unhurried drinks. With no strict licensing hours, you don't feel the need to drink everything before eleven o'clock. As for clublife, *"it can be hard to get in."* You have to be *"dressed in the latest Versace. And having lots of women with you really helps."* When you get in you'll find clubs are *"more classy, more themed and the most smoky places anywhere."* If you get to know Parisians (*"it takes slightly longer, but when you do it's less superficial"*), dinner parties will feature strongly in your diary.

accommodation: The Left Bank is a popular area with trainees, though locations of apartments vary widely. One trainee, after finding out that he was going to 'Gay Paris', found himself living in a gay quarter. The area was *"a lot of fun"* he said.

advice from trainees

• Try to forget the 'holiday image' of Paris; you are there to work.
• Don't expect to get into clubs in jeans and t-shirts. Take your designer stuff.

the verdict: If you're going to Paris remember that you will probably work on big corporate transactions, which means it won't be a doss. Once out of the office you step into romantic Paris, so if you haven't already found the love of your life, find him/her for the duration of your stay.

best of the rest

Frankfurt: This is likely to offer finance-related work, so more of a business and transaction driven seat than six months with black letter law. Socially there is an ex-pat scene and there is certainly a tendency to mix with other English speakers. There is a list in circulation detailing the numbers of UK trainees in the city. **best things:** *"It's quite close to London!"* so your friends can visit easily. The standard of living is good. You can get by with English in many offices. Good parks. **worst things:** It's not as glamorous as other overseas secondments. Lots of people live outside the city and consequently it could be a bit livelier. There's not much pre-war history as the city was bombed to blazes.

Madrid: You need to be a Spanish speaker as this is the language of business here. There's a sizeable contingent from the UK firms in Madrid. Spanish firms operate around the two hour siesta from 2pm to 4pm. This means that the official working day stretches for a whopping ten and a half hours from 9.30am–8pm. (But you do get a snooze.) *"It takes a while to get used to the day. It's nice but at 4pm in London you'd be thinking of leaving relatively soon. Here you still have half a day left."* Cultural influences are strong and you will definitely adopt the Spanish way of doing things, such as eating out at 10pm. **best things:** A wicked social scene. Plaza Santa Ana is the hub of the city's nightlife. *"It's full of everyone from abroad. Not necessarily lawyers... It's very international... vibrant and full of bars and clubs."* Tapas. Abandoning the Anglo way of doing things and learning Latin habits. Living in a city that never sleeps (except at siesta time). **worst things:** hmmm...living in a city that never sleeps.

Singapore: Desperately popular with UK trainees. The lure of Asia is intense. Shipping is a common area of work for those lucky enough to secure a secondment here. English is spoken in all offices as it is the official language in this polyglot society. The working week, like in Hong Kong, is Monday to Saturday lunchtime. **best things:** a big, fun social scene. High standard of living and a tropical environment. Proximity to the pleasure zones of Malaysia, Bali and the South Pacific. Everyone will want to visit. Food is an eclectic mix of Chinese, South Indian and Malaysian. Shopping is fabulous – great electronic goods, you can get clothes tailor-made. **worst things:** Singapore is known to be a highly regulated society and some people find it too 'sanitised'. Known as the 'Fine City', you can be fined for jaywalking, importing more than 10 packets of chewing gum and not flushing the toilet. The weather – it feels like 95% humidity all year round.

Piraeus, Greece: *"People don't want to go to Piraeus"* – or so we kept hearing. It's Greek and it's shipping. We assume that it's the latter which is the main turn-off. It may also be the fact that you're unlikely to be in a big gang of trainees from your firm – usually you'll be the only one posted. A handful of firms have offices out there so it ought to be possible to hook up with other UK trainees. Small offices like those found in Piraeus allow you to develop relationships with more senior staff, which will get you out of a trainee rut (if you feel stuck in one). Many who go will be Greek speakers but it's not absolutely essential. **best things:** Greek food and culture. Mediterranean climate. The social scene is not known for being ruinous though. Island-hopping. Yachts. **worst things:** You may miss the buzz of London and your social circle. Greece is a summer country – winter is short but miserable as everything closes down. You may not like shipping work.

Prague: Way better in the summer. A beautiful City with stunning ballet and theatre but sometimes you miss the buzz of London and having your friends around. The architecture and culture are fabulous but the food is dire and it's virtually impossible to get a decent coffee.

Tokyo: Becoming ever more popular amongst City trainees. You must love noise, karaoke and pachinko. Space is at a real premium in Tokyo, so flats are never spacious. Be prepared for complete culture shock. A unique experience if you can get it.

Moscow: If you're a Russian speaker and your firm has a Moscow office you are in the frame for a secondment there, whether you like it or not. It may be difficult to convince HR that you are best suited to New York or Singapore. Not a large number of trainees in the city but the chance to really get to know colleagues and the workings of a small office as well as your clients' business needs in eastern Europe. Take your long johns in winter and invest in a fur hat, whatever your feelings about it. Temperatures of -18º are quite usual in winter.

Gulf (Bahrain, Abu Dhabi, Dubai): These secondments will not throw you into a totally unfamiliar environment as the expat scene is so very strong in these Gulf locations. Female secondees may notice more of a difference than their male counterparts, as Islamic tradition and laws do need to be respected and this will often require modification of dress and behaviour between men and women. If you're unhappy about the prospect of making these adjustments, don't go.

US firms in london

The US firms with London offices are struggling to become better known. They vie with top City firms for the best candidates. In many cases they now headhunt trainees directly from the magic circle. Most US firms are still young and small in the London marketplace. Many do not have developed graduate recruitment programmes. But they are recognising the value of 'growing their own,' i.e. training their own solicitors.

Many US firms already receive up to 2000 speculative applications for one or two places per year. It's important not to be blinded by high salaries or the prospect of international travel. These offices are UK outposts of US firms. They service a particular work-type, which is mainly corporate and finance work. Applicants should be sure that this work type genuinely interests them.

One of the main advantages of the London office of a US firm is that it offers a friendly, informal small office culture with the opportunity to be noticed, with backup and work of a huge international network of offices.

Cleary, Gottlieb, Steen & Hamilton
Number of Trainees: 4

One of the leading US firms in Europe. With ten offices worldwide, the firm's London office has been established for almost 30 years. The firm has

leading corporate finance, banking and competition practices. The London office works very closely with New York. It is staffed by US and local lawyers in roughly equal proportions. Trainees usually spend one year in London doing M&A, capital markets, tax and regulatory work. This is followed by a compulsory six month seat in Brussels, primarily to gain experience in EU competition law. The final seat is usually back in London.

Trainees are treated as equivalent to full first year associates in other European offices, with considerable independence and autonomy. The "*good learning environment*" is attributed to a combination of its "*interesting, diverse and international*" people, the sophisticated nature of the work and the firm culture ("*the London office is small but you get the feeling that it is very much part of a huge firm*"). The downside of the smaller office with the heavy workload may be insufficient feedback at times. Hours can be extreme because of the nature of work. The firm looks for relevant US experience and a second career which demonstrates a greater level of maturity. Undertaking the NY Bar Exam is compulsory for trainees who do not already hold the qualification. Language training is also available.

Coudert Brothers
Number of Trainees: 8

A New York firm with 27 offices worldwide. Very well-established in the UK, with a broader practice than many US offices currently aspire to. Training is split into four six-month seats with a guaranteed seat abroad, usually in Brussels. Placements in Paris and Hong Kong and secondments to major commercial and institutional clients are arranged on a case by case basis. Trainees agree that training is not formalised or structured – "*there is less spoon-feeding. You need to be proactive and organise your own training to some extent.*" Quality of work can be "*hit or miss*" depending on what's going on but trainees "*are not as far down the food chain as you might think.*"

There is a strong perception that the office is *"New York controlled, everything has to be cleared by them."* Trainees describe the working environment as *"competitive, commercial and professional"* but *"everyone gets along with each other"* and there is *"lots of dialogue between people."* Typical trainees tend to be more 'complete' as individuals as opposed to being straight out of an educational establishment.

LeBoeuf, Lamb Greene & McRae
Number of Trainees: 6

Less high profile than the other US firms in London, it nevertheless possesses one of the most well-rounded practices with both corporate and finance transactional work as well as insurance, commercial litigation and commercial property. Best known for its international energy work and international projects work.

Trainees spend up to 12 months doing contentious work, with the remaining twelve in non-contentious. The practice is not heavily departmentalised and rather than simply *"dropping work"* when rotating into the next seat, trainees tend to carry over matters and see them to completion. With a *"nice cultural blend of US/ UK"* staff, the atmosphere is described as *"studious, not frenetic."* There is no pecking order (*"the partners are very laid back"*). Working hours tend to be regular unless the workload dictates otherwise, most notably, in the corporate department sphere. There is a *"varied intake"* of trainees who tend to be older with a broad experience of life. *"This is not a place for shrinking violets"* or those who are inclined to *"wait for something to happen."*

Mayer Brown & Platt
Number of Trainees: 4

A top Chicago firm with a strong New York office and a City presence going back 20 years. Although it has only recently developed an English law capability, the practice is growing fast with particularly strong banking and international securitisation practices. Core practice areas are corporate, banking and finance and specialist work in CIS/ Russian matters. There are opportunities for in-house placements with some of the firm's clients, such as a major investment bank. A three month litigation seat is undertaken by placement with UK City firm, Stephenson Harwood. There may be future opportunities for litigation placements in one of the firm's US offices. There is *"lots of variety"* in the work and tasks such as proof-reading are *"rare."* Trainees are given a high level of responsibility. Ideal candidates appear to be those with strong personalities who seek responsibility and are quite confident. They may well be older or have had previous work experience.

McDermott Will & Emery
Number of Trainees: 1 (and looking to increase)

Not a typical 'Wall Street' outfit, this Chicago based firm with branches throughout the US has a diverse range of clients with US and European interests and main strengths in cross-border banking, capital markets and projects. With a clear objective to compete directly with its UK City counterparts, the firm has attempted to establish a full service English law firm from scratch over the last couple of years.

Within Law Society rules, trainees can choose the practice areas they cover over four six-month seats, namely, corporate and corporate finance, litigation, tax, banking and finance, IT and IP, telecoms and employment. Trainees can expect to be constructively involved in deals right from the beginning, undertaking a variety of interesting tasks. *"You are given a lot more responsibility and expected to know your stuff and apply what you've learned."* They are expected to work hard to complete tasks as necessary but without the *"macho experience"* of *"staying on every night for the sake of it."*

The London office is unusual in that there are very few US attorneys based there. It is more like a high profile City firm with big US backup.

Shearman & Sterling
Number of Trainees: 7
See main True Picture section

Sidley & Austin
Number of Trainees: 10

Dual US/English law firm recommended for securitisation, derivatives and telecommunications. Training is organised into five training seats split into three six-month seats and two three-month seats covering corporate, international finance and banking, property, tax and the information industry (IP, IT and telecoms). The Law Society requirements for experience in contentious work are currently met by carrying out theoretical case work in London culminating in a mock trial at the firm's Chicago office. This is currently under review with potential scope for placement with a barristers' chambers.

Fewer trainees means a more sociable environment with an absence of cliques. Trainees come from a broad age group (between 23 to 30 years) and diversity of backgrounds (approximately 50% law to non law graduates). A relaxed attitude prevails, with dress down Fridays. The *"newness"* of the atmosphere, as opposed to *"entrenched"* attitudes perceived in City firms, and the prevailing US ethos which discourages hierarchy (*"you can talk to the partners"*) are considered a bonus.

Weil Gotschal & Manges
Number of Trainees: 9

One of the largest offices of a US firm in London, with a predominance of UK qualified lawyers. Leading securitisations and derivatives teams. As is the case with other firms of its kind, the atmosphere is very young (*"there are no old or unapproachable people"*) and casual – they dress down every day. The atmosphere is industrious – *"everyone is here to work,"* yet it's *"small enough for people to socialise."* Having observed its size doubling over the past

two years, one trainee commented that this must be one of the fastest growing offices of its kind – *"full of opportunities."* Practice areas covered in London include corporate, litigation, capital markets, banking, IP, property. A seat in New York is available, where securitisation, tax and property are likely areas of practice.

Trainees are seen as *"all very different in personality,"* and the general feeling is that aside from academic prerequisites, candidates are assessed as to whether they would fit in. They are all quite ambitious – one noted that there *"doesn't appear to be a glass ceiling for women"* with the male to female ratio estimated as approaching 50:50. This is a place where *"you have the chance to shine"* but by the same token *"you can't hide either."*

White & Case
Number of Trainees: 13

Training is divided into four six-month seats usually including a foreign seat in Paris, Brussels, Singapore or Hong Kong. There is some choice in practice areas which include corporate, banking, litigation, competition, project finance and IP.

Trainees can expect to be involved in high profile matters at levels which are appropriate to their experience. They are given a high level of responsibility (*"they will let you run with things and take charge"*) and generally *"feel an integral part"* of the team. There is consistent comment that none have *"felt out of depth"* in handling those cases which have been allocated to them single-handedly. An *"exciting"* atmosphere comprises roughly 50:50 US to UK/European staff working in different languages, integrating UK work with that from the firm's other overseas offices. There is a prevalence of those with language skills and Oxbridge graduates are thought to have *"an edge."* With emphasis on individuality among trainees, there is a variety of *"personalities"* who have *"done something a bit unusual"* before joining.

prospects for newly qualifieds

Trainees looking to move firms on qualification are *"chronically insecure and desperate people."* So says a Chambers and Partners recruitment consultant. *"They are high maintenance and you have to be like a therapist for them."*

Surely these people have got it made? The economy is strong and newly-qualifieds are in great demand. Salaries have soared. US firms are crying out for new blood trained at someone else's expense. So why the trauma?

We asked our legal recruitment specialists the questions you have all been asking us about qualification....

private practice

The market is strong for newly qualifieds. Corporate is *"buoyant."* Finding good commercial property lawyers is *"like looking for hen's teeth."* Banking and finance are doing well. It's not too bad if you're looking for corporate tax or shipping. Commercial is *"OK but not brilliant for newly qualifieds although it's booming further up."* But litigation is *"flat,"* insolvency *"thin"* and there are never enough employment or IP/IT vacancies to fulfil the demand for jobs.

who is recruiting? The large City firms. Big surprise. It's a popular move for newly-qualifieds from small firms to 'upsize.' Such is the market right now that *"candidates can get into firms on qualification that rejected them for a training contract."* The biggest practices might consider candidates from firms just outside the top 50 as well as inside. Typically, trainees from the magic circle and second tier firms will stay within that range or move to respected niche practices.

If I train at the biggest firms will I have more options? *"There's a good deal of truth in that. You'll have a greater number of options if you go to the most blue chip firm that you can."* But small West End firms may be sceptical about someone leaving the magic circle. *"They may think that the candidate doesn't know what a culture shock is in store for them. They may be a high risk from the firm's point of view."* Those leaving the magic circle may feel more comfortable going into another big or mid-sized firm.

Moving to a small firm from a big one on qualification or soon afterwards is making a statement loud and clear. It's an indication that you did not enjoy the big firm culture. *"It's not a one-way street. You could move back up to a bigger firm, but you've made a very big statement."* You could go back to a big firm but perhaps not the magic circle.

What do recruiters look for in a newly-qualified lawyer? *"At that level, it's hard to judge who's good and who isn't. Newly qualified solicitors have to sell themselves on personality not expertise. They have to show that they are sparky, bubbly and charming."* Experience of your chosen field is important, but no one is going to have a huge amount of experience at the time they qualify.

Should you switch firms on qualification or wait until a couple of years PQE? *"If you get an offer from a better firm you would be mad not to take it. If you don't, stay put."* The main message if you are ambitious is: *"Just get to the firm with the best reputation as early as possible. These days there are no brownie points for staying put."* Moving on qualification is acceptable but it's unwise to keep moving around after that.

Are the US firms my best option? *"US firms take on the odd newly-qualified. When certain key acquisitions hit the headlines every newly qualified lawyer thinks they can command an £80k salary."* The numbers recruited are still relatively small. Generally US firms take individuals from the magic circle or those on the fringes of it. *"Some have made the move from medium-sized firms, including regional practices."* But these jobs are few and far between and not available to everyone. Not all US firms pay New York salaries!

How easy is it to get a job in London if you have trained in the regions? In property you are highly marketable as the work is essentially the same nationwide. In corporate, if you have trained at a strong regional corporate practice you will perceive no real disadvantage. You can also move from a relatively small practice if it is well-regarded as a commercial player.

industry and banking

It's not hard to see the allure of the in-house culture. More predictable working hours. More opportunity to become commercially involved. Incentivised pay structures which translate into potential for large bonus payments or share options. But lack of infrastructure and hands-on supervision may deter some.

Who would be considered for a job with a bank? There are always a few positions for newly qualifieds within the banking industry, almost always for those with experience in banking and/or capital markets. So successful applicants will come from the magic circle or second tier banking firms. These jobs tend to come up throughout the year rather than in March and September when training contracts end. Secondments to industry during training or afterwards are very useful for making contacts and may give additional insight into recruitment opportunities.

How do you get jobs in banks? International investment banks recruit more in general as they are bigger. There are a few opportunities at the retail banks and the commercial banks but it would be very unusual indeed for the private banks to take on a NQ. Jobs in finance houses tend to occur in the regions and seem to be much less well-paid. There aren't many NQ banking and finance jobs cropping up in any one year. Candidates are at their most marketable at 2-4 years PQE. You will almost only hear about opportunities in banking through recruitment consultancies.

Outside banking the best experience that you can gain to increase your prospects of getting a job in industry is in general company/commercial work. This may have a specialist slant, for example, corporate M&A, IP/ IT or employment. Opportunities for property lawyers are increasing. Those for litigators are more limited.

What about dot.coms? *"There's almost no chance of a newly-qualified moving to the in-house legal team of a dot.com. Those teams are small and want people with experience."* You'll have more chance of a job with larger hi-tech companies. Experience of IT matters often tips the balance in a candidate's favour.

What sort of person is most sought after? Much of a candidate's success has to do with his or her attitude. Teams are small and employers are keen to find the right 'fit.' This will often take precedence over experience. Commercial awareness is an important attribute which can be cultivated by keeping abreast of developments in industry-related publications such as the *Financial Times* and *Wall Street Journal*. Candidates must be able to demonstrate an interest and understanding of the in-house legal environment.

qualifying in other jurisdictions

In an increasingly competitive international legal and business world, many lawyers view dual or foreign qualification as a desirable addition to their professional skill-set. Such qualifications enable them to offer a broader and more comprehensive service.

the US bar

Qualification at one of the US Bars permits solicitors to practise freely in New York as attorneys or to represent American clients in the UK. Some feel this makes them more marketable to the growing number of US firms based in London and beyond. City of London law firms based in New York may also look favourably upon this additional qualification.

There are only a small number of course providers authorised in the UK to prepare for and administer the examination. Central Law Training is a Birmingham-based legal education and training organisation. The New York Bar lecture programme and examinations are conducted from its London facilities. To be eligible for the NY Bar exam you must hold a three year full-time or four year part-time LLB degree qualification. There is the option of a five-month lecture programme or home study course. The former is the more popular option as it allows close contact and communication with the lecturer and other course students.

A California Bar programme is also offered, although less interest has been shown in this, as it additionally requires 12 months experience in practice as a solicitor and is only available via the home study method.

NY Bar exams are conducted twice yearly. The lecture programme commencing in February prepares for a bar exam in July and a September lecture programme leads to final examination the following February. All lectures take place on Friday evenings and Saturdays (drinkers and socialites beware!) at the Café Royal on Regent Street.

Pass rates on the lecture programme run at around 70-80%. Bar-Bri legal texts are used, the preparatory papers used by most US students. Central Law is also considering a placement scheme where all participants spend four weeks with a US law firm, although this remains embryonic at this stage.

The University of Holborn also offers two courses in preparation for the New York Bar Exam. Students must have completed the equivalent of a three year degree course, based on English common law, at a recognised law school or university. Students can opt for the eight week review course or part-time fifteen week course, both of which take place at the college in London on Friday evenings and at weekends, preparing them for the twice-yearly examinations in New York.

The review course covers an eight week period starting in October for the February examinations or in March for the July examinations. The courses are held on weekends. Students are taught by qualified American attorneys, many of whom were initially British barristers and several of whom practise in New York.

Any eligibility queries should be addressed to the New York State Board of Examiners, 7 Executive Centre Drive, Albany, New York 12203, USA.

qualifying as an australian solicitor

Increasingly, the sun-drenched climate and laid-back charm of Australia offers an attractive alternative to over-stressed northern hemisphere professionals seeking a lifestyle-driven career change. Australia's federal system supports several states with different legal jurisdictions and varying rules governing admission requirements to the professional bodies of solicitors and barristers.

Below, we provide brief information for one popular choice – the state of New South Wales incorporating the principal city of Sydney. Contact details for solicitors' professional associations in Victoria and Queensland are also listed.

"Australia offers an attractive alternative to over-stressed northern hemisphere professionals."

new south wales

In New South Wales, a person is admitted as a Legal Practitioner to the Supreme Court of New South Wales. Once they have obtained a practising certificate from the state's Law Society, they are free to practise as a solicitor or barrister.

The Legal Practitioners Admission Board is the appropriate admitting authority in New South Wales and is responsible for administering the application process. English solicitors are required to apply for admission under Rule 100 of the Legal Practitioners Transitional Admission Rules 1994 which advises as to the requirements for transfer.

These requirements may necessitate further academic and practical legal training. But certain academic exemption clauses and practical exemptions exist dependent upon prior qualifications and relevant work experience. These courses can be studied at either the Legal Practitioners Admission Board itself or various educational establishments in New South Wales. A series of fees for registration, processing, admission etc. are payable to the board .

Contact: The Legal Practitioners Admission Board, Level 4 ADC Elizabeth Building, Corner King and Elizabeth Streets, Sydney, NSW 2000, Australia. **Tel:** 02 9392 0300. **Fax:** 02 9392 0315

Contact: The Law Society of New South Wales, 170 Philip Street, Sydney, NSW 2000, Australia. **Tel:** 61 2 9926 0333. **Fax:** 61 2 9231 5809. **Website:** www.lawsocnsw.asn.au. **Email:** lawsociety@lawsocnsw.asn.au

Contact: Law Institute Of Victoria, 470 Bourke St, Melbourne, Victoria 3000, Australia. **Tel:** 61 3 9607 9311. **Fax:** 61 3 9602 5270. **Website:** www.liv.asn.au

Contact: Queensland Law Society Inc. Law Society House, 179 Ann St, Brisbane, Queensland 4000, Australia. **Tel:** 61 7 3842 5888. **Fax:** 61 7 3842 5999. **Website:** www.qls.com.au

law society of scotland

Qualified solicitors from England and Wales seeking to practise in Scotland firstly need to be fully admitted to the roll in England and Wales. A certificate of good standing is required from the Law Society to The Law Society of Scotland.

There are no structured preparatory lectures or organised tuition programmes for the inter-UK transfer test held in Edinburgh, an examination consisting of 3x2 hour papers. The Law Society Of Scotland and Strathclyde University administer and oversee a home study programme, providing learning texts and communication support.

On successful completion of the transfer test, solicitors will be eligible to be admitted to the roll of Scottish solicitors, and thereby can practise freely. A £250 administration fee is required, payable to The Law Society Of Scotland. Additionally, examination fees are charged at £50 each.

Contact: The Law Society Of Scotland, 26 Drumsheugh Gardens, Edinburgh EH3 7YR. **Tel:** 0131 226 7411, **Fax:** 0131 225 2934.

overseas lawyers

becoming an english lawyer

Lawyers from Europe, Africa, the Caribbean and Australasia are among the main groups of overseas professionals who annually seek to add their name to the Roll of Solicitors of England and Wales.

The QLTT (Qualified Lawyers Transfer Test) is a Law Society accredited conversion test that permits lawyers qualified in selected countries outside the UK, as well as UK barristers to retrain and requalify as solicitors. The test covers four heads: Property, Litigation, Principles of Common Law and finally Professional Conduct and Accounts.

The Law Society determines which heads candidates must pass, dependent on their primary professional qualification. Candidates need to apply for a certificate of eligibility from the Law Society before applying to sit the test. Foreign qualified lawyers will usually have to pass sections of the test in conjunction with a two year experience requirement. This may be reduced if they have already completed an 'articles-style' training scheme overseas.

A full list of jurisdictions that fall under the umbrella of the Qualified Lawyers Transfer Regulations (QLTR) and the appropriate subjects and experience requirements can be obtained from the Law Society or via their website.

The Law Society confirms those types of previous experience which may be taken into account during the application process. Evidence of dates, written confirmation from employers, head of chambers etc. need to be submitted with any application, such as:

- Up to 12 months pupillage certified as satisfactory by the pupil master.
- Any period spent in practice at the Bar (i.e. – tenancy or squatting).
- A period spent in legal employment in the office of a solicitor or lawyer in private practice.
- Any period spent in legal employment with the Crown Prosecution Service or with the Magistrates/Court Service.
- Any period spent in legal employment in the Civil Service, Local Government, a public authority, commerce or industry provided that the employment is in a legal department which is headed by a solicitor, barrister or lawyer of at least five years standing.

For barristers, the experience must have been gained in England, Wales or Northern Ireland. Experience gained overseas may count if it occurred in a common law jurisdiction and in all cases, should be within the last five years.

Any unusual requests which do not fit into the above category requirements are usually considered by the Transfer Casework Committee.

test and study providers

There are two official test 'providers' – recognised educational establishments who offer the examination service and preparatory training and tuition courses. The Law Society refer potential participants to both.

The College of Law administers and runs the test but also offers a range of preliminary tuition options to prepare candidates for examination. These fall under three different categories; Distance Learning Courses, Evening Lectures/Weekend Courses, Revision Sessions.

BPP Law School runs the test twice yearly after focused study courses and sessions on key areas. Face to face methods or distance learning are available.

SPECIALIST PRACTICE AREAS

banking

In modern parlance 'banking' covers basic commercial loan agreements, constituted by contracts between borrowers and lenders, together with capital markets work. This covers the issuance of debt or equity securities and related areas such as securitisation, repackaging and structured finance, plus the whole range of derivatives products. A banking lawyer's work might vary from the preparation, negotiation and drafting of a syndicated loan agreement – considered 'pure' banking – to the structuring of a foreign exchange currency or interest rate swap. Increasingly, banking work involves tax efficient deal structures, requiring the setting up of special purpose companies in jurisdictions which have sympathetic tax regimes, such as the Cayman Islands.

Banking lawyers in 'straight' banking work will be responsible for drafting all the major terms of loan contracts including the taking of security, events of default and the covenants. Basically, they are concerned with the documentation of lending money, and arranging its signing and completion. In capital markets work they will often actually assist with the structuring of the commercial terms of a deal and advise on whether a proposed transaction breaches any securities laws. A typical capital markets transaction might involve a company raising several million sterling via an issue of a bond sold into say Europe or a public offering of equity. The proceeds are then swapped into dollars and perhaps used for an acquisition. In this way banking obviously overlaps with corporate finance work, particularly M&A. Banking lawyers should have a broad knowledge of these areas. This area of practice is now completely global and much of the work is international.

Banking is strictly regulated, though not prohibitively so. Financial services regulation now employs ever greater numbers of compliance lawyers. As credit risk departments and capital adequacy requirements become increasingly important so does their advisory role. In London they will primarily be concerned to ensure compliance with the Financial Services Authority which regulates the UK market.

type of work

Top level banking and capital markets work is highly polarised and concentrated in the world financial centres. "You get to work in a handful of glamorous cities like New York, Hong Kong and Paris." said one senior banking lawyer. Within the UK, there is a chasm between work done by the inner core of top City specialists, such as **Allen & Overy**, **Clifford Chance**, **Linklaters** and **Freshfields Bruckhaus Deringer**, and other firms. The complexity and value of the transactions are greater at the larger City firms, whose clients tend to be international merchant and investment banks. There are also prominent and reputable national firms based in the northern financial centres such as **Addleshaw Booth & Co** and **DLA**.

At the leading City firms with strong banking practices – such as **Allen & Overy** and **Clifford Chance** – deals are cutting edge and clients are prestigious. Reflecting the global nature of the practices themselves, top City banking deals can span continents and cover the front pages of the Financial Times. Stephen Lucas at **Clifford Chance** believes that this creates a "culture of high level support and a great degree of sophistication." Modern technology and the use of precedents frequently means a time-critical deal can be pulled off quickly instead of having to reinvent the wheel every time.

Regional firms with well-developed banking practices see a very different type of work. Their client base may consist of smaller retail banks or building societies. As Richard Papworth from

Addleshaw Booth & Co in Leeds explains, "the reality is that you won't see a huge number of multi-billion pound international financings. However the quality of the work can be high and young lawyers have a lot of opportunities to get actively involved."

Banking involves less 'pure law' than other practice areas – "there is more emphasis on the preparation of contracts and the financial side of things than on legality – the satisfaction tends to come from the delivery and completion of projects, seeing something through from start to finish." The work is dominated by transactions but there is a fast turnaround. This can be an attractive feature to those with short attention spans; "you don't get bogged down in things which go on for years. You see things through relatively quickly."

Although perceived as a niche area, banking overlaps with many other disciplines. Invariably lawyers will be involved in financing a range of things – property, corporate acquisitions or a power project for example. Stephen Lucas from **Clifford Chance** described this spread – "you are very often managing a transaction involving a number of different specialisms. You become the focus for that because you represent the deliverer or the recipient of the finance so you have to manage a large team." Banking is not a support department. It occupies a frontal position facing the clients – the providers of the money.

Among the more complex structured banking transactions, you will touch on a cross-section of almost all basic legal knowledge and will need to know how these areas work. Stephen Lucas describes how it involves a peripheral knowledge of many other areas – "If a company wants to buy another publicly listed company but doesn't have the money to do so, it borrows from banks, it will secure that borrowing on its assets and on the assets of the target company – its shares, its intellectual property and real estate. When the financing and the loan agreement are underway, you need to understand the corporate regime that will allow company A to buy company B because that is what you're funding. Although you're not documenting that corporate sale purchase agreement you need to understand the way it works, because it has to tie in with the financing."

Banking law is definitely placed at the glamorous end of the profession. Prestigious high finance deals and international travel are common. "The banking lawyer is always more glamorous than his tax counterpart!" said one categorically. Another lawyer enjoyed the travel and exposure to other cultures.

"I've been able to travel to Moscow and other exotic cities taking advantage of several working opportunities!" However it is also hard work and you should enter banking law for the right reasons. One lawyer loved his area but was understated and philosophical. "Some people will say there is nothing glamorous about international travel, hotels or getting on the front page of the FT. Sometimes you're exhausted."

There are certain macho stereotypes associated with banking lawyers. The practitioners interviewed were keen to stress that these are unfair caricatures of a small minority. Like the banking profession itself, lawyers are frequently outgoing and dynamic and sometimes exhibit a certain bravado. Salary rewards are high, however, and the 'work hard, play hard' maxim is never far from the norm.

a day in the life of....

On a day to day level, banking lawyers operate in small transaction management teams spanning the range of seniority. It is a meeting intensive environment involving a lot of documentation, managing several supporting aspects of the transaction such as the availability of funding. There is a high premium placed on technical ability and judgement. At **Addleshaw Booth & Co**, juniors would be permitted to handle the documentation for a straightforward bank or building society loan from very early on. More complex transactions require additional experience and supervision but this is an area of law where early responsibility is common. "I love doing what I do," said one young lawyer enthusiastically, "sealing big transactions and negotiating contracts. Banking law is the pivot which allows you do that."

Newly qualified banking lawyers will usually see a good deal of the work – mainly because they will be given a lot of drafting and asked to attend a lot of meetings. This has its rewards: "the interaction with the business world is excellent – banking law gives such a good understanding of financial markets." On a new deal, banking lawyers will assist on structuring issues, give advice and work on the completion of a deal, culminating in the drafting and signing of a loan agreement. One young lawyer summed up the appeal: "I really enjoy the big deals" and contact with "very on the ball clients!"

The lifestyle implications for banking lawyers can be tough and days rarely predictable. One lawyer humorously confirmed its commonly held reputation for long and strenuous hours – "banking could certainly be recognised as being at the stickier end of quality of life," but the pay-off can be huge. "There is so much adrenalin in deal completion." The demands are intensive because of the cyclical nature of transactional management – peaks and troughs rather than core repeat business is the norm. A normal 50 hour week can easily rise to 75 or 100 hours as a deal nears completion. Working into the early hours is not uncommon, even in the early stages of a career. However, banking lawyers universally speak of the buzz of completing a deal – a major motivational force.

Dedication is a fundamental requirement as transactions vary from the very simple to very complicated ones. Some keep you in the office from 9-6 pm, some keep you there from 9-6 am and you can gravitate towards the type of complexity and deal that suits you – often dependent on the firm or its specialist area.

skills needed

Strong practical intelligence...analytical skills...keen interest and understanding of business and international finance...the ability to dedicate to the task, to see it through to completion...commitment...sense of humour...diligence, accuracy and care...the capacity to do routine work in the early stages of your career....

career options

Many young lawyers at City firms view banking law as an ideal platform for the financial markets with the potential to open up future doors. There is frequently an overlap and fluidity with the banking world itself. It is relatively common for lawyers with a couple of years PQE to move to an investment banking or corporate finance role. With slightly more legal experience, movement to an in-house legal position within a bank is another common option. However, Stephen Lucas from **Clifford Chance** warns against making the wrong career move – "If you want to become a banker, become a banker not a lawyer. It's really that simple. Don't spend time at university studying law, CPE, LPC, articles etc. – you'd be a four year qualified banker by the same stage. However, if you want to be a banking lawyer, but decide it's not for you, there is ample opportunity soon after qualification to move into banking." This is a big-money world. Salary levels in all related areas are similarly placed, if not even higher. Even at very junior levels, secondments to international banks are made available by most firms and can provide a taster of things to come.

leading banking firms

All information on leading firms comes from the Chambers Guide to the Legal Profession 2000-2001.
Allen & Overy: Perceived to have retained the *"qual-*

ity edge" over **Clifford Chance** on the domestic scene, this *"first class"* firm's banking output is described as *"top products produced by focused and tough negotiating players"* who *"never make mistakes."* The bulk of the firm's work is for lenders, with around 20% of the client base consisting of large borrowers such as GEC and British Aerospace. One of the major features of the firm which our market research revealed was the *"great lengths the firm goes to to teach the juniors what is in the documents,"* there thus being *"no reason to suspect the quality of A&O lawyers."* This junior level, which is encouraged to develop a portfolio of specialisms, also benefits from the firm's willingness to promote quickly to partner level, which has allowed the firm to develop as the market expands. Split into five groups, the *"balanced and constructive"* London banking team has around 150 lawyers whose total billings increased by over 20% in 1999, advising 800-plus banking and borrower clients. London is still the centre of gravity for financial transactions in Europe. The firm has seen fit to reinforce Continental offices (particularly Paris and Frankfurt) with highly rated partners as it attempts to gain global banking hegemony. Already, over 40% of the firm's banking partners are based outside the UK, a number that is set to increase. This translated into acting on over 40 cross-border deals worth over $100bn in the past year. These deals include advising an 11-bank syndicate financing a Euro30bn loan for Vodafone's hostile bid for Mannesmann.

Clifford Chance: *"They are still the firm with the broadest spread of office and as a result have the geographical edge on A&O."* A practice which has grown dramatically and keeps on growing, enabling the firm to have a base of specialists, a depth of practice and a range which keeps them at the top of the pile. This range and depth has been further developed with the addition of strong US and German banking capabilities. Added to this is expertise in other financial areas – Rogers & Wells includes a leading finance litigation practice whilst Pünder has an active securi-

ties practice. The volume of business has thus risen dramatically as has the deal size. With the mergers, finance as a whole (including asset finance and capital markets) now takes up 35% of the firm's workload (of which banking is half). The market perceives the upper echelons of CC's banking practice to be peopled with *"charmers."* Whilst the firm has outstanding partners, reservations were expressed as to consistency of quality throughout the *"vast"* banking practice. Nevertheless, it was widely accepted that *"when they dedicate themselves to a task and resource it properly"* they *"get it right and don't mess around."* With the vast majority of deals now being of a cross-border nature, large deals include the bond issue in Olivetti, and acting for Deutsche in financing Mannesmann purchases from Olivetti. The majority of the firm's clients are financials, with Chase Manhattan, Citibank, Merrill Lynch and Morgan Stanley among its largest sources of fees. Other deals in which the team advised on financings include Cable & Wireless' investment in the One2One network. Buy-out activity saw the firm active on Findus European frozen fish and Thomson Directories buy-outs. The firm is becoming more active in new areas such as telebanking, e-commerce and intra-day trading, and has introduced an online deal room.

Freshfields Bruckhaus Deringer: Known for its borrower client base, the firm is widely respected for its work on large cross-border lending work, including Repsol's acquisition of YPF, Air Liquide's joint bid for BOC, Thomson-CSF for Racal and Generali's bid for INA. Two factors contribute to the Freshfields' reputation as a banking team concentrated on borrowers – the immense reputation of the corporate (M&A, competition and tax) teams and the firm's historic relationship with the Bank of England, a relationship which seemed to preclude them from developing close relationships with private lenders. However, although heavily involved in acquisitions generated from the corporate side, the banking practice is very much standalone, with lending clients such as Citibank and Chase, and borrower clients such as One2One, who have no relationship with the corporate team. Not regarded as a volume outfit, the firm does an *"excellent job"* on complex transactions, including tax-driven work.

Linklaters: Making inroads into lender work, the *"supremely competent"* banking team is seen to have *"come on apace"* to such an extent that most see them *"slightly ahead of the rest"* yet still below the two London banking giants. The practice has hired during the year and team members are *"a good crowd to deal with."* As a whole, work for the lenders takes up around 60% of the practice's workload, yet due to the leading corporate side, borrowers tend to dominate in M&A related financings (the firm advised Vodafone on corporate and financing issues for its Airtouch and Mannesmann bids). In 1999 the team acted on 54 M&A related financings totalling $93.8bn. With a strong corporate side and respected alliance partners throughout Western Europe (the team also has US capacity in London), the practice has been increasingly involved in cross-border financings, advising US and continental based banks and venture capital houses. On the borrower side, as well as the Vodafone financings, the team advised Jazz Telecom, a Spanish start-up telecoms provider, on a Euro300m secured syndicated loan facility.

Lovells: The practice is *"excellent"* on MBOs and general acquisition finance. Additionally it has an active retail banking and bank regulatory practice, advising Dresdner Kleinwort Benson on the £114m take-private of Sanderson Group Plc by Alchemy Partners.

Norton Rose: The firm takes a *"precision bombing approach"* to banking, concentrating resources on specific financial areas. Although the banking team is perceived to be a large one, it does not consider itself to have the resources for 'commodity' (i.e. high volume) lending work. Main areas of work include acquisition finance, bid financing and telecoms financing, with additional competence in trade finance, export credit work, sovereign and regulatory work. Perceived to be pulling the international side together, the finance team has 40 partners in total around the world. Correspondingly, the proportion of international work is increasing. The market considers that the firm's complementary finance areas, such as asset finance and capital markets are moving ahead thereby boosting the banking practice.

Slaughter and May: Whilst the corporate firm tag sticks to Slaughters it does *"high quality"* and *"effective"* banking work – *"everything they do is good."* It is a testament to this ability that, although not perceived by peers as *"having the volume"* of the more banking-centric City firms, the team has nevertheless acted on some of the largest financings of the year, including acting for Telecom Italia's banks on the defence to Olivetti's takeover. Acting at the top end of acquisition finance work, the practice has also been involved on legal developments in the bank lending area, as part of the LMA's working group on loan agreements alongside its magic circle rivals. The strength of the firm's domestic and international client base means that it has experience dealing at the highest end of acquisition finance deals. Large deals where the firm advised the banks include a Euro13bn facility for KPN (for the E-Plus acquisition) and a Euro2.6bn facility for companies within the Royal Numico Group. Major lending clients include JP Morgan, CSFB and ABN AMRO. On the borrower side the firm worked on raising £1bn for Punch Tavern's bid for Allied Domecq's retailing business, and the firm has advised borrowers including British Steel, Hunstman and Mannesman on financing activities. The firm also acts for the corporate treasury function of major corporates, including Diageo and Bunzl. The practice is particularly strong on cross-discipline transactions, requiring lawyers with corporate, banking and capital markets knowledge, and is seen on tax-driven transactions.

Burges Salmon, Bristol: *"They divide the market with Osborne Clarke."* The banking practice is deemed to *"have momentum"* and for peers outside the region is a practice which *"can deliver."* Up to half of the practice's work is sourced from London, and it is growing its lenders client base. Core work is acquisition finance where the firm works for a relatively even mix of borrowers and lenders. The team is also active in asset finance, trade finance, treasury work and property finance.

Osborne Clarke OWA, Bristol, Reading: Acquisition finance is the practice's bread and butter, working for senior lenders as well as management and venture capital companies (the firm has a strong corporate practice). Involved in property, corporate restructuring and insolvency. Appreciated for its *"get on with it attitude,"* the team is highly rated, and seen to be *"pulling in the higher grade work"* with the help of the London office.

Pinsent Curtis, Birmingham: An excellent reputation in banking is ascribed to the *"size of their team"* and their *"dedicated senior quality."* Public to privates this year include Pemberstone plc and Epwin Group. The practice works mainly for the large regional lenders, but also advises borrowers in conjunction with a strong corporate team. Over half of the team's work has a London component. Also works on legal opinions for US-based and other foreign clients.

Wragge & Co, Birmingham: Highly rated for its *"hands-on, cooperative"* approach. It works on City-generated, national and international deals from its Birmingham base, for a mixed base of borrowers and lenders. Corporate lending (including acquisition finance) takes up a third of the practice's time, with restructuring and insolvency taking a third and property and projects the remainder. Within pure banking, the bulk of work is in acquisition finance.

Dickinson Dees, Newcastle: *"Broad, strong and dominant."* The practice deals for a majority of lending clients, although the strong corporate side brings in more than a fair share of borrower work, which has enabled the practice to gain solid acquisition finance experience. A full time banking assistant works in the team with two to three other associates working part time in the department. On property finance these are joined by pure lending lawyers in the property department.

Addleshaw Booth & Co, Leeds, Newcastle: *"The best all-round team."* With trans-Pennine strength and an office in London, the firm is now more of a national player. Relationships with such clients as Yorkshire Bank and 3i Group ensure that the firm is still seen as being dominant in the Leeds market for *"general"* banking work. However, market perception is that local rivals Hammond Suddards have caught up in acquisition finance. With 3i less dominant in acquisition finance in Leeds, the firm has been doing more recent work on the lending side. Other significant business areas include property finance, housing association finance, building society and treasury and capital markets work, where the firm works principally for issuers.

Hammond Suddards Edge, Leeds: Regarded as *"top in acquisition finance."* The firm's premier reputation in acquisition finance is seen to rest solely on the shoulders of its partner. Although not regarded as having as much strength in other areas, the firm is also involved in housing association, reconstruction and property finance work, working for banks, building societies and corporates.

Eversheds, Leeds, Newcastle: A team with a broad spread of banking expertise, the practice's work ranges from corporate treasury matters to Muslim banking products. In finance the firm is known more for its PFI work, but the banking side is seen as a *"cracking general practice which knows what it's doing."* Areas of activity have included property and telecoms financing, and e-commerce business.

LEADING FIRMS

LONDON	BANKING	LONDON	BANKING
Allen & Overy	******	Lovells	****
Ashurst Morris Crisp	***	Macfarlanes	**
Clifford Chance	******	Norton Rose	****
CMS Cameron McKenna	**	Shearman & Sterling	***
Denton Wilde Sapte	***	Simmons & Simmons	**
DLA	*	Slaughter and May	****
Freshfields Bruckhaus Deringer	*****	Taylor Joynson Garrett	**
Gouldens	*	Travers Smith Braithwaite	**
Herbert Smith	***	Watson, Farley & Williams	*
Linklaters	*****	Weil, Gotshal & Manges	**

SOUTH AND SOUTH WEST	BANKING	SOUTH AND SOUTH WEST	BANKING
Blake Lapthorn, *Fareham*	***	CMS Cameron McKenna, *Bristol*	****
Bond Pearce, *Bristol, etc*	*****	Lester Aldridge, *Bournemouth*	***
Burges Salmon, *Bristol*	******	Osborne Clarke OWA, *Bristol*	******

WALES, MIDLANDS & E. ANGLIA	BANKING	WALES, MIDLANDS & E. ANGLIA	BANKING
Edwards Geldard, *Cardiff*	*****	Hammond Suddards Edge, *Birmingham*	***
Eversheds, *Cardiff*	******	Martineau Johnson, *Birmingham*	****
Morgan Cole, *Cardiff*	*****	Pinsent Curtis, *Birmingham*	******
Browne Jacobson, *Nottingham*	**	Shoosmiths, *Northampton*	**
DLA, *Birmingham*	***	Wragge & Co, *Birmingham*	******
Eversheds, *Birmingham, Nottingham*	*****	Eversheds, *Cambridge, Ipswich, Norwich*	******
Gateley Wareing, *Birmingham*	****	Mills & Reeve, *Cambridge, Norwich*	*****

THE NORTH	BANKING	THE NORTH	BANKING
Addleshaw Booth & Co, *Manchester*	*****	Dickinson Dees, *Newcastle upon Tyne*	******
Chaffe Street, *Manchester*	****	Eversheds, *Newcastle upon Tyne*	*****
Cobbetts, *Manchester*	***	Robert Muckle, *Newcastle-upon-Tyne*	****
Davies Wallis Foyster, *Liverpool, Manc.*	***	Ward Hadaway, *Newcastle upon Tyne*	*****
DLA, *Liverpool, Manchester*	******	Addleshaw Booth & Co, *Leeds*	******
Eversheds, *Manchester, Leeds*	******	DLA, *Leeds*	***
Garretts, *Manchester*	***	Hammond Suddards Edge, *Leeds*	*****
Halliwell Landau, *Manchester*	******	Pinsent Curtis, *Leeds*	***
Hammond Suddards Edge, *Manchester*	***	Walker Morris, *Leeds*	***
Kuit Steinart Levy, *Manchester*	**		

corporate law

All commercial law firms are keen to be involved in corporate work. Transactions in this area command large fees and receive coverage in the national and regional press. Experienced corporate lawyers are much in demand and are among the highest paid in the profession, earning six figure salaries in some instances.

The core of corporate work relates to mergers and acquisitions (M&A) and corporate restructurings. Requiring large amounts of capital, this type of work is often interdependent with finance (banking and capital markets work) and thus often comes under the umbrella name of corporate finance. Companies fund their acquisitions by a variety of means. They may restructure, disposing of certain assets not considered essential to their core business in order to raise capital. If they are privately held, they may decide to raise finance by 'going public.' This involves an offering of their shares to the public (an equity offering), including institutional investors like pension funds, on any of the public stock exchanges such as the London or New York Stock Exchanges. If they are already public companies, they may make a rights issue (offer of new shares). They may also raise money via debt. This may take the form of loans from the 'market' (bonds) or from banks or other specific financial institutions (see banking). Finance is often raised by a combination of these methods for a complex high value deal.

Other areas of corporate practice are joint ventures and buy-outs. Buy-outs can be simply the present management raising capital to take control of their company (an MBO). Buy-out companies like 3i often fund this type of deal. Often the buy-out company will itself pinpoint the deal and take a controlling interest in the target. These sorts of deals can involve the buy-out company borrowing a large amount of capital proportionate to its underlying value, hence the term 'leveraged buy-outs.' Companies can bring in other buy-out companies to spread the risk and the values of the buy-outs can be as large as any public take-over. **Ashurst Morris Crisp** for example, advised Cinven and Citicorp Venture Capital on the £825m acquisition of William Hill. Joint ventures can be structured in the form of a partnership through the formation of a new company or under a contractual arrangement. These can be as huge as the £800m HMV Media Group joint venture (advised by **Rowe & Maw**) which includes the HMV, Dillons and Waterstones music and book retail outlets.

type of work

Corporate work depends on the size and location of the firm. Large City firms act for listed companies on the stock exchange, and deal with household names such as BT, BP and Tesco. Smaller City and regional firms tend to advise leading regional private companies and a handful of FTSE 250 companies.

The distinction between stock exchange and private company work is more than just the size of the company. Private companies' M&A work is amicable because the deal can only proceed if all parties agree to it, whereas stock market companies can be subject to hostile take-overs.

Lawyers advising on private company acquisitions will help draft the sale and purchase agreements, arrange the financing for the deal and carry out a process known as 'due diligence.' The sale, purchase and financing negotiations are usually carried out between company board members and lawyers. Trainees are not expected to take a lead role in negotiating the agreement, although they may be asked to attend the meetings. A private company sale takes about a month to complete. Whereas a trainee can expect to be involved in one or two deals at a time, newly qualifieds can expect to be working on several at once under the supervision of different partners.

Trainees and students on work experience tend to carry out due diligence work – a time consuming but necessary task to ensure honesty between a purchaser (known as a bidder) and a company being purchased (known as a target). If a target claims to be the largest widget manufacturer in the country, then it could be the trainee's job to check this is true. Trainees will also be expected to check that the target is not involved in outstanding litigation and does not have damaging 'change of control' clauses, which could harm profitability after a takeover.

Stock exchange deals are different. Private companies have few shareholders (owners). Stock exchange-registered companies can have millions. This makes them vulnerable to hostile takeover bids from rival companies who can buy shares and thereby obtain a controlling stake.

To help public companies combat this threat, the stock exchange has developed a detailed takeover code to govern both friendly and hostile M&A activity. The code sets a strict timetable for companies to make and respond to potential bidders and sets out detailed guidelines for the treatment of shareholders. Lawyers advising these companies know this code inside out, and will explain what company directors should be doing at every stage of a potential acquisition. If a merger or acquisition is agreed, corporate lawyers will advise on the formation of the new or modified company and any required financing.

a day in the life...

The hours a trainee is expected to work depends on the type of deal and the individual managers. A partner in a medium-sized London firm said trainees could expect to work an average of five-and-a-half days a week. Working three 20 hour days in a row may be unusual, but should not be dismissed

out of hand. In public company takeover work strict timetables under the yellow and blue books must be adhered to. This often results in 'all-nighters' to ensure that all the due diligence exercise is watertight and that all the necessary final agreements and documentation are prepared according to the timetables. Private company work can be equally time pressured with the client pushing for the best deal in the shortest time.

However, trainees and newly qualifieds who excel in company work seem to thrive in pressured situations where the need to have an eye for detail is paramount.

Because corporate work is often a whole new world for trainees, they can find it takes time to adjust. But Mark Rawlinson, corporate partner with **Freshfields**, would urge trainees not to be put off in their first few months. "I hated my first six months in the corporate department and found it difficult," says Rawlinson." But a senior property lawyer who had been a captain in the marines said to me that I'd make a good corporate lawyer, so I went back and tried it again. After the first 18 months, it began to get more interesting. The trouble is as a trainee everything moves at 100mph and there's such a lot to take in."

skills needed...

....not for the fainthearted...ability to work long hours under extreme pressure...media-friendliness...you enjoy seeing the deals you do in the newspapers and meeting high quality, high profile people on deals where there's a lot of money at stake...good presentation skills...ability to think on your feet...decisiveness...confidence, tact and clear communication skills...a good eye for detail... patience and understanding....

career options

Currently the corporate world is expanding, particularly boosted by the growth in IT/e-commerce. This has benefited many of the smaller City firms and those in the regions. Although the work undertaken by the regional firms is often of a lower value, it can still involve tricky cross-border negotiations. At the smaller end of the market, transactions tend to focus on private equity financing, AIM (Alternative Investment Market) or Ofex flotations, often following the specialisms of the firms. Watch out also for the growing influence of US law firms acting out of their London office. Whilst at the moment only a small number of these firms (e.g **Weil Gotshal & Manges**, **Shearman & Sterling**) are running deals without the support of their big brothers across the pond, the ability to leverage US style relationships with major investment banks should not be overlooked.

The reward for working in a large commercial department of a smaller firm (both in the regions and in London) is often involvement in a client's affairs at an earlier stage. These larger regional firms also provide the opportunity, like their City counterparts, for qualified lawyers to be seconded to major clients. **Osborne Clarke OWA** has had a corporate lawyer at South Western Electricity plc for example.

A sound grounding in corporate finance makes an excellent springboard for working in industry. Many lawyers move in-house to major companies at an early stage of their careers, tempted by salaries comparable with private practice, but more predictable hours.

Moves in-house do occur at partner level, but they are less common.

Another popular move among young corporate finance lawyers is to join the banking world, either as an in-house lawyer or as a corporate finance executive or analyst. This is a chance to move from 'lawyer' to 'client.' Those who have made the transition seem to enjoy the dynamic pace of life and are glad to have shed the advisory role. Such moves generally occur early on, but high profile moves of senior partners to investment banks is not uncommon.

Becoming a company secretary and advising board members on their internal legal compliance procedures is an alternative route. This position is suitable for senior lawyers with a general range of company and commercial skills and salaries can be in excess of £100,000.

Although an in-house career is increasingly common for corporate lawyers, the majority of lawyers are happy working in private practice. Nigel Boardman originally trained at **Slaughters** in 1973 and has remained in the corporate department – apart from a two year break working for a major bank – ever since. If you enjoy corporate work, it seems you are reluctant to leave the lifestyle behind.

leading firms

All information on leading firms comes from the Chambers Guide to the Legal Profession 2000-2001.

Freshfields Bruckhaus Deringer: European M&A opportunities are said to be behind the merger with Bruckhaus Westrick Heller Lober and this has strengthened the firm's expansionist policy, setting out its stall to be the pre-eminent European firm. This fits well with market perception of it *"leading the global domination charge."* A *"centrally-led, tight management structure"* has led *to "rigorous quality"* at partner level and a collegiate atmosphere which encourages its younger partners to gain invaluable experience on big ticket deals. Recent transactions include advising EMI on the merger between its music businesses and Time Warner, advising Royal Bank of Scotland on its £25.5 bn bid for NatWest and advising Mannesmann on the £80bn hostile takeover bid by Vodafone Airtouch.

Linklaters: Currently facing a massive management challenge as it spreads its *"philosophy of control and seduction"* throughout the Alliance partners, yet perceived by the market to have already *"achieved amazing inroads, acting on a global scale."* The firm has a culture of commerciality with *"lawyers bred to think about the client first."* However, it is occasionally felt to have too heavily pursued a cult of the personality which overshadows its junior partners. The team has partners focusing on specialist industry groups such as healthcare, telecoms and IT, utilities and transport. Major deals of the year include acting for Vodafone on its hostile bid for Mannesmann, as well as its merger with Airtouch, and the defence of NatWest from a hostile bids from RBS (£21bn) and the Bank of Scotland (£25bn).

Slaughter and May: "*Traditionally the best franchise of the* [big] *three*" with an enviable dominance of the global plc market. The question most posed by the market is the credibility of its 'Best Friends' policy. This international strategy has divided opinion with the firm seen as "*conservative,*" "*uniquely British, holding a dominant position*" and "*certainly no fool*" in its relationships with highly regarded firms such as Hengeler Mueller Weitzel Wirtz (Germany) and Uria y Menendez (Spain). However, the huge consolidation in the European corporate market has led concerned competitors to opine that a strong marriage will be more effective than friendships in the long run. Recent major deals include acting for Orange on its sale to France Telecom, advising Unilever on its proposed acquisition of Bestfoods and for Glaxo Wellcome on its merger with SmithKline Beecham.

Allen & Overy: A firm which had "*made a fortune with its remarkable banking and securities practice*" is perceived to be moving out of that shadow with heavy investment in the corporate team. More often seen acting as counsel for the financials in the largest M&A transactions, such as the finance arrangers for Vodafone's bid for Mannesmann. The international network, particularly strong in Germany, France, Italy and Spain, has led to extensive "*impressive, deal-generating capabilities*" both in cross border transactions and those requiring multi-jurisdictional advice. Acted for Heineken on the acquisition of Cruzcampo (Spain's largest brewer, value $1 bn) and for CSFB and Morgan Stanley on Bank of Scotland's £22bn bid for NatWest.

Clifford Chance: "*Proud of what they have done for the London profession,*" is a universally reflected view of the firm's international strategy. Its multi-jurisdictional capabilities and, in particular, the merger with Rogers & Wells (US) and Pünder (Germany), has strengthened the international M&A resource also providing an essential securitisation facility. A prime example of this transatlantic approach appeared in the integrated US and UK advice given to Lend Lease Corporation on the acquisition of Bovis from P&O. However, overall perception is of increased volume rather than value. Advised CGU on its merger with Norwich Union and Morgan Stanley on the formation of Allied Zurich into a single holding company valued at £24bn.

Herbert Smith: "*Refocused well and made great strides.*" The firm is praised across the board for promoting "*hard working, fine individuals*" into the driving seat of its major deals, thereby producing a "*bright, intelligent*" team who are "*fired up.*" Big-ticket deals have been abundant this year, particularly "*out of the ordinary cross border transactions*" in the IT sector (advised CSFB on the QXL.com's IPO). However, the lack of a clearly-defined international strategy is considered by many to be a drawback for the firm's future prospects, and it is felt that "*it will be difficult for them to sustain growth in a primarily international field.*" Advised Publicis on its £4bn acquisition of Saatchi & Saatchi, acted for Time Warner on EU aspects of its merger with AOL and advised Olivetti on its successful hostile bid for Telecom Italia.

leading regional firms

Osborne Clarke OWA, Bristol, Reading: "*A good firm with quality people,*" and generally recognised to be "*the benchmark for other firms.*" The judicious poaching of leading lawyers from rival firms and a dynamic management team is increasingly taking OC into a league of its own. High-fliers can expect a fast track to partnership. In Bristol, the corporate finance team has recently "*pulled ahead of Burges Salmon*" to take the number one slot. Meanwhile, the

Reading team "*has made quite a big impact*" on the Thames Valley and "*is seen to be there, or just about there, in everything which comes up.*" The fundamental question is whether Osborne Clarke is now a regional firm with a London office, or a London firm with regional offices. Commentators have already noted that "*there's not enough work for them in the South West,*" and that "*they're slowly moving the balance of their work to their London office.*"

Burges Salmon, Bristol: "*Along with Osborne Clarke, they are head and shoulders above the rest.*" Generally considered to be more conservative and locally focused than OC, the firm has a particularly strong transport client base. Typical work handled over the last year includes acting for Newco in its $60m cross border buyout of the US and UK operations of Spear Group, and acting for Bridport plc on its take-over by West Washington in a £30m public to private transaction. Recently acted for Orange on its acquisition of Ananova for £95m.

Wragge & Co, Birmingham: This firm retains its premier rating as the "*number one firm*" for corporate finance work in the Midlands. The firm is the largest single site corporate practice outside London, and has a strategy of being a 'City' firm based in Birmingham. There are four limbs to the firm's transactional practice. The first is acting for major national and international corporations on M&As. The second is acting for plcs with significant Midlands presence. The third is acting for IT/telecom businesses, and the fourth is acting in the private equity arena for both investor and investee clients. Overall the firm is seen to be "*very commercial*" and "*willing to get the job done.*" The one-office approach seems to be "*paying handsome dividends for them*" at present, although there has been comment in the market that eventually the firm will need to expand into other regions in order to better service its ever-growing client base, which is situated all around the country and increasingly on the Continent. The firm recently advised on a £500m outsourcing project by British Airways and acted for Preussag AG in its £700m plus joint venture with West LB and Carlson Inc to form the Thomas Cook Group.

Addleshaw Booth & Co, Manchester: This firm is still seen as the "*undisputed leader*" for corporate finance work in the North West, particularly in terms of resources and client base, although it is not as far ahead of the field as in previous years. Possessing a "*treasure trove of plc lawyers,*" and strong on private equity, the firm has "*the clients that everyone else wants.*" The firm recently acted for Airtours plc in the £852m share exchange offers for the whole of the ordinary and convertible preference share capital of First Choice Holidays plc. Another highlight for the firm was acting for BWI plc on the £85.2m recommended takeover of the company by a German purchaser.

LEADING FIRMS

LONDON	CORPORATE FINANCE: 60+ SOLICITORS IN CORPORATE TEAM	CORPORATE FINANCE: 30-60 SOLICITORS IN CORPORATE TEAM	CORPORATE FINANCE: FEWER THAN 30 SOLICITORS IN CORP TEAM
Allen & Overy	*****		
Ashurst Morris Crisp	***		
Baker & McKenzie		****	
Beachcroft Wansbroughs			**
Berwin Leighton		****	
Biddle			****
Bird & Bird			*****
Charles Russell			**
Clifford Chance	*****		
CMS Cameron McKenna	*		
Coudert Brothers			**
D J Freeman		**	
Dechert		**	
Denton Wilde Sapte	*		
DLA		***	
Eversheds		**	
Field Fisher Waterhouse			*****
Fox Williams			**
Freshfields Bruckhaus Deringer	******		
Gouldens		****	
Hammond Suddards Edge			******
Harbottle & Lewis			****
Herbert Smith	*****		
Hobson Audley			**
Howard Kennedy			***
Lawrence Graham			*****
Laytons			**
Lewis Silkin			***
Linklaters	******		
Lovells	***		
Macfarlanes		******	
Manches			*
Marriott Harrison			**
Memery Crystal			****
Middleton Potts			*
Nabarro Nathanson		****	
Nicholson Graham & Jones			****

LONDON	CORPORATE FINANCE: 60+ SOLICITORS IN CORPORATE TEAM	CORPORATE FINANCE: 30-60 SOLICITORS IN CORPORATE TEAM	CORPORATE FINANCE: FEWER THAN 30 SOLICITORS IN CORPORATE TEAM
Norton Rose	****		
Olswang		****	
Osborne Clarke OWA			******
Paisner & Co			******
Pinsent Curtis			*****
Radcliffes			*
Rakisons			*
Richards Butler			*****
Rowe & Maw		******	
Simmons & Simmons	**		
Sinclair Roche & Temperley			****
SJ Berwin & Co		*****	
Slaughter and May	******		
Stephenson Harwood		**	
Taylor Joynson Garrett		***	
Theodore Goddard		***	
Travers Smith Braithwaite		*****	
Warner Cranston			*****
Watson, Farley & Williams			****
Wedlake Bell			**

THE SOUTH	CORPORATE FINANCE	THE SOUTH	CORPORATE FINANCE
Argles Stoneham Burstows, *Crawley*	****	**Paris Smith & Randall,** *Southampton*	****
Blake Lapthorn, *Fareham, Portsmouth, Southampton*	******	**Rawlison & Butler,** *Crawley*	****
		Shadbolt & Co, *Reigate*	****
Bond Pearce, *Southampton*	******	**Shoosmiths,** *Solent*	****
Brachers, *Maidstone*	***	**Stevens & Bolton,** *Guildford*	*****
Clyde & Co, *Guildford*	***	**Thomas Eggar Church Adams,** *Chichester, Horsham, Reigate, Worthing*	***
Cripps Harries Hall, *Tunbridge Wells, Kent*	****		
DMH, *Brighton, Crawley*	****	**Thomson Snell & Passmore,** *T. Wells*	****
Lester Aldridge, *Bournemouth*	***		

THAMES VALLEY	CORPORATE FINANCE	THAMES VALLEY	CORPORATE FINANCE
B P Collins, *Gerrards Cross*	**	Morgan Cole, *Oxford, Reading*	***
Clarks, *Reading*	*****	Mundays, *Esher*	****
Garretts, *Reading*	***	Nabarro Nathanson, *Reading*	****
Kimbell & Co, *Milton Keynes*	****	Osborne Clarke OWA, *Reading*	******
Manches, *Oxford*	*****	Pitmans, *Reading*	****

SOUTH WEST	CORPORATE FINANCE	SOUTH WEST	CORPORATE FINANCE
Bevan Ashford, *Bristol, Exeter*	****	Laytons, *Bristol*	**
Bond Pearce, *Exeter, Plymouth*	****	Lyons Davidson, *Bristol*	*
Bretherton Price Elgoods, *Cheltenham*	*	Michelmores, *Exeter*	**
Burges Salmon, *Bristol*	*****	Osborne Clarke OWA, *Bristol*	******
Cartwrights, *Bristol*	**	Stephens & Scown, *Exeter, St Austell, Truro*	**
Charles Russell, *Cheltenham*	**		
Clark Holt, *Swindon*	**	TLT Solicitors, *Bristol*	****
CMS Cameron McKenna, *Bristol*	**	Veale Wasbrough, *Bristol*	**
Foot Anstey Sargent, *Exeter, Plymouth*	***		

WALES	CORPORATE FINANCE	WALES	CORPORATE FINANCE
Berry Smith, *Cardiff*	***	Hugh James Ford Simey, *Cardiff*	**
Bevan Ashford, *Cardiff*	***	M&A Solicitors, *Cardiff*	***
Edwards Geldard, *Cardiff*	*****	Morgan Cole, *Cardiff*	******
Eversheds, *Cardiff*	****		

MIDLANDS	CORPORATE FINANCE	MIDLANDS	CORPORATE FINANCE
Browne Jacobson, *Nottingham*	***	Harvey Ingram Owston, *Leicester*	*
DLA, *Birmingham*	****	Hewitson Becke + Shaw, *Northampton*	*
Edwards Geldard, *Nottingham*	*	Howes Percival, *Northampton*	*
Eking Manning, *Nottingham*	**	Kent Jones and Done, *Stoke-on-Trent*	*
Eversheds, *Birmingham*	*****	Knight & Sons, *Newcastle-under-Lyme*	*
Freethcartwright, *Nottingham*	**	Lee Crowder, *Birmingham*	**
Garretts, *Birmingham*	*	Martineau Johnson, *Birmingham*	***
Gateley Wareing, *Birmingham*	***	Pinsent Curtis, *Birmingham*	*****
George Green & Co, *Warley*	*	Shoosmiths, *Northampton, Nottingham*	**
Hammond Suddards Edge, *Birmingham*	***	Wragge & Co, *Birmingham*	******

EAST ANGLIA	CORPORATE FINANCE
Ashton Graham, *Bury St Edmunds*	****
Birketts, *Ipswich*	*****
Eversheds, *Ipswich, Norwich*	******
Garretts, *Cambridge*	*****
Greene & Greene, *Bury St. Edmunds*	****
Greenwoods, *Peterborough*	****

EAST ANGLIA	CORPORATE FINANCE
Hewitson Becke + Shaw, *Cambridge*	******
Mills & Reeve, *Cambridge, Norwich*	******
Prettys, *Ipswich*	*****
Steele & Co, *Norwich*	***
Taylor Vinters, *Cambridge*	******

NORTH WEST	CORPORATE FINANCE
Aaron & Partners, *Chester*	*
Addleshaw Booth & Co, *Manchester*	******
Brabner Holden Banks Wilson, *Liverpool*	**
Chaffe Street, *Manchester*	***
Cobbetts, *Manchester*	**
Davies Wallis Foyster, *Liverpool, Manchester*	**
DLA, *Liverpool, Manchester*	*****

NORTH WEST	CORPORATE FINANCE
Eversheds, *Manchester*	*****
Garretts, *Manchester*	*
Halliwell Landau, *Manchester*	****
Hammond Suddards Edge, *Manchester*	****
Kuit Steinart Levy, *Manchester*	*
Pannone & Partners, *Manchester*	*
Wacks Caller, *Manchester*	*

YORKSHIRE	CORPORATE FINANCE
Addleshaw Booth & Co, *Leeds*	******
Andrew M. Jackson & Co, *Hull*	*
DLA, *Leeds, Sheffield*	****
Eversheds, *Leeds*	*****
Garretts, *Leeds*	*
Gordons Cranswick Solicitors, *Bradford, Leeds*	*
Gosschalks, *Hull*	*

YORKSHIRE	CORPORATE FINANCE
Hammond Suddards Edge, *Leeds*	*****
Irwin Mitchell, *Leeds, Sheffield*	**
Lupton Fawcett, *Leeds*	**
Pinsent Curtis, *Leeds*	***
Read Hind Stewart, *Leeds*	**
Rollit Farrell & Bladon, *Hull*	**
Walker Morris, *Leeds*	***

NORTH EAST	CORPORATE FINANCE
Dickinson Dees, *Newcastle upon Tyne*	******
Eversheds, *Middlesbrough, Newcastle upon Tyne*	*****

NORTH EAST	CORPORATE FINANCE
Robert Muckle, *Newcastle upon Tyne*	***
Ward Hadaway, *Newcastle upon Tyne*	****
Watson Bouton, *Newcastle upon Tyne*	****

SPECIALIST PRACTICE AREAS CORPORATE FINANCE

crime

General criminal lawyers act for defendants in magistrates' courts, Crown Courts and courts martial. Whatever the seriousness of the charge, the basic process is the same. The difference is in the detail. Less serious offences are dealt with in the magistrates' courts, with the accused usually represented by a solicitor. More serious cases are tried in the Crown Courts. Though solicitors can now take exams to enable them to work as advocates in the Crown Courts, most still prefer to use a barrister.

In addition to expertise in criminal law and procedure, lawyers need to be familiar with mental health, immigration and extradition issues. This chapter deals mainly with general criminal law.

type of work

It's hard work but it can be fun. Unlike in many legal careers, you are not office-bound, and there are plenty of opportunities for advocacy. Dealing with criminal clients can often be challenging, but is not as hard as you might think. "Major criminals can be very, very interesting people" says Gerry McManus of Manchester firm **Burton Copeland**. "A lot of them have a number of problems; drugs, drink, health and psychiatric problems" says Mark Studdert, partner in Camden practice **Hodge, Jones & Allen** "but in the general scheme of things they are easy people to deal with, because they are unwilling participants in the system and want the case to go away as soon as possible."

The immediacy of the work is another plus, and criminal lawyers are often able to see the fruits of their advice and work within a relatively short time. This is particularly true for lawyers who are accredited to work as duty solicitors at magistrates' courts. Their role is to provide advocacy for those who cannot afford representation. Clients often have no idea

of how the process works and are very grateful for their intervention, which can often lead to immediate results. Because the work is date driven, cases have a quick turnover, and even murder cases are dealt with in under a year. "There is a lovely rhythm to criminal work" says Girish Thanki, partner with niche firm **Thanki Novy Taube**. "You finish it, you bill it, you get the money within a couple of months. Whether you're upbeat because you got the desired result or annoyed because you failed to, it's all over quickly and things are moving on."

Criminal law is in flux, with the Access to Justice reforms, Government Legal Aid reforms and the Human Rights Act likely to impact strongly on the present system. One major change and by far the biggest issue facing the criminal defence lawyer will be the advent of block contracting of criminal legal services. This will result in legally aided criminal defence work only being carried out by a limited number of franchised firms that can demonstrate their ability to handle the work. This may have the effect of ending high street criminal practice and concentrating criminal work in the hands of larger, specialist practices. There is some unease in the profession over the likely effect of this development; that everything will be done with an eye to costs, reducing the system to a conveyor belt. These worries are compounded by the loss of the automatic right to a jury trial – it will now be for the magistrate's court to decide whether jury trial is appropriate or not.

The precise effects of the Human Rights Act are uncertain as yet, but all courts will have to take its provisions into account in all cases. With specific articles dealing with, amongst others, the right to privacy, the right to a fair trial and freedom of expression, this will mean extra tools in the hands of the defence lawyer at every stage of the criminal process.

All this change makes it a very interesting time to become a criminal lawyer. As Mark Studdert, points out: "there have been major pieces of legislation every year that I've been in practice. Not only changing specific laws, but also the whole procedural approach. You are very much at the cutting edge of legislative changes, and of how society is dealing with its problems."

a day in the life...

Criminal lawyers lead a hectic life, particularly in small practices, where administrative pressures are greater. You might get into the office at 8.30 am, having already spent some of the night at the police station as duty solicitor. At 9.30 am, it's off to the magistrates' court for procedural and remand hearings, or a plea in mitigation. Lunch is on the hoof. The afternoon is spent interviewing clients and conferring with counsel. There is still paperwork to deal with and you could be back in the police station tonight. When at last you get home, you'll have to spend some of your 'free' time preparing for the next day's court hearing.

As a criminal trainee you will be thrown in at the deep end, with your own caseload and appearances in the magistrates' courts from day one. One of the most important elements of your training will be attending police station interviews or listening to tapes of them. You will also get to assist senior lawyers and barristers in more serious assault, rape and murder cases, and may get to sit through major trials. This breadth of opportunity and responsibility is one of the main attractions of the training.

skills needed

....an eye for fine detail...strong understanding of the law...ability to be sharp and resolute on your feet...finely honed social skills...flair...imagination ...client-handling skills..."Those with prior experience in psychology or counselling usually make excellent criminal lawyers"...empathy...good organi-

sational, administrative and IT skills...you'll need to love your work and be 100% committed to it...ability to work without reward....

career options

At the moment most high street practices handle criminal work, though, as explained above, this may change with increasing specialisation. For those seeking a good general criminal practice, Greg Powell of **Powell Spencer & Partners** has a tip. "Ask a senior probation officer, social worker or the Citizens Advice Bureau which firms they have a good relationship with."

Specialist criminal firms offer high profile criminal and civil rights work. However, training contracts in these firms are scarce as some are unable to offer experience in all areas of law required by the Law Society. Advancement for assistants may be slow as they usually have a small number of partners.

Aspiring criminal lawyers often have a preference for Legal Aid work. Many firms specialising in family and child care also have criminal departments, enabling trainees to handle the full range of Legal Aid work during training. In terms of quality, such firms are often regarded as highly as specialist criminal practices. The Crown Prosecution Service does not take trainees but recruits qualified solicitors.

leading criminal law firms

All information on leading firms comes from the Chambers Guide to the Legal Profession 2000-2001.

Bindman & Partners: This *"impressive"* practice, has a widespread reputation for civil liberties work and crime with political facets, namely race-related crimes, cases against environmental and animal rights activists, extradition, and terrorist charges. Recently represented a number of journalists and media clients against charges of violating the Official Secrets Act.

Birnberg Peirce & Partners: *"Has a corner of the market sewn up"* for high profile political and terrorist cases. It is widely felt *"you couldn't get a better lawyer* for terrorist offences" than "pre-eminent" Gareth Peirce.

Edward Fail Bradshaw & Waterson: A "top firm" particularly noted for armed robbery cases. Handle a large volume of heavyweight crime including murders, large drug cases, corruption, and bigamy.

Hodge Jones & Allen: A large team which represented a defendant in Stephen Lawrence murder case.

Kingsley Napley: Although better known for its serious fraud practice, the firm also handles a substantial number of high profile general crime cases for private clients. Well-known for defending General Pinochet, the team is also active in the Bloody Sunday Inquiry and Marchioness disaster inquiry.

Offenbach & Co: General criminal practice with an emphasis on civil liberties. Particularly noted for expertise in drug related conspiracies. Recently defended an academic researcher against computer obscenity charges.

Powell Spencer & Partners: A busy north-west London practice handling a volume of traditional crime for a community client base. Maintains dedicated police station and youth justice teams.

Saunders & Co: Criminal practice with a "reputation for quality work." Handle heavyweight drugs, murder, rape and arson cases. Involved in leading case relating to voluntary bills of indictment.

Taylor Nichol: A "committed" team with a recognised niche in cases involving miscarriage of justice. Handle "ground breaking appellate work" and defend offenders with mental disorders. One of their assistants is "the leading youth lawyer in the country."

Thanki Novy Taube: An "avant-garde" practice known for its extradition work and actions against the police. Handled Mardi Gras bomber and Regent's Canal twins murder cases.

T.V. Edwards: A volume practice with "an intelligent approach to court." Team includes two solicitor advocates with higher court rights.

Whitelock & Storr: This small practice maintains a "high standard of client care and preparation." Covers the range of traditional crime with noted expertise in extradition work.

Burton Copeland, Leeds: remains the "premier" firm in the region for both fraud work and serious traditional crime. The general crime unit contains a "fund of talent."

Sugaré & Co, Leeds: maintains a solid reputation for general crime, with a specialism in road traffic matters.

LEADING FIRMS

LONDON	CRIME	LONDON	CRIME
Alistair Meldrum & Co	****	Kingsley Napley	******
Andrew Keenan & Co	*****	Magrath & Co	****
Bindman & Partners	******	McCormacks	****
Birnberg Peirce & Partners	******	Offenbach & Co	******
Christian Fisher	*****	Powell Spencer & Partners	******
Claude Hornby & Cox	****	Russell Jones & Walker	****
Darlington & Parkinson	****	Russell-Cooke, Potter & Chapman	*****
Dundons	****	Saunders & Co	******
Duthie Hart & Duthie	*****	Simons Muirhead & Burton	*****
Edward Fail Bradshaw & Waterson	******	Taylor Nichol	******
Fisher Meredith	*****	Thanki Novy Taube	******
Hallinan, Blackburn, Gittings & Nott	*****	Tuckers	****
Henry Milner & Co	*****	TV Edwards	******
Hickman & Rose	*****	Venters Reynolds	*****
Hodge Jones & Allen	******	Victor Lissack & Roscoe	*****
J.B. Wheatley & Co	****	Whitelock & Storr	******
Joy Merriam & Co	****		

SOUTH WEST	CRIME	SOUTH WEST	CRIME
Bobbetts Mackan, *Bristol*	******	Stephens & Scown, *Exeter*	*****
Crosse & Crosse, *Exeter*	*****	Stones, *Exeter*	*****
Douglas & Partners, *Bristol*	******	Wolferstans, *Plymouth*	*****
John Boyle and Co, *Redruth*	******	Woollcombe Beer Watts, *Newton Abbot*	*****

WALES	CRIME	WALES	CRIME
Gamlins, *Rhyl*	******	Martyn Prowel Solicitors, *Cardiff*	******
Graham Evans & Partners, *Swansea*	******	Robertsons, *Cardiff*	******
Huttons, *Cardiff*	******	Spiro Grech & Co, *Cardiff*	******

MIDLANDS	CRIME	MIDLANDS	CRIME
Banners Jones Middleton, *Chesterfield*	******	Kieran & Co, *Worcester*	******
Barrie Ward & Julian Griffiths, *Nottingham*	******	Nelsons, *Nottingham*	******
		Parker & Grego, *Birmingham*	*****
Brethertons, *Rugby*	*****	Purcell Parker, *Birmingham*	*****
Eddowes Waldron, *Derby*	*****	Rees Page, *Wolverhampton*	*****
Elliot Mather, *Chesterfield*	*****	Silks, *Oldbury*	*****
Fletchers, *Nottingham*	******	The Johnson Partnership, *Nottingham*	******
George, Jonas & Co, *Birmingham*	*****	The Smith Partnership, *Derby*	******
Glaisyers, *Birmingham*	******	Tyndallwoods, *Birmingham*	*****
Hawley & Rodgers, *Loughborough*	*****	Woodford-Robinson, *Northampton*	******

EAST ANGLIA	CRIME	EAST ANGLIA	CRIME
Belmores, *Norwich*	*****	Hunt & Coombs, *Peterborough*	******
Copleys, *Huntingdon*	******	Lucas & Wyllys, *Great Yarmouth*	*****
David Charnley & Co, *Romford*	*****	Overbury Steward Eaton & Woolsey, *Norwich*	******
Fosters, *Norwich*	*****		
Gepp & Sons, *Chelmsford, Colchester*	******	Thomson Webb Corfield, *Cambridge*	*****
Gotelee & Goldsmith, *Ipswich*	*****	Twitchen Musters & Kelly, *Southend-on-Sea*	******
Hatch Brenner, *Norwich*	******		
Hegarty & Co, *Peterborough*	*****		

NORTH WEST	CRIME	NORTH WEST	CRIME
Betesh Fox & Co, *Manchester*	****	Jones Maidment Wilson incorp	*****
Brian Koffman & Co, *Manchester*	****	Hatton Scates Horton, *Manchester*	
Burton Copeland, *Manchester*	******	Linskills Solicitors, *Liverpool*	***
Cunninghams, *Manchester*	****	Maidments, *Manchester*	*****
Draycott Gibbon Moore & Wright, *Manchester*	***	R.M. Broudie & Co, *Liverpool*	****
		Russell & Russell, *Bolton*	*****
Farleys, *Blackburn*	***	The Berkson Globe Partnership, *Liverpool*	****
Forbes, *Blackburn*	****		
Garstangs, *Bolton*	*****	Tuckers, *Manchester*	*****
Jackson & Canter, *Liverpool*	***		

NORTH EAST	CRIME	NORTH EAST	CRIME
David Gray & Company, *Newcastle upon Tyne*	*****	Irwin Mitchell, *Sheffield*	*****
		Levi & Co, *Leeds*	*****
Grahame Stowe, Bateson, *Leeds*	*****	Myer Wolff & Manley, *Hull*	****
Henry Hyams & Co, *Leeds*	****	Sugaré & Co, *Leeds*	******
Howells, *Sheffield*	*****	The Max Gold Partnership, *Hull*	*****

employment law

If you are fascinated by human nature, curious about the internal workings of corporate Britain and want to be involved in the cases provoking legislative and social changes affecting everyone who has ever had a job, then perhaps you should think about employment law.

The work of an employment lawyer is a rich and varied mix of advisory, pre-emptive, contractual and litigious work. Contentious work may be in an employment tribunal, County Courts or the High Court. Many employment cases which start in the employment tribunal become test cases which are appealed to the higher courts so they may end up in the Court of Appeal, House of Lords or even the European Court of Justice. In tribunals employees ('applicants') may claim for redundancy pay, unfair and wrongful dismissal, sex, race and disability discrimination against their employers ('respondents'). Claims for breach of contract may also be made in the High Court or County Courts depending on the value of the claim.

Specialist employment teams are divided along partisan lines. The 'fat cat' firms (City firms with a corporate client base and high charge-out rates) work for employers and highly-paid senior executives. The 'right on' firms act mainly for Trade Union clients and other individuals. They often have allied practices in defendant personal injury.

type of work

'Employment law guru' Janet Gaymer is head of the leading London employment team at **Simmons & Simmons**. The firm acts primarily for employers although it does handle cases for senior executives and individuals with particularly complex cases. Janet spends much of her time building relationships with clients and developing an understanding of their businesses. "Long-term client relationships are hugely important," she states, "because so much of employment law is a question of industrial relations, communications and strategy planning." Lawyers acting for trade unions tend to be more ideologically motivated. Michael Short, head of employment at **Rowley Ashworth**, obviously relishes his battles on behalf of union members. He represented several hundred thousand employees from various manufacturing unions in their campaign to reduce the engineering industry's working week. "I suggested they set up a fund and all contribute a small amount. Then selected 'stormtroopers' in certain key areas went on strike, backed by resources from the fund. Eventually we got a challenge from British Aerospace and were served with affidavits. The last of these arrived at about midnight, with a hearing set for ten the next morning. We stayed up all night to draft our responses, but it was worth it – the working week was reduced from 39 to 37 hours." For Michael Short, this was far more satisfying than a 'big money' case.

Corporate cases can prove equally satisfying, particularly when acting for the individual. Chris Booth, a partner in the employment department at **Pinsent Curtis** in Leeds, represented the former finance director of Magnet Ltd in his claim for wrongful dismissal. "Very few cases actually go to trial," he says, "but this one lasted six weeks. In the end, we won a £500,000 settlement." Chris Booth adds, "it felt good helping the small fish win and sometimes you go beyond mere professional relationships. The FD is quite a good pal of mine now, because he thinks I did a good job."

Employment, or labour law, is by its nature highly politicised, regulating as it does the power struggle between workers and employers. Naomi Feinstein, employment partner at City firm **Lovells** says, "with the Labour Government in power and more and more European law in this area things are likely to be very lively in employment law for some time to come."

a day in the life....

8.30am: arrive in office nursing hangover and facing pile of urgent paperwork. First draft Notice of Appearance in Employment Tribunal proceedings, setting out employer's side of story in 'drunken sacking' unfair dismissal case. Make and inhale large cup of strong coffee. Consider recent instructions to draft contract of employment for senior executive.

Next turn (slightly depressed) to considering implications of Transfer of Undertakings Regs on business sale being handled by corporate colleagues. Corporate partner in charge thinks himself rather an expert on TUPE and has written detailed note on his understanding of position; i.e. TUPE does not apply. Tactfully but firmly (in view of your junior position and partner's greater ego) break it to him that TUPE does apply. All seller's employees will transfer automatically to purchaser of company. Draft letter of advice to client about potential redundancies. Client will panic. Include advice on how best to break news and consult with employees while avoiding major public relations disaster.

Receive any number of phone calls from clients' personnel managers throughout day. What do fiendish Working Time Regulations say about paid holiday? Appropriateness or otherwise of taking disciplinary action against employee in love triangle with two colleagues. Love triangle not a problem. Threatening colleagues outside work is.

8.30pm: Leave office having stayed late to prepare submissions for Employment Tribunal. No need to instruct counsel so will do own advocacy, not just sit behind barrister and fall asleep. If witnesses perform well, satisfaction of seeing evidence hit home, expertly followed up by (own) strong submissions on law. If not, rise manfully to challenge of pulling things round in closing speech or, (last resort) settling with applicant.

skills needed

....need to like and be interested in people...sensitivity...sense of humour...versatility...flexibility...practicality...ability to assimilate quick changes in strategy and advice...detailed knowledge of relevant statutes and case-law....

career options

First of all you have to make the choice between acting for applicants or respondents. The larger commercial firms act for respondents or employers. Smaller, more affordable firms act for individual employees or applicants. It is theoretically possible to cross over but rare as the decision to go to one or the other tends to be based on personal politics.

There are options to go in-house but very few companies have a large enough legal team to include a full-time employment lawyer. However Reuters has recently recruited an employment specialist because of the volume of EU legislation and the complications arising from the Human Rights Act. Towards the top end of the professional scale, lawyers may apply to chair employment tribunals; many partners in leading employment practices combine their practice with part-time tribunal chairs.

Remaining in private practice seems to be the popular choice among the lawyers we interviewed and they expressed confidence in the choice of employment law as a career. Like most litigation, the volume of work increases in times of recession.

leading employment firms

All information on leading firms comes from the Chambers Guide to the Legal Profession 2000-2001.

Simmons & Simmons: A "*quality practice that can't be ignored*" remains the market leader in London for respondent employment work. Disruptions affecting the rest of the firm have made no impact on this "*well structured and well managed department which delivers results.*" The group maintains its "*top of the tree*" position largely thanks to its "*first class client list*" on employers in FTSE and plc companies, financial services, arts organisations, and high profile public bodies.

Baker & McKenzie: Has ably weathered the loss of its star Fraser Younson over a year ago to **McDermott Will & Emery** but is still seen to be lacking a big hitter personality. The practice acts for major UK and multi-national companies and has a developed European dimension. Members are frequently called upon to advise clients in connection with European Works Council issues.

National firm **Eversheds** has links throughout the UK and is a recognised leader for employment work. The practice operates from the firm's highly rated London, Cardiff, Birmingham, Norwich, Ispwich, Manchester, Leeds, and Newcastle branches. In addition to a fair share of heavyweight contentious work, the practice advises clients on impending EU legislation and business risk analysis. A large team gives them the capability to act on large corporate mergers overseeing the project management employment aspects of change management. The team has a reputation for a *"confrontational"* approach to litigation and rates highly for its *"national coverage."* Over the past year the group was active in advising on the employment aspects of the creation of the Financial Ombudsman Scheme.

Lovells' employment team maintains a good balance and spread of work for a number of quality blue-chip clients. The practice is divided equally between contentious tribunal work, corporate support and advisory work. The firm's German connections has also increased the group's activity in pan-European employment projects. This *"energetic"* group is reputed to be *"committed to providing good client service"* and has been involved in the employment aspects of a number of corporate transactions including the merger between Trinity and Mirror.

The leading employee practice in London is **Pattinson & Brewer**. The *"first port of call"* for applicant work, these *"collective labour law specialists"* are *"good people to have batting for you"* in the employment tribunal. Team members have extensive experience of executive severances, disability discrimination cases, human rights and transfer regulation issues. This *"innovative"* team handles a large volume of work for trade unions, voluntary associations, charities and senior executive applicants. The firm also maintains an employment practice in its Chatham office. Other leaders in London include **Rowley Ashworth** and **Thompsons**. The **Rowley Ashworth** group *"thinks about problems and drafts helpful instructions."* They have acted in a substantial number of claims for holiday pay calculated in accordance with Working Time Regulations. **Thompsons** is an *"approachable"* team acting exclusively for trade unions and trade union members.

DMH, Brighton: Has a *"well-organised department"* that is seen to have the *"inside track"* on a range of employment matters. Clients range from individual employees to national chains to NHS trusts. The group acts for both sides in Disability Discrimination Act cases before the Employment Appeals Tribunal and is frequently instructed by employers in multi-applicant cases and large scale redundancy situations.

Morgan Cole, Oxford, Reading: Remains pre-eminent in the Thames Valley due to a *"breadth of expertise rarely found outside City firms."* The group acts for institutional clients including universities and NHS trusts. Corporate clients include a number of hi-tech and computer companies. Also undertakes a significant amount of work on behalf of senior executives. Recently acted in a House of Lords decision on redundancy payments, indirect discrimination and community law in Barry v Midland Bank plc.

Complex and high profile employment work in the South West is shared between **Bevan Ashford**, **Bond Pearce**, **Burges Salmon**, and **Osborne Clark OWA**. **Bevan Ashford** is *"pre-eminent in public sector work"* and renowned for advising NHS trusts throughout the South West on employment issues. This *"realistic"* team *"talks the right language"* and is highly rated for having both "resources in terms of numbers" to draw on, and a varied client base that includes multi-national and nationally based companies.

Bond Pearce, Plymouth, Southampton: Geared primarily towards employers and undertakes a substantial amount of work in retail and education sectors.

Burges Salmon, Bristol: Possesses an employer-oriented department acting for bigger plcs and some public sector organisations. This *"sensible"* team *"gives effective advice and looks after clients well"* and was noted for its *"clear, commercial way of putting things forward."*

Osborne Clarke OWA, Bristol, Reading: Acts for employers in the transport, energy, financial services, IT and technology sectors. Receiving a substantial amount of employment work from the firm's corporate departments, the team handles a fair share of deal-oriented transactional work. This *"professional"* team, *"always on top of the facts,"* was particularly noted for its drafting skills.

In Birmingham **Wragge & Co**'s fast growing employment team is able to call on an enormous commercial client base, which has led some to suggest that they are in fact a support facility for the corporate team. The group has advised on a variety of unfair dismissal and discrimination claims, and has niche strength in TUPE, restrictive covenants, maternity and working time.

In East Anglia **Hewitson Beck + Shaw**'s employment practice is spread over its Cambridge and Northampton offices. The group acts predominantly for employers and some senior executives.

Mills & Reeve, Cambridge, Norwich: Maintains a *"lawyerly"* group with the *"strength and depth to allocate their resources"* to address a range of employment concerns for local businessmen, plcs, education institutions, local authorities and NHS trusts.

Addleshaw Booth & Co, Manchester: A *"household name"* in employment law. The firm commands a *"sizeable team"* with a *"good spread"* of clients across the leisure, pharmaceuticals, banking, media, retail, and healthcare sectors.

DLA, Manchester, Liverpool: Possesses a *"quality team with a high calibre reputation."* The practice is recommended for discrimination advice, reorganisation and executive termination issues. Practitioners reportedly know how to be *"tough without being difficult"* in acting for a client base of plcs, professional partnerships, local and national government organisations, TECs and education bodies.

Hammond Suddards Edge, Manchester: Profile is said to have grown rapidly over the past few years due to energetic marketing and a varied employer client base of banks, manufacturing companies and airlines. Sometimes described as *"confrontational"* in approach, the employment unit is the largest in the North West.

The leader in Yorkshire, *"few can touch"* **Pinsent Curtis**' *"first-class"* team of *"sound and courteous"* practitioners. Deemed to be strongest in the area in terms of manpower and technical experience. The group acts for a number of universities and blue-chip UK and international corporates, and conducts Working Time training seminars. Particularly distinguished in the field of European Works Councils, the practice was instrumental in setting up and advising on the second wave of voluntary European Works Councils for major multi-national companies prior to the December 1999 implementation deadline.

Dickinson Dees, Newcastle: Recommended as an *"efficient"* practice with evident strength and depth. Acts primarily for employers in plcs and health and local authorities. The group offers comprehensive human resources services and has particular expertise in TUPE, employee incentives and collective bargaining issues.

Short Richardson & Forth: Maintains a *"boutique image,"* acting for both individual employees and employers in a range of companies from plcs to small owner managed businesses. Team members are *"courteous, civilised and easy to deal with."*

Thompsons: The leading applicant firm in the region, acting on behalf of trade unions and their members in matters of equal pay, redundancy and consultancy requirements.

LEADING FIRMS

LONDON	EMPLOYMENT: MAINLY RESPONDENT	EMPLOYMENT: MAINLY APPLICANT
Allen & Overy	***	
Baker & McKenzie	*****	
Beachcroft Wansbroughs	**	
Bindman & Partners		****
Boodle Hatfield	*	
Charles Russell	**	
Clifford Chance	**	
CMS Cameron McKenna	***	
Dechert	*	
Denton Wilde Sapte	**	
Eversheds	*****	
Fox Williams	****	
Freshfields Bruckhaus Deringer	*	
Herbert Smith	***	
Hodge Jones & Allen		***
Irwin Mitchell		***
Langley & Co	*	
Lawfords		***
Lewis Silkin	***	
Linklaters	**	
Lovells	*****	
Macfarlanes	*	
McDermott, Will & Emery	**	
Norton Rose	*	
Olswang	*	
Osborne Clarke OWA	**	
Paisner & Co	*	
Pattinson & Brewer		******
Pinsent Curtis	**	
Richards Butler	*	
Rowe & Maw	****	
Rowley Ashworth	`	*****
Russell Jones & Walker		****
Salans Hertzfeld & Heilbronn HRK	*	
Simmons & Simmons	******	
Slaughter and May	**	
Speechly Bircham	*	
Stephenson Harwood	**	
Theodore Goddard	*	
Thompsons		*****
Travers Smith Braithwaite	*	

LEADING FIRMS *continued*

THE SOUTH	EMPLOYMENT	THE SOUTH	EMPLOYMENT
Argles Stoneham Burstows, *Crawley*	****	**DMH,** *Brighton*	******
Blake Lapthorn, *Portsmouth*	*****	**Paris Smith & Randall,** *Southampton*	*****
Brachers, *Maidstone*	****	**Pattinson & Brewer,** *Chatham*	****
Clarkson Wright & Jakes, *Orpington*	****	**Stevens & Bolton,** *Guildford*	****
Cripps Harries Hall, *Tunbridge Wells, Kent*	*****		

THAMES VALLEY	EMPLOYMENT	THAMES VALLEY	EMPLOYMENT
Clarks, *Reading*	*****	**Pickworths,** *Watford*	***
Henmans, *Oxford*	*****	**Underwoods,** *St Albans*	****
Morgan Cole, *Oxford, Reading*	******		

SOUTH WEST	EMPLOYMENT	SOUTH WEST	EMPLOYMENT
Bevan Ashford, *Bristol*	******	**Pattinson & Brewer,** *Bristol*	****
Bond Pearce, *Plymouth*	******	**Stephens & Scown,** *Exeter*	***
Burges Salmon, *Bristol*	******	**Stone King,** *Bath*	***
Cartwrights, *Bristol*	*****	**Thompsons,** *Bristol*	*****
Eversheds, *Bristol*	*****	**Thrings & Long,** *Bath*	***
Michelmores, *Exeter*	***	**TLT Solicitors,** *Bristol*	***
Osborne Clarke OWA, *Bristol*	******	**Veale Wasbrough,** *Bristol*	****

WALES	EMPLOYMENT	WALES	EMPLOYMENT
Edwards Geldard, *Cardiff*	****	**Morgan Cole,** *Cardiff, Swansea*	*****
Eversheds, *Cardiff*	******	**Palser Grossman,** *Cardiff Bay*	***
Hugh James Ford Simey, *Cardiff*	***		

MIDLANDS	EMPLOYMENT	MIDLANDS	EMPLOYMENT
Browne Jacobson, *Nottingham*	***	**Martineau Johnson,** *Birmingham*	****
DLA, *Birmingham*	****	**Mills & Reeve,** *Birmingham*	***
Eversheds, *Birmingham*	******	**Pinsent Curtis,** *Birmingham*	*****
Hammond Suddards Edge, *Birmingham*	*****	**Shakespeares,** *Birmingham*	***
Hewitson Becke + Shaw, *Northampton*	******	**Shoosmiths,** *Nottingham*	***
Higgs & Sons, *Brierley Hill*	****	**Wragge & Co,** *Birmingham*	******

EAST ANGLIA	EMPLOYMENT	EAST ANGLIA	EMPLOYMENT
Eversheds, *Ipswich, Norwich*	★★★★★★	Prettys, *Ipswich*	★★
Greenwoods, *Peterborough*	★★★	Steele & Co, *Norwich*	★★★★★
Hewitson Becke + Shaw, *Cambridge*	★★★★★★	Taylor Vinters, *Cambridge*	★★★★
Mills & Reeve, *Cambridge, Norwich*	★★★★★★		

NORTH WEST	EMPLOYMENT	NORTH WEST	EMPLOYMENT
Addleshaw Booth & Co, *Manchester*	★★★★★★	Halliwell Landau, *Manchester*	★★★
Beachcroft Wansbroughs, *Manchester*	★★	Hammond Suddards Edge, *Manchester*	★★★★★★
Cobbetts, *Manchester*	★★★★	Mace & Jones, *Liverpool, Manchester*	★★★★★
Davies Wallis Foyster, *Liverpool, Manchester*	★★★	Pannone & Partners, *Manchester*	★★
		Thompsons, *Liverpool, Manchester*	★★★★
DLA, *Liverpool, Manchester*	★★★★★★	Whittles, *Manchester*	★★★★★
Eversheds, *Manchester*	★★★★★★		

YORKSHIRE	EMPLOYMENT	YORKSHIRE	EMPLOYMENT
Addleshaw Booth & Co, *Leeds*	★★★★	Irwin Mitchell, *Sheffield*	★
Beachcroft Wansbroughs, *Sheffield*	★★★	Lupton Fawcett, *Leeds*	★
DLA, *Leeds, Sheffield*	★★★★	Nabarro Nathanson, *Sheffield*	★★
Eversheds, *Leeds*	★★★	Pinsent Curtis, *Leeds*	★★★★★★
Ford & Warren, *Leeds*	★★	Read Hind Stewart, *Leeds*	★★★
Gordons Cranswick Solicitors, *Bradford*	★	Rollit Farrell & Bladon, *Hull*	★★
Hammond Suddards Edge, *Leeds*	★★★★★	Walker Morris, *Leeds*	★★★

NORTH EAST	EMPLOYMENT	NORTH EAST	EMPLOYMENT
Crutes, *Newcastle upon Tyne*	★★★	Thompsons, *Newcastle upon Tyne*	★★★★★★
Dickinson Dees, *Newcastle upon Tyne*	★★★★★★	Ward Hadaway, *Newcastle upon Tyne*	★★★★
Eversheds, *Newcastle upon Tyne*	★★★★★★		
Short Richardson & Forth, *Newcastle upon Tyne*	★★★★★★		

environmental law

Don't assume that to be an environmental lawyer you must be a fully paid up member of Greenpeace and passionate about saving the planet. There certainly are careers for the passionate and crusading, but these are unlikely to be in private practice as a solicitor. Most environmental lawyers are instructed by corporate clients. Their role is primarily damage limitation and pre-emptive advice, the avoidance of damaging negative publicity and defence from prosecution when mistakes are made. It also includes considerable involvement in transactional work, ensuring that environmental liability arising out of corporate acquisitions and disposals is fully apportioned and understood. A small minority of lawyers act for the Environment Agency, environmental pressure groups and private individuals.

type of work

The caseload of an environmental lawyer will be split between contentious and non-contentious matters. Unusually for work often carried out in commercial firms contentious work may involve criminal law such as defending clients from criminal prosecution for breach of regulations. On the civil side it may involve tortious claims ('toxic torts') from those who suffer loss as a result of environmental impact as well as disputes as to liability following a mishap. On transactional work the environmental lawyers have a vital input where there is a sale or purchase of a business or land, drafting contractual provisions for the allocation of risk. There is also 'stand alone' work; advice to clients, perhaps on the likely extent of their obligations following a change in the law or the introduction of new EC Regulations. This may cover issues such as waste, pollution control, water abstraction and nature conservation.

Most environmental litigators have wider practices. A number are commercial litigators with experience of environmental defence work, others do a mix of contentious and non-contentious work. Chris Papanicolaou, partner at **Gouldens**, says that there is plenty of scope for getting involved in defending clients against prosecution by the regulatory authorities. He has seen an upturn in the numbers of prosecutions since the authorities really began to flex their muscles a couple of years ago. "In the magistrates court I might find myself running an argument on abuse of process. Or I might argue that the regulator has interpreted the law incorrectly." He points out that if there are still arguments being run over the 1954 Landlord and Tenant Act then it's going to take years before the environmental legislation of 1990/91 and onwards is interpreted properly. This means a lot of argument in court.

This is a key point. The fact that the area of law is relatively new means a substantial amount of research and interpretation to be carried out. A trainee can really come into his or her own in their environment seat, given that they might, almost by accident, become the most expert person in the team on a new piece of legislation or EC Directive. Chris Papanicolaou told us that this was how his career in environmental law took off. "In 1989 the Environmental Protection Bill came out. I was the one who read it and did the report for the senior partner." Ross Fairley, senior associate at **Allen & Overy**, agrees. "There's far more of a role to play for a trainee in advising on the law because the area is so new. I think the appeal is that someone can come in and, if a piece of legislation is in development, their views can be as valid as people who have been in the area for five or six years."

Many specialists approach non-contentious work from a property or planning base. The government recently introduced its contaminated land regime which is set to provide increased opportunities to offer environmental-related advice, particularly for property based lawyers.

Others at the largest firms may be kept more than busy in a support role to the corporate lawyers. Environmental insurance is another niche, and there are firms such as **Leigh, Day & Co** who have cornered the market for claimants in multi-party environmental tort litigation.

skills needed

"You have to be a jack of all trades"...versatility...a sound knowledge of how business and corporate structures work...an interest in environmental matters...a basic knowledge of science...research, interpretation and presentation skills...ability to work as part of a team.

career options

A decade ago solicitors suddenly saw environmental law as a new emerging practice area and got pretty excited about it. A generation of new partners, now in their thirties, have firmly established themselves from their roots as original pioneers and vanguards of environmental law. Commercial reality has tempered that excitement and lawyers now understand that it is not the growth area that everyone perceived it to be. Only the large London firms and a few large regional firms can offer specialism in environmental law. However, if you are lucky enough to become a specialist you will gain experience fast and be much in demand.

The local authority route is an alternative to starting out in private practice. A training contract with a L.A. may put you into contact with regulatory work, environment-related planning issues, waste management and air pollution cases and a role in advising the L.A. of its own liability in relation to property and business activities.

In-house positions are few and far between. Whilst it might be more common in the US for a company to have a lawyer responsible for environmental/health and safety issues, over here an in-house lawyer is more likely to have a general corporate counsel role. Paul Kelly at Northumbria Water, for example, deals with environmental law matters, commercial contracts, civil and criminal litigation as well as water and drainage law. Certain environmental pressure groups such as Greenpeace have their own lawyers.

The Department of the Environment, Transport and the Regions employs over 80 lawyers, generally recruited from within the Government Legal Service but with a small number coming from private practice. There are opportunities for trainees on GLS funded schemes in the Department. Chris Muttukumaru, the department's director of legal services, points out that the variety of work available for lawyers in the department allows for a flexible career. Work covers litigation, the drafting of subordinate legislation, preparation of bills, straight advisory work and contract drafting. He stresses that someone with a real interest in the way government operates would be best suited for such a role.

Another career option is with the Environment Agency for England and Wales. The Agency has responsibility for protecting and enhancing the environment through the regulation of the most potentially polluting corporate activities. It also protects water resources, flood defence and fisheries. The legal workload is diverse and includes the prosecution of environmental crime, civil litigation, the maintenance of the Thames Barrier and regulating the disposal of radioactive waste. Peter Kellett of the Agency's Head Office legal staff observes "The work is stimulating, highly politicised and vital. Our goal is firm but fair regulation to safeguard the environment for current and future generations." The Agency employs 56 solicitors and two trainees, seven barristers and five legal executives who work from eight regional offices and a head office in Bristol. Opportunities exist for further progression into management. Vacancies are generally advertised in the legal press. Anyone interested should contact the regional solicitor in the relevant office.

leading environmental firms

All information on leading firms comes from the Chambers Guide to the Legal Profession 2000-2001.
Several of London's top commercial firms have well-established environmental departments. The capabilities of smaller and regional firms are often shaped by the individual expertise of perhaps one or two lawyers.

Freshfields Bruckhaus Deringer: has consistently threatened to establish itself as *the* leading environmental practice. It is considered by some to offer the most comprehensive full-service team. Famed both for defence litigation and big-ticket transactional work, the contentious and non-contentious departments were recently fused to create an integrated internal structure. The large team's caseload is increasingly multinational and comprises a number of cross-border litigation matters and major international projects.

Allen & Overy: is also felt to be operating at the highest level, muscling in on an increasing number of major transactions for corporate and banking clients. Positioned in the corporate department, the practice exploits a vast quantity of M&A-driven work, as well as the firm's advantages in banking and lender liability. It is also complemented by environmental litigation and some stand-alone work. Advice to the chemical industry, for clients such as ICI, is a forte.

Simmons & Simmons: is the original 'pure' environmental City practice and still a favourite amongst other lawyers. Not quite competing with the corporate and transactional might of their principal competitors, the firm is perceived to offer the best balance between transaction support, contentious and stand alone regulatory and advisory work. The workload of the practice extends from waste, contaminated land and litigation to water, landfill and human rights. Clients are drawn primarily from the industrial, waste and energy sectors

CMS Cameron McKenna: is felt to possess a superior stand-alone practice, not excessively shaped by ties to either corporate or property departments. Although some corporate support is a feature of the practice, the firm's chief expertise rests in advising medium-sized plcs on a stand-alone basis. Increasing work on contamination-related civil litigation has been evident recently, as well as advice on regulatory and compliance matters in the waste and water fields. The firm also has a specialist environmental information service which provides advice to European multi-nationals.

The mainstay of the **Ashurst Morris Crisp** practice is the provision of advice on corporate transactions – the majority stemming from the manufacturing, industrial and chemical sectors. There is additionally some pure regulatory work and a separate contentious department dealing with environmental litigation. Energy to waste advice is an area of particular expertise.

Denton Wilde Sapte: is most commonly recommended for a substantial regulatory stand-alone component with particular expertise in the energy industry and on PFI projects. Landfill and packaging waste are also additional strings to the bow.

The environmental practice at **Lawrence Graham** is recognised for its litigation strength and for transactional support to the corporate and property departments. Half of the **Linklaters** environment practice profits from large numbers of premium corporate transactions. The remainder is composed of litigation and environmental planning.

For those after a more radical human rights tinged firm, a number of small claimant practices specialise in individual and group actions. **Leigh, Day & Co** (London), **Richard Buxton** (Cambridge) and **Public Interest Lawyers** (Birmingham) fit into this category.

In The North, the Leeds office of **Eversheds** is considered to be one of the leading regional practices, home to large amounts of environmental defence litigation and portions of corporate support.

The South West, home of the Environment Agency, has a particularly buoyant market. Firms such as **Bond Pearce, Burges Salmon** and **Osborne Clarke OWA** contain a number of individual specialists.

LEADING FIRMS

LONDON	ENVIRONMENT	LONDON	ENVIRONMENT
Allen & Overy	******	Linklaters	****
Ashurst Morris Crisp	****	Lovells	***
Barlow Lyde & Gilbert	***	Nabarro Nathanson	***
Berwin Leighton	***	Nicholson Graham & Jones	**
Clifford Chance	***	Norton Rose	***
CMS Cameron McKenna	*****	Rowe & Maw	**
Denton Wilde Sapte	****	Simmons & Simmons	******
Freshfields Bruckhaus Deringer	******	SJ Berwin & Co	**
Gouldens	**	Slaughter and May	***
Herbert Smith	***	Stephenson Harwood	**
Lawrence Graham	****	Theodore Goddard	**
Leigh, Day & Co	****	Trowers & Hamlins	**

THE SOUTH	ENVIRONMENT	THE SOUTH	ENVIRONMENT
Bevan Ashford, *Bristol*	*****	DMH, *Brighton*	******
Blake Lapthorn, *Portsmouth, Southampton*	******	Fynn & Partners, *Bournemouth*	*****
Bond Pearce, *Plymouth, Southampton*	******	Lyons Davidson, *Bristol*	****
Brachers, *Maidstone*	******	Osborne Clarke OWA, *Bristol*	******
Burges Salmon, *Bristol*	******	Stephens & Scown, *Exeter*	******
Clarke Willmott & Clarke,		Stevens & Bolton, *Guildford*	****
Bristol, Taunton	*****	Veale Wasbrough, *Bristol*	****

WALES, MIDLANDS, E. ANGLIA	ENVIRONMENT	WALES, MIDLANDS, E. ANGLIA	ENVIRONMENT
Edwards Geldard, *Cardiff*	******	Mills & Reeve, *Cambridge, Norwich*	******
Eversheds, *Cardiff, Birmingham, Norwich*	******	Morgan Cole, *Cardiff*	******
Hammond Suddards Edge, *Birmingham*	*****	Pinsent Curtis, *Birmingham*	******
Hewitson Becke + Shaw, *Cambridge*	*****	Richard Buxton, *Cambridge*	******
Kent Jones and Done, *Stoke-on-Trent*	****	Wragge & Co, *Birmingham*	******

THE NORTH	ENVIRONMENT	THE NORTH	ENVIRONMENT
Addleshaw Booth & Co, *Leeds, Manchester*	*****	Leigh, Day & Co, *Manchester*	******
Dickinson Dees, *Newcastle upon Tyne*	****	Masons, *Manchester*	*****
DLA, *Manchester, Sheffield*	******	Nabarro Nathanson, *Sheffield*	******
Eversheds, *Leeds, Manchester*	******	Pinsent Curtis, *Leeds*	***
Hammond Suddards Edge, *Leeds, Manchester*	*****	Wake Dyne Lawton, *Chester*	******

european union/competition

Covers both domestic and EU competition law and non-competition EU law. Many firms handle work spanning all these departments although most have particular strengths. The practice is mainly about the implications of EU Articles 81 and 82 . These contain the prohibitions on anti-competitive agreements and the abuse of a dominant market position.

Merger control and clearance is a major area of activity within the competition sphere – the regulation of both UK and European mergers which may have a bearing on competition in member state countries. Domestic competition law brings practitioners into close contact with regulatory bodies such as the Office of Fair Trading and the Department of Trade and Industry. Non-competition EU law covers the general principles of EU law and specialist areas such as the anti-discrimination provisions of the EU treaty.

The volume of work generated by the EU is huge. It is now so pervasive that almost any practice area has to consider the impact of European law.

type of work

All areas within competition are growing fast – it is a fairly specialised field in its own right and few junior lawyers would expect to sub-specialise initially. A senior lawyer from a reputable regional firm outlined the broad flavour of the work. "Many of the regional and smaller City firms try and deal with most things. Our main areas are merger control, UK competition law (Competition Act), EU Articles 81 and 82, state aids, sectorial regimes such as gas and telecoms and also public procurement."

Ralph Cohen from City firm **SJ Berwin & Co** described the spread at his practice. "It could involve dealing with merger clearances, acting as general counsel and reviewing all forms of agreement with respect to competition laws, assisting companies in getting deals approved by regulators and explaining to clients why they are required to be competitive."

Slaughter and May has a heavily M&A-related practice. Much of its work concerns obtaining approval in the relevant jurisdiction for the merger to take place. There is also significant stand-alone monopoly work – investigation of those companies that are alleged to have abused their market power. Michael Rowe, one of the firm's young competition lawyers, believes the proportion of work in these areas tends to reflect the client base of the firm. "Many of our clients are number one or two in their market, so monopoly and merger work frequently surfaces."

There are areas of competition where smaller niche firms tend to predominate. These include anti-competitive agreements, anti-trust measures and compliance agreements, review of industrial agreements and licence and supply agreements.

There is an increasingly significant regulatory aspect to competition work which exhibits different characteristics and involves a sizeable level of contact with officialdom in the EU cities. "You have to be prepared to talk to officials!" says Ros Kellaway from **Eversheds**. The amount of regulatory involvement will depend on the firm – some large City firms have made a specialisation out of it. One regional lawyer describes its growth – "Ten years ago no-one knew anything about regulation, now there are people in top City firms who do nothing but telecoms regulation."

Competition work can fall under both contentious and non-contentious umbrellas. The emphasis is usually on providing strategic and preventative advice to avoid recourse to litigation. One lawyer stressed the importance of these services. "Although litigation is increasing, contentious work is a small part, probably under 10% of our business.

In a sense, if you get to court you've been defeated."

EU/competition law demands a greater knowledge of how markets operate than other corporate practice areas. Michael Rowe says. "I actually spend a lesser proportion of my time researching black letter law or doing things that are strictly legal. I focus more time on reading into markets, developing an understanding of how markets operate, of how competition operates within those markets." Ralph Cohen makes a similar point. "It's unlike usual commercial practice in that the objective being sought is very different. There is no deal-making, it's all about commercial transactions complying with the regulators."

One senior partner believes it is technically more exacting. "As a corporate lawyer you need a lot of skills but you don't need to be quite as intellectually rigorous as you do in an area like competition. It is quite complex." Ros Kellaway stresses that it is "qualitatively different" to other practice areas because it is fundamentally about how markets work and the economics of these arrangements. "It is very different to a straightforward legal understanding. You have to understand a very different body of law, a different legal order – the final analysis is an economic market analysis."

There is major exposure to power and politics in the work of a competition lawyer and you will be immersed in industries that have their own sensitivities. The work involves the exercise of advocacy skills, either in written form when putting together a brief or arguing a case – the aim being to tell a story that is credible and persuasive when appearing before the regulators.

Within competition law, client contact and meetings are frequently undertaken. Although it is a specialist area of law, positions of autonomy and greater responsibility are soon awarded with ability.

a day in the life...

"The workload might include assisting with a merger filing, analysing products and businesses,

advising on drafting agreements and attending an OFT meeting with a partner." Juniors are often involved when instructed on a new case and are required to research the background to the market, absorb information and become an expert very quickly – "the ability to see the wood from the trees is important," says Ralph Cohen.

Most competition firms have a Brussels office ("it would be difficult to function successfully without one,") and are keen to send junior lawyers on placements there. Although some UK firms do the majority of active work on-site domestically, presence in Belgium is useful for "keeping eyes and ears open" and maintaining close contacts with the politicians and power-brokers! Anti-dumping and trade law is still one area of competition which remains very heavily Brussels-driven.

The transnational nature of competition law brings with it a high degree of glamour, frequent travel and prestigious clients. Overseas trips and high-profile cases are common. According to one lawyer, "we certainly to and fro a lot more, not just to Brussels but all over, you do pick up a fairly international clientele." The highlight for her is "working in an area of law that it is very rapidly developing. You open the paper every day and there are two or three stories that are of crucial relevance to something you're working on. Its a very immediate area – so it can be glamorous!"

Michael Rowe is pleased with his career choice and supports this view: "there are so many options – you're more likely to travel, you're more likely to get a greater degree of responsibility at an earlier stage in your career. But as with any other practice area, there will be times when you're in the office late and you're churning out something that has to be done. At those moments, it feels very unglamorous!"

Lifestyle-wise "You don't have to sell your soul to being here 24 hours a day," said one lawyer. The hours can be cyclical in that they are governed by the number of transactions that are in the office at any one time, however they are becoming more regular as new areas of competition open up. Another competition expert believes the specialist areas give you more control over your life. "It is better in that it is far less meeting driven than corporate, you're more in control of your own destiny. There is flexibility to take time out during the day and make it up later."

skills needed

...adaptability...a broad understanding...an interest in business and markets and how competition functions...strong technical skills...clear analytical mind...top-level academic credentials...attention to detail, thoroughness...good mediation and lobbying skills...persuasiveness...effective communication skills...decisiveness...linguistic ability...enthusiasm...

career options

At the bottom end, EU/competition can be competitive and difficult to break into – more so perhaps than other areas of law, but there are still opportunities to be had. Ros Kellaway says the irony is, "that although there are enormous volumes of work generated by the EU, there are still relatively few practices with large departments and only a small number of niche practices." She receives a large number of unsolicited CVs from students keen to break into this area of practice but only some have the right mix of ability and practical experience. Don't be put off. The number of active firms and size of competition departments are set to carry on growing – this is very much an upwardly moving area of law. High academic credentials, technical and communication skills top the requirement list. Failing to qualify into an EU department, Ros Kellaway offers some alternative entry routes. "The best method is to enter a mainstream corporate department and work towards specialisation or go for employment which is hugely dominated by an EU dimension."

Competition is a specialist area but there are a reasonable number of options available as more companies take on in-house competition lawyers. The skills you develop in industry analysis and understanding of markets could well be employed in a broader business context. There is not a huge transference or movement out of private practice to in-house or mainstream business at the moment although success in this practice area certainly provides great potential for it.

leading EU firms

All information on leading firms comes from the Chambers Guide to the Legal Profession 2000-2001.

Freshfields Bruckhaus Deringer: Clearly an anti-trust powerhouse with *"corporate professionalism an overriding feature of the firm."* Lead partners are *"major players"* who *"cut to the quick."* Brussels-based partners still command immense market respect. Economists find the London team *"particularly easy to deal with, they get you involved early and don't tell you your job."* First appearances would seem to suggest that highly rated London-based partners are few compared to the competition, yet the practice still gets the *"chunky high profile transactions."* Whilst some perceive the work to be *"skewed to M&A,"* the team is nevertheless considered to have *"many strengths apart from merger work."* Merger work includes the GEC Marconi/British Aerospace, RBS/NatWest and Telewest/Flextech link-ups. Non-merger work includes Competition Commission inquiries into grocery retailing and milk, and work in the financial services, brewing, media, telecoms and railway sectors. The practice has also worked on most major European cartel cases in sectors such as banking, cement, gas, graphite electrodes, media, newsprint, steel beams and pipes.

Herbert Smith: Following heavy market recommendation the popular and *"extremely strong"* practice moves into the top tier this year. A broad and balanced team, the partners all do a range of work. The firm additionally has partners well respected for newspaper regulation and transport work, and clients are impresssed with the junior ranks. A wide range of competition and regulatory work is dealt with, including mergers and takeover battles such as those of First Choice with Kuoni and Airtours and NatWest with Bank of Scotland and RBS. In the newspaper industry, the firm advised Trinity Plc on the competition aspects of its proposed acquisition of the Mirror Group. Other work includes defending BSkyB's exclusive contract to televise live Premier League football, advising the FIA on the Formula One investigation and advising the Indian and Armenian governments on trade issues.

Linklaters: Whilst many in the market commented that the recent departure of two key partners left *"two pretty big holes,"* clients and outside observers commented on the *"strength in depth"* of the team. Partners and young associates alike are *"all impressive,"* and whilst *"there are no superstars, that is part of their attraction." "They are a collection of very good people," "there are no glitzy individuals, but they all have drive and application."* Thus whilst waning in terms of heavyweight hitters compared to previous years, the team nevertheless retains its leading status this year. The Alliance operates an integrated European practice group, and the market commented on the strength of some of its Brussels players. Well known for its merger work, the practice advised on the link-ups of BAT/Rothmans, Vodafone/Airtouch, Vodafone/Mannesmann, Lafarge/Blue Circle, Scottish & Newcastle/Kronenbourg, BP Amoco/Castrol, BAe/GEC Marconi, NatWest/RBS and other multi-jurisdictional mergers. Cartel work, and trade law work are also an important feature of the practice, with a recent arrival boosting the WTO practice.

Slaughter and May: This year the team received the most recommendations and also the most commentaries. The practice is *"not everyone's cup of tea,"* with many lawyers finding the team *"tricky to deal with,"* principally due to a perceived *"confrontational"* approach and an *"overbearing self-confidence."* However, all agree that the practice is *"extremely good at representing a client"* – it *"instils trust"* and is *"tough and often right."* Clients themselves have *"no difficulty dealing with the team."* The Brussels office continues to generate market respect. Like all firms with top

M&A practices, the competition team is sometimes seen to be a merger shop. Whilst being *"extremely experienced at merger work,"* however, the practice is also considered to be *"top on behavioural work,"* which makes it one of the more rounded practices of the leading tier. In a typical year, around half of the practice's work is M&A related. Rothmans/BAT, Kingfisher/Asda and the three-way aluminium merger are included in the list of year's deals. Inquiry work includes advice in the ice cream, supermarkets, public medical insurance and hospital services industries.

Lovells: London operates as one group with Brussels, where the practice remains a key player unanimously regarded as one of the more *"balanced"* practices, they are *"nice to work with"* and *"commercial." "Top for behavioural work,"* with *"strength in trade matters"* and a *"pre-eminent shipping competition practice,"* the practice is indeed *"well rounded."* However, the practice is perceived to be less involved than its foremost competitiors on merger and utilities work, which means the team has had a reduced profile this year. Work this year includes advising on the attempted Telia/Telenor merger, on a joint venture between Alsthom and ABB with a disposal to General Electric. Inquiry work includes advising Mars in the ice cream 'wars,' and working on appeals subsequent to the commission steel tubes and steel beams investigation.

leading regional firms

All information on leading firms comes from the Chambers Guide to the Legal Profession 2000-2001.

Burges Salmon, Bristol: With a *"good press and a good corporate practice"* behind it, to say that this is Bristol's premier competition practice would be *"a fair reflection of the market."* Adding to an impressive transport work portfolio (particularly in the bus and rail sectors) the practice advised on clearing the CHC Helicopter Corporation/HSG link-up. Inquiry and review work includes successfully reducing undertakings for FirstGroup/SB Holdings.

Bond Pearce, Plymouth: Among what one client descibed as the firm's *"exceptionally diverse range of esoteric legal skills,"* lies the EU and competition team. Most of the work is of a behavioural nature, though mergers do form part of the practice's capability. Sectoral expertise is in retail, transport (maritime and aviation), pharmaceuticals, chemicals and defence work. Recent activity has seen the firm involved on contentious activity, and the firm was instructed in relation to intended High Court proceedings against Birdseye Walls Ltd, alleging breaches of EC Competition law and claiming compensation under the Commercial Agents' Regulations.

Pinsent Curtis, Birmingham, Leeds: The Birmingham office works alongside the London and Leeds offices in what is a national competition team with a *"fine reputation."* Around a third of the practice's work is on mergers and this year the team was active advising Arriva plc on transactions in the bus and rail sectors. The rest of the team's work is oriented to the behavioural side, with a substantial amount of procurement work (e.g. for the procurement arm of the NHS) and post-Competition Act advisory work.

Wragge & Co, Birmingham: A *"solid and ambitious practice,"* which has gone against a perceived trend (where Brussels is leaving more work to the individual member states) by recently opening a Brussels office. The strength of the corporate client base gives the competition team a steady flow of merger work and this year the team acted for HJ Heinz Europe on its acquisition of United Biscuits Frozen & Chilled Foods Ltd. Other areas of activity have been in the energy, automotive and aviation sectors. Public procurement, regulatory, anti-dumping, complaint work and compliance programme work are also busy.

Eversheds, Birmingham: The benefits of the national practice were exemplified by the Birmingham office's ability to advise clients of the Competition Commission's car inquiry as a direct result of the involvement of the London group. Regular corporate support work includes mergers (Partco/Unipart) and commercial contract (distribution agreements) work. The team has been particularly active in the motor manufacturing and airport sectors this year. The practice has also been busy on compliance programme work subsequent to the Competition Act.

Addleshaw Booth & Co, Manchester: *"Technical"* and have the *"expert touch."* The competition team is part of the wider trade and regulatory group. The firm's blue chip client base means that it has been involved on merger control issues, commercial agreements, investigations and compliance work in the light of the Competition Act. More than half of the practice's work is of a non-merger nature – behavioural work, procurement and state aid matters. Work includes being appointed by a major utility (Kelda) to advise on periodic price reviews and regulatory matters generally.

Eversheds, Leeds: The practice works on mergers, commercial arrangements, investigatory, compliance and contentious work. The utility sector has been an area of particular activity. As well as advising clients on their multi-jurisdictional mergers, the firm advises third parties to transactions. eg American Securities LP, a US merger arbitrage firm, in connection with the hostile bid by Vodafone Airtouch for Mannesmann, and the proposed merger of United News & Media and Carlton.

Dickinson Dees, Newcastle: Known for its strong base of active corporate clients. Merger work has seen it act on merger clearances at EU and OFT level for Go-Ahead, and on disposals and acquisitions for other clients. Transport, particularly trains and buses, is a busy area. Like all practices, the firm has been busy following the Competition Act, working on compliance programmes for clients such as Go-Ahead and Arriva Plc.

LEADING FIRMS

LONDON	COMPETITION/ ANTI-TRUST	LONDON	COMPETITION/ ANTI-TRUST
Allen & Overy	****	Herbert Smith	******
Ashurst Morris Crisp	****	Linklaters	******
Baker & McKenzie	**	Lovells	*****
Bristows	*	Norton Rose	***
Clifford Chance	****	Richards Butler	*
CMS Cameron McKenna	*	Simmons & Simmons	***
Denton Wilde Sapte	****	SJ Berwin & Co	****
Eversheds	*	Slaughter and May	******
Freshfields Bruckhaus Deringer	******	Theodore Goddard	**

SOUTH WEST & WALES	COMPETITION/ ANTI-TRUST	SOUTH WEST & WALES	COMPETITION/ ANTI-TRUST
Bond Pearce, *Plymouth*	*****	Eversheds, *Cardiff*	******
Burges Salmon, *Bristol*	******	Morgan Cole, *Cardiff*	******
Edwards Geldard, *Cardiff*	******		

MIDLANDS	COMPETITION/ ANTI-TRUST	MIDLANDS	COMPETITION/ ANTI-TRUST
Eversheds, *Birmingham*	*****	Wragge & Co, *Birmingham*	******
Pinsent Curtis, *Birmingham*	******		

THE NORTH	COMPETITION/ ANTI-TRUST	THE NORTH	COMPETITION/ ANTI-TRUST
Addleshaw Booth & Co, *Leeds, Manchester*	******	Eversheds, *Leeds, Manchester, Middlesbrough, Newcastle upon Tyne*	******
Dickinson Dees, *Newcastle upon Tyne*	*****	Pinsent Curtis, *Leeds*	*****

family law

Family law includes the law relating to divorce and any resulting financial settlements, domestic violence and child law. This also covers the growing area of the breakdown of unmarried relationships ('co-habitation'), while child law includes private issues relating to children (such as residence, parental contact, surrogacy and adoption) and public law work (where children are taken into care by local authorities or otherwise have contact with social services). While many lawyers practise in all of these areas, the increasing specialisation of the profession means that there is a growing divide between those who do largely financial/matrimonial and some private child work, and those who specialise in children and public law work. The division is often dependent on where the firm is situated, with high street and specialist legal aid firms doing the majority of public law work.

Of course all family lawyers require an up to date knowledge of family law, but there is more to the practice than that. Those working on the financial side also require an understanding of property, tax, trusts and pensions. Those on the public law side may need a grounding in criminal law, welfare law, education law and mental health issues.

type of work

Divorce is one of the most stressful life events. One of the tasks of a family lawyer is to offer support through it. Their clients are often emotional, bitter and oblivious to logical argument and the lawyer must be able delicately to circumvent this emotion. They must assist them to articulate their true concerns, and to ensure that they can see the bigger picture. Clients range from 'high net worth' individuals with substantial property and assets to people with very little money, but a painful contact battle to fight. The well-known London firms acting for wealthy and often high-profile clients must also learn how to deal with the media interest in their cases. **Mishcon de Reya**, for example, represent the Duchess of York and Jerry Hall.

High income matrimonial work often involves complex commercial, financial and tax problems, often with an international aspect. "An element of my work is looking at balance sheets, trust documents, pension funds and property transfers," says Richard Sax of **Manches**. A typical day may include meeting a new client who wishes to divorce her wealthy Italian husband and is worried about gaining custody of her children and calling the Cayman Islands to sort out another client's tax problem. For Mark Harper, partner at **Withers**, the most interesting cases are those involving competing jurisdictions in several different countries, which may make the finances harder to sort out on divorce, or may mean that a divorce cannot be obtained in another jurisdiction.

Public childcare work can be the most disturbing of all types of family law. It comes into play when a local authority has concerns about the welfare of a child and applies to the court to have the child taken into care. Childcare lawyers will thus represent either the parents, the local authority or the guardian appointed by the court to look after the child's interests. Parents in these cases often have a history of violence, alcoholism or mental illness while the children themselves could have the same problems and could also be victims of mental, physical or sexual abuse. Philip Kidd of Exeter firm **Tozers** once had to interview two children with armed police standing by because the father was looking for them with a gun. Acting for children, he says, requires particular skill. "You have to remember you're acting for a vulnerable human being," says Kidd, "My youngest child client was just seven days old, and the rest range from toddlers to teenagers. I see older children more often to check whether they continue to give the same instructions as their guardians. You can get into close relationships with them – but not too close, obviously, because you walk away at the end of the case."

Most newly-qualified solicitors who specialise in childcare will start by representing parents, as at the moment you need to be at least three years' qualified (and have experience doing childcare work) before you can apply to get on the Law Society's Children Panel, from which most representatives for children are selected.

a day in the life...

West End Firm: As a trainee in a West End family department, your job will involve taking notes in client interviews, drafting documents, researching points of law and court work. The court work can vary from preparing bundles, to running to court to lodge documents in time, to attending court with counsel. In addition you will usually have a structured training programme, plenty of supervision and support and earn a reasonable salary.

High Street Firm: Family work in a small or high street practice often involves both divorce and childcare work. A typical day will be very different from a day spent at **Withers**, **Manches** or **Mishcon de Reya**. In a high street practice you are more likely to be thrown in at the deep end and given more responsibility early on. Your first client of the morning may walk in off the street with her children, having fled from her violent husband. She needs an emergency loan, temporary accommodation and an injunction to prevent her husband from attacking her and her children. Your second client has a first appointment to discuss his potential divorce. The first interview in divorce cases is often a challenge. "The impact of the emotional consequence of a marriage breakdown is huge," comments Peter Jones, of Leeds firm **Jones Myers Gordon**, "I've had clients in front of me who have been in physical shock when their spouse has walked out. You need a lot of patience, you need a lot of understanding, but you still need to move them foward." The afternoon may involve assisting counsel on your own.

skills needed

Matrimonial...understanding of human weakness...ability to be non-judgmental...sympathy and objectivity...non-confrontational skills...*"the ability to negotiate from strength but without making it litigious"*...listening skills...commercial acumen...numeracy

Childcare work...humanity...a fair amount of medical knowledge...conversance with the legal aid system...determination...level-headedness...counselling skills...ability to separate any emotional response from your professionalism

career options

In the prestigious London firms, and in some large regional outfits, trainees may be able to do a family seat as part of their training. The work will generally be for wealthy private clients and will focus on divorce and financial disputes. In the high street, work will be a mixture of private and legal aid cases. Some high street family departments are mixed with conveyancing or criminal departments, so you will receive a grounding in several areas. There will be the opportunity to handle childcare work from day one.

There is no typical career path into family law, and some lawyers come to it after working for several years in City firms. However, because it is such an emotional and demanding field, most family lawyers have been committed to it from very early on in their careers. According to Mark Harper, it certainly helps to have gained some prior experience in counselling or dealing with people. "If you've only studied law through books, it can be quite overwhelming dealing with all this raw emotion."

Many family lawyers derive their vocation from the cutting edge element of much of the work and the pace of legislative change. As Peter Jones puts it, "Its developments attempt to reflect, perhaps faster than most areas of law, the change of views of society." At present the main issues under the microscope are no-fault divorce, pension sharing and the rights of co-habitees and gay and lesbian couples. "The next five years are not going to be complacent" says Jones. "It stops you from being bored."

The alternatives to private practice are limited, but qualified lawyers can work in-house for local authorities and charities such as the NSPCC. In rare cases, those with good advocacy skills might go to the Bar, but this is preferably done at an early stage in their career. Family lawyers occasionally move into mediation or social work, but the remuneration in these fields is poor and the pressure can be just as great as in private practice.

leading firms

All information on leading firms comes from the Chambers Guide to the Legal Profession 2000-2001.

Manches: Very well-known and *"exceedingly well-resourced"* firm which receives widespread praise from its peers. The size and strength of the team means that its big money clients are able to receive a *"luxury service."* The firm consequently remains in the front rank. The team specialises in complex and high value financial cases, and high profile highlights of last year included acting for Sir Ian McEwan and continued involvement in the Paloma Picasso divorce. This was the biggest ever in the UK, with an estimated target value of £250m, although it settled for an undisclosed amount. They also handle the full range of private children work and abduction as well as cohabitation issues and pre-nuptial agreements.

Withers: Seen by the market as a *"pre-eminent"* team in the field, offering *"a better spectrum of service"* with leading partners supported by *"competent assistants."* The firm continues to vie with Manches for the leading position. High value, high profile and often international ancillary relief is the focus of the

practice, with clients able to take advantage of the firm's complementary tax and trust expertise. Other increasing areas of practice include cohabitation, surrogacy and pre-nuptial agreements.

One particular highlight of the last year was the team's involvement in the landmark 'stolen' sperm case 'Von Schonburg v London Gynaecology and Fertility Centre.' They are retained by a large number of wealthy and high profile clients and have particular expertise in complex financial settlements and children's issues, pre-nuptial agreements and work with an international dimension.

Blandy & Blandy, Reading: The team's strength and depth mean it maintains its top band position. Equally strong in public and private children work and high net worth financial settlements, the practice is also making a name for itself on the mediation front with its 'STEPahead' counselling program.

Manches, Oxford: This branch office has strong connections with the main London office which give this Oxford branch a high profile in complex and high level ancillary relief cases. Also handles financial and private child care matters for a private client base of medics, academics, media professionals and marketing directors.

Lester Aldridge, Bournemouth: Active on the London circuit, this Bournemouth practice handles big money cases with assets ranging from £1m to £10m. They act in a substantial number of international cases and have carved a particular niche in handling ancillary relief for expatriots in the Tokyo money markets. They also operate a mediation practice.

Bond Pearce, Plymouth: A team of specialists handling heavyweight financial settlements. Acts for a range of professional clients from senior civil servants to farmers, business owners and company chairmen. Also handles private children matters relating to divorce.

Burges Salmon, Bristol: Financially focused practice receives referrals from the firm's large private client base. Act mainly for farming clients and entrepreneurs, frequently advising clients on the implications of pension sharing legislation. One associate has particular expertise in co-habitation issues.

Foot Anstey Sargent, Plymouth, Exeter: A February 2000 merger combined the strengths of the Foot & Bowden and Anstey Sargent teams. The firm has a "formidable" reputation for child care work as well as the capacity for heavyweight financial cases.

TLT Solicitors, Bristol: Trumps recently merged with Lawrence Tucketts to form a sizeable family practice with a considerable reputation in the area. The team focuses primarily on high net worth ancillary relief cases for professionals, gentry, and celebrities in the southwest. A substantial proportion of work involves international assets or foreign partners. However, the team is also active in mediation and has recruited one new partner to undertake public law children cases.

Hugh James Ford Simey, Cardiff: Operating a number of offices throughout the region, the firm is a recognised presence in South Wales. Has taken the lead in mediation in Wales through the team's involvement in the mediation pilot scheme. The group maintains a domestic violence hotline and acts frequently for women's aid refuges. Have a niche speciality in international child abduction and receive referrals through membership on the Reunite panel in Wales.

Challinors Lyon Clark, West Bromwich: A young and diverse team at this West Bromwich firm covers the full range of family law which undertakes both high net and legal aid ancillary relief cases. Has considerable expertise in public and private children work with particular experience in adoption, abduction, and Hague Convention cases. The firm possesses a legal aid block contract and offers advice to domestic violence victims at the local women's refuge. Also very involved in training for police officers and guardians *ad litem*.

Nelsons, Nottingham: A recent merger with Trumans has increased the firm's presence throughout the East Midlands. The firm's main work is for higher value ancillary relief cases in excess of £1m. Niches are in divorces for British nationals abroad and advice on the relevance of new pensions regulations. They also act for children in public care cases.

Tyndallwoods, Birmingham: This 'right-on' firm has a strong reputation for child care work, acting for guardians and occasionally parents. An unusual amount of international adoption cases come via the top class immigration practice. The practice is largely legal aid-focused but also undertakes high value ancillary relief.

Mills & Reeve, Cambridge, Norwich: Considered *"big players"* in high net worth ancillary relief cases involving landed estates and large farming businesses. Have a commanding experience of tax, trust, chattel, and pension problems associated with divorce settlements. The team also has a specialist in international child abduction and offers mediation services.

Pannone & Partners, Manchester: Viewed by many as *"clear market leaders,"* the practice has just risen to the leading firm spot to reflect its acknowledged size, strength, client base and reputation for *"good service and good results."* Ancillary relief and private children work is provided by a large team in a *"tightly controlled house style"* for a range of clients which include many high value professional and business individuals and some media personalities.

Addleshaw Booth & Co, Leeds: This is a predominantly commercial firm which nevertheless retains a *"strong, well-resourced and extremely experienced"* practice. It has achieved a *"pre-eminence"* in the region and *"gets all the mega stuff."* Work focuses largely on ancillary relief and private children work for high net worth clients including local landed gentry, business and professional people. Many instructions come in from elsewhere in the UK and abroad.

LEADING FIRMS

LONDON	FAMILY/ MATRIMONIAL	LONDON	FAMILY/ MATRIMONIAL
Anthony Gold, Lerman & Muirhead	*	International Family Law Chambers	**
Barnett Sampson	**	Kingsley Napley	***
Bates, Wells & Braithwaite	****	Levison Meltzer Pigott	*****
Bindman & Partners	**	Manches	******
Charles Russell	*****	Miles Preston & Co	*****
Clintons	***	Mishcon de Reya	***
Collyer-Bristow	**	Osbornes	*
Dawson & Co	**	Payne Hicks Beach	*
Dawson Cornwell	***	Reynolds Porter Chamberlain	**
Farrer & Co	*****	Russell-Cooke, Potter & Chapman	**
Fisher Meredith	*	Sears Tooth	****
Forsters	*	Stephenson Harwood	**
Goodman Ray	**	The Family Law Consortium	***
Gordon Dadds	*****	The Simkins Partnership	*
Hodge Jones & Allen	**	Withers	******

THE SOUTH & THAMES VALLEY	FAMILY	THE SOUTH & THAMES VALLEY	FAMILY
Brachers, *Maidstone*	****	Blandy & Blandy, *Reading*	******
Coffin Mew & Clover, *Portsmouth*	****	Boodle Hatfield, *Oxford*	***
Cripps Harries Hall, *Tunbridge Wells, Kent*	****	Darbys Mallam Lewis, *Oxford*	*****
DMH, *Brighton*	****	Henmans, *Oxford*	****
Lester Aldridge, *Bournemouth*	******	Iliffes Booth Bennett, *Uxbridge*	****
Max Barford & Co, *Tunbridge Wells*	****	Linnells, *Oxford*	****
Paris Smith & Randall, *Southampton*	*****	Manches, *Oxford*	******
Thomson Snell & Passmore, *Tunbridge Wells*	*****	Morgan Cole, *Oxford*	*****
		Rowberry Morris, *Reading*	***

SOUTH WEST	FAMILY	SOUTH WEST	FAMILY
Bond Pearce, *Plymouth*	******	Stephens & Scown, *Exeter*	*****
Burges Salmon, *Bristol*	******	Stone King, *Bath*	**
Clarke Willmott & Clarke, *Taunton, Yeovil*	*****	Stones, *Exeter*	***
E. David Brain & Co, *St. Austell*	***	TLT Solicitors, *Bristol*	******
Foot Anstey Sargent, *Exeter*	******	Tozers, *Exeter, Plymouth, Torquay*	******
Gill Akaster, *Plymouth*	******	Veale Wasbrough, *Bristol*	**
Hartnell & Co, *Exeter*	***	Withy King, *Bath*	**
Hooper & Wollen, *Torquay*	****	Wolferstans, *Plymouth*	******
Hugh James Ford Simey, *Exeter*	**	Woollcombe Beer Watts, *Newton Abbot*	**
Ian Downing Family Law Practice, *Plymouth*	****		

WALES, MIDLANDS & E. ANGLIA	FAMILY	WALES, MIDLANDS & E. ANGLIA	FAMILY
Granville-West, *Newbridge (nr. Newport)*	****	Varley Hibbs, *Coventry*	***
Harding Evans, *Newport*	****	Wace Morgan, *Shrewsbury*	*****
Hugh James Ford Simey, *Cardiff*	******	Warren & Allen, *Nottingham*	***
Larby Williams, *Cardiff*	******	Young & Lee, *Birmingham*	****
Leo Abse & Cohen, *Cardiff*	****	Buckle Mellows, *Peterborough*	****
Martyn Prowel Solicitors, *Cardiff*	******	Cozens-Hardy & Jewson, *Norwich*	***
Nicol, Denvir & Purnell, *Cardiff*	******	Eversheds, *Cambridge, Norwich*	****
Robertsons, *Cardiff*	****	Fosters, *Norwich*	****
Wendy Hopkins & Co, *Cardiff*	*****	Greenwoods, *Peterborough*	******
Blair Allison & Co, *Birmingham*	******	Hatch Brenner, *Norwich*	***
Blythe Liggins, *Leamington Spa*	***	Hunt & Coombs, *Peterborough*	******
Challinors Lyon Clark, *West Bromwich*	******	Leonard Gray, *Chelmsford*	****
Freethcartwright, *Nottingham*	*****	Miller Sands, *Cambridge*	*****
Hadens, *Walsall*	****	Mills & Reeve, *Cambridge, Norwich*	******
Lanyon Bowdler, *Shrewsbury*	****	Overbury Steward Eaton & Woolsey, *Norwich*	***
Morton Fisher, *Kidderminster*	****		
Nelsons, *Derby, Grantham*	******	Rudlings & Wakelam, *Thetford*	***
Rupert Bear Murray Davies, *Nottingham*	******	Silver Fitzgerald, *Cambridge*	******
Tyndallwoods, *Birmingham*	******	Ward Gethin, *King's Lynn*	****

THE NORTH	FAMILY	THE NORTH	FAMILY
Addleshaw Booth & Co, *Manchester*	****	Gordons Cranswick Solicitors, *Bradford, Leeds*	****
Burnetts, *Carlisle*	***		
Cobbetts, *Manchester*	****	Grahame Stowe, Bateson, *Leeds*	****
Cuff Roberts, *Liverpool*	****	Henry Hyams & Co, *Leeds*	***
Farleys, *Blackburn*	*****	Irwin Mitchell, *Sheffield*	*****
Forbes, *Blackburn*	***	Jones Myers Gordon, *Leeds*	*****
Green & Co, *Manchester*	****	Kirbys, *Harrogate*	***
Jones Maidment Wilson inc Hatton Scates Horton, *Manchester*	****	Lee & Priestley, *Leeds*	****
		Zermansky & Partners, *Leeds*	*****
Laytons, *Manchester*	*****	Askews, *Redcar*	***
Morecroft Urquhart, *Liverpool*	***	Dickinson Dees, *Newcastle upon Tyne*	******
Pannone & Partners, *Manchester*	******	Hay & Kilner, *Newcastle uponTyne*	****
Rowlands, *Manchester*	***	Jacksons, *Stockton-on-Tees*	***
Stephensons, *Leigh*	****	Mincoffs, *Newcastle upon Tyne*	*****
Addleshaw Booth & Co, *Leeds*	******	Samuel Phillips & Co, *Newcastle upon Tyne*	****
Andrew M. Jackson & Co, *Hull*	****	Sinton & Co, *Newcastle upon Tyne*	*****
Crombie Wilkinson, *York*	***	Ward Hadaway, *Newcastle upon Tyne*	***

intellectual property

Intellectual property lawyers divide the field into two broad areas: patent work (hard IP) i.e. the protection of inventions; and non-patent work (soft IP) i.e. trade marks, design rights, copyright, passing off, anti-counterfeiting and confidential information. Hard IP has links with product liability work. Both types of IP overlap with IT (information technology), telecommunications, broadcasting and internet work.

type of work

IP clients include manufacturers and suppliers of hi-tech and engineering products, leading brand owners, teaching hospitals, universities, scientific institutions and media clients (including broadcasters, newspapers, publishers and artists). IP work can be contentious and non-contentious. Disputes usually revolve around an allegation of infringement of one or more intangible property rights existing in an invention, a literary/artistic work, a trade mark or a product.

"You'll be instrumental in defending a leading brand and fighting off competitors in the market place," says Vanessa Marsland, an IP partner at **Clifford Chance**. "One of my clients is Kimberley Clark which owns the Andrex brand of toilet paper. Last year their competitor, Fort Sterling, started packaging its rival Nouvelle eco-toilet paper with the message that softness was guaranteed. If customers disagreed, they could exchange the product for a packet of Andrex. Kimberley Clark felt the offer was confusing, and that people might believe that Nouvelle was endorsed by Andrex." **Clifford Chance** carried out a number of street surveys to see if people really were confused. "I've got an interesting job," Marsland jokes, "I show people packets of toilet paper." But she won the case.

Richard Kempner, a partner in the Leeds office of **Addleshaw Booth & Co**, handled the supermarket 'look-alike' case, defending Asda, makers of Puffin biscuits, against United Biscuits, makers of Penguin chocolate biscuits. United claimed that Asda was passing off the Puffin as the Penguin, and that the Puffin name and picture breached its Penguin trade marks. The case ended in a draw. Asda won on trade mark infringement, but United Biscuits won on passing off, forcing Asda to alter its packaging.

Asima Khan, a newly qualified solicitor with **Addleshaw Booth & Co**, worked on the Puffin-Penguin case as a trainee. "IP lets you see the corporate side of work but in a more interesting way," she says. "I was surprised there was such high-profile work outside London. Before starting my IP seat, I helped produce market research questionnaires which were part of Asda's defence. At the beginning of my IP seat, I attended the closing speeches of the case at the Royal Courts of Justice. It was so exciting playing a part in a case like that."

Internet IP law is a fledgling area of work, constantly throwing up new issues. **Clifford Chance**'s Vanessa Marsland is involved in a variety of cases concerning trade mark infringement on the internet. Many cases, she says, involve complex international issues. "If you're trading globally on the internet and infringe someone else's rights, are you guilty of infringement all over the world or just in the country where you're physically located?"

Few students know much about IP when they begin their training contracts, which is why most large firms with an IP specialism send trainees on a course in Bristol run by the Intellectual Property Lawyers' Association. The residential course counts as half an MA and is taught by partners from major IP firms.

a day in the life...

An IP lawyer's day might begin with an early morning hearing in the Patents Court. Your client, a French company, has brought an action for patent infringement. The other side's applying to strike it out on a technical ground. They fail. By mid-morning, you're on the phone to the client to tell them the good news and discuss possible options for a settlement. When you get back to the office, there's a message waiting for you from an American biotech company. They're forming a joint venture with a multi-national pharmaceutical company, and want you to draft various licensing agreements. They have to be finished within 48 hours. You've been working at it for an hour when the phone rings. It's one of your most important clients. They have evidence that their goods are being counterfeited, and want to know what steps they can take to protect their trade marks. You advise them to commence proceedings immediately, and apply the next day for an order preventing the other side from destroying evidence. You get on the phone to counsel's clerk and say you'll need one of his top barristers the next morning. Then you spend the rest of the evening taking evidence from your client and preparing the affidavit in support of the next day's application. You get home late, slump into bed and wake up in the middle of the night worrying about those licensing agreements. There's another long day ahead of you tomorrow . . .

skills needed

Patent law...a basic understanding of science (at least science A-levels)

General IP...curiosity in things artistic and technological...quirky and eccentric characters...all-round ability...

career options

Many IP lawyers began their careers as litigators or general commercial lawyers and only started to specialise as they saw niche areas opening up. Constantly developing technology keeps this field moving and there are ever-increasing opportunities to specialise in IP from early on in your career. If you choose the right firm, you'll probably be able to do at least one IP seat during training.

IP knowledge is equally valuable outside private practice. Manufacturing, pharmaceutical and research companies employ patent specialists and there are in-house legal teams at Proctor & Gamble, Reckitt & Benckiser and Unilever. Non-patent lawyers find their way into the media world: all major publishers and television companies have in-house IP lawyers.

Alternatives to strictly legal practice include more general business/management posts within the organisations mentioned above. Many broadcasting companies now employ lawyers in positions such as Head of Business and Legal Affairs. Additionally firms of trademark agents and patent attorneys are often keen to recruit those with a legal training.

leading IP firms

All information on leading firms comes from the Chambers Guide to the Legal Profession 2000-2001.

Bird & Bird: *"No rubbish or time-wasting"* from this powerhouse of IP. Perceived to be edging more to a technology base by some whilst also acknowledged to have a growing commercial side to the firm. Litigation, however, is what the team is best known for and they sit without question at the top of both the Patent and General league tables. Why? One expert explained it quite simply in terms of *"quality of solicitors and quality & quantity of work. It is a whole firm dedicated to this area of law."* Bird & Bird were in on IP ahead of almost everyone else in the game and the same can be said of the emerging technology sectors. Any talk in the market about a diminished profile is largely explained by the fact that some of their really big patent cases in the last couple of years have now settled. The well known focus areas of biotech, hi-tech and pharmaceuticals belie a thoroughly impressive client list across the board.

Conducted trade mark and passing off litigation for Associated Newspapers in relation to the METRO trade mark against the Guardian Group and Modern Times Group.

Bristows: If Bird & Bird are still perceived as a niche firm, Bristows are doubly so. Finally free of the *"old family firm image,"* Bristows has emerged once more as an all round leader and a truly *"class act."* It occupies the position of overall joint leader despite the fact that it does not have a giant-sized commercial practice behind it and as a result has an overwhelming bias towards litigation. A common sentiment of the department's work is that it is *"first rate and you know it will always be incredibly thorough."* The fact that so many of their lawyers are so well known speaks volumes. Plenty of grey goods actions and a thriving brands prosecution practice has helped see the non-patent work increase at an even faster pace in the last year than the patent work. The numbers of overseas clients instructing on litigation continues to grow. Advising United Distillers & Vintners on brand protection, transactions and co-ordination of foreign litigation.

Simmons & Simmons: As strong as ever. Traditionally very good on soft IP, on the patents side, it is now recognised as an equally potent force and is involved in plenty of big cases. The pharmaceuticals sector is clearly behind much of Simmons' success but chemicals and electronics are also significant. The practice now manages big-ticket European litigation rather than concentrating purely on domestic bound disputes. The firm has a TM filing practice. Acted for Proctor & Gamble on the CA interlocutory hearing concerning disclosure in the patent amendment action with Kimberley-Clark.

Taylor Joynson Garrett: Seen to be really *"holding their own"* and working on *"great cases."* A large department which has come from a smaller base than the other three leaders, the style is seen as distinctively aggressive, and for this reason a few practitioners commented that they were not always the easiest opponents. Others went no further than

acknowledging a *"firm but fair"* approach. Litigation is the engine room to the IP practice and there is a self proclaimed preoccupation with winning. All the assistants on the patent side have science or technology qualifications. Clients vary enormously from tobacco, food and pharmaceuticals manufacturers through to charities, oil and computer games. The emphasis is on contentious work, but the broader nature of the firm also ensures a modest helping of corporate support work.

Wragge & Co incorporating Needham & James: Until its recent merger with Birmingham powerhouse Wragge & Co, Needham & James was an established boutique firm. It was felt to be *"excellent at handling small to medium sized litigation,"* particularly patents, with a really *"sensible"* approach. That market perception didn't quite factor in the size of many of the clients. In terms of size they may have been *"a minnow"* but they were swimming with the big fish daily. Big City players were often surprised that Wragge & Co didn't have a London presence. Their activity in Birmingham rippled through anyway and the marriage with Needham & Grant looks set to provide each of the two firms with what they were looking for. Acting for Unilever in the action against Nestlé & Ors, the Birmingham office was such a strong practice across the spectrum of IP work that many London opposition thought Wragges was a City firm anyway. There appears to be little in the way of competition in the Midlands for them. They *"get on with it and conduct business pleasantly."* The Midlands provides a ready-made client base in the engineering and manufacturing sectors and the firm has enhanced its skills in the pharmaceuticals and agrochemical sectors through the recruitment of specialists at degree and PhD level. In the last year, the firm worked on a huge brand-splitting exercise for Heinz and saw the completion of *Hadley Industries* v *Metal Sections*.

Willoughby & Partners: *"A lovely practice"* with a *"pretty impressive range of clients."* This firm has *"an element of sexiness to it,"* with its Docklands location and collection of ex-City lawyers now working together purely on IP for big brand names. Willoughby leads a band of youngsters deemed to be *"competent and enthusiastic."* Acted in the parallel imports litigation between SmithKline Beecham and GlaxoWellcome and in the well publicised Mont Blanc pens litigation. The team additionally includes two full time senior consultants and a barrister.

Osborne Clarke OWA, Reading, Bristol: Significant corporate and commercial deals and a new thrust in branding work has characterised the IP activities of the firm this year. Strong showing from IT clients, media, retail, motor and sports sectors.The firm won work from motor manufacturer Morgan and acted for Ryder Cup Ltd dealing with injunctive proceedings in relation to TM infringement, particularly on the internet.

Hewitson Becke + Shaw, Cambridge: In a region that is bursting into life with new technology, HB+S remain clearly at the top of the pile in the Cambridge area for IP work. The firm is now targeting US clients. The team has attained a superb reputation for litigation and has been involved in many recent important decisions. Particularly active on biotech patent litigation in the last year, it also acted on landmark TM disputes relating to product shape and labelling issues. Partners and assistants are confirmed to operate out of the Cambridge or Norwich offices depending on client requirements.

Mills & Reeve, Cambridge: This strong commercial practice is well positioned to use its wider strengths to make the best of the requirement to link funders with those developing new technology. Long held relationships with Cambridge colleges provide the route into many new spin-out companies arising from academic research. Clients reach nation-wide and are not pooled exclusively around Cambridge, despite rich seams of work locally.

Hill Dickinson (incorporating Philip Woods), Stockport: A practice little understood by the market and operating as an IP oasis in Stockport, away from the firm's main offices in Manchester. There is little that the team doesn't take on and the client base ranges from TV companies to textiles. It has been advising on hi-tech joint ventures between universities and hospitals.

LEADING FIRMS

LONDON	IP: PATENT	IP: GENERAL
Allen & Overy	*	***
Ashurst Morris Crisp		**
Baker & McKenzie	**	****
Bird & Bird	******	******
Briffa		*
Bristows	******	******
Charles Russell		*
Clifford Chance	***	*****
CMS Cameron McKenna		**
Dechert		*
Denton Wilde Sapte		***
DLA		**
Eversheds	**	****
Field Fisher Waterhouse		**
Freshfields Bruckhaus Deringer		**
Gouldens		*
H2O (Henry Hepworth Organisation)		*
Hammond Suddards Edge	*	**
Herbert Smith	****	****
Linklaters	****	*****
Llewelyn Zietman		***
Lovells	****	****
Macfarlanes		*
Norton Rose		*
Olswang		***
Roiter Zucker	*	**
Rowe & Maw		**
Simmons & Simmons	*****	*****
SJ Berwin & Co		*
Slaughter and May		***
Stephenson Harwood		***
Stringer Saul	*	
Taylor Joynson Garrett	*****	*****
Willoughby & Partners		****
Wragge & Co	****	***

THE SOUTH	IP	THE SOUTH	IP
DMH, *Brighton*	★★★★★	**Lochners Technology Solicitors,** *Godalming*	★★★★★★
Lester Aldridge, *Bournemouth*	★★★★		

THAMES VALLEY	IP	THAMES VALLEY	IP
Garretts, *Reading*	★★★★	**The Law Offices of Marcus J. O'Leary,** *Bracknell*	★★★★★★
Manches, *Oxford*	★★★		
Nabarro Nathanson, *Reading*	★★★★★	**Willoughby & Partners,** *Oxford*	★★★★★★
Osborne Clarke OWA, *Reading*	★★★		

SOUTH WEST	IP	SOUTH WEST	IP
Beachcroft Wansbroughs, *Bristol*	★★★★	**Humphreys & Co,** *Bristol*	★★★★
Bevan Ashford, *Bristol*	★★★★★	**Laytons,** *Bristol*	★★★★
Burges Salmon, *Bristol*	★★★★	**Osborne Clarke OWA,** *Bristol*	★★★★★★

WALES, MIDLANDS & E. ANGLIA	IP	WALES, MIDLANDS & E. ANGLIA	IP
Edwards Geldard, *Cardiff*	★★★★★★	**Pinsent Curtis,** *Birmingham*	★★★★★
Eversheds, *various*	★★★★★	**Shoosmiths,** *Northampton*	★★★
Morgan Cole, *Cardiff*	★★★★★	**Wragge & Co,** *Birmingham*	★★★★★★
Browne Jacobson, *Nottingham*	★★	**Greenwoods,** *Peterborough*	★★★
Freethcartwright, *Nottingham*	★★★	**Hewitson Becke + Shaw,** *Cambridge*	★★★★★★
Hammond Suddards Edge, *Birmingham*	★★★★	**Mills & Reeve,** *Cambridge, Norwich*	★★★★★
Hewitson Becke + Shaw, *Northampton*	★★★	**Taylor Vinters,** *Cambridge*	★★
Martineau Johnson, *Birmingham*	★★★★★		

NORTH WEST	IP	NORTH WEST	IP
Addleshaw Booth & Co, *Manchester*	★★★★★★	**Hill Dickinson,** *Stockport*	★★★★★
DLA, *Liverpool, Manchester*	★★★★	**Kuit Steinart Levy,** *Manchester*	★★★
Eversheds, *Manchester*	★★★	**Lawson Coppock & Hart,** *Manchester*	★★★
Halliwell Landau, *Manchester*	★★★★★★	**Philip Conn & Co,** *Manchester*	★★
Hammond Suddards Edge, *Manchester*	★★★★	**Taylors,** *Blackburn*	★★★

NORTH EAST	IP	NORTH EAST	IP
Addleshaw Booth & Co, *Leeds*	★★★★★★	**Irwin Mitchell,** *Leeds*	★★★
Dickinson Dees, *Newcastle upon Tyne*	★★	**Lupton Fawcett,** *Leeds*	★★★★
DLA, *Leeds, Sheffield*	★★★★★★	**Pinsent Curtis,** *Leeds*	★★★★★★
Eversheds, *Leeds*	★★★★★★	**Walker Morris,** *Leeds*	★★★★
Hammond Suddards Edge, *Leeds*	★★★★★		

SPECIALIST PRACTICE AREAS INTELLECTUAL PROPERTY

275

IT, e-commerce & telecoms

The boundaries between IT, telecoms, IP, broadcasting, e-commerce and digital media are growing ever more blurred as internet 'convergence' issues tighten their grip over the broader communications industry. With IP enjoying a section in its own right and broadcasting and digital media covered under media, this section will focus on IT, e-commerce and telecommunications law. IT work (including e-commerce) consists principally of outsourcing (where outside IT specialists are brought in to set up and run a company's computer systems), systems development, IT contract drafting and on-line/internet advice. Telecoms largely revolves around proffering advice on the regulatory statutes which govern telecommunications companies and are designed to protect the interests of consumers. Competition law is also of ever growing importance in the telecoms field, as mega-mergers bring monopoly issues to the forefront.

The transactional side of telecoms, highlighted this year by several major mergers within the industry, differs little from standard M&A work, though a certain knowledge of regulatory matters is of course necessary.

Digital media is an increasingly important aspect of media law which relates to information disseminated in a digitised format. This is a heavily internet-oriented practice area sometimes dubbed 'multimedia.' A dynamic new area of practice, with both regulatory and transactional aspects, digital media is at the very forefront of 'convergence' issues. Most digital media lawyers originally hailed from an IP/copyright background, though others started out in telecommunications (principally on the regulatory side) and data protection. Clients are very varied, including internet service providers, internet industry bodies, software developers, games designers and banks providing on-line services.

a day in the life...

A typical day for an IT lawyer might include advising on a new software development contract, reading through a system integration contract, advising on an internet issue and popping down to court for a hearing on a major system. **Osborne Clarke OWA**'s Paul Gardner specialises in computer games. He is currently advising a games publisher on what copyright allows you to depict in terms of club strips in football games and several games console manufacturers on how close to the Sony games console they can design their products.

For internet and communications lawyer David Naylor of US firm **Weil Gotschal & Manges** there is no such thing as a 'typical day.' A week's work might consist of advising internet and communications startups on all aspects of internet law from content liability to on-line contracting through to advising more mature internet companies on building business networks across Europe and acting for telecoms companies on UK and EU commercial and regulatory matters. He would be in frequent contact with the firm's US and Brussels offices in relation to cross-border work for US and EU clients and collaborating with the corporate department on funding issues and acquisitions in commercial internet deals. Foreign travel is not as frequent as you might think, as London is a major hub for the telecoms industry anyhow and "our office is so phenomenally busy."

skills needed

IT/e-commerce...ability to be a "deal-maker"...an excellent understanding of "hard" regulatory matters...a good grasp of the commercial world...ability to keep up to speed...sensitivity to the needs of artists...a willingness to "roll up your sleeves"...real mental dexterity...gut feel for the issues...feel challenged and thrilled by change....

Telecoms...general grounding in corporate... some industry knowledge...background in economics...comfort with technical language or jargon ...innovative...knowledge of competition law....

Digital media...basic understanding of copyright matters...up to date understanding of new media, both technically and as an industry...flexibility to clients' needs...a "sensible approach to risk"....

leading IT firms

All information on leading firms comes from the Chambers Guide to the Legal Profession 2000-2001.

Baker & McKenzie is a *"well-known, established practice"* that is indisputably one of London's finest and is seen to benefit from a *"good European geographic spread,"* especially in Germany. Said to treat IT as *"less of a corporate service arm than many other large firms."* Active across the entire span of IT work, the practice's centres of excellence are in outsourcing agreements, IT litigation, digital media and IT/telecommunications convergence matters. The major part of their extensive client portfolio are large soft and hardware suppliers, many of them from the US.

Bird & Bird has a *"focused"* team with a massive reputation in the field and *"strong US connections."* They are at the head in public sector procurement work, especially when it comes to telecoms-related project finance and for their superb technical expertise. The team was picked this year to act as preferred counsel to Sema Group, one of the world's leading IT and business services companies. The firm scores highly once again in the related field of internet/e-commerce law, being hailed as a *"true convergence practice"* and counting well-known names such as Demon Internet amongst its clients.

Clifford Chance is seen to be equally at home dealing with regulatory and corporate matters, though clients are principally major corporate users within the financial and trading sectors. With *"great all-round expertise"* across the 'convergence' spectrum (IT, e-commerce, telecoms, media and corporate), the City leviathan certainly has *"the power*

to make it" in the cut-and-thrust IT battlefield, where it has long been a distinguished combatant. While some see the IT practice to be intimately linked to the firm's corporate activities (though less so than at other 'magic circle' firms), the overall market view was summarised as: *"You can never, never discount them – they have a lot of clients in the field."*

Olswang is an *"extremely go-ahead, trendy"* firm with an impressive depth and breadth of experience in 'convergence' practice areas. Commonly perceived to be the *"media darling,"* the firm has successfully expanded beyond its media roots into 'pure' IT, Internet/e-commerce, digital mixed media and telecoms work. Active across the entire IT spectrum, the firm's clients include both suppliers and users, both national and international. Work conducted ranges from procurement contracts and software distribution agreements to outsourcing and IT litigation. Clients include Freeserve and BSkyB.

leading digital media firms

Niche media firm The Simkins Partnership has advised NTL on 'internet liability' (whether a provider is responsible for illegal material accessible via their search vehicle) and is currently advising Sony on setting up a 'digital dance site.' IP/media boutique H2O is acting for Ulster unionist leader David Trimble in his defamation suit against Amazon.com, the first libel action against an internet web-based bookshop.

leading IT firms outside London

The Law Offices of Marcus J. O'Leary is a 'boutique' practice in Bracknell with a *"wonderful reputation"* and a *"traditional focus on M4 corridor IT firms"* (*"a strategy that has worked"*). Active across the IT spectrum (software, hardware, outsourcings etc...), the firm is increasingly involved in Internet/E-commerce matters and has an emerging specialism in IT/music convergence issues. Clients are drawn from across the IT/Internet/multimedia spectrum and include numerous household names.

Nabarro Nathanson's Reading outpost is seen to enjoy *"pride of place"* in the Thames valley. Known for both contentious and non-contentious work, the practice is admired for its *"unrivalled"* advice when it comes to IT project work. The national IT practice's strength is still seen to lie in Reading, with the London office languishing in its shadow. Clients comprise IT suppliers and services (very rarely users), with a niche in acting on behalf of venture capitalists investing in the IT industry. E-commerce and IT sector joint ventures are areas of growth. The firm has been advising Deloitte Consulting on a major systems implementation project.

DMH of Brighton is an *"expanding"* IT practice that rules the roost unchallenged in Kent and Sussex. At home in both the contentious and non-contentious spheres, the bulk of the practice's workload stems from 'hard' IT systems supply agreements. Internet/e-commerce is also a major new focus, accounting for roughly three fifths of the practice's current clients. Have recently been acting for Eyretel in connection with a system supply agreement with a major telecoms company.

Osborne Clarke OWA in Bristol is a *"hugely energetic and aggressive"* firm that has *"made a big impact"* in the IT and internet/e-commerce field this year. The practice is principally occupied with systems sales purchases, outsourcing agreements, corporate support and internet/e-commerce issues (especially US start-ups in the UK). Clients include both users and suppliers. Highlight transactions include advising on the sale of Aethos Communication Systems to Logica plc for c.£40m and of Knowledge Technology to Sysnstar plc for c.£12m.

With *"the best commercial department in the Midlands,"* **Eversheds, Birmingham** is now *"looking to build up"* its IT/IP department, which is already held to be *"out on its own after Wragges."* Offering a full service on the IT front, the practice's strengths are in public sector IT work, e-commerce, IT outsourcings (for both the public and private sectors), and 'e-government' matters including IT PFIs. Clients range

from suppliers and software processors to banks and venture capitalists looking to invest in e-business start-ups. The firm has recently been advising Lincolnshire County Council on a large, complex outsourcing and the business process consequences thereof.

Wragge & Co in Birmingham is *"technically very good"* and has a *"substantial client-base."* Our interviewees were split between those who no longer see them as a clear leader and those who continue to view Wragges as in a league of its own amongst the regional IT firms. Outsourcing and IT-related corporate, commercial, insurance, telecoms and financial services work form the bulk of the practice's workload. E-commerce and internet start-up transactions, especially those with a private equity component, are another area of expertise. Is advising BA on the outsourcing of its Next Steps IT system, reportedly one of the largest in the private sector in the UK.

Edwards Geldard is Cardiff's premier IT practice, with particular fortes in facilities management and IT public procurement contracts. Clients include software developers, IT service providers, plcs, broadcasters, software and hardware suppliers and the Welsh Development Agency.

Masons: A firm with a niche IT practice with an especially good name for government IT projects and data protection matters. Whilst Leeds is seen to have an edge over Manchester, the gap has definitely closed, with the latter office acknowledged to be *"competent if low profile."* In addition to public sector PFI/PPP work, Leeds is known for its expertise in global data flows and e-commerce, while Manchester has a good reputation for IT outsourcings. The northern offices share the national practice's high profile for IT litigation. The firm has been advising numerous public and private clients and government agencies on compliance with the new Data Protection Act . It is also involved in the divestments of the polyurethanes, tioxide and petrochemical business of ICI to Huntsman Group and the ICI Acrylics business to Ineos.

LEADING FIRMS

LONDON	IT	E-COMMERCE	TELECOMS
Allen & Overy	****		*****
Ashurst Morris Crisp	*		***
Baker & McKenzie	******	****	****
Berwin Leighton	*		
Bird & Bird	******	******	******
Bristows	*		
Charles Russell			**
Clifford Chance	******	*****	******
CMS Cameron McKenna	*		
D J Freeman	*		
Denton Wilde Sapte	***	****	****
DLA	*		
Field Fisher Waterhouse	***	****	***
Freshfields	**		****
H2O (Henry Hepworth Organisation)		***	
Hammond Suddards Edge	*		
Harbottle & Lewis		***	
Herbert Smith	**	***	
Kemp & Co	***	***	
Linklaters	**		****
Lovells	*****		
Masons	****		
Nabarro Nathanson	*		
Olswang	*****	******	****
Osborne Clarke OWA	****	**	
Paisner & Co		***	
Pinsent Curtis		**	
Rakisons			**
Rowe & Maw	**		**
Simmons & Simmons	*		****
Slaughter and May	**		
Tarlo Lyons	**		
Taylor Joynson Garrett	****	***	***
Theodore Goddard	*	**	

LEADING FIRMS *continued*

THE SOUTH	IT/TELECOMS	THE SOUTH	IT/TELECOMS
Clyde & Co, *Guildford*	*****	Lester Aldridge, *Bournemouth*	*****
DMH, *Brighton*	******		

THAMES VALLEY	IT/TELECOMS	THAMES VALLEY	IT/TELECOMS
Boyes Turner & Burrows, *Reading*	***	Osborne Clarke OWA, *Reading*	*****
Garretts, *Reading*	*****	The Law Offices of Marcus	
Manches, *Oxford*	*****	J. O'Leary, *Bracknell*	******
Nabarro Nathanson, *Reading*	******	Willoughby & Partners, *Oxford*	*****

SOUTH WEST	IT/TELECOMS	SOUTH WEST	IT/TELECOMS
Beachcroft Wansbroughs, *Bristol*	****	Foot Anstey Sargent, *Exeter*	****
Burges Salmon, *Bristol*	****	Laytons, *Bristol*	*****
Clark Holt, *Swindon*	****	Osborne Clarke OWA, *Bristol*	******

MIDLANDS & EAST ANGLIA	IT/TELECOMS	MIDLANDS & EAST ANGLIA	IT/TELECOMS
Eversheds, *Birmingham, Nottingham*	******	Pinsent Curtis, *Birmingham*	*****
Hewitson Becke + Shaw, *Cambridge, Northampton*	*****	Wragge & Co, *Birmingham*	******

WALES	IT/TELECOMS	WALES	IT/TELECOMS
Edwards Geldard, *Cardiff*	******	Morgan Cole, *Cardiff*	*****
Eversheds, *Cardiff*	*****		

THE NORTH	IT/TELECOMS	THE NORTH	IT/TELECOMS
Addleshaw Booth & Co, *Leeds, Manchester*	****	Halliwell Landau, *Manchester*	****
		Irwin Mitchell, *Leeds*	***
DLA, *Leeds, Manchester, Sheffield*	**	Masons, *Leeds, Manchester*	******
Eversheds, *Leeds*	*****	Pinsent Curtis, *Leeds*	***

litigation

Litigation lawyers – or litigators – act for clients involved in disputes. There are three ways in which disputes can be pursued. Litigation itself involves recourse to the courts. This can be an expensive and time-consuming process. For this reason, contracts often provide for disputes between the parties to be referred to binding arbitration, normally by an expert in the field. Unlike court proceedings, arbitrations are confidential. They are particularly common in the shipping, insurance and construction industries. Alternative Dispute Resolution (ADR) is a cheaper alternative to both litigation and arbitration. Although it can take various forms, ADR often involves structured negotiations between the parties directed by an independent mediator. This form of ADR is known as mediation. There are other less common forms such as neutral evaluation, expert determination and conciliation. The parties retain the right to litigate if they find it impossible to reach an agreement.

If you think that contentious work is all about court-room drama, think again. Many disputes settle before commencement of proceedings. If proceedings are commenced, the odds are that the case will never reach trial. Parties to commercial litigation are not, as a rule, interested in having their 'day in court' although there may be matters of principle which need to be determined. The emphasis, therefore, is on reaching a commercial settlement. "If you can keep your clients out of court, they will love you much more than if you get them into a scrap," says Neil Fagan, leading litigation partner at **Lovells**. "Most of our work involves trying to stop people litigating."

type of work

General commercial litigators handle a variety of business disputes. Most cases will be contractual – everything from a dispute over the sale of a multi-million pound business, to an argument over the meaning of a term in a photocopier maintenance contract. They might also deal with negligence claims by companies against their professional advisors. Some litigators specialise in certain industry sectors – for example, construction, shipping, insurance, property or media. But most of the litigator's skills are common to all areas of commercial litigation, according to Christopher Style of **Linklaters**. "The procedure in running a court action or an arbitration, and the skill in negotiating an agreement is the same, whether you're talking about a dispute between the manufacturers of widgets or between accountants, stockbrokers or bankers," he says.

Litigation is a process. Once a case has been commenced, it follows a pre-determined course laid down by the rules of court – statement of case, disclosure of documents, various procedural applications and, in a small number of cases, trial. In a major case, this process can take several years. The mutual disclosure of relevant documents can be a particularly protracted and expensive affair, although new rules which came into force in April 1999 are intended to limit this process.

Managing this process is the litigator's primary role. This requires not only a mastery of the rules of court, but also a keen appreciation of tactics. If you're acting for a defendant, for example, you might ask the claimant for more information about its claim by means of a request for further information. Obtaining the information might not be your primary aim. You might know perfectly well the main thrust of the claim. But your request may expose weaknesses in the claimant's case. It also has a nuisance value, forcing the claimant to spend time and money in providing you with further information. If you're lucky, the request may persuade the claimant to settle a case. Disclosure can also be used as a tactical ruse, with parties taking advantage of their disclosure obligations to swamp their opponents with largely irrelevant documents. The Woolf reforms to the civil justice system, implemented in April 1999 have reduced the scope for such tactical games by simplifying procedures.

The range of the litigator's work has increased over the last few years, thanks largely to the extension of High Court rights of audience to solicitors. Although solicitors could always draft statements of case – the formal documents setting out the claimant's claim and the defendant's response – and act as advocates in High Court procedural hearings, they rarely did so. Instead, such work was normally referred to barristers. This is now changing. There hasn't been a flood of solicitor-advocates into the High Court. But the possibility of a career as an advocate, together with potential costs savings for the client, is encouraging solicitors to keep more work in-house. This phenomenon is particularly marked in the large City firms. **Herbert Smith** and **Lovells** for example have advocacy policies where solicitor advocates are used in all cases other than major hearings or full trials. The Woolf reforms are likely to accelerate this trend since they put a greater emphasis on written advocacy and have introduced the preliminary hearing – the case-management conference – which is dealt with by the solicitors with the day-to-day handling of the case.

a day in the life...

As a trainee, a proportion of your time will be spent researching points of law and procedure. Depending on your firm, specialist group you sit in and timing, you could be involved on one massive case with an important role in running the organisation of all the documents to be disclosed. Or you could be running a caseload of small county court cases in which you may be making small applications before a district judge. In a large City firm, a qualified litigator may sometimes work on no more than two or three big cases at a time. The caseload will probably be more varied in smaller litigation departments.

Paul Williams, a five-year qualified litigator at **Lovells**, says his days can be quite varied. You might start your day preparing for a procedural hearing in the Commercial Court at which you will be the advocate, arriving at court to find you are opposed by an experienced barrister instructed by the other side. (The firm has a policy of instructing counsel only in limited circumstances and litigators are encouraged to undertake as much advocacy as possible.) After a discussion outside the court with the other side's counsel, you reach agreement on a number of points but there is one matter on which you cannot agree. Your opponent insists that his client is entitled to ask your client to produce certain documents. You disagree.

You enter court and the judge asks a number of questions about the conduct of the proceedings. You have to explain the reasons for delays in taking certain procedural steps. However, after some argument the judge agrees with you and refuses to order your client to produce the documents. After the judge has given directions dealing with the disclosure of documents and witness statements, the hearing ends. You look at your watch to see that the hearing has lasted over an hour, although it only felt like a few minutes.

You rush back to the office, listen to a number of voicemail messages from clients and other lawyers, check your e-mails, then see you have received a fax from a client requesting an urgent response. You are already running late for lunch with another client but have to stay to deal with the enquiry. After twenty minutes or so you arrive at the restaurant where the client and your supervising partner are having lunch to celebrate a successful mediation in which you were involved. The client, an insurer, is pleased because the mediation resulted in the settlement of a £7m claim for less than £1m and avoided the time and expense of a trial. "Mediation is a cost-effective and constructive way of resolving commercial disputes," says Williams "and clients favour it because they are fully involved in the process, unlike a trial, where the lawyers control what happens."

Back to the office after lunch for a meeting with a witness. You are preparing his witness statement. This is hard work because his recollection of events is poor. This is not surprising because the events in question happened over five years ago. This is not uncommon in litigation. Luckily you are able to use the firm's document database to locate a letter written by the witness which jogs his memory. "Computer databasing of documents is the way forward in litigation," says Williams. "It allows you to view images of documents on screen, and searches for documents which would have taken hours now take a matter of seconds. Trainees who would previously have carried out manual searches can do something more productive."

Finally it is time for a conference call with clients in the USA. Due to the time difference the call is arranged for 6pm. You and your supervising partner update the clients on procedural matters. The client wants to discuss strategy and the possibility of bringing other parties into existing litigation. After discussing this you raise the question of mediation. The client, a US insurer, has participated in numerous mediations and expects you to be familiar with the mediation process. Luckily your recent mediation experience allows you to discuss the different approaches to mediation in the UK and the USA. The client is clearly impressed by your experience. By 7.30pm the conference call is over. The client has asked for a letter of advice. You consider whether to start this now but decide instead to write it first thing the next morning when you can approach the matter fresh. Your department is having drinks at the local wine bar and, after a busy day, you are only too glad to join them at 8pm.

skills needed

....drive...commercial-mindedness...grasp of tactics...natural toughness...competitiveness...drive –

"You need to like to win"...the ability to assimilate information quickly and see the big picture..."The best litigators are those with strong commercial awareness and an ability to think laterally around the immediate dispute"...strong negotiating skills... "Verve and panache"...a hard edge..."Charm takes you a long way but clients and opponents need to know that you can bite."

career options

All commercial practices in London and the provinces have litigation departments. Law Society rules require that all trainees do a contentious element in their training contract. **Herbert Smith** has the leading general commercial litigation practice in the City, followed by **Freshfields Bruckhaus Deringer**, **Clifford Chance** and **Lovells**. Among the specialist industry sectors, Masons leads the field in construction litigation. The insurance and shipping firms such as **Barlow Lyde & Gilbert**, **Clyde & Co**, **Ince & Co** and **Davies Arnold Cooper** are strong, not only in insurance litigation, but also in professional negligence work and shipping litigation.

In-house opportunities are less common than for corporate lawyers. Banks, insurance, construction and shipping companies sometimes employ specialist litigators. Only the very largest in-house departments need general commercial litigators.

leading litigation firms

All information on leading firms comes from the Chambers Guide to the Legal Profession 2000-2001.

Herbert Smith: Seemingly untouchable as the premier team, producing consistently high quality across a very large department. Its reputation has definitely changed. *"It used to be the endless letters on a Friday afternoon, but not now."* It can still *"generate a situation which you just can't get out of,"* but whilst *"the letters are tough"* they are *"realistic, clever formidable litigators,"* not offering a plain *"red meat"* diet all of the time. A good choice of firm, *"particularly for cases where the cost is not an issue and requires a team to be working on it."* There is no shortage of 50+ aged partners, who are felt by some to be *"very individualistic"* and certainly the most senior figures have almost unmatched standing. Key matters have included Bairds v Marks & Spencer and instructions from the Law Society concerning Kamlesh Bahl. Clients include Vodafone; BSkyB; Royal & Sun Alliance.

Lovells: *"First class – we enjoy working with them"* was a fairly representative comment of the good-natured and *"gentlemanly"* Lovells litigators. Barristers gush about the quality of instructions and support given. *"They do a huge amount of work and allow the bar to get on with the barristering."* Achieved a swift decision on Young v Robson Rhodes, where it acted for the defendant in this case examining the erection of Chinese walls.

Freshfields Bruckhaus Derringer: *"Involved in lots of areas"* and *"really motoring."* The bar confirms that they give *"fantastic back up"* and overall, the team is seen to be *"more consistent than some others"* with a *"stronger intellect."* The established names are joined by the newly recommended and *"somewhat dry"* Paul Lomas, who *"has the ability to turn his hand to a whole range of disputes."* Acting for the Government of Brunei in matters including claims against Prince Jefri.

Barlow Lyde & Gilbert: *"A phenomenal amount of work and they do it well."* For a firm which *"does nothing else but litigate – their whole attention is turned to it,"* a lesser reputation would be a problem. Insurance/reinsurance/professional negligence is still a clear focus. Of the firms of the insurance ilk, it is perceived to be more broad based. Although one interviewee implied that a team of Amazon warriors dwelt at Barlows, others felt that its litigators had *"changed their style of late."* The team handle both professional negligence and insurance work in addition to more general commercial litigation. Currently acting for the principal defendant in the Metro Trading case.

SJ Berwin & Co: *"Lots of good clients with money – a really different firm."* It *"understands and respects litigation as a key part of the practice."* The team is *"big on*

personality" and displays a *"tough, no nonsense attitude with the right level of aggression turned on and off as required."* Plenty of international work and good links with the US. It acts in the Nigerian Noga litigation for the Abacha family and in the Eastern Agents matter in which it is bringing a claim for five companies against Eastern Electricity plc concerning the application and construction of Commercial Agents regulations.

Pinsent Curtis, Birmingham, Leeds: Field leaders in the Midlands and in Yorkshire. The Birmingham team is well-thought of and held to be *"organised, sensible, good-quality and professional."* Typically undertakes multi-million breach of warranty claims, financial services mis-selling cases, IT disputes and claims under the Restrictive Trade Practices Act. Recently acted on a breach of EC directive on free movement of goods case against the Secretary of State for Trade and Industry and the Secretary of State for Health. The Leeds practice has regained lost ground conceded over the last few years and is *"now well and truly back as a contender."* Key strengths include expertise in the retail sector, IT disputes, regulatory work, the food industry and competition issues. A large number of multi-million pound IT disputes have been handled in the last year, including advice given to some major retailers in respect of highly-publicised web-site retailing issues.

Eversheds, nationwide: With stand-out practices in Wales, Yorkshire, East Anglia, North East and the North West, as well as highly-regarded teams in the Midlands and South West, Eversheds is extremely visible on the regional litigation scene. In Manchester, its mainstream reputation in broad commercial litigation is beefed up with expertise in contentious construction, IP and defamation. In contrast, the Midlands teams (in Birmingham and Nottingham) have consolidated traditionally strong areas of practice such as transport, manufacturing and engineering, while expanding newer areas in litigation: IT, telecoms and education. They recently handled a dispute with a rail operator for the sum of £65m. The Yorkshire team is sizeable and runs the gamut of litigation from corporate and shareholder matters to IT and negligence disputes. Large single quality pieces of litigation are best exemplified by the team's involvement in the Bloody Sunday Inquiry. The Newcastle outfit handles a variety of contractual disputes and has recently been involved in several contentious intellectual property matters including advice given in relation to cross-jurisdictional questions of ownership, copyright infringement and passing off.

Addleshaw Booth & Co, Manchester, Leeds: A dominant firm in the North West and North East. The Leeds practice is powered by a *"fundamentally great corporate client base,"* and boasts a clutch of individual litigators, who *"work effectively in teams, with lots of hands-on input."* It has a broad litigation practice with particular expertise in computer/IT and construction disputes. Although the Manchester team is felt to adopt a lower-key stance than some of its tougher Leeds counterparts, it too boasts some fine individual reputations and a perennially healthy corporate client base. It fields an active defamation and media/television practice and brings additional specialist expertise in financial services litigation, pensions, pharmaceuticals, minerals and railways.

DLA, Manchester, Liverpool, Leeds, Birmingham: Among the leaders in the North West and North East, DLA also has a well-regarded outfit in Birmingham. The high quality Manchester/Liverpool team, is involved in substantial disputes and demonstrates a tangible litigation ethos. It is active in a number of large corporate, shareholder, company law and civil fraud disputes. The large Leeds team boasts many ex-City lawyers and is felt to be expanding its litigation profile and building on its *"red-meat"* litigation ethos of the 90s, while tempering it with a more conciliatory post-Woolf approach. It recently acted for Newcastle United plc in a claim by UEFA Sports GmbH (German/European television broadcaster) in a dispute over broadcasting rights for UEFA Cup games.

LEADING FIRMS

LONDON	LIT (COMMERCIAL): 40+ LITIGATORS	LIT (COMMERCIAL): FEWER THAN 40 LITIGATORS
Allen & Overy	***	
Ashurst Morris Crisp		******
Baker & McKenzie		******
Berwin Leighton		**
Biddle		*
Charles Russell		**
Clifford Chance	***	
Clyde & Co		*****
CMS Cameron McKenna	**	
D J Freeman		*****
Dechert		****
Denton Wilde Sapte	*	
DLA	*	
Eversheds		*****
Freshfields Bruckhaus Deringer	*****	
Gouldens		*****
Hammond Suddards Edge		***
Herbert Smith	******	
Lawrence Graham		****
Lewis Silkin		**
Linklaters	****	
Lovells	*****	
Macfarlanes		*
Memery Crystal		**
Mishcon de Reya		**
Nabarro Nathanson		*****
Nicholson Graham & Jones		*****
Norton Rose	**	
Reynolds Porter Chamberlain		****
Richards Butler	*	
Rowe & Maw		*
Simmons & Simmons	**	
SJ Berwin & Co		******
Slaughter and May	*	
Stephenson Harwood		******
Taylor Joynson Garrett		**
Theodore Goddard		*
Travers Smith Braithwaite		****

THE SOUTH	LIT (COMM)	THE SOUTH	LIT (COMM)
Argles Stoneham Burstows, *Crawley*	****	DMH, *Brighton*	*****
Barlows, *Chertsey*	***	Lester Aldridge, *Bournemouth*	**
Blake Lapthorn, *Fareham*	******	Paris Smith & Randall, *Southampton*	***
Bond Pearce, *Southampton*	*****	Thomas Eggar Church Adams, *Chichester, Worthing*	*****
Brachers, *Maidstone*	****		
Cripps Harries Hall, *Tunbridge Wells*	******	Thomson Snell & Passmore, *Tunbridge Wells*	***

THAMES VALLEY	LIT (COMM)	THAMES VALLEY	LIT (COMM)
Boyes Turner & Burrows, *Reading*	*****	Morgan Cole, *Oxford, Reading*	******
Clarks, *Reading*	******	Nabarro Nathanson, *Reading*	*****
Garretts, *Reading*	*****	Shoosmiths, *Reading*	*****

SOUTH WEST	LIT (COMM)	SOUTH WEST	LIT (COMM)
Beachcroft Wansbroughs, *Bristol*	*****	Foot Anstey Sargent, *Exeter, Plymouth*	****
Bevan Ashford, *Bristol*	*****	Laytons, *Bristol*	****
Bond Pearce, *Bristol, Exeter, Plymouth*	*****	Lyons Davidson, *Bristol*	***
Burges Salmon, *Bristol*	******	Osborne Clarke OWA, *Bristol*	******
Cartwrights, *Bristol*	****	TLT Solicitors, *Bristol*	*****
Clarke Willmott & Clarke, *Yeovil*	***	Veale Wasbrough, *Bristol*	*****
Eversheds, *Bristol*	*****		

WALES	LIT (COMM)	WALES	LIT (COMM)
Edwards Geldard, *Cardiff*	******	Morgan Cole, *Cardiff, Swansea*	******
Eversheds, *Cardiff*	******	Palser Grossman, *Cardiff Bay*	*****
Hugh James Ford Simey, *Cardiff*	******		

MIDLANDS	LIT (COMM)	MIDLANDS	LIT (COMM)
Bell Lax Litigation, *Birmingham*	**	Lee Crowder, *Birmingham*	***
Browne Jacobson, *Nottingham*	****	Martineau Johnson, *Birmingham*	*****
Challinors Lyon Clark, *West Bromwich*	**	Moran & Co, *Tamworth*	**
DLA, *Birmingham*	****	Pinsent Curtis, *Birmingham*	******
Eversheds, *Birmingham, Nottingham*	*****	Shakespeares, *Birmingham*	**
Freethcartwright, *Nottingham*	***	Shoosmiths, *Northampton*	**
Gateley Wareing, *Birmingham*	***	The Wilkes Partnership, *Birmingham*	**
Hammond Suddards Edge, *Birmingham*	****	Wragge & Co, *Birmingham*	******
Kent Jones and Done, *Stoke-on-Trent*	**		

LEADING FIRMS *continued*

EAST ANGLIA	LIT (COMM)	EAST ANGLIA	LIT (COMM)
Birketts, *Ipswich*	★★★	Mills & Reeve, *Cambridge, Norwich*	★★★★★★
Eversheds, *Ipswich, Norwich*	★★★★★★	Prettys, *Ipswich*	★★★★
Greenwoods, *Peterborough*	★★★★	Taylor Vinters, *Cambridge*	★★★★★
Hewitson Becke + Shaw, *Cambridge*	★★★★★		

NORTH WEST	LIT (COMM)	NORTH WEST	LIT (COMM)
Addleshaw Booth & Co, *Manchester*	★★★★★★	Eversheds, *Manchester*	★★★★★★
Berg & Co, *Manchester*	★★	Halliwell Landau, *Manchester*	★★★★★
Berrymans Lace Mawer, *Liverpool, Manchester*	★★	Hammond Suddards Edge, *Manchester*	★★★★
		Hill Dickinson, *Liverpool*	★★★
Brabner Holden Banks Wilson, *Liverpool, Preston*	★★	Kershaw Abbott, *Manchester*	★
		Mace & Jones, *Liverpool*	★
Chaffe Street, *Manchester*	★★	Pannone & Partners, *Manchester*	★
Cobbetts, *Manchester*	★★★★★	Rowe & Cohen, *Manchester*	★
Cuff Roberts, *Liverpool*	★	Wacks Caller, *Manchester*	★
Davies Wallis Foyster, *Liverpool*	★★	Weightmans, *Liverpool*	★
DLA, *Liverpool, Manchester*	★★★★★★		

YORKSHIRE	LIT (COMM)	YORKSHIRE	LIT (COMM)
Addleshaw Booth & Co, *Leeds*	★★★★★★	Gosschalks, *Hull*	★★
Andrew M. Jackson & Co, *Hull*	★★★	Hammond Suddards Edge, *Leeds*	★★★★★★
Beachcroft Wansbroughs, *Leeds*	★★★	Irwin Mitchell, *Sheffield*	★★★★★
Brooke North, *Leeds*	★★	Keeble Hawson, *Leeds, Sheffield*	★★★
DLA, *Leeds*	★★★★★★	Lupton Fawcett, *Leeds*	★★★★
Eversheds, *Leeds*	★★★★★★	Pinsent Curtis, *Leeds*	★★★★★★
Ford & Warren, *Leeds*	★★★	Rollit Farrell & Bladon, *Hull*	★★★★
Gordons Cranswick Solicitors, *Bradford, Leeds*	★★★★	Russell & Creswick, *Sheffield*	★★
		Walker Morris, *Leeds*	★★★★★

NORTH EAST	LIT (COMM)	NORTH EAST	LIT (COMM)
Dickinson Dees, *Newcastle upon Tyne*	★★★★★	Robert Muckle, *Newcastle upon Tyne*	★★★★
Eversheds, *Newcastle upon Tyne*	★★★★★★	Ward Hadaway, *Newcastle upon Tyne*	★★★★★★
Hay & Kilner, *Newcastle upon Tyne*	★★★★	Watson Burton, *Newcastle upon Tyne*	★★★★★

media

We have divided this chapter into three categories: Advertising and Marketing, Defamation and Entertainment law. Entertainment is further subdivided into Film and Broadcasting, Music, Theatre and Publishing. According to Nigel Bennett, partner in the Film & Television Department at leading media firm **The Simkins Partnership**, students should ask themselves one fundamental question. Do you want to be in the world of money or the world of ideas? If you want the former then join a big City firm. If you want something more flexible and less institutionalised, then entertainment law may just be for you.

area of law

advertising & marketing: Firms with advertising and marketing clients specialise in both 'pure' and general advertising law. 'Pure' advertising law is copy clearance for ad agencies, marketing, PR, advertisers and other media clients. It requires a knowledge of broadcasting and publishing self regulatory codes such as the Advertising Standards Authority code and the Independent Television Commission code as well as statutes such as the Obscene Publications Act. An understanding of defamation and intellectual property law is also required.

General advertising law means advising your advertising client base on commercial contracts with suppliers, clients and the rest of the media, employment issues, corporate transactions and litigation. It is more likely that having gone to a firm with a client base in this industry you will tend to specialise one way or the other. The complete all-rounder is a rare creature.

'Talent contracts' are a specialism in themselves and require a depth of industry knowledge to do well. This is where an advertising lawyer acts on behalf of an ad agency client to negotiate a contract for the 'talent' to appear in a magazine, radio or TV ad. Clients will deal with the more routine ones themselves, but lawyers get called in for the bigger stars when the contracts become more complex.

"It's not a document intensive area of law," said Dominic Farnsworth, an assistant at West End firm **Lewis Silkin**, specialising in pure advertising advice to a number of agencies. "It's more of a mind game. You simply don't have the time to do hours of research....it's fast in and fast out. That keeps it fresh and fun."

a day in the life....

Dominic tells us, "at 2pm I might get a call from an agency with a legal problem for an ad with a 5pm print deadline. They need immediate and robust copy clearance advice. The key legal risks that I have to assess are trademark and copyright infringement, passing off issues, defamation, regulatory codes, whether or not any consents are required from personalities, whether the ad is misleading and whether or not there are comparative advertising considerations. You've got to think really fast to identify the problems." He then has to find a way to minimise these. Any letter of advice has to be written with the agency's own clients in mind as his advice will normally be passed on to the advertiser as well and needs to be diplomatically presented.

skills needed

...a fast, practical and commercial mind... an understanding of and sensitivity to the industry...quick turnaround time...readiness to innovate...detailed knowledge of copyright law....

defamation: One of the most high-profile and arguably most 'glamorous' areas of legal practice. A person can be defamed by written word, which is libel, or by spoken word, which is slander. The majority of actions taken are for libel. On the contentious side, lawyers act for either individuals or companies (claimants) seeking to sue publishers or broadcasters for damaging their reputation or for the individuals or companies being sued (defendants). On the non-contentious side, work includes pre-publication or pre-broadcast advice to authors, editors and TV companies.

Defamation is a fascinating field of law to work in, hinging as it does on questions of personal honour and the right to freedom of expression. Clients can range from high profile politicians or popstars to unknown businessmen. A libel lawyer will therefore gain experience of people from all walks of life and numerous different professions. Client contact is likely to begin at a much more junior level than in the corporate sector. Many see it as 'critical to career progression' to build up personal links to clients and in-house lawyers as quickly as possible. A typical day might involve a client meeting – hearing a claimant's story for the first time and giving advice on the best course of action; planning how to run an action; making an application to court on a procedural matter; persuading a reluctant witness to give evidence in court and possibly investigating an obstruse point of law. Many people think libel is all about trials, but in fact most libel lawyers have only one or two full trials per year. Trainees will probably spend more time in court than qualified solicitors, because they are encouraged to shadow barristers on short hearings and they may also undertake advocacy themselves. Up and coming libel star Katherine Rimell of **Theodore Goddard** sees it as "a very interesting career, especially as it relates to freedom of expression. And it certainly has its glamorous moments!"

Unlike most areas of law principles or public image often matter more than money. This means that clients may insist on taking a case to court for reasons of personal 'honour' even where they have a near hopeless case. "Principles are awfully expensive," said Rupert Grey of **Crockers Oswald Hickson**, "but they drive the whole game."

skills needed

...people skills...ability to understand what makes people tick...an interest in language (many are English graduates or former journalists) and current affairs...a keen understanding of human nature...flexibility...sensitivity...understanding of psychology....sharp, analytical mind...creative approach...working knowledge of copyright, confidentiality, contempt of court and the relevant industry codes of practice....

entertainment: We divide entertainment law into Film and Broadcasting, Music, Theatre and Publishing. Clients range from film studios and television production companies to theatre groups and individual artists. Work varies from the financing of West End productions to clearance and classification advice for the British Board of Film Classification. Equally, clients of all types will need contract, employment and litigation advice. Key to almost everything is an understanding of commercial law and intellectual property and how these apply to the entertainment industry.

According to Nigel Bennett of **The Simkins Partnership**, the entertainment lawyer often fulfills a traditional role as a general commercial advisor, as well as providing technical legal services. "You are providing solutions to a whole range of problems. Someone may require a co-producer in Spain. Another client may wish to buy the film rights to John Le Carré's latest novel. Another may ask you to find the finance for a project. You have a broader brief. It is fascinating work."

As opposed to a lot of City work, entertainment law is not mainly a matter of standard form procedures. In the early stage of your career you must learn quickly how the industry works. Clients value experience and want lawyers who have done it before. You play a prominent role and are much more than a small cog in a huge corporate wheel.

You therefore need the confidence to stand up and be counted.

film & broadcasting: According to Nigel Bennett, from a lawyer's point of view, you can look at a film or a television programme as any other commercial product. First you have to develop the product, then you have to finance it, then you have to produce it and then you have to sell it. All of these elements require legal advice of one kind or another. The work can be roughly summarised as a combination of commercial contract law (with an element of banking and secured lending) and the law of copyright. The film lawyer would normally see the process through from start to finish.

music: Clients come from all sectors of the music industry including record labels, production companies, managers and the artists themselves. Some firms lean more towards acting for talent, others to the record labels. Central to the work of each type of practice is contract work. High profile litigation sometimes arises when there is a dispute over contract terms or ownership of rights in compositions. Sometimes when band members split with each other or with their management, as happened with the Spice Girls and Robbie Williams, lawyers find that they are brought in to fight their client's corner in the process of sorting out who is entitled to what. Whether specialising in contentious or non-contentious work, music lawyers have to be fully versed in all aspects of copyright as well as contract law. Specialist music firms may also advise on the incorporation and development of new record labels and joint venture agreements between larger and smaller labels.

theatre: There are a few practitioners in London who thrive off the theatrical world. Some work with broader media firms, others attract clients by virtue of their own reputation. Clients include theatre and opera companies, producers, theatrical agents and actors. Theatre lawyers will spend a lot of time in contract negotiations for their clients. Relationships between the constituent parties to a new production all need to be established and regulated through these contracts. A lawyer will usually find himself involved from the inception of the idea for a production right through to the opening curtain and beyond. Increasingly, lawyers will become involved in arrangements for the funding of a new production.

publishing: Work in this sector includes contractual, licensing, copyright and libel work for publishing houses. Most of this work is carried out in-house or by libel lawyers, so there are only a few London firms who can be said to specialise in publishing law. As with libel, an interest in language and literature are obvious requirements.

skills needed

...social skills...same outlook and language as clients...understanding of the way creative people work...understanding of the industry...a thorough working knowledge of contract and copyright law...communication skills... creativity in problem solving...be prepared to immerse yourself in the business...commercial aptitude...patience...methodical nature...inquisitiveness....

career options

Increasingly there is crossover between private practice and working in-house for media and entertainment organisations. Lawyers transfer between the two more readily than they did a few years ago. Money is generally perceived to be better in-house and the hours are considered more favourable – you do not need to go out looking for new clients, for example. However, one should remember that in recessionary times, in-house counsel are normally the first to go as their legal work can quite easily be outsourced.

Michael Griffiths works for the legal department of Paramount Home Entertainment International, having initially been in private practice. His colleagues have come from a variety of places, both specialist media firms and general commercial firms. Mike's workload is very varied and all manner of things land on his desk. In addition to the film work, the company requires its lawyers to give them a range of advice, just like any other large organisation.

Working in-house can have distinct advantages over private practice. A lack of stiffness and formality is characteristic of the entertainment industry generally and Mike says that this translates through to his working environment. Casual dress, less hierarchy and involvement in a fair degree of non-legal business management tasks can make for a refreshing contrast to the usual experience of a commercial lawyer. Just after we interviewed him Mike was going to the screening of a film for two hours. Just part of the job!

leading advertising & mkt. firms

All information on leading firms comes from the Chambers Guide to the Legal Profession 2000-2001.
Most advertising lawyers are London-based. **Lewis Silkin** and **Macfarlanes** and **Osborne Clarke OWA** are the leaders, but close behind is **The Simkins Partnership**. Outside of London, **Hammond Suddards Edge** in the Midlands, **Eversheds** in Birmingham and **Lester Aldridge** in Bournemouth are regarded highly.

leading defamation firms

Farrer & Co: Top-flight outfit whose behind-the-scenes, commercial approach has given it a reputation for being *"discreet enough to act both for the News of the World and the royal family."* On the defendant side, the team acts for several major newspaper titles and publishing groups, while claimant clients include high-profile individuals, institutions and corporations. Recent work has included an increasing number of cases with an international element, particularly in relation to e-mail and internet libel issues. Clients include NewsGroup, Daily Telegraph and Haymarket Publishing.

Olswang: Despite a year marked by fewer front-page cases than in previous years, this *"small but perfectly formed"* team maintains its reputation for *"getting on with it"* for its large bank of *"extremely loyal clients."* The firm is most notable for its formidable defendant practice, with major clients including national newspapers, magazine groups, companies and charities. In addition, the team has a strong reputation in issues relating to the nascent field of internet and e-mail libel and content, and has a smaller claimant practice. Acted for The Guardian and The Sunday Times in the libel action brought by Keith Schellenberg, the former laird of the Scottish Isle of Eigg. Clients include Julie Andrews, Guardian Newspapers Ltd and Freeserve plc.

Peter Carter-Ruck and Partners: Large team still thought to be *"in a class of its own"* for claimant work in terms of sheer volume, profile and quality. Many in the market praised the team's *"entrepreneurial approach,"* the most notable example being the continuing success of the firm's conditional fee system for certain defamation cases. On the defendant side, the team acts for book, magazine and newspaper publishers and television companies. Acted for Victor Kiam in his successful action against Mirror Group Newspapers. Clients include United Broadcasting and Entertainment, Express Newspapers, National Magazine Company.

Wiggin and Co, Cheltenham: Continue to build up a first-class reputation at this largely defendant practice, with an expanding client base. Seen to be competing increasingly with London firms. Handles a wide range of work including corporate defamation, TV clearance and cases referred from insurers.

Foot Anstey Sargent, Exeter: Long established defamation practice which acts for a large number of regional newspapers and is *"particularly good at reporting restricted material."* Some work is also handled for book publishers and radio stations. Recently defended a libel action based on 110 articles.

leading entertainment firms

SJ Berwin & Co: The film finance practice now appears unassailable in its top ranking position. Major sale and leaseback work and a mass of traditional bank lending has allowed a team packed with great partners to shine. On the production side the team advises on both TV and film projects. The firm advised Société Générale on the funding arrangements for the Anglo-French-Hungarian co-production of 'The Luzhin Defence' and acted for The Britt Allcroft Company on its new film production of 'Thomas the Tank Engine.'

Richards Butler: A strong and long-held link with the BBC is viewed as the cornerstone of the broadcasting practice. Instructions range from copyright and content issues through to distribution and transmission matters in both TV and radio. Production advice is split evenly between film and TV clients, whilst on the finance side, the firm sees sale and leaseback transactions as well as bank and gap/mezzanine finance. Instructed by Société Générale on an insurance-backed revolving credit facility for Intermedia Film Equities, the makers of 'Sliding Doors' and 'Enigma'.

Olswang: Top of the range for production and broadcasting work. A perception that clients pay handsomely but get the best quality advice. *"Very corporate, as opposed to a west end approach"* some felt, whilst others commented that the firm now has to work hard to live up to the reputation is has acquired. Act for terrestrial, cable and satellite broadcasters. Recent work includes the launch of ITN's 24 hour news channel, a joint venture with NTL. On the production and finance side much of the work has been for the distributors and studios, such as the production work on 'The Talented Mr. Ripley' for Miramax.

Davenport Lyons: *"A great, classic entertainment firm"* with music as one of its assets. This year, work has ranged from the conclusion of The Clash's new publishing deal with Universal Music to Copyright Tribunal references. *"Commercially sensible and techni-cally knowledgeable"* on film finance and production work this is a firm seen to offer good value advice with a *"responsive"* style. The team has seen a high volume of bank lending for several major players, has advised insurers and acted on sale and lease-backs and EIS schemes. The production caseload is felt to have increased in volume and profile. The partners are said to be nurturing some real talent at junior level. Acted for the Arts Council of England on their funding of a number of films, including 'Love's Labours Lost.' Advised the British producer of 'Vatel,' the largest Anglo-French co-production in history.

Denton Wilde Sapte: Superlative for broadcasting, particularly in pay TV, very strong in finance and well regarded in production work. The Denton Hall/Wilde Sapte merger is perceived to have brought particular advantage on the funding side. With ample resources and international reach, DWS is recognized as being amongst the more capable players with real industry background. Its documentation is praised as well as its top lawyers. Advised on the launch of The Money Channel including digital distribution and transmission arrangements with BSkyB and others. Very well known for its involvement in M&A work for media businesses, the team is seen far more for its corporate, particularly international, expertise. Represented Windswept Pacific Entertainment Co (USA) and Windswept Pacific Music Limited (UK) on the disposal of a large part of their publishing catalogue to EMI. Pulling away from the pack in publishing. The rise of e-publishing has added to the group's strengths rather than challenged them. Last year, the firm helped Britannica.co.uk bring Britannica's content online.

Russells: Still number one for music. The explanations are clear, consistent and frequent. With this firm clients get *"great ability and no weak links," "you can't ignore them and they are good to do business with."* While there may be litigators to compete on an equal footing, the non-contentious crown remains firmly planted on the collective head of the Russells team. The work handled by the firm is comprehensive from artist deals through to management disputes and corporate acquisitions.

Tarlo Lyons: Some feel that the reputation of the theatre practice rests quite heavily on its main client Cameron Mackintosh, but such a view fails to take into account scores of other top productions on which the firm works each year. Recent shows have included 'Witches of Eastwick', 'Gumboots', 'Tap Dogs' and 'Happy Days'

Wiggin and Co, Cheltenham: *"Outstanding"* to the extent that *"no one else in the regions compares."* A number of its media partners work from both the Cheltenham and London offices. It has a focus in newer media and television but also publishing expertise. Acts for an increasing number of independent film and TV production companies.

Hammond Suddards Edge, Birmingham: Coming at media and entertainment work primarily from two angles; sports broadcasting and venue ownership. Both have as a common thread the exploitation of live entertainment. Have also become involved in film financing and negotiations for clients who wish to exploit rights pertaining to TV and radio performances and concepts. Advised Aston Villa FC on broadcasting deal with NTL.

McCormicks, Leeds: Has the strongest profile in the region. There is a strong sports broadcasting bias to the firm's work. The firm advised FAPL on problems concerning the overseas broadcasting contract with Canal+ and on current and future broadcasting arrangements with, inter alia, BSkyB and the BBC. Also acts for a number of TV personalities and comedians.

LEADING FIRMS

LONDON	ADV & MKTNG	DEF	MEDIA & ENTERTAINMENT:				
			FILM	B'CASTNG	MUSIC	THEATRE	PUB'G
Allen & Overy				*			
Ashurst Morris Crisp				****			
Babbington Bray and Krais					**		
Baker & McKenzie	*						
Bates, Wells & Braithwaite						***	
Beachcroft Wansbroughs	*						
Biddle		****					
Bindman & Partners		**					
Campbell Hooper						*****	
Clifford Chance	*	*		*****			
Clintons					*****	*****	
CMS Cameron McKenna	***						
Crockers Oswald Hickson		****					
D J Freeman		*****		***			
Davenport Lyons		*****	*****	**	*		
David Price & Co		****					
Denton Wilde Sapte			****	******	*		******
Eatons					***		
Eversheds					*		
Farrer & Co		******					
Field Fisher Waterhouse	****			**			
Finers Stephens Innocent		*					
Goodman Derrick		***		****			
H2O (Henry Hepworth Organisation)		***	***				***
Hamlins					*		
Hammond Suddards Edge	****						
Harbottle & Lewis		**	*****	**	**	***	****
Harrison Curtis			***		*	****	
Herbert Smith				*			
Lawrence Graham	**						
Lee & Thompson			*****		****		
Lewis Silkin	******	*					
Lovells	*	***		*			
Macfarlanes	******						
Manches		*					
Mishcon de Reya		*					
Olswang	*	******	******	******			
Osborne Clarke OWA	******						

LONDON	ADV & MKTNG	DEF	MEDIA & ENTERTAINMENT:				
			FILM	B'CASTNG	MUSIC	THEATRE	PUB'G
Peter Carter-Ruck and Partners		******					
Reynolds Porter Chamberlain		****					
Richards Butler			*****	****			
Rowe & Maw	**						
Russells							
Russell Jones & Walker		***					
Schilling & Lom and Partners		*****	***				
Searles					*		
Sheridans					***		
Simons Muirhead & Burton		***					
SJ Berwin & Co			******	**			
Spraggon Stennett Brabyn					*		
Statham Gill Davies					**		
Swepstone Walsh		***					
Tarlo Lyons						******	
Taylor Joynson Garrett	**				*****		
The Simkins Partnership	*****		****	**	**	****	***
Theodore Goddard	***	****	*****		**	**	
Townleys	*						
Travers Smith Braithwaite				*			
Wiggin & Co				*****			

REGIONS	DEFAMATION
Bevan Ashford, *Bristol*	****
Brabner Holden Banks Wilson, *Liverpool*	*****
Cobbetts, *Manchester*	*****
Foot Anstey Sargent, *Exeter*	******
Pannone & Partners, *Manchester*	***
Wiggin & Co, *Cheltenham*	******
Wragge & Co, *Birmingham*	***

personal injury & clinical negligence

As related areas of practice, personal injury and clinical negligence work are often undertaken in the same department or sometimes by specialist firms. Claimant firms are instructed by private individuals, legal expenses insurers and trade unions. Clients of defendant firms include private individuals, health authorities, hospitals, trusts, insurance companies, public bodies and self-insuring companies. Firms acting for both claimants and defendants are on the decrease, mainly as a result of major insurers shrinking their panels of firms which represent them.

Personal injury cases range from simple "slip and trip" cases (such as falling over uneven paving stones) to fatal accidents, major disaster litigation (the Paddington Rail crash) and complex group ("multi-party") actions, often in the environmental or industrial disease context. Examples of these include the asbestos-related disease actions brought on behalf of the South African miners, the tobacco litigation and the Gulf War Syndrome cases.

Clinical negligence actions include those arising from treatment of medical conditions or injuries. Among the most complex and serious cases which carry the highest potential amount of compensation are those arising from birth, such as brain-damaged babies.

type of work

PI and clinical negligence lawyers spend the majority of their time gathering information from clients as evidence to support their cases, obtaining expert evidence, researching the technicalities of their cases and generally preparing for litigation. Pre-litigation advice includes advising the client on the strength of their case, and if it is strong enough to take forward, taking the client through aspects of funding the case and general case strategy. Only a very small percentage of cases reach trial as most set-

tlements are reached out of court to avoid unecessary costs – an imperative objective under the recent reforms to the legal system (commonly referred to as "the Woolf reforms").

personal injury: Road traffic accident ("RTA") claims are generally routine in nature ("high volume, low value claims") but are the staple diet of many high street and general practices. The most efficient practices will have dedicated IT resources to deal with the substantial amount of standard documentation and paperwork generated by this type of work. Other claimant firms which are more specialist in nature have lawyers with expertise in a variety of niche areas. **Leigh, Day & Co** specialises in multi-party actions with an environmental aspect such as asbestos-related diseases work and gas poisonings. They also have expertise in aviation disasters and horse-riding accidents. **Russell Jones & Walker** handle deafness cases, for example, representing police officers deafened by motorcycle and gunfire noise, and an office worker deafened by a faulty fire alarm. They also have a special unit for victims of sexual assault.

Defendant firms are often instructed by insurers, but they require as much specialist knowledge as their claimant counterparts. "Shortly after qualifying I bought myself a Teach Yourself Anatomy book and read it from cover to cover," says Steve Daykin, head of defendant PI at **Nabarro Nathanson** in Sheffield. He is has been defending British Coal in the "Vibration White Finger" (a condition where vibrating machinery causes fingers to turn white and go numb) litigation in the Court of Appeal, and in a group respiratory disease claim. He obviously needs to be fully aware of the medical conditions allegedly suffered by the claimants.

This type of work takes lawyers from the factory floor to the coal mine, from the scene of an accident to the hospital, and from the home to the sports field. They become mini-experts in a number of activities. Terry Lee, partner with **Evill & Coleman**, had to learn the ins and outs of the rules of rugby as well as draw on his knowledge of head and spinal injuries, when he represented the rugby player, Ben Smolden, in his ground-breaking action against two rugby referees. Smolden sustained severe injuries during a match and one of the referees was held liable for those injuries.

clinical negligence: Like PI, clinical negligence work ranges from simple injuries to actions worth millions of pounds in damages. The more complex cases require an in-depth knowledge of medical technicalities. Katie Hay, a consultant with the defendant firm, **Capsticks**, explains that the doctors and experts can tell you much of what you need to know, but that with most specialist cases, "you just have to sit down and learn it for yourself."

Hay defended Merton, Sutton and Wandsworth Health Authority in an action brought by a patient who became pregnant after she had supposedly been sterilised. Following detailed gynaecological, histological and video evidence, it was established that the doctor who performed the sterilisation had not been at fault. The lawyers knew as much about the medical complications as the doctors by the end of the trial.

An awareness of mental as well as physical illness is often required by the lawyers. Specialist claimant firm, **Pritchard Englefield**, acted for Mr and Mrs Tredget in their test case against Bexley Health Authority, which established that a father who witnessed the mismanaged birth of his son (who died shortly afterwards) could recover damages for his own psychological injury.

Magi Young, partner with claimant firm, **Parlett Kent**, recently achieved a settlement of £1.2 million for a psychiatric patient who managed to take an overdose while under one-to-one observation. For 12 hours, the hospital failed to realise that she had lapsed into a coma.

These cases are at the top end of the scale and a trainee or recently qualified solicitor would obviously play only a junior role in such matters. Nevertheless, this role could still involve liaising with clients and doctors. As a trainee with Parlett Kent points out: "I already have a lot of client contact, and give advice and support on the 'phone, as well as taking witness statements and attending consultations with counsel." He also undertakes advocacy for his firm and sometimes finds himself up against a partner on the other side.

Clinical negligence and PI are intense and absorbing fields and require hard work and long hours just to keep up to speed with advances in medicine and technology. According to Steve Daykin, those at the top of the profession routinely work a 60-70 hour week.

skills needed

...an interest in medical issues...knowledge of anatomy and medical conditions...understanding of how the NHS works...awareness of the professional relationships between doctors, nurses, managers and patients...non-squeamish nature...good communication skills...sensitive and sympathetic approach...great strength of character...empathy...tact and sensitivity...assertiveness...confidence, tenacity and common sense...emotional commitment and dedication....

career options

Magi Young has always acted for claimants. She trained in a small legal aid practice where she tackled personal injury, clinical negligence, mental health, housing, immigration, crime and family law. She then moved to Pannone Napier (now **Pannone & Partners**), where she immediately specialised in personal injury and clinical negligence and became a partner after four years. She has been a partner with **Parlett Kent** for the past eight years and recently set up a branch of the firm in Exeter.

After training with **Robert Muckle**, Steve Daykin joined British Coal as an assistant solicitor to experience the public sector. In 1986, he became British Coal's area solicitor for the north east and was in charge of 20 lawyers. In 1990, **Nabarro Nathanson** took over part of British Coal's legal department and Daykin moved to join the firm. He now heads their PI department. He had this to say of his field: "You talk to commercial lawyers who think their jobs are more demanding because they earn more money, but acting for defendants in PI is a hell of a challenge and no less intellectually demanding."

There are very few in-house options for lawyers in this field. When pressed, Steve Daykin suggested that there may be openings for defendant solicitors with health authorities and the Post Office, but commented that "such opportunities are getting rarer all the time, with the majority of work being referred to specialist practices." Magi Young knows of no in-house lawyers in this field and stressed that as it is such a demanding and highly-focused area. "It is only for those whose commitment is total and career changes on the inside are extremely rare." Katie Hay agrees: "This is a popular area of law as it involves commercial decision-making in a human context. Those who succeed in breaking into it tend to be here to stay."

Their advice is to make focused applications to specialist firms, because the trend within private practice is towards increasing specialisation in a small number of niche firms.

leading personal injury firms

All information on leading firms comes from the Chambers Guide to the Legal Profession 2000-2001.
claimant: – Russell Jones & Walker, London: Historically a Trade Union firm, and well known for its work for the Police Federation, the team has *"gone from strength to strength"* this year, with a number of defendant firms recognising the practice as *"the best of the bunch."* Effective marketing has raised its profile, but new institutional clients such as the Royal College of Nursing, and the doubling in size of the firm's dedicated private client unit suggests that there is substance behind the *"very positive, proactive"* image presented. **Thompsons, London:** The biggest claimant personal injury practice nationwide, the London office retains a loyal following of Trade Union clients which generate over 75% of the practice's workload. The firm is strong in both the public sector and manufacturing, working with UNISON, the GMB, the MSF and a number of Civil Service unions. The London office received mixed reviews this year, with many commentators noting that it is *"not the force of old,"* and it is generally held that the firm has *"geared up for volume"* and has *"lost a number of its quality practitioners."* Nevertheless, the firm remains popular with its principal clients, and has been active in a number of high profile cases, such as the Paddington Rail Inquiry. **Evill and Coleman, London:** Received recommendations from a large number of claimant and defendant firms, this practice is known for handling high value claims, particularly head injuries. **Irwin Mitchell, London:** Part of a widely respected national practice, the London office has established a formidable reputation in its own right. Catastrophic injuries, particularly road traffic-related, form the mainstay of the practice, with individual settlements of up to £2m reached in the past year. **Leigh, Day & Co, London:** Referred to as a *"passionate outfit,"* this firm is known for taking on those claims deemed too risky by more orthodox claimant firms. In particular, the firm has a reputation for conditional fee Multi-Party actions, and is currently heavily involved in an asbestos case on behalf of South African miners. The London office also has a traditional PI team, acting principally for private clients, which specialises in RTA, horseriding and sports injury related cases.
defendant: – Barlow Lyde & Gilbert, London: A rapidly growing practice which covers a broad spectrum of personal injury work. Best-known for working with local authorities and their insurers, defending claims of bullying, stress, child abuse and

failure to educate. BLG has recently taken on **Davies Arnold Cooper**'s highly respected motor unit and are now able to do volume work alongside more complex and catastrophic claims. **Beachcroft Wansbroughs, London:** *"The leading player nationwide,"* the firm is *"expanding and expanding"* to meet the needs of the large composite insurers that provide 80% of the practice's caseload. While fast-track work provides the volume, the firm has a balanced practice and has retained some quality individuals. **Berrymans Lace Mawer, London:** While this practice continues to grow, the team does not yet dominate the PI defence market. A broad-based practice, with a balance of fast-track and multi-track work, the London team maintains a particularly high profile in industrial disease-related work such as stress, asbestos and RSI.

claimant: – Shoosmiths, Northampton: The newly opened 'Claims Compensation Division' is principally focused on processing fast-track claims for legal expense insurers and motoring organisations. The division's focus is national rather than regional, and there are few firms capable of competing with this large outfit. *"They will always secure a settlement quickly and cheaply."*

Irwin Mitchell, Birmingham: A large broad-based practice, which mixes expertise in high-value claims with a volume RTA practice for legal expense insurers. Multi-track PI team recently secured one of the highest awards handed out in a personal injury case (£5.1m). The department is also strong on travel and tourism cases. **Leeds, Sheffield:** Retains its reputation as *"the leading claimant practice in the North."* Best known for acting on behalf of private clients with severe injuries, the firm also has experience in multi-party claims, including the vibration white finger and respiratory disease cases against British Coal. There is also a motor division, which, when combined with the Birmingham Motor practice, provides the only serious competition to Shoosmiths nationally. Also handles some trade union work.

defendant: Bond Pearce: Although better known for defence work, the team is recognised as having *"a large PI practice with good people on the claimant side."* The firm acts for various Trade Unions, major credit-hire companies and private clients. Particular niche strengths include occupational disease work, RTA claims and employers/public liability.

Eversheds, Norwich: Works with a range of clients but with particular strength in local authority work and with self-insured plcs. Areas of expertise include sexual abuse claims, RSI, sports law and police work. **Newcastle:** Not traditionally known for acting for composite insurers, the team is nonetheless on the panel for the Royal & Sun Alliance and Norwich Union. Also has an unrivalled client base in the self-insured market. Particular expertise in industrial diseases.

leading clinical negligence firms

All information on leading firms comes from the Chambers Guide to the Legal Profession 2000-2001.

claimant: – Leigh Day & Co, London: Continues as the *"first port of call for claimant clinical negligence"* with its members *"at the spearhead of driving initiatives."* Maintains a *"heavyweight"* caseload in undiagnosed cancer claims, infectious disease work, and cerebral palsy cases. Involved in RAGE claims, securing an award of £465,000 for damages resulting from excessive radiotherapy following a lumpectomy.

defendant: – Capsticks, London: Described as *"leaders in the field,"* outstanding recommendations keep this *"well organised team"* offering *"high quality service across the board"* at the top of the defendant tables.

claimant: – Blake Lapthorn, Southampton: Covers a wide range of clinical negligence work with particular specialisms in misdiagnosis of breast cancer, obstetric, and orthopaedic negligence.

Freethcartwright, Nottingham: Clinical negligence practice spread over three franchised offices. Group includes a barrister, allowing the team to do their own advocacy. Continues to act in high profile cases, including MMR children's vaccine cases, and pursued a claim on behalf of a patient who contracted malaria in a hospital.

Pannone & Partners, Manchester: A *"fair and sensible"* group who *"drives a claim hard for the client."* A *"solid, thorough team."* Involved in Alder Hey inquiry into a Liverpool hospital's retention of body parts of dead children.

Irwin Mitchell, Leeds: A *"well set-up, dedicated department"* known for *"getting results for claimants."* Handles all mainstream clinical negligence cases, but maintains a high profile in birth trauma, medical products, and multi-party cases. Currently representing the nvCJD family at the BSE Inquiry.

other leading defendant firms

All information on leading firms comes from the Chambers Guide to the Legal Profession 2000-2001.

Beachcroft Wansboroughs, nationwide: A *"large and reputable"* team with acknowledged expertise in high value claims. Group advises on risk management, issues of consent, confidentiality and access to records. Acts for a number of NHS Trusts.

Bevan Ashford, Bristol: A large *"formidable"* team well known throughout the UK as a *"huge player"* for defendant clinical negligence work. The practice is divided into teams covering all the regions. Team members are commended for their *"up to date knowledge of the law"* and *"aggressive"* approach to litigation. **Cardiff:** *"A good firm with tentacles everywhere,"* it remains the only private firm handling a substantial amount of clinical negligence defence work in Wales. **Mills & Reeve, Birming-**

ham: A very large and ever-expanding team, sometimes described as *"patchy,"* but retaining a recognised stronghold on clinical negligence defendant work in the area. The team employs a number of dual qualified medical specialists on the team. **Cambridge, Norwich:** A practice with *"a long track record"* in the area which is sometimes perceived as excessively *"systematic"* in approach. Acts for large number of acute units and health and community trusts in East Anglia. **Scrivenger Seabrook:** Praised for their *"creative and pro-active approach"* the *"innovative deal-makers"* at this firm have an acknowledged expertise in complex and high value clinical negligence cases. **Hempsons:** A large *"well managed practice"* maintains its position as the leading *"specialist defendant firm"* in the area. Covers the full range of medical negligence work, including mental health and dental negligence, regularly settling cases with damages over the £1m mark. Received much publicity for its defence of Dr. Harold Shipman.

Le Brasseur J Tickle: Widely recommended as a team of *"good technicians"* with a *"dogged"* approach to clinical negligence litigation. The only firm in Leeds on the NHSLA panel. Specific specialisms include brain damage baby cases, neurosurgical, paediatric, and cancer claims.

Eversheds, nationwide: Practice looks to be on an upswing. Increased involvement in the mediation pilot scheme and training on mediation involvement. Practice acted in over 100 clinical negligence cases with damages in the region of £1m.

LEADING FIRMS

LONDON	CLINICAL NEG: CLAIMANT	CLINICAL NEG: DEFENDANT	PI: CLAIMANT	PI: DEFENDANT
Alexander Harris	****			
Anthony Gold, Lerman & Muirhead			**	
Barlow Lyde & Gilbert				******
Beachcroft Wansbroughs		*****		******
Berrymans Lace Mawer				******
Bindman & Partners	*****			
Bolt Burdon			*	
Capsticks		******		
Charles Russell	****			
David Levene & Co			*	
Davies Arnold Cooper				*****
Evill and Coleman	****		****	
Field Fisher Waterhouse	****			
Hempsons		*****		
Hextall Erskine				****
Hodge Jones & Allen			***	
Irwin Mitchell			****	
Kennedys				*****
Kingsley Napley	*****			
Le Brasseur J Tickle		*****		
Leigh, Day & Co	******		****	
O.H. Parsons & Partners			**	
Parlett Kent	*****			
Pattinson & Brewer			****	
Rowley Ashworth			****	
Russell Jones & Walker			******	
Stewarts			***	
Thompsons			*****	
Vizards, Staples & Bannisters				*****
Watmores				****

THE SOUTH	CLINICAL NEG: CLAIMANT	CLINICAL NEG: DEFENDANT	PI: CLAIMANT	PI: DEFENDANT
AE Wyeth & Co, *Dartford*				*****
Amery-Parkes, *Basingstoke*			*****	
Beachcroft Wansbroughs, *Winchester*		******		******
Berrymans Lace Mawer, *Southampton*				******

THE SOUTH	CLINICAL NEG: CLAIMANT	CLINICAL NEG: DEFENDANT	PI: CLAIMANT	PI: DEFENDANT
Blake Lapthorn, *Portsmouth*	******		*****	
Bond Pearce, *Southampton*				******
Brachers, *Maidstone*		*****		
Davies Lavery, *Maidstone*				******
Ensor Byfield, *Southampton*				******
George Ide, Phillips, *Chichester*			*****	
Keoghs, *Southampton*				*****
Lamport Bassitt, *Southampton*			*****	
Palser Grossman, *Southampton*				*****
Pattinson & Brewer, *Chatham*			*****	
Penningtons, *Godalming*	*****			
Shoosmiths, *Basingstoke*			******	
Thomson Snell & Passmore, *Tunbridge Wells*	******	******	*****	
Warner Goodman & Streat, *Fareham*			*****	

THAMES VALLEY	CLINICAL NEG: CLAIMANT	CLINICAL NEG: DEFENDANT	PI: CLAIMANT	PI: DEFENDANT
Boyes Turner & Burrows, *Reading*	******		*****	
Fennemores, *Milton Keynes*			*****	
Henmans, *Oxford*			*****	*****
Morgan Cole, *Reading*				******
Osborne Morris & Morgan, *Leighton Buzzard*	*****		******	

SOUTH WEST	CLINICAL NEG: CLAIMANT	CLINICAL NEG: DEFENDANT	PI: CLAIMANT	PI: DEFENDANT
Barcan Woodward, *Bristol*	******			
Beachcroft Wansbroughs, *Bristol*		*****		******
Bevan Ashford, *Bristol*		******		*****
Bobbetts Mackan, *Bristol*			****	
Bond Pearce, *Plymouth*			******	*****
Cartwrights, *Bristol*				*****
David Gist & Co, *Bristol*			****	
Hugh James Ford Simey, *Exeter*				*****
John Hodge & Co, *Weston-super-Mare*	*****			

SOUTH WEST	CLINICAL NEG: CLAIMANT	CLINICAL NEG: DEFENDANT	PI: CLAIMANT	PI: DEFENDANT
Lyons Davidson, *Bristol*			******	
Over Taylor Biggs, *Exeter*	******			
Palser Grossman, *Bristol*				*****
Preston Goldburn, *Falmouth*	******			
Rowley Ashworth, *Exeter*			*****	
Russell Jones & Walker, *Bristol*	*****		*****	
Thompsons, *Bristol*			******	
Tozers, *Exeter*	****			
Veale Wasbrough, *Bristol*			******	
Veitch Penny, *Exeter*				*****
Withy King, *Bath*	*****			
Wolferstans, *Plymouth*	*****		*****	
Woollcombe Beer Watts, *Newton Abbot*	****			

WALES	CLINICAL NEG: CLAIMANT	CLINICAL NEG: DEFENDANT	PI: CLAIMANT	PI: DEFENDANT
Bevan Ashford, *Cardiff*		******		
Dolmans, *Cardiff*				*****
Edwards Geldard, *Cardiff*	*****			
Eversheds, *Cardiff*				****
Hugh James Ford Simey, *Cardiff, Merthyr Tydfil*	*****		******	******
Huttons, *Cardiff*	******			
John Collins & Partners, *Swansea*	*****			
Leo Abse & Cohen, *Cardiff*			******	
Loosemores, *Cardiff*			*****	
Morgan Cole, *Cardiff*				******
Palser Grossman, *Cardiff Bay*				******
Smith Llewelyn Partnership, *Swansea*	*****		*****	
Thompsons, *Cardiff*			******	

MIDLANDS	CLINICAL NEG: CLAIMANT	CLINICAL NEG: DEFENDANT	PI: CLAIMANT	PI: DEFENDANT
Anthony Collins Solicitors, *Birmingham*	****			
Barratt Goff & Tomlinson, *Nottingham*			****	

MIDLANDS	CLINICAL NEG: CLAIMANT	CLINICAL NEG: DEFENDANT	PI: CLAIMANT	PI: DEFENDANT
Beachcroft Wansbroughs, *Birmingham*		*****		******
Browne Jacobson, *Birmingham, Nottingham*		****		******
Buller Jeffries, *Birmingham*				*****
Challinors Lyon Clark, *Birmingham*	****			
Chapman Everatt, *Birmingham*				****
Everatt & Company, *Evesham*				*****
Freethcartwright, *Derby, Nottingham*	******		*****	
Hammond Suddards Edge, *Birmingham*				****
Irwin Mitchell, *Birmingham*	*****		******	
Mills & Reeve, *Birmingham*		******		
Nelsons, *Nottingham*			****	
Rowley Ashworth, *Birmingham*			******	
Russell Jones & Walker, *Birmingham*			******	
Thompsons, *Birmingham*			******	
Weightmans, *Birmingham*				******

EAST ANGLIA	CLINICAL NEG: CLAIMANT	CLINICAL NEG: DEFENDANT	PI: CLAIMANT	PI: DEFENDANT
Cunningham John, *Thetford*	******		******	
E. Edwards Son & Noice, *Ilford*			*****	*****
Eversheds, *Norwich*				******
Gadsby Wicks, *Chelmsford*	*****			
Greenwoods, *Peterborough*				*****
Leathes Prior, *Norwich*			*****	
Merricks, *Ipswich*				*****
Mills & Reeve, *Cambridge, Norwich*		******		******
Morgan Jones & Pett, *Great Yarmouth*	*****		*****	
Prettys, *Ipswich*	****			*****
Scrivenger Seabrook, *St. Neots*		******		
Taylor Vinters, *Cambridge*			*****	

NORTH WEST	CLINICAL NEG: CLAIMANT	CLINICAL NEG: DEFENDANT	PI: CLAIMANT	PI: DEFENDANT
Alexander Harris, *Altrincham*	*****			
Beachcroft Wansbroughs, *Manchester*				*****

LEADING FIRMS *continued*

NORTH WEST	CLINICAL NEG: CLAIMANT	CLINICAL NEG: DEFENDANT	PI: CLAIMANT	PI: DEFENDANT
Berrymans Lace Mawer, *Liverpool, Manchester*				******
Donns Solicitors, *Manchester*			***	
George Davies, *Manchester*		****		
Halliwell Landau, *Manchester*				****
Hempsons, *Manchester*		******		
Hill Dickinson, *Liverpool, Manchester*		*****		*****
James Chapman & Co, *Manchester*				******
John Pickering & Partners, *Oldham*			*****	
Jones Maidment Wilson, *Manchester*	*****			
Keoghs, *Bolton*				******
Leigh, Day & Co, *Manchester*	****		*****	
Linder Myers, *Manchester*	*****		***	
Pannone & Partners, *Manchester*	******		******	
Russell Jones & Walker, *Manchester*			****	
Thompsons, *Liverpool*			****	
Weightmans, *Liverpool, Manchester*				******
Whittles, *Manchester*			*****	

YORKSHIRE	CLINICAL NEG: CLAIMANT	CLINICAL NEG: DEFENDANT	PI: CLAIMANT	PI: DEFENDANT
Beachcroft Wansbroughs, *Leeds, Sheffield*		******		******
DLA, *Leeds, Sheffield*				*****
Hempsons, *Harrogate*		******		
Heptonstalls, *Goole*	*****			
Irwin Mitchell, *Leeds, Sheffield*	******		******	****
Le Brasseur J Tickle, *Leeds*		******		
Nabarro Nathanson, *Sheffield*				****
Pattinson & Brewer, *York*			*****	
Praxis Partners, *Leeds*				****
Rowley Ashworth, *Leeds*			*****	
Russell Jones & Walker, *Leeds, Sheffield*			*****	
Stamp Jackson and Procter, *Hull*	*****			

NORTH EAST	CLINICAL NEG: CLAIMANT	CLINICAL NEG: DEFENDANT	PI: CLAIMANT	PI: DEFENDANT
Beecham Peacock, *Newcastle upon Tyne*			****	
Browell Smith & Co, *Newcastle upon Tyne*			****	
Crutes, *Newcastle upon Tyne*		*****		****
Deas Mallen, *Newcastle upon Tyne*				****
Eversheds, *Newcastle upon Tyne*		******		******
Hay & Kilner, *Newcastle upon Tyne*	*****		****	****
Jacksons, *Stockton-on-Tees*				******
Marrons, *Newcastle upon Tyne*			*****	
Peter Maughan & Co, *Gateshead*	******			
Samuel Phillips & Co, *Newcastle upon Tyne*		****		
Sinton & Co, *Newcastle upon Tyne*				*****
Thompsons, *Newcastle upon Tyne*			******	
Ward Hadaway, *Newcastle upon Tyne*		****		

private client

'Private clients' are private individuals as opposed to corporate entities. The definition of 'private client' work really depends on what sort of firm you're thinking of applying to. In a commercial practice, the term generally refers to advice on tax and trusts to high net worth individuals who are prepared to pay hundreds of pounds an hour for top specialist advice and personal service. For a high street firm it could mean any member of the public, wealthy or otherwise and would include advice on divorce, conveyancing and drawing up wills. In this chapter we refer to the work carried out in commercial firms.

Private client work has become synonymous with certain services provided to individuals. These include trusts, tax and probate advice and associated services connected with the acquisition, disposal and management of personal assets.

Solicitors who have developed a niche in trust law may find that their expertise is sought after by charitable organisations and so need an understanding of the rules governing charities. Work is generally purely advisory and non-contentious although litigation is always a possibility.

type of work

trusts and personal tax: Any solicitor must respect client confidentiality. With private clients the reasons for doing so are more acutely apparent. The solicitor is often drawn into a very detailed examination of a client's family life and finances. The solicitor has to respect the client's privacy whilst maintaining impartiality and giving the best possible practical advice. The solicitor must also hear the most private details of family circumstances and finances with understanding but without judgment.

David Long, partner at City firm **Charles Russell**, sees UK trusts law as a very portable product internationally. He is confident that firms will find

their private client lawyers becoming more in demand in the future by foreign clients. "The beauty of our English language is that it is world-wide, and English corporate and commercial law is worldwide, ranking with New York law as the dominant law. Trusts and the tax planning work is also an important invisible export. The trust is a wonderfully flexible tool for planning." Surprisingly, Andrew Young of **Lawrence Graham** sees the trust as a fashionable tool for the internationally wealthy. "Rich people in foreign countries know their friends have trusts so they want one too. It is the ultimate fashion accessory for the seriously rich."

Trusts are a very popular way of holding assets and avoiding tax (rather than evading tax, which is illegal) often by holding funds in off-shore jurisdictions. Trusts allow family members access to funds whilst also allowing the donor a degree of control over the manner in which the funds are accessed.

The creation of trusts in other jurisdictions often means that the lawyer will have to spend time ensuring that his client understands the system of law behind the setting up of a trust. David Long told us, "In the off-shore world you get a culture clash between people brought up in Napoleonic Code countries which have certain heirship rights for children which don't fit at all well with our common law system. So you get rich men in Italy or Spain taking their money to the Bahamas or Bermuda and creating trusts. Then you may have litigation in the original country to determine whether the trust works to defeat the interest of the children who would otherwise have inherited." A lawyer must be very careful to appraise the client of all the possible foreign law implications.

As well as handling off-shore trusts in conjunction with overseas lawyers and trust companies, private client lawyers find that they advise an increasing number of overseas clients seeking to invest in the UK. Off-shore and private banks may also need advice about their clients' UK interests.

A private client lawyer will be consulted on a range of different issues from immigration and employment questions through to share transactions and property deals. The most experienced individuals have the breadth of experience to give an answer to these diverse questions. However, in a large multi-service law firm there is plenty of opportunity to turn to the expertise of colleagues.

Says David Long: "Some private clients get very close to you and don't do anything major without asking or discussing it with you. You are often a trustee or executor looking after their money for the next generation and that's tremendous. It's very flattering to be asked to be a trustee." He likes the fact that aside from having some money the clients are all very diverse. "I would not wish my practice to have only rich farmers or aristocrats or businessmen. I like the variety because human beings are so different all the time. That's the beauty of it! And you do get to know them quite well when you're advising them on this sort of thing."

charities: A related area of practice is charities law, where clients range from well known national charities to low profile local private charitable trusts. Work consists of charity registration and reorganisation, Charity Commission investigations, the development of trading subsidiaries and advising charitable clients on any other issues necessary such as tax, trust or property matters. Many firms, especially the smaller ones, frequently specialise in advising particular types of charity, for example religious or environmental charities.

skills needed

...good all round legal skills...good 'bedside manner'...facilitation skills...flexibility...enormous tolerance....strong grounding in trusts and tax...innovative yet well-organised thinker...ability to see the bigger picture...

career options

Training at an established private client firm such as **Withers, Farrers** and **Boodle Hatfield** will give the best possible start. City firms such as **Allen & Overy** and **Macfarlanes** have continued to offer these services to their clients, allowing trainees to combine private client work with a corporate training. Following the 90's trend for hiving off private client departments from large corporate practices, very recently firms are recognising the value of private client lawyers to service the new breed of 'e-trepreneurs.'

In-house opportunities are limited although some off-shore trust companies and private banks do have in house legal advisers. For those who fancy working abroad, banks in the Bahamas, Cayman Islands and Jersey may employ lawyers in advisory or risk control positions.

For charities specialists there is less scope in terms of law firms specialising in this area, but with the opportunity to make strong contacts with clients there is always the possibility of moving into a more general role within the industry.

leading trusts/personal tax firms

All information on leading firms comes from the Chambers Guide to the Legal Profession 2000-2001.

Macfarlanes: Seen by many as the *"golden practice"* with an *"outstanding combination of intellect and clients,"* it edges to the top of the rankings this year. The team is respected for its commercial approach and quality across the board, with work ranging from UK and offshore tax and trust advice to heritage property, corporate support, the Lloyd's insurance market and trust litigation. Its major clients include landed individuals, entrepreneurs (including Richard Branson and Sir Paul Getty) and institutions and the practice is particularly rated for the strength of its international private client base.

Allen & Overy: Retains its reputation as a *"strong, high value private client practice."* The team advises UK and foreign-domiciled individuals and families on all aspects of trust and tax planning and is increasingly known for its corporate support role. The group advised on the creation of a discretionary trust as part of the securitisation of a large portfolio of trading assets. Noted by the market for its international capability and offshore work.

Lawrence Graham: Respected practice whose broad UK, offshore and commercial expertise is supplemented by an investment management unit. The department counts leading private banks, trust companies and UK and foreign-domiciled families amongst its clients. The full range of non-contentious and contentious tax, trusts and probate work is handled, with particular strengths in offshore and institutional private client work. Highlights of the last year include continuing administration of the estate of the late Diana, Princess of Wales.

Withers: The largest private client practice in the country, its *"vast client base and accumulation of collective knowledge"* ensures its continuing position in the top league. The practice acts for around 15% of individuals in *The Times Rich List* in addition to trust companies and private banks, while its international client base has continued to expand, particularly in the Middle East, the USA and Europe. On top of the strength of its trusts and tax, commercial, international and probate groups, the group is seen to be at the forefront of trust litigation, and has acted in several multi-jurisdictional trust disputes.

leading private client firms

Boodle Hatfield: Remains the top practice in the region with accountants recommending it for *"the more complex tax and trusts work,"* which includes reorganising UK and offshore trusts, complex probates and trust and probate litigation. Strong links with the London office ensure a healthy national and international client base including landed estates, entrepreneurs, expatriates and members of the Oxford arts and academic community.

Hewitson Becke + Shaw, Birmingham: Well-regarded practice with *"breadth of experience"* which

specialises in tax and trust advice for landed and investor clients, often with international connections. Also handles administration of deceased estates and family trusts, with 300 trusts currently under administration. **Norwich:** An *"extremely responsive and extremely professional"* outfit, which retains its top-flight reputation. The team handles all aspects of tax and trust work for a substantial client base including landed estates, farmers, local businessmen and an increasing number of wealthy London clients.

Dickinson Dees, Newcastle: Large team which *"has been around a long time"* and is highly rated throughout the region for its expertise and *"large and diverse client base,"* which includes many of the major private land-owning families in the North. In addition to the full range of offshore and onshore tax and trust work, wills and probate, the team is well-versed in landed estate administration, pension scheme administration, trust litigation and contentious probate.

Halliwell Landau, Manchester: *"A strong team"* which provides wills and probate work, estate planning and trust creation and administration for a broad client base which includes wealthy private families and Barclays Bank Trust Corporation (non-litigious legal work). A recent lateral hire has strengthened the offshore practice. Recently awarded national contract to advise the partners of J Rothschild Assurance Plc on tax planning.

leading agriculture firms

Farrer & Co: Three hundred years old next year, this *"outstandingly good"* practice continues to grow. They have had *"a spectacular year"* acting for the Duchy of Cornwall in the purchase of the 28,000 acre Prudential land portfolio, and the core of their work remains acquisitions and sales for large landed estates. Also highly rated for heritage work, they have niche expertise on such diverse matters as treasure, commons rights and the law of the manor.

Macfarlanes: *"Thoroughbred"* firm with *"a marvel-*

lous selection of private clients." It represents pension funds alongside landed estates and wealthy foreign owners. Considered to be more commercial than the other two leading London firms, the team is developing a particular expertise advising on EU regulations and environmental law. Acted last year in the acquisition of 1,800 acres of the Wilton Castle Estate, including a golf club, nursery, aerial sites, agricultural tenancies and the greater part of a village.

Withers: Acting for over 130 landed estates, this strong practice claims a large share of the market in farm and estate conveyancing. The core of the business remains transactional work but the team is also particularly strong on agricultural holdings issues. Team *"always knows precisely what they're on about."* Last year dealt with green field development sites worth over £75m.

leading charities firms

Bates, Wells & Braithwate: Remains the leading firm, and *"its profile is still growing."* Known particularly for its large number of voluntary sector clients who appreciate the team's *"approachability"* and understanding of the sector. Charity work is one of the firm's core businesses. Work ranges from constitutional and restructuring issues through to intellectual property and employment. Recent work included a major constitutional overhaul for the Civil Servants' Benevolent Fund. Acts for Tate Gallery, British Red Cross

Farrer & Co: Renowned in the market for its royal connections and heritage and endowed clients. Areas of expertise include incorporating charities, setting up trading companies and tax issues. Clients include museums, literary companies, independent schools and quasi-governmental bodies.

Paisner & Co: This *"high profile"* practice is traditionally known for its Jewish, Islamic and Christian charities and heritage work, but clients also extend to new government appointed education agencies, active charities and not for profit organisations such as Credit Unions and Friendly Societies. Specialisms include mergers, re-organisations and complex Charity Commission investigations.

Withers: The practice's *"integrated"* approach takes it up a band this year. Its traditional skills in legacy and NHS charity work remain recognised and it has been expanding and picking up clients over the last year. Combining traditional constitutional and tax advice with other services, including a specialist charity litigation team, the firm is also well-versed in issues relating to government 'hive off' organisations. Acts for Macmillan Cancer Relief, Salvation Army, RSPCA.

Stone King, Bath: Remains *"way ahead"* in the region. The firm is renowned for its Roman Catholic charity clients and acts for a growing number of service provider and educational charities. Particular work specialisms include constitutional issues, mergers, joint ventures, Charity Commission investigations and quasi-governmental charities. One notable highlight is ongoing advice to the three national charities who are combining to promote the Petroleum Geology Conference 2003. Acts for LSU College Trustees, Royal Photographic Society.

Wrigleys, Leeds: With the recent addition of Eversheds' Leeds private client practice bolstering its strength further, this exclusively private client/charities practice firm rises to the top band this year. This was confirmed by the firm's August 2000 merger with rival top firm, Malcolm Lynch. Known in the market for its portfolio of *"all sorts of interesting clients,"* Wrigleys has a large number of significant heritage, religious, educational charities and private family charitable trusts under its belt. Recent *"cutting edge"* work includes lottery-funded and conservation projects. Acts for Major heritage, educational and religious charities.

LEADING FIRMS

LONDON	TRUSTS & PERSONAL TAX	AGRICULTURE	CHARITIES
Allen & Overy	*****		****
Bates, Wells & Braithwaite			******
Bircham & Co.	***		***
Boodle Hatfield	****	***	
Charles Russell	****		****
Claricoat Phillips			***
Currey & Co	****	***	
Dawson & Co	*	*****	
Dechert	*		
Farrer & Co	****	******	*****
Field Fisher Waterhouse			*
Forsters	***	****	
Gouldens	*		
Harbottle & Lewis			***
Herbert Smith			*
Hunters	**		
Lawrence Graham	*****		**
Lee & Pembertons	**	*****	*
Lee Bolton & Lee			**
Linklaters	*		*
Macfarlanes	******	******	**
May, May & Merrimans	*	****	
Nabarro Nathanson			****
Nicholson Graham & Jones	***		
Paisner & Co	**		*****
Park Nelson	*		
Payne Hicks Beach	***	*****	
Radcliffes	*		**
Rooks Rider	*		
Simmons & Simmons	**		
Sinclair Taylor & Martin			****
SJ Berwin & Co			*
Speechly Bircham	***		***
Taylor Joynson Garrett	***		
Trowers & Hamlins	*		***
Wedlake Bell	**		
Winckworth Sherwood			**

THAMES VALLEY	AGRICULTURE	CHARITIES	TRUSTS & PERSONAL TAX
B P Collins, *Gerrards Cross*			***
Blandy & Blandy, *Reading*			*****
Boodle Hatfield, *Oxford*			******
Boyes Turner & Burrows, *Reading*			**
BrookStreet Des Roches, *Witney*		*****	
Clarks, *Reading*			***
Henmans, *Oxford*	*****	****	*****
Iliffes Booth Bennett, *Uxbridge*		****	****
Linnells, *Oxford*		****	
Manches, *Oxford*		******	
Matthew Arnold & Baldwin, *Watford*			***
Morgan Cole, *Oxford*	******		
Mundays, *Esher*			***
Pictons, *Hemel Hempstead*			***
Pryce Collard Chamberlain, *Abingdon*	****		
Stanley Tee & Co, *Bishop's Stortford*	****		***
Winckworth Sherwood, *Oxford*		******	

THE SOUTH	AGRICULTURE	CHARITIES	TRUSTS & PERSONAL TAX
Adams & Remers, *Lewes*			*****
Barlows, *Chertsey*		*****	**
Blake Lapthorn, *Portsmouth*		******	****
Brachers, *Maidstone*	******		***
Buss Murton, *Tunbridge Wells*			**
Charles Russell, *Guildford*			*
Cripps Harries Hall, *Tunbridge Wells*	****	*****	******
DMH, *Brighton*			***
George Ide, Phillips, *Chichester*			*
Griffith Smith, *Brighton*		*****	*
Humphries Kirk, *Wareham*	*		
Knights, *Tunbridge Wells*	***		
Lester Aldridge, *Bournemouth*		*****	***
Moore & Blatch, *Lymington*			****
Paris Smith & Randall, *Southampton*			****
Penningtons, *Godalming*	***		***
Staffurth & Bray, *Bognor Regis*			**

SPECIALIST PRACTICE AREAS   PRIVATE CLIENT

THE SOUTH cont'd	AGRICULTURE	CHARITIES	TRUSTS & PERSONAL TAX
Stevens & Bolton, *Guildford*			****
Thomas Eggar Church Adams, *Chich.*	****	******	******
Thomson Snell & Passmore, *T. Wells*		******	*****
White & Bowker, *Winchester*	*****		***
Whitehead Monckton, *Maidstone*			*

SOUTH WEST	AGRICULTURE	CHARITIES	TRUSTS & PERSONAL TAX
Battens (with Poole & Co), *Yeovil*	**		
Bevan Ashford, *Bristol*	***		
Beviss & Beckingsale, *Chard*	*		
Bond Pearce, Exeter, *Plymouth*	***	*****	*****
Burges Salmon, *Bristol*	******	*****	******
Charles Russell, *Cheltenham*			*****
Clarke Willmott & Clarke, *Taunton*	****	**	****
Coodes, *St. Austell*			***
Eversheds, *Bristol*		**	
Every & Phillips, *Honiton*	*		
Foot Anstey Sargent, *Exeter*			*****
Hooper & Wollen, *Torquay*			***
Meade-King, *Bristol*			***
Michelmores, *Exeter*		***	***
Osborne Clarke OWA, *Bristol*	*	*****	******
Pardoes, *Bridgwater*	**		
Parker Bullen, *Salisbury*		***	
Porter Dodson, *Yeovil*	*		
Rickerby Watterson, *Cheltenham*		**	***
Stephens & Scown, *Exeter, Liskeard, Truro*	****		**
Stone King, *Bath*		******	
Stones, *Exeter*			**
Thrings & Long, *Bath*	***	***	
TLT Solicitors, *Bristol*			****
Tozers, *Exeter*		****	
Veale Wasbrough, *Bristol*		****	***
Wiggin & Co, *Cheltenham*			******
Wilsons, *Salisbury*	*****	****	******
Woollcombe Beer Watts, *Newton Abbot*			**

WALES	AGRICULTURE	CHARITIES	TRUSTS & PERSONAL TAX
Bevan Ashford, *Cardiff*			★★★★
Edward Harris & Son, *Swansea*	★★★★★		
Edwards Geldard, *Cardiff*		★★	★★★★★★
Eversheds, *Cardiff*			★★★★
Gabb & Co, *Abergavenny*	★★★★		
Hugh James Ford Simey, *Cardiff*			★★★★★
Margraves, *Llandrindod Wells*	★★★★★★		★★★★
Morgan Cole, *Cardiff*	★★★★		

MIDLANDS	AGRICULTURE	CHARITIES	TRUSTS & PERSONAL TAX
Anthony Collins Solicitors, *Birmingham*		★★★★★★	
Arnold Thomson, *Towcester*	★★★★★		
Browne Jacobson, *Nottingham*			★★★★★
Chattertons, *Horncastle*	★★		
Freethcartwright, *Nottingham*			★★★★
Gabb & Co, *Hereford*	★★★		
Gateley Wareing, *Birmingham*		★★★★★	★★★
Gwynnes, *Wellington*	★★★		
Hewitson Becke + Shaw, *Northampton*	★★★★	★★★★★	★★★★★
Higgs & Sons, *Brierley Hill*			★★★★
Knight & Sons, *Newcastle-under-Lyme*	★★★★		
Lanyon Bowdler, *Shrewsbury*	★★★		
Lee Crowder, *Birmingham*		★★★★★	★★★★★
Lodders, *Stratford-upon-Avon*	★★★		★★★★
Manby & Steward, *Wolverhampton*	★★★		
Martineau Johnson, *Birmingham*	★★★★	★★★★★★	★★★★★★
Morton Fisher, *Worcester*	★★★★		
Pinsent Curtis, *Birmingham*			★★★★
Roythorne & Co, *Nottingham, Spalding*	★★★★★★		★★★
Shakespeares, *Birmingham*		★★★★★★	★★★★
The Wilkes Partnership, *Birmingham*			★★★
Wilkin Chapman, *Louth*	★★		
Willcox Lane Clutterbuck, *Birmingham*			★★★
Wragge & Co, *Birmingham*		★★★★★★	★★★★★
Wright Hassall, *Leamington Spa*	★★★★★		

EAST ANGLIA	AGRICULTURE	CHARITIES	TRUSTS & PERSONAL TAX
Ashton Graham, *Bury St Edmunds, Ipswich*	***		***
Barker Gotelee, *Ipswich*	*****		
Birketts, *Ipswich*	****		
Cozens-Hardy & Jewson, *Norwich*		******	****
Eversheds, *Cambridge, Norwich*	****	*****	*****
Greene & Greene, *Bury St. Edmunds*	**		***
Greenwoods, *Peterborough*		*****	
Hewitson Becke + Shaw, *Cambridge*	****	*****	******
Hood Vores & Allwood, *Dereham*			***
Howes Percival, *Norwich*	***		****
Leathes Prior, *Norwich*		*****	
Mills & Reeve, *Cambridge, Norwich*	******	*	******
Prettys, *Ipswich*	***		***
Rustons & Lloyd, *Newmarket*	**		
Taylor Vinters, *Cambridge*	*****	******	****
Ward Gethin, *King's Lynn*			***
Willcox & Lewis, *Norwich*			***

NORTH WEST	AGRICULTURE	CHARITIES	TRUSTS & PERSONAL TAX
Addleshaw Booth & Co, *Manchester*			*****
Birch Cullimore, *Chester*	****	******	*****
Brabner Holden Banks Wilson, *Liverpool*		******	******
Cartmell Shepherd, *Carlisle*	******		
Cobbetts, *Manchester*			*****
Cuff Roberts, *Liverpool*			****
Davies Wallis Foyster, *Liverpool*			****
Halliwell Landau, *Manchester*		****	******
Mason & Moore Dutton, *Chester*	****		
Napthen Houghton Craven, *Preston*	****		
Oglethorpe Sturton & Gillibrand, *Lanc.*	*****		
Oswald Goodier & Co, *Preston*		*****	
Pannone & Partners, *Manchester*		****	****
Walker Smith & Way, *Chester*	*****		

YORKSHIRE	AGRICULTURE	CHARITIES	TRUSTS & PERSONAL TAX
Addleshaw Booth & Co, *Leeds*	*****	****	*****
Andrew M. Jackson & Co, *Hull*	****		****
Armitage Sykes, *Huddersfield*			**
Brooke North, *Leeds*			***
Gordons Cranswick Sols, *Brad., Leeds*			***
Grays, *York*	*****	*****	***
Irwin Mitchell, *Sheffield*		****	***
Keeble Hawson, *Sheffield*		***	
Lupton Fawcett, *Leeds*			***
McCormicks, *Leeds*		***	
Pinsent Curtis, *Leeds*		***	****
Rollit Farrell & Bladon, *Hull*	******		***
Stamp Jackson and Procter, *Hull*	****		
Walker Morris, *Leeds*			**
Wrigleys, *Leeds*	*****	******	******

NORTH EAST	AGRICULTURE	CHARITIES	TRUSTS & PERSONAL TAX
Askews, *Redcar*			**
Dickinson Dees, *Newcastle upon Tyne*	******	****	******
Eversheds, *Newcastle upon Tyne*		***	
Jacksons, *Stockton-on-Tees*	***		
Latimer Hinks, *Darlington*	****		
Ward Hadaway, *Newcastle upon Tyne*	*****		***

projects

project finance: The structuring, financing, construction and operation of infrastructure developments such as roads, power stations, bridges and telecommunications networks – is now considered a 'sexy' area for many of the UK's leading law firms. Several of these now have stand-alone project groups. Certainly, the high profile, international nature of the work attracts many of the most talented lawyers in the UK and overseas. Projects are located throughout the world and projects lawyers hail from every major jurisdiction. However, the major projects are dominated by a few City firms and the largest US practices.

PFI/PPP: In the UK, the Private Finance Initiative (PFI), a part of the Public Private Partnerships (PPP) introduced under the Conservative Government and relaunched by Labour, has provided an important source of work. The objective of PFI is to introduce private funding and management into areas which were previously the domain of government, such as the building and operation of roads and hospitals. Through PFI, many smaller London firms and regional practices have become involved in projects work for the first time. That said, it is the City firms who are at the forefront of a current trend towards exporting the principle of PFI to governments abroad.

energy: Some energy projects fall within the heading 'Project Finance' – e.g. the development of the Manah power plant in Oman – but 'energy' is a much wider field. Examples of general energy work include **CMS Cameron McKenna** advising several Indian states on the restructuring and privatisation of their electricity boards and **Lovells** conducting specialist international joint venture work on production-sharing contracts to secure exploration rights in North Africa and Russia.

construction: The physical building of infrastructure projects is only a small, if vital, part of project finance. Similarly, for most construction departments, project finance developments are only one of several sources of work. There are two aspects to construction work: developing the contractual arrangements prior to building work starting (negotiating the contracts between the employer, the contractor, sub-contractors, architects, engineers, surveyors, interior designers, etc.) and litigating when it all goes horribly wrong. Most construction practices do both contentious and non-contentious work. Some, however, are better known for one or the other. **Fenwick Elliott** is renowned for litigating when buildings are defective or late, while **CMS Cameron McKenna**'s reputation rests on its building work.

type of work

Projects vary from telecoms links in Tanzania, oil pipelines in the Caucasus and Sahel, power projects in China and India, port developments in Yemen and Oman, toll roads in Israel and gold mines in Indonesia, to PFI hospital projects in Greenwich and sewage plants in Birmingham. The exact nature of the work depends on the type, size and location of the project. However, almost all the major infrastructure projects in which regional firms are involved will be PFI projects of one sort or another. In addition to PFI and PPP other common acronyms include BOO (build, own and operate), BOOT (build, own, operate, transfer) and DBFO (design, build, finance, operate) to name but a few.

Projects work also varies depending on the type of client a firm is acting for. There are a number of parties in a project finance development. There is the project company – usually a special purpose company established to build, own and operate (hence BOO) the power station or whatever the project is.

SPECIALIST PRACTICE AREAS   PROJECTS

Often the project company is a joint venture between a number of project sponsors who contribute equity to part-fund the project. Project sponsors could include the manufacturer of the gas turbines to be installed in the power station, the construction company that will erect the plant, and the power company that will buy the electricity produced. The company could also be partially owned by a government body or banks.

The project promoter is the organisation that commissions the project. It could be an NHS Trust that wants a new hospital built, or a host government which thinks a privately financed motorway would be a great idea. Funders provide the finance to build the project. Funders include banks, guarantors, export credit agencies, governments, and international funding agencies and they operate in consortiums and individually. Other categories of client are the contractors, operators, and so on. Each party requires its own legal representation.

A common feature of most major projects is the tender process. A public authority or major corporation (the procurer) will invite interested parties (bidders) to tender on the design, building, financing and operation (i.e. DBFO) of a project. At the end of this tender process – which can last up to two years – the winning company or consortium will be selected to manage the project. This company will then have to secure the finance, obtain the necessary planning permission and agree construction, service and employment contracts. Lawyers advising on any of these contracts must understand the big picture. They have to see how changing one contractual term will have a knock-on effect throughout the entire transaction.

Charles Robson, a partner in **Lovells'** projects department, acted for the banks in one of the PFI's flagship hospital projects, the £300m Norfolk and Norwich. "A commercial deal was struck between the project company and the NHS Trust. In the deal, the Trust promised to pay for the delivery of a new building and the services within it." says Robson.

"There were two main parts to our role. We assessed how the principal parties had apportioned the risk in the project, and advised the bank on any amendments to their documents." This function can sometimes include a renegotiation of the deal. The firm's other primary role was drafting the credit agreement between the project company and the banks, and the security documentation that supports it.

International transactions are generally larger, more complex and can appear more glamorous. Jeremy Gewirtz of **Linklaters** recently advised the project sponsors financing an LNG tanker to transport gas from Muscat to the Dhabol power station in Maharashtra, India. Though the tanker financing was stand alone, it was also intimately linked to the complex and high profile Dhabol Power Project. The most complex issue involved the co-ordination of arrangements between the lenders to the tanker project and the lenders to Dhabol.

skills needed

...be prepared to travel overseas several times a year or even live abroad for a time...all-round commercial awareness...patience...resilience...tact and diplomacy...strong client skills...broad general legal knowledge...

career options

Lawyers used to specialise in major projects after gaining several years' experience in a relevant discipline. Whilst a lot of people continue to enter projects work via this route, many take a more direct approach. It is now possible to specialise in projects work on qualification.

Nearly all international projects are governed (to varying degrees) by English law or New York law, so experience in this field is internationally marketable. American law firms in particular are recruiting experienced English lawyers, which has forced up salaries to make international projects work one of the highest paid specialisms in the legal world.

leading projects firms

All information on leading firms comes from the Chambers Guide to the Legal Profession 2000-2001.

Allen & Overy: Projects: A *"stunningly brilliant"* projects team packed with *"big personalities."* This practice is seen to be pulling away from the chasing pack with a successful leverage of banking superiority and moves into the sponsor market. The firm advises on all industry sectors with particular strengths in power, energy and transport. It has a truly international penetration. Advised Japan Bank for International Co-operation on its involvement in the US$1.6bn limited recourse financing of oil and gas reserves in Brazil. **PFI:** The PFI/PPP side of the practice has a good mix of clients with the traditional A&O bias towards lenders, but also including sponsors and concession granting authorities. Growth areas are health, defence, accommodation and transport. Acted for lenders on resurrected Treasury Building projects including refurbishment and subsequent facilities management.

Clifford Chance: Projects: *"Impressive"* practice praised for its *"flexibility and cohesion,"* has an enviable reputation acting mainly for sponsors and the banks. Acted as local counsel for lenders in the US$575m Flag Atlantic telecoms deal in the US and as foreign sponsor counsel for Phillips Petroleum on the US$1bn Q Chem petrochemical project in Quatar. **PFI:** Perceived by the market as a balanced practice in terms of UK domestic PFI and International projects, the practice has been involved in high profile deals such as advising the consortium (Rotch Property Group Ltd and J. Henry Schroder & Co Ltd) on the Chichester NHS Trust project. Prominence across the board including defence (MoD Tornado Simulator Project), accommodation (advice to bidding consortium on transfer of Inland Revenue and Customs & Excise property portfolio STEPS) and transport (A13 Thames Gateway).

Linklaters: Projects: Recommended for the *"consistent"* quality of its work and its smooth operating process. With a well-balanced client base this practice has strengths in power generation and distribution, transport, water telecoms and infrastructure work. Acted for sponsors on US$2.5bn Dabhol Power projects in India which closed Phase II in 1999 and included the financing for the LNG and Shipping Infrastructure and advised Greek Government on US$2.5bn project financing of ringroad around Athens. **PFI:** Regarded as having a good focus on the domestic PFI market but perhaps overshadowed by the success within international project finance.Growth area for the practice this year include defence (MoD Skynet 5 projects) and education (Glasgow Schools).

Freshfields: Projects: A significant practice in project finance, however it is perceived by the market to be dwarfed by its PFI activity. The team is said to be *"slicker than most"* with a strong international presence acting on both the sponsor and lender side with its leading stars complimented on their financial acumen. Strengths include transport: advised Derech Eretz Highways on the US$ 1.35bn financing of the Cross-Israel Toll Road project, the largest in Israel and energy: acted for OPIC on the financing of US$600m Cuiaba Integrated Power project. **PFI:** With major clients in all sectors of the market and firm grip on the domestic scene, this side of the practice is seen as particularly impressive (*"top-drawer PFI team"*). Advised Warburg Dillon Read with the financing of Section 2 of the Channel Tunnel Rail Link and over the last three years has advised London Underground on the Connect (digital communication) project.

Norton Rose: Projects: *"Delightful"* projects team praised across the board for its international presence and pre-eminence in the energy and infrastructure market, with a balanced client base acting for financiers, multi-laterals and developers. However the firm is perceived to suffer from a lack of US capacity and a weakness in the capital markets which sets it apart from our top three leading firms. Acted for AES Corporation and achieved financial close of the acquisition of Drax power station from

National Power Plc (£1.875bn) and for Paribas in connection with the TotalFina SA, Tractabel SA consortium bid for Taweelah A1 independent power and water project. Advising the project company in the Athens Ring Road project (US$3bn). **PFI:** Perceived by the market as a minor focus for the projects finance team, PFI activity has included a number of high profile clients. Acted for Bank of America, RBS, Toronto-Dominion and Bayerische Landesbank in the funding of the London Underground Project Connect.

leading energy firms

Denton Wilde Sapte: Many say *"it's the best energy firm in London."* With energy forming almost 20% of the firm's workload, this is a key focus. Respected for its *"breadth and depth,"* this large team is encountered at every turn: on technical and industrial as well as corporate matters. Financing aspects are felt to have benefited from February's merger with Wilde Sapte. In short, it is a *"very, very solid practice, difficult to knock."* Strength in the power sector centre on regulatory and restructuring matters. The team's recent work in the sector includes advising OFGEM on the new electricity trading arrangements, notably drafting the new balancing and settlement code. Extensive regulatory and restructuring work has also been done for the Governments of Ireland & Lesotho and the Sultanate of Oman, while corporate work included advising London Electricity on its £160m acquisition of SWEB and involvement in EDF's acquisition of London Electricity. A broad upstream oil practice, which is also strong on gas issues, comprises a host of established names. During the year the firm set up a new independent UKCS gas company, Consort Resources. The team advised Petronas on its investment in Premier Oil (with Amerada Hess) and acted for Premier Oil on the West Natuna gas production and pipeline project. Downstream, the firm has advised on the introduction of the New Gas Trading Arrangements (effective from 1 October 1999) and continued to advise British Gas on the Network Code. Abroad, there has been a notable role in advising the sub-Caucasus states and Central Asian republics on the legal requirements of the Energy Charter Treaty.

It has been a successful year for the firm's work in the water sector. This included acting for the Ministry of Defence on Project Aquatrine, the largest water/sewerage project underway in the UK.

Herbert Smith: *"Undoubtedly right up at the top"*, this is one of the best all-round energy firms. Of special note are its power expertise, a healthy O&G practice, a leading profile in water and a litigation track record which stands alone. The energy team is felt to combine *"know-how with bloody hard work."* The client base includes many electricity companies. *"At the heart of the new trading arrangements,"* the team is currently acting for the 14 PES's on the introduction of supply competition in the UK, and for 10 REC's concerning the new wholesale trading arrangements to replace the Electricity Pool. Other recent work includes advice to Northern Ireland Electricity/Viridian on the restructuring of the electricity industry in the Republic of Ireland. Clearly, the department has an outstanding litigation profile, and has capitalised on the recent upturn in oil and gas litigation to act in some high-profile cases. Among them was one for BP Amoco concerning litigation arising from a drilling contract for the world's largest jack-up rig. Traditionally strong in North Sea oil financing, the team recently advised Chase Manhattan on a number of deals, including a US$220m refinancing facility for Intrepid Energy North Sea. M&A work remains a focus: Davey advised Petroplus on its Cressier oil refinery acquisition and Bond represented Amerada Hess in its strategic alliance with Petronas for a £136m equity stake in Premier Oil. A leading water practice spans pure regulatory work, corporate and commercial matters and international water projects. The firm's water team has been advising on numerous domestic restructurings, including that of British Water. On the corporate side the team advised Bechtel Enterprises on the sale of its 50% stake in the International Water Group. Overseas, the firm has advised on water projects in the Philippines and South Africa for International Water. Clients include St Clements Services; Enterprise Oil plc; Yorkshire Water.

CMS Cameron McKenna: *"One has to hand it to them; they have a great profile."* The energy team won widespread accolades and is now ranked alone just behind the two market leaders. Known for technical expertise, the department is considered to have *"made a virtue out of energy – especially power."* Strong on industry market structures, and act for a number of transmission companies. The power work for the past year has been seasoned with international highlights. In Canada, the team represented the municipal and distribution utilities in preparation for the new Ontario electricity markets, while it advised the Mexican regulator on the development of that country's new electricity trading system. The group has also acted for developers in power projects in Africa. Now held to possess *"a sound mainstream North Sea practice,"* the firm has been aided by an office in Aberdeen. The team worked on the Catchment Area Project to finalise the Neptune Field Agreements. In contentious matters, the firm has acted in North Sea litigation concerning the Banff Field. Closely involved with the International Private Water Association, the water team are strong on international water projects, public and private, such as Bulgaria's goundbreaking Sofia Water & Sewerage Project (for the Municipality and EBRD).

leading construction firms

All information on leading firms comes from the Chambers Guide to the Legal Profession 2000-2001.

Masons Nationwide: *"Construction juggernauts"* Masons are still so far ahead of any of the other firms that one really must ask what's behind the sucess of the *"brickies"* firm. In a nutshell, it has focused itself like no other of its size. Its army of clients are those with core activities in construction and engineering and the firm seeks to service the clients' primary needs. Masons is at the epicentre of construction disputes in the UK and is spreading its sphere of influence overseas. It represented the joint venture company in arbitration proceedings against the Government of Hong Kong arising out of its Strategic Sewage Disposal Scheme. The Masons style appears to be to spare no effort and opponents confirm that *"you are put on your mettle"* by the firm. *"Vast expertise"* and *"absolute excellence"* are shown at partner level, although one or two of our interviewees indicated that the lawyers are *"not all black belts as they are not all big, old and ugly enough."* Advised Arrow Light Rail Ltd as project sponsor on the £270m Nottingham Light Rail PFI.

CMS Cameron McKenna London: The three separate units within the group are perceived to adhere to strict divisions but it is now recognised that, for the first time in a number of years, the group is achieving a good balance between dispute resolution and non-contentious work. Its reputation is enhanced by the firm's strength in PFI, property and health and safety. The firm has a reputation as the voice of the employer. The contentious team bats for the contractor as much as it does for the employer. Acted for Panatown in 'Alfred McAlpine Construction v Panatown' which went to the House of Lords in October 1999.

Rowe & Maw London: Truly overwhelming endorsement for this group of practitioners with whom *"you can identify the real issues."* Partners and assistants display ambidextrous qualities in that they handle both contentious and non-contentious matters for both employers and contractors. There is a distinct impression that the department retains its own character within a firm that is becoming increasingly 'City' in its focus and that the ethos of the place is right for the brave new world of construction dispute resolution. *"They are reflective litigators – thinking practitioners."* The firm represented VHE in 'VHE Construction plc v RBSTB Trust Co. Ltd', a case concerning the effect of an adjudicator's decision on set-offs.

LEADING FIRMS

LONDON	CONSTRUCTION	ENERGY	PROJECTS/PFI
Allen & Overy	*	****	******
Ashurst Morris Crisp	**	**	**
Baker & McKenzie	*	*	*
Barlow Lyde & Gilbert	*		
Beachcroft Wansbroughs		*	
Beale and Company	*		
Berrymans Lace Mawer	*		
Berwin Leighton	***		*
Bird & Bird			*
Clifford Chance	**	****	*****
Clyde & Co		*	
CMS Cameron McKenna	*****	*****	***
Coudert Brothers		**	
Davies Arnold Cooper	*		
Denton Wilde Sapte	*	******	***
DLA			*
Eversheds		*	
Fenwick Elliott	****		
Field Fisher Waterhouse		*	
Freshfields Bruckhaus Deringer	**	***	****
Glovers	*		
Hammond Suddards Edge	***		
Herbert Smith	****	******	***
Holman Fenwick & Willan		*	
Ince & Co		*	
Lawrence Graham		**	
LeBoeuf, Lamb, Greene & MacRae		*	
Linklaters	***	****	*****
Lovells	***	**	**
Masons	******	*	*
Milbank, Tweed, Hadley & McCloy			**
Nabarro Nathanson		**	
Nicholson Graham & Jones	***		
Norton Rose	***	****	****
Richards Butler		*	
Rowe & Maw	*****		*
Shadbolt & Co	****		
Shearman & Sterling			**

LONDON	CONSTRUCTION	ENERGY	PROJECTS/PFI
Simmons & Simmons	*	**	*
SJ Berwin & Co	*		*
Slaughter and May		***	**
Taylor Joynson Garrett	**		
Trowers & Hamlins	*		*
Vinson & Elkins LLP		**	
Warner Cranston	*		
Watson, Farley & Williams		*	
Wedlake Bell	*		
Weil, Gotshal & Manges			*
White & Case			**
Winward Fearon	***		

THE SOUTH	CONSTRUCTION	ENERGY	PROJECTS/PFI
Blake Lapthorn, *Portsmouth*	****		
Cripps Harries Hall, *Tunbridge Wells*	*****		
Shadbolt & Co, *Reigate*	******		

THAMES VALLEY	CONSTRUCTION	ENERGY	PROJECTS/PFI
Clarks, *Reading*	******		
Corbett & Co, *Teddington*	*		
Deborah Mills Associates, *Marlow*		*****	
Linnells, *Oxford*	******		
Morgan Cole, *Oxford*	******		

SOUTH WEST	CONSTRUCTION	ENERGY	PROJECTS/PFI
Beachcroft Wansbroughs, *Bristol*	***		
Bevan Ashford, *Bristol, Exeter*	*****		******
Bond Pearce, *Plymouth*	**	******	
Burges Salmon, *Bristol*	**		*****
Laytons, *Bristol*	****		
Masons, *Bristol*	******		******
Osborne Clarke OWA, *Bristol*	**		
Veale Wasbrough, *Bristol*	***	*****	

WALES	CONSTRUCTION	ENERGY	PROJECTS/PFI
Eversheds, *Cardiff*	*****		*****
Hugh James Ford Simey, *Cardiff*	*****		
Morgan Cole, *Cardiff*	******		*****

MIDLANDS	CONSTRUCTION	ENERGY	PROJECTS/PFI
Browne Jacobson, *Nottingham*	*		
DLA, *Birmingham*	****		******
Edwards Geldard, *Derby*		*****	
Eversheds, *Birmingham, Derby, Nottingham*	**	*****	******
Freethcartwright, *Nottingham*	**		
Garretts, *Birmingham*	*		
Gateley Wareing, *Birmingham*	****		
Hammond Suddards Edge, *Birmingham*	*****	*****	
Kent Jones and Done, *Stoke on Trent*		*****	
Knight & Sons, *Newcastle under Lyme*		*****	
Lee Crowder, *Birmingham*	**		
Martineau Johnson, *Birmingham*		******	
Merricks, *Birmingham*	**		
Pinsent Curtis, *Birmingham*	***	*****	******
Shoosmiths, *Northampton*	*		
Wragge & Co, *Birmingham*	******	******	****

EAST ANGLIA	CONSTRUCTION	ENERGY	PROJECTS/PFI
Eversheds, *Ipswich, Norwich*	****		
Greenwoods, *Peterborough*	****		
Hewitson Becke + Shaw, *Cambridge*	*****		
Mills & Reeve, *Cambridge*	******		*****

NORTH WEST	CONSTRUCTION	ENERGY	PROJECTS/PFI
Addleshaw Booth & Co, *Manchester*	****		******
DLA, *Liverpool, Manchester*	****		
Elliotts, *Manchester*	**		
Eversheds, *Manchester*			*****

NORTH WEST cont'd	CONSTRUCTION	ENERGY	PROJECTS/PFI
Halliwell Landau, *Manchester*	***		
Hammond Suddards Edge, *Manchester*	*****		
Hill Dickinson, *Liverpool*	**		
Kirk Jackson, *Manchester*	****		
Masons, *Manchester*	******		
Pannone & Partners, *Manchester*	***		
Wake Dyne Lawton, *Chester*		****	

YORKSHIRE	CONSTRUCTION	ENERGY	PROJECTS/PFI
Addleshaw Booth & Co, *Leeds*	******		******
Denison Till, *York*	*		
DLA, *Leeds, Sheffield*	****		
Eversheds, *Leeds*	***	*****	
Hammond Suddards Edge, *Leeds*	*****		
Irwin Mitchell, *Sheffield*	*		
Masons, *Leeds*	****		
Nabarro Nathanson, *Sheffield*	*	******	***
Pinsent Curtis, *Leeds*	**	****	******
Walker Morris, *Leeds*	***		***
Wrigleys, *Leeds*		****	

NORTH EAST	CONSTRUCTION	ENERGY	PROJECTS/PFI
Dickinson Dees, *Newcastle upon Tyne*	*****	****	****
Eversheds, *Newcastle upon Tyne*	******		
Robert Muckle, *Newcastle upon Tyne*	****		
Watson Burton, *Newcastle upon Tyne*	*****		

property

A property lawyer's tools are land law and contract law. Most work involves a blend of the two. The acquisition and disposal of land and the creation and termination of relationships between investors, land owners and land users are, in the main, contractual issues. Add to this a body of common law and a swathe of statutes and you have the nuts and bolts of property law. Overlaying all of this is the property market, the most significant ingredient of all.

Clients vary widely in terms of their level of involvement with the property market. At one end of the scale is the residential conveyancing client who may only be involved in one property transaction in his whole life. At the other is the large institution whose representative is a property professional himself. In between are the users and owners of property. Each client requires a different style of service. The one-off user may need plenty of hand-holding, whilst the professional may simply need action without detailed explanation.

The firm you choose will determine what type of client base you'll be working with and increasingly the type of transaction you'll encounter. Some in the City believe that commercial property work is going through a sea change and that at the largest firms routine lease drafting and more conventional property work has had its day. Clients will look to smaller and medium sized firms and to the regions for this kind of service. The big City property practices will concentrate on the newer ways of investing in property through joint ventures, limited partnerships and investment trusts. The City firms will specialise in complex property finance and become more like corporate lawyers whose deals have a property asset base.

The work of the property solicitor leans against other disciplines – company law, finance, revenue law and trusts to name but three. You may encounter areas such as liquor licensing, health and safety, telecommunications, environmental law, agricultural law, insolvency, project finance and planning. You will come to learn about the role of surveyors and property agents. You will interact with the Inland Revenue, local authorities, the Land Registry, Companies House, property agents, building surveyors, architects, banks and mortgage lenders, brokers, designers and the list goes on. Think about how much real property there is in this country and how many different relationships there are between owners, users, investors, sellers and buyers. You will see how much property work there is and how varied it is.

type of work

Property work is basically transaction driven and involves a huge amount of documentation to be considered and amended. In an average day you'll spend a considerable amount of time in negotiations either on the phone or in meetings with clients, other lawyers and property professionals in related areas.

An example of a standard piece of commercial property work would be the business lease. Typically you might receive instructions for a new lease from a client who has negotiated the basics with the help of a commercial agent. The main structure of the deal will be established but many points require further negotiation. A fifteen year lease of one floor in an office block, for example, could involve a provision for one party to bring the lease to an end after a certain number of years. It could involve the right for the tenant to sub-let or transfer the lease to a third party. It could involve a major re-fit of the premises or a period which is rent free. During the lease period major issues between the parties include the review of rent at set times and the level of annual service charge payments to cover the costs of maintenance and services to the building. All of these issues must be dealt with before the lease is signed and the parties commit to the long-term relationship. Clients always want certainty from you; it's your job to give them the nearest possible thing to that. They expect you, the experienced professional, to anticipate what might go wrong and to protect them ahead of time. Whilst a property lawyer generally works on a deal in which both sides have the same goal, the trick is to get the very best deal for your client and to get it done within the time scale that the client sets for you.

Victoria Sutcliffe is an assistant solicitor at **Lovells**. Property took her by surprise – as it does for a good majority of those who end up making a career of it. She liked the fact that, from her first day as a trainee she felt she was productive, in control and running her own files. "From day one the phone was ringing. As I walked in the door a client rang to say they were ready to complete and from then on the telephone didn't stop ringing. The clients don't stop asking lots of questions so you build up a very good relationship with them. More than in almost any other department you are responsible for your own destiny at a very junior level. There is an end product which you can see. You can drive through any city centre and say I bought that, I sold that, I leased that."

skills needed

...verbal and written negotiating skills...attention to detail...ability to think through a potential problem and give clear advice to clients...pro-active time and case management...ability to communicate well and forge professional relationships...knowledge of wide scope of client businesses.

career options

Just as the fortunes of the property market have been cyclical, the fortunes of property lawyers rise and fall accordingly. A decade ago, the market dealt a serious blow to this part of the legal profession and it is only in more recent years that there has been a strong demand for property lawyers. For those qualifying into and gaining experience in commercial property work during the leaner years, the present up turn in the market has put them in a strong position and the salaries commanded have begun to match those in other core commercial areas.

After a while in private practice or perhaps as a result of other commitments, some lawyers look for change. In-house jobs in industry and commerce are popular. Such positions offer the chance to work for a single 'client' on essentially the same types of transactions as contemporaries in private practice.

The Land Registry or the Law Commission provide career options for those with a more academic bent and, increasingly, know-how lawyers play a prominent role in the education and on-going training of property lawyers in larger practices. In addition to keeping their teams up to speed on developments in the law the know-how specialist would be responsible for periodically updating the firm's standard documentation and producing news updates for clients.

leading commercial property firms

All information on leading firms comes from the Chambers Guide to the Legal Profession 2000-2001.

In London the large City firms with broad commercial practices are at the top of the pile.

The *"Rolls Royce"* of property firms, **Linklaters** leads the field due to the group's *"international coverage"* and *"client list to die for."* Said to have *"quality and consistency at all levels,"* **Linklaters** members are known for their *"responsiveness"* and ability to *"come up with radical solutions."* The group has a particular niche in corporate headquarters and rent review work and is seen to be increasingly active on property finance. Other top practices include **Berwin Leighton** whose noted commitment to property as a core area of practice gives it the reputation of having *"the most eggs in the property basket."* This is a *"classic property firm with a strong local authority practice"* considered *"brilliant"* for *"large projects and innovative tax* *and planning schemes."* By comparison with other City property firms, Berwin Leighton is seen as more UK-based and some voiced concern that the nature of the practice might lead them towards more and more commoditised property work. Nevertheless, the are recognised *"unbeatable for sheer hitting power in the retail shopping area"* and public sector work.

"Geared for mega-transactions," **Clifford Chance** are seen as having *"pound for pound more resources devoted to property than anyone else."* The property group is in a *"superb position for picking up work that spins off the corporate side."* As one interviewee noted, he is *"not sure there is another firm who could have handled the Canary Wharf transactions."* The team has considerable expertise in real estate finance and recent mergers with firms Pünder, Volhard, Weber & Axster and Rogers & Wells promise to give the team an increasing share of the international market. The only criticism leveled at the team was that is was sometimes *"patchy"* – *"there are some who get too bogged down in detail."*

Although better known in the market for PFI and litigation work, **Herbert Smith** maintains a solid reputation for pure property work, built largely on work for institutional clients such as Standard Life and Greycoat. Recent reorganisation of the firm's management committee has fed the perception that the firm's commitment to property is weakening under the pressures exerted by the corporate department. The group nevertheless receives strong recommendations from peers and clients alike for *"quality service"* and *"an eye for detail,"* and has recognised strengths in planning and public sector development projects.

"Well-organised" **Lovells** *"clearly has a quality system in place."* The practice is recommended for having a *"spread and depth across a number of related specialisms"* including property finance and private partnering. The firm recently achieved a major coup when instructed by the Inland Revenue/Customs and Excise in connection with the STEPS transaction,

with a total value of £4bn. Seen to be *"making a play for corporate PFI work,"* **Lovells** is also expanding into the European market following its merger with Boesebeck Droste.

A *"property-led firm"* **Nabarro Nathanson** has an enormous team dedicated to property work for investors and developers across a range of sectors and has a widely-acknowledged expertise in property finance. The department receives mixed reviews from the market. Often described as *"needlessly aggressive,"* the team is aid to suffer from *"quality control"* problems at more junior levels. The group nevertheless *"clearly handles a great volume of complex transactions"* including large securitisation deals and city centre regeneration projects. Amongst the smaller firms, **Fosters** and **Maxwell Batley** maintain strong reputations in the field for high-level property work.

leading property firms

All information on leading firms comes from the Chambers Guide to the Legal Profession 2000-2001.

In the South, **Blake Lapthorne** are the *"undoubted kings of the Solent."* Praised for its *"uniformity of standards"* the team is highly rated for its retail and development work for leading regional and national clients. Localised strengths include secured lending and waterfront development. **Bond Pearce** also has a strong regional presence in the South and South West. The team is particularly active in out of town retail developments and has niche expertise in offshore cable estate laying for the Crown Estate Marine. A small but *"quality"* property team of *"good pedigree"* and *"high intellect"* receives excellent instructions by way of corporate support.

Top firms in the Thames Valley include **Denton Wilde Sapte** who concentrate chiefly on large scale retail and leisure portfolio management and development advice in relation to English Partnership's property. In Reading and Oxford, **Morgan Cole** have key strengths in commercial development, insolvency , property finance and portfolio management for clients including energy multinationals and hi-tech businesses. Also in Reading, **Pitmans** is noted as a *"busy"* practice with a heavy presence in the residential and commercial development sectors. Said to take a *"broad-brush strategic approach,"* the Pitmans' team is *"good at thinking laterally and getting things done."*

In Wales, **Eversheds** clearly *"dominate the scene"* in terms of size and clientele, with institutional work seen as the core areas of strength. Other leaders in the area include niche property firm **Berry Smith**, **Edwards Geldard**, noted for its expertise in public/private sector relationships, and the public sector, health trust and institutional oriented **Morgan Cole**.

A national firm with tentacles throughout the UK, **Eversheds** also ranks as a regional giant in the Midlands, considered to be the strongest link in the Eversheds chain. The group is heavily involved in large local schemes and rates highly for inward investment and development work. The firm handles quality property work from its Birmingham, Nottingham, Norwich, Ipswich, Cambridge, Manchester, and Newcastle offices. In the Midlands, its chief competitor in the region is **Wragge & Co** said to be *"on the top for consistency."* The Wragges crew

maintain a highly *"technical and commercial approach"* and have seen sustained growth in residential development. In East Anglia, **Mills & Reeve** has a strong health and university client base which remains the core of the practice, but acts increasingly for developers and hi-tech occupiers.

In the Northwest, **Addleshaw Booth & Co**, **Cobbetts**, **DLA**, and **Halliwell Landau** share the lead for property work. Addleshaw's has particular expertise in town centre redevelopment schemes. The firm rates highly on the property front for both its Manchester and Leeds offices. **Cobbetts** has a national reputation in the licensed and unlicensed food and drink retail sector. **DLA** are considered a *"good outfit"* with a *"national presence"* acting for commercial, industrial and retail developers and occupiers, institutional investors and lenders. *"Positive and proactive,"* the team at **Halliwell Landau** undertakes joint venture work, funding and enterprise zone transactions and is strongly development-oriented. **Dickinson Dees** are the clear leaders in the North East. The group has expertise in urban regeneration projects for local authorities and developers and is also involved in volume conveyancing for builders and lenders.

LEADING FIRMS

LONDON	PROPERTY	LONDON	PROPERTY
Allen & Overy	*	Lawrence Graham	*
Ashurst Morris Crisp	**	Linklaters	******
Berwin Leighton	*****	Lovells	****
Boodle Hatfield	*****	Macfarlanes	**
Clifford Chance	*****	Manches	*****
CMS Cameron McKenna	***	Maxwell Batley	******
Coudert Brothers	***	McGuinness Finch	**
D J Freeman	**	Mishcon de Reya	**
Dechert	**	Nabarro Nathanson	****
Denton Wilde Sapte	**	Norton Rose	**
DLA	*	Olswang	*
Eversheds	*	Park Nelson	**
Finers Stephens Innocent	****	Simmons & Simmons	*
Fladgate Fielder	****	SJ Berwin & Co	***
Forsters	******	Slaughter and May	*
Freshfields Bruckhaus Deringer	***	Speechly Bircham	****
Gouldens	*	Stepien Lake Gilbert & Paling	*****
Hamlins	**	Teacher Stern Selby	**
Herbert Smith	****	Thomas Eggar Church Adams	**
Julian Holy	**	Trowers & Hamlins	****

THE SOUTH	PROPERTY (COMMERCIAL)	THE SOUTH	PROPERTY (COMMERCIAL)
Blake Lapthorn, *Fareham*	******	Penningtons, *Basingstoke, Godalming, Newbury*	***
Bond Pearce, *Southampton*	*****		
Brachers, *Maidstone*	***	Rawlison & Butler, *Crawley*	***
Clyde & Co, *Guildford*	****	Sherwin Oliver Solicitors, *Portsmouth*	****
Coffin Mew & Clover, *Portsmouth*	***	Shoosmiths, *Solent*	***
Cripps Harries Hall, *Tunbridge Wells, Kent*	****	Steele Raymond, *Bournemouth*	***
DMH, *Brighton*	****	Stevens & Bolton, *Guildford*	*****
GCL Solicitors, *Guildford*	***	Thomas Eggar Church Adams, *Chichester, Horsham, Reigate, Worthing*	****
Lester Aldridge, *Bournemouth*	****		
Moore & Blatch, *Southampton*	***	Thomson Snell & Passmore, *Tunbridge Wells*	****
Paris Smith & Randall, *Southampton*	****		

THE SOUTH	PROPERTY	THE SOUTH	PROPERTY
B P Collins, *Gerrards Cross*	★★★	Iliffes Booth Bennett, *Uxbridge*	★★★★
BrookStreet Des Roches, *Witney*	★★★★★	Laytons, *Surrey*	★★★
Clarks, *Reading*	★★★★★	Linnells, *Oxford*	★★★
Colemans, *Maidenhead*	★★	Matthew Arnold & Baldwin, *Watford*	★★
Denton Wilde Sapte, *Milton Keynes*	★★★★★★	Morgan Cole, Oxford, *Reading*	★★★★★★
Fennemores, *Milton Keynes*	★★	Pictons, *St. Albans*	★★
Harold Benjamin Littlejohn, *Harrow*	★★★	Pitmans, *Reading*	★★★★★★
Beachcroft Wansbroughs, *Bristol*	★★★★★	Foot Anstey Sargent, *Exeter, Plymouth*	★★★
Bevan Ashford, *Bristol, Exeter*	★★★★★	Lyons Davidson, *Bristol*	★★★
Bond Pearce, *Bristol, Exeter, Plymouth*	★★★★★	Michelmores, *Exeter*	★★★★★
Bretherton Price Elgoods, *Cheltenham*	★★★	Osborne Clarke OWA, *Bristol*	★★★★★★
Burges Salmon, *Bristol*	★★★★★★	Rickerby Watterson, *Cheltenham*	★★★
Cartwrights, *Bristol*	★★★	Stephens & Scown, *Exeter, St Austell*	★★★
Charles Russell, *Cheltenham*	★★★	TLT Solicitors, *Bristol*	★★★★
Clarke Willmott & Clarke, *Bristol, Taunton*	★★★★★	Townsends, *Swindon*	★★★
Davies and Partners, *Gloucester*	★★★★	Veale Wasbrough, *Bristol*	★★★★★

WALES	PROPERTY	WALES	PROPERTY
Berry Smith, *Cardiff*	★★★★★	Morgan Cole, *Cardiff, Swansea*	★★★★★
Edwards Geldard, *Cardiff*	★★★★★	Palser Grossman, *Cardiff Bay*	★★★★
Eversheds, *Cardiff*	★★★★★★	Robertsons, *Cardiff*	★★
Hugh James Ford Simey, *Cardiff*	★★★		

MIDLANDS	PROPERTY	MIDLANDS	PROPERTY
Browne Jacobson, *Nottingham*	★★	Knight & Sons, *Newcastle-under-Lyme*	★★★
DLA, *Birmingham*	★★★★	Lee Crowder, *Birmingham*	★★★★
Eversheds, *Birmingham, Nottingham*	★★★★★★	Manby & Steward, *Wolverhampton*	★★
Freethcartwright, *Leicester, Nottingham*	★★★	Martineau Johnson, *Birmingham*	★★★
Hammond Suddards Edge, *Birmingham*	★★★★★	Pinsent Curtis, *Birmingham*	★★★★★
		Shoosmiths, *Northampton, Nottingham*	★★★
Harvey Ingram Owston, *Leicester*	★★	Wragge & Co, *Birmingham*	★★★★★★
Higgs & Sons, *Brierley Hill*	★★	Wright Hassall, *Leamington Spa*	★★

EAST ANGLIA	PROPERTY	EAST ANGLIA	PROPERTY
Ashton Graham, *Bury St Edmunds, Ipswich*	***	Mills & Reeve, *Cambridge, Norwich*	******
Birketts, *Ipswich*	*****	Prettys, *Ipswich*	**
Ellison & Co, *Colchester*	**	Taylor Vinters, *Cambridge*	****
Eversheds, *Cambridge, Ipswich, Norwich*	******	Tolhurst Fisher,	
H. Montlake & Co, *Ilford*	**	*Chelmsford, Southend-on-Sea*	**
Hewitson Becke + Shaw, *Cambridge*	*****	Wollastons, *Chelmsford*	***
Kenneth Elliott & Rowe, *Romford*	**		

NORTH WEST	PROPERTY	NORTH WEST	PROPERTY
Aaron & Partners, *Chester*	**	Field Cunningham & Co, *Manchester*	****
Addleshaw Booth & Co, *Manchester*	******	Gorna & Co, *Manchester*	**
Beachcroft Wansbroughs,		Halliwell Landau, *Manchester*	******
Manchester	****	Hammond Suddards Edge,	
Bermans, *Liverpool*	*	*Manchester*	*****
Berrymans Lace Mawer, *Liverpool*	**	Hill Dickinson, *Chester, Liverpool*	**
Brabner Holden Banks Wilson,		Jones Maidment Wilson,	
Liverpool	**	*Altrincham, Manchester*	***
Bullivant Jones, *Liverpool*	*****	Kuit Steinart Levy, *Manchester*	**
Chaffe Street, *Manchester*	*	Mace & Jones, *Liverpool, Manchester*	***
Cobbetts, *Manchester*	******	Pannone & Partners, *Manchester*	***
Cuff Roberts, *Liverpool*	**	Wacks Caller, *Manchester*	*
Davies Wallis Foyster, *Liverpool*	****	Walker Smith & Way, *Chester*	*
DLA, *Liverpool, Manchester*	******	Weightmans, *Liverpool, Manchester*	*
Eversheds, *Manchester*	******		

YORKSHIRE & NORTH EAST	PROPERTY	YORKSHIRE & NORTH EAST	PROPERTY
Addleshaw Booth & Co, *Leeds*	******	Irwin Mitchell, *Sheffield*	***
Andrew M. Jackson & Co, *Hull*	***	Keeble Hawson, *Sheffield*	*
Denison Till, *York*	*	Nabarro Nathanson, *Sheffield*	***
DLA, *Leeds, Sheffield*	****	Pinsent Curtis, *Leeds*	****
Eversheds, *Leeds, Newcastle upon Tyne*	*****	Read Hind Stewart, *Leeds*	***
Gordons Cranswick Solicitors,		Rollit Farrell & Bladon, *Hull*	*
Bradford, Leeds	**	The Frith Partnership, *Leeds*	*
Gosschalks, *Hull*	**	Wake Smith, *Sheffield*	*
Hammond Suddards Edge, *Leeds*	****	Walker Morris, *Leeds*	*****
Archers, *Stockton-on-Tees*	***	Robert Muckle, *Newcastle-upon-Tyne*	****
Dickinson Dees, *Newcastle upon Tyne*	******	Ward Hadaway, *Newcastle upon Tyne*	****
Jacksons, *Stockton-on-Tees*	***	Watson Burton, *Newcastle upon Tyne*	****

SPECIALIST PRACTICE AREAS

PROPERTY

public interest law

Public interest law concerns the relationship between state and citizen. Whilst each area of law grouped under this heading is a separate subject in its own right, requiring particular skills and personal qualities, all areas concern the activities of public bodies, and in particular whether their actions are lawful. Challenging their decisions by way of judicial review is an important thread in civil liberties, immigration and education work. Lawyers involved in local government law see the other side of the coin. They advise public authorities on their powers and how to defend their decisions.

Each of these areas will be heavily affected by the implementation of the Human Rights Act, which enshrines the European Convention of Human Rights in British law. This came into effect in October 2000. All legislation and court judgments will then have to be read in the light of provisions of the Act. It is likely that this will 'open the floodgates' and mean interesting and busy times ahead for lawyers in these fields.

type of work

human rights/civil liberties: Civil liberties is a broad concept covering suspected miscarriages of justice, actions against the police, prisoners' rights, public order, discrimination and free speech issues. Redress will often be sought by judicial review, and there is considerable cross-over between civil liberties and areas such as crime and immigration.

As all these areas are covered under provisions of the new Human Rights Act, the volume of judicial review is likely to increase at an alarming pace over the next few years. Lawyers and campaign groups practising in this field have attempted to train fellow lawyers and professionals in the implications of the Act for other areas of law, including commercial disciplines.

At **Bindman & Partners**, Stephen Grosz's work is characterised by its variety. A morning's work might include studying a European directive on freedom of access to information on the environment, advising a client on a school closure, meeting a student who failed exams because of insufficient provision for dyslexia, and considering new instructions from a homosexual naval officer.

An imaginative legal mind, an ability to adapt to different areas of law and an interest in using the law creatively and strategically are all important qualities in a civil liberties lawyer, according to Stephen Grosz. "You need to try and push back the boundaries, and if you're working with campaigning organisations, as you frequently are, you have to understand their needs and priorities." Grosz also looks for a sympathetic and understanding nature and a broad world view, as opposed to a narrow legalistic outlook.

career options

Places at the few firms which do civil liberties work and offer training are incredibly competitive. Such firms often prefer older trainees who have worked in relevant fields to students fresh from university. It is vital, then, to get involved in voluntary or campaign work at an early stage if you wish to train in this area.

There are a number of organisations which are particularly known for their campaigning work in civil liberties and human rights, such as Amnesty International and Justice. All can be joined, for a fee and amongst other benefits will send you newsletters with up to date information about their campaigns and recent changes in the law. For hands-on experience, it is best to contact your local law centre or relevant voluntary organisations.

A career as a civil liberties lawyer may be interesting but is unlikely to be lucrative. Law Centres, campaigning groups and voluntary organisations offer alternatives to private practice.

type of work

immigration: There are two types of immigration work: personal and business. Personal immigration clients are private individuals seeking advice. Work includes political asylum cases, nationality issues, marriage applications and family reunion cases. Much of this is legally aided and is carried out by small firms. In business immigration clients are often employers seeking advice on behalf of employees or, more usually, future employees. Work includes advising national and multinational corporations on work permits and investor applications and advising employers on avoiding breaches of the immigration acts. Large and medium-sized commercial firms undertake this work.

a day in the life....

A typical day, says Peter Alfandary, head of Corporate Immigration at **Warner Cranston**, might involve advising the English arm of a foreign company wanting to bring staff from New York to work in the UK, drafting an application for a work permit on behalf of a multi-national client, advising a foreign investor on setting up a business in the UK, advising a human resources department on whether a potential employee has a legal right to work in the UK and telephoning the British Embassy in Beijing to sort out entry clearance for the wife of a Chinese executive.

A typical day for personal immigration expert Wesley Gryk could involve encounters with a whole range of clients. He may spend the morning with a lesbian couple advising them on same sex immigration issues, followed by an emergency meeting with a foreign wife abandoned by her husband. The afternoon could involve simple work permit advice to someone who is not likely to have a problem, then more complicated advice to someone who has virtually no legal right to be in the country and has been

"underground" for twenty years. A junior lawyer's day may be just as varied – they may start the morning filing, but then be sent off on their own for a five hour interview at Gatwick airport or the Home Office, in sole charge of looking after the interests of an asylum seeker.

skills needed

....communication...tact, diplomacy and patience...good drafting and advocacy skills...an interest in current affairs and politics...liberalism (for personal immigration)...scepticism...presentation skills...a team player....

career options

Personal immigration does not offer the financial rewards enjoyed by those in more commercial disciplines, or those specialising in business immigration. But would-be personal immigration specialists are unlikely to be motivated by financial gain. Alternatives to private practice include working for a Law Centre or bodies such as the UN or Joint Council for the Welfare of Immigrants. Leading immigration lawyer Alison Stanley, for example, was articled at **Winstanley-Burgess**, then spent several years as the solicitor to the JWCI before returning to private practice with **Bindman & Partners**. It is also possible to come to this type of work from a more commercial background. Wesley Gryk began his career as a corporate lawyer with large US firm Shearman & Sterling.

type of work

local government: Most firms with a dedicated public sector or local authority department will act on behalf of the authorities in a defensive or preemptive capacity attempting to stave off potential judicial review or advising on the liabilities and of proposed new methods of service delivery. Other firms will represent the claimant(s) actively seeking to challenge the decisions of the local authority.

Although local authorities have their own inhouse legal teams, they will frequently outsource work to private practice on a whole range of matters from development and urban regeneration projects, planning appeals, local government finance and vires (powers) to housing stock transfers and the implementation of "best value" techniques.

Niche specialists **Leonie Cowen & Associates**, for example, have been advising The London Borough of Tower Hamlets on the legal structuring of a charitable trust regarding the £20m-£30m multi-purpose Mile End Park millennium project. **Rowe & Maw**, for example, acted for the Westminster City Council Auditor in the 'homes for votes' case. They also act for local authorities concerning PFI, social services and human rights advice. **Sharpe Pritchard** act for a whole raft of councils defending them against judicial challenges to their policies on childcare, education, and health.

a day in the life of ....

A typical day for Tony Curnow, head of the Public Sector Group at **Ashurst Morris Crisp**, might include drafting heads of terms for a local authority regeneration project, meeting with clients to discuss a housing transfer agreement, reviewing a compulsory purchase order case and chasing the Department of Transport for the issue of a draft road closure order.

skills needed

....ability to get on with people at all levels...flexibility...political awareness...understanding of the relationship between central and local government...head for statutory interpretation...ability to master a complex regulatory regime ...self-motivation...common sense approach....

career options

The obvious starting point for someone wishing to specialise in local government law is to apply for a training contract with a local authority legal department. You then have the option to stay at the authority or move into private practice. "Somebody who'd done their training in a local authority, stayed on for a year or so, and then applied to us would be an

attractive package." Says Tony Curnow "they might be more attractive than someone who'd been solely in the private sector, but it depends on the individual."

On the other hand, firms like **Nabarro Nathanson**, **Eversheds** or **Ashurst Morris Crisp** may be able to offer broader commercial experience during training, as well as good quality local government work. A wider range of options may then remain open on qualification. You could continue in a commercial private practice, transfer into more general public law work or move into a local authority.

Salaries are generally higher in private practice, but hours are often longer to match. The good news about local authorities is that pay and conditions are perceived to be improving.

type of work

education: There are two kinds of client in education work: institutions and individuals. Commercial firms tend to act for institutions including universities, schools, colleges and funding organisations. Smaller, niche firms act for individuals, including pupils and their parents, university students and children with special needs.

Advice to institutional clients covers more than just education law. Eversheds, for example, advises universities and colleges on employment law, industrial relations, constitutional issues, funding matters, student relations and discipline. At **Beachcroft Wansbroughs**, Julian Gizzi was involved in the Dearing Committee inquiry into the running of Further Education colleges and is also involved in funding and franchising issues.

David Ruebain, meanwhile, at **David Levene & Co**, might spend his morning with the parents of a disabled child trying to sort out funding for transport to school. His afternoon could be spent on the telephone arguing against an examining board on behalf of a 'special needs' pupil. Jack Rabinowicz at **Teacher Stern Selby** may have to deal with the parents of a child bully one day and the parents of a child who has been bullied the next.

skills needed

institutions:...commercial outlook...aptitude for statutory interpretation...the self-confidence to stick your neck out and take a view....

individuals:...a rights-based perspective..."you've got to have decided that earning as much money as possible is not your priority"...a head for statute and case law...a feel for the way public policy is developing....

career options

There are a number of opportunities to practice education law outside private practice. Joining a local authority legal department is one obvious option – a significant part of local authority legal work involves educational institutions. There are also posts within the Department for Education, and some universities now have their own legal units.

leading human rights firms

All information on leading firms comes from the Chambers Guide to the Legal Profession 2000-2001.

Bindman & Partners: The breadth and quality of its work for applicants gives it an edge over others and an unrivalled human rights perspective. Its resources are deployed in a range of areas including immigration, criminal, mental health, judicial review, animal rights, inquest, discrimination and freedom of speech. Recent high profile cases include acting for Amnesty International in the Pinochet case and for Greenpeace concerning genetically modified crop tests.

Bhatt Murphy: This dedicated civil law firm has won widespread praise for its police and prisons work. It is considered top rate for actions against the police or public authorities. Caseload includes judicial review, deaths in custody, and challenges under the new Human Rights Act.

Birnberg Peirce & Partners: has an emphasis on crime work but related strengths in immigration, discrimination and prisoners' rights issues. Historically, have maintained a fine reputation for Irish terrorist cases, most notably on behalf of the Guildford Five.

Currently acting for an individual claiming physical abuse and wrongful imprisonment on the grounds of racism.

Christian Fisher: Well known for its work on disasters such as the Marchioness and the Ladbroke Grove rail crash. In the latter, they are acting for eight bereaved families with lost children. Also rated for its more broad ranging actions against the police, deaths in custody, inquests, and asylum refugee work.

Deighton Guedalla: has a reputation for actions against the police, discrimination, human rights work, immigration and crime. Represented a former policewoman in a leading case against the Metropolitan Police. It achieved the highest award (£300,000) of damages.

Birmingham's **Tyndallwoods** are recognised as leading players. Human rights flavoured family and immigration work is the order of the day. Liverpool's **AS Law** has a reputation for prisoner's rights, asylum, housing and mental health work. Also act closely with women's and prisoners support groups such as Justice for Women and UNLOCK. **Harrison Bundey** in Leeds also works on deaths in police and prison custody cases. Recently represented a same-sex couple in relation to a child custody case whilst one partner was in prison. **Howells** in Sheffield are involved primarily in human rights work for legal aid funded individuals. Likewise, **Robert Lizar** are a nationally renowned Manchester based criminal firm praised for its human rights work.

leading business immigration firms

CMS Cameron McKenna: London's most high profile and productive business immigration team with a spread of international office links. The team is one of the largest in the country, and acts for corporate and financial clients, processing high volumes of work permit applications for 'inter-company transferees' – businesspeople seeking to relocate to another country. Also act for entrepreneurs, and wealthy individual foreign investors. The practice has advised Premier League and first division football clubs on a number of urgent immigration matters. **Kingsley Napley:** offers one of London's best mixtures of experience, knowledge and team strength. The practice acts for the range of business clients including a number of e-commerce enterprises seeking to introduce staff to the UK. **Bates, Wells & Braithwaite:** has a varied immigration department acting for both business and personal clients, particularly complex applications. Work stretches from corporate work permits for large oil multi-nationals to US e-commerce start-ups to self-employed artists. Involved in the deportation issue surrounding Lennox Lewis' Ghanaian right-hand man. **Magrath & Co:** A large West End practice with a prestigious client list of corporate, banking and media clients seeking work permit services. **Warner Cranston:** Commercial practice offering work permit and investor application services to client base of US, Japanese and Middle Eastern corporations and financial institutions. Processed permits for a number of international Hitachi executives, an American millionaire investor and a US mobile telecoms service expanding its European operations. Several smaller firms engage in both personal and business immigration issues and are usually suitable for less run-of-the-mill applications. Examples in London include **DJ Webb & Co**, **Pulig & Co** and **Penningtons**.

leading personal immigration firms

Bindman & Partners has an enviable reputation acting on a range of asylum, refugee, nationality and family work. They have a lawyer specialising in India/Bangladeshi cases and family reunions. **Birnberg Peirce & Partners** continually praised for their handling of asylum, detainee and habeas corpus work, and focus on *"esoteric"* student cases and illegal overstayers. A full time Turkish caseworker handles Kurdish asylum cases. **Deighton Guedella** is home to a small team known for asylum and children's cases. Turkish Kurd community work is a noted speciality. **Wesley Gryk:** An individually driven and pioneering practice closely associated with high pro-

file AIDS and gay rights work, as well as asylum cases. **Winstanley-Burgess** is a large personal immigration practice with a fine reputation for asylum and human rights cases.

Many northern human rights/crime practices also engage in large chunks of asylum and other immigration work. The North East is home to **David Gray & Co** who are involved in asylum, family settlements and deportations. Clients include Kosovans, Croatians and Afghanis. Sheffield legal aid firm **Howells** has immigration practitioners straddling civil, family and housing law, and are well equipped to handle large numbers of asylum cases. **AS Law** in Liverpool, **Harrison Bundey & Co** (Leeds) and **James & Co** in Bradford all contain noted practitioners engaging in the human rights/crime/immigration mix.

In the South, **Eric Robinson & Co** handle asylum cases for Kosovan, S. American and Indonesian applicants, while in the same town **Trethowans** conduct business work permit applications for S African and Zimbabwean clients. **Darbys Mallam Lewis** in Oxford is a well-respected practice dealing in family reunion and asylum cases drawn heavily from the Kosovan, Syrian and Sudanese community. Commercial firm **Linnells** act for charities, university colleges and technology companies. Bristol community firm **Bobbetts Mackan** advises on asylum and family reunion matters, many drawn from the area's local Somali population. **Tyndallwoods** is the Midlands premier immigration practice, with a reputation that stretches nationwide. Workload is mainly asylum, with clients originating from Africa, Eastern Europe and Asia. The rest is split between family, student and business work permits. Suffolk based general practice **Gross & Co.** offers business immigration services to a national and international clientele including the INVESTEC banking group, ING Barings and wealthy individuals. **Leathes Prior** in Norwich offers business immigration services to its commercial clients while also handling East European refugee cases.

leading local government firms

Nabarro Nathanson: London's pre-eminent local authority practice with a bulging roster of public sector clients. Quality services are offered in property, town centre regeneration, education/schools, NHS trusts and PFI projects. Recently acted for the London Borough of Lewisham on the unique Pathfinder project providing schools, social services and catering facilities. Also completed major housing regeneration projects for the London Borough of Hackney. **Rowe & Maw:** Regarded as a leading firm for 'vires' and local authority powers matters. Its reputation as leaders for audit law and local government finance is also supported by work in regeneration, housing, PFI and social services. Many local authority clients and district auditors continue to use the firm for due diligence and audit opinion. **Sharpe Pritchard:** Well known as an agency litigation practice. They possess an extensive public sector client base, and act for large numbers of local authorities in judicial review proceedings as well as advising on vires, planning and community governance. **Ashurst Morris Crisp:** Has a comprehensive team with inter-related expertise in planning, urban development and public law advice. Prominent in private and public sector tie-ups, allowing them to draw upon expertise in regeneration, land disposals and planning inquiries. Acted for Bath and North East Somerset Council on the Southgate town centre leisure and housing redevelopment.

Eminent planning and property firm **Berwin Leighton** has local authority expertise, as do **Lawrence Graham**. Much smaller but noted for their high individual quality, niche practice **Leonie Cowen & Associates** act for several local authorities requiring sophisticated advice and innovative service delivery solutions. Social housing and stock transfer experts **Trowers & Hamlins** and **Jenkins & Hand** inevitably have a great deal of contact with local authorities.

The Leeds branch of **Eversheds** is arguably the nations dominant local authority practice. They were the original pioneers and one of the first private firms to welcome ex local authority solicitors. Ahead of the game, they offer the latest cutting edge service delivery solutions and can compete freely with the London competition.

In the South West, **Bevan Ashford** and **Bond Pearce** are rated as the region's leading practices. Post devolution, Wales has a buoyant public sector market, with all of **Eversheds**, **Morgan Cole** and **Edwards Geldard** containing experienced local authority practitioners. Likewise in the Midlands, **Wragges**, **DLA** and **Pinsent Curtis** have notable ex local authority lawyers on their teams.

leading education firms

institutions – Eversheds: The largest education practice in the country with an extensive roster of further and higher education institutional clients. The team's core education services include university and college governance, employment, student issues and higher education franchising/overseas collaboration. Recently advised the University of Surrey and Roehampton University on the establishment of a new federal structure. **Beachcroft Wansbroughs:** A well-known education practice which acts for a large number of public bodies, particularly on the funding side, in addition to several higher education institutions. **Winckworth Sherwood:** Has a strong reputation for acting for Church voluntary-aided schools and foundation schools. **Lawford & Co:** Wide-ranging practice based mainly in the FE and HE sectors which receives referrals on specialist education issues from a number of universities and colleges. **Lee Bolton & Lee:** Highly rated schools team covering charity and governance issues, property, employment, student issues and setting up trading subsidiaries.

Manches in Oxford is particularly known in the H.E. sector for its large number of college clients. Also acts for F.E. colleges, independent schools and scientific research councils. Services offered include student and staff discipline matters, employment and property work. In the same city, **Morgan Cole** has particular experience in outsourcing and funding arrangements, college take-overs and setting up hi-tech companies. **Bond Pearce**, **DMH**, **Steele Raymond** and **Thomas Eggar Church Adams** in the South of England have acknowledged specialists on board.

Bristol's **Veale Wasbrough** boasts a pre-eminent national reputation for their independent schools practice. Acting for 600 independent schools, specialist advice is available on pastoral policy, rebuilding internal structures and regulatory authority compliance. **Stone King** in Bath is a recognised force in the independent and maintained schools sector.

Birmingham's **Martineau Johnson** has a highly rated education practice which competes strongly in the national H.E. market, in addition to acting for schools and examination boards. In East Anglia, **Mills & Reeve** is the dominant player. Acted for the University of Cambridge in its joint venture with Massachusetts College of Technology.

With a string of offices based around its Manchester and Newcastle hubs, national firm **Eversheds** is the leading northern practice. They are skilled in acting for LEAs in schools work and handle everything from employment, student issues, governance and commercial issues to sensitive governor issues and major PFI/PPP schemes.

leading education firms

individuals – Teacher Stern Selby: A leading firm owing to its size and expertise in the area. Receives large numbers of referrals from other London and regional solicitors. Known to act for pupils and parents on matters such as admissions, bullying and special education needs. Involved in several high profile cases over the last year, including the landmark education negligence case 'Phelps v LB Hillingdon'. **Bindman & Partners:** Ubiquitous and distinguished human rights practice handles admissions and exclusions issues for pupils/parents, disputes over exam results and funding for higher education students. **David Levene & Co:** Highly respected for its involvement in special education needs and related community care and disability discrimination issues. All aspects of education litigation are covered, from admissions, exclusion and bullying to educational negligence and curriculum matters. **Gills:** Represents individuals in education disputes, particularly for HE students. Areas of expertise include quality of education issues, educational negligence and judicial review. **John Ford Solicitors:** Acts primarily for parents and children in special needs matters, often with a community care overlap.

AE Smith & Son in Stroud is a *"first stop for parents"* and receives many referrals from solicitors throughout the region. Have expertise in the area of special needs, particularly dyslexic children, exclusion, admission appeals and educational negligence. Recently acted for the applicant in the test case of 'G v Bromley' deciding whether local authorities can be sued for educational negligence. **Bobbetts Mackan** in Bristol is well known for its judicial review expertise and work for H.E. students. **Young & Lee** in Birmingham handles special education needs tribunals and exclusions/admissions judicial reviews for pupils, parents and some local authorities.

In Wales, **Hugh James Ford Simey** is recommended for special education needs, admissions and educational negligence work for parents. **Russell Jones & Walker** and **Sinclairs** are also regarded names.

Young & Lee in Birmingham handle special education needs tribunals and exclusions/admissions judicial reviews for pupils, parents and some local authorities. Up north, niche Lancaster education practice **Elaine Maxwell & Co** acts for the claimants in exclusions, admissions and disciplinary disputes. **Ridley Hall** in Huddersfield and **Campbell Smith** in Edinburgh also come recommended for pupil disabilities and special needs work.

LEADING FIRMS

LONDON	HUMAN RIGHTS	EDUCATION	IMMIGRATION	LOCAL GOVERNMENT
Ashurst Morris Crisp				****
Baker & McKenzie			***	
Bates, Wells & Braithwaite			*****	
Beachcroft Wansbroughs		*****		
Berwin Leighton				****
Bhatt Murphy	*****			
Bindman & Partners	******	*****	******	
Birnberg Peirce & Partners	****		******	
Campbell Hooper			*	
Christian Fisher	****		***	
Clifford Chance				**
CMS Cameron McKenna			******	
Coker Vis Partnership			*****	
D J Freeman				*
David Levene & Co		*****		
Dechert				*
Deighton Guedalla	****		******	
Denton Wilde Sapte				***
DJ Webb & Co			**	
Eversheds		******	****	
Farrer & Co		**		
Fisher Meredith		****		
Fox Williams			**	
Gherson & Co			****	
Gill & Co			****	
Glazer Delmar			*****	
Gulbenkian Harris Andonian			***	
Harbottle & Lewis			*	
Herbert Smith				**
Hickman & Rose	**			
Irwin Mitchell	*			
Jenkins & Hand				**
John Ford Morrison		*****		
Kingsley Napley			******	
Lawfords		****		
Lawrence Graham				****
Lee Bolton & Lee		****		
Léonie Cowen & Associates				****

LEADING FIRMS *continued*

LONDON	HUMAN RIGHTS	EDUCATION	IMMIGRATION	LOCAL GOVERNMENT
Luqmani Thompson			****	
Magrath & Co			*****	
Mishcon de Reya			***	
Nabarro Nathanson				******
Norton Rose			***	
Penningtons			**	
Powell & Co			****	
Pullig & Co			***	
Reynolds Porter Chamberlain		***		
Rowe & Maw				*****
Sharpe Pritchard				*****
Simons Muirhead & Burton	**			
Stuart Miller			***	
Sturtivant & Co			****	
Taylor Nichol	*			
Teacher Stern Selby		******		
Thanki Novy Taube	*			
Trowers & Hamlins				****
Warner Cranston			*****	
Wesley Gryk			******	
Wilson & Co			***	
Winckworth Sherwood		*****		*
Winstanley-Burgess	***		******	
Witham Weld		***		

THE SOUTH	HUMAN RIGHTS	EDUCATION	IMMIGRATION	LOCAL GOVERNMENT
Bartram & Co, *Hounslow*			****	
Coningsbys, *Croydon*		****		
Darbys Mallam Lewis, *Oxford*			******	
Gills, *Southall*		*****		
Linnells, *Oxford*			******	
Manches, *Oxford*		***		
Morgan Cole, *Oxford*		***		
Winckworth Sherwood, *Oxford*		**		

THE SOUTH	HUMAN RIGHTS	EDUCATION	IMMIGRATION	LOCAL GOVERNMENT
Bond Pearce, *Southampton*		******		
DMH, *Brighton*		***		
Eric Robinson & Co, *Southampton*			******	
Steele Raymond, *Bournemouth*		***		
Thomas Eggar Church Adams, *Chichester*		***		
Trethowans, *Southampton*			******	
A.E. Smith & Son, *Stroud*		****		
Bevan Ashford, *Bristol, Exeter*		**		******
Bobbetts Mackan, *Bristol*		***	******	
Bond Pearce, *Bristol, Exeter, Plymouth*		**		*****
Michelmores, *Exeter*		****		
Osborne Clarke OWA, *Bristol*		**		
Rickerby Watterson, *Cheltenham*		****		
Stone King, *Bath*		*****		
Tozers, *Exeter*		***		
Veale Wasbrough, *Bristol*		******		

WALES, MIDLANDS & E. ANGLIA	HUMAN RIGHTS	EDUCATION	IMMIGRATION	LOCAL GOVERNMENT
Edwards Geldard, *Cardiff*				*****
Eversheds, *Cardiff, Nottingham*		*****	******	******
Hugh James Ford Simey, *Cardiff*		***		
Morgan Cole, *Cardiff*		*****		*****
Russell Jones & Walker, *Cardiff*		***		
Sinclairs, *Penarth*		***		
Anthony Collins Solicitors, *Birmingham*				****
DLA, *Birmingham*				*****
Martineau Johnson, *Birmingham*		******		
McGrath & Co, *Birmingham*	*****		*****	
Nelsons, *Nottingham*			*****	
Pinsent Curtis, *Birmingham*				*****
Shakespeares, *Birmingham*		****		
Tyndallwoods, *Birmingham*	******		******	
Wragge & Co, *Birmingham*		****		******
Young & Lee, *Birmingham*		****		

WALES, MIDLANDS & E. ANGLIA	HUMAN RIGHTS	EDUCATION	IMMIGRATION	LOCAL GOVERNMENT
Birkett Long, *Colchester*		***		
Eversheds, *Ipswich, Norwich*		*****		
Gross & Co., *Bury St. Edmunds*			******	
Leathes Prior, *Norwich*			******	
Mills & Reeve, *Cambridge, Norwich*		******		******
Steele & Co, *Norwich*				******
Wollastons, *Chelmsford*		***	******	

THE NORTH	HUMAN RIGHTS	EDUCATION	IMMIGRATION	LOCAL GOVERNMENT
A S Law, *Liverpool*	******		*****	
Addleshaw Booth & Co, *Manchester*		****		
David Gray & Company, *Newcastle upon Tyne*	*****		******	
Davis Blank Furniss, *Manchester*			****	
DLA, *Leeds, Liverpool, Sheffield*		****		
Elaine Maxwell & Co, *Lancaster*		******		
Eversheds, *Leeds, Manchester, Middlesbrough, Newcastle upon Tyne*		*****		******
Harrison Bundey & Co., *Leeds*	******		*****	
Howells, *Sheffield*	******		******	
Irwin Mitchell, *Sheffield*	******			
Jackson & Canter, *Liverpool*			*****	
James & Co, *Bradford*			*****	
Masons, *Leeds*				****
Pannone & Partners, *Manchester*				***
Pinsent Curtis, *Leeds*		****		*****
Ridley & Hall, *Huddersfield*		*****		
Robert Lizar, *Manchester*	******			
Samuel Phillips & Co, *Newcastle upon Tyne*			****	
Thornhill Ince, *Manchester*			****	
Walker Morris, *Leeds*				***

shipping

definition of terms

P&I Club – 'Protection and indemnity' Club: a marine insurance club run mutually by and for ship-owners.

Charterparty – Commercial instrument, essentially a contract for the hire of an entire ship for the purpose of import or export of goods.

Bill of Lading – a certificate of undertaking by the master of a ship to deliver goods on payment of the named sum to a named party.

Salvage – reward payable by owners of ships and goods saved at sea by 'salvors.'

Underwriter – an individual who agrees to indemnify an assured person against losses under a policy of insurance.

MOA – Memorandum of Agreement.

area of law

Suggest shipping law as a practice area to the majority of law students and you may well be met by a glazed look and a swift exit. At best you will call to mind images of Greek shipping magnates chewing on vast Havanas and news coverage of dramatic collisions at sea. In fact shipping law is an exciting, complex and unpredictable area of practice, involving many cutting edge principles of law.

Shipping law can be defined as "the law relating to all aspects of carriage by sea and international trade." It involves both contentious and non-contentious work.

Contentious work is divided into 'Wet' and 'Dry'. The difference, in essence, is that 'Wet' (traditionally known as Admiralty) work concerns disputes arising from mishaps at sea, i.e. collision, salvage, total loss etc. whilst 'Dry' (traditionally known as Marine) arises from disputes over contracts made on dry land; charterparties, bills of lading, cargo and sale of goods contracts. Non-contentious includes registra-tion of ships and re-flagging yet mainly relates to ship finance advice, which is essentially corporate in nature.

Other niche practice areas include yachting and fishing (often regulatory advice).

type of work

Shipping lawyers have a choice of non-contentious and contentious work available to them on qualification. On the non-contentious side advice is given on shipbuilding contracts, sale and purchase agreements, ship finance, contracts of employment for crew members and contracts of affreightment etc. Contentious work includes ad hoc 'consultancy' advice on day to day matters for regular clients, arrest of ships, together with conduct of High Court and arbitration cases from the time of the initial dispute through issuing of pleadings and interlocutory proceedings to final hearing and enforcement. Clients range from owners, operators, traders and charterers to P&I Clubs, other insurers and hull underwriters.

Very few lawyers will advise on both sides and those that do are generally located in smaller overseas offices where they are often required to turn their hands to most shipping related matters. Moreover, the type of firm you train with will normally pre-determine your eventual specialism.

There are a number of specialist firms in London such as **Ince & Co**, **Holman Fenwick & Willan** and **Clyde & Co** where you will concentrate to a large degree on contentious shipping work for the duration of your training contract. Other corporate firms such as **Norton Rose** and **Watson, Farley Williams** are known predominantly for their non-contentious work (namely ship finance) yet will also offer seats in other practice areas. Gina Power, four years qualified shipping lawyer at **Lawrence Graham**, started her career at medium sized City firm **Penningtons** precisely because she was not entirely sure which area of law she intended to specialise in. She was immediately attracted to commercial litigation and had a chance to do a six month seat in shipping. A broad choice of seats may prove vital if a trainee decides after six months that shipping is not for them.

Clare Matthews, shipping lawyer at **AUS P&I** in Sydney, urges prospective trainees to obtain vacation work placements prior to deciding which firms to apply to. She decided to commence her training at **Ince & Co** after taking a placement there one summer. If you are unable to obtain work experience then try to talk to lawyers at the firms. They will invariably be happy to discuss any queries you may have and will largely welcome your interest and initiative.

Trainees at the bigger London firms are occasionally offered the chance to take a seat abroad and this is definitely something you should consider. Don't despair if this is not the policy of your chosen firm or if they do not actually have any overseas offices. Gina Power, for example, speaks fluent Greek, and pestered her partners at **Penningtons** to be allowed to do a three month stint with a Greek shipping firm. It was up to her to arrange this, yet she managed to gain valuable international experience with a top firm in the port of Piraeus.

Many cultures are still male oriented when it comes to business and prefer to deal 'man to man.' Indeed, within shipping law there is still quite a high drop-out rate amongst women and most of the top shipping partners are male. Nonetheless, all lawyers interviewed agreed that this should not dissuade female applicants. Many top female shipping lawyers are now coming through the ranks and achieving partnership staus at a relatively young age. According to Gina Power, "although some shipping clients can be difficult at first, they all show enormous respect once they realise you are as effective, hard working and persistent as your male counterparts."

a day in the life....

All shipping lawyers interviewed baulked at the idea of describing a typical day; nothing about this area of law is typical – "expect the unexpected" is the catchphrase. Due to the global nature of your client base you are acutely aware of all the different time zones that you are working to on any one day. "Organisation is the key", says Power, who admits it is sometimes difficult for shipping lawyers to juggle their day.

Oliver Weiss from leading firm **Ince & Co**. describes how on one occasion he received a call from a client to say that a barge had capsized in the South China Sea leaving many casualties. By 10 that night he was on a flight to Singapore (with a team including trainees) to take statements from all surviving crew members. This kind of occurrence may not be a run of the mill occurrence for trainees but it is not unusual for shipping lawyers at a senior level.

Many cases are high profile, attracting media interest for both their factual and legal content. Consider the shipping casualties which have hit the headlines over the last 10 years; The Marchioness, Herald of Free Enterprise, the Braer oil spillage and the Sea Empress – all have involved lawyers in various capacities. Consider too, the cases you learn in contract law – many of the leading cases are complex shipping matters.

skills needed

dry/wet:...no place for shrinking violets...abreast of legal developments and industry trends ...extremely familiar with contract, tort and court procedure...extremely flexible in terms of hours and availability to travel...good communicators...good sense of humour, common sense, team spirit and self motivation...

wet:...previous knowledge of sea life...(many 'wet' speciality lawyers are either ex-mariners or naval officers).

career options

Those interested in shipping law should be aware that jobs outside London are relatively few and far between. Shipping work is limited to towns with ports. After London, Plymouth, Liverpool and Newcastle are most important. In the larger firms with overseas offices there are opportunities for assistants to gain experience working abroad for a few years or even permanently. All interviewees considered this to be a good career move, particularly with regard to future partnership prospects back home. According to Gina Power, you are likely to undertake greater responsibility in a smaller overseas office where you are working in the same time zone and culture as your clients. This immediacy of contact is great for personal PR and you could end up returning to London with a host of new clients which you would not have otherwise obtained. Oliver Weiss is now based in the Greek port of Piraeus after lengthy stints in the firm's London and Hong Kong offices.

If, after qualification, you decide that shipping is not for you then your skills and solid grounding as a commercial litigator should allow you to qualify into another contentious department within or outside your present firm.

If private practice does not appeal, there is of course the possibility of going in-house. Ship owners, P&I clubs, operators and marine insurers all have openings for specialist lawyers. Clare Matthews, for example, completed her training at **Ince & Co.** before joining **Watson, Farley & Williams** as a shipping lawyer in Singapore. She now works for **AUS P&I** Club in Sydney, Australia as a correspondent for many of the major international P&I Clubs. She feels that her knowledge of the day to day running of the shipping industry has increased substantially since working in-house. "The advice is more immediate and quite exciting," she says, "although in the long term you are not likely to make as much money as a top London partner." The hours and working conditions are widely perceived to be much more attractive than life in private practice. The predominance of English law in international shipping matters also make it relatively easy for in-house shipping lawyers to return to private practice in the future.

Some shipping lawyers choose to go it alone as sole practitioners or are setting up niche firms. One such lawyer is Nicola Ellis (Plymouth) who set up on her own in 1994. Her background was in general litigation, but she 'fell into' marine work on qualification after a spell at **Clyde & Co** in Guildford during which she handled some cargo claims. Having gained that experience she found herself handling similar work in subsequent jobs and being encouraged to specialise by one particular yacht-building client. She now deals with mainly yachting work, representing the insured rather than the insurer in the majority of cases.

leading shipping firms

All information on leading firms comes from the Chambers Guide to the Legal Profession 2000-2001.

Holman Fenwick & Willan: Perceived as a *"supremely confident"* outfit, the firm's individual litigators are perceived as *"getting to the merits of a dispute quickly."* Whilst its worldwide reputation for salvage work is viewed as *"beyond compare"*, the team have recently been involved in some heavyweight foreign litigation. The firm's continuing global expansion (particularly the recent opening of the Shanghai office) has noticeably lifted its profile in this area. The firm is known to be well connected within the German, Far East and Greek owner markets and to have strong ties with the Scandinavian P&I Club market. Has offices in China, France, Greece, Hong Kong and Singapore.

Ince & Co: An international commercial law firm with an unusual structure being non-departmentalised. All work stems from its origins as a shipping and commercial firm. Shipping and international trade constitute about 40% of its workload and well over half the fee-earners handle shipping work. Ubiquitous shipping practice which *"seems to be everywhere at the moment."* The firm has a *"big reputa-*

tion and some very loyal clients." The market views the firm's ability to secure both *"volume and quality "* from a diverse client-base as the main driving force behind its success. The practice is seen by many to be *"more rounded"* than the immediate competition. Because of its unusual structure, trainees at this firm do not sit in different seats. Instead they sit with different partners and compete for work from all parts of the firm. Ex-trainee Clare Matthews, comments that *"you are a file handler from day one which is both exciting and daunting."* Has offices in London, Singapore, Piraeus and Hong Kong.

Clyde & Co: Has a similar structure to Ince & Co and is particularly rated for its cargo expertise. An extremely diverse practice which, although historically aligned with cargo interests, has a substantial owner and banking client base. However, whilst the firm is clearly a major shipping force (*"ignore them at your peril"*) its sustained push into corporate work has led to the market opinion that it is not quite the force of old in purely shipping matters. Nonetheless, the quality of the individual partners is beyond any doubt. Has offices in France, Greece, Hong Kong, Russia, Singapore, United Arab Emirates and Venezuela.

Hill Taylor Dickinson: A shipping, insurance and international trade firm in the City. Smaller than the leaders, with only two international offices in Dubai and Greece, it nevertheless is highly respected in the market for the *"absolute quality"* of its litigators.

Richards Butler: Felt to be *"in the ascendancy"*, the shipping group has recovered its strong reputation within the London market. Although known historically as a dry practice, the team are making a play for a greater share of wet work. The team has been involved in major collision and salvage work, including the *Sea-land Mariner* and *Maersk Tokyo* cases. On the dry side, the team are respected for *"making a point properly and not being unduly aggressive."* Strong owner and club connections are especially notable in Italy, and the team gets a lot of spin-off litigation work from the firm's established ship financing arm. Acting for the liquidators, the team has handled all the disposals, selling and arresting relating to the liquidation of the Romanian state shipping fleet Navron.

Curtis Davis Garrard: An interesting niche practice. Relaxed outfit of ex-City lawyers who wanted out of the rat race; they have a dress-down policy and encourage home-working. Its been a *"turbulent year"* for this Heathrow-based firm which has made a number of partner hires, as well as well-publicised defections. Known particularly for the quality of its off-shore shipping and commodities practice, the team have been involved in big-ticket projects and disputes. The large City firms with shipping capability include **Norton Rose**, particularly active in non-contentious work and particularly recommended for finance work.

Davies Johnson & Co, Plymouth: A respected niche practice consisting of ex-City lawyers. Known to have strong Greek, Dutch and Norwegian connections, the firm are involved in dry shipping and related commodities work. Strong Scandinavian P&I connections drive the dry practice which is active in charterparty disputes.

Hill Taylor Dickinson, Liverpool: The team consists of several very highly rated individuals split between Manchester (Cargo) and Liverpool (Owners.) Perceived to have superb P&I club relationships, the team are considered *"top tier"* for both wet and dry work. The team acts for many of the major composite insurers in the UK.

Eversheds, Newcastle: Seen to be on the rise this year. Perceived to be an *"outstanding shipping firm, wet or dry."* The team have had a busy year, notably representing tanker companies in response to oil contamination claim and pumping warranties. The team's good market profile for marine personal injury work has been consolidated.

LEADING FIRMS

LONDON	SHIPPING: DRY	SHIPPING: WET
Barlow Lyde & Gilbert	*	
Bentleys, Stokes & Lowless	**	**
Clifford Chance	**	***
Clyde & Co	*****	*****
Constant & Constant	**	**
Fishers	*	
Hill Taylor Dickinson	****	****
Holman Fenwick & Willan	******	******
Holmes Hardingham	**	***
Ince & Co	******	******
Jackson Parton	**	
Lawrence Graham	*	
Middleton Potts	*	
More Fisher Brown	**	
Norton Rose	***	***
Richards Butler	****	***
Shaw and Croft	*	**
Sinclair Roche & Temperley	***	***
Stephenson Harwood	***	**
Thomas Cooper & Stibbard	**	**
Waltons & Morse		**
Watson, Farley & Williams	**	

THE REGIONS	SHIPPING: DRY	SHIPPING: WET
Curtis Davis Garrard, *Feltham*	*	
Davies, Johnson & Co, *Plymouth*	******	
DMH, *Brighton*	******	
Foot Anstey Sargent, *Plymouth*	******	
Grant & Horton Marine, *Plymouth*	******	
Dale & Co Solicitors, *Felixstowe*	******	
Eversheds, *Ipswich, Newcastle upon Tyne*	******	
John Weston & Co, *Felixstowe*	******	
Andrew M. Jackson & Co, *Hull*	*****	******
DLA, *Liverpool, Manchester*	*****	*****
Hill Dickinson, *Liverpool*	******	******
Mills & Co, *Newcastle upon Tyne*	******	
Rayfield Mills, *Newcastle upon Tyne*	******	******

sports law

The term 'sports law' used to be a convenient umbrella denoting an amalgam of separate legal disciplines both contentious and non-contentious for sporting clients. The lawyer had to apply these general legal principles within a sporting context. But all lawyers interviewed agreed that a separate body of law relating to specific sports- related issues is now developing at an ever-increasing pace.

According to Andy Korman, Head of Sponsorship at sports specialists **Townleys**, this is best illustrated when national law and particular sports regulations collide. He gives the example of the well known Bosman Case, in which football regulation governing the transfer of players were at odds with European employment legislation. Regulatory bodies are increasingly being taken to court for imposing rules which are at odds with the prevailing laws of the land. Parul Patel, assistant solicitor at **Clarke Willmott & Clarke**, agrees and comments that increased professionalism and the globalisation of sporting concerns will inevitably lead to increased legislation nationally and across Europe. She points to the creation of a Minister for Sport and the fact that sport is now such a major global industry as an indication of the inevitability of further specific industry regulation.

The areas of law which retain particular importance in sports-related work remain intellectual property (the protection and exploitation of rights); EU and competition law (looking at the sports industry to see whether it is restrictive of competition); media and entertainment law (covering broadcasting, sponsorship, advertising); commercial/corporate law; crime & personal injury.

type of work

The area we call 'sports law' can be divided into three main aspects:

1. The regulatory, disciplinary, criminal and personal injury advice given to individuals, teams and ruling bodies.
2. Media/sponsorship and advertising.
3. Corporate and commercial advice, e.g. the stock market listing of a football club.

In addition, students should also determine whether they envisage a career in litigation or as a non-contentious lawyer. There is increasingly a greater willingness to litigate among sporting clients.

However one defines sports law it is obvious that prospective trainees should think carefully before deciding which firms to approach. Firms fall broadly into one category or another although most handle a cross-section of sports-related work as required by their clients.

Townleys advise exclusively on sports law matters and offer trainees four sports-related seats to be chosen from the areas of broadcasting, commercial, New Media, dispute resolution, governance, IP and sponsorship. The team works on sports as varied as triathlon, squash, football, rugby and bob-sleigh and last year worked on the sponsorship of the Rugby World Cup legal programme; Fulham FC's Commercial and player matters; Six Nations merchandising and Formula One brand protection work.

Denton Wilde Sapte, meanwhile, has a strong media bias to their sports work advising individuals on their intellectual property rights and sponsorship. They advised Tracey Edwards (skipper of the first all-woman crew attempting to sail round the world) on various trademark registrations, on a publishing deal and on setting up her own website. The team is also involved in regulatory and disciplinary issues and recently defended Restrictive Practices court proceedings brought by the Director General of Fair Trading regarding Premier League Rules and broadcast agreements.

Another firm known for regulatory and disciplinary work is **Farrer & Co.** Karena Vleck advised the British Athletics Federation in the long running Diane Modahl case and is a non-executive director of UK Athletics. As well as dealing with constitutional issues she has been negotiating TV rights and sponsorship, agency and event agreements.

Nicholson Graham & Jones was probably the first City firm to establish a sports department and to approach the sector from a corporate angle. Many sporting disciplines are covered by their client base, including football, rugby and cricket as well as minor sports such as greyhound racing and snow boarding. Their involvement in acquisitions of businesses, competition law, property, insolvency, sponsorship agreements, players' contracts and constitutional advice shows the breadth of the team's work.

a day in the life...

'Sporadic' is the description most used by practitioners to describe the nature of the job. A typical day for rugby specialist Parul Patel might involve a lengthy contract negotiation for a player, advising a major international name on personal injury litigation and attempting to find clubs for out of contract clients. All agreed that, although their chosen field was considered by most to be a 'sexy' area to work in, sports law is by no means a soft option. The day to day legal work is as exhausting (and at times mundane) as any other specialism. Nonetheless, the high profile nature of the job was viewed favourably by all sport lawyers interviewed. Andy Korman, for example, gets a "kick" when watching a football team whose shirt sponsorship he has negotiated. Moreover, if commenting on your cases for television, fending off reporters and watching major events from the comfort of the directors' box interests you then you are likely to enjoy the discipline.

skills needed

"It is not enough to be passionate about sport" claims Andy Korman. "You need to be able to grasp many aspects of law quickly, and to understand how they impact on each other." Particularly important is a good commercial grounding, a knowledge of contract, media and intellectual property law and an awareness of EU and competition law. He cites the example of a trainee at **Townleys** whose Masters in intellectual property law and IT law made him particularly suited to the firm's New Media department.

However it is vital to show a proven track record of interest in the area. If students are offered the chance to do a dissertation at University then they should pick a topic with a relevance to sport. Trainees who can relate to the sporting issues of the day and understand the inherent legal implications are precisely what Townleys are looking for.

Parul Patel, meanwhile, considered language skills important, and pointed to the increasing globalisation of sport in this respect. Her ability to speak French and Italian is proving invaluable in her negotiations with European clubs on behalf of her rugby playing clients.

Unfortunately, for the majority of people, this is an area where good contacts can easily sway job interviews. A sports department will be much more likely to look at you if you have played rugby for your country or if your father is a premiership football manager. Jonny Searle, lawyer with **Ashurst Morris Crisp** and Olympic oarsman, also suggests that clients tend to treat you with less suspicion when they know you can empathise with them as a sports player. Despite increased professionalism many sportsmen and women are still cynical about lawyers and the business of making money out of sport.

Students should not despair if they fail to get a training contract offering a sports law seat. Andy Korman, for example, trained at a well known corporate firm in the City before joining **Townleys** on qualification. Likewise, Parul Patel joined **Clarke**

Willmott & Clarke as a sports lawyer after qualification from leading regional firm Eversheds. Although Eversheds was not known for its sporting client base she harassed the partners for anything sports-related that came in, managing to build up her own portfolio of experience. "You will only get work if you ask for it" she says. "Be persistent, use your initiative and be up front about your interest in sport from day one."

skills needed

...strong personal skills...not for prima donnas...people skills as well as paper skills... vibrant team players...energy...determination to succeed...knowledge of the business of sport...technical appreciation of key sports...

career options

In private practice, sports specialists move into this area both by accident and design. Sports lovers often try to steer their careers in this direction, while corporate, litigation, intellectual property or personal injury lawyers who have acquired a sporting clientele may suddenly find themselves referred to as sports lawyers.

There are various in-house opportunities in the the sports world. Brian Clarke (ex-**Nabarro Nathanson**) is the European head of sports management agency IMG. You could work for a governing body such as the FA or the the RFU; for a sports broadcaster negotiating rights, or as an agent for individual sports personalities or teams. Lawyer Mel Stein has made a name for himself in this respect with his work for Paul Gascoigne.

leading sports firms

All information on leading firms comes from the Chambers Guide to the Legal Profession 2000-2001.

Townleys: Remains the only law firm in the country with an exclusive sports focus. Its lawyers are considered "young, entrepreneurial and dedicated." Although some query the firm's ability to take on the bigger-ticket competition and corporate work, the sheer breadth of their involvement in sport is considered to be "beyond compare." Work for the 'Super 12' UK racecourses has been characterised as "groundbreaking." Much of their work concerns the commercial exploitation of sporting and cultural events. During 1999 they worked on events such as the Five Nations Championship, the Rugby World Cup 1999, the Commonwealth Games 2002, the Boat Race 1999 and Formula One motor racing. Much of their work is international and foreign language skills are useful. Some of the staff are former professional sports people.

Denton Wilde Sapte: This is a large commercial firm with a well-developed sports practice. Considered "a great sports brand" by the market, the team's "deep industry knowledge" sets it apart. The firm has the requisite corporate, competition and litigation strength to "handle anything." Its successful defence of The FA Premier League Limited in the Restrictive Practices Court was a headline case last year. The team drafted all the commercial and organisational agreements for the Cricket World Cup 1999. Advised on both the Linford Christie and Douggie Walker doping inquiries. There are overlaps with the firm's entertainment practice and with the planning department (whose clients include Chelsea Football Club). Other clients include the England and Wales Cricket Board; IAAF; The F.A Premier League Limited.

Bird & Bird: A large sports group, whose combination of "technical brilliance" and "commercial savvy" is admired by the market. Work covers the spectrum of industry-related matters on behalf of corporate entities, governing bodies, sports rights agencies and high net worth individuals. The firm's entrenched reputation for IP, IT and e-commerce advice has aided the sports group's growth in these areas. A highlight was the team's advice to Europ@web on its $50m lead investment in Sportal, the European Internet company. The team advised SEGA Europe Limited on the sponsorships of Arsenal, St.Etienne and Sampdoria Football Clubs.

Nicholson Graham & Jones: This medium commercial firm is heavily involved in the corporate element of sports work. The breadth of their practice enables them to handle 'big ticket stuff' including the competiton element and also heavyweight corporate work. Heavily involved in new media type deals, advising rights owners. They are well-rounded, handling a broad range of sports including rugby, greyhound racing and ladies beach volleyball. Also have some players as clients, such as Harry Kewell.

Clarke Willmott & Clarke, Bristol: Number one in the region, having acquired a ready-made sports practice from Alsters with whom they merged last year. The team is especially noted for its advice on behalf of individual players. The team successfully defended Jeremy Guscott against well- publicised assault charges in 1999.

Osborne Clarke OWA, Bristol: Lauded for its client base, the team undertakes a variety of work for institutions, clubs and individuals. Sponsorship deals, players' contracts, and wide-ranging litigation matters have constituted the group's recent caseload. The team advised the Professional Event Riders' Association on the formation and launch of sponsorship deals with MasterCard, Credit Suisse and Husky.

Hammond Suddards Edge, Birmingham: The only serious player in the region, this Birmingham firm has a national reputation for the quality of its regulatory and constitutional advice. Advised the British Athletics Federation (In Administration) on the successful defence of claims made by Diane Modahl in the House of Lords. New media, internet and e-commerce advice have also flourished.

James Chapman & Co, Manchester: Viewed historically as a one client firm (its work on behalf of Manchester United is legendary) it has been commended for a much greater depth this year (*"they understand commercial reality"*). Have recently recruited a specialist in sports rights, who advises governing bodies, sports marketing companies and sporting clubs in all areas of rights protection and exploitation. The team was appointed sole adviser to a leading multi-national company on its staging of a proposed round the world challenge, and advised Manchester United on its ground-breaking £30m sponsorship deal with Vodafone.

McCormicks, Leeds: An eclectic sports practice, which has received strong client recommendations this year. The team has a pivotal role in advising the F.A. Premier League and has negotiated the new television contracts up for renewal in 2001/2002. Acted for boxer Richie Woodhall in a successfully mediated dispute with Frank Warren.

LEADING FIRMS

LONDON	SPORT	LONDON	SPORT
Ashurst Morris Crisp	*	Max Bitel, Greene	****
Bird & Bird	*****	Memery Crystal	**
Charles Russell	**	Mishcon de Reya	**
Clintons	**	Moorhead James	*
Collyer-Bristow	***	Nicholson Graham & Jones	*****
Denton Wilde Sapte	******	Olswang	**
Farrer & Co	****	Russell Jones & Walker	**
Field Fisher Waterhouse	*	Simmons & Simmons	*
Freshfields Bruckhaus Deringer	**	SJ Berwin & Co	****
Grower Freeman & Goldberg	**	The Simkins Partnership	*
Harbottle & Lewis	***	Theodore Goddard	*
Herbert Smith	***	Townleys	******

SOUTH WEST	SPORT	SOUTH WEST	SPORT
Clarke Willmott & Clarke, *Bristol*	******	Stones, *Exeter*	*****
Osborne Clarke OWA, *Bristol*	******		

MIDLANDS	SPORT	MIDLANDS	SPORT
Hammond Suddards Edge, *Birmingham*	******		

THE NORTH	SPORT	THE NORTH	SPORT
Addleshaw Booth & Co, *Manchester*	****	McCormicks, *Leeds*	******
George Davies, *Manchester*	*****	Walker Morris, *Leeds*	*****
Gorna & Co, *Manchester*	****	Zermansky & Partners, *Leeds*	***
James Chapman & Co, *Manchester*	******		

tax

A significant percentage of a company's income is paid out in tax, so it's not hard to see why tax lawyers are so valuable to their clients. Good advice can result in a tax saving that can reap enormous financial benefits for the client. Even the most costly lawyers' fees are money well spent. In a nutshell, it's the tax adviser's job to tell the client exactly how to structure its business activities so as to be most tax efficient.

type of work

Corporate tax lawyers are widely seen as 'anoraks.' In fact they need to be extremely commercial animals. Tax law is not a refuge for those who want to screen themselves from client involvement behind towers of statute books. There's no room for those who want to theorise about technicalities of 'black letter law' in isolation from the real world for which it was written. That said, if it is the thrill of the chase you are after, and the adrenalin of the all-night meeting, you may be unfulfilled.

Steve Edge (a "seriously able practitioner"), partner at **Slaughter and May** and probably the UK's most well-known tax lawyer comments: "Sometimes I'm the first lawyer to be involved on a big deal. But as the job is done, I'll see people who have been up all night on negotiations and have the tremendous satisfaction that they've moved mountains. More often than not the tax people will have been more remote in the latter stages of the deal unless a problem arises. When a problem does arise you have to react like the fire brigade and sort things out quickly!" One thing in tax law is certain – no one has any patience with tax advisers who make a meal of things.

There is tremendous satisfaction in being able to come in and provide a positive solution under pressure in such circumstances and that obviously produces its own form of adrenalin. You certainly have to regard yourself as an ideas person and a problem solver, but you are unlikely to get the champagne and the glory for driving the deal to completion.

A good lawyer absorbs himself in the world of his clients. Be they corporate finance, banking or property-based he needs to understand these areas of law and the culture, constraints and regulations affecting the sector. So, as in all commercial areas of law, you need to be a business adviser, with a particular expertise in tax.

skills needed

....be more than just an 'anorak'...detailed knowledge of tax laws...ability to communicate extremely complex ideas in layman's language...a keen eye for detail...a forensic mind...laser-like precision...absolute confidence in your own judgment...common sense....

career options

Specialist tax lawyers are not two-a-penny so after just a few years of bedding down into the practice area you will become a very marketable commodity. In the last few years there has been a degree of movement of senior figures between tax departments in banks, accountancy firms, law firms and also to the Bar and to and from the Inland Revenue or Customs and Excise.

Some of the most respected tax barristers have only been called to the bar for a couple of years but had previously been successful solicitors. The knowledge and skills developed in practice are so transferable that you then become free to select the context in which you deliver a service to clients or advise those who make policy decisions concerning tax legislation.

leading tax firms

Freshfields Bruckhaus Deringer: Most solicitors clearly regard the practice as London's number one, due to the *"sheer number of quality people." "They have the full range, talent is widespread and there are no weak links in the chain."* The first team to spring to mind amongst the City practices, particularly for cross-border work. It remains the first among equals of tax practices in the Square Mile, although without a concerted effort by rivals, it will soon be first without equals. *"They work hard, are knowledgeable, thorough and professional."* The growing London practice is involved on the majority of high profile UK and cross-border M&A and specialist financing transactions. High profile merger work this year includes the EMI music business merger with Time Warner (£12bn).

Slaughter and May: Whilst rival solicitors suggested that the firm was *"missing out on the big finance deals,"* or that it was *"not keeping up on the international side,"* all conceded that the practice was exceptionally strong for major City work. As well as M&A-related tax, where *"they are top,"* the practice is highly regarded for structured finance work, particularly asset finance and financial product development work, the 'big finance' areas which are tax-dependent. This is a smaller team than its immediate rivals and is perceived to be dependent on the individuals rather than the team. Clients and other interested parties suggested that this was an advantage; *"they were always different from the other magic circlers," "the fact that you've got the individuals means that that you have more than a team, which is why you go to them."* A broad-front practice which, as well as providing advice for the firm's well-known UK clients, also advises US and other international corporates and financials. A high proportion of the team's work is pure tax consulting work and the practice includes an ex-Inland Revenue investigation team for investigatory and litigation work. High profile M&A transactions this year include the BAT/Rothmans and Carlton/ United News & Media link-ups. Other corporate transactions include the disposals involving Allied/Punch and Guardian Royal Exchange/ Aegon.

Clifford Chance: *"Up at the top, they have the brand,"* the team offers a *"technically good and never less than reasonable service."* Whilst some view the large practice as *"a bit of a sleeping giant,"* clients and solicitors alike commented on the *"very strong range of experts at partner level."* This is especially seen on the finance side, where the practice's *"range of expertise"* means that it is regarded as *"the first choice for finance."* In particular, the practice is seen as having *"a huge share of the securitisation market."* The team is recognised by clients for its commercial awareness. Advice is generally seen as *"sound, cautious rather than aggressive."* Viewed as a *"cutting edge and client friendly"* practice, who's *"secret is in the team."* Financial work this year includes the Barclays Credit Card securitisation and the Formula One securitisation. The tri-partite merger has encouraged an increasing number of instructions across the network, advising on the Merrill-Lynch and HSBC joint venture in internet private banking being an example.

Linklaters: Whilst involved on the major corporate deals of the year, the practice is generally viewed by the market to have *"weakened a bit."* Tony Angel's move to managing partner last year is considered to have *"damaged the practice's flair"* in the medium to long term, such was his status. The firm is also perceived to have a practice skewed more towards the M&A side as opposed to structured finance (asset finance and securitisation), when compared to Slaughters and especially Freshfields (*"they are not at the Freshfields level"*). The practice is considered to be *"strong and steady,"* with *"good individuals"* and it is *"still there for the top deals."* Internationally, clients praise the firm's *"expertise and resource at the top level."* They admire the *"ideas and strength in implementation"* of the practice, and praise the team for *"getting it right with the drafting."* The *"consistent quality"* of the team, its *"user friendliness and commercial aware-*

ness" meant that a lot of clients brushed aside reservations to declare that the practice was *"still my cup of tea."* Corporate work includes Vodafone / Airtouch / Mannesmann and Lloyds TSB's acquisition of Scottish Widows. Major restructuring work includes those of Allied Domeqc, Cable & Wireless Communications, Unigate, BAe and Tarmac.

Allen & Overy: Seen to have *"gone for it in a big way,"* the tax practice has *"beefed up and considerably raised its profile."* It is especially well regarded for finance work (although corporate work makes up nearly half of the practice's workload), but is not yet considered to possess the profile of its most direct competitor in tax finance work, Clifford Chance, and the firms are thus separated in the rankings. The practice has a reputation for *"very professional, technically good and conservative advice."* Having traditionally been seen as a *"firefighting tax group,"* in the past few years competitors have observed *"a lot of effort"* in building the practice and view it as *"climbing fast."* Corporate work includes advising in the Punch Taverns saga and on sales for Cable & Wireless. Financial work includes advising on financing for the Drax power station acquisition and the Vodafone/Airtouch/Mannesman deal, advising on the Broadgate and London City airport securitisations and on British Aerospace exchangeables into Orange. The rounded practice also advises on investigation and litigation work. Another growing area is in VAT. The team has been busy working on e-business and outsourcing issues for clients such as NatWest. The year has also witnessed a steady stream of property, securitisation and financial services work for the VAT team as well as work on the private client side. Clients include ING Barings, Cable & Wireless, Morgan Stanley, Goldman Sachs, Bank of America.

Burges Salmon, Bristol: Advises a wide range of listed and international corporates, private companies, private equity groups, entrepreneurs and property consortia. The team plays a strong hand in asset finance and syndicated loans. Other non-mainstream areas of activity include litigation, investigations, human rights and indirect tax work.

Osborne Clarke OWA, Bristol: *"They all have experience and they know what they're talking about."* The team's main work is in supporting the corporate practice, and it has strengths in property and asset finance. The firm has increasingly been advising on venture capital fund raising issues and on e-commerce related issues.

Pinsent Curtis, Birmingham: A well respected team providing a range of direct and indirect corporate tax advice, as well as share scheme advice, for clients ranging from corporates to entrepreneurs. A sizeable consultancy practice, with around half of the team's work being independently generated. The team has a significant specialism in property. The team has been appointed to the panel advising on the tax and VAT aspects of the construction of the £475m new Wembley Stadium.

Leeds, Manchester: A high profile corporate tax team with a cutting edge profile in employee share schemes work. Has a national reputation for tax work. Advises corporates and wealthy individuals and entrepreneurs. International work, property and projects are strengths of the team.

Wragge & Co, Birmingham: A range of high quality corporate transaction work characterises this *"solid team."* Aside from mainstream corporate the team also advises on inward investment, employee incentives, indirect tax and litigation. The VAT, property and share scheme sides of the practice are reported to be growing. Work this year includes advising AT&T on its joint venture with BT.

Addleshaw Booth & Co, Leeds, Manchester: *"They are at the top, you'd expect nothing less."* Strong in both Northern offices, the growing practice is well regarded for advice on mainstream corporate and financial work as well as property, employee benefits and venture capital issues. Work this year includes advising the Stadium Group on the disposal of the Meadowhall Centre to British Land.

LEADING FIRMS

LONDON	TAX	LONDON	TAX
Allen & Overy	****	Lovells	***
Ashurst Morris Crisp	***	Macfarlanes	***
Berwin Leighton	**	McDermott, Will & Emery	*
Clifford Chance	*****	Nabarro Nathanson	**
Clyde & Co	*	Norton Rose	***
CMS Cameron McKenna	**	Olswang	**
Denton Wilde Sapte	**	Simmons & Simmons	**
DLA	*	SJ Berwin & Co	***
Field Fisher Waterhouse	*	Slaughter and May	******
Freshfields Bruckhaus Deringer	******	Theodore Goddard	**
Hammond Suddards Edge	*	Travers Smith Braithwaite	*
Herbert Smith	***	Watson, Farley & Williams	*
Linklaters	*****		

THE SOUTH	TAX	THE SOUTH	TAX
Blake Lapthorn, *Fareham*	*****	Osborne Clarke OWA, *Bristol*	******
Burges Salmon, *Bristol*	******	Wiggin & Co, *Cheltenham*	*****

MIDLANDS & EAST ANGLIA	TAX	MIDLANDS & EAST ANGLIA	TAX
DLA, *Birmingham*	*****	Pinsent Curtis, *Birmingham*	******
Eversheds, *Norwich, Nottingham*	*****	Wragge & Co, *Birmingham*	******
Mills & Reeve, *Cambridge*	****		

THE NORTH	TAX	THE NORTH	TAX
Addleshaw Booth & Co, *Leeds, Manchester*	******	Hammond Suddards Edge, *Leeds, Manchester*	*****
Dickinson Dees, *Newcastle upon Tyne*	***	Pinsent Curtis, *Leeds*	******
Eversheds, *Leeds, Manchester*	****	Walker Morris, *Leeds*	***

A-Zs

cardiff law school

Centre For Professional Legal Studies PO Box 294 Cardiff CF10 3UX
Tel: (029) 2087 4964 Fax: (029) 2087 4984
Email: Selley@Cardiff.ac.uk
Website: www.cf.ac.uk/claws/cpls

contact name
Mrs Zoe Selley

university profile

Cardiff Law School is long established, well-resourced and enjoys an international reputation for its teaching and research. In the most recent assessment of research quality conducted by the Higher Education Funding Council, Cardiff achieved a grade 5 rating, placing it in the top dozen law schools in the country. Cardiff offers opportunities for students to pursue postgraduate study by research leading to the degrees of M.Phil and Ph.D. In addition, taught Masters degrees in the areas of canon, commercial, criminal justice and medical law are offered in full and part-time mode.

legal practice course and bar vocational course

Within the Law School, the Centre for Professional Legal Studies is validated to offer both the Legal Practice Course and the Bar Vocational Course. Students are taught by experienced solicitors and barristers who have been specifically recruited for this purpose. All students pursuing the vocational courses are guaranteed placements with solicitors' firms or sets of chambers, while students studying the Bar Vocational Course additionally enjoy a one week placement with a Circuit or District Judge. Cardiff's Legal Practice Course has twice been rated "Excellent" by the Law Society; one of only five out of the 30 providers of this course to achieve the top ranking.

facilities

Recent developments within the Law School include extensive IT provision together with dedicated accommodation for the vocational courses which house a practitioner library, courtroom facilities, fixed and movable audio visual equipment for recording interactive practitioner skills activities. In addition, the main law library contains a substantial collection of primary and secondary material.

The Law School is housed in its own building at the heart of the campus, itself located in one of the finest civic centres in Britain and only a short walk from the main shopping area. The University has its own postgraduate centre, together with a full range of sporting and social facilities.

CARDIFF
UNIVERSITY
PRIFYSGOL
CAERDYĐ

university of central england in birmingham

Faculty of Law & Social Sciences Franchise Street Perry Barr Birmingham B42 2SU
Tel: (0121) 331 6600 Fax: (0121) 331 6622
Email: lss@uce.ac.uk
Website: www.uce.ac.uk

contact

Please apply to:
Admissions Officer,
Faculty of Law & Social
Sciences,
Perry Barr,
Birmingham B42 2SU

Tel: (0121) 331 6600
Fax: (0121) 331 6622
Email: lss@uce.ac.uk
Website: www.uce.ac.uk

college profile

Based in Birmingham, the School of Law has been a major centre for legal education and training in the city for over 30 years, and its close links to the city's legal community ensure its courses reflect the modern needs of the profession.

A wide range of high quality courses is taught by experienced and well qualified staff, in a law school noted for its friendly and approachable atmosphere. Its facilities include a legal practice resource centre, fully-equipped IT workrooms, and a court room and solicitor's office, both with audio-visual recording.

legal practice course/postgraduate diploma in legal practice (full or part-time)

The LPC course is designed to give you an advantageous start to your career as a solicitor in a competitive professional environment. It offers a wide range of commercial and private client options. The interactive teaching and learning methods replicate the typical transactions which you will encounter in practice and are designed to develop the self-sufficiency and confidence necessary when embarking on your training contract. The course can be studied by 4 days' attendance over one year or by two evenings' attendance over two.

cpe/postgraduate diploma in legal studies (full or part-time)

The course places emphasis on the development of legal skills by use of interactive teaching and learning methods and problem solving techniques. Successful students are guaranteed a place on the LPC.

main legal practice/legal studies (part-time)

These courses are designed for students who have completed the LPC or CPE respectively and wish to acquire further specialisation in an aspect of legal practice or law. They are research based courses that can be completed in substantial part by distance learning, and can be completed in six months to two years.

city university, london

The Law Department Northampton Square London EC1V 0HB
Tel: (020) 7477 8301 Fax: (020) 7477 8578
Email: cpe@city.ac.uk or law@city.ac.uk
Website: www.city.ac.uk/law

college profile

City University, London, was granted a Royal Charter in 1966. The University is located within walking distance of the Law Society, the major City firms of solicitors, the Bar Council, Inns of Court, Royal Courts of Justice and Central Criminal Court. The Law Department has close ties with the professions and the Inns of Court School of Law is affiliated to the University. The Department places special emphasis on careers advice and there is an active mooting programme including an Inns of Court sponsored competition. Guaranteed places are available for both the BVC and the LPC.

cpe/diploma in law (full-time or part-time)

The City CPE is unashamedly academic in the way it is taught. The original CPE, it is the largest University CPE/Diploma course and benefits from specialist staff with unrivalled experience, including visiting academics from Oxford, Cambridge and other established Universities. It can be converted into an LLB by completing additional course units on a part-time basis and may be converted into an MA by thesis.

graduate entry llb honours degree

City's graduate entry LLB is a programme designed for non-law graduates who want a broader two-year course leading to a qualifying law degree. The course is designed to provide both a general knowledge of the central areas of the law and to allow special interests to be developed. The academic work and examinations are of first degree standard and the course is taught jointly with the Department's three year undergraduate LLB degree. Separate tutors and tutorials give this course its own special identity within the Department.

llm environmental law (full-time or part-time)

The need to protect the environment is one of the key issues of our time. This taught Masters course provides an opportunity to study environmental law at an advanced level.

llm anglo-american law (full-time or part-time)

This taught Masters course enables students with a civil law background to study key features of the Anglo-American legal tradition and to develop an advanced understanding of the UK and US legal systems.

CITY City University London

the college of law

Braboeuf Manor Portsmouth Road Guildford GU3 1HA
Tel: 0800 3280153 Fax: (01483) 460 460
Email: info@lawcol.co.uk
Website: www.lawcol.org.uk

contact name
Freephone: 0800 3280153
Email: info@lawcol.co.uk

college profile

The College of Law, the largest legal training establishment in Europe, has branches in Guildford, London, Chester, York and in Birmingham from September 2001. The College has an excellent reputation with law firms and chambers and its teaching staff are professionally qualified as solicitors or barristers. The College's specialist knowledge and extensive contacts are coupled with its careers advisory service, specifically geared towards law students, to help students gain training contracts and pupillages. It offers the following courses:

postgraduate diploma in law (full-time, part-time or distance learning)

The PgDL is the law conversion course for graduates of disciplines other than law who wish to become solicitors or barristers. Students will receive in-depth tuition in seven foundation subjects from tutors with a proven track record in providing legal education. Successful students receive a Diploma in Law and are guaranteed a place on the College's Legal Practice Course.

legal practice course (full-time, part-time, or block learning)

The LPC is the vocational stage of training for prospective solicitors. The College's LPC has been developed in consultation with both City and provincial firms to address the real needs of today's legal profession, and ensure the course meets the demands of life in practice.

bar vocational course (full-time)

The BVC is the vocational stage of training for prospective barristers and is available at the College's site in Chancery Lane, London. It has been developed in conjunction with practising barristers to prepare students for life in their early years at the Bar. Practitioners from highly respected sets of chambers also contribute to the delivery of the course.

For further information about courses at any of the College's branches please contact Admissions.

The College of Law
of England and Wales

de montfort university

Department of Professional Legal Studies The Gateway Leicester LE1 9BH
Tel: (0116) 257 7177 Fax: (0116) 257 7186
Email: aaarseth@dmu.ac.uk Website: www.dmu.ac.uk

contact names
leicester
Tel: (0116) 257 7177
Fax: (0116) 257 7186
Email:
aaarseth@dmu.ac.uk

birmingham
Tel: (0121) 414 6870
Fax: (0121) 414 6871
Email:
bathersr@lpc.bham.ac.uk

bristol
Tel: (0117) 954 5361/2
Fax: (0117) 954 6717
Email:
nmarshallea@dmu.ac.uk

Application form and
information about distance
and open-learning courses:
ITC
Tel: (01234) 844305
Fax: (01234) 844342
Email:
j.marshall@ilex-tutorial.ac.uk

college profile
De Montfort University is an experienced provider of first class legal education and train-ing. A range of courses is offered, including the Legal Practice Course, the Postgraduate Diploma in Law, the Professional Skills Course and the LLM in Advanced Legal Practice. The Legal Practice Course is at a choice of three sites: De Montfort University in Leicester, Bristol in association with the University of Bristol, and Birmingham in association with the University of Birmingham. All students on the Legal Practice Courses are provided with a laptop computer, pre-installed with specialist legal software. The excellent teaching team are all qualified solicitors who maintain links with private practice. The open and distance learning courses are provided by De Montfort University in association with ILEX Tutorial College.

legal practice course (full-time or by open learning)
This is the vocational course for law graduates (or those who otherwise satisfy the acade-mic requirements of the Law society) who wish to become solicitors. Students study the compulsory subjects of Business Law and Practice, Conveyancing and Litigation before choosing from an extensive range of commercial and private client options. The open learning LPC is studied over two years, and the face-to-face tuition takes place mainly at weekends.

postgraduate diploma in law (full-time or by distance learning)
This is the 'conversion' course for non-law graduates who wish to become solicitors or bar-risters. The distance learning course is of two years duration. Learning is supported by face-to-face tuition over four long weekends in each year.

professional skills course
A fast track Professional Skills Course will run in Leicester from 2001. The course will have two intakes each year, in February and August.

masters degree in advanced legal practice
The Masters Degree programme is run in association with Central law training Ltd. The programme is aimed at qualified solicitors who wish to enhance their knowledge and skills in their field of professional practice.

university of exeter

The Centre for Legal Practice Amory Building
Rennes Drive Exeter EX4 4RJ
Tel: (01392) 263157 Fax: (01392) 263400
Email: Jenny.L.Cook@exeter.ac.uk Website: www.exeter.ac.uk

college profile

The Centre for Legal Practice was established in 1992 to provide postgraduate programmes relevant to the practice of law. Its main activities are the provision of the Legal Practice course, which is recognised by the Law Society for the purposes of vocational training for solicitors, and the Diploma in Law programme which is recognised by both the Law Society and the Council of Legal Education as covering the academic stage of training for graduates in a subject other than Law.

The Centre is validated by the Law Society and was awarded their top rating of 'Excellent' at their assessment visit in 1999. The Centre offers dedicated postgraduate facilities, small teaching classes, a consistently high pass rate and excellent links with local and national firms – all in a beautiful location.

legal practice course (full-time)

The programme is of 33 weeks duration beginning with a three-week Core Areas Foundation course. The course provides instruction in the practical legal skills of client interviewing, advocacy, drafting and legal research and in the pervasive subjects of Professional Conduct, Financial Services, Accounts and Human Rights. The three compulsory subjects of Business Law, Conveyancing and Litigation are studied over a sixteen-week teaching block. Students then choose three elective subjects from the following list: Corporate Finance, Commercial Contracts, Commercial Leases, Housing & Welfare Law, Employment Law, Family Law, Insurance Law and Private Client. The emphasis of the programme is on participative learning and subjects are taught on a practical transactional basis.

diploma in law course (full-time)

Students will follow a programme of study for 36 weeks, beginning with a structured introductory reading course for two weeks before coming into residence. A residential Foundation course takes place over four weeks preceding the commencement of the Michelmas Term. Thereafter students will observe the normal ten-week terms of the University. Students will study the following subjects from the LLB syllabus: Criminal Law, Contract Law, Law of Torts, Public Law of the EU & UK II, Land Law, Constitutional Principles of the EU & UK, Trusts Law. Students also submit a 4000 word dissertation on an area of legal study not covered within the seven foundation subjects.

contact name
Jenny L.Cook
Centre for Legal Practice,
Amory Building ,
Rennes Drive,
Exeter University,
EX4 4RJ

Tel (01392) 263157
Email:
Jenny.L.Cook@exeter.ac.uk
Website:
www.exeter.ac.uk/law/
centprac.htm

A-Z UNIVERSITIES AND LAW SCHOOLS

inns of court school of law

4 Gray's Inn Place Gray's Inn London WC1R 5DX
Tel: (020) 7404 5787 Fax: (020) 7831 4188
Email: bvc@icsl.ac.uk or 1pc@icsl.ac.uk or llm@icsl.ac.uk
Website: www.icsl.ac.uk

contact name
Please apply to
Admissions at the address
above for further details or
to request a prospectus.

college profile

The Inns of Court School of Law is the leading provider of postgraduate legal training for both solicitors and barristers and has a well-established CPD programme including the PSC. The BVC has been redesigned with provision made for home access via a PC to course materials, CD-ROMs and online databases. Recently a Pro Bono project was launched giving vocational course students the opportunity to work with live clients at the School's Advice Clinic or to work with a voluntary partner.

bar vocational course (full-time or part-time)

The ICSL seeks to train lawyers that will be well-equipped for the future, it is the only institution to offer the BVC in part-time mode. The course provides training in seven skill areas: advocacy; conference skills; negotiation; opinion writing; drafting; fact managemet and legal research. Places offered: 750 full-time; 100 part-time (per year).

legal practice course (full-time)

The LPC has been highly tailored to meet students' future needs in practice, with a heavy emphasis on learning via the use of IT resources. The foundation course consists of: Ethics, Skills, The European Context and Taxation, followed by compulsory subjects of Business Law and Practice, Litigation and Advocacy and Conveyancing, with a choice of three out of six electives.
Places offered: 100 full-time

llm in criminal litigation (full-time or part-time)

Run in association with City University, this LLM is the only postgraduate degree course in the country to be devoted exclusively to Criminal Litigation. It allows students to examine critically the four key subjects that underpin the criminal justice system – criminal procedure, sentencing, criminal evidence and criminal advocacy.

INNS OF COURT SCHOOL OF LAW
PIONEERS IN PROFESSIONAL
LEGAL TRAINING

keele university

Law Department Keele ST5 5BG
Tel: (01782) 583229 Fax: (01782) 583228
Website: www.keele.ac.uk

college profile

Keele University is a friendly campus community located in attractive surroundings in the Midlands, with easy access to Manchester and Birmingham. The Law Department is dynamic, lively and research-active, with a strong emphasis on interdisciplinary studies, and is firmly committed to graduate study. The campus offers excellent IT facilities, a sports centre and thriving students' union.

diploma in legal studies/cpe course (full-time or part-time)

Enables non-law graduates to complete the first stage of professional training at an established university with small group teaching. Students are taught by experienced law staff; there are modules on mooting and client interviewing, and a chance to upgrade to a Master's degree. A link with Chester College of Law provides guaranteed places on the LPC.

llm in child law/ma in child care law & practice

These courses concentrate upon issues concerned with children, parents, human rights, the professions and the state. The LLM is offered full-time or part-time; the MA is taught part-time only in four teaching blocks per year. The MA is accredited for Law Society CPD points.

llm in general legal studies & research (full-time or part-time)

Offers an opportunity to study a variety of different areas of law in depth, together with a research training course. Assessment is by a variety of methods, including a research dissertation.

m.phil/ph.d supervision

Research supervision is offered in many fields. Areas of expertise include; professional negligence; criminal law; health care law; civil liberties; constitutional & administrative law; European Union law; legal history; gender, sexuality and law; property & taxation; planning; legal theory; child & education law; international human rights.

contact name
Eileen Farne
Department of Law,
Keele University,
Keele,
Staffordshire ST5 5BG

Tel: (01782) 583229
Fax: (01782) 583228
E-mail:
lab07@law.keele.ac.uk
Website: www.keele.ac.uk/
depts/la/home.htm

A-Z UNIVERSITIES AND LAW SCHOOLS

KEELE
UNIVERSITY

london guildhall university

Department of Law 84 Moorgate London EC3M 6SQ
Tel: (020) 7320 1616 Fax: (020) 7320 1163
Email: enqs@lgu.ac.uk
Website: www.lgu.ac.uk

contact name
Robert Hawker

college profile

London Guildhall University was one of the first providers to obtain accreditation to run professional law courses. The teaching style of these courses is considered to be one of the friendliest and most thorough available. The University prides itself on giving students personal and individual attention; it is committed to keeping class numbers low; and its IT facilities include MIMICS and other software programs that are found in practice. Students receive training that is relevant, professional and with the right level of assistance to ensure success on their course.

Its location in the heart of the City of London means there is easy access to underground and mainline stations.

legal practice course (full or part-time day and evening)

Many of the teaching staff are either recently out of practice, or still in practice, and therefore the emphasis is on the provision of professional training. Welfare and commercial electives are offered, including some rare subjects such as Immigration and International Trade.

Class sizes are deliberately limited and skills training is provided in smaller groups to ensure personal and individual attention. Computers are utilised within the classrooms along with video cameras to ensure that all the latest training and practitioner tools are made available to students.

A unique (to London) part-time day course is offered to provide flexibility in training modes.

common professional examination (full-time or part-time day or evening)

Training is by both lectures and tutorials with an emphasis on the seven foundations of legal knowledge. The course prides itself on an intimate atmosphere with personal and individual attention offered to all students. A variety of teaching and assessment methods are utilised including research assignments, case and statute analysis, and oral presentations.

Fee assistance is provided to those students wishing to continue with the LPC at London Guildhall University. The University also offers a flexible mode of study that helps students commit when considering undertaking a professional course.

manchester metropolitan university

School of Law Elizabeth Gaskell Campus Hathersage Road Manchester M13 OJA
Tel: (0161) 247 3050 Fax: (0161) 247 6309
Email: law@mmu.ac.uk

contact name
Contact the Admissions Tutor for the relevant course.

college profile

The School of Law is one of the largest providers of legal education in the UK, and enjoys an excellent reputation for the quality and range of its courses. The School's courses are well designed and taught, combining rigorous academic standards with practical application. Giving you the best possible start for your career.

bar vocational course (full-time)

This course provides the vocational stage of training for intending practising barristers. Adopting a Syndicate Group approach, the BVC is activity based and interactive. Extensive IT and audio visual facilities combine with dedicated, well equipped premises to provide an enjoyable and stimulating experience. Excellent student support is provided including mentoring by practising barristers and an Additional Professional Programme which is designed to bridge the gap betweeen student and professional life.

legal practice course (full-time or part-time)

This course is for those wishing to qualify as a solicitor. Offering a full range of commercial and private client electives the Legal Practice Course, taught by professionally qualified staff, prepares you for every day practice. There is a dedicated Resource Centre and an excellent pastoral care programme for LPC students. Consistently recognised by the Law Society for its high quality.

postgraduate diploma in law/cpe (full-time or part-time)

An increasing number of graduates enter the legal profession this way, with employers attracted by the applicant's maturity and transferable skills. The course places emphasis on the acquisition of legal research and other relevant legal skills. The School guarantees a place on the LPC, subject to satisfactory performance, and gives favourable treatment for the BVC.

the
MANCHESTER
METROPOLITAN
UNIVERSITY

middlesex university

Middlesex University Business School The Burroughs Hendon London NW4 4BT
Tel: (020) 8411 5090 Fax: (020) 8411 6069
Email: headmissions@mdx.ac.uk
Website: http://mubs.mdx.ac.uk

contact name

Sheila Sharp
Admissions Manager
The Burroughs
London NW4 4BT

Tel: (020) 8411 5090
Fax: (020) 8411 6069
Email:
headmissions@mdx.ac.uk
Website:
http://mubs.mdx.ac.uk

college profile

Middlesex University Business School (MUBS) is the largest business school in London, and is located at the Hendon campus, within 30 minutes of Central London by Underground rail.

The law group has been offering both undergraduate and postgraduate programmes for over 25 years, and hosts the Centre for Research into Industrial and Commercial law, with current projects in: Employment law (whistleblowing), Environmental law, European law and Compliance of Football League clubs with racism legislation.

undergraduate programmes

BA (Hons) Law and LLB (Hons) are offered at undergraduate level. There are opportunities to train in legal skills, IT and specialise with a wide range of optional modules on offer for those wishing to combine law with another field of study such as business. Both programmes provide exemption from the first stage of professional legal education for those seeking a professional career in law.

postgraduate programmes llm in employment law

Designed for practising lawyers, human resource practitioners, trade union officials and advice workers. Students without a background in law are admitted and undertake a pre-course block on Legal principals & methods.

pg diploma in law/cpe (full-time and distance learning)

Designed for law & non-law graduates who wish to have an in-depth understanding of English and European Union laws and/or wish to pursue a career in law. The distance learning option is run in partnership with Semple Piggot Rochez Ltd (SPR).

All programmes are recognised by the Law Society and the General Bar council, while the CPE board approves the CPE programmes.

university of northumbria at newcastle

School of Law University of Northumbria
Sutherland Building Newcastle-upon-Tyne NE1 8ST
Tel: (0191) 227 4494
Fax: (0191) 227 4557
Email: muriel.theillere@northumbria.ac.uk
Website: www.northumbria.ac.uk

contact name
Ms. M. Theillere

college profile

The School of Law at the University of Northumbria is known for its excellence in the provision of academic and professional legal education. Situated in central Newcastle the School has over 60 full-time teaching staff and is one of the largest departments in the University. Full-time, part-time and distance learning modes of study are available. The School is validated to run the Bar Vocational Course, the Legal Practice Course and the Common Professional Examination/Diploma in Law Course. It also offers the Professional Skills Course and an extensive LLM programme, including courses in Mental Health Law, Medical Law, Commercial Law, European Law and new for September 2001 LLM courses in International Trade Law and Commercial Property (subject to validation). The Law School has dedicated lecture and workshop accommodation together with its own Law Skills Centre which includes a large practitioner library, court room and offices with full CCTV facilities plus open access IT equipment.

lpc (full-time or part-time)

- the vocational training course for students who wish to qualify as solicitors
- a wide range of corporate and private client electives
- practical workshops

bvc (full-time)

- the vocational training course for students who wish to qualify as barristers
- practical skills training in dedicated accommodation
- strong practitioner participation

cpe

- the academic stage of training for non-law graduates who wish to qualify as solicitors or barristers
- structured study materials
- opportunity to obtain a law degree with an additional study programme
- guaranteed places for successful students either on our Legal Practice Course or, subject to the requirements of the General Council of the Bar, on our Bar Vocational Course.

UNIVERSITY *of*
NORTHUMBRIA *at* NEWCASTLE
Promoting Excellence in Higher Education

A-Z UNIVERSITIES AND LAW SCHOOLS

nottingham law school

Nottingham Law School
Belgrave Centre Nottingham NG1 5LP
Tel: (0115) 848 6871 Fax: (0115) 848 6878

contact
Nottingham Law School,
Belgrave Centre,
Chaucer Street,
Nottingham NG1 5LP

bar vocational course

Nottingham Law School has designed its BVC to develop to a high standard a range of core practical skills, and to equip students to succeed in the fast-changing environment of practice at the Bar. Particular emphasis is placed on the skill of advocacy. Advocacy sessions are conducted in groups of six and the School uses the Guildhall courtrooms for most sessions. The BVC is taught entirely by recently practising barristers, and utilises the same integrated and interactive teaching methods as all of the School's other professional courses. Essentially, students learn by doing and Nottingham Law School provides a risk-free environment in which students are encouraged to realise, through practice and feedback, their full potential.

legal practice course

The LPC is offered by full-time and part-time block study. This course has been designed to be challenging and stimulating for students and responsive to the needs of firms, varying from large commercial to smaller high street practices.

Nottingham Law School's LPC features: integration of the transactions and skills, so that each advances the other, whilst ensuring the transferability of skills between different subject areas. Carefully structured inter-active group work which develops an ability to handle skills and legal transactions effectively, and in an integrated way. A rigorous assessment process that nevertheless avoids 'assessment overload', to maintain a teaching and learning emphasis to the course. A professionally qualified team, retaining substantial links with practice. An excellent rating from The Law Society's Assessment Panel in every year of its operation.

the postgraduate diploma in law (full-time)

The Nottingham Law School PgDL is a one year conversion course designed for any non-law graduate who intends to become a solicitor or barrister in the UK. The intensive course effectively covers the seven core subjects of an undergraduate law degree in one go. It is the stepping stone to the LPC or the BVC at Nottingham Law School, and a legal career thereafter. It is a postgraduate Diploma (Dip Law) in its own right, which can be presented to employers. It operates on a similar basis to the LPC (see above), though inevitably it has a more academic bias.

Nottingham Law School

semple piggot rochez

Lower Ground 62 Blenheim Crescent Notting Hill London W11 1NZ
Tel: (020) 7229 1016 Fax: (020) 7229 1104
Website: www.spr-law.com

college profile

Semple Piggot Rochez acquired the legal division of Wolsey Hall in 1998. Working with their partner, The Law Group at Middlesex University, SPR delivers a two year part-time distance learning Postgraduate Diploma in Law (CPE) accredited by the CPE Board – the first CPE in the UK to be fully supported online on the internet.

first cpe to be supported fully on the internet

While it is not necessary to have internet access to do the course – as the course is self contained – those with access will be able to use the purpose designed website (www.spr-law.com). Students will be given free online access over the net to LAWTEL, WESTLAW, The Official Law Reports, All England Law Reports, Weekly Law Reports, Halsbury's Laws, Legislation Direct, Law Direct, Law Reports Digest, PLC Magazine and European Counsel magazine. The Virtual Workstation on the SPR website provides a range of additional services; mail service, notice boards, conferencing, text based real time communication channels, SPR 'netcasts', online debate forum, links to over 4500 legal and other resources on the net.

two centres: oxford and london

SPR is accredited by the CPE board to enrol 100 students in each year. The programme held over 4 extended study weekends (Friday-Sunday) is fully supported by detailed course manuals written by members of the lecturing team. Teaching will be held in two centres: Oxford and London. Students may choose either the Oxford Centre or the London Centre to suit their convenience. Students attending the Oxford course will be given access to the Bodleian Library. Students attending the London Centre will be provided with reader cards to a London Library.

spr reverses the fees trend by reducing the tuition fees

The fee for the course is now £1950, reduced from £2262 last year. If you are interested in joining this innovative net supported course, please visit the website. You will be able to download a prospectus and review the many services online. SPR also provides, free of charge to all students, some 2000 pages of legal course notes and other materials – online. Alternatively call Jane O'Hare, the Course Director on (01865) 201546 or Mike Semple Piggot on (020) 7229 0820. SPR is always pleased to meet students who wish to make an appointment to see them at their London office.

contact
Jane O'Hare Course Director
Tel: (01865) 201546

prospectus
Online
www.spr-law.com
Printed
Semple Piggot Rochez,
173b Cowley Road,
Oxford OX4 1LT

Tel: (01865) 201546
Email: msp@spr-law.com

CONSILIO
Online Magazine
www.spr-consilio.com

SEMPLE PIGGOT ROCHEZ

A-Z UNIVERSITIES AND LAW SCHOOLS

staffordshire university

Staffordshire University Law School Leek Road
Stoke on Trent ST4 2DF
Tel: (01782) 294689/294452 Fax: (01782) 294335
Email: ph3@staffs.ac.uk Website: www.staffs.ac.uk/schools/law/welcome.html

contact names
Pat Holdcroft
CPC Administrator

Tel: (01782) 294689
Fax: (01782) 294335
Email: ph3@staffs.ac.uk

Julie Gingell
LPC Administrator
Tel: (01782) 294452
Email: jg5@staffs.ac.uk

college profile

Staffordshire University Law School offers a comprehensive range of academic and professional postgraduate courses. An enthusiastic team of well qualified staff with a commitment to academic development, legal research and publication is able to offer a breadth and depth of specialist legal knowledge and experience. This is complemented by a £3 million purpose-built state-of-the-art Law School building which exemplifies the University's commitment and approach to legal education and support. The spacious building with its exciting design, set in an attractive setting, is based on a central law library surrounded by teaching and study rooms. It includes two mock courtrooms, staff rooms, study areas and extensive information
technology provision. The combination of dedicated staff and a purpose-built building provide an unrivalled resource for law
students, providing a focus for legal practitioners, and a centre of excellence for legal education and professional training. Its library and Legal Information Technology Cenre provide access to wide ranging information sources, expertise and facilities.

legal practice course (full-time or part-time)

The course offers:

- unique practitioner-student mentoring scheme
- comprehensive support in securing training contracts
- excellent, dedicated LPC facilities
- full range of Masters top-up awards
- dedicated teaching staff involved in professional practice

common professional examination/postgraduate diploma in legal studies (full-time or part-time)

The course offers:

- a postgraduate legal qualification ('upgrade' to Masters)
- completion of the academic stage of legal training (equivalent to LLB)
- Certificate in Social Welfare Law and Practice on completion of the CPE '8th Subject'
- 'credits' towards further degrees or vocational courses
- guaranteed Staffordshire University Legal Practice Course place (full or part-time routes)
- mentoring scheme and assistance with work experience

university of the west of england

Faculty of Law Frenchay Campus Coldhabour Lane Bristol BS16 1QY
Tel: (0117) 976 2171 Fax: (0117) 976 3841
Email: law@uwe.ac.uk Website: www.uwe.ac.uk

contact name
Gabriel Fallon
Tel: (0117) 344 3769
Fax: (0117) 976 3841
Email: Gabriel.Fallon

college profile

The Bristol Institute of Legal Practice, which is part of the Faculty of Law at the University of the West of England, Bristol, is one of the largest providers of professional legal education in the United Kingdom. The Law Society has recognised the quality of its Legal Practice Courses by awarding them an 'Excellent' rating. It is also proud to be one of only seven providers outside London to be validated by the Bar Council to run the Bar Vocational Course. Moreover, the Higher Education Funding Council for England and Wales rated teaching across the Faculty as a whole as 'excellent'.

The Bristol Institute of Legal Practice offers the following courses:

legal practice course – lpc (full-time and part-time)

The Institute's Legal Practice Courses have a national reputation for quality, which has been recognised by the Law Society with its award of an 'excellent' rating. Moreover, it currently offers more elective subjects (13) than any other provider in the country. The Faculty has very good links with both local and national firms of solicitors.

bar vocational course – bvc (full-time)

In 1966 the UWE Faculty of Law, and Cardiff University, were jointly honoured by the Bar Council in being validated to run the Bar Vocational Course. When validating the course the Chairman of the Bar Council remarked among other factors taken into account was: 'the standard of the facilities to be made available for the Course and the strength of support from the local Bar'.

common professional examination (full-time and part-time)

The Faculty has run CPE courses for over 20 years. Both the full-time and part-time versions of the course are recognised nationally as being high quality. They are also very popular and highly respected by the Legal Profession. The courses have very high pass rates and, on the successful completion of the Bristol CPE, students also receive a Postgraduate Diploma in Law.

university of wolverhampton

School of Law Molineux Street Wolverhampton WV1 1SB
Tel: (01902) 321000 Fax: (01902) 321570

college profile

Based in Wolverhampton and offers courses for students intending to become solicitors.
The law school has been offering these courses for over 20 years. Their LPC programme
has had consistently good ratings. The lecturers are drawn from ex-solicitors, barristers,
academics and individuals from business and industry. There are excellent IT facilities, a
well-stocked library and a sports centre.

legal practice course (full/part-time)

The vocational training course for those intending to practise as solicitors. The core subjects of Business, Litigation and Conveyancing are taught, together with a range of
commercial and private client options. Professional skills courses,
practical workshops and seminars are all part of the training. Close links with local practitioners, mentoring, and CV distribution. Purpose built courtroom. Exclusive LPC
resources room.

Group social activities.

common professional examination (full/part-time)

The academic stage of training for non-law graduates wishing to become solicitors or barristers. A full programme of lectures and tutorials is offered on this demanding course.
Students are taught by ex-solicitors and barristers. Places on the LPC are guaranteed for
successful students. Flexible studying choices are under review.

contact name
Lynn Leighton-Johnstone
Recruitment and
Admissions
(01902) 321 999

UNIVERSITY OF
WOLVERHAMPTON

addleshaw booth & co

Sovereign House PO Box 8 Sovereign Street Leeds LS1 1HQ
Tel: (0113) 209 2000 Fax: (0113) 209 2060
100 Barbirolli Square Manchester M2 3AB
Tel :(0161) 934 6000 Fax: (0161) 934 6060
60 Cannon Street London EC4N 6NP
Tel: (020) 7982 5000 Fax: (020) 7982 5060
Email: grad@addleshaw-booth.co.uk
Website: www.addleshaw-booth.co.uk

firm profile

Addleshaw Booth & Co is a leading UK law firm, operating nationally and with an international capability. We provide commercial advice and legal solutions to a wide range of clients in the corporate, financial, public and private sectors.

main areas of work

Banking and Financial Services; Commercial; Commercial Property; Corporate Finance; Litigation and Dispute Resolution; Private Client; enact (Housing).

trainee profile

Graduates of all disciplines who are capable of achieving a 2:1, can demonstrate commercial awareness, a flexible attitude and a willingness to learn. Non-academic interests and achievements will also be taken into account and applications from mature applicants are welcomed.

training environment

During each six-month seat, there will be regular two-way performance reviews with the supervising partner or solicitor. Trainees are given the opportunity to spend a seat in one of the other offices and there are also a number of secondments to the in-house legal departments of various clients such as Astra Zeneca, British Aerospace and Airtours. The on-the-job training received within teams is complemented by a programme of lectures and residential courses, many designed specifically for trainees. The firm has a reputation of being a friendly and pleasant place to work and particular emphasis is placed upon building relationships and valuing everybody's contribution towards the success of the business.

benefits

Corporate membership of gyms, season ticket loan.

vacation placements

Places for 2001: 40; Duration: 2 weeks; Remuneration: £150 p.w.; Closing Date: 23 February 2001.

sponsorship & awards

CPE and LPC fees are paid, together with a maintenance award of £3,500.

Partners	111
Assistant Solicitors	393
Total Trainees	60

contact
Simran Gill, Graduate Manager

method of application
Application form

selection procedure
Interview, assessment day

closing date for 2003
27 July 2001

application
Training contracts p.a.
40 approx
Applications p.a. **2,000**
% interviewed p.a. **6%**
Required degree grade: **2:1**

training
Salary:
1st year (2000)
£18,000-£18,500
(Manchester & Leeds)
£22,000-22,500 (London)
2nd year (2000)
£19,000-19,500
(Manchester & Leeds)
23,500-24,000 (London)
Holiday entitlement:
25 days
% of trainees with
a non-law degree p.a.
40%

post-qualification
Salary (2000)
£29,000
(Manchester & Leeds)
£40,000 (London)
% of trainees offered job
on qualification (2000): **85%**

other offices
Leeds, London,
Manchester

A-Z SOLICITORS

379

allen & overy

One New Change London EC4M 9QQ
Tel: (020) 7330 3000 Fax: (020) 7330 9999
Website: www.allenovery.com

firm profile

Allen & Overy is one of the world's premier global law firms, with major strengths in banking, international capital markets and corporate work. All departments work closely together to meet the needs of clients which include governments, financial institutions, businesses and private individuals.

main areas of work

Banking; International Capital Markets; Corporate; Litigation; Property; Private Client; Tax; Employment and related areas.

trainee profile

Intellectual ability is a prerequisite but as Allen & Overy is a commercial firm it also looks for people with a good level of business understanding. The firm looks for creative, problem solving people who can quickly identify salient points without losing sight of detail. You will need to be highly motivated, demonstrate initiative and the ability to alternate between leading and being part of a team.

training environment

Within a highly pressurised environment, trainees obtain a balance of practical and formal tuition. You will experience at least four different areas of work, but will spend a significant amount of time in at least two of the following departments: banking, corporate and international capital markets. Your preferences will be balanced with the firm's needs. Seminars provide practical advice and an introduction to each area of law. Placements abroad are available. A positive, open and co-operative culture is encouraged both professionally and socially. A range of sporting activities are available.

benefits

PPP scheme, private medical insurance, season ticket loans, gym membership, subsidised restaurant, 6 weeks unpaid leave on qualification.

vacation placements

Places for 2001: 60-70; Duration: 3 weeks; Remuneration: £200 p.w.; Closing Date: 31 January 2001.

sponsorship & awards

CPE and LPC fees and £5,000 maintenance p.a. (£4,500 outside London, Oxford and Guildford).

Partners	305*
Associates	922*
Total Trainees	321*

denotes world-wide figures

contact
Graduate Recruitment

method of application
Application form

selection procedure
Assessment centre

closing date for 2003
CPE candidates:
Early February 2001;
Law students:
Early August, 2001

application
Training contracts p.a. 120
Applications p.a. 4,000
% interviewed p.a. 10%
Required degree grade: 2:1

training
Salary:
1st year (2000) £25,000
2nd year (2000) £28,000
Holiday entitlement:
25 days
% of trainees with a
non-law degree p.a. 40%
No. of seats available
abroad p.a. 25

post-qualification
Salary (2000): £42,000
% of trainees offered job
on qualification (2000): 90%
% of partners (as at 1/9/00)
who joined as trainees:
60%

overseas offices
Amsterdam, Bangkok,
Beijing, Brussels,
Bratislava, Budapest,
Dubai, Frankfurt, Hong
Kong, Luxembourg,
Madrid, Milan, Moscow,
New York, Paris, Prague,
Rome, Singapore, Tirana,
Tokyo, Turin, Warsaw.

ashurst morris crisp

Broadwalk House 5 Appold St London EC2A 2HA
Tel: (020) 7638 1111 Fax: (020) 7972 7800
Email: isabelle.sorgo@ashursts.com
Website: www.ashursts.com

firm profile

An international City practice, smaller than its principal competitors yet consistently ranked amongst the top few firms in the country in terms of the work in which it is involved and clients for whom it acts.

main areas of work

Company 45%; Property 25%; Litigation 15%; Banking 10%; Tax 5%.

trainee profile

Candidates should want to be involved in the highest quality work that a City firm can offer. The firm wants high achievers academically as the work is intellectually demanding. Candidates should show common sense, good judgement, a willingness to take on responsibility, a sense of humour and an outgoing nature. Language skills and an international perspective on life will impress.

training environment

The training contract comprises four or five seats including six months in each of three of the principal departments. Opportunities exist to work in Brussels, Paris, Frankfurt, Milan, Singapore and Tokyo, or on secondment to a client. A fast-track two week PSC course run in partnership with the College of Law, covers the compulsory core elements and there is an extensive in-house training programme. The firm gives trainees as much responsibility as they can manage, and a full role in servicing clients' needs. Trainees are encouraged to take on pro bono work.

benefits

Season ticket loan, medical cover, life cover, membership of a gym/squash club.

vacation placements

Places for 2001: 60; Duration: 2 placements of 3 weeks; Remuneration: £200 p.w.(2000); Closing Date: 16 February 2001.

sponsorship & awards

CPE and LPC funding and £4,500 maintenance allowance p.a. (£4,000 outside London and Guildford). LPC Distinction Award of £500.

Partners 105*
Assistant Solicitors 335*
Total Trainees 109
denotes world-wide figures

contact
Isabelle Sorgo
Graduate Recruitment

method of application
Handwritten or typed letter and CV

selection procedure
Interviews with 1 assistant and 2 partners

closing date for 2003
10 August 2001

application
Training contracts p.a.
45–50
Applications p.a.
3,000
% interviewed p.a.
15%
Required degree grade:
2:1

training
Salary: 2000
1st seat (First 6 months):
£25,000
2nd seat (6-12 months):
£26,000
3rd seat (12-18 months):
£27,000
4th seat (after 18 months):
£28,000
Holiday entitlement:
25 days
% of trainees with a
non-law degree p.a.: 50%
No. of seats available
abroad p.a.: 16

post-qualification
Salary (2000): £42,000
% of trainees offered job
on qualification (2000): 95%

overseas offices
Brussels, Delhi, Frankfurt, Paris, Singapore, Tokyo, Milan, and New York.

baker & mckenzie

100 New Bridge Street London EC4V 6JA
Tel: (020) 7919 1000 Fax: (020) 7919 1999
Email: london.graduate.recruit@bakernet.com
Website: www.ukgraduates.bakernet.com

firm profile

Baker & McKenzie is the law firm with the greatest global reach – 61 offices in 35 countries. The London office is a leading City practice with a domestic and foreign client base. It provides business and financial legal services to corporations, financial institutions, governments and entrepreneurs.

main areas of work

Corporate/Finance/EC/Tax/Commercial 47%; Litigation/ Construction 23%; Employment/Pensions/Immigration 13%; Intellectual Property 10%; Commercial Property 7%.

trainee profile

Baker & McKenzie are looking for trainees who are stimulated by intellectual challenge and want to be 'the best' at what they do. Effective communication together with the ability to be creative but practical problem solvers, team players and to have a sense of humour are qualities which will help them stand out from the crowd. Language and IT skills are also valued. The firm encourages their trainees to take time out before commencing their training contract whether just to travel or undertake further studies.

training environment

Four six-month seats which include corporate and litigation together with the possibility of a secondment abroad or with a client. During each seat you will have formal and informal reviews to discuss your progress as well as subsequent seat preferences. Your training contract commences with a highly interactive and practical induction programme which focuses on key skills including practical problem solving, interviewing, presenting and the application of information technology. The firm's training programmes include important components on management and other business skills, as well as seminars and workshops on key legal topics for each practice area. They run the Professional Skills Course in-house – two modules of which are undertaken at the start of your training contract. There is a Trainee Solicitor Liaison Committee which acts as a forum for any new ideas or problems which may occur during the training contract. Trainees are actively encouraged to participate in a variety of pro bono issues and outside of office hours there is a varied sporting and social life.

benefits

Permanent health insurance, life insurance, private medical insurance, group personal pension plan, gym membership, luncheon vouchers, interest-free season ticket loan.

Partners	68
Assistant Solicitors	165
Total Trainees	55

contact
Joanna Darby /
Natalie Stacey

method of application
Letter and application form

selection procedure
Candidates to give a short oral and written presentation, interview with 2 partners, meeting with a trainee

closing date for 2003
Non-law: 18/2/01;
Law: 28/7/01

application
Training contracts p.a. 30
Applications p.a. 2,000
% interviewed p.a. 6%
Required degree grade 2:1

training
Salary:
1st year (2000) £25,000
2nd year (2000) £28,000
Holiday entitlement
25 days
% of trainees with a
non-law degree p.a.
approx 50%
No. of seats available
abroad p.a. Variable

post-qualification
Salary (2000)
£43 – £45,000
% of trainees offered job
on qualification (2000) 80%
% of partners (as at 1/9/00)
who joined as trainees
40%

vacation placements

Places for 2001: 30; Duration: Summer (3 weeks); Remuneration: £250 p.w.; Closing Date: 31 January 2001

sponsorship & awards

CPE Funding: Fees paid + £5,000 maintenance.
LPC Funding: Fees paid + £5,000 maintenance.

additional information

As mentioned, trainees have the opportunity to spend three months working in one of our overseas offices. Trainees have already been seconded to our offices in Sydney, Palo Alto and Riyadh. In addition they also operate an Associate Training Programme which enables lawyers with 18–24 months pqe to spend between 6–24 months working in an overseas office. In recent years the firm has had associates spend time in Palo Alto, Chicago, Moscow, Hong Kong and Sydney. Baker & McKenzie have a very extensive know-how practice both in London and globally which is ably assisted by BakerWeb, the firm's intranet.

trainee comments

"Training at B&M has given me precisely the experience I was hoping for from a City law firm with a global reputation – stimulating work, a challenging environment and high quality training. However, B&M has gone a step further and provided a relaxed atmosphere in an office where people can be counted on to enjoy themselves both during and after work." (Sunny Mann, first seat trainee, King's College London).

"One year after joining the firm I look back and can't believe how much I have learnt! It has been a steep but very rewarding learning curve, where you are given as much responsibility as you can handle. On-the-job training is supplemented by a programme of first class lectures and workshops with a practical bias – a world away from university and law school!" (Penny Hunt, second seat trainee, London Guildhall University).

"At Baker & McKenzie, you realise early on in your training that you are considered a valuable member of a team – the work that I have done has often been integral to the projects on which I am working and, in many instances, my own ideas and opinions have been sought after and implemented by more senior lawyers." (David Chmiel, second seat trainee, University College London).

overseas offices

Almaty, Amsterdam, Bahrain, Baku, Bangkok, Barcelona, Beijing, Berlin, Bogotá, Brasilia, Brussels, Budapest, Buenos Aires, Cairo, Caracas, Chicago, Dallas, Frankfurt, Geneva, Hanoi, Ho Chi Minh City, Hong Kong, Houston, Hsinchu, Juarez, Kiev, Madrid, Manila, Melbourne, Mexico City, Miami, Milan, Monterrey, Moscow, Munich, New York, Palo Alto, Paris, Prague, Rio de Janeiro, Riyadh, Rome, St Petersburg, San Diego, San Francisco, Santiago, São Paulo, Singapore, Stockholm, Sydney, Taipei, Tijuana, Tokyo, Toronto, Valencia, Warsaw, Washington DC, Zurich.

A - Z

SOLICITORS

barlows

Guildford House 66 Guildford St Chertsey KT16 9B
Tel: (01932) 568245 Fax: (01932) 562650
Email: sheilanewey@barlows.co.uk
Website: www.barlows-legal.com

firm profile

Barlows is a flourishing, fast growing, mixed practice with offices in Guildford, Godalming and Chertsey, all within easy reach of London. With around 120 staff the firm is large enough to provide a full range of experience for its trainees, whilst maintaining a family atmosphere.

main areas of work

Civil Litigation (including Employment, Family and Personal Injury); Company and Commercial; Property; Private Client.

trainee profile

Barlows requires trainees of a high academic calibre, preferably but not necessarily law graduates, who have a broad range of interests. Successful candidates will be ambitious and react positively to pressure.

training environment

Trainees are given a large degree of responsibility and client involvement from an early stage. Trainees normally spend six months in four departments across the three offices, usually sharing an office with a supervising partner who ensures access and involvement with a wide variety of cases and clients. Training is highly personalised. When considered competent and sufficiently confident in their own capabilities, trainees are allowed to handle their own cases. Trainees are actively encouraged to get involved with marketing and developing their IT skills. Formal training is mainly undertaken through Law South, a group of 10 legal practices that combine resources to provide PSC and other training. The Training Partner and HR Manager take joint responsibility for regularly monitoring trainees' progress. Trainees are seen as an investment for the future growth and development of the firm and those that prove themselves can expect excellent long-term prospects. Five current partners were trainees with the firm.

Partners	12
Assistant Solicitors	30
Total Trainees	8

contact
Sheila Newey
HR Manager

method of application
Letter, application form and CV

selection procedure
Interview with partners and HR Manager

closing date for 2003
31 August 2001

application
Training contracts p.a. 3-4
Required degree grade 2:1

training
Salary:
1st year(2000) £13,500
reviewed every six months
Holiday entitlement:
20 days

beale and company

Garrick Hse 27-32 King St Covent Garden
London WC2E 8JD
Tel: (020) 7240 3474 Fax: (020) 7240 9111
Email: a.bruce@beale-law.com
Website: www.beale-law.com

firm profile

Beale and Company is a long-established commercial practice with offices in Covent Garden in Central London. The firm provides a comprehensive range of legal services to commercial clients drawn from a wide range of business sectors. The firm has particular experience in construction, insurance, IT, corporate and commercial, employment, and international business where its expertise has long been recognised.

main areas of work

Litigation and dispute resolution; corporate and commercial; other non-contentious (including private client and property).

trainee profile

Trainees should have an excellent academic backgound and be eager to make their mark. Commercial awareness and experience or an interest in construction, insurance or IT will assist.

training environment

The firm offers excellent prospects to the right candidate. The training period generally consists of four six-month seats in partners rooms, two in litigation and dispute resolution and the remainder in corporate and commercial, employment, private client or property. Each trainee is supervised by the partner for whom the trainee works on a daily basis and progress is reviewed regularly by another partner. There is a formal induction procedure and in-house lectures and training on legal matters relevant to the firm's practice are given. The offices are fully computerised. The firm has a friendly and informal working environment and regular social events.

benefits

Season ticket loan (after 6 months), private health insurance (after 2 years), discretionary entertainment and social events.

Partners	9
Assistant Solicitors	9
Total Trainees	6

contact
Mrs Alexandra Bruce
Training Partner

method of application
CV with covering letter
(typed or hand written)
and SAE

selection procedure
Two interviews with
partners

closing date for 2003
Submit between 1 August
2001 and 31 October 2001

application
Training contracts p.a. **3**
Applications p.a. **1500**
% interviewed p.a. **1.5%**
Required degree grade **2:1**

training
Salary:
1st year(2003)
to be determined
(not less than 18,500)
2nd Year(2004)
discretionary review
every six months
Holiday entitlement:
23 days
% of trainees with a
non-law degree p.a. **60%**

post-qualification
Salary (2000) **£33,000**
% of trainees offered job
on qualification (2000)
100%
% of partners (as at 1/9/00)
who joined as trainees
89%

berwin leighton

Adelaide House London Bridge London EC4R 9HA
Tel: (020) 7760 1000 Fax: (020) 7760 1111
Email: traineerecruit@berwinleighton.com
Website: www.berwinleighton.com

firm profile

Berwin Leighton is a top 20 City firm. Founded in 1970, the firm is a modern growing practice that puts a premium on commercial, as well as technical advice, client relations and quality transactional care. They are entrepreneurial, tenacious and innovative.

main areas of work

The firm is highly regarded for their Corporate, Commercial Property, Finance and Litigation and Dispute Resolution departments.

trainee profile

Berwin Leighton is looking for intelligent trainees who are motivated, creative, interested in business and demonstrate strong communication skills.

training environment

Training starts with an induction covering all the practical aspects of working in a law firm from billing to client care. Comprehensive technical education programmes have been developed for each department and trainees attend weekly seminars supplemented by trainee lunches and skill sessions. You will undertake a tailor made PSC course which the firm is accredited to run in-house. Trainees spend six months in four seats, and your progress will be reviewed every three months. The firm operates an open door policy and trainees can enjoy early responsibility secure in the knowledge that there is a safety net of supervision.

benefits

Private health insurance, subsidised gym membership, season ticket loan, life assurance.

vacation placements

Places for 2001: Open Days in the Easter Vacation, application by CV and covering letter before 28 February 2001. Attendance at an Open Day could lead to a one week placement in the Summer Vacation.

sponsorship & awards

CPE funding: Fees paid + £4,000 maintenance LPC funding: Fees paid + £4,000 maintenance.

Partners	69
Assistant Solicitors	131
Total Trainees	38

contact
Claire Benson
Graduate Recruitment
Manger

method of application
Firm application form

selection procedure
Assessment centre +
partner interview

closing date for 2003
31 July 2001

application
Training contracts p.a. 25
Applications p.a. 2,000
% interviewed p.a. 5%
Required degree grade 2:1

training
Salary:
1st year (2000) £25,000
2nd Year (2000) £28,000
Holiday entitlement:
22 days
% of trainees with
a non-law degree p.a. 40%
No. of seats available
abroad p.a. 4

post-qualification
Salary (2000) £42,000
% of trainees offered job
on qualification (2000): 95%
% of assistants (as at
1/9/00) who joined as
trainees: 38%
% of partners (as at 1/9/00)
who joined as trainees:
22%

overseas offices
Brussels

sj berwin & co

222 Gray's Inn Road London WC1X 8HB
Tel: (020) 7533 2222 Fax: (020) 7533 2000
Email: info@sjberwin.com
Website: sjberwin.com

firm profile

Since its formation in 1982, S J Berwin & Co has established a strong reputation in corporate finance. It also has a number of niche specialisms in areas such as film finance and private equity. Much work is international and clients range from major multi-national business corporations and financial institutions to high net worth individuals.

main areas of work

Corporate 50%; Commercial Property 20%; Litigation 17%; EU / competition 10%; Tax 3%

trainee profile

The firm wants ambitious, commercially-minded individuals who seek a high level of involvement from day one. Candidates must be bright and determined to succeed. They should be likely to achieve a 2:1 or first.

training environment

Four seats of six months each will be completed, and the seats are set, ideally, to the needs of the trainee. Two seats will be in the corporate finance arena, which includes Frankfurt and Madrid. The firm has a dedicated training department and weekly training schedules coupled with training designed specifically for trainees allows a good grounding in legal and non-legal skills and knowledge. Language tuition is available to those with a European language.

benefits

PRP, corporate sports membership, free lunch, health insurance

vacation placements

Places for 2001: 60; Duration: 2 weeks; Remuneration: £200 p.w.; Closing Date: 2 March 2001.

sponsorship & awards

CPE and LPC Fees paid and £4,000 maintenance p.a.

Partners	80
Assistant Solicitors	160
Total Trainees	70

contact
Charlotte Bishop

method of application
Letter and CV

selection procedure
Interview (early September)

closing date for 2003
3 August 2001

application
Training contracts p.a. **40**
Applications p.a. **2,000**
% interviewed p.a. **10%**
Required degree grade **2:1**

training
Salary:
1st year(2000) **£25,000**
2nd Year (2000) **£28,000**
Holiday entitlement:
· **50 days over 2 years**
% of trainees with
a non-law degree p.a. **40**
No. of seats available
abroad p.a. **6**

post-qualification
Salary (2000) **£42,000**
% of trainees offered job
on qualification (2000): **90%**
% of assistants (as at
1/9/00) who joined as
trainees: **30%**
% of partners (as at 1/9/00)
who joined as trainees:
16%

overseas offices
Brussels, Frankfurt, Madrid

bevan ashford

35 Colston Avenue Bristol BS1 4TT
Tel: (0117) 918 8992 Fax: (0117) 929 1865
Email: j.brierley@bevanashford.co.uk
Website: www.bevanashford.co.uk

firm profile

Bevan Ashford is one of the largest regional practices in the UK with a network of 7 offices in Bristol, Cardiff, Exeter, London, Plymouth, Taunton and Tiverton. With 74 experienced partners, each of whom is a specialist in their field, and a total staff of over 500, the firm is able to provide clients with an efficient, professional and cost-effective service. Its national reputation means that the firm's client base ranges from multi-national corporations and institutions through to smaller businesses, partnerships and individuals. Its success in attracting and keeping quality clients is achieved by the firm's complete commitment to total client care. By recruiting, training and keeping top quality personnel the firm believes it can continue its culture of client care and offer its clients the individual standards of service they require.

main areas of work

Healthcare 27%; Commercial Property 20%; Commercial Litigation 15%; Company & Commercial 16%; Private Client 17%; Other Work 5%.

trainee profile

Bevan Ashford is only as strong as its people. The firm's success is achieved by attracting and keeping enthusiastic, bright people with sound common sense, plenty of energy and the ability to work and communicate well with others plus a sense of humour! Language and IT skills are also desirable.

training environment

The core of your training will be practical work experience in conjunction with an extensive education programme consisting of talks, lectures and a residential weekend seminar to back-up the practical work. The training is aimed at developing attitudes, skills and legal and commercial knowledge essential for your career success. Your practical work experience will be reviewed on a regular basis by your supervising partner and you will be encouraged to take on as much work, and responsibility, as you wish. The firm is friendly with an open door policy with a wide range of social, sporting and cultural activities plus an active social club.

vacation placements

Places for 2001: 75

sponsorship & awards

Available for LPC only

Partners	74
Assistant Solicitors	126
Total Trainees	40

contact
Jean Brierley

method of application
Application form
and covering letter

closing date for 2003
31 July 2001

application
Training contracts p.a. 20
Required degree grade 2:1

post-qualification
% of trainees offered job
on qualification (2000): 90%

other offices
Bristol, Cardiff, Exeter,
(London), Plymouth,
Taunton, Tiverton.

biddle

1 Gresham St London EC2V 7BU
Tel: (020) 7606 9301 Fax: (020) 7606 3305
Email: gradrecruit@Biddle.co.uk
Website: www.Biddle.co.uk

firm profile

A progressive, medium-sized business law practice based in the City. Clients range from institutional investors, pension funds and international companies, to newspapers, publishers and new technology businesses. They are a member of LOGOS, a group of law firms with offices throughout the European Union.

main areas of work

Corporate/Commercial 33%; Litigation 20%; Pensions 14%; Media & IT 14%; Property 8%; Insolvency 4%; Employment 7%.

trainee profile

The firm values, above all, first-class intelligence, common-sense, willingness to learn and commercial awareness. They are not looking for specific character traits. Their aim is to build a team of varied yet complementary personalities where, for example, the more bookish are balanced by the charismatic. A second language is an asset but not essential.

training environment

On-the-job training is supplemented with in-house seminars and courses. Coaching in IT is also given. Trainees spend three to four six-month placements in varying departments: corporate/commercial, litigation, media and IT, pensions, property, taxation, private client, and employment law. The final seat is likely to be in the area in which you wish to specialise. Trainees sit with partners and progress during each seat is closely monitored by the relevant partner. The company culture is open-door and informal.

benefits

Bonus up to 25% of salary, BUPA, life assurance, season ticket loan.

sponsorship & awards

CPE and LPC fees paid and maintenance grant offered.

Additional Information

The firm's website has a special Graduate Section developed by current trainees. Find it at www.Biddle.co.uk.

Partners	32
Assistant Solicitors	33
Total Trainees	11

contact
Martin Webster

method of application
2 page CV and covering letter

selection procedure
1 interview

closing date for 2003
31 August 2001

application
Training contracts p.a. 4-6
Applications p.a. 1,500
% interviewed p.a. 2.5%
Required degree grade 2:1

training
Salary:
1st year (2000) £22,500
2nd year (2000) £24,000
Holiday entitlement:
4 weeks
% of trainees with
a non-law degree p.a. 50%

post-qualification
Salary (2000) £37,000
% of trainees offered job on qualification (2000): 100%
% of assistants (as at 1/9/00) who joined as trainees: 51%
% of partners (as at 1/9/00) who joined as trainees: 40%

bird & bird

90 Fetter Lane London EC4A 1JP
Tel: (020) 7415 6000 Fax: (020) 7415 6111
Website: www.twobirds.com

firm profile
Bird & Bird is an international commercial law firm with offices in London, Brussels, Paris and Hong Kong. The firm maintains a strong sectoral focus and has an enviable reputation in each of its key practice areas: e-commerce; communications; IT; IP; media; sports; pharmaceuticals and biosciences. Within these sectors, advice is also offered for corporate and commercial law, employment, banking and financial services, litigation and tax.

main areas of work
Company 55%; Intellectual Property 22%; Litigation 14%; Property 8%; Private Client 1%.

trainee profile
The firm looks for high calibre recruits – confident individuals capable of developing expert legal skills and commercial sense.

training environment
Following an introduction course, you will undertake four seats of six months, three of which are spent in company, litigation and property. The choice of final seat is yours. You will share an office with a partner or senior assistant who will guide and advise you. You will hone drafting and legal research skills and gain familiarity with legal procedures. The firm encourages you to make an early contribution to case work and to meet clients immediately. Internal seminars and external lectures are arranged to cover the PSC. Trainees are welcome to join the number of sports teams at the firm and to attend various social events and outings.

benefits
BUPA, season ticket loan, subsidised sports club membership, life cover, PHI.

vacation placements
Places for 2001: 12; Duration: 3 weeks; Remuneration: £180 p.w.; Closing Date: March 2001.

sponsorship & awards
LPC and CPE fees paid and a yearly maintenance grant of £3,500.

Partners 64*
Assistant Solicitors 160*
Total Trainees 21*
* denotes world-wide figures

contact
Lynne Walters

method of application
Application form

selection procedure
Assessment mornings

closing date for 2003
July 2001

application
Training contracts p.a. **12**
Applications p.a. **2,500**
% interviewed p.a. **10%**
Required degree grade **2:1**

training
Salary:
1st year(2000) **£22,500**
2nd year (2000) **£24,000**
Holiday entitlement:
20 days
% of trainees with
a non-law degree p.a.
varies

post-qualification
Salary (2000) **£37,000**
% of trainees offered job
on qualification (2000): **90%**
% of assistants (as at
1/9/00) who joined as
trainees: **20%**
% of partners (as at 1/9/00)
who joined as trainees:
17%

overseas offices
Brussels, Hong Kong,
Paris.

blake lapthorn

Harbour Court Compass Road North Harbour
Portsmouth PO6 4ST
Tel: (023) 92 221122 Fax: (023) 92 221123
Website: www.blakelapthorn.co.uk

firm profile

Founded in 1869 and one of the largest and most progressive regional law firms in the south of England, the firm's main activities are centred in two large purpose built out of town offices on the M27 – one providing commercial and litigation services and the other private client services. In addition there are offices in Southampton and London and all the offices are equipped with state of the art information technology. The size of the firm means that it is able to offer clients the same range and level of service expected from the best London firms. There are 47 partners, many of whom were trainees with the firm and a total staff of over 400.

main areas of work

Company/Commercial 24%; Commercial Property 17%; Litigation 26%; Private Client (PI, Property, Family, Crime, Probate, Finance) 33%.

trainee profile

In addition to excellent academic achievements, the firm values previous experience, which has developed maturity and a wider perspective. Commercial awareness, team-working and well-developed communication skills are also an advantage as well as familiarity with the use of IT.

training environment

Five trainees are recruited each year and have a minimum of four placements lasting three or six months. Trainees' preferences are taken into account as far as possible, but the firm believes in providing well-rounded training supplemented with in-house education and regular appraisals and reviews with the Training Principal. Trainees are also allocated a 'mentor', normally a senior solicitor.

sponsorship & awards

LPC: loan of £4,000 repayable from salary.

Partners	45
Assistant Solicitors	70
Total Trainees	21

contact
Ruth Little
Director of Personnel &
Training

method of application
Firm's Application form
(on website) plus c.v.

selection procedure
Interview with Partners,
including giving a
presentation plus
group exercise.

closing date for 2003
31 July 2001

application
Training contracts p.a. 5
Applications p.a. 750
% interviewed p.a. 8/10%
Required degree grade 2.1

training
Salary:
1st year(2000) £14,000
2nd year(2000) £15,000
Holiday entitlement:
22 days

post-qualification
Salary (2000) £23,500
% of trainees offered job
on qualification (2000):
80%

bond pearce

Ballard House West Hoe Road Plymouth PL1 3AE
Tel: (01752) 266633 Fax: (01752) 225350
Email: tlh@bondpearce.com
Website: www.bondpearce.com

firm profile
Major commercial law firm. With offices in Bristol, Exeter, Plymouth and Southampton they are one of the largest commercial legal practices in southern England.

main areas of work
The size of Bond Pearce and the full range of legal services provided ensures trainee solicitors gain unrivalled experience with training in four separate specialist seats. Specialist groups within Bond Pearce, backed up by effective support services, provide the highest quality of services to a broad range of clients: Commercial Group (Corporate, Banking & Insolvency, Commercial Litigation); Insurance Group; Property Group (Commercial Property, Planning & Environment, Private Client); Personal Injury and Family Group

trainee profile
Successful candidates may come from various backgrounds and enjoy a wide range of interests, but will have in common the desire to excel at their work and get the most out of life. Personal qualities are paramount. The firm looks for bright and enthusiastic individuals who can demonstrate initiative, commercial acumen, team working skills and a sense of humour.

training environment
Trainee solicitors have their own desks in the same office as the partner, associate or senior solicitor with whom they are working. They become an integral part of each team, closely involved in the diversity of their work and whilst fully supervised, trainees are encouraged to take on as much responsibility as possible. Technology plays a vital role in Bond Pearce. Their offices are linked by a networked computer system, the accounts and time recording systems are fully computerised and all staff, including trainee solicitors, are equipped with a fully networked PC on their desks. There are close links between the firm's offices and trainee solicitors join together in all training and many social activities. Bond Pearce has a thriving sports and social club.

vacation placements
Closing Date: Deadline for summer placement scheme 31 March 2001.

sponsorship & awards
LPC financial assistance

Partners	51
Assistant Solicitors	90
Total Trainees	31

contact
Tina Hosken

method of application
Application form,
handwritten letter,
CV and photograph

selection procedure
Interviews and vacation
placement scheme

closing date for 2003
31 July 2001

application
Training contracts p.a.
10-15
Applications p.a. **500**
% interviewed p.a. **10%**

training
Salary:
1st year (2000)
Depending on location
up to £16,250
Holiday entitlement:
20 days
% of trainees with
a non-law degree p.a. **25%**

post-qualification
Salary (2000):
Depending on location
up to £28,000
% of trainees offered job
on qualification (2000): **93%**
% of assistants (as at
1/9/00) who joined as
trainees: **38%**
% of partners (as at 1/9/00)
who joined as trainees:
37%

boyes turner

10 Duke St Reading RG1 4RX
Tel: (0118) 959 7711 Fax: (0118) 957 3257
Email: hbarnett@b-t-b.co.uk
Website: www.btb-solicitors.co.uk

firm profile

Boyes Turner is a leading Thames Valley practice, renowned for its Insolvency and Medical Negligence work and well respected for Corporate and Commercial, Commercial Property, Intellectual Property, Employment, Personal Injury, Family Law and Private Client. While the focus for growth has been commercial work, the firm retains a commitment to acting for individuals and also to civil legal aid.

main areas of work

Company / Commercial (including Employment) 20%; Commercial Property 20%; Medical Negligence / Personal Injury 20%; Litigation 15%; Insolvency 10%; Family 5%; Private Client 10%.

trainee profile

Boyes Turner regards its trainees of today as its assistant solicitors and beyond of tomorrow and expects a high level of commitment, hard work and resourcefulness. Trainees must be responsive to the firm's mission to provide an excellent quality of service to both commercial and individual clients and also contribute to the team-working philosophy.

training environment

The programme is structured so that trainees spend six months in each of four areas: property, litigation, private client and commercial. Work covers both individual and commercial clients, with as much client contact as possible, supervised by a partner or a senior solicitor. The training principal oversees all aspects of the programme, while each trainee is assigned a tutor (one of the partners) who reviews their progress monthly. This is on two levels – first in assessing how the trainee is developing as a lawyer and secondly how the trainee is developing as an individual, including communication and negotiating skills.

benefits

Free medical insurance.

sponsorship & awards

CPE and LPC loan of £3,000 and only one loan per applicant. Interest free and re-paid over training contract.

Partners	**16**
Assistant Solicitors	**15**
Total Trainees	**6**

contact
Helen Barnett

method of application
Letter and CV

selection procedure
2 interviews

closing date for 2003
18 August 2001

application
Training contracts p.a. **3/4**
Applications p.a. **2200**
% interviewed p.a. **1%+**
Required degree grade **2:2**

training
Salary:
1st year (2000) £17,000
2nd year (2000) £18,000
Holiday entitlement:
22 days
% of trainees with
a non-law degree p.a.
Varies

post-qualification
Salary (2000) **£26,000**
% of trainees offered job
on qualification (2000):
100%
% of assistants (as at
1/9/00) who joined as
trainees: **33%**
% of partners (as at 1/9/00)
who joined as trainees:
20%

A-Z SOLICITORS

brachers

Somerfield House 59 London Road Maidstone ME16 8JH
Tel: (01622) 690691 Fax: (01622) 681430
Email: name@brachers.co.uk
Website: www.brachers.co.uk

firm profile

Founded 100 years ago, Brachers is a general regional practice, which has links with Kent's agricultural community. It also has an expanding London office.

main areas of work

General litigation, medical negligence, commercial property, trusts and personal tax, company/commercial, family, employment.

trainee profile

Candidates need to have a strong academic background, common sense and be a team player. Both graduates in law and non-law subjects are considered as well as more mature candidates.

training environment

Trainees have four six-month seats out of company/commercial, property, general civil litigation, defendant insurance, medical negligence, family, employment, and corporate commercial. Two appraisals are carried out, one halfway through and one at the end of each seat. The firm has an open door policy and is committed to developing a long term career structure. Social events are organised.

sponsorship & awards

LPC/CPE £1,000 discretionary award.

Partners	21
Assistant Solicitors	26
Total Trainees	8

contact
Mary Raymont

method of application
Handwritten letter and CV

selection procedure
Interview day with partners

closing date for 2003
31 August 2001

application
Training contracts p.a. **6**
Required degree grade **2:1**

training
Salary:
1st year (2000) £13,500
2nd Year (2000) £14,500
Holiday entitlement:
20 days

post-qualification
Salary (2000) £22,500
% of trainees offered job on qualification (2000): 100%
% of assistants (as at 1/9/00) who joined as trainees: 27%
% of partners (as at 1/9/00) who joined as trainees: 26%

bristows

3 Lincoln's Inn Fields London WC2A 3AA
Tel: (020) 7400 8000 Fax: (020) 7400 8050
Email: info@bristows.com
Website: www.bristows.com

firm profile
Bristows is a leading commercial practice in Central London, pre-eminent in intellectual property law including IT, e-business, brands and biotechnology. It has a substantial practice in company and commercial law and strong complementary practices in commercial litigation, employment, competition, tax, environmental and property law.

main areas of work
Intellectual Property 54%; Company/Corporate Finance/ Commercial/Tax 15%; Computer and IT 16%; Commercial Litigation 10%; Commercial Property 5%.

trainee profile
Bristows recruits graduates of all disciplines. As well as academic ability, they look for practical intelligence, the capacity to communicate well and the ability to assimilate complex materials while still seeing the wood for the trees.

training environment
Trainees receive a high level of individual attention, spending each of their four or five seats with either a partner or senior solicitor. This, plus the opportunity of secondments to multinational clients, gives trainees closer involvement in cases and greater contact with partners and clients alike. Continuous and formal assessment by seat holders, regular review sessions with the training partner and a comprehensive in-house training programme all provide additional support for trainees to develop the skills gained from this excellent hands on experience. Working in small teams, with each team headed by a partner, trainees play an active role from very early on in their training, seeing assignments through from start to finish.

benefits
Excellent career prospects, a competitive package, firm pension scheme, life assurance and health insurance.

vacation placements
Places for 2001: 36; Duration: Summer – 2 weeks, Christmas/Easter – 1 week; Remuneration: £200 p.w.; Closing Date: Christmas – 17/11; Easter/Summer – 28/2.

sponsorship & awards
CPE/LPC fees plus £4,000 maintenance grant for each.

Partners	26
Assistant Solicitors	49
Total Trainees	13

contact
Graduate Recruitment Officer

method of application
Application form

selection procedure
2 individual interviews

closing date for 2003
31 January 2001 for February interviews, 31 August for September interviews

application
Training contracts p.a. **10**
Applications p.a. **2,000**
% interviewed p.a. **6%**
Required degree grade **2.1 (Preferred)**

training
Salary:
1st year (2000) £21,200
2nd year (2000) £23,200
Holiday entitlement:
4 weeks
% of trainees with a non-law degree p.a. **75%**

post-qualification
Salary (2000) **£36,000**
% of trainees offered job on qualification (1999): **72%**
% of assistants (as at 1/9/99) who joined as trainees: **50%**
% of partners (as at 1/9/99) who joined as trainees: **47%**

burges salmon

Narrow Quay House Narrow Quay Bristol BS1 4AH
Tel: (0117) 902 2725 Fax: (0117) 902 4400
Email: lisa.head@burges-salmon.com
Website: www.burges-salmon.com

firm profile

Burges Salmon is one of the largest regional commercial law firms based in Bristol, with all staff located in impressive waterfront offices. Over fifty per cent of the firm's client base is located outside the south west with whom the firm maintains constant contact through hi-tech mobility including web cam links and touch-down facilities across Europe. Additionally, a facility in Holborn Gate was established two years ago to meet the requirements of the firm's London clients.

main areas of work

Providing a diverse range of services, the four core areas include: Company Commercial and Corporate Finance; Litigation; Property and Tax and Trusts. Working for both commercial and private clients, the firm's niche areas include: agribusiness, food, transport, land use and environment, e-commerce, IP and IT, human resources and banking.

trainee profile

Candidates must demonstrate high levels of analytical ability, communication skills, resilience and a clear understanding of client service.

training environment

Attracting and retaining excellent trainee solicitors is central to Burges Salmon's business. The firm's 100% trainee retention rate is attributed in part to its Law Society accredited training programme and its unusual training contract structure. As opposed to a traditional six-month seat system, Burges Salmon operates a four-month system to give trainees maximum exposure to all areas of the firm's work and the opportunity to revisit departments of their choice.

benefits

Annually reviewed competitive salary, bonus and pension.

vacation placements

Places for 2001: 32; Duration: 2 weeks; Remuneration: £125 p.w.; Closing Date: 23 February 2001.

sponsorship & awards

In addition to CPE and LPC tuition fees at the institution of your choice, maintenance grants of £3,500 to LPC students and £4,000 to students studying for both CPE and LPC (£2,000 p.a.) are paid.

Partners	44
Assistant Solicitors	160
Total Trainees	31

contact
Lisa Head
Graduate Recruitment &
Development Manager

method of application
Employer's Application
Form & covering letter

selection procedure
Penultimate year law students, final year non-law students, recent graduates or mature candidates are asked to apply for open days, vacation placements and/or training contracts.

closing date for 2003
10 August 2001

application
Training contracts p.a. 20
Applications p.a. **1,000**
% interviewed p.a. **10%**
Required degree grade **2:1**

training
Salary:
1st year (2000) **£17,500**
2nd Year (2000) **£18,500**
Holiday entitlement:
24 days
% of trainees with
a non-law degree p.a. **50%**

post-qualification
Salary (2000) **£30,000**
% of trainees offered job
on qualification (2000):
100%
% of assistants (as at
1/9/00) who joined as
trainees: **40%**
% of partners (as at 1/9/00)
who joined as trainees:
20%

cadwalader, wickersham & taft

55 Gracechurch Street London EC3V 0EE
Tel: (020) 7456 8573 Fax: (020) 7456 8600
Email: hrdept@cwt-uk.com
Website: www.cadwalader.com

firm profile
Cadwalader, Wickersham & Taft is a major New York based law firm, recognised for its innovative approach to legal and commercial matters. The London office, established in September 1997, is renowned for its expertise in capital markets, financial restructuring, corporate, project finance, litigation, real estate and tax. The office services clients interested in capitalising on the European and worldwide markets, as well as those seeking US-style investment banking services and access to American capital markets.

main areas of work
Capital markets, financial restructuring, project finance, corporate, litigation, real estate and tax.

trainee profile
Candidates need to demonstrate that they are intellectually bright and ambitious, have good communications skills and a commitment to the law. The firm looks for well-rounded individuals with a desire to succeed and a robust and resilient personality.

training environment
Training consists of four six-month seats taking into account trainees' preferences. Responsibility and exposure to client meetings will take place at an early stage. Trainees share an office with a partner or associate, who supervise, review performance and provide feedback on a regular basis. Formal reviews will be carried out every six months. Elements of the PSC will occur at the start of the training contract; the remainder will take place over the following two years. The firm is friendly and supportive with an open door policy, operating a strict "dress down code" all year round. There is also a varied sporting and social calendar.

benefits
Permanent health insurance, season ticket loan, BUPA and life assurance.

vacation placements
Places for 2001: 6; Duration: 4 wks (3 in London and 1 in New York); Remuneration: £225 p.w.; Closing Date: 31 January 2001.

sponsorship & awards
CPE Funding: Fees paid + £4,500 maintenance
LPC Funding: Fees paid + £4,500 maintenance

Partners	6
Assistant Solicitors	21
Total Trainees	2

contact
HR Manager

method of application
CV and covering letter

selection procedure
2 interviews

closing date for 2003
31 August 2001

application
Training contracts p.a. 4
Applications p.a. 500
% interviewed p.a. 2-3%
Required degree grade 2:1

training
Salary:
1st year (2000) £25,000
2nd Year (2000) £28,000
Holiday entitlement:
24 days

post-qualification
Salary (2000) £54,000
% of trainees offered job on qualification (2000):
100%

Overseas Offices
New York, Washington and Charlotte

campbell hooper

35 Old Queen St London SW1H 9JD
Tel: (020) 7222 9070 Fax: (020) 7222 5591
Email: humanresources@campbellhooper.com
Website: www.campbellhooper.com

firm profile
With over 200 years' experience, Campbell Hooper is well equipped to face the requirements of today's ever changing market and adopts a modern and dynamic management style with high investment in IT and training and development. The firm's clients are involved in a variety of industries including information technology, telecoms, banking, advertising, construction, property investment and development, media, manufacturing, a number of service industries and local government and government departments. Membership of Proteus, a European network of independent law firms, provides an invaluable international aspect to the firm.

main areas of work
High standards of client service are delivered through four departments: company/commercial; commercial property; commercial litigation and private client. The principal areas of work are charities; company; construction; defamation; domestic conveyancing; employment; environmental; european; family; immigration; insurance; litigation; media; planning; property; rating; tax; trust and estate planning and wills and probate.

trainee profile
Applications are welcomed from those with a keen commercial focus complimented by a solid academic history. Motivation, enthusiasm and professional commitment are equally important.

training environment
You will develop your commercial acumen and legal flair through exposure in each of the four departments. Equal emphasis is placed on providing you with both professional and personal career support. This is facilitated through day to day coaching from either a partner or solicitor, constructive feedback on performance through mid and end of seat reviews and mentoring from the trainee partner who will take a personal interest in your professional development. In addition the firm is committed to continuous development and you will be encouraged to attend client seminars, be actively involved in practice development initiatives as well as participating in other training and development activities including the compulsory professional skills course.

benefits
Season ticket loan.

Partners	14
Assistant Solicitors	16
Total Trainees	4

contact
Vikki Weller Human Resources Manager

method of application
CV with covering letter. Brochures available on request.

closing date for 2003
31 July 2001

application
Training contracts p.a. 2-3
Applications p.a. 500
% interviewed p.a. 4%
Required degree grade
2:1 any discipline

training
Salary:
1st year (2000) £20,000
2nd Year (2000) £22,500
Holiday entitlement:
20 days

capsticks

77-83 Upper Richmond Road London SW15 2TT
Tel: (020) 8780 2211 Fax: (020) 8780 4811
Email: career@capsticks.co.uk
Website: www.capsticks.com

firm profile
One of the leading legal advisers to the National Health Service, the firm handles litigation, administrative law, commercial and property work for NHS Trusts and health authorities, as well as other public sector bodies, charities and regulatory bodies.

main areas of work
Clinical Law 54%; Commercial 6%; Commercial Property 15%; Dispute Resolution 7%; Employment Law 18%.

trainee profile
Successful candidates possess intellectual agility, good interpersonal skills and are capable of taking initiative.

training environment
Four six-month seats, which may include clinical negligence/personal injury; commercial property; contract and commercial; employment law and commercial/property litigation. Trainees take responsibility for their own caseload and are involved in client meetings from an early stage. There are also opportunities to contribute to the firm's marketing and management processes. There are numerous in-house lectures for all fee earners. There is an open door policy, and trainees receive informal feedback and supervision as well as regular appraisals. Despite the firm's rapid expansion, it has retained a friendly atmosphere and a relaxed working environment. There are numerous informal social and sporting activities.

benefits
Bonus scheme, PHI, death in service cover, interest-free season ticket loan.

vacation placements
Places for 2001: yes; Duration: 2 weeks; Closing Date: 28 February 2001.

sponsorship & awards
Scholarship contributions to CPE and LPC courses.

Partners	24
Assistant Solicitors	30
Total Trainees	12

contact
Sue Laundy

method of application
Application form and CV

selection procedure
Candidates are encouraged to participate in the firm's summer placement scheme. Final selection is by interview with the Training Principal and other partners.

closing date for 2003
31 July 2001

application
Training contracts p.a. **6–8**
Applications p.a. **1000+**
% interviewed p.a. **5%**
Required degree grade
2:1 or above

training
Salary:
1st year (2000) c. £22,000
2nd year(2000) c. £24,000
Holiday entitlement:
22 days p.a.
(increased by 1 day p.a.
to max 25 days)
% of trainees with
a non-law degree p.a. **40%**

post-qualification
Salary (2000):
£33,000 + bonus scheme
% of trainees offered job
on qualification (2000): **60%**
% of assistants (as at
1/9/00) who joined as
trainees: **20%**
% of partners (as at 1/9/00)
who joined as trainees: **8%**

charles russell

8–10 New Fetter Lane London EC4A 1RS
Tel: (020) 7203 5000 Fax: (020) 7203 5307
Graduate Recruitment Line: (020) 7203 5353
Website: www.cr-law.com

firm profile

Charles Russell is a progressive City law firm with regional offices in Cheltenham and Guildford and a network of close professional contacts throughout the world. A rapidly growing law firm, it offers a wide range of legal services for both corporate and private clients. The firm recruits a small number of trainees for a firm of its size as it believes it enables them to provide the best possible training. The firm is committed to its clients and their demands. It also respects the fact that its staff need to have a life of their own.

main areas of work

Whilst the commercial division offers the opportunity for involvement in major corporate transactions, the firm's commitment to private clients and charities remains unshaken. Charles Russell is particularly well known for media and communications, commercial property, company/commercial, charities, insurance and reinsurance and offers clients specialist expertise in employment and pensions, corporate finance, tax, intellectual property, family, computer law, sports regulation, planning and environmental law.

trainee profile

Trainees should be balanced, rounded achievers with a solid academic background. Outside interests are fundamental.

training environment

Trainees spend six months in four of the following training seats – litigation, company/commercial, property, private client, family, employment and intellectual property. Wherever possible the firm will accommodate an individual preference. You will be seated with a partner/senior solicitor. Regular appraisals are held to discuss progress and direction. Trainees are encouraged to attend the extensive in-house training courses. The PSC is taught both internally and externally. All trainees are expected to take on as much responsibility as possible. A social committee organises a range of activities from quiz nights through to sporting events.

benefits

BUPA immediately, PHI and Life Assurance after six months service, 25 days holiday.

sponsorship & awards

CPE and LPC fees paid and annual maintenance of £4,000.

Partners	72
Assistant Solicitors	127
Total Trainees	22

contact
Eileen Moran
Graduate Recruitment
Line: 020 7203 5353

method of application
Hand written letter and
application form

selection procedure
Assessment days to
include an interview and
other exercises, designed
to assess identified
performance criteria

closing date for 2003
31 July 2001

application
Training contracts p.a.
10–12
Applications p.a. 2,000
% interviewed p.a. 3%
Required degree grade 2:1

training
Salary:
1st year (2000) £23,000
2nd year (2000) £24,500
Holiday entitlement:
25 days

post-qualification
Salary (2000) £39,000

regional offices
Also offer training contracts
in its Cheltenham and
Guildford offices.
Applications are dealt with
by the London Office.

clarks

Great Western House Station Rd Reading RG1 1JX
Tel: (0118) 958 5321 Fax: (0118) 960 4611
Email: inmail@clarks-solicitors.co.uk
Website: www.clarks-solicitors.co.uk

firm profile

Founded in 1913, Clarks is a commercial law firm with a proven track record across the UK and overseas (with 17 partners and 5 associates). Clients range from small to medium sized enterprises to multi-national companies. Clarks is particularly recognised for the number of international FTSE 250 clients who have chosen to use its services. Based in Reading, Clarks has taken full advantage of the rapid commercial and professional expansion of this thriving 'capital' of the Thames Valley.

main areas of work

Commercial Property; Corporate; Litigation; Employment; Planning; IP/IT; Insolvency; Private Client.

trainee profile

Candidates must have a good academic record and should have good interpersonal skills. Language skills are an advantage.

training environment

On joining Clarks, trainees will receive a full induction programme. Trainees immediately become part of a team and are encouraged to have direct involvement with clients and to play a part in building long term relationships with them. Training usually consists of seats of 6 months in four of the following teams: Property, Corporate, Litigation, Employment and IP/IT. Within each seat you will have a mentor (a partner or an associate) who will have responsibility for guiding and encouraging you through that seat. In addition to training within a workgroup you are also encouraged to attend our in-house weekly seminars. Clarks also supports you in your professional skills courses. Clarks is a classic yet innovative firm with an open, friendly culture. It retains a high number of trainees upon qualification and a significant number have progressed through the firm to become associates or partners.

benefits

Pension, free conveyancing.

vacation placements

Places for 2001: On application.

Partners 17
Assistant Solicitors 37
Total Trainees 10

contact
Sarah Moore HR Manager

method of application
Application form (from brochure or website)

selection procedure
Open day/interview plus second interview (with limited written tests).

closing date for 2003
no closing date

application
Training contracts p.a. 5-6
Applications p.a. 5-600
% interviewed p.a. 10%
Required degree grade usually 2:1 or above (but will consider lower grade subject to explanation)

training
Salary:
1st year (2000) £15,500
2nd Year (2000) £17,000
Holiday entitlement:
20 days

post-qualification
% of trainees offered job on qualification (2000): 90%
% of assistants (as at 1/9/00) who joined as trainees: 35%
% of partners (as at 1/9/00) who joined as trainees: 40%

overseas offices
Affiliated to TagLaw worldwide - ability to second to foreign office possible, subject to appropriate language skills.

cleary, gottlieb, steen & hamilton

City Place House 55 Basinghall Street London EC2V 5EH
Tel: (020) 7614 2200 Fax: (020) 7600 1698
Website: www.cgsh.com

firm profile

Founded in the United States in 1946, from its inception the firm has maintained a strong international presence. It now has over 780 lawyers in 10 offices worldwide with more than 250 lawyers in Europe with offices in Paris (opened 1949), Brussels (1961),Frankfurt (1991) and Rome (1998) in addition to London (1971). It is common for lawyers to spend time in offices other than their home office.

main areas of work

Mergers and acquisitions (takeovers, cross-border mergers, joint-ventures), securities (equity offerings, debt offerings, bond issues, privatisations, global offerings, private placements), banking and finance, tax, EU and competition law.

trainee profile

Candidates must have an excellent academic background including at least a 2.1 law degree from a top U.K. university and have an open and outgoing personality. They must have a flexible approach to work, I.T. and language skills are an advantage.

training environment

There are no departments. Trainees sit with partners and senior solicitors and will do a mix of M&A, capital markets, tax and regulatory work. Seats change every six months. One seat will be in Brussels and there will be opportunities to travel and work in other offices. Ongoing legal training is provided by regular training talks covering all areas of law practiced at the firm. I.T. training is also provided. Trainees will be required to take the New York bar exam. Assistance will be given with this. Trainees will work on a wide range of matters many governed by Laws other than English Law. Trainees will in most respects be fulfiling the same roles as first year lawyers do in our other offices.

benefits

Pension, health insurance, long-term disability insurance, health club, employee assistance programme.

sponsorship & awards

LPC funding; Fees paid plus £4,500 maintenance award.

Partners	10
Assistants	36
Total Trainees	4

contact
Penny Cave

method of application
Letter and C.V.

selection procedure
2 interviews

closing date for 2003
30 Sept 2001

application
Training contracts p.a.
up to 4
Required degree grade 2.1

training
Salary:
1st year (2000) £33,000
2nd year (2000) £39,000
Holiday entitlement:
20 days

post-qualification
Salary varies from office
to office

overseas offices
Brussels, Frankfurt, Hong Kong, Moscow, New York, Paris, Rome, Tokyo, Washington DC.

clifford chance

200 Aldersgate Street London EC1A 4JJ
Tel: (020) 7600 1000 Fax: (020) 7600 5555
Email: graduate.recruitment@cliffordchance.com
Website: www.cliffordchance.com

firm profile
Clifford Chance is one of the largest law firms in the world with 29 offices throughout Europe, Asia and America. It delivers legal services to powerful and influential businesses and financial institutions around the globe, working across international borders to shape the deals that make the news. As a trainee this means you will gain breadth and depth in your experiences.

main areas of work
Banking & Finance; Capital Markets; Corporate; Litigation & Dispute Resolution; Real Estate; Tax, Pensions & Employment.

trainee profile
Consistently strong academic profile (minimum 2:1 degree), a broad range of interpersonal skills and extra-curricular activities and interests.

training environment
The Clifford Chance Training Contract has been devised to provide you with the technical skills and experience you need to contribute to the firm's success on a day-to-day basis, to achieve your professional qualification and to progress to a rewarding career. Your two year training contract consists of four six-month seats. About 75% of trainees will spend a seat on a secondment at an international office or with a client. In each seat you will be working alongside senior lawyers. Trainees are encouraged to use initiative to make the most of expertise and resources available to the firm. Three monthly appraisals and monitoring in each seat ensures trainees gain a range of work and experience.

benefits
Prize for first class degrees and distinction in LPC, interest free loan, private health insurance, subsidised restaurant, fitness centre, life assurance, occupational health service, and permanent health assurance.

vacation placements
Places for 2001: Easter and summer break. Visits to City institutions are organised and there is a strong social element to the programme; Duration: 2 weeks; Remuneration: £240 pw; Closing Date: 9 February 2001.

sponsorship & awards
CPE and LPC fees paid and £5,000 maintenance p.a. (£4,500 outside London, Guildford and Nottingham).

Partners 453
Assistant Solicitors 2082
Total Trainees 327

contact
Katrina Thomas
Graduate Recruitment

method of application
Application form

selection procedure
Assessment day comprising an interview with a partner and senior solicitor, a group exercise and a verbal reasoning test

application
Training contracts p.a. 130
Applications p.a. 2,000
% interviewed p.a. 30%
Required degree grade 2:1

training
Salary:
1st year (2000) £25,000
2nd Year (2000) £28,000
Holiday entitlement:
25 days
% of trainees with a non-law degree p.a. 35%
No. of seats available abroad p.a. 98

post-qualification
Salary (2000) £42,000
% of trainees offered job on qualification (2000): 97%

overseas offices
Amsterdam, Bangkok, Barcelona, Beijing, Berlin, Brussels, Budapest, Dubai, Dusseldorf, Frankfurt, Hong Kong, Leipzig, Luxembourg, Madrid, Milan, Moscow, Munich, New York, Padua, Paris, Prague, Rome, Sao Paulo, Shanghai, Singapore, Tokyo, Warsaw, Washington DC.

A-Z SOLICITORS

clyde & co

51 Eastcheap London EC3M 1JP
Tel: (020) 7648 1580 Fax: (020) 7623 5427
Email: careers@clyde.co.uk
Website: www.clydeco.com

firm profile

A major international commercial firm with over 700 personnel world-wide and a client base spanning more than 100 countries. It is a leading practice in international trade, insurance, reinsurance, shipping and energy, and has experienced a high level of growth in corporate and finance. UK offices are in London, Guildford and Cardiff, with trainee solicitors recruited for London and Guildford.

main areas of work

Insurance/Reinsurance 26%; Banking, Corporate Commercial and Tax 26%; Marine and Transport 21%; Other Commercial Litigation 10%; Property 7%; Employment 3%.

trainee profile

The firm has no stereotypical trainee. Non-law graduates are welcome, especially those with modern languages or science degrees. The firm places as much importance on finding candidates with an outgoing, interesting personality as it does on academic credentials.

training environment

Trainees become immediate 'casehandlers' and usually have their own office. They are encouraged to take on as much responsibility and client contact as possible, and are involved in developing business relationships. The PSC is run in-house and there is a full programme of lectures, seminars, courses, workshops and educational visits.

benefits

Subsidised sports club, interest free ticket loan, staff restaurant and weekly free bar (London); monthly staff lunch and monthly free bar (Guildford).

Legal Work Experience

Further information upon request. Closing Date: 28 February 2001. Please telephone for details.

sponsorship & awards

CPE and LPC Fees paid and maintenance grant. Sponsorship provided where no LEA funding available.

Partners	104
Assistant Solicitors	120
Total Trainees	37

contact
Georgia de Saram
Graduate Recruitment and
Development Officer

method of application
Application form
and covering letter

selection procedure
Individual interview with
Georgia de Saram,
followed by interview with
two partners

closing date for 2003
31 August 2001

application
Training contracts p.a. 20
Applications p.a. 2,000
% interviewed p.a. varies
Required degree grade 2:1

training
Salary:
1st year (2000) £22,000
2nd year (2000) £24,000
Holiday entitlement:
22 days
% of trainees with
a non-law degree p.a.
varies
No. of seats available
abroad p.a. varies

post-qualification
Salary (2000) £36,000
% of trainees offered job
on qualification (2000): 82%

overseas offices
Caracas, Dubai, Hong
Kong, Paris, Piraeus,
Singapore,
Associate office –
St Petersburg.

cms cameron mckenna

Mitre House 160 Aldersgate Street London EC1A 4DD
Tel: (020) 7367 3000 Fax: (020) 7367 2000
Email: cameronmckenna@bnbi.com
Website: www.cmck.com/gradrec

firm profile

CMS Cameron McKenna is a major full service UK and international commercial firm advising businesses and governments on transactions and projects particularly in the UK, continental Europe, the Asia Pacific region, North America and Southern Africa. They have particular strengths in a number of industry sectors such as banking and finance, corporate, construction, projects, energy, healthcare, bioscience, insurance and property. The firm is modern, entrepreneurial and innovative and are strong on achievement. (They believe the key to success is clear communication and entrepreneurial flair).

main areas of work

Banking; Corporate; Insurance; Energy; Projects & Construction; Property; Commercial.

trainee profile

The firm looks for high-achieving team players with good communication, analytical and organisational skills. You will need to show initiative and be able to accept personal responsibility, not only for your own work, but also for your career development. You will need to be resilient and focused on achieving results.

training environment

The firm is friendly and supportive and puts no limits on a trainee's progress. It offers four six month seats, three of which will be in the firm's main area of practice. In addition you may gain experience of a specialist area or opt for a secondment to national or international clients. In each seat you will be allocated high quality work on substantial transactions for a range of government and blue-chip clients. Regular appraisals will be held with your seat supervisor to assess your progress, skills and development needs. The three compulsory modules of the PSC will be completed before joining, allowing trainees to become effective and participate on a practical level as soon as possible. The Professional Skills Course is complemented by a comprehensive in-house training programme that continues up to qualification and beyond.

vacation placements

Places for 2001: 55; Duration: 2 weeks; Remuneration: £200 p.w.; Closing Date: 28 February 2001.

sponsorship & awards

CPE and LPC Funding: Fees paid and a maintenance grant of £4,500 (London and Guildford), £4,000 (elsewhere)

Partners	157
Assistant Solicitors	434
Total Trainees	90

contact
Graduate Recruitment
Team 0845 3000 491

method of application
Employer's application form.

selection procedure
Two-stage selection procedure. Initial interview followed by assessment centre.

closing date for 2003
By September 2001

application
Training contracts p.a. **80**
Applications p.a. **1,500**
% interviewed p.a. **27%**
Required degree grade **2:1**

training
Salary:
1st year (2000) **£25,000**
2nd Year (2000) **£28,000**
Holiday entitlement:
25 days
% of trainees with
a non-law degree p.a. **40%**
No. of seats available
abroad p.a. **(currently) 12**

post-qualification
Salary (2000) **£42,000**
% of trainees offered job
on qualification (2000): **90%**

cms cameron mckenna continued

Additional Information

Every trainee has a PC on their desk with email connection and access to legal and business databases. The firm financially supports trainees who wish to learn or improve a foreign language. There will be the opportunity to become involved in a number of sporting and social events.

trainee comments

"I spent half of my second seat in Almaty, the capital of Kazakhstan, working with 30 others to establish companies to develop the country's oil, gas and gold reserves. In a previous seat, I had to complete and hand over title on a £10 million deal myself. It was an incredible amount of responsibility and a valuable experience." (Simon Mead, trainee solicitor).

"Compared to other firms where I have friends it's very friendly and unstuffy here. It has retained the smaller firm environment even though we're now a top ten firm. Some firms pay lip service to the 'open door' idea but it really happens here. My best moment so far was helping the team who pitched against four of the top ten City firms for one of two places to do work for the Post Office - and we were appointed." (Jamie Butler, trainee solicitor).

"The most rewarding thing about the international opportunities here, whether it's before or after qualification, is the sheer scope the firm can offer you. There is no doubt that an international perspective is a massive selling point for law firms. Clients don't want to be dealing with one firm in London and any number of others overseas. And that's great news when you're a trainee because you have more chance to travel during your training contract, and then after qualification. My overseas experience was an invaluable part of my contract. I completed a seat in Hong Kong in our Corporate Recovery Group and worked in Orissa, India on the restructuring of the electricity industry. I doubt I'd get those kind of opportunities elsewhere". (Gill Meller, assistant solicitor).

branch offices
Aberdeen, Almaty, Amsterdam. Arnhem, Beijing, Berlin, Bristol, Brussels, Bucharest, Budapest, Capetown, Chemnitz, Dresden, Dusseldorf, Frankfurt, Hamburg, Hilversum, Hong Kong, Johannesburg, Kazakhstan, Leipzig, Moscow, Munich, Prague, Russia, Singapore, Slovakia, Stockholm, Stuttgart, Tashkent, Toronto, Utrecht, Uzbekistan, Vienna, Warsaw, Washington DC, Zurich.

cameron mckenna

cobbetts

Ship Canal House King Street Manchester M2 4WB
Tel: (0161) 833 3333 Fax: (0161) 833 3030
Email: lawyers@cobbetts.co.uk
Website: www.cobbetts.co.uk

firm profile

Cobbetts is one of Manchester's most long-established firms with a staff of 260 including 41 partners. The firm has successfully managed to remain at the forefront of commercial law practice without sacrificing the professionalism by which it earned its reputation. The recent dual accreditation of Investors In People and Lexcel provide national recognition of the firm's outstanding commitment to quality.

main areas of work

The firm is divided into two main divisions. The corporate division deals with the following areas of work: corporate; commercial; intellectual property; IT; banking and private client. The commercial property division is one of the largest under one roof in the North and includes specialist expertise in environmental law, planning, licensing, property litigation, Housing Associations, and construction. Cobbett's client base includes both PLCs and owner-managed businesses, banks and financial institutions, public-sector organisations, property companies and retail and licensed operators.

trainee profile

Law and non-law graduates.

training environment

Four 6 month seats are available. Typically, these include one property, one litigation and one commercial/corporate seat. There is an opportunity for one trainee each year to spend 3 months in Brussels.

benefits

Social Club and LA Fitness Pool and gym.

vacation placements

Places for 2001: A small number of placements are available during July and August.

sponsorship & awards

CPE and LPC grant available.

trainee comments

"A challenging environment......."
"The training offered is hands on.............the firm is renowned for being a friendly place to work, a reputation that is justly and richly deserved."

Partners	41
Assistant Solicitors	70
Total Trainees	22

contact
Simon Jones
Trainee Partner

method of application
Application form (available on request)

selection procedure
Half day assessments

closing date for 2003
31 July 2001

application
Training contracts p.a. 8
Applications p.a. 700
% interviewed p.a. 10%
Required degree grade 2:1

training
Salary:
1st year (2000) £16,250
2nd Year (2000) Reviewed each year
Holiday entitlement:
20 days
% of trainees with a non-law degree p.a. 30%
No. of seats available abroad p.a. 1

post-qualification
% of trainees offered job on qualification (2000): 100%
% of assistants (as at 1/9/00) who joined as trainees: 75%
% of partners (as at 1/9/00) who joined as trainees: 60%

overseas offices
Brussels

coudert brothers

60 Cannon Street London EC4N 6JP
Tel: (020) 7248 3000 Fax: (020) 7248 3001
Email: info@london.coudert.com
Website: www.coudert.com

firm profile

Founded in 1853, Coudert Brothers is a global partnership with 27 offices in 14 countries worldwide. In London the firm was one of the first English multi-national partnerships of English solicitors and registered foreign lawyers. The firm advises on all aspects of national and international business law.

trainee profile

The quality and complexity of legal work undertaken by the firm demands that it recruits only individuals of the highest calibre. It is essential that trainees are enthusiastic, confident and outward going individuals, able to perform in a fast-moving and challenging environment. Early responsibility is routine and broadbased experience guaranteed. Coudert Brothers accepts law and non-law graduates. Applicants should have at least three A-level passes at Grades A and B and a 2:1 degree. In view of the international nature of the firm's work and clients, language skills are an advantage, but not essential.

training environment

The training at Coudert Brothers comprises four six-month placements. Three of these will be with the firm's core practices: corporate and commercial, banking and finance, litigation, and property. The fourth will be drawn from one of the firm's other disciplines: energy and utilities, telecom-munications, tax and funds and competition law. There is an opportunity for a secondment to one of our foreign offices. Partners and senior assistants ensure that trainees gain practical experience in research, drafting, procedural and client-related skills by working closely with them during each placement. There are regular appraisals during the two year training contract. Legal and professional training is provided through an in-house training programme and external conferences.

benefits

Pension, health insurance, subsidised gym membership, season ticket loan.

sponsorship & awards

CPE Funding: Fees paid + £4,000 p.a. maintenance
LPC Funding: Fees paid + £4,000 p.a. maintenance

Partners	11
Assistant Solicitors	19
Total Trainees	8

contact
Christine de Ferrars Green
Graduate Recruitment
Partner

method of application
Letter and CV

selection procedure
2 interviews with partners

closing date for 2003
15 August 2001

application
Training contracts p.a. 4
Required degree grade 2:1

training
Salary:
1st year (2000) £25,000
2nd year (2000) £28,000
Holiday entitlement:
20 days

post-qualification
Prospects are good as the firm only takes a small number of trainees each year

overseas offices
Almaty, Antwerp, Bangkok, Beijing, Berlin, Brussels, Denver, Frankfurt, Ghent, Hong Kong, Jakarta, Los Angeles, Milan, Munich, Montréal, Moscow, New York, Palo Alto, Paris, San Francisco, San José, Singapore, St Petersburg, Sydney, Tokyo, Washington DC.

associated offices:
Budapest, Prague, Stockholm and Mexico City.

cripps harries hall

Windsor House 6-10 Mount Ephraim Road Tunbridge Wells, Kent TN1 1EE
Tel: (01892) 515121 Fax: (01892) 506069
Email: aol@crippslaw.com
Website: www.e-cripps.co.uk

firm profile

Established almost 150 years ago, Cripps Harries Hall has progressed steadily towards being regarded as the leading law firm in the South East outside London. It is an innovative and young firm; most of the partners are in their thirties or forties and the atmosphere is friendly and outgoing. The firm achieved the Lexcel quality mark in January 1999, the first 'Top 100' firm to do so. In addition to its headquarters in Tunbridge Wells, there are offices in London and Crowborough, East Sussex.

main areas of work

Commercial Litigation: 25% Corporate & Commercial Property: 23%; Finance and Investment Services: 23% Private Client: 14% Residential conveyancing and agriculture: 9%; General Litigation: 6%.

trainee profile

Cripps Harries Hall is looking for talented, confident, capable people who want to make a contribution during their period of training and who will want to stay with us as assistant solicitors and potential partners. You will be expected to integrate expert legal advice with a highly developed use of information technology.

training environment

The two year training contract is divided into six periods, spent in different departments where you receive a thorough grounding in the relevant practice and have frequent one-to-one reviews of your progress. You will usually share a room with a partner, and work as an integral member of a small team. The Director of Education will arrange your continuing education to include seminars, courses and training in business, presentation, IT and marketing skills.

benefits

PPP, DIS, PHI, Pension.

sponsorship & awards

Discretionary LPC Funding: Fees - 50% interest free loan, 50% bursary.

Partners	32
Assistant Solicitors	44
Total Trainees	14

contact
Annabelle Lawrence,
Personnel Manager

method of application
Handwritten letter and
firm's application form
available on website.

selection procedure
1 interview with Managing
Partner and Personnel
Manager

closing date for 2003
31 July 2001

application
Training contracts p.a. 8
Applications p.a. Up to
1,000
% interviewed p.a. 5%
Required degree grade 2.1

training
Salary:
1st year (2000) £14,500
2nd Year(2000) £16,000
Holiday entitlement:
25 days
% of trainees with
a non-law degree p.a. 25%

post-qualification
Salary (2000) £25,000
% of trainees offered job
on qualification (2000):
100%
% of assistants (as at
1/9/00) who joined as
trainees: 42%
% of partners (as at 1/9/00)
who joined as trainees:
30%

associated firms
A network of independent
law firms in 18 European
countries.

cumberland ellis peirs

Columbia House 69 Aldwych London WC2B 4RW
Tel: (020) 7242 0422 Fax: (020) 7831 9081
Email: nicolawaldman@cep-law.co.uk
Website: www.cep-law.co.uk

firm profile

A Central London firm of solicitors with a varied practice. The firm has a broad base of commercial and institutional clients including those involved in the media and information technology, quasi government councils, sporting associations, charities, City Livery companies, housing associations and landed estates, as well as having an established reputation for its private client services.

main areas of work

Company/Commercial; Commercial Property; Litigation; Private Client and Financial Services.

trainee profile

Law and non-law graduates who have a consistently strong academic record. Individuals who can work with and relate well to others; who are commercially aware, with an ability to think creatively and to make a contribution to the firm. The firm is looking for candidates who have presence and enthusiasm, who are outgoing and articulate and who have a broad range of outside interests. IT skills are important.

training environment

Trainees spend six months in each of the Company Commercial, Litigation, Private Client and Property departments under the supervision of a Partner or Senior Assistant. Trainees are fully involved in all aspects of the work of the department. Client contact and early responsibility for handling your own caseload are encouraged, subject to necessary guidance and supervision. There are a number of social, sporting and marketing activities going on during the course of the year and life outside the office is encouraged. An open door policy applies and the firm has a friendly and informal environment. Where possible the firm aims to recruit its trainees at the end of the training contract. The PSC is taught externally at the College of Law.

benefits

Season ticket loan, luncheon vouchers.

sponsorship & awards

It is not the firm's policy to offer vacation placements or sponsorship.

Partners	12
Assistant Solicitors	8
Total Trainees	3

contact
Nicola Waldman

method of application
Handwritten letter and covering CV (adding reference to 'Chambers')

selection procedure
Two interviews with partners

closing date for 2003
To be submitted between 1 July and 30 September 2001

application
Training contracts p.a.
1 or 2
Applications p.a. 600
% interviewed p.a. 3%
Required degree grade 2:1

training
Holiday entitlement:
20 days

davies arnold cooper

6–8 Bouverie Street London EC4Y 8DD
Tel: (020) 7936 2222 Fax: (020) 7936 2020
Email: daclon@dac.co.uk
Website: www.dac.co.uk

Partners	46
Total Fee-earners	176
Total Trainees	28
Total Staff	357

contact
Graduate Recruitment

method of application
DAC application form

selection procedure
Open day and individual interviews

closing date for 2003
31 July 2001

required degree grade
2:1 capability

firm profile

Davies Arnold Cooper are a leading practice in Dispute Resolution (including all forms of litigation, arbitration and alternative dispute resolution), Corporate Risk and Commercial Property Services. They look for the issues of the future and have recently been at the forefront of issues such as Trans-national Litigation, Rehabilitation, Human Rights, E-Risks, Occupational Health and Employee issues, Reputation Management, Corporate Accountability and Health and Safety. They have taken a lead in their firm wide usage of ADR and technological advances such as paperless litigation. They remain the number one choice for multi-party actions arising in the UK and internationally relating to product liability or physical disasters and accidents. Examples of high profile litigation include actions arising out of the collapse of the Maxwell empire, Barings, Polly Peck, Banesto, Piper Alpha, Haemophilia and Heathrow Tunnel collapse.

main areas of work

Insurance, financial services, construction, commercial property, pharmaceutical, healthcare, manufacturing and retailing.

trainee profile

Davies Arnold Cooper look for people who can demonstrate a strong intellect combined with analytical and problem solving skills. Well organised, flexible and self motivated you must be a strong communicator and able to work effectively with a variety of different people. You will thrive in a fast moving, commercial environment with plenty of opportunity for early responsibility. The firm welcomes applications from all age groups and backgrounds, from people who want to make a positive difference.

training environment

One of the only two law firms listed in the 'Britain's Best Employers' Directory. Their induction and training schemes are widely admired and trainees receive a comprehensive grounding in core legal skills. As a medium-sized firm they offer a flexible training programme with the opportunity for early responsibility within a supportive environment. They offer a career not just a training contract and they see their trainees as the future of their business.

sponsorship & awards

CPE and LPC: grants covering course and examination fees. Discretionary interest-free loans for maintenance are available.

davies wallis foyster

37 Peter Street Manchester M2 5GB
Tel: (0161) 228 3702 Fax: (0161) 835 2407
5 Castle Street Liverpool L2 4XE
Tel: (0151) 236 6226 Fax: (0151) 236 3088
Email: trainees@dwf-law.com
Website: www.dwf.law.co.uk

firm profile

Davies Wallis Foyster is one of the leading law firms in the North West, providing a full range of services for corporate and commercial clients and insurance clients. Over the years, the firm has recruited market leaders in all its service areas and has built substantial, multi-skilled teams around them. It is, therefore, capable of delivering a menu of world-class services to help clients achieve a competitive edge. The firm has a reputation for the quality, style and energy of its people and its willingness to provide client references. DWF is a member of EU-LEX, a network of international law firms handling cross-border work.

main areas of work

Services for corporate and commercial clients 65%; Services for insurance clients 35%.

trainee profile

DWF wants trainees to play a part in building on its success. The firm is looking for trainees who enjoy working as part of a busy team, who respond positively to a challenge and think they have what it takes to deliver results for clients. The firm is looking for its partners of the future.

training environment

All trainees commence life at DWF with a welcome programme designed to provide a clear picture of the firm and its services before moving to their first seat. The firm provides a flexible seat rotation including corporate, property, commercial litigation and insurance with agreed options which focus on post-qualification aspirations. This is supplemented by general training as well as specific training relevant to the particular seat which may be run in-house or using external courses. Appraisals are carried out during each seat to review progress and development. Trainees will have the opportunity to join in the busy social life within the office and with local trainee solicitors' groups.

benefits

Life Assurance. Pension Scheme to be introduced.

vacation placements

Places for 2001: Open day events at each office.

sponsorship & awards

LPC funding.

Partners	44
Assistant Solicitors	50
Total Trainees	11

contact
Mrs Lynn Davies
Training Administrator
(Manchester address)

method of application
Handwritten letter and C.V.
or DWF application form

selection procedure
Two stage
interview/selection process

closing date for 2003
31 July 2001

application
Training contracts p.a.
at least 6
Applications p.a. c.1000
% interviewed p.a. 5%
Required degree grade:
2:1 in any subject
preferred

training
Salary:
1st year (2000) £16,000
Holiday entitlement:
23 days p.a. minimum

post-qualification
% of trainees offered job
on qualification (2000):
100%

dechert

2 Serjeants' Inn London EC4Y 1LT
Tel: (020) 7583 5353 Fax: (020) 7775 7322
Email: info@dechertEU.com
Website: www.titmuss-sainer-dechert.com

firm profile

Following a six year alliance Titmuss Sainer Dechert and US law firm Dechert Price & Rhoads merged on 1 July 2000 to form a new law firm, Dechert. The London office is organised into three core areas: Business Law, Litigation and Property. Within these departments there are specialist lawyers in areas such as Banking and Insolvency, Commercial, Customs and Excise, Defamation, Employment, Financial Services, Insurance, Intellectual Property, Investigations, Securitisation, Tax and Trademarks. The London Office has a total complement of 370 lawyers and supporting staff. In total, the firm has in the region of 600 lawyers in its ten offices throughout Europe and the US. The offices are: Boston; Brussels; Harrisburg; Hartford; London; New York; Paris; Philadelphia; Princeton and Washington.

main areas of work – London

Commercial (including Trademarks) 5%, Corporate 23%, Employment 4%, Financial Services 13%, Litigation 18%, Property 34% and Tax & Private Client 3%.

trainee profile

Candidates should be able to empathise with a wide range of people, as their clients come from all walks of life. Dechert looks for enthusiasm, intelligence, an ability to find a practical solution to a problem and for powers of expression and persuasion. Also wanted are those with a desire and ability to promote the firm's business at every opportunity. Dechert want people who will remain on qualifying and make their careers with the firm. They take fewer trainees than comparable firms because they regard as paramount the quality of training and opportunities for individual progression.

training environment

Unusually training is divided into six four-monthly periods, giving trainees the chance to sample a wide range of work. Your supervisor will participate with you and a Trainee Panel Partner (who will be responsible for your well-being throughout your training contract) in a formal oral and written assessment of your work towards the end of each seat. Trainees have the opportunity to spend four months in the firm's office in Brussels and the firm expects that some trainees may now spend a period in their second year in one of the US Offices. The greater number of seats makes it easier to fit in with any special requests to work in specific areas of the firm. Prior to the recent merger, the London office was the first English firm to appoint a training director in the early 1980s and their most recent appointee is a senior educator and the former director of the College of Law in London.

Partners	47
Assistant Solicitors	86
Total Trainees	24

contact
Lynn Muncey

method of application
Letter and application form

selection procedure
1 interview with at least 2 partners

closing date for 2003
17 August 2001

application
Training contracts p.a. up to 15
Applications p.a. over 1,000
% interviewed p.a. 12%
Required degree grade 2:1 (or capability of attaining a 2:1)

training
Salary:
1st year (2000) £25,000
2nd Year (2000) £28,000
(to be reviewed in October 2001)
Holiday entitlement:
20 days
% of trainees with a non-law degree p.a.
Varies
No. of seats available abroad p.a. 3

post-qualification
Salary (2000) £40,000
(to be reviewed October 2001)
% of trainees offered job on qualification (2000): 100%
% of partners (as at 1/9/00) who joined as trainees: 30%

A-Z SOLICITORS

dechert continued

The PSC is provided in a tailored format by the firm, with some modules taking place in-house. That apart there is an extensive training programme in which trainees are encouraged to participate (numerous aspects being particularly aimed at trainees).

benefits

Free permanent health and life assurance, subsidised membership of local gym and interest-free season ticket loans.

vacation placements

Places for 2001: 8; Duration: 9 July to 20 July 2001; Remuneration: no less than £190 p.w.; Closing Date: Applications considered between: 1 November 2000 and 28 February 2001. Open Day for Law Undergraduates; 24 April 2001; Places 20-30. Open Days for Non-Law Graduates; 3 July 2001 and 2nd date in October 2001 TBC; Places 20-30 on each day.

sponsorship & awards

LPC fees paid and £4,000 maintenance p.a. for those living in London and £3,750 for those outside (where local authority grants unavailable).

trainee comments

"The firm provides both a friendly and fun place to work together with a sound legal training which is gained both on the job and through lectures and seminars. The system of six four month seat rotations has given me the flexibility of gaining experience in four practice areas while also having the advantage of being able to get a year's experience in my chosen specialism which has set me up perfectly for qualification". (Susanna Beeson, newly qualified solicitor, read Geography at Edinburgh)

"I found my training extremely interesting and rewarding. The 4 month seat rotation is a system that I particularly like because this way you are able to experience a wider variety of work enabling you to make a more informed decision as to what area of law suits you best". (Stephen Diosi, newly qualified solicitor, read Law at University of Wales, Cardiff)

"The introduction of a Director of Training has been of enormous benefit to trainees. Bernard George is independent from the departments and always available for a confidential chat. As I knew early in my training contract that I wanted to qualify into Litigation, I have been given experience of 4 different areas of Litigation". (Sarah Lockyer, newly qualified solicitor, read Law and French at Birmingham).

denton wilde sapte

Emma Hooper.
Grad Recruitment.

Five Chancery Lane Clifford's Inn London EC4A 1BU
Tel: (020) 7242 1212 Fax: (020) 7404 0087
Email: info@dentonwildesapte.com
Website: www.dentonwildesapte.com

firm profile

Denton Wilde Sapte is a large international law firm, with particular strengths in banking and finance, energy and infrastructure, media and technology, property, retail and aviation as well as in construction, environment, financial services, insurance and reinsurance, local government, rail, roads, and shipping. The firm has offices in 13 jurisdictions covering Europe, Central and South East Asia and the Middle East. In addition the firm is a founder member of Denton International, a network of leading law firms.

main areas of work

Corporate 34% (including Tax, Media, Energy, Employment and Pensions); Litigation 25%; Banking and Finance 23%; Property 18%.

trainee profile

The firm looks for candidates from any degree discipline with a strong academic and extra curricular record of achievement. The firm looks for good team players with excellent interpersonal skills and the flexibility to grow with the firm. Languages are an advantage, but not essential.

training environment

Four six-month seats, one of which may be spent in one the firm's overseas offices. Two-week induction at the beginning of contract. PSC core modules completed by October with remaining electives completed by the end of the first year. The firm has many social and sporting activities.

benefits

Holiday entitlement commences at 21 days rising by one day for every full year served, meal away from home allowance, private health cover, season ticket loan, subsidised sports club membership, permanent health insurance, death in service cover.

vacation placements

Places for 2001: 120 places available on information weeks/open days during Summer; Closing Date: Applications accepted during January to 30 March 2001 with interviews taking place during March/April 2001.

sponsorship & awards

CPE and LPC funding: fees and a maintenance grant (less any local authority funding).

Partners	196*
Assistant Solicitors	401*
Total Trainees	127

contact
Reina McGovern

method of application
Application form

selection procedure
First interview; Selection test; Second interview

closing date for 2003
Law/Non-law:
17 August 2001

application
Training contracts p.a. 50
Applications p.a. 3,000
% interviewed p.a. 10%
Required degree grade 2:1

training
Salary:
1st year (2000) £25,000-£26,000
2nd Year(2000) £27,000-£28,000
Holiday entitlement: 21 days
% of trainees with a non-law degree p.a. 40% max.
No. of seats available abroad p.a. currently 10

post-qualification
Salary (2000) £42,000
% of trainees offered job on qualification (2000): 97%

overseas offices
Almaty, Beijing, Brussels, Cairo, Dubai, Gibraltar, Hong Kong, Istanbul, Moscow, Paris, Singapore, Tokyo. Associated offices: Abu Dhabi, Barcelona, Berlin, Chemnitz, Cologne, Copenhagen, Dar es Salaam, Dresden, Düsseldorf, Frankfurt, Gothenburg, Hamburg, Madrid, Malmö, Muscat, Oslo, Stockholm, Vienna.

dickinson dees

St. Ann's Wharf 112 Quayside
Newcastle-upon-Tyne NE99 1SB
Tel: (0191) 279 9000 Fax: (0191) 279 9100
Email: law@dickinson-dees.co.uk
Website: www.dickinson-dees.com

firm profile

The largest firm in the north east, Dickinson Dees offers both commercial and private client services. The firm has new premises on Newcastle's Quayside and in the Tees Valley. The firm has an associated office in Brussels with opportunities for trainees to spend time on secondment there.

main areas of work

Corporate 30%; Property 30%; Private Client 20%; Litigation 20%.

trainee profile

Good academic and analytical ability. Good commercial and business sense. Confident, personable and adaptable with good communication skills. Able to fit into a team.

training environment

Trainees are relatively few for the size of the practice. You are fully integrated into the firm and involved in all aspects of firm business. The training contract consists of four seats. One seat is spent in each of the commercial property, company/commercial and litigation departments. You are able to specialise for the fourth seat. This is encouraged so that personnel rise through the firm rather than being recruited from outside. Trainees sit with partners or associates and training is reviewed every three months. The firm has its own Training Manager. There are in-house induction courses on each move of department and opportunities for trainees to get involved in the in-house training programme. The professional skills course is run in conjunction with Northumbria University and the firm has played a key role in the development and implementation of this course. The working environment at Dickinson Dees is supportive and friendly. You will lead a busy life with sporting and social events organised by the office.

vacation placements

Places for 2001: 24; Duration: 1 week; Remuneration: £100 p.w.; Closing Date: 28 February 2001. Application forms are available.

open days

Open days will be held in the summer of 2001. Application forms are available on request. Closing date: 30 April 2001.

sponsorship & awards

CPE/LPC fees paid and £2,000 interest free loan.

Partners	51
Assistant Solicitors	72
Total Trainees	22

contact
Jamie Pass

method of application
Application form and letter

selection procedure
Interview

closing date for 2003
31 July 2001

application
Training contracts p.a. **14**
Applications p.a. **700**
% interviewed p.a. **10%**
Required degree grade **2:1**

training
Salary:
1st year (2000) **£16,000**
2nd year (2000) **£17,000**
Holiday entitlement:
4 weeks
% of trainees with
a non-law degree p.a. **50%**
No. of seats available
abroad p.a. **1**

post-qualification
Salary (2000) **Under review**
% of trainees offered job
on qualification (2000):
100%
% of assistants (as at
1/9/00) who joined as
trainees: **60%**
% of partners (as at 1/9/00)
who joined as trainees:
29%

branch office
Rond Point Schuman 9 -
Box 13 B-1040 Brussels
Tel: +32 2 233 3747
Fax: +32 2 233 3740

trainee comments

"I wanted to work for a leading commercial firm with a progressive outlook and an excellent training record; Dickinson Dees is the law firm that fulfils all their criteria." (Elizabeth Allen, first year trainee in 1998/99, read English at University of London and LLB at Northumbria University)

"I wanted to work for an expanding and developing commercial firm that invested time and effort in its trainees. Dickinson Dees offers all of the above with an enthusiastic and friendly approach." (Edward Meikle, second year trainee in 1998/99, read Art History at University of East Anglia)

"After completing a week of work experience at Dickinson Dees I felt that I would get a thorough training at a leading commercial firm and great future prospects." (Sara Brody, second year trainee in 1999/2000, read law at Hull University)

"Dickinson Dees offers trainees the highest level of training. Trainees are involved at all levels and have a high degree of client contact. Overall a great place to work in a friendly and relaxed environment." (Ian Hornby, second year trainee in 1999/2000, read Law at Newcastle University)

"If you are looking for a leading commercial firm that provides nationally recognised training, and real longer term opportunities, Dickinson Dees cannot be overlooked." (Ben Butler, first year trainee in 1999/2000 read Ancient History at Newcastle University)

d j freeman

43 Fetter Lane London EC4A 1JU
Tel: (020) 7583 4055 Fax: (020) 7353 7377
Email: aem@djfreeman.co.uk
Website: djfreeman.co.uk

firm profile

An innovative firm whose lawyers work in multi-disciplinary teams concentrating on specific business sectors. It is one of the leading firms in the property, insurance and media/ communications industries, and has a strong commercial litigation department. It also has more women partners than any other City law firm.

main areas of work

Property Services 42%; Insurance Services 26%; Commercial Litigation 20%; Media & Communications 12%.

trainee profile

Clear and creative thinkers who work well under pressure and as part of a team.

training environment

Trainees spend six months in the firm's major practice areas, and once a month are able to discuss their progress in each seat with a partner. Believing supervised experience to be the best training, the firm soon gives trainees the chance to meet clients, be responsible for their own work and join in marketing and client development activities. Regular workshops in each seat help develop basic skills in the different departments. Any suggestions or concerns can be voiced at a trainee solicitors' committee. The firm has an active social committee which organises events from quiz evenings to wine tasting, as well as a theatre club.

benefits

Subsidised meals in staff restaurant; BUPA after three months; a variety of social and sporting events.

vacation placements

Places for 2001: 16; Duration: 3 weeks; Remuneration: £150 p.w.; Closing Date: 14 March 2001.

sponsorship & awards

LPC Funding.

Partners	56
Assistant Solicitors	71
Total Trainees	25

contact
Anne Mellars
(020) 7556 4181

method of application
Application form

selection procedure
Interview

closing date for 2003
July 2001

application
Training contracts p.a.
12–15
Applications p.a. **600**
% interviewed p.a. **10%**
Required degree grade **2:1**

training
Salary (2000)
1st six months £25,000
2nd six months £26,000
3rd six months £27,000
4th six months £28,000
Holiday entitlement:
20 days

post-qualification
Salary (2000): £37,000

dla

125 London Wall London EC2Y 5AE
Tel: (020) 7796 6677 Fax: (0121) 212 5792

firm profile

This ambitious firm thinks of itself as a business as much as a law firm. Its expansion has been meteoric. In 1989, it was below the top 35 UK firms in terms of size – it is now the seventh largest. It has offices in eight major cities in the UK, but still operates as one partnership. The full range of corporate and commercial services is offered.

main areas of work

Corporate 25%, Insurance 9%, Real Estate 17%, Litigation 17%, Business Support & Restructuring 6%, Human Resources 7%, Business Services 6%, Banking 7%, Reinsurance, Marine & Aviation 5% and Law Training 1%.

trainee profile

The firm only wants exceptional people. Good academic ability is no longer sufficient. It wants people with different backgrounds and skills. The successful candidates will believe in themselves, relate well to other people, have an appetite for life and a desire to succeed in business.

training environment

The firm deliberately takes on a relatively small number of trainees for its size. This enables it to offer in-depth experience and excellent prospects on qualification. Trainees will spend four six month seats in different commercial areas. They will sit with a partner or associate and learn through practice and observation. There is an ongoing commercial skills training programme and the PSC is run in-house. Good sports and social facilities.

benefits

Pension, health insurance, life assurance, 23 days holiday.

vacation placements

Places for 2001: 180; Duration: 1 week; Remuneration (2001): £185 p.w. London, £140 p.w. regions; Closing Date: 28 February 2001.

sponsorship & awards

Full CPE and LPC fees are paid and a maintenance grant is offered for both years.

Partners 250*
Assistant Solicitors 400*
Total Trainees 100
denotes world-wide figures

contact
Sally Carthy
National Graduate
Recruitment Manager

method of application
Application form

selection procedure
First interview, assessment afternoon including second interview with 2 partners

closing date for 2003
31 July 2001

application
Training contracts p.a. 70+
Applications p.a. 2,200
% interviewed p.a. 10%
Required degree grade 2:1

training
Salary:
1st year (2000)
£25,000 (London)
£18,000 (regions)
2nd year(2000)
£28,000 (London)
£20,000 (regions)
Holiday entitlement:
23 days
% of trainees with
a non-law degree p.a. 40%

post-qualification
Salary (2000)
£40,000 (London)
£28,500 (regions)
% of trainees offered job
on qualification (2000): 93%

dla continued

trainee comments

"Growing up in Liverpool and having spent all my academic life here, it was not a question of where I wanted to start my professional career but who I wanted to start it with. I applied to a number of firms in Liverpool but it was Dibb Lupton Alsop which impressed me the most. Dibb Lupton Alsop provided an opportunity to do high quality commercial work in my home town and showed commitment and dedication to my training and future career which was second to none." (Clare Tickle, second year trainee in the Liverpool office, read law at Liverpool University)

"I had lived in London for three years on and off before starting work and I had long wanted to work in a City firm. I chose Dibb Lupton Alsop for their obvious ambition - particularly evidenced around the time I applied for a training contract by the well documented merger and their expansionist ideas. I was influenced greatly by the unstuffy attitude I perceived at interview. This was a marked difference from some other firms who interviewed me." (Guy Sheppard, second year trainee in the London office, read Latin at Exeter University)

"As a truly national firm Dibb Lupton Alsop offers me a City reputation, excellent quality of work and a commitment to training without being in London. As a trainee with a past 'non legal life' Dibb Lupton Alsop is a firm with a modern culture that recognises the added value that alternative disciplines can offer. As business lawyers with a reputation for being pro-active, ambitious and competitive in the market, Dibb Lupton Alsop are always looking to be better and committed to be the best." (Joely Richardson, newly qualified in the Birmingham office, studied Business Studies at Leeds Business School)

"Once I started applying for training contracts it became obvious that Dibb Lupton Alsop, as a truly national firm, would be able to offer me the best quality work and training. However, the main factor that influenced me was that despite rapid growth in the last decade, the firm were still very ambitious and had such clear objectives of the position they wanted to be in in the near future and how they planned to achieve it. This expansion was something that I wanted to be a part of." (Jamie Gamble, first year trainee in the Sheffield office, studied law at Nottingham University).

Overseas Offices
Brussels, Hong Kong

**associated offices
(DLA & Partners)**
Paris, Barcelona, Brussels

DLA

dmh

100 Queens Road Brighton BN1 3YB
Tel: (01273) 329 833 Fax: (01273) 747 500
Email: admin@dmh.co.uk
Website: www.dmh.co.uk

firm profile

DMH offers expertise and service comparable to City firms to a range of commercial organisations, non-profit institutions and private clients. The firm also undertakes international work and is fast developing a reputation for its work in the TMT sector. Its main commercial offices are at Brighton and Crawley. Client focused, the firm is open, approachable and innovative.

main areas of work

Corporate Finance; Commercial Property; Planning & Environmental; Employment; Intellectual Property/IT; Litigation; Residential Conveyancing; Personal Injury; Private Client.

trainee profile

The firm looks for intelligent and motivated graduates with a sound academic background, enthusiasm and good communication skills. In addition to this, those candidates who are able to demonstrate a high level of business acumen will impress.

training environment

Usually four six-month seats taken from the following areas: Employment, Innovation & Media, Commercial, Corporate, Planning, Commercial Property, Litigation, Personal Injury, Civil Litigation, Residential Conveyancing and Private Client work. Trainees are closely supervised by the partner to whom they are attached but have every opportunity to work as part of a team and deal directly with clients. The majority of seats are in Brighton and Crawley.

vacation placements

Places for 2001: limited number, priority given to trainee interviewees and Sussex University; Duration: 1-2 weeks; Remuneration: £100.00 p.w. expenses; Closing Date: 31 March 2001.

Partners	28
Assistant Solicitors	24
Total Trainees	8

contact
Jean Clack

method of application
CV and covering letter

closing date for 2003
December 2001

application
Training contracts p.a. 4-5
Applications p.a. 350-450
% interviewed p.a. 3%
Required degree grade 2:1

training
Salary:
1st year (2000) £14,500
2nd Year (2000) £17,000
Holiday entitlement:
20 days
% of trainees with
a non-law degree p.a. 50%

post-qualification
Salary (2000) £25,000
% of trainees offered job
on qualification (2000):
100%
% of assistants (as at
1/9/00) who joined as
trainees: 36%
% of partners (as at 1/9/00)
who joined as trainees:
50%

eversheds

Senator House 85 Queen Victoria Street London EC4V 4JL
Tel: (020) 7919 4500 Fax: (020) 7919 4919
Email: gradrec@eversheds.com
Website: www.eversheds.com

firm profile
A European law firm, Eversheds has over 1,750 legal and business advisers in 19 locations. Its distinctive approach gives clients access to a large team of lawyers who combine local market knowledge with an international perspective.

main areas of work
Corporate, commercial, litigation and dispute management, commercial, property and employment. In addition to these core areas each office provides expertise in a further 30 business and industry sectors.

trainee profile
Eversheds' people are valued for being straightforward, enterprising and effective. The firm listens to its clients. It likes to simplify rather than complicate. It expects trainees to be business-like, unstuffy and down-to-earth. You will need to display commercial acumen, imagination and drive, and above all you will need to be results-driven.

training environment
You will be encouraged to play a major part in the direction your training and development takes, with advice and supervision always available. In each department you will sit with a partner or a senior assistant and participate from an early stage in varied, complex and high-value work. Eversheds aims to retain as many trainees as possible on qualifying, and many of the partners were trainees with the firm. A steep learning curve begins with a month of basic training followed by departmental seats - three of which will cover the firm's main practice areas. During your training you will also complete an Eversheds-designed Professional Skills Course, and, on qualification, follow a progressive career structure.

benefits
Regional variations

vacation placements
Places for 2001: 120; Duration: 2 weeks; Remuneration: regional variations; Closing Date: 31 January 2001.

sponsorship & awards
CPE/LPC fees and maintenance grants.

Partners	350+
Assistant Solicitors	630+
Total Trainees	224

contact
Andrew M Looney
Graduate Recruitment Officer

method of application
Application form and covering letter to be returned to London address

selection procedure
Selection days include group and written exercises, presentations and interview.

closing date for 2003
31 July 2001

application
Training contracts p.a. 100-110
Applications p.a. **3,000**
% interviewed p.a. **15%**
Required degree grade **2:1**

training
Salary:
1st year (2000) £15,500 to £24,000
2nd Year (2000) £16,500 to £27,000
Holiday entitlement: **23 days**
% of trainees with a non-law degree p.a. **45%**
No. of seats available abroad p.a. **Up to 12**

post-qualification
Salary (2000)
Regional variations
% of trainees offered job on qualification (2000): **90%**

overseas offices
Amsterdam*, Birmingham, Bristol, Brussels, Cambridge, Cardiff, Copenhagen*, Derby, Ipswich, Leeds, London, Manchester, Monaco, Newcastle, Norwich, Nottingham, Paris, Sofia*, Teesside. (* Associate offices)

farrer & co

66 Lincoln's Inn Fields London WC2A 3LH
Tel: (020) 7242 2022 Fax: (020) 7831 9748
Email: trainees@farrer.co.uk
Website: www.farrer.co.uk

firm profile
Farrer & Co is one of the UK's leading law practices. It provides a range of specialist advice to private, institutional and corporate clients.

main areas of work
The firm's breadth of expertise is reflected by the fact that it has an outstanding reputation in fields as diverse as matrimonial law, offshore tax planning, employment, heritage work, charity law and defamation.

trainee profile
Trainees are expected to be highly motivated individuals with keen intellects and interesting and engaging personalities. Those applicants who appear to break the mould – as shown by their initiative for organisation, leadership, exploration, or enterprise – are far more likely to get an interview than the erudite, but otherwise unimpressive, student.

training environment
The training programme involves each trainee in the widest range of cases, clients and issues possible in a single law firm. This provides a broad foundation of knowledge and experience and the opportunity to make an informed choice about the area of law in which to specialise. A high degree of involvement is encouraged under the direct supervision of solicitors and partners. Trainees attend an induction programme and regular internal lectures. The training principal reviews trainees' progress at the end of each seat and extensive feedback is given. The firm has a very friendly atmosphere and regular sporting and social events.

benefits
Health and life insurance, subsidised gym membership, season ticket loan.

vacation placements
Places for 2001: 18; Duration: 2 weeks at Easter, 3 weeks in summer; Remuneration: £200 p.w.; Closing Date: 31 January 2001.

sponsorship & awards
CPE Funding: Fees paid + £4,000 maintenance. LPC Funding: Fees paid + £4,000 maintenance.

Partners	43
Assistant Solicitors	48
Total Trainees	12

contact
Graduate Recruitment Manager

method of application
Firm's application form and covering letter

selection procedure
Interviews with Graduate Recruitment Manager and Partners

closing date for 2003
31 July 2001

application
Training contracts p.a. 6
Applications p.a. 1,500
% interviewed p.a. 2.5%
Required degree grade 2:1

training
Salary:
1st year (2000) £24,000
2nd year (2000) £26,000
Holiday entitlement:
20 days
% of trainees with
non-law degrees p.a. 42%

post-qualification
Salary (2000) £36,000
trainees offered job
on qualification (2000):
100%
% of assistants (as at 1/9/00) who joined as trainees: 72%
% of partners (as at 1/9/00) who joined as trainees: 70%

A-Z

SOLICITORS

423

fenners

15 New Bridge Street London EC4V 6AV
Tel: (020) 7936 8000 Fax: (020) 7936 8100
Email: info@fenners.co.uk

firm profile

Fenners is a City based firm specialising in company/commercial law, corporate finance, technology, commercial property, and town planning. The firm has a broad client base, including listed and unquoted companies, financial advisers, brokers, banks and other institutions.

main areas of work

Commercial Property 50%; Corporate/Commercial 50%.

trainee profile

Candidates will demonstrate academic excellence combined with commitment and motivation to pursuing a career in a specialist City firm. In addition, extra curricular activities and interests are highly regarded as evidence of a balanced and well rounded candidate.

training environment

Training consists of seats within the firm's commercial property and corporate/commercial departments, with an option for a further contentious seat. You will sit with a Partner or an experienced solicitor who will provide you with daily tasks and support. In addition, you will have an opportunity to receive feedback and discuss your progress with your training principal every three months. Fenners' trainees are highly valued and their development within the firm is encouraged by providing a challenging, supportive and enjoyable environment in which to work.

benefits

Health insurance, season ticket loan.

vacation placements

Places for 2001: 10; Duration: 2 weeks; Remuneration: competitive rates; Closing Date: 30 April 2001.

sponsorship & awards

CPE and LPC funding to be discussed with candidates.

Partners	3
Assistant Solicitors	7
Total Trainees	4

contact
Robert Fenner

method of application
Handwritten letter and CV. Brochures available on request

selection procedure
2 interviews with partners. The firm does not require completion of an application form. Candidates should submit CVs

closing date for 2003
Applications should preferably be received by 1 September 2001.

application
Training contracts p.a. 3
Applications p.a. 400
% interviewed p.a. 5%
Required degree grade 2:1

training
Salary:
1st year Market for City
2nd year Market for City
Holiday entitlement:
22 days
% of trainees with a non-law degree p.a.
variable

post-qualification
Salary: Market for City

field fisher waterhouse

35 Vine Street London EC3N 2AA
Tel: (020) 7861 4000 Fax: (020) 7488 0084
Email: kmd@ffwlaw.com
Website: www.ffwlaw.com

firm profile

Field Fisher Waterhouse is a progressive City firm with a reputation for providing a quality service to an impressive list of UK and international clients. The firm has particular strengths in its core practice areas of Corporate/Finance, Property, Litigation and IP/IT. It is also highly regarded for its expertise in specialist areas including e-commerce, medical litigation, communications & media, travel & tourism, and employment. The firm prides itself on its collegiate atmosphere, its creative and commercial approach to the law and its constructive approach to career development.

main areas of work

Property 24%; IP/IT 20%; Corporate 16%; Litigation 14%; Banking, Finance & Commercial 11%; Professional Regulation 9%; Employment 4%; Other 2%.

trainee profile

The firm is looking to recruit ambitious individuals with ability, enthusiasm and determination, who will be able to respond creatively and commercially to its clients' needs. It values strong personal qualities as well as academic achievement and welcomes applications from both law and non-law students.

training environment

Training will be split into five seats. Four will be in the firm's core practice areas and your fifth seat is yours to choose in the department which interests you most. In each seat you will work with several partners and assistants to gain a broad experience of the department. You will participate in a formal assessment at the end of each seat. The firm aims to develop your grasp of legal principles and to foster your commercial awareness. Your training will combine practical hands on experience and a comprehensive training programme of in-house lectures and external seminars. Staff enjoy the benefits of a thriving sports and social committee which organises many trainee and FFW events throughout the year.

benefits

25 days annual holiday, season ticket loans, health insurance, private medical healthcare.

vacation placements

Places for 2001: A summer vacation scheme will be run during July 2001. Application by CV and covering letter, by 31 March 2001.

sponsorship & awards

Tuition fees and maintenance grant paid for CPE and LPC.

Partners	66
Assistant Solicitors	101
Total Trainees	20

contact
Karen Danker

method of application
Firm's own application
form and covering letter

selection procedure
Interview

closing date for 2003
31 August 2001

application
Training contracts p.a. **10**
Applications p.a. **2,500**
Required degree grade **2:1**

training
Salary:
1st year (2000) £23,000
2nd Year (2000) £24,000
Holiday entitlement:
25 days
% of trainees with a
non-law degree p.a. **50%**

post-qualification
Salary (2000) **37,000**
% of trainees offered job
on qualification (2000): **80%**
% of assistants (as at
1/9/00) who joined as
trainees: **40%**
% of partners (as at 1/9/00)
who joined as trainees:
40%

A-Z

SOLICITORS

425

finers stephens innocent

179 Great Portland St London W1N 6LS
Tel: (020) 7323 4000 Fax: (020) 7580 7069
Email: admin@fsilaw.co.uk
Website: www.fsilaw.co.uk

firm profile

Finers Stephens Innocent was formed in 1999 by the merger of West End property and commercial practice Finers with City niche media and litigation practice Stephens Innocent. The environment of the firm is friendly and forward thinking, and it is known for being client focussed and having an entrepreneurial and practical approach to its work. The firm is a member of the Network of Leading Law Firms and of LAWROPE, a European network of law firms.

main areas of work

Commercial Property, Litigation, Media, Family, Defamation, Company/Commercial. Private Client. See the firm's website for further details.

trainee profile

The firm looks for academic excellence in applicants and prefers those with a law degree. It also looks for maturity, an interesting personality, strong communication skills, ability to think like a lawyer and an indefinable 'it' which shows that you have the potential to become a long-term member of the firm's team.

training environment

After your induction programme, you will complete four six-month seats, sharing a room with either a Partner or Senior Assistant. The firm has two Training Partners who keep a close eye on the welfare and progress of trainees. There are regular group meetings of trainees and an appraisal process which enables you to know how you are progressing as well as giving you a chance to provide feedback on your view of your training.

benefits

20 days holiday, private medical insurance, life insurance, long term disability insurance, subsidised gym membership, season ticket loan.

open day

Held in June/July 2001 for 2003 training contract applicants. For further details, please write during April/May 2001 with an up to date CV including your most recent exam results.

sponsorship & awards

Contribution of £3,000 towards LPC course fees.

Partners	40
Assistant Solicitors	29
Total Trainees	12

contact
Personnel Director

method of application
CV and covering letter.

selection procedure
Two interviews, each with two Partners usually including one of the Training Partners, Robert Craig and Carolyn Brown.

closing date for 2003
31 July 2001

application
Training contracts p.a. 3-6
Applications p.a. 1500
% interviewed p.a. 5%
Required degree grade 2:1

training
Salary:
1st year (2000) £20,000
2nd year (2000) £22,000
Holiday entitlement:
20 days
% of trainees with
a non-law degree p.a.
0-33%

post-qualification
Salary (2000) £33,000
% of trainees offered job
on qualification (2000):
75%

forbes

Marsden House 28-32 Wellington Street (St. Johns) Blackburn BB1 8DA
Tel: (01254) 662831 Fax: (01254) 681104
Email: siobhanh@f-p.co.uk

firm profile

A leading North-West practice with nine offices and 290 staff, Forbes is progressive and forward looking in all aspects of its business. Underlying the practice is the strongest commitment to quality, both in its service to clients and as an employer, with strong emphasis being placed on staff training and career development - a fact confirmed by Forbes being one of the first firms to be recognised as an Investor in People. Offering a wide range of legal expertise, Forbes is noted, in particular, for excellence in company/commercial, civil litigation, defendant insurer, crime, family and employment services. Three partners are qualified Higher Court Advocates and the firm holds many Legal Aid franchises as well as an ISO9001 accreditation.

main areas of work

Company/commercial, civil litigation, defendant insurer, crime, family and employment services.

trainee profile

Forbes looks for high-calibre recruits with strong local connections and good academic records, who are keen team players.

training environment

A tailored training programme involves six months in four of the following crime, civil litigation, defendant insurer, matrimonial, and non-contentious/company commercial.

Partners	23
Assistant Solicitors	44
Total Trainees	8

contact
Siobhan Hardy

method of application
Handwritten letter and CV

selection procedure
Interview with partners

closing date for 2003
31 July 2001

application
Training contracts p.a. **3**
Applications p.a. **350**
% interviewed p.a. **varies**
Required degree grade **2:1**

training
Salary:
1st year (2000) **£12,000**
Holiday entitlement:
20 days

post-qualification
Salary (2000):
highly competitive
% of trainees offered job
on qualification (2000):
100%

freshfields bruckhaus deringer

65 Fleet Street London EC4Y 1HS
Tel: (020) 7936 4000 Fax: (020) 7832 7001
Email: graduaterecruitment@freshfields.com
Website: www.freshfields.com

firm profile
Freshfields Bruckhaus Deringer is a leading international firm with a network of 30 offices in 19 countries. The firm provides first-rate legal services to corporations, financial institutions and governments around the world.

main areas of work
Corporate; Mergers and Acquisitions; Banking; Litigation; Arbitration; Jt Ventures; Employment, Pensions and Benefits; Asset Finance; Comm Property; Tax; Capital Mrkts; Intellectual Property and Information Technology; Project Finance; Private Finance Initiative; US securities; EU/Competition; Communications and Media; Construction and Engineering; Energy; Environment; Financial Services; Restructuring and Insolvency; Insurance; International Tax; Investment Funds.

trainee profile
Good academic qualifications, good record of achievement in other areas, common sense and creative thinking. Language and computer skills are also an advantage.

training environment
At least three months in each of the corporate, finance and litigation departments, and seats in the property, intellectual property/information technology, employment, and tax departments also available. Trainees may also have the option of spending 6 months in another office or in the legal department of a client. High priority is given to trainees' preferences. A comprehensive programme of technical legal training and skills training, as well as the PSC, is provided.

benefits
Life Ass; permanent health insurance; group personal pension; interest-free loan for a season travel ticket; free membership of the firm's private medical insurance scheme; subsidised staff restaurant; gym.

vacation placements
Places for 2001: 100; Duration: 2 weeks; Remuneration: £450 (total); Closing Date: 14 February 2001 but apply as quickly as possible after 1 December 2000 as there may not be places left by the deadline.

sponsorship & awards
CPE and LPC fees paid and £5,000 maintenance p.a. for those studying in London and Oxford and £4,500 p.a. for those studying elsewhere.

Partners	441*
Assistant Solicitors	
	1,850*
Total Trainees	155

contact
Maia Lawson

method of application
Application form

selection procedure
1 interview with 2 partners

closing date for 2003
24 August 2001

application
Training contracts p.a. 95
Applications p.a. c.3,500
% interviewed p.a. c.11%
Required degree grade 2:1

training
Salary:
1st year (2000) £25,000
2nd Year (2000) £28,000
Holiday entitlement:
25 days
% of trainees with
a non-law degree p.a.
c40%
No. of seats available
abroad p.a. c.40

post-qualification
Salary (2000) £42,000
% of trainees offered job
on qualification (2000):
100%

overseas offices
Amsterdam, Bangkok, Barcelona, Beijing, Berlin, Bratislava, Brussels, Budapest, Cologne, Dusseldorf, Frankfurt, Hamburg, Hanoi, Ho Chi Minh City, Hong Kong, Leipzig, Madrid, Milan, Moscow, Munich, New York, Paris, Prague, Rome, Shanghai, Singapore, Tokyo, Vienna, Washington DC.

garretts

180 Strand London WC2R 2NN
Tel: (020) 7344 0344 Fax: (020) 7438 2518
Email: pr@glegal.com
Website: kspace.arthurandersen.com

firm profile

Garretts was founded in 1993 and is a fast growing, entrepreneurial law firm, which provides commercial advice from the major business and financial centres around the country to both UK and foreign countries. It is associated in Scotland with Dundas & Wilson and, together, currently ranks in the UK's top 25 law firms by size and fee income. The firm provides a full range of high quality legal services to business and private clients. Multi-jurisdictional transactions are facilitated through its membership of Anderson Legal, the global legal services network associated with Anderson Worldwide SC, which now has over 2900 lawyers operating in 35 countries around the world.

main areas of work

Banking; capital markets and IPO's; collective investments; commercial litigation; construction; corporate and commercial; EC and competition; employment; employee share schemes; environmental law; financial services; hospitality and leisure; immigration; intellectual property; mergers and acquisitions; new media and IT; pensions; pharmaceuticals and biotechnology; planning; projects; private client and real estate.

trainee profile

Successful candidates will have a strong academic background, outgoing personality, relevant work experience and an interest in extra-curricular activities.

training environment

Trainees spend six months in four different seats, in a variety of departments. Formal training consists of a residential induction course, two day courses at the start of each new placement and professional in-house lectures. Social and sporting activities are encouraged.

benefits

BUPA; subsidised gym membership; S.T.L

vacation placements

Places for 2001: 60 throughout the UK; Duration: 3 weeks; Remuneration: £225 p.w. (2000) (London); Closing Date: 5 February 2001.

sponsorship & awards

CPE + LPC fees paid and £3,750-£4,000 grant p.a.

Partners	51
Assistant Solicitors	129
Total Trainees	52

contact
Kate Henry

method of application
Application form or covering letter and CV

selection procedure
1 hour interview in London, second interview held in regional office of choice

application
Training contracts p.a. 40
Applications p.a. 2,000
% interviewed p.a. c.20%
Required degree grade 2:1

training
Salary:
1st year (2000)
£25,000 (London)
Holiday entitlement:
20 days

additional information
SECONDMENT PROGRAMME
There are opportunities to spend time abroad. Currently the firm has trainees on secondment to Anderson Legal in Sydney, Rajah & Tann in Singapore, Archibald Anderson in Paris and Studio di Consulenza Legale e Tributeria in Milan. The firm is actively looking into secondments to other countries.

goodman derrick

90 Fetter Lane London EC4A 1PT
Tel: (020) 7404 0606 Fax: (020) 7831 6407

firm profile

Founded in 1954 by Lord Goodman, the firm now has a broad commercial practice and is
well known for its media and defamation work, particularly relating to television.

main areas of work

Media 35%; Commercial and General Litigation 25%; Corporate 20%; Property 15%;
Charities/Private Client 5%.

trainee profile

Candidates must show that they will quickly be able to handle responsibility and deal
directly with clients. They must be suited to the firm's work environment, present themselves confidently and be quick thinking and practically-minded.

training environment

Training at the firm is based on direct and active involvement with the work of the practice. The PSC is partly carried out at the start of the training contract, with some courses
taking place over the following two years, coupled with the firm's general training programme. Trainees are in addition expected to initiate personal research if specialist
knowledge needs to be gained for a particular piece of work. Four periods of six months
are spent in litigation, property, media (contentious and non-contentious) and com-
pany/commercial law. Work groups within these main departments allow trainees to
experience further specialist fields. For example, litigation includes employment work.
Trainees' own preferences and aptitude will be monitored by the supervising partner and
discussed at monthly meetings and at three-monthly appraisals. The firm has a very
friendly and informal environment.

benefits

Medical Health Insurance, season ticket loan.

sponsorship & awards

LPC fees plus maintenance grant.

Partners 20
Assistant Solicitors 9
Total Trainees 5

contact
Nicholas Armstrong

method of application
CV and covering letter

selection procedure
2 interviews

closing date for 2003
End August 2001

application
Training contracts p.a. 3
Applications p.a. 1200
% interviewed p.a. 2%
Required degree grade:
min. 2:1

training
Salary:
1st year (2000) £19,000
2nd year (2000) £20,000
Holiday entitlement:
20 days
% of trainees with a
non-law degree p.a. 0%

post-qualification
Salary (2000) £31,500
% of trainees offered job
on qualification (2000)
100%
% of assistants (as at
1/9/00) who joined as
trainees: 40%
% of partners (as at 1/9/00)
who joined as trainees:
26%

gouldens

10 Old Bailey, London, EC4M 7NG
Tel: (020) 7583 7777 Fax: (020) 7583 6777
Email: recruit@gouldens.com
Website: www.gouldens.com

firm profile

Gouldens is a leading commercial firm based in the City of London with a high quality client base in the UK and abroad. It provides a full range of legal services to major commercial clients from the UK and overseas.

main areas of work

Company/Commercial (incl Corporate Tax) 42%; Property (inc. Planning) 23%; Litigation (incl IP) 20%; Banking/Capital Markets 12%; Personal/International Tax Planning 3%.

trainee profile

Candidates should have obtained or are predicted a 2:1 degree in any discipline. They should be willing to accept the challenge of responsibility in an atmosphere where not only technical expertise but flair, originality and enthusiasm are rewarded.

training environment

The firm operates a non-rotational system of training which is unique in the City. Trainees receive work simultaneously from all departments in the firm and see matters through from start to finish. They are encouraged to assume their own workload which allows for early responsibility and development of potential at a faster rate than might otherwise be the case, and more extensive client contact. Work will vary from small cases which you may handle alone (with appropriate supervision) to larger matters where you will assist a partner or an assistant solicitor. Practical experience is supported by a full training programme, including twice-weekly seminars as well as regular sessions. Provided performance during training has been good, the firm aims to offer jobs to all trainees on qualification.

benefits

BUPA, season ticket loan, subsidised sports club membership, group life cover.

vacation placements

Places for 2001:
Summer (law): 35 : 2 weeks: £225 : closing date 28/2
Easter (non-law): 7 : 2 weeks: £225 : closing date 28/2
Christmas (non-law): 14 : 2 weeks : £225 : closing date 30/10

sponsorship & awards

CPE and LPC fees paid and £4,500 maintenance p.a.

Partners	37
Assistant Solicitors	75
Total Trainees	26

contact
Jeanette Ryan

method of application
Letter and CV

selection procedure
2 interviews with partners

closing date for 2003
30 October 2001

application
Training contracts p.a. 20
Applications p.a. **2,500**
% interviewed p.a. **10%**
Required degree grade **2.1**

training
Salary:
1st year (2000) £27,000
Salary:
2nd year (2000) £29,000
Holiday entitlement:
4 weeks
% of trainees with
a non-law degree p.a. **25%**

post-qualification
Salary (2000) £45,000
% of trainees offered job
on qualification (2000):
100%
% of assistants (as at
1/9/00) who joined as
trainees: **55%**
% of partners (as at 1/9/00)
who joined as trainees:
52%

halliwell landau

St. James's Court Brown St Manchester M2 2JF
Tel: (0161) 835 3003 Fax: (0161) 835 2994
Email: info@halliwells.com

firm profile

Halliwell Landau is the largest independent commercial law firm in the North West. Over the last few years the firm has increased substantially in both size and turnover and now has in excess of 180 fee earners. This development leads to a continuing requirement for solicitors and has given rise to more internal promotions to partnerships.

main areas of work

Corporate/Banking 24%; Commercial Litigation 20%; Commercial Property 17%; Insolvency 12%; Insurance Litigation 12%; Planning/Environmental law 4%; Trust and Estate Planning 4%; Intellectual Property 4%; Employment 3%.

trainee profile

Candidates need to show a good academic ability but do not necessarily need to have studied law at University. They should demonstrate an ability to fit into a hardworking team. In particular Halliwell Landau is looking for candidates who will develop with the firm after their initial training.

training environment

Each trainee will spend six months in at least three separate departments. These will usually include commercial litigation, corporate and property. So far as possible if an individual trainee has a particular request for experience in one of the more specialist departments then that will be accommodated. In each department the trainee will work as a member of one of the teams within that department as well as being able to assist other teams. Specific training appropriate to each department will be given and in addition trainees are strongly encouraged to attend the firm's regular seminars on legal and related subjects. There is also a specific training programme for trainees. Each trainee will be assessed both mid-seat and at the end of each seat.

benefits

A subsidised gym membership is available.

vacation placements

Places for 2001: 30; Duration: 2 weeks; Remuneration: £100 p.w.; Closing Date: 31 March 2001.

sponsorship & awards

A contribution will be made to either CPE or LPC fees.

Partners	54
Assistant Solicitors	138
Total Trainees	16

contact
Paul Rose

method of application
CV and application form

selection procedure
Open days or summer placements

closing date for 2003
31 July 2001

application
Training contracts p.a.
8-10
Applications p.a. **1000**
% interviewed p.a. **5%**
Required degree grade **2:1**

training
Salary:
1st year (2000) £16,750
2nd year (2000) £17,750

post-qualification
Salary (2000):
£26,000-£28,000
% of trainees offered job on qualification (2000): **80%**
% of assistants (as at 1/9/00) who joined as trainees: **12%**
% of partners (as at 1/9/00) who joined as trainees: **9%**

hammond suddards edge

7 Devonshire Square Cutlers Gardens London EC2M 4YH
2 Park Lane Leeds LS3 1ES
Trinity Court 16 Dalton Street Manchester M6O 8HS
Rutland House 148 Edmund Street Birmingham B3 2JR
Tel: (020) 7655 1000 Fax: (020) 7655 1001
Website: www.hammondsuddardsedge.com

firm profile

Hammond Suddards Edge is a leading commercial law firm with offices in London, Birmingham, Leeds, Manchester and Brussels. They have nearly 2,000 staff, including 185 partners, 720 solicitors and 94 trainees, and are regarded as innovative, opportunistic and highly successful in the markets in which they operate. The firm has resulted from the merger of Hammond Suddards and Edge Ellison on 1 August 2000.

main areas of work

Banking; Corporate Finance; Commercial Dispute Resolution; Construction; Employment; Financial Services & Corporate Tax; Insolvency; Intellectual Property; Insurance; Pensions; Property.

trainee profile

Hammond Suddards Edge seek applications from all disciplines for both vacation work and training contracts. They look for three characteristics: strong academic performance, work experience in the legal sector and significant achievement in non-academic pursuits.

training environment

Around 45 trainee solicitors are recruited each year who each carry out six four-month seats during their training contract. All trainees are required to move around a minimum of three offices during their training and subsidised trainee accommodation is provided in all locations to facilitate this process. Trainees can choose their seats as they progress through the training contract.

benefits

Subsidised accommodation in all locations. Flexible benefits scheme which allows trainees to choose their own benefits from a range of options.

vacation placements

Places for 2001: 48; Duration: 3 weeks; Remuneration: £220 p.w. (London), £170 pw (Leeds, Manchester and Birmingham); Closing Date: 28 February 2001.

sponsorship & awards

CPE and LPC fees paid and maintenance grant of £4,100 p.a.

Partners 185
Assistant Solicitors 720
Total Trainees 94

contact
Alison Archer
Graduate Recruitment
Manager
(London office)

method of application
Application form

selection procedure
Two Interviews

closing date for 2003
31 July 2001

application
Training contracts p.a. 45
Applications p.a. 1,500
% interviewed p.a. 3%
Required degree grade 2:1

training
Salary:
1st year (2000) £19,500 +
accommodation
2nd year (2000) £20,500+
accommodation
Holiday entitlement:
23 days
% of trainees with
a non-law degree p.a. 25%
No. of seats available
abroad p.a. 3

post-qualification
Salary (2000):
London £40,000
Other £28,000-30,000
% of trainees accepting
job on qualification (2000):
90%

overseas offices
Brussels.

harbottle & lewis

Hanover House 14 Hanover Square London W1R 0BE
Tel: (020) 7667 5000 Fax: (020) 7667 5100
Email: kbeilby@harbottle.co.uk
Website: www.harbottle.co.uk

firm profile
Harbottle & Lewis is recognised for the unique breadth of its practice in the entertainment, media, travel (including aviation) and leisure industries. It undertakes significant corporate commercial and contentious work for clients within these industries including newer industries such as digital mixed media.

main areas of work
Music, film and television production, theatre, broadcasting, computer games and publishing, sport, sponsorship and advertising, aviation, property investment and leisure.

trainee profile
Trainees will have demonstrated the high academic abilities, commercial awareness, and initiative necessary to become part of a team advising clients in dynamic and demanding industries.

training environment
The two year training contract is divided into four six months seats where trainees will be given experience in a variety of legal skills including company commercial, litigation, intellectual property and real property working within teams focused on the firm's core industries. The firm has a policy of accepting a small number of trainees to ensure they are given relevant and challenging work and are exposed to and have responsibility for a full range of legal tasks. The firm has its own lecture and seminars programme in both legal topics and industry know-how. An open door policy and a pragmatic entrepreneurial approach to legal practice provides a stimulating working environment.

benefits
Lunch provided; season ticket loans.

sponsorship & awards
LPC fees paid and interest free loans towards maintenance.

Partners 18
Assistant Solicitors 55
Total Trainees 10

contact
Kathy Beilby

method of application
CV and letter

selection procedure
Interview

closing date for 2003
31 July 2001

application
Training contracts p.a. 3
Applications p.a. 800
% interviewed p.a. 5%
Required degree grade 2:1

training
Salary:
1st year (2000) £21,500
2nd year (2000) £23,000
Holiday entitlement:
in the first year - 21 days
in the second year - 26 days
% of trainees with
a non-law degree p.a. 40%

post-qualification
Salary (2000) £37,000
% of trainees offered job
on qualification (2000): 40%

henmans

116 St. Aldates Oxford OX1 1HA
Tel: (01865) 722181 Fax: (01865) 792376
Email: welcome@henmans.co.uk
Website: www.henmans.co.uk

firm profile

Henmans is a well-established Oxfordshire based practice with a strong national reputation serving business and private clients. Henmans philosophy is to be extremely client focused to deliver exceptional levels of service. The firm achieves this through an emphasis on teamwork to ensure clients always have access to a specific partner with specialist support, and through an ongoing program of training to guarantee clients optimum advice and guidance. The firm's policy of bespoke services and controlled costs ensure that both corporate and private clients benefit from City level litigation standards at competitive regional prices.

main areas of work

The firms core service of litigation is nationally recognised. The Personal Injury and Clinical Negligence Litigation is strong, as is Professional Negligence work.   Personal Injury 26%; Professional Negligence and Commercial Litigation 29%; Corporate / Employment 12%; Property 17%; Private Client (including Family) Charities and Trusts 16%.

trainee profile

Commercial awareness, sound academic accomplishment, intellectual capability, IT Literacy, teamworking, good communication skills

training environment

Trainees are introduced to the firm with a detailed induction and overview of its client base. Experience is likely to be within the PI, Property, Family, Commercial Litigation, and Private Client departments. The firm values commitment and enthusiasm both professionally and socially as an integral part of its culture. The firm provides an ongoing programme of in-house education and regular appraisals within its supportive and friendly environment.

Partners	19
Assistant Solicitors	30
Total Trainees	5

contact
Viv J Matthews MA FCIPD
Human Resources
Manager

method of application
Handwritten letter + CV

selection procedure
Interview with HR Manager
and partners

closing date for 2003
30 July 2001

application
Training contracts p.a. 3
Applications p.a. 500

training
Salary:
1st year (2000) £13,500
2nd Year (2000) £14,600
Holiday entitlement:
20 days
% of trainees with a
non-law degree p.a. 30%

post-qualification
Salary (2000) £24,000
% of assistants (as at
1/9/00) who joined as
trainees: 35%
% of partners (as at 1/9/00)
who joined as trainees:
15%

herbert smith

Exchange House Primrose Street London EC2A 2HS
Tel: (020) 7374 8000 Fax: (020) 7374 0888
Email: graduate.recruitment@herbertsmith.com
Website: www.herbertsmith.com

firm profile

A major City firm with an international dimension, Herbert Smith has particular strengths in international M&A, corporate finance and international projects with a strong profile in litigation and arbitration. The working environment is strongly team-orientated, friendly and informal, probably as a result of the diverse backgrounds of the firm's partners and staff.

main areas of work

International M&A; Corporate Finance and Banking (including Capital Markets); Energy; Projects and Project Finance; Competition; Property; International Litigation; Arbitration.

trainee profile

Trainees need common sense, self-confidence and intelligence to make their own way in a large firm. They are typically high-achieving and intelligent, numerate and literate with general and legal work experience.

training environment

Structured training and supervision are designed to allow trainees to experience a unique range of both contentious and non-contentious work and take on responsibilities as soon as they can. You will work within partner-led teams and have your own role. Individual strengths will be monitored, developed and utilised. On-the-job training is divided into four six-month seats: three in the firm's major areas of practice and one abroad or in a specialist area. Lectures and case studies will take up 30 days of the contract and the firm runs its own legal development programme. There are good social and sporting activities and a life outside work is positively encouraged.

benefits

Profit Share, permanent health insurance, private medical insurance, season ticket loan, life assurance, gym, group personal accident insurance and matched contributory pension scheme.

vacation placements

Places for 2001: 95
Duration: 1x1 week (final year non-law students only) (Christmas); 1x2 weeks (Easter); 3x3 weeks (Summer). Remuneration: £200 p.w.; Closing Date: 24 Nov 2000 for Christmas scheme; 16 Feb 2001 for Easter and Summer scheme.

sponsorship & awards

CPE and LPC fees paid and £5,000 maintenance pa.

Partners 168*
Assistant Solicitors 446*
Total Trainees 150*
* denotes world-wide figures

contact
Sharon Stelling

method of application
Application form

selection procedure
Interview

closing date for 2003
31 August 2001

application
Training contracts p.a. 90
Applications p.a. 2,000
% interviewed p.a. 20%
Required degree grade 2:1

training
Salary:
1st year (2000) £25,000
2nd year(2000) £28,000
Holiday entitlement:
25 days
% of trainees with
a non-law degree p.a.
c. 40%

post-qualification
Salary (2000) £42,000
% of trainees offered job
on qualification (2000): 90%

overseas offices
Bangkok, Beijing, Brussels,
Hong Kong, Moscow,
Paris, Singapore, and
Tokyo.

hewitson becke + shaw

42 Newmarket Road Cambridge CB5 8EP
Tel: (01604) 233 233 Fax: (01223) 316511
Email: mail@hewitsons.com (for all offices)
Website: www.hbslaw.co.uk (for all offices)

firm profile

Established in 1865, the firm handles mostly company and commercial work, but has a growing body of public sector clients. The firm has three offices: Cambridge, Northampton and Saffron Walden.

main areas of work

Four sections: Corporate, Technology, Property and Private Client.

trainee profile

The firm is interested in applications from candidates who have achieved a high degree of success in academic studies and who are bright, personable and able to take the initiative.

training environment

The firm offers four six-month seats.

benefits

The PSC is provided by the College of Law during the first year of the Training Contract. This is coupled with an extensive programme of Trainee Solicitor Seminars provided by specialist in-house lawyers.

vacation placements

Places for 2001: a few placements are available, application is by way of letter and CV to Caroline Lewis; Duration: 1–2 weeks.

sponsorship & awards

Funding for the CPE and/or LPC is not provided.

Partners	51
Assistant Solicitors	41
Total Trainees	18

contact
Caroline Lewis
7 Spencer Parade
Northampton NN1 5AB

method of application
Firm's application form

selection procedure
Interview

closing date for 2003
End of August 2001

application
Training contracts p.a. 15
Applications p.a. 1,400
% interviewed p.a. 10%
Required degree grade:
2:1 min

training
Salary:
1st year (2000) £15,750
2nd year (2000) £16,750
Holiday entitlement:
22 days
% of trainees with a
non-law degree p.a. 50%

post-qualification
Salary (2000): Under review
% of trainees offered job
on qualification (2000): 63%
% of assistants (as at
1/9/00) who joined as
trainees: 48%
% of partners (as at 1/9/00)
who joined as trainees:
14%

hill dickinson

Pearl Assurance House 2 Derby Square Liverpool L2 9XL
Tel: (0151) 236 5400 Fax: (0151) 236 2175
Email: law@hilldicks.com
Website: www.hilldickinson.com

firm profile
The firm is one of the largest in the North West, with offices in Liverpool, Manchester, Chester and London. It adopts a pragmatic and personal approach with clients on a local, national and international level.

main areas of work
Litigation (Insurance/Construction/Professional Negligence/Commercial Litigation/Insolvency) 50%; Commercial Property, Planning and Environmental 15%; Shipping 15%; Health/Medical Negligence 10%; Company, Commercial, Pensions, Tax, Intellectual Property, PFI 10%.

trainee profile
Consistent achievers of a high intellectual calibre, possessing team skills, commercial acumen, resilience and a sense of humour. The firm recruits people who vary greatly in terms of personality and values outside interests.

training environment
Trainees spend six months in each of the four departments (insurance, mercantile, health, and commercial) and will be given the chance to specialise in specific areas. You will be given the opportunity to learn and develop communication and presentation skills, legal research, drafting, interviewing and advising, negotiation and advocacy. Trainees are encouraged to accept responsibility and are expected to act with initiative. The practice has an active social committee and a larger than usual selection of competitive sporting teams.

vacation placements
Places for 2001: yes; Duration: 1 week; Remuneration: no; Closing Date: 1 April 2001.

sponsorship & awards
Discretionary LPC funding.

Partners	72
Assistant Solicitors	63
Total Trainees	17

contact
Ruth Lawrence
Partner

method of application
CV and passport-sized photograph with supporting letter

selection procedure
Assessment day

closing date for 2003
1 October 2001

training
Salary:
1st year (2000) £15,000
2nd Year (2000) £16,000
Holiday entitlement:
4 weeks

post-qualification
% of trainees offered job on qualification (2000): **89%**

hill taylor dickinson

Irongate House Duke's Place London EC3A 7HX
Tel: (020) 7283 9033 Fax: (020) 7283 1144
Email: gradrec@htd-london.com
Website: www.htd.co.uk

firm profile

Hill Taylor Dickinson can trace its origins back over 170 years. Best known for its expertise in shipping and marine insurance work, the firm has also developed a wide and diverse commercial practice. As a medium sized firm with a genuine open door policy it can offer a training environment which is renowned for its approachability, friendliness and lack of bureaucracy.

main areas of work

Shipping & Commodities: 56%; Commercial Transactional: 17%: Insurance and Reinsurance: 18%; Personal Injury & Employment: 8%; Other: 1%.

trainee profile

Intellectual ability and effective communication skills are a pre-requisite. Beyond this the firm seeks to recruit a cross section of trainees of different ages, backgrounds and experience with a personality suitable to the rigours of professional practice with the potential to become a partner at this firm. Good foreign languages are an advantage due to the international nature of the firm's work. Previous travel, work experience, voluntary work or interests are also taken into account.

training environment

Trainees spend six months in four different professional groups within the firm and sit with either a partner or senior solicitor. Whenever possible, trainees are given a chance to nominate which seats they would prefer. Trainees are given ample opportunity to develop their legal and client service skills through being given early responsibility and client contact. Learning through work experience is regularly supplemented by a pre qualification programme which includes in-house seminars, lectures and workshops developed especially for the firm's trainees.

benefits

STL; Private Health Insurance; gym loan.

sponsorship & awards

£5,000 scholarship for LPC plus a £2,500 interest free loan (repayable over training contract).

Partners	24
Assistant Solicitors	28
Total Trainees	8

contact
Graduate Recruitment
Department

method of application
application form. Call or
email the Graduate
Recruitment department
from 1 April to 30 July

selection procedure
Interview/Assessment
Day held early to mid
September

closing date for 2003
31 July 2001

application
Training contracts p.a. **4**
Applications p.a. **400-500**
% interviewed p.a. **5%**
Required degree grade **2:1**

training
Salary:
1st year (2000) **£21,000**
2nd Year (2000) **£23,000**
Holiday entitlement:
20 days
% of trainees with a
non-law degree p.a. **varies**
No. of seats available
abroad p.a. **none**

post-qualification
Salary (2000) **£36,000**
% of trainees offered job
on qualification (2000): **50%**
% of assistants (as at
1/9/00) who joined as
trainees: **60%**
% of partners (as at 1/9/00)
who joined as trainees:
63%

overseas offices
Greece, Dubai.

A-Z

SOLICITORS

439

hodge jones & allen

Twyman House 31-39 Camden Road London NW1 9LR
Tel: (020) 7482 1974 Fax: (020) 7267 3476
Email: hja@hodge-jones-allen.co.uk
Website: www.hodge-jones-allen.co.uk

firm profile

Hodge Jones & Allen was founded in 1977 with the intention of providing high quality legal help, mainly under the Legal Aid Scheme, for those who have suffered injustice. The firm has grown to 21 partners and over one hundred staff and is led by managing partner Patrick Allen. It has been involved in a number of high profile and leading cases, notably personal injury cases arising from the King's Cross fire and the Marchioness disaster, and is also handling 3 major group claims, including Gulf War Syndrome.

main areas of work

Personal Injury 35%; Crime 28.5%; Family 21%; Housing 7.5%; Property & Employment 7%.

trainee profile

Ideally candidates should have strong IT skills together with a proven commitment to and/or experience of working in Legal Aid/Advice sectors.

training environment

Trainees have a full induction on joining HJA covering the work of the firm's main departments, procedural matters and professional conduct. Training consists of four six-month seats and trainees normally share an office with a partner who assists them and formally reviews their progress at least once during each seat.

benefits

Pension, life assurance, permanent health insurance, quarterly drinks, summer outing, christmas party.

Partners	21
Assistant Solicitors	24
Total Trainees	10

contact
Sarah Firth Personnel Manager

method of application
By application form only - one year in advance

selection procedure
Interview and selection tests in previous October

closing date for 2003
September 2002

application
Required degree grade: 2:1 degree preferred

holman fenwick & willan

Marlow House Lloyds Avenue London EC3N 3AL
Tel: (020) 7488 2300 Fax: (020) 7481 0316
Email: grad.recruitment@hfw.co.uk

firm profile

Holman Fenwick & Willan is an international law firm and one of the world's leading specialists in maritime transportation, insurance, reinsurance and trade. The firm is a leader in the field of commercial litigation and arbitration and also offers comprehensive commercial and financial advice. Founded in 1883, the firm is one of the largest operating in its chosen fields with a team of over 200 lawyers worldwide, and a reputation for excellence and innovation.

main areas of work

Their range of services include marine, admiralty and crisis management, insurance and reinsurance, commercial litigation and arbitration, international trade and commodities, energy, corporate and financial.

trainee profile

Applications are invited from commercially minded under-graduates and graduates of all disciplines with good A-levels and who have, or expect to receive, a IIi degree. Good foreign languages or a scientific or maritime background are an advantage.

training environment

During your training period they will ensure that you gain valuable experience in a wide range of areas. They also organise formal training supplemented by a programme of in-house seminars and ship visits in addition to the PSC. Your training development as an effective lawyer will be managed by our Recruitment & Training Partner, Ottilie Sefton, who will ensure that your training is both successful and enjoyable.

benefits

Private medical insurance, permanent health and accident insurance, subsidised gym membership, season ticket loan.

vacation placements

Places for 2001: 12; Duration: 2 weeks. Dates: 25 June – 6 July/16 July – 27 July; Remuneration: £250 p.w.; Closing Date: Applications accepted 1 Jan – 14 Feb. 2001

sponsorship & awards

CPE Funding: Fees paid + £4,500 maintenance. LPC Funding: Fees paid + £4,500 maintenance.

Partners	76
Assistant Solicitors	152
Total Trainees	18

contact
Graduate Recruitment Officer

method of application
Handwritten letter and typed CV

selection procedure
Two interviews with partners
and written exercise

closing date for 2003
31 July 2001

application
Training contracts p.a. 7
Applications p.a. 1,200
% interviewed p.a. 5%
Required degree grade 2:1

training
Salary:
1st year (2000)
1st six months £23,000
2nd six months £23,750
3rd six months £24,500
4th six months £25,000
Holiday entitlement:
22 days
% of trainees with
a non-law degree p.a. 50%

post-qualification
Salary (2000) £38,000
% of trainees offered job
on qualification
(Sept 2000): 100%

overseas offices
Hong Kong, Nantes, Paris, Piraeus, Rouen, Shanghai and Singapore.

A-Z SOLICITORS

howes percival

Oxford House Cliftonville Northampton NN1 5PN
Tel: (01604) 230400 Fax: (01604) 620956
Email: law@howes-percival.co.uk
Website: www.howes-percival.co.uk

firm profile

Howes Percival is a 27 partner commercial law firm with a committed view to exceeding clients' expectations well into the 21st century. It has four offices throughout the East Midlands and East Anglia. Areas of outstanding strength within the firm include: company commercial (with particular emphasis on corporate finance), commercial property, commercial litigation, employment, tax and private client. The client profile is to be envied by any city firm.

main areas of work

Company Commercial 30%; Commercial Property 25%; Commercial Litigation 20%, Insolvency 10%; Employment 10%; Private Client 5%.

trainee profile

Beyond excellent academic qualifications and technical and professional skills, the firm is looking for those with a proven track record in team working, who are commercially aware, innovative, adaptable to change and high on conceptual thinking, analysis and decision making. In addition candidates will be able to demonstrate excellent interpersonal skills.

training environment

As the practice is departmentalised, trainees will spend a maximum of six months in four departments (see "main areas of work"). At the Norwich office trainees may also gain experience in agriculture and licensing. Trainees are assigned a departmental training supervisor who, in addition to providing day to day guidance' will formally assess the trainee at three and six month intervals. In addition to PSC training, trainees will receive a tailored in-house training programme, including CPD accredited courses, the firm's own Client Care Programme and IT training.

benefits

Payment of LPC & PSC course fees.

Partners	27
Assistant Solicitors	27
Total Trainees	9

contact
Mrs K Collyer

method of application
Letter and firm's form

selection procedure
Assessment centres including second interview with training principal and partner

closing date for 2003
31 July 2001

application
Training contracts p.a. 6
Applications p.a. 300
% interviewed p.a. 13%
Required degree grade 2:1

training
Salary:
1st year (2000) £15,500
2nd year (2000) £16,750
Holiday entitlement:
23 days

post-qualification
% of trainees offered job on qualification (2000): 100%
% of assistants (as at 1/9/00) who joined as trainees: 22%
% of partners (as at 1/9/00) who joined as trainees: 7.5%

A-Z

SOLICITORS

hugh james ford simey

Arlbee House Greyfriars Rd Cardiff CF10 3QB
Tel: (029) 2022 4871 Fax: (029) 2038 8222
Email: trainingcontracts@hjfs.co.uk
Website: www.hjfs.co.uk

firm profile

Hugh James Ford Simey is one of the UK's leading regional law firms. The firm has experienced phenomenal growth and success since it was formed in 1960 and has for many years been one of only a handful of firms to dominate the legal scene in Wales. As Hugh James Ford Simey, the firm is placed high in the table of the top 100 law firms in the UK. The firm offers its clients a comprehensive service covering the whole of South Wales and the West Country through its network of twelve offices.

main areas of work

The main areas covered by the firm are Commercial Litigation, Commercial Services, Commercial Property and Private Client. In response to demand for specific services, a number of specialist groups have been established which include construction, debt recovery, e-business, employment, head injury, housing associations, insurance, lender services and sports law. The breakdown of the main areas of work is as follows: Claimant Personal Injury 30%; Commercial and Insurance Litigation 25%; Commercial Services 13%; Commercial Property 12%; Private Client 10%; Construction and Professional Indemnity 10%.

trainee profile

Hugh James Ford Simey welcomes applications from law and non-law undergraduates with a good class degree. Candidates must exhibit first class legal and practice skills and good interpersonal and IT skills are essential. The firm seeks to retain its trainees upon qualification and sees them as an integral part of the future of the firm. Hugh James Ford Simey is proud of the fact that the majority of the firm's present partners were trained at the firm.

training environment

Trainees generally undertake four seats of not less than six months which may be in any of the firm's offices. Broadly, experience will be gained in all four main work categories. The breadth of work dealt with by the firm enables us to ensure that over-specialisation is avoided.

benefits

Company pension scheme

vacation placements

Places for 2001: available.

Partners	60
Assistant Solicitors	51
Total Trainees	14

contact
Jane O'Rourke
HR Manager

method of application
Application form available
from HR Manager

selection procedure
Assessment Day

closing date for 2003
31 July 2001

application
Training contracts p.a. **7**
Applications p.a. **350**
% interviewed p.a. **30%**
Required degree grade **2:2**

training
Salary: 1st year(2000)
**Competitive and
reviewed annually**
Salary: 2nd Year(2000)
**Competitive and
reviewed annually**

other offices
Cardiff, Merthyr Tydfil,
Bargoed, Talbot Green,
Blackwood, Treharris,
Pontlottyn, Bristol, Exeter,
Exmouth, Sidmouth.

ince & co

Knollys House 11 Byward Street London EC3R 5EN
Tel: (020) 7623 2011 Fax: (020) 7623 3225
Email: claire. kendall@ince.co.uk

firm profile
Since its foundation in 1870, Ince & Co has specialised in international commercial law and is best known for its shipping and insurance work.

main areas of work
Shipping & International Trade 40%; Insurance/Reinsurance 40%; Professional Indemnity 10%; Company, Commercial Property 10%.

trainee profile
Hard-working competitive individuals with initiative who relish challenge and responsibility within a team environment. Academic achievements, positions of responsibility, sport and travel are all taken into account.

training environment
Trainees sit with four different partners for six months at a time throughout their training. Under close supervision, they are encouraged from an early stage to meet and visit clients, interview witnesses, liaise with counsel, deal with technical experts and handle opposing lawyers. They will quickly build up a portfolio of cases from a number of partners involved in a cross-section of the firm's practice and will see their cases through from start to finish. They will also attend in-house and outside lectures, conferences and seminars on practical and legal topics.

benefits
STL, corporate health cover, PHI.

vacation placements
Places for 2001: 16; Duration: 2 weeks; Remuneration: £200 p.w.; Closing Date: 16th February 2001.

sponsorship & awards
LPC fees, £4,000 grant for study in London, £3,500 grant for study elsewhere.

Partners	56*
Assistant Solicitors	72*
Total Trainees	23
*denotes world-wide figures	

contact
Claire Kendall

method of application
Typed/handwritten letter and CV

selection procedure
Interview with 2 partners from Recruitment Committee and a written test

closing date for 2003
3 September 2001

application
Training contracts p.a. **11**
Applications p.a. **2,000**
% interviewed p.a. **5%**
Required degree grade **2:1**

training
Salary:
1st year (2000) £23,000
2nd year (2000) £25,000
Holiday entitlement:
22 days
% of trainees with a non-law degree p.a. **55%**

post-qualification
Salary (2000) **£36,500**
% of trainees offered job on qualification (2000): **91%**
% of assistants (as at 2000) who joined as trainees: **66%**
% of partners (as at 2000) who joined as trainees: **76%**

overseas offices
Hong Kong, Singapore, Shanghai, Piraeus (consultancy)

irwin mitchell

St. Peter's House Hartshead Sheffield S1 2EL
Recruitment line: (0114) 274 4580 Fax: (0114) 272 9346
Email: enquiries@irwinmitchell.co.uk
Website: www.irwinmitchell.co.uk

firm profile

Irwin Mitchell is a rapidly expanding 76 partner practice with over 1300 employees and offices in Sheffield, Leeds, Birmingham and London. The firm is particularly well known for commercial law, commercial litigation, insurance law, business crime and plaintiff personal injury litigation. Their strong reputation for dealing with novel and complex areas of law and handling developmental cases (such as the vibration white finger and CJD cases and the Matrix-Churchill 'arms to Iraq' affair) means that they can offer a broad range of experience within each of their specialist departments, giving trainees a high standard of training.

main areas of work

Corporate Services 37%; Plaintiff Personal Injury 28%; Insurance Litigation 17%; Private Client 12%; Police Prosecutions 6%.

trainee profile

Irwin Mitchell is looking for well motivated individuals with a real commitment to the law and who can demonstrate above average academic and social ability. Law and non-law graduates are recruited. Foreign languages and IT skills are an asset. The firm believes that trainees are an investment for the future and as such they prefer to keep their trainees once they qualify.

training environment

The two-year Training Contract consists of 4 seats. Our trainees also benefit from an Induction programme, monthly training meetings and the Professional Skills Course which is organised and financed by the firm. Each trainee has a review every 3 months with their supervising partner. There are numerous other activities in which trainees are encouraged to participate, eg. team skills challenges, conferences, mock trials.

vacation placements

Places for 2001: 30; Duration: 2 weeks; Remuneration: £75 p.w.; Closing Date: 1 March 2001.

sponsorship & awards

CPE and LPC fees paid and £3,000 maintenance grant.

Partners	76
Assistant Solicitors	148
Total Trainees	30

contact
Sue Lenkowski/
Tracey Easton

method of application
Brochures and application forms are available from the Human Resources Dept. Call the recruitment line between 1 March and 30 July

selection procedure
Assessment centres and interviews are held in late August and early September and successful candidates are invited to a second interview with 2 partners

closing date for 2003
31 July 2001

application
Training contracts p.a. 15
Applications p.a. 1,000
% interviewed p.a. 8%

training
Salary:
1st year (2000) £16,000
2nd year (2000) £18,000
Holiday entitlement:
23 days
% of trainees with a non-law degree p.a. 44.5%

post-qualification
% of trainees offered job on qualification (2000): 64%
% of assistants (as at 1/9/00) who joined as trainees: 32%
% of partners (as at 1/9/00) who joined as trainees: 16%

A-Z SOLICITORS

jeffrey green russell

Apollo House 56 New Bond Street London W1Y OSX
Tel: (020) 7339 7000 Fax: (020) 7339 7001
Email: jgr@jgrlaw.co.uk
Website: www.jgrweb.com

firm profile

Jeffrey Green Russell is a medium-sized commercial law firm with strong international connections based in New Bond Street, London. The firm is determined to excel on its clients' behalf. It works hard to find the best and most cost effective solutions to their problems. The firm tries to be innovators not imitators, providing a rapid and constructive response to its clients' increasingly specialised needs. JGR is a founder member of ACL International, an association of commercial lawyers, providing members with access to an effective global legal service, beneficial for international business requirements.

main areas of work

JGR has a diverse client base and specialises in company/commercial and taxation, litigation, white-collar crime, insurance litigation, property, gaming, licensing and leisure, and private client. Most of its clients are in commerce, finance and industry, and range in size from small businesses to multinational corporations. Their activities are wide-ranging and include banking, finance, technology, leisure and the licensed trade, insurance, and property.

trainee profile

The firm welcomes intelligent, enthusiastic, and ambitious individuals, who are not afraid of responsibility, and are keen to learn from experienced lawyers who will guide them through their training period. Not only should they undertake work with diligence and care, and strive to develop negotiating skills, but should consider the variety of needs of both individual and corporate clients.

training environment

Trainees are supervised through the various departments, including company/commercial, litigation, property, and licensing. To maximise our efficiency and productivity, and to provide cost effective services, the firm has for many years been making major investments in sophisticated office technology. Accordingly trainees should have a keen interest in utilising office technology and be willing to develop these skills alongside their legal training to encourage the highest-quality service with speed. Visit the firm's website for further information.

Partners	22
Assistant Solicitors	32
Total Trainees	4

contact
Jacqueline Rook

method of application
CV with covering letter

selection procedure
Room will be made available for exceptional candidates.

closing date for 2003
No time limits because the firm has no specific vacancies to fill.

application
Training contracts p.a. 4

kennedys

Longbow House 14-20 Chiswell Street London EC1Y 4TW
Tel: (020) 7614 3771 Fax: (020) 7638 2212
Email: personnel@kennedys-law.com
Website: www.kennedys-law.com

firm profile

Kennedys is a medium-sized international City firm which has grown considerably in recent years. The firm is primarily known as an insurance-driven commercial litigation practice, although it is also recognised for its skills in the non-contentious commercial field. The firm has 49 partners and over 300 staff located in four offices in the UK, including two in London and separate practices in Belfast and Hong Kong. The firm's associated offices in New York, San Francisco, Paris, Madrid, New Delhi, Karachi, Beirut and Dublin, together with its in-house European lawyers in London, ensure that it can advise its clients on all their commercial problems within most jurisdictions.

main areas of work

Insurance Litigation 83%; Company/Commercial 6%; Employment 6%; Construction (non-contentious) 3%; Commercial Property 2%.

trainee profile

Kennedys are looking for ambitious people with creative practical, problem-solving skills. Successful candidates will be those who combine independence of thought with the ability to work as part of a team. Requirements are a minium 2:1 degree which may or may not be in law. Fluency in a major European language is a positive asset.

training environment

At Kennedys the emphasis will be on commercial litigation but trainees will also undertake non-contentious work in company/commercial and commercial departments. Trainees may also spend some time in the construction, medical negligence, personal injury, banking and employment teams. There may also be opportunities for training abroad, particularly France and Germany.

benefits

Life assurance, PHI, private medical insurance, season ticket loan, subsidised gym membership.

vacation placements

Places for 2001: 10

sponsorship & awards

£9,000 towards fees and assistance for LPC only.

Partners	49
Assistant Solicitors	64
Total Trainees	14

contact
Rob Hind
Personnel Director

method of application
Handwritten letter, CV and application form.

selection procedure
Minimum of one interview with two Partners and Personnel Director

closing date for 2003
17 August 2001

application
Training contracts p.a. **6-8**
Applications p.a. **1500**
% interviewed p.a. **3%**
Required degree grade **2:1**

training
Salary:
1st year (2000) **£20,000**
2nd year (2000) **£22,000**
Holiday entitlement:
25 days

post-qualification
Salary (2000) **£33,000**
% of trainees offered job on qualification (2000): **95%**

overseas offices
Hong Kong

associated offices
New York, San Francisco, Paris, New Delhi, Karachi.

klegal

Ludgate House 107-111 Fleet Street London EC4A 2AB
Tel: (020) 7694 2500 Fax: (020) 7694 2501
Website: www.klegaltrainees.co.uk

firm profile

KLegal is the UK associated firm of KPMG and was founded in July 1999. The firm exists to provide legal services as part of KPMG's multi-disciplinary approach to client service. The firm has a unique opportunity to help develop a top-quality legal practice on an international basis alongside one of the top global professional services providers.

main areas of work

The firm's focus is on developing its legal expertise in practice areas that complement the services offered by KPMG. These include banking and finance, corporate, commercial, e-commerce, IT and telecoms, employment, financial services, intellectual property, projects/PFI, property, tax litigation, competition and trade & customs.

trainee profile

KLegal is looking for top-quality candidates with ambition who share its vision and who are capable of helping us to achieve it. The firm is a constantly changing environment and its rapid growth rate is set to continue apace. The firm is looking to those who see the opportunities this provides both for themselves as individuals and for their colleagues generally.

training environment

KLegal's training is based upon a conventional rotation of seats of 6 months in 4 main practice areas. The firm provides opportunities for its trainees to learn their legal skills as part of multi-disciplinary teams and secondment opportunities within KPMG may also be available, enabling them to become amongst the best commercially minded lawyers in the City. And its personal development training is second to none. The firm's commitment is to provide an enjoyable experience, allowing individuals to maximise both their own personal and professional development.

benefits

Non-contributory pension, life assurance, free lunch, Flextra, 25 days holiday.

vacation placements

Places for 2001: 12; Duration: 4 weeks; Remuneration: £220 p.w.; Closing Date: 31 April 2001.

sponsorship & awards

CPE Funding: Fees paid + maintenance.
LPC Funding: Fees paid + maintenance.

Partners 11
Assistant Solicitors 10
Total Trainees 9

contact
Patrick Martin Graduate Recruitment Partner

method of application
On-line application. Visit www.klegaltrainees.co.uk

selection procedure
2 interviews + assessment exercises

closing date for 2003
31 August 2001

application
Training contracts p.a. 30-40
Applications p.a. c.750
Required degree grade 2:1

training
Salary:
1st year (2000) £25,000
Holiday entitlement:
25 days

overseas offices
Member of KLegal International.

knight & sons

The Brampton, Newcastle under Lyme ST5 0QW
Tel: (01782) 619 225 Fax: (01782) 717 260
Email: ttpc@knightandsons.co.uk
Website: www.knightandsons.co.uk

firm profile

Knight & Sons is a medium sized, commercially orientated firm with a strong private client department. The firm was founded in 1767 and it has 15 partners and approximately 130 members of staff.

main areas of work

The firm's main areas of work are Commercial Property 30%; Corporate and Commercial 27%; Commercial Litigation 26%; Tax, Trust and Private Client 11%; Brewery and Licensing 6%.

trainee profile

The firm is keen to recruit trainees who will stay on once they have qualified. Successful candidates are commercially aware, proactive and outgoing in character. Languages, computer literacy and outstanding academic achievement are desirable.

training environment

Trainees generally spend six months in each of the four main departments (litigation, commercial property, company commercial and tax, trusts and private client), but may also gain experience in the specialist units such as development planning and environmental, employment, personal injury, agriculture and charity. The firm runs in-house skills-based programmes designed to enhance business and client care skills for all fee-earners. The atmosphere is lively and a social committee organises events throughout the year ranging from a summer ball to a quiz night.

benefits

Subsidised gym membership.

vacation placements

Applications to be received by :
31 October for the following Christmas
28 February for the following Easter
30 April for the following Summer

sponsorship and awards

Interest free loans may be available but are strictly subject to individual negotiation.

| Trainees | 7 |
| Partners | 15 |

contact
Zoe Theofilopoulos

method of application
Please make a handwritten application supported by CV.

closing date for 2003
By 31 July each year to begin two years hence.

application
Training contracts p.a. 3-4

Starting salary
Above Law Society minimum with a review each six months

Minimum qualifications
2.1 degree

Offices
Newcastle under Lyme.

lawrence graham

190 Strand London WC2R 1JN
Tel: (020) 7759 6694 Fax: (020) 7379 6854
Email: graduate@lawgram.com
Website: www.lawgram.com

firm profile

Lawrence Graham is a growing firm with a broad client base, which includes many UK and international public and private companies, pension funds, financial institutions, shipping companies, small businesses and private individuals. The firm's business is divided into four main practice areas: Commercial Property, Company & Commercial, Litigation and Tax & Financial Management. Each of the four main practice areas is organised into specialised teams. The firm has associations with many law firms throughout the world, including North America, Europe and the Far East. It also has an office in the Ukraine where the firm has had clients since the 1920s.

main areas of work

Property 35%; Company & Commercial 29%, Litigation (inc Shipping) 23%, Tax & Financial Management 13%.

trainee profile

The firm purposely recruits a fewer number of trainees for its size to enable comprehensive, hands on training. Candidates, who are normally of 2.1 calibre, should demonstrate strong technical and interpersonal skills, the ability to understand a client's commercial priorities and objectives and the judgement to deal with complex problems.

training environment

Trainees are given the opportunity to learn both formally and practically. Seminars are regularly held throughout the two years. Training consists of four six-month seats including a seat in each of the Company & Commercial, Litigation and Property departments. The fourth seat can be in either Tax & Financial Management or back to one of the main departments. Each trainee is assigned a mentor. All work is supervised but independence and responsibility increases with experience. Social events including sporting events are also organised.

benefits

Season ticket loan, on-site gym.

vacation placements

Places for 2001: 40; Duration: 2 weeks during Easter break and 4x2 weeks between June-August; Remuneration: £200 p.w.; Closing Date: 31 January 2001.

sponsorship & awards

CPE Funding: Course Fees and £3,750 maintenance grant.
LPC Funding: Course Fees and £3,750 maintenance grant.

Partners	80
Assistant Solicitors	98
Total Trainees	30

contact
The Graduate Recruitment Officer

method of application
Firm's application form.
For Law: After 2nd year results
For Non-Law: After final results

selection procedure
Interview and written exercise

closing date for 2003
31 July 2001

application
Training contracts: 16
Applications p.a. 1,000
Required degree grade 2:1

training
Salary:
1st year (2000) £25,000
2nd year (2000) £28,000
% of trainees with a non-law degree p.a. 40%

post-qualification
Salary (2000) £40,000
% of trainees offered job on qualification (2000): 100%
% of assistants (as at 1/9/00) who joined as trainees: 42%
% of partners (as at 1/9/00) who joined as trainees: 32%

laytons

Carmelite 50 Victoria Embankment Blackfriars London EC4Y 0LS
Tel: (020) 7842 8000 Fax: (020) 7842 8080
Email: london@laytons.com
Website: www.laytons.com

firm profile

Layton assigns a core legal team to each client who knows its business and can advise directly or by deploying the specialist skills of colleagues. The approach to legal issues is practical, creative and energetic, providing high quality advice founded on a range of complementary specialist skills relevant to the firm's primary fields of focus. The firm is a single national team operating through its four offices, each of which draws on the strengths of the whole with the benefit of excellent IT and communications.

main areas of work

Company/Commercial 33%; Commercial Property/Land Development 20%; General Litigation 19%; Building Litigation 11%; Employment 8%; Private Client 5%; Insolvency 4%.

trainee profile

All trainees have contact with clients from an early stage, working on a wide variety of transactions. Trainees will soon be responsible for their own files, although they are always supported and have regular appraisals throughout the training contract. The firm recruits with a view to retaining trainees to assistant level. Trainees are also encouraged to participate in the firm's business development activities.

training environment

Trainees are placed in four six-month seats in each of the firm's principal departments: · Company Commercial, Property, Litigation and Private Client.

vacation placements

Places for 2001: 6; Duration: 1 week; Closing Date: 31 March 2001.

sponsorship & awards

CPE Funding: yes; LPC Funding: yes.

Partners	28
Assistant Solicitors	43
Total Trainees	15

contact
Ian Burman

method of application
Application form

selection procedure
2 interviews

closing date for 2003
31 August 2001

application
Training contracts p.a. 8
Applications p.a. 2,000
% interviewed p.a. 5%
Required degree grade:
1 or 2:1

training
Salary:
1st year (2001) Market rate
2nd Year (2001) Market rate
Holiday entitlement:
22 days

post-qualification
Salary (2001) Market rate
% of trainees offered job on qualification (2000): 80%
% of assistants (as at 1/9/00) who joined as trainees: 90%
% of partners (as at 1/9/00) who joined as trainees: 20%

le brasseur j tickle

Drury House 34–43 Russell Street London WC2B 5HA
Tel: (020) 7836 0099 Fax: (020) 7831 2215
Email: enquiries@lbjt.co.uk
6–7 Park Place Leeds LS1 2RU
Tel: (0113) 234 1220 Fax: (0113) 234 1573
Windsor House Windsor Lane Cardiff CF10 3DE
Tel: (029) 2034 3035 Fax: (029) 2034 3045

firm profile

Le Brasseur J Tickle has an enviable reputation for tradition and excellence. The firm has 29 partners and approximately 135 members of staff. The firm is located in three major commercial and legal centres, London, Leeds and Cardiff, from which legal expertise is provided to all types of clients from multi-national corporations to individuals.

main areas of work

Health Care: 50%; Personal Injury: 5%; Employment: 10%; Company Commercial: 15%; Commercial Property: 10%; Commercial Litigation: 10%.

trainee profile

Le Brasseur J Tickle looks to recruit trainees from a broad academic background with good intellectual ability and an assured outgoing personality who will prove to be responsive to the needs of the firm's clients. When recruiting trainees, the partners look to the future and to appointing trainees as assistant solicitors following qualification. Indeed a significant number of partners trained with the firm.

training environment

The firm provides an extensive legal and skills training programme for trainee solicitors and other qualified staff in addition to on-the-job training. Trainees are introduced to the firm with an induction programme covering the work of the firm's departments, the major clients, procedural matters and professional conduct. Training consists of four six-month seats in the following areas: Company Commercial; Commercial Property; Health Care Law; and General Litigation. Every endeavour is made to allocate the final seat, following discussion, in the area of law in which the trainee wishes to specialise after qualification. You will share an office with a partner, who will assist you and formally review your progress at the end of your seat. The PSC is taught externally. The firm is friendly with an open-door policy and there are various sporting and social events organised throughout the year.

Partners	29
Assistant Solicitors	47
Total Trainees	8

contact
Training Partner

method of application
Letter and CV

selection procedure
2 interviews

closing date for 2003
31 July 2001

application
Training contracts p.a. 4
Applications p.a. 1,500
% interviewed p.a. 2%

training
Salary:
1st year (2000)
(London) £18,000
(Leeds) £14,250
2nd year (2000)
(London) £20,000
(Leeds) £15,000
Holiday entitlement:
4 weeks
% of trainees with a
non-law degree p.a. 50%

post-qualification
Salary (2000):
(London) £30,000
(Leeds) £22,500
% of trainees offered job
on qualification (2000):
100%
% of assistants (as at
1/9/00) who joined as
trainees: 60%
% of partners (as at 1/9/00)
who joined as trainees:
50%

lee bolton & lee

1 The Sanctuary Westminster London SW1P 3JT
Tel: (020) 7222 5381 Fax: (020) 7222 7502
Email: enquiries@1thesanctuary.com

firm profile

Founded in 1855 Lee Bolton & Lee is a successful medium sized firm based in Westminster. It is closely associated with parliamentary agents and solicitors, Rees and Freres, who provide a specialist service in parliamentary, public and administrative law.

main areas of work

Commercial; Property; Private Client; Litigation; Charity; Education Work.

trainee profile

They seek to recruit trainees with a good degree (2:1 or above), first class communication skills, motivation, professionalism, initiative, enthusiasm, and a sense of humour.

training environment

Trainees spend six months in each of four seats: Private Client, Property, Litigation and Commercial Property, sitting with either a senior solicitor or a Partner. Training is comprehensive and covers a full induction programme, participation in internal seminars and training sessions and attendance at external courses, including the Professional Skills Course. Trainees are given responsibility for their own files from the beginning, and whilst this might at first seem daunting, the firm operates an open door policy and help is never far away. Progress is reviewed monthly by your elected Supervisor and every three months by the Training Principal. There are various sporting and social events.

benefits

Season ticket loan, non-guaranteed bonus.

sponsorship & awards

A contribution towards LPC funding but dependent upon being offered a training contract.

Partners 14
Assistant Solicitors 10
Total Trainees 4

contact
Susie Hust

method of application
Letter and CV

selection procedure
Panel interview

closing date for 2003
End July 2001

application
Training contracts p.a. 2
Applications p.a. 800
% interviewed p.a. 3%
Required degree grade 2:1

training
Salary:
1st year £18,500
2nd year £19,500
Holiday entitlement:
22 days
% of trainees with a
non-law degree p.a. 50%

post-qualification
Salary (2000) £29,000
% of trainees offered job
on qualification (2000):
100%
% of assistants (as at
1/9/00) who joined as
trainees: 40%
% of partners (as at 1/9/00)
who joined as trainees:
15%

lester aldridge

Russell House Oxford Road Bournemouth BH8 8EX
Tel: (01202) 786161 Fax: (01202) 786110
Email: enquiries@lester-aldridge.co.uk

firm profile

Lester Aldridge is one of the largest law firms in central Southern England. It is a progressive and innovative practice, which has adopted a corporate style management structure. The firm is market led with an emphasis on the development of specialist units offering expert advice on specific aspects of the law from lawyers who are familiar with a particular industry. Lawyers are encouraged and trained to adopt a commercial approach, seeking legal solutions to business problems. The firm has taken the innovative step of employing non-solicitors e.g. accountants to develop certain areas of the business.

main areas of work

Litigation: 34%; Corporate & Banking and Finance: 26%; Private Client Services: 19%; Commercial Property: 15%; Investment Services: 6%.

trainee profile

Candidates should have strong intellectual capabilities, be resourceful and be able to relate easily to other people. IT skills and a team approach are also required.

training environment

Trainees receive an extended version of the firm's induction procedure which covers the firm's aims, values and structure, administration and support. Training consists of four six month seats in the private client, banking and finance, commercial and litigation areas of work, and trainees are fully integrated members of the teams they work within. About half way through each seat, trainees discuss their preferences for the next seat with the partner responsible for allocations and every attempt is made to match aspirations to the needs of the firm. Trainees have a training principal for the duration of the contract who will discuss progress every month. They receive a comprehensive formal appraisal from their team leader towards the end of each seat, and the managing partner also meets all trainees as a group every three months.

benefits

Life assurance scheme.

vacation placements

Places for 2001: 8; Duration: 2 weeks; Remuneration: £60 pw; Closing Date: 31 March 2001.

sponsorship & awards

Discretionary

Partners	31
Assistant Solicitors	17
Total Trainees	10

contact
Ms Juliet Milne

method of application
Letter, CV and completed application form

selection procedure
Interview by a panel of partners

closing date for 2003
31 August 2001

application
Training contracts p.a. 5
Applications p.a. 300
% interviewed p.a. 5%
Required degree grade 2:1

training
Salary:
1st year (2000) £15,000
2nd year (2000) £16,500
Holiday entitlement:
20 days
% of trainees with
a non-law degree p.a. 20%

post-qualification
Salary (2000) £24,500
% of trainees offered job
on qualification (2000):
100%
% of assistants (as at
1/9/00) who joined as
trainees: 30%
% of partners (as at 1/9/00)
who joined as trainees:
25%

lewis silkin

Windsor House 50 Victoria Street London SW1H 0NW
Tel: (020) 7227 8000 Fax: (020) 7222 4633
Email: info@lewissilkin.com

firm profile

Lewis Silkin places the highest priority on its relationship with clients, excellent technical ability and the commercial thinking of its lawyers. As a result, it is a profitable and distinctive firm, with a friendly and lively style.

main areas of work

The firm has a wide range of corporate clients and provides services through three main departments: corporate, litigation and property. The major work areas are: construction; corporate services, which includes company, commercial and corporate finance; commercial litigation and dispute resolution; employment; housing and project finance; marketing services, embracing advertising and marketing law; property; technology and communications, which includes IT, media and telecommunications.

trainee profile

The firm looks for trainees with keen minds and personality, who will fit into a professional but informal team. Law and non-law degrees considered.

training environment

Lewis Silkin provides a comprehensive induction and training programme, with practical "hands-on" experience in four six-month seats, three of which will be in one of the main departments. The fourth seat can be in one of the specialist areas. Trainees usually sit with a partner who can give on-going feedback and guidance and progress is formally reviewed every three months. Trainees have the opportunity to get involved in the firm's social and marketing events and also to represent the firm at local trainee solicitors' groups and Law Centres.

benefits

Life assurance, critical illness cover, health insurance, season ticket loan, group pension plan.

vacation placements

Places for 2001: None.

sponsorship & awards

Full fees paid for LPC.

Partners 31
Assistant Solicitors 40
Total Trainees 12

contact
Ruth Willis
Personnel and Training
Manger

method of application
Covering letter and C.V.

selection procedure
Assessment day, including an interview with two partners and an analytical exercise.

closing date for 2003
31 July 2001

application
Training contracts p.a. **6**
Applications p.a. **1,000**
Required degree grade **2:1**

training
Salary:
1st year (2000) £22,000
2nd year (2000) £23,000
Holiday entitlement:
25 days

post-qualification
Salary (2000) **£36,000**

A-Z

SOLICITORS

linklaters (a member firm of linklaters & alliance)

One Silk Street London EC2Y 8HQ
Tel: (020) 7456 2000 Fax: (020) 7456 2222
Email: graduate.recruitment@linklaters.com
Website: www.linklaters.com

firm profile

Linklaters is one of the premium global commercial law firms based in the City of London. The firm is a member of Linklaters & Alliance which brings together six of Europe's leading law firms.

main areas of work

There are three core practice areas: corporate, global finance (includes securities, banking, projects and asset finance) and specialist groups (includes commercial real estate, litigation, construction and engineering, employee incentives, employment, EU competition and regulation, financial markets, IP, investment funds, pensions, tax, technology and trusts.)

trainee profile

High academic achievers with outside interests, confidence and commitment to thrive in a strong client centred, commercial environment. Desire for early involvement and responsibility. Language skills are advantageous. All degree disciplines considered.

training environment

Your training will be tailored in line with business needs and your individual aspirations. It will be geared to providing you with high quality experience and early responsibility so that you qualify with confidence. During your training you will have four seats covering all three core practice areas. The majority of trainees spend time either on a client secondment or in one of the firm's overseas offices. A couple of months into your training, your interests and experience will be discussed with you in order to develop your individual seat plan.

benefits

PPP medical insurance, life assurance, pension, season ticket loan, in-house gym and corporate membership of Holmes Place, in-house dentist, doctor and physio, 24 hour subsidised restaurant.

vacation placements

Places for 2001: 120 Places available at Christmas, Easter and Summer; Remuneration: £225 p.w.

sponsorship & awards

CPE and LPC fees paid in full. A maintenance grant is also provided of £4,500 - £5,000 per annum. Language bursaries are also offered, upon completion of the LPC.

Partners	250
Assistant Solicitors	741
Total Trainees	257

contact
Sarah Emmott

method of application
Application form

selection procedure
2 Interviews (same day)

application
Training contracts p.a. **150**
Applications p.a. **2,500**
% interviewed p.a. **20%**
Required degree grade **2:1**

training
Salary:
1st year (2000) £25,000
2nd Year (2000) £28,000
Holiday entitlement:
25 days
% of trainees with
a non-law degree p.a. **45%**
No. of seats available
abroad p.a. **100**

post-qualification
Salary (2000) **£42,000**
% of trainees offered job
on qualification (2000):
100%

**overseas offices of
linklaters & alliance**
Alicante, Amsterdam, Antwerp, Bangkok, Berlin, Bratislava, Brussels, Bucharest, Budapest, Cologne, Frankfurt, Gothenburg, The Hague, Hong Kong, Leipzig, London, Luxembourg, Madrid, Malmo, Milan, Moscow, Munich, New York, Padua, Paris, Prague, Rome, Rotterdam, Sao Paulo, Shanghai, Singapore, Stockholm, St Petersburg, Tokyo, Warsaw, Washington D.C.

lovells

65 Holborn Viaduct London EC1A 2DY
Tel: (020) 7296 2000 Fax: (020) 7296 2001
Email: recruit@lovells.com
Website: www.lovells.com

firm profile

One of the leading international law firms based in the City of London, Lovells has 24 offices located across Asia, Europe and North America. The breadth of the practice, and a pre-eminence in so many practice areas sets the firm apart from most of its competitors.

main areas of work

Corporate Finance; Banking; EC and Competition Law; Insurance Litigation; Intellectual Property; Insolvency; Commercial Property.

trainee profile

Individualists, not clones, whose keen intelligence extends beyond an excellent degree. A practical and commercial mind is vital, and so is a talent for analytical thinking.

training environment

Six-month seats in the four key sectors: corporate, litigation, property and one other specialised commercial sector. In each department you will be assigned a partner or senior solicitor who will supervise your work. During each seat, you will have formal and informal reviews to discuss your progress and preferences for subsequent seats. The third seat can be spent in an international office or on secondment to the in-house legal department of a major client. Trainees can help with Lovells' pro bono work such as part-time work at law centres or in a Citizens Advice Bureau. Numerous social and sporting activities help staff unwind together.

benefits

PPP, PHI, season ticket loan, corporate gym membership at Homes Place, staff restaurant, life assurance, in-house dentist and doctor.

vacation placements

Places for 2001: Christmas 2000 - 2 weeks, closing date: 10 November 2000; Easter 2001 - 2 weeks, Summer 2001 - 3 weeks, closing date: 12 February 2001.

Partners	247*
Assistant Solicitors	800*
Total Trainees	125

contact
Clare Walton
Recruitment Manager

method of application
Application form

selection procedure
Assessment day: critical thinking test, group exercise, interview

closing date for 2003
End of October 2001

application
Training contracts p.a. 80
Applications p.a. 1,500
% interviewed p.a. 30%
Required degree grade
2:1 minimum

training
Salary:
1st year (2000) £25,000
2nd Year (2000) £28,000
Holiday entitlement:
25 days
% of trainees with a
non-law degree p.a. 30%
No. of seats available
abroad p.a. 20

post-qualification
Salary (2000) £42,000

overseas offices
Alicante, Beijing, Berlin, Brussels, Chicago, Dresden, Düsseldorf, Frankfurt, Hamburg, Ho Chi Minh City, Hong Kong, Milan, Moscow, Munich, New York, Paris, Prague, Rome, Singapore, Tokyo, Warsaw, Washington DC. Associated offices: Budapest, Vienna, Zagreb.

lovells continued

sponsorship & awards

CPE and LPC course fees are paid, as well as a maintenance grant (in 2000/01) of £5,000 for London and Guildford and £4,500 elsewhere; £1,000 advance in salary on joining; £500 bonus; £250 for distinction for LPC; £250 for a 1st class degree result.

additional information

Lovells has a number of support systems which ensure you are getting the help you need. You are assigned a 'contact partner' during training, who will meet with you regularly, to monitor your progress and help you plan your future. Formal training is also vital during your Training Contract because you will be working in specialised areas. You will also gain an overview of the numerous areas of Lovells' practice. The courses are given by a combination of external and in-house training and have been adapted for, or developed by, the firm. You will also participate in the Professional Skills Course.

trainee comments

"The variety of the work and the amount of client contact really appealed to me - as did Lovells' culture" (Paul Brown, qualified lawyer, read law at Nottingham).
"Despite its size, Lovells constantly impresses me with the remarkable level of efficiency and speed with which it goes about its business"(Thomas Harding, second year trainee, read Archaeology and Anthropology at Peterhouse, Cambridge).

mace & jones

19 Water Street Liverpool L2 0RP
Tel: (0151) 236 8989 Fax: (0151) 227 5010
Email: donal.bannon@maceandjones.co.uk
14 Oxford Court, Bishopsgate, Manchester M2 3WQ
Tel: (0161) 236 2244 Fax: (0161) 228 7285
Email: phil.farrelly@maceandjones.co.uk
Website: www.maceandjones.co.uk

firm profile

Mace & Jones is a leading regional practice in the North West and remains a full service firm while enjoying a national reputation for its commercial expertise, especially in employment, litigation/insolvency, corporate and property. The firm's clients range from national and multinational companies and public sector bodies to owner managed businesses and private individuals, reflecting the broad nature of the work undertaken. Sound practical advice is given always on a value for money basis.

main areas of work

Commercial Litigation/Insolvency 15%; Commercial Property 15%; Company/Commercial 15%; Employment 35%; Personal Injury/Private Client/Family 20%.

trainee profile

The firm seeks to recruit highly motivated trainees with above average ability and the determination to succeed. The right calibre of trainee will assume responsibility early in their career. The firm provides a comprehensive internal and external training programme.

training environment

Trainees complete an induction course to familiarise themselves with the work carried out by the firm's main departments, administration and professional conduct. Training consists of four six month seats in the following departments: Company/Commercial, Employment, Commercial Litigation/Personal Injury Litigation, Property Law, Family Law. Strenuous efforts are made to ensure that trainees are able to select the training seat of their choice. A trainee will normally be required to share an office with a partner who will supervise their work and review the trainee's progress at the end of the seat. The PSC is taught externally. The firm operates an open door policy and has various social events.

benefits

Health Insurance

Partners	28
Assistant Solicitors	45
Total Trainees	12

contact
Liverpool office: Donal Bannon Manchester Office: Phil Farrelly

method of application
Covering letter and typed C.V. which should indicate individual degree subject results

selection procedure
Interview with partners

closing date for 2003
31 March 2002

application
Training contracts p.a. **12**
Applications p.a. **1500**
% interviewed p.a. **1%**
Required degree grade **2:1**

training
Salary:
1st year (2000) £13,000
2nd year (2000) £13,500
Holiday entitlement:
20 days
% of trainees with a non-law degree p.a. **40%**

post-qualification
Salary (2000) **negotiable**
% of trainees offered job on qualification (2000): **20%**
% of assistants (as at 1/9/00) who joined as trainees: **80%**
% of partners (as at 1/9/00) who joined as trainees: **40%**

A-Z

SOLICITORS

459

macfarlanes

10 Norwich Street London EC4A 1BD
Tel: (020) 7831 9222 Fax: (020) 7831 9607
Email: gs@macfarlanes.com
Website: www.macfarlanes.com

firm profile

A leading City firm serving national and international commercial, industrial, financial and private clients.

main areas of work

Company, Commercial and Banking 45%; Property 25%; Litigation 15%; Tax and Financial Planning 15%.

trainee profile

Any degree discipline. Actual or predicted 2:1 or better.

training environment

Macfarlanes divides the training contract into four six-month periods. You will usually spend time in each of the firm's four main departments (Company, Commercial and Banking; Litigation; Property; Tax and Financial Planning). There is an extensive in-house training programme. Trainees have responsibility for real work and make a contribution that is acknowledged and appreciated.

benefits

Twenty-one working days holiday in each calendar year (rising to 26 days upon qualification); interest free season ticket loan; free permanent health insurance[*]; free private medical insurance[*]; subsidised conveyancing; subsidised health club/gym membership; subsidised firm restaurant; subscription paid to the City of London Law Society or the London Trainee Solicitors' Group.

[*]After 12 months service.

vacation placements

Places for 2001: 40; Duration: 2 weeks; Remuneration: £200 p.w.; Closing Date: 28 February 2001 but applications considered and places offered from the beginning of January 2001.

sponsorship & awards

CPE and LPC fees paid in full and a £4,500 maintenance allowance for courses studied in London and Guildford and £4,000 for courses studied elsewhere. Prizes for those gaining distinction or commendation for the LPC.

Partners	52
Assistant Solicitors	105
Total Trainees	37

contact
Graham Stoddart

method of application
Application form and letter

selection procedure
Assessment Day

closing date for 2003
31 July 2001

application
Training contracts p.a. 20
Applications p.a. **1,500**
% interviewed p.a. **15%**
Required degree grade **2:1**

training
Salary:
1st year (2000) £25,000
2nd year (2000) £28,000
Holiday entitlement:
21 days
% of trainees with a
non-law degree p.a. **40%**

post-qualification
Salary (2000) **£42,000**
% of trainees offered job
on qualification (2000):
100%
% of assistants (as at
1/9/00) who joined as
trainees: **53%**
% of partners (as at 1/9/00)
who joined as trainees:
65%

overseas offices
Brussels

manches

Aldwych House 81 Aldwych London WC2B 4RP
Tel: (020) 7404 4433 Fax: (020) 7430 1133
Email: personnel@manches.co.uk
Website: www.manches.com

firm profile

Manches is a full service London commercial law firm at the forefront in a number of specialist legal practice areas and industrial sectors. It has a prestigious family law practice and an Oxford office. It emphasises a plain speaking, straightforward approach and is run along corporate lines with all non-legal functions handled by the Chief Executive.

main areas of work

Corporate 22%; Commercial Property 20%; Commercial Litigation 20%; Family Law 12%; Intellectual Property 8%; Banking and Insolvency 7%; Social Housing; 4%; Employment 4%; Personal Estate Planning 3%

trainee profile

The firm looks for candidates with a sound academic background, commercial acumen, enthusiasm and commitment. It wants engaging and outgoing personalities who will contribute to its development and help achieve its business goals. Clear and persuasive communication skills and tenacity are a must.

training environment

The firm provides high quality, individual training. Training is generally divided into four periods of 6 months (usually one in a niche practice area). Its comprehensive in-house training programme enables trainees to take responsibility from an early stage ensuring that they become confident and competent solicitors. Trainees are also encouraged to participate in departmental meetings and briefings and receive regular appraisals.

benefits

Season ticket loan, BUPA after 6 months, permanent health insurance, life insurance, pension after 6 months.

vacation placements

Places for 2001: 24; Duration: 2 weeks; Remuneration: £150 p.w.; Closing Date: 31 January 2001.

sponsorship & awards

CPE and LPC Funding: tuition fees and maintenance.

Partners	48
Assistant Solicitors	62
Total Trainees	20

contact
Sheona Clark
Tel: 020 7872 8690
(Graduate Recruitment line)

method of application
Application form

selection procedure
Individual interview with
2 partners. Possible 2nd
interview.

closing date for 2003
31 July 2001

application
Training contracts p.a. 7-8
Applications p.a. 1000
% interviewed p.a. 5%
Required degree grade 2:1

training
Salary:
1st year (2000)
London £22,000
2nd Year (2000)
London £24,600
Holiday entitlement:
22 days

post-qualification
Salary (2000)
London £36,180
% of trainees offered job
on qualification (2000):
90%

martineau johnson

St. Philips House St. Philips Place Birmingham B3 2PP
Tel: (0121) 200 3300 Fax: (0121) 200 3330
Email: emily.dean@martjohn.co.uk
Website: www.martineau-johnson.co.uk

firm profile

Forward thinking and on the leading edge of commercial practice, Martineau Johnson is a substantial law firm with offices in Birmingham and London. As one of the most innovative and progressive commercial law firms, it is a recognised market leader in many areas of practice and has a high reputation. The firm recently strengthened its name and reputation by launching four brand values: Know-How, Plain Speaking, Passion and Done Deals. These encapsulate both the service provided to clients and the culture within the firm.

main areas of work

Corporate 18%; Property 16%; Litigation 20%; Private Client 15%; Education 5%; Intellectual Property 5%; Employment 4%; Banking and Insolvency 7%; Trade and Energy 10%.

trainee profile

Martineau Johnston seeks to recruit 14 trainees in the year 2003. Successful candidates must have a good degree, not necessarily in law, be motivated, outgoing, with commercial flair and business skills, and be capable of original and creative thought.

training environment

The firm is committed to the personal supervision and training of trainees. Each trainee has a personal mentor. There is a unique system of seat rotation – seats are of four months duration and can be combined so that time can be spent in six different seats or longer if preferred. The firm offers a structured training programme and in addition to the above, trainees are encouraged to take part in the firm's varied sporting and social activities.

benefits

Pension; private health; life assurance; permanent health insurance; interest free travel loans; critical illness cover; Birmingham Hospital Saturday Fund; domestic conveyancing; will drafting and subscription fees.

vacation placements

Places for 2001: Open days held at Easter and during the summer months.; Closing Date: 28 February 2001.

sponsorship & awards

CPE - discretionary loan; LPC - grant for fees and maintenance.

Partners	35
Assistant Solicitors	100
Total Trainees	19

contact
Emily Dean

method of application
Application form

selection procedure
Assessment centre - half day

closing date for 2003
31 July 2001

application
Training contracts p.a. 14
Applications p.a. 500
% interviewed p.a. 10%
Required degree grade 2:1

training
Salary:
1st year (2000) £16,000
2nd Year (2000) £17,500
Holiday entitlement:
23 days
% of trainees with a
non-law degree p.a. 38%

post-qualification
Salary (2000) £30,000
% of trainees offered job
on qualification (2000):
100%
% of assistants (as at
1/9/00) who joined as
trainees: 56%
% of partners (as at 1/9/00)
who joined as trainees:
61%

masons

30 Aylesbury Street London EC1R 0ER
Tel: (020) 7490 4000 Fax: (020) 7490 2545
Email: graduate.recruitment@masons.com
Website: www.masons.com

firm profile

Masons is not a traditional law firm. It is entrepreneurial and highly responsive to change. It is also driven by a strategic vision aimed at strengthening its reputation as one of the most highly regarded and successful law firms in Europe and the Far East.

main areas of work

A training contract with Masons will give you access to first class resources combined with hands on experience in a highly focused and exciting environment. You will be part of an expanding international team that is well known for its advice to the Information and Technology, Construction & Engineering, and Energy & Infrastructure industries. Masons also provides Project Finance, Property, Commercial, Environmental Planning, Employment, Pension and Tax services.

trainee profile

Applications are welcome from individuals with quality legal or non-legal degrees, a minimum of 2:1.

training environment

In London, trainees spend four months in six seats. You will receive early exposure to the day to day work of the firm. You will learn at first hand what it takes to deal with clients, resolve complex problems and deliver consistent results. This invaluable experience will be underpinned by a comprehensive training programme designed around a range of formal training.

benefits

Life assurance, private health care, subsidised restaurant and season ticket loan (London).

vacation placements

Places for 2001: 36 (London), 5 (Manchester); Duration: 2 weeks in 2 different departments, June–end of August; Closing Date: 12 Feb 2001.

sponsorship & awards

All fees paid for CPE and LPC, plus a bursary of £4,000 for the year.

Partners 91*
Assistant Solicitors 283*
Total Trainees 45
denotes world-wide figures

contact
Kelcy Davenport

method of application
Firm's own application form

selection procedure
Assessment day followed by an interview

closing date for 2003
31 July 2001

application
Training contracts p.a. 30
Applications p.a. 1200
% interviewed p.a. 10%
Required degree grade 2:1

training
Salary:
1st year (2000)
£25,000 (London)
2nd year (2000)
£28,000 (London)
Holiday entitlement:
23 days

post-qualification
Salary (2000):
£42,000 (London)
% of trainees offered job on qualification (2000): 94%
% of partners (as at 1/9/00) who joined as trainees: 29%

overseas offices
Brussels, Dublin, Guangzhou (PRC), Hong Kong, Singapore

may, may & merrimans

12 South Square Gray's Inn London WC1R 5HH
Tel: (020) 7405 8932 Fax: (020) 7831 0011
Email: mmm@link.org

firm profile
May May & Merrimans is an old established Inns firm with a broad based practice which has a particularly strong reputation for its work with private clients, including landed estates and their related trusts.

main areas of work
Private client including tax and estate planning for UK and offshore clients, Wills, Settlements and Probate; Charity law; agricultural, commercial and residential property; civil litigation and family law; business law for private clients and unquoted companies.

trainee profile
The firm welcomes applications from law and non-law graduates with a first class academic record. The qualities it looks for in its trainees are initiative, enthusiasm, a practical turn of mind and good communication skills.

training environment
The firm's approach to training is to offer active involvement in good quality work and to maintain a careful balance between exercising supervision and encouraging trainees to accept as much responsibility as possible. The firm is not strictly departmentalised and trainees normally spend the first few months of their training contract concentrating on litigation and family law and the remainder working on a variety of non-contentious matters, principally private client and property.

sponsorship & awards
Discretionary loans for LPC.

Partners	11
Assistant Solicitors	5
Total Trainees	2

contact
Alexandra Sarkis

method of application
Letter and CV

selection procedure
Interview

closing date for 2003
31 July 2001

application
Training contracts p.a. **1**
Applications p.a. **200**
% interviewed p.a. **3%**
Required degree grade **2.1**

training
Salary:
**Competitive with
similar size/type firms**
Holiday entitlement:
20 days

post-qualification
% of trainees offered
job on qualification
(1997-2000): **100%**
% of assistants (as at
1/9/00) who joined
as trainees: **60%**
% of partners (as at 1/9/00)
who joined as trainees:
55%

mayer, brown & platt

Bucklersbury House, 3, Queen Victoria Street,
London EC4N 8EL
Tel: (020) 7246 6200 Fax: (020) 7329 4465
Email: tknights@mayerbrown.com
Website: www.mayerbrown.com

firm profile

Mayer, Brown & Platt is an international law firm headquarted in Chicago, there are over 850 lawyers throughout offices across the United States, Mexico and Europe. MBP's London office, established in 1974, has approximately 40 lawyers and is the flagship of MBP's European and CIS network.

main areas of work

The principal practice areas of the firm's London offices are comprised of: Conventional finance; Project finance; Leasing and asset finance; Capital markets, Securities and derivatives; Mergers and acquisitions; and General corporate matters.

trainee profile

The firm seeks outstanding candidates with academic excellence and a flexible attitude with business acumen, along with a sense of humour, good judgement, common sense and motivation.

training environment

Trainees are inducted into the firm's culture and environment. Training seats are offered in the following departments: Civil litigation; Commercial; Company; and Banking. The litigation seat is covered by secondment for three months to a City law firm or one of the firm's international offices. Trainees usually move from seat to seat, sharing an office with a supervising senior associate. The Professional Skills Course is run externally and a programme of monthly in-house lectures is run for lawyers and trainees. At least three formal appraisals are carried out during the training contract, and ongoing progress is monitored at all times. MBP has a friendly, sociable environment with an open door policy. Regular evening social events are organised for all members of staff.

benefits

Private medical insurance, season ticket loan, life assurance (4x basic salary), long term disability insurance.

vacation placements

Places for 2001: Not offered at present.

sponsorship & awards

100% funding for CPE and LPC plus maintenance grant.

Partners 10
Assistant Solicitors 26
Total Trainees 4

contact
Tracy Knights

method of application
Application Form

selection procedure
Two interviews with partners, associates and often a current trainee

closing date for 2003
31 August 2001

application
Training contracts p.a. 2
Applications p.a. 600
% interviewed p.a. 2%
Required degree grade:
High 2:1

training
Salary:
1st year (2000) £26,000+
2nd year (2000) £27,000+
Holiday entitlement:
25 days
% of trainees with a
non-law degree p.a. 50%

post-qualification
Salary (2000) £54,000
% of trainees offered job
on qualification (2000):
100%

overseas offices
Chicago, Charlotte,
Houston, Köln, Los
Angeles, New York,
Washington.

Representative offices:
Ashgabat, Bishkek,
Tashkent. Independent
correspondent offices:
Mexico City and Paris.

A-Z SOLICITORS

mccormicks

Britannia Chambers 4 Oxford Place Leeds LS1 3AX
Tel: (0113) 246 0622 Fax: (0113) 246 7488
Email: mccormicks@btinternet.com
Wharfedale House 37 East Parade Harrogate HG1 5LQ
Tel: (01423) 530630 Fax: (01423) 530709

firm profile

McCormicks is a high profile, progressive and highly regarded firm offering a full range of legal services to both corporate and private clients. It is regarded as one of the leading firms in the North of England and has been described by the Yorkshire Post as 'a law firm in the top rank' and by Yorkshire Television as 'one of the Region's top law firms.' The average age of the partners is 35 and the firm has a reputation for a vibrant and dynamic atmosphere.

main areas of work

(alphabetically) Charities; Commercial Litigation; Company and Commercial; Corporate Crime including VAT and Inland Revenue Investigation work and tribunals; Debt Collection and Mortgage Repossessions; Defamation; Employment; Family; General Crime (especially Road Traffic); Insolvency; Intellectual Property; Media/ Entertainment; Sports Law; Personal Injury; Private Client – the firm is regarded as one of the leading commercial, litigation, fraud, media and sports law practices in the North.

trainee profile

A McCormicks trainee will combine intellectual achievement, sense of humour, commitment to hard work and a pro-active disposition to achieving the best possible outcome for the firm and its clients.

training environment

You will be assigned to the appropriate department and will be supervised by a mentor. Your work and development will be constantly reviewed by your mentor together with regular file and progress reviews both by your team supervisor and by the Training Partner. This framework provides for your maximum development within a friendly, progressive and supportive environment. There is an open-door policy and a great team spirit.

vacation placements

Places for 2001: Available in summer vacation. Application forms by 1 Jan 2001.

Partners 8
Assistant Solicitors 12
Total Trainees 7

contact
Mark Burns,
Training Partner

method of application
Application Form

selection procedure
Selection day and interview with Training Partner

closing date for 2003
31 July 2001

application
Training contracts p.a. 4
Applications p.a. 1000
% interviewed p.a. 10%
Required degree grade 2:1

training
Salary:
1st year (2000)
Highly competitive

post-qualification
Salary (2000):
Highly competitive
% of trainees offered job on qualification (2000): 100%
% of partners (as at 1/9/99) who joined as trainees: 70%

mcdermott, will & emery

7 Bishopsgate London EC2N 3AQ
Tel: (020) 7577 6900 Fax: (020) 7577 6950
Website: www.mwe.com

firm profile

Founded in 1934 in Chicago, McDermott, Will & Emery is an international law firm with over 850 lawyers in 12 offices worldwide. The Firm's legal practice in London encompasses a broad range of practice groups, including corporate and commercial, mergers and acquisitions, securities and finance, restructuring and workouts, tax, arbitration, employment, intellectual property and environmental. The London office, which opened in November of 1998, is growing rapidly and as at September 2000, was 60 lawyers strong.

main areas of work

International and Commercial; Mergers and Acquisitions; Corporate Finance; International Taxation; Litigation; E-commerce; Intellectual Property; Information Technology; Telecoms; Employment; Pensions and Banking and Finance.

trainee profile

Applications are invited from commercially aware candidates who have an outstanding academic record and who possess a high degree of initiative and confidence.

training environment

Four seats over a two year period of traineeship. Comprehensive in-house training in Corporate and Litigation, plus 2 of the Firm's other practice areas will enable you to experience hands-on work in each of these departments. The trainee will share an office with an experienced solicitor and will be formally reviewed at the end of each period. MW&E aims to provide trainees with a high level of responsibility and work related experience, thereby allowing the trainee to fully understand the scope of the work carried out by the Firm. Trainees participate in training lectures and seminars with other solicitors to further acquaint themselves with the Firm's culture and expectations. Scope does exist for the trainee to work on U.S. secondment and on secondment to UK clients. MW&E is proud of its friendly and open working environment, whilst maintaining the highest levels of professional responsibility to clients.

benefits

Private Medical and Dental Insurance, Life Assurance, Permanent Health Insurance, Non-Contributory Pension, Interest-Free Season Ticket Loan, Gym Membership.

sponsorship & awards

CPE and LPC funding; Tuition for relevant courses.

Partners	465*
Assistant Solicitors	372*
Total Trainees	1

*denotes world-wide figures

contact
Human Resources
Manager

method of application
Application form

closing date for 2003
31 July 2001

training
Salary:
1st year (2000) £29,000

mills & reeve

Francis House 112 Hills Road Cambridge CB2 1PH
Tel: (01223) 364422 Fax: (01223) 355848
Email: stephen.trowbridge@mills-reeve.com
Website: www.mills-reeve.com

firm profile

Mills & Reeve is one of the largest UK commercial law firms. They operate throughout England and Wales from offices in Birmingham, Cambridge, London and Norwich.

main areas of work

The firm offers a full range of corporate, commercial, property, litigation and private client services to a mix of regional and national businesses. They are regional leaders in corporate and commercial work, national specialists in the sectors of Health, Insurance, Higher Education and Agriculture and specialists in Hi-tech and Bio-tech work.

trainee profile

Lively personalities who listen and communicate effectively. Accuracy, attention to detail and a solid academic background are also important to the firm.

training environment

Trainees are offered four five-month seats followed by a final seat of four months. This final seat allows the trainees to revisit the area of law into which they are going to qualify, or experience a new area of law. During each seat, trainees sit with a partner or experienced solicitor. Early responsibility is encouraged and performance is reviewed via a mix of formal appraisals and informal reviews. Staff at all levels are friendly and approachable. The firm operates a full induction programme to integrate trainees immediately. Practical training is complemented by a series of in-house lectures and the PSC.

benefits

Life assurance at two times pensionable salary and a contributory pension scheme.

vacation placements

Places for 2001: 25; Duration: 2 weeks; Remuneration: £110 p.w.; Closing Date: 1 March 2001.

sponsorship & awards

The firm pays the full costs of the LPC fees and offers a maintenance grant for the LPC year. Funding for the CPE is also available.

Partners	59
Assistant Solicitors	185
Total Trainees	25

contact
Stephen Trowbridge
Graduate Recruitment &
Development Manager

method of application
Firm's application form

selection procedure
Interview and assessment

closing date for 2003
15 August 2001

application
Training contracts p.a.
25-30
Applications p.a. 500
% interviewed p.a. 16%
Required degree grade 2:1

training
Salary:
1st year (2000) £15,750
2nd year (2000) £16,750
Holiday entitlement:
25 days
% of trainees with
a non-law degree p.a.
Approx 30%

post-qualification
Salary (2000) £28,000
% of trainees offered job
on qualification (2000):
92%
% of assistants (as at
1/9/00) who joined as
trainees: 48%
% of partners (as at 1/9/00)
who joined as trainees:
38%

mishcon de reya

21 Southampton Row London WC1B 5HS
Tel: (020) 7440 7000 Fax: (020) 7404 5982
Email: graduate.recruitment@mishcon.co.uk
Website: www.mishcon.co.uk

firm profile

An unconventional commercial firm with a substantial reputation, Mishcon de Reya provides legal services to a wide range of corporate, entrepreneurial and individual clients. It is run by lawyers who understand business and its partnership with clients extends beyond office walls. Organised departmentally into litigation, corporate & commercial, property and family, the firm has developed specially client-focused groups composed of lawyers from various departments. Groups currently include: art, banking, technology, e-commerce & communications, employment, fraud, retail & leisure, immigration and sport. The practice is run by young partners with an open culture.

main areas of work

Litigation 37%; Company Commercial 26%; Property 27%; Family 10%.

trainee profile

Those who read nothing but law books are probably not the right trainees for this firm. The firm want people who can meet the highest intellectual and business standards, while maintaining outside interests. Candidates should be cheerful, enterprising and ambitious - they should see themselves as future partners.

training environment

Trainees have four six-month seats. Three of these are usually in the litigation, property and company commercial departments, with an opportunity to specialise in the fourth seat. Trainees share a room with an assistant solicitor or a partner and the firm style is friendly and informal. Computer literacy is encouraged and access to on-line legal and business databases is available. Trainees are encouraged to participate in voluntary work at Law Centres.

benefits

Health cover, subsidised gym membership, season ticket loan, permanent health insurance, life assurance and pension.

vacation placements

Places for 2001: 12; Duration: 3 weeks; Remuneration: £150 p.w.; Closing Date: 30 March 2001.

sponsorship & awards

CPE and LPC funding with bursary.

Partners	30
Assistant Solicitors	33
Total Trainees	19

contact
Human Resources Department

method of application
Application form

closing date for 2003
31 July 2001

application
Training contracts p.a. 6
Applications p.a. 800+
% interviewed p.a. 6%
Required degree grade 2:1

training
Salary:
1st year (2000) £22,000
2nd Year (2000) £24,000
Holiday entitlement:
22 days p.a.
No. of seats available
abroad p.a. Occasional
secondments available

post-qualification
% of trainees offered job
on qualification (2000):
75%
% of assistants (as at
1/9/00) who joined as
trainees: 38%
% of partners (as at
1/9/00) who joined as
trainees: 22%

morgan cole

Buxton Court 3 West Way Oxford OX2 0SZ
Tel: (01865) 262600 Fax: (01865) 262670
Email: louise.pye@morgan-cole.com
Website: www.morgan-cole.com

firm profile

Morgan Cole is one of the leading independent law practices in the country, providing a full range of legal services to both individual and corporate clients in both the public and private sectors. The firm has a reputation for excellence and therefore attracts the highest quality of staff from all fields. The firm is a founder member of the Association of European Lawyers, one of the five leading UK law firms responsible for establishing a network of English speaking lawyers throughout Europe, thus ensuring that clients with business interests in Europe are provided with expert legal advice. The practice consists of five main divisions: business services, property, litigation, insurance litigation and specialist insurance services. As a modern practice, it strives to meet the legal needs of clients in all sectors of industry and commerce. The firm's areas of work are acquisitions and disposals; commercial; corporate finance; employment; energy, european and competition; information technology; insolvency; intellectual property; joint ventures; management Buy-outs and Buy-ins; PFI; sports law; agricultural and commercial property; construction; environment/planning/health and safety; medical negligence; personal injury; professional indemnity; commercial litigation; licensing; family and alternate dispute resolution.

trainee profile

Successful candidates should be commercially aware, proactive, outgoing and able to apply a logical and common-sense approach to solving client problems. The firm is seeking applications from graduates/undergraduates in both law and non-law subjects, preferably with at least a 2.2 degree.

training environment

Trainees spend not less than six months in at least three different divisions, and since each division handles a wide variety of work within its constituent teams, there is no danger of over-specialisation.

vacation placements

Places for 2001: Offered.

sponsorship & awards

The firm offers full funding of fees for attendance on the LPC for those trainees who will commence training with the firm. Funding for CPE is currently under review.

Partners 96
Assistant Solicitors 246
Total Trainees 36

contact
Paul Rippon

method of application
Applicants should complete the firm's application form which is available from the HR department in Oxford.

selection procedure
Assessment Centre and interview

closing date for 2003
31 July 2001

application
Required degree grade 2.2

training
Salary:
1st year (2000)
competitive for the London, Thames Valley and South Wales regions and reviewed annually in line with market trends
2nd Year (2000)
competitive for the London, Thames Valley and South Wales regions and reviewed annually

other offices
Croydon, London, Reading, Swansea.

nabarro nathanson

Lacon House Theobald's Road London WC1X 8RW
Tel: (020) 7524 6000 Fax: (020) 7524 6524
Email: graduateinfo@nabarro.com
Website: www.nabarro.com

firm profile

One of the UK's leading commercial law firms with offices in London, Reading and Sheffield. The firm is known for having an open but highly professional culture and expects its lawyers to have a life outside work.

main areas of work

Company and commercial law; commercial property; planning; pensions and employment; corporate finance; IP/IT; commercial litigation; construction; PFI; environmental law

trainee profile

Nabarro Nathanson welcomes applications from law and non law undergraduates. Candidates will usually be expecting a minimum 2:1 degree. As well as strong intellectual ability graduates need exceptional qualities. These include: enthusiasm, drive and initiative, common sense and strong interpersonal and teamworking skills.

training environment

Trainees undertake six four-month seats which ensures maximum exposure to the firm's core practice areas (company commercial, commercial property and litigation). The firm aims to retain all trainees on qualification. In addition to the core seats, trainees have the opportunity to gain further experience by spending time in specialist areas (eg pensions, IP/IT, tax, employment), possibly in Paris or Brussels, or completing a further seat in a core area. In most cases trainees will return to the seat they wish to qualify into for the remaining four months of their contract. This ensures a smooth transition from trainee to qualified solicitor.

benefits

Trainees are given private medical insurance, 25 days holiday entitlement per annum, a season ticket loan and access to a subsidised restaurant and subsidised corporate gym membership. Trainee salaries are reviewed annually.

vacation placements

Places for 2001: Places available; Duration: 3 weeks - between mid-June and end of August; Closing Date: 28 February 2001.

sponsorship & awards

Full fees paid for CPE and LPC and a maintenance grant. London and Guildford: £4,500. Elsewhere: £4,000.

Partners	102
Assistant Solicitors	203
Total Trainees	56

contact
Jane Drew

method of application
Application form

selection procedure
Interview and assessment day

closing date for 2003
31 July 2001

application
Training contracts p.a. 30
Applications p.a. 1,500
Required degree grade 2:1

training
Salary:
1st year (2000)
London & Reading £25,000
Sheffield £18,000
2nd Year (2000)
London & Reading £28,000
Sheffield £20,000
Holiday entitlement:
25 days

post-qualification
Salary (2000)
London £40,000
(reviewed annually)

overseas offices
Brussels; Associated offices: Dubai, Paris.

nicholson graham & jones

110 Cannon Street London EC4N 6AR
Tel: (020) 7648 9000 Fax: (020) 7648 9001
Email: info@NGJ.co.uk
Website: www.ngj.co.uk

firm profile
A successful mid-sized practice, offering strength across a number of key disciplines to a broad range of corporate clients.

main areas of work
Company, Commercial, Litigation, Property, Construction & Engineering, Banking & Insolvency, Private Client, Intellectual Property, Planning & Environmental, Employment, Sport, Travel.

trainee profile
The firm recruits both law and non-law graduates with excellent degrees and a practical approach.

training environment
Training is broad-based with six months in each of the main departments: Company/Commercial, Litigation and Property and a six month seat of your choice. The emphasis is on-the-job training with personal supervision from partners. There is also a comprehensive induction and in-house training programme for each department and on a firmwide basis. The firm encourages individual development through early responsibility and client contact. Trainees participate in all activities including business development and marketing. The atmosphere is genuinely friendly and supportive and trainees' contributions are valued.

benefits
Life assurance, season ticket loan, subsidised gym membership, BUPA, 25 days holiday a year, salaries reviewed every year.

vacation placements
Places for 2001: 2 July and 6 July 2001. 4 students per fortnight; Remuneration: TBA.

sponsorship & awards
CPE and LPC full Fees and £3,500 maintenance for each.

Partners	56
Assistant Solicitors	43
Total Trainees	20

contact
Gail Harcus

method of application
Application form

selection procedure
Interview and assessment

closing date for 2003
31 July 2001

application
Training contracts p.a. **10**
Applications p.a. **1000**
% interviewed p.a. **4%**
Required degree grade **2:1**

training
Salary:
1st year (2000) **£25,000**
2nd year (2000) **£28,000**
Holiday entitlement:
25 days
% of trainees with a
non-law degree p.a. **Varies**

post-qualification
Salary (2000) **£40,000**
% of trainees offered job
on qualification (2000): **90%**

overseas offices
Brussels

norton rose

Kempson House Camomile Street London EC3A 7AN
Tel: (020) 7283 6000 Fax: (020) 7283 6500
Email: grad.recruitment@nortonrose.com
Website: www.nortonrose.com

firm profile
A leading City and international law firm specialising in large-scale corporate and financial transactions. Strong in asset, project and ship finance. More than two thirds of the firm's work has an international element.

main areas of work
Corporate Finance 27%; Banking 27%; Litigation 26%; Property, Planning & Environmental 9%; Taxation 5%; Competition 3%; Employment, Pensions + Incentives 2%; Intellectual Property + Technology 1%.

trainee profile
Successful candidates will be commercially aware, focused, ambitious and team-orientated. High intellect and international awareness are a priority, and language skills are appreciated.

training environment
Norton Rose's seat system is innovative. In the first 16 months of the 24-month training contract, trainees will have a seat in each of the core departments of banking, commercial litigation and corporate finance, plus one in a more specialist area. The remaining time can be spent in one of three ways: all eight months in one chosen seat; or four months in one department and four months in the department in which they want to qualify; or four months abroad and four in their chosen department. In-the-field experience is considered as important as formal training at Norton Rose, and trainees are expected to learn by observing experienced lawyers at work, interacting with clients and solicitors, handling sensitive issues and organising their time as well as attending external courses. Internal competition among trainees is discouraged, as great store is placed on team-working.

benefits
Life assurance (25+), private health insurance (optional), season ticket loan, subsidised gym membership.

vacation placements
Places for 2001: 45 Summer, 15 Christmas; Duration: Summer: 3 weeks, Christmas: 2 weeks; Remuneration: £225 p.w.; Closing Date: 2 February 2001 for Summer, 3 November 2000 for Christmas. 5-6 open days per year are also held.

sponsorship & awards
£1,000 travel scholarship, £800 loan on arrival, 4 weeks unpaid leave on qualification.

Partners	154*
Assistant Solicitors	535*
Total Trainees	103

denotes world-wide figures

contact
Brendan Monaghan

method of application
Employer's application form

selection procedure
Interview and group exercise

closing date for 2003
3 August 2001

application
Training contracts p.a.
65-75
Applications p.a. 2,500+
% interviewed p.a. 10%
Required degree grade 2:1

training
Salary:
1st year(2000) £25,000
2nd year (2000) £28,000
Holiday entitlement:
22 days
% of trainees with a
non-law degree p.a. 40%
No. of seats available
abroad p.a. 12

post-qualification
Salary (2000) £42,000
% of trainees offered job
on qualification (2000):
97%

overseas offices
Bahrain, Bangkok*,
Brussels, Greece, Jakarta*,
Milan, Moscow, Paris,
Prague, Singapore,
Warsaw

Associate Office

olswang

90 Long Acre London WC2E 9TT
Tel: (020) 7208 8888 Fax: (020) 7208 8800
Email: olsmail@olswang.com
Website: www.olswang.com

firm profile
Olswang is different. Forward thinking, progressive. Olswang is about realising the potential of its clients, of all of its people and the potential within every situation in which its clients find themselves. The firm's aim is simple. To be the preferred law firm of leading companies in the Technology, Media and Telecommunications sectors. Olswang knows the players, knows the business and above all, understands the issues. Being different has brought rapid growth. Olswang is a 400+ strong team committed to providing innovative solutions through legal excellence.

main areas of work
Advertising; Banking; Commercial Litigation; Corporate and commercial; Defamation; E commerce; Employment; EU and Competition; Film and TV (finance / production);Information Technology; Intellectual Property; Music; Private Equity; Property; Sport; Tax; Telecommunications; TV/Broadcasting.

trainee profile
Being a trainee at Olswang is both demanding and rewarding. The firm is interested in hearing from individuals with a 2:1 degree and above, exceptional drive and relevant commercial experience. In addition, it is absolutely critical that trainees fit well into the Olswang environment which is challenging, robust, busy, demanding, individualistic and fun.

training environment
Olswang want to help trainees match their expectations and needs with those of the firm. Training consists of four six-month seats in the company, entertainment, litigation or property groups. You will be assigned a mentor, usually a partner, to assist and advise you throughout your training contract. In-house lectures supplement general training and six monthly appraisals assess development. Regular social events with the other trainees not only encourages strong relationship building but adds to the fun of work.

benefits
After six months: pension contributions, medical cover, life cover, dental scheme, subsidised gym membership.

vacation placements
Places for 2001: 10 (July) 10 (August); Duration: 3 weeks; Remuneration: £190 pw; Closing Date: 14 February 2001.

Partners	46
Assistant Solicitors	98
Total Trainees	22

contact
Helen Turnbull
Human Resources Director

method of application
Firm's application form –
Online preferred.

selection procedure
Interview; Psychometric tests.

closing date for 2003
31 July 2001

application
Training contracts p.a. 18
Applications p.a. 3,000+
% interviewed p.a. 3%
Required degree grade: 2:1+

training
Salary:
1st year (2000) £23,500
Holiday entitlement:
23 days
% of trainees with a non-law degree p.a. 50%

post-qualification
Salary (2000) £40,000
% of trainees offered job on qualification (2000):
100%
% of assistants (as at 1/9/00) who joined as trainees: 26%
% of partners (as at 1/9/00) who joined as trainees: 2.2%

overseas offices
Brussels.

osborne clarke owa

50 Queen Charlotte Street Bristol BS1 4HE
Tel: (0117) 917 4322 Fax: (0117) 917 4323
Email: recruitment@osborneclarke.com
Website: www.osborneclarke.com

firm profile
In the past five years the firm has grown by more than 20 per cent per year and is now dominant in the South of England. It also competes with the largest City and national firms in its chosen international practice areas - corporate finance, private equity, M&A, technology media and telecoms. In Europe, its strategic alliance (Osborne Westphalen Alliance - OWA) with leading firms in Germany, France, Spain, Holland and Denmark gives clients access to over 450 lawyers in 16 cities. It has strong links with the US, particularly North America, where it has over 250 clients. In the City, Osborne Clarke's corporate lawyers have seen a surge in work undertaken for clients in the technology, media and telecoms sectors and have advised on some of the groundbreaking deals of 2000. The firm has an enviable reputation in advertising and marketing, litigation, commercial property, construction, corporate banking, competition, tax, environmental and pensions. The employment team is one of the UK's largest and most highly regarded groups of employment advisors.

main areas of work
Corporate finance, employment, venture capital, IT, telecoms and media.

trainee profile
The firm values personality, enthusiasm, the ability to provide practical commercial solutions and the communication skills to deal with clients at all levels. A non-law degree and/or time spent travelling are viewed positively.

training environment
Trainees will spend six months in three core departments, either in Bristol, London, the Thames Valley or in Europe, before choosing to specialise in a particular area. They are expected to take on responsibility at an early stage. There is a structured timetable of external and internal training, with three and six monthly reviews. The firm encourages a wide variety of social and sports activities.

benefits
None until qualified

vacation placements
Places for 2001: 20; Duration: 1 week; Remuneration: £130-150 p.w.; Closing Date: 28 February 2001.

sponsorship & awards
LPC fees paid. CPE fees paid. Maintenance grant of £2,500 for each.

Partners	70
Assistant Solicitors	190
Total Trainees	45

contact
Joanne Moody

method of application
application form and brochure available on request or through the firm's website
www.oc4jobs.com

selection procedure
Individual interviews and group exercises.

closing date for 2003
31 July 2001

application
Training contracts p.a. 20
Applications p.a. 1000-1200
% interviewed p.a. 10%
Required degree grade: 2:1 preferred

training
Salary:
1st year (2000) £17,000-£22,000
2nd Year(2000) £18,000-£23,000
Holiday entitlement: 21 days
% of trainees with a non-law degree p.a. 30%
No. of seats available abroad p.a. 3

post-qualification
Salary (2000):
£30,000-£40,000
% of trainees offered job on qualification (2000): 90%

overseas offices
Barcelona, Brussels, Copenhagen, Cologne, Frankfurt, Hamburg, Lyon, Milan, Paris, Rotterdam.

paisner & co

Bouverie House 154 Fleet St London EC4A 2JD
Tel: (020) 7353 0299 Fax: (020) 7583 8621
Email: gradrectmt@paisner.co.uk
website: www.paisner.co.uk

firm profile

Based in the City, Paisner & Co is a broadly-based commercial firm handling all aspects of legal work for commercial clients both national and international. Clients include UK and international listed and smaller companies from a wide range of industry sectors, in particular leisure, retail and mail order, health, communications, manufacturing, high-technology, property development, insurance and financial services.

main areas of work

The firm's three core practice areas are corporate/commercial, commercial property and commercial litigation. Specialist areas include: computer, media and intellectual property; asset and consumer finance; charities; construction and engineering; corporate tax; employment and pensions; EU/UK competition; property litigation; regulatory law; reinsurance/insurance; trusts and estate planning. Company/Commercial (including e-commerce, IP and Media) 37%; Property 20%; Litigation (including insurance & reinsurance) 19%; Trusts & Estate Planning 10%; Employment 8%; Construction & Engineering 6%.

trainee profile

Intelligent, energetic, positive and hard working team players. Individuals who gain a sense of achievement from finding solutions and providing services.

training environment

Trainees spend six months in four of the following departments- company and commercial, commercial litigation, commercial property, employment and trusts. You will often work in cross-departmental teams, but will have one-to-one supervision from a partner or senior solicitor. Development is monitored with an assessment every six months. Internal and external lectures, carrying Law Society Continuing Education Points, are given twice a day. Trainees are given library research and Lexis induction courses. Staff are encouraged to get to know each other- partners and senior solicitors are accessible and willing to teach. The office environment is relaxed and informal. Social and sporting events are organised and there is a daily internal e-bulletin.

vacation placements

Places for 2001: 20; Duration: 4 weeks; Remuneration: £200 p.w.; Closing Date: 15 Feb. 2001.

sponsorship & awards

LPC Funding: Yes; CPE Funding: No.

Partners	52
Assistant Solicitors	58
Total Trainees	19

contact
Diane Austin
Human Resources
Manager

method of application
Firm's application form

selection procedure
Application form and interview

closing date for 2003
31 July 2001

application
Training contracts p.a.
10 – 12
Applications p.a. **2,000**
% interviewed p.a. **3%**
Required degree grade **2:1**

training
Salary:
1st year (2000) £22,000
2nd year (2000) £24,000
Holiday entitlement:
21 days
% of trainees with
a non-law degree p.a.
10%

post-qualification
Salary (2000) **£40,000**
% of trainees offered job
on qualification (2000): **75%**
% of assistants (as at
1/9/00) who joined as
trainees: **10%**
% of partners (as at 1/9/00)
who joined as trainees:
10%

pannone & partners

123 Deansgate Manchester M3 2BU
Tel: (0161) 909 3000 Fax: (0161) 909 4444
Email: julia.jessop@pannone.co.uk
Website: www.pannone.com

firm profile

A high profile Manchester firm continuing to undergo rapid growth. The firm prides itself on offering a full range of legal services to a diverse client base which is split almost equally between personal and commercial clients. The firm was the first to be awarded the quality standard ISO9001 and is a founder member of Pannone Law Group - Europe's first integrated international law group.

main areas of work

Commercial Litigation 22%; Personal Injury 24%; Corporate 11.5%; Commercial Property 7%; Family 11%; Clinical Negligence 9.5%; Private Client 9.5%; Employment 5.5%.

trainee profile

Selection criteria include a high level of academic achievement, teamwork, organisation and communication skills, a wide range of interests and a connection with the North West.

training environment

An induction course helps trainees adjust to working life, and covers the firm's quality procedures and good practice. Regular trainee seminars cover the work of other departments within the firm, legal developments and practice. Additional departmental training sessions focus in more detail on legal and procedural matters in that department. Four seats of six months are spent in various departments and trainees' progress is monitored regularly. Trainees have easy access to support and guidance on any matters of concern. Work is tackled with gusto here, but so are the many social gatherings that take place.

vacation placements

Places for 2001: 50; Duration: 1 week; Remuneration: 0; Closing Date: 9 March 2001.

Partners	57
Assistant Solicitors	41
Total Trainees	17

contact
Julia Jessop

method of application
Application form and CV

selection procedure
Individual interview, second interview comprises a tour of the firm and informal lunch

closing date for 2003
10 August 2001

application
Training contracts p.a. 8
Applications p.a. 500
% interviewed p.a. 12%
Required degree grade 2:2

training
Salary:
1st year (2000) £16,000
2nd year (2000) £18,000
Holiday entitlement:
20 days
% of trainees with a non-law degree p.a. 50%

post-qualification
Salary (2000) £25,000
% of trainees offered job on qualification (2000): 86%
% of assistants who joined as trainees: 35%
% of partners who joined as trainees: 37%

payne hicks beach

10 New Square Lincoln's Inn London WC2A 3QG
Tel: (020) 7465 4300 Fax: (020) 7465 4400
Email: a-palmer@payne-hicks-beach.co.uk

firm profile

Payne Hicks Beach is a medium-sized firm based in Lincoln's Inn. It primarily provides specialist tax, trusts and probate advice to individuals and families. It also undertakes corporate and commercial work.

main areas of work

Private Client 33%; Commercial Litigation 13%; Commercial Property 12%; Matrimonial and Family Law/ Litigation 10%; Residential/Agricultural Property 10%; Tax (business and corporate) 10%; Corporate/Commercial 10%; General, Miscellaneous 2%.

trainee profile

The firm looks for law and non-law graduates with a good academic record, a practical ability to solve problems, enthusiasm and an ability to work hard and deal appropriately with their colleagues and the firm's clients.

training environment

Following an initial induction course, trainees usually spend six months in four of the firm's departments. Working with a partner, they are involved in the day to day activities of the department, including attending conferences with clients, counsel and other professional advisers. Assessment is continuous and you will be given responsibility as you demonstrate ability and aptitude. To complement the PSC, the firm runs a formal training system for trainees and requires them to attend lectures and seminars on various topics.

benefits

Season travel ticket loan, life assurance 4 x salary, permanent health insurance.

sponsorship & awards

Fees for the CPE and LPC are paid.

Partners	20
Assistant Solicitors	11
Total Trainees	4

contact
Mrs Alice Palmer

method of application
Handwritten letter and CV

selection procedure
Interview

closing date for 2003
11 August 2001

application
Training contracts p.a. **2**
Applications p.a. **1,000**
% interviewed p.a. **3%**
Required degree grade **2:1**

training
Salary:
1st year (2000) **£21,000**
2nd year (2000) **£23,000**
Holiday entitlement:
4 weeks
% of trainees with a
non-law degree p.a. **50%**

post-qualification
Salary (2000) **£34,000**
% of trainees offered job
on qualification (2000): **67%**
% of assistants (as at
1/9/00) who joined as
trainees: **35%**
% of partners (as at 1/9/00)
who joined as trainees:
20%

penningtons

Bucklersbury House 83 Cannon Street London EC4N 8PE
Tel: (020) 7457 3000 Fax: (020) 7457 3240

firm profile
An international law firm, with offices in the City, Basingstoke, Godalming, Newbury and Paris. There are four main departments. Specialist units cover industry sectors and key overseas jurisdictions.

main areas of work
Property 33%; Litigation (including Shipping and Family) 29%; Corporate/Commercial 21%; Private Client 17%.

trainee profile
Penningtons is looking for bright, enthusiastic, highly motivated and well rounded individuals with a keen interest in the practice of law.

training environment
Six-month seats are provided in three or four of the following departments: corporate/commercial, property, litigation, and private client. Individual preference is usually accommodated in the second year. Trainees are given a thorough grounding in the law. International opportunities do arise. There are in-house lectures and reviews and appraisals occur regularly. The firm aims to utilise trainees' talents to their full, but is careful not to overburden them. All staff are supportive and the atmosphere is both professional and informal.

benefits
Subsidised sports and social club, life assurance, season ticket loan.

vacation placements
Places for 2001: 60 on London Open Days at Easter; Remuneration: expenses; Closing Date: 15 February 2001. Some summer vacation placements out of London. Closing date 30 April 2001.

sponsorship & awards
LPC Funding is available. Awards are given for commendation or distinction in LPC.

Partners	48*
Assistant Solicitors	65*
Total Trainees	21

denotes world-wide figures

contact
Lesley Lintott

method of application
Handwritten letter, CV and application form

selection procedure
1 interview with a partner and director of studies

closing date for 2003
15 August 2001

application
Training contracts p.a.
10/11
Applications p.a. **2,000**
% interviewed p.a. **5%**
Required degree grade **2:1**

training
Salary:
1st year (2000)
£21,000 (London)
2nd year (2000)
£23,000 (London)
Holiday entitlement:
22 days
% of trainees with a non-law degree p.a. **40%**

post-qualification
Salary (2000):
£34,000 (London)
% of trainees offered job on qualification (2000): **60%**
% of assistants (as at 1/9/00) who joined as trainees: **45%**
% of partners (as at 1/9/00) who joined as trainees: **49%**

overseas offices
Paris

A-Z SOLICITORS

479

pinsent curtis

Dashwood House 69 Old Broad Street London EC2M 1NR
Tel: (020) 7418 7097 Fax: (020) 7418 7050
3 Colmore Circus Birmingham B4 6BH
Tel: (0121) 626 5731 Fax: (0121) 626 1040
1 Park Row Leeds LS1 5AB
Tel: (0113) 244 5000 Fax: (0113) 244 8000
Email: nimisha.gosrani@pinsent-curtis.co.uk
Website: www.pinsents.com

firm profile

Pinsent Curtis is a major national commercial firm. It has a first class reputation based on its work for a substantial list of quality corporate clients. The firm also has strong contacts with merchant banks, underwriters and insurers, and has the largest tax department outside London.

main areas of work

Litigation & Professional Indemnity; Corporate; Commercial; Property; Tax; Employment.

trainee profile

The firm seeks applications from both law and non-law graduates with a good honours degree. However, not only is a good academic background required, but also personality, commitment and common sense. Given that the bulk of work is business oriented, trainees need to communicate with the business community, be interested in its problems and have the ability to give positive commercial advice.

training environment

Trainees sit in four seats of six months ranging from corporate, property, litigation, commercial, tax and employment. Hands-on experience is seen as an essential part of the learning process, so early responsibility and contact with clients are encouraged. Partners or associates oversee your work and are on hand to help and advise. The PSC is taught in-house, and there is an internal structured development programme to broaden your knowledge. The firm has an open-door policy and informal atmosphere, and there are many social and sporting activities for its staff.

vacation placements

Easter and Summer schemes.
Places for 2001: 140; Duration: 1 week; Closing Date: 28 February 2001.

sponsorship & awards

CPE/ LPC fees are paid. In addition to this, maintenance grants of £2,500 for CPE and £4,500 for LPC are offered.

Partners	135
Assistant Solicitors	240
Total Trainees	66

contact
Miss Nimisha Gosrani
Recruitment Hotline:
(020) 7418 7097

method of application
Application form

selection procedure
Assessment centre
including interview

closing date for 2003
31 July 2001

application
Training contracts p.a.
25-30
Applications p.a. 4000
Required degree grade 2:1

training
Salary:
1st year (2000) £23,000
2nd year (2000) £25,000
Holiday entitlement:
22 days
No. of seats available
abroad p.a. 1

overseas offices
Brussels

pritchard englefield

14 New St London EC2M 4HE
Tel: (020) 7972 9720 Fax: (020) 7972 9722
Email: po@pritchardenglefield.co.uk

firm profile

A medium-sized City firm practising a mix of general commercial and non-commercial law with many German and French clients. Despite its strong commercial departments, the firm still undertakes family and private client work and is known for its clinical negligence and PI practice and its strong international flavour.

main areas of work

All main areas of commercial practice including litigation, company/commercial (UK, German, French and some Italian), employment also private client/probate, personal injury, clinical negligence and some family.

trainee profile

Normally only high academic achievers with a second European language (especially German and French) are considered. However, a lower second degree coupled with exceptional subsequent education or experience could suffice.

training environment

An induction course acquaints trainees with the computer network, library and administrative procedures and there is a formal in-house training programme. Four six-month seats make up most of your training. You can usually choose some departments, and you could spend two six-month periods in the same seat. Over two years, you learn advocacy, negotiating, drafting and interviewing, attend court, use your language skills and meet clients. Occasional talks and seminars explain the work of the firm, and you can air concerns over bi-monthly lunches with the partners comprising the Trainee panel. PSC is taken externally over two years. Quarterly drinks parties, musical evenings and ten-pin bowling number amongst popular social events.

benefits

Some subsidised training, luncheon vouchers.

sponsorship & awards

£2,000.

Partners	26
Assistant Solicitors	11
Total Trainees	8

contact
Marian Joseph

method of application
Standard application form available from Graduate Recruitment

selection procedure
1 interview only in September

closing date for 2003
31 July 2001

application
Training contracts p.a. 4
Applications p.a. 300–400
% interviewed p.a. 10%
Required degree grade: generally 2:1

training
Salary:
1st year (2000) £19,000
2nd year (2000) £19,250
Holiday entitlement
25 days
% of trainees with a non-law degree p.a.
Approx 50%

post-qualification
Salary (2000)
Approx £30,000
% of trainees offered job on qualification (2000) 75%
% of assistants (as at 1/9/00) who joined as trainees 75%
% of partners (as at 1/9/00) who joined as trainees: 50%

overseas offices
Frankfurt, Hong Kong

A-Z SOLICITORS

481

radcliffes

5 Great College Street Westminster London SW1P 3SJ
Tel: (020) 7222 7040 Fax: (020) 7222 6208
Email: marie.o'shea@radcliffes.co.uk
Website: www.radcliffes.co.uk

firm profile

A distinctive, highly accomplished law firm, Radcliffes combines traditional values like integrity and prompt response with a client-focused approach to everything it does. From its offices in the heart of Westminister, the firm handles commercial matters and private client work with equal skill, empathy and understanding of clients' individual needs.

main areas of work

The firm is organised into five departments: Company/Commercial, Litigation and Dispute Resolution, Commercial Property, Tax and Private Client, and Family Law. Experts within these departments integrate their knowledge in the firm's specialist groups: Growing Businesses, Property Investment and Development, Private Client, Charity and Health.

trainee profile

Its aim is to recruit trainee solicitors who have a real prospect of becoming future partners. The firm seeks not just academic but also extra curricular activities, self-confidence, determination and a sense of humour.

training environment

Trainees are introduced to the firm with a full induction week.

benefits

Health insurance, season ticket loan, life assurance, PHI.

vacation placements

Places for 2001: 10; Duration: 2 weeks; Remuneration: £130 p.w.; Closing Date: 31 March 2001.

Partners	33
Assistant Solicitors	20
Total Trainees	8

contact
Marie O'Shea
Administration Secretary

method of application
CV and covering letter or EAF

selection procedure
2 Interviews with partners

closing date for 2003
27 July 2001

application
Training contracts p.a. 4
Applications p.a. 1016
% interviewed p.a. 9%
Preferred degree grade 2:1

training
Salary:
1st year (2000) £20,000
2nd year (2000) £21,500
Holiday entitlement:
22 days p.a.

post-qualification
Salary (2000) £33,000
% of trainees offered job on qualification (2000): 100%
% of assistants (as at 1/9/00) who joined as trainees 50%
% of partners (as at 1/9/00) who joined as trainees: 50%

reynolds porter chamberlain

Chichester House 278-282 High Holborn London WC1V 7HA
Tel: (020) 7306 3509 Fax: (020) 7242 1431
Email: pt1@rpc.co.uk
Website: www.rpc.co.uk

firm profile

Reynolds Porter Chamberlain is a leading commercial law firm with over 170 lawyers. In addition to its main offices in Holborn, the firm has an expanding office at Leadenhall Street in the City which serves its insurance clients. Best known as a major litigation practice, particularly in the field of professional negligence, RPC also has thriving corporate, commercial property, private client and construction departments. Another rapidly expanding part of the firm is its media and technology unit. This handles major defamation actions and has dealt with some of the biggest internet deals to date.

main areas of work

Litigation 60%; Corporate 10%; Commercial Property 10%; Construction 10%; Media & Technology 5%; Family/Private Client 5%.

trainee profile

The firm appoints ten trainees each year from law and non-law backgrounds. Although proven academic ability is important (they require a 2.1 or above), RPC also values flair, energy, business sense, commitment and the ability to communicate and relate well to others.

training environment

As a trainee you will receive first rate training in a supportive working environment. You will work closely with a Partner and be given real responsibility as soon as you are ready to handle it. At least six months will be spent in each of the three main areas of the practice and they encourage trainees to express a preference for their seats. This provides a thorough grounding and the chance to develop confidence as you see matters through to their conclusion. In addition to the externally provided Professional Skills Course they provide a complimentary programme of in-house training.

benefits

Four weeks' holiday, bonus schemes, private medical insurance, income protection benefits, season ticket loan, subsidised gym membership, active social calendar.

vacation placements

Places for July 2001: 12; Duration: 2 weeks; Remuneration: £175 p.w.; Closing Date: 28 February 2001.

sponsorship & awards

CPE Funding: Fees paid + £4,000 maintenance. LPC Funding: Fees paid + £4,000 maintenance.

Partners	51
Assistant Solicitors	80
Total Trainees	17

contact
Sally Andrews
Head of Personnel

method of application
Hand-written covering letter and application form

selection procedure
Assessment Days held in September

closing date for 2003
17 August 2001

application
Training contracts p.a. 10
Applications p.a. 600
% interviewed p.a. 7.5%
Required degree grade 2.1

training
Salary:
1st year (2000) £22,000
2nd year (2000) £24,000
Holiday entitlement:
20 days
% of trainees with a non-law degree p.a. 25%

post-qualification
Salary (2000) £36,000
% of trainees offered job on qualification (2000): 57%
% of assistants (as at 1/9/00) who joined as trainees: 50%
% of partners (as at 1/9/00) who joined as trainees: 35%

A-Z SOLICITORS

richards butler

Beaufort House 15 St. Botolph Street London EC3A 7EE
Tel: (020) 7247 6555 Fax: (020) 7247 5091
Email: law@richardsbutler.com

firm profile

Established in 1920, Richards Butler is noted for the exceptional variety of its work. It has acknowledged strengths in shipping, commodities, company/commercial, commercial disputes, property, insurance, media/entertainment, competition and energy law, in each of which it has international prominence.

main areas of work

Corporate/Commercial/Banking/Finance 31%; Shipping/International Trade & Commodities/Insurance 29%; Commercial Disputes 24%; Commercial Property 16%.

trainee profile

Candidates should be players rather than onlookers, work well under pressure and be happy to operate as a team member or team leader as circumstances dictate. Candidates from diverse backgrounds are welcome, including mature students with commercial experience and management skills.

training environment

Richards Butler provides practical experience across as wide a spectrum of the law as possible. Training is divided into four periods of five months and one period of four months. Trainees start in general corporate, litigation and commercial property seats, however there are opportunities to work in other additional specialised areas such as shipping, media law, or international trade in later seats.

benefits

Performance related bonus, Life insurance, Private Patients' Plan, interest free season ticket loan, subsidised staff restaurant, staff conveyancing allowance.

vacation placements

Places for 2001: 45; Duration: 2 weeks; Remuneration: £200 p.w.; Closing Date: 28 February 2001. In addition, the firm offers overseas scholarships to 4 students.

sponsorship & awards

CPE and LPC fees and maintenance paid.

Partners	102*
Fee earners	365*
Total Trainees	56*

* denotes world-wide figures

contact
Jill Steele

method of application
Firm's application form

selection procedure
1 interview

closing date for 2003
31 July 2001

application
Training contracts p.a. **20**
Applications p.a. **2,000**
% interviewed p.a. **5%**
Required degree grade: **2:1**

training
Salary:
1st year (2000) £25,000
2nd year (2000) £28,000
Holiday entitlement:
22 days
% of trainees with a
non-law degree p.a. **33%**
No. of seats available
abroad p.a. **10**

post-qualification
Salary (2000):
£38,000 plus bonus
% of trainees offered job
on qualification (2000): **84%**
% of assistants who
joined as trainees: **59%**
% of partners who
joined as trainees: **48%**

overseas offices
Abu Dhabi, Beijing, Brussels, Doha, Hong Kong, Muscat, Paris, Piraeus, São Paulo, Warsaw.

rowe & maw

20 Black Friars Lane London EC4V 6HD
Tel: (020) 7248 4282 Fax: (020) 7248 2009
Email: roweandmaw@roweandmaw.co.uk
Website: www.roweandmaw.co.uk

firm profile

Founded 100 years ago, Rowe & Maw is a leading commercial firm, with offices in London, including one at Lloyd's, and in Brussels. Its strength lies in advising companies and businesses on day-to-day work and special projects.

main areas of work

Corporate 34%, Litigation 22%, Property 11%, Pensions 8%, Intellectual Property 8%, Construction 7%, Banking and Projects 6%, Employment 4%.

trainee profile

The firm is interested in students with a good academic record and a strong commitment to law. Commercial awareness gained through legal or business work experience is an advantage. Extra-curricular activities are taken into consideration. The firm wants trainees to become future partners. The current senior partner trained with the firm.

training environment

There are September and March intakes. Training divides into four six-month seats. All trainees spend time in the corporate, litigation and property departments, frequently working for blue chip clients. Secondments to Brussels or to clients in the UK or abroad are an option for some. The firm has a professional development and training programme which covers subjects like EU law and the workings of the City. Advocacy and drafting skills are also taught. Trainees are encouraged to join in the sports and social life.

benefits

Interest free season ticket loan, subsidised membership of sport clubs, private health scheme.

vacation placements

Places for 2001: 25; Duration: 2 weeks; Remuneration: £200 p.w.; Closing Date: 28 February 2001.

sponsorship & awards

CPE and LPC fees paid and £4,000 (£4,500 for London/Guildford) maintenance p.a.

Partners	79
Assistant Solicitors	130
Total Trainees	42

contact
Sophie Wood

method of application
Application form

selection procedure
Selection workshops including an interview and a business exercise

closing date for 2003
15 August 2001

application
Training contracts p.a. **25**
Applications p.a. **1,250**
% interviewed p.a. **10%**
Required degree grade **2:1**

training
Holiday entitlement:
25 days
% of trainees with a non-law degree p.a. **50%**
No. of seats available abroad p.a. **2**

post-qualification
Salary (2000) **£40,000**
% of trainees offered job on qualification (2000): **75%**
% of assistants (as at 1/9/00) who joined as trainees: **50%**
% of partners (as at 1/9/00) who joined as trainees: **40%**

russell-cooke

2 Putney Hill London SW15 6AB
Tel: (020) 8789 9111 Fax: (020) 8785 4286
Email: traineeapplications@russell-cooke.co.uk

firm profile

A medium-sized practice with three offices in the London area. The City office deals primarily with commercial and contentious property. The Putney office has a range of specialist departments including company/commercial, crime, judicial review, commercial and construction litigation, matrimonial, French property and tax, domestic and commercial conveyancing, personal injury litigation, private client and trusts. The Kingston-upon-Thames office runs a specialist child-care department plus matrimonial, domestic conveyancing and crime.

main areas of work

Commercial Property: 20%; Company Commercial: 10%; Commercial Litigation: 15%; Public Law: 10%; Private Client: 10%; Domestic Conveyancing: 10%; Matrimonial: 10%; Crime 10%; Personal Injury: 5%.

trainee profile

Trainees will need at least two A grades and a B grade at A Level and a 2:1 degree, though not necessarily in law. You will also need to be good at the practical business of advising and representing clients. Intellectual rigour, adaptability and the ability, under pressure, to handle a diverse range of people and issues efficiently and cost-effectively are vital attributes.

training environment

Trainees are usually offered four seats lasting six months each. Photocopying and researching points of law will not take up all your time in the firm. You will have the chance to manage your own case work and deal directly with clients, with supervision suited to your needs and the needs of the department and clients. Internal training and an annual executive staff conference supplement the externally provided PSC. Social events include quiz nights, wine tasting, summer and Christmas parties and thriving cricket and netball teams.

Partners	24
Assistant Solicitors	28
Total Trainees	10

contact
Julie Brown

method of application
Application form

selection procedure
First and second interviews.

closing date for 2003
10 August 2001

application
Training contracts p.a. 4
Applications p.a. 500
% interviewed p.a. 7%
Required degree grade 2:1

training
Salary:
1st year (2000) £18,500
2nd year (2000) £20,000
Holiday entitlement:
22 days
% of trainees with a
non-law degree p.a. 50%

post-qualification
Salary (2000) Market
% of trainees offered job
on qualification (2000):
100%
% of assistants (as at
1/9/00) who joined as
trainees: 40%
% of partners (as at 1/9/00)
who joined as trainees:
50%

russell jones & walker

Swinton House 324 Gray's Inn Road London WC1X 8DH
Tel: (020) 7837 2808 Fax: (020) 7837 2941
Email: enquiries@rjw.co.uk
Website: www.rjw.co.uk

firm profile

Russell Jones & Walker was founded in London in the 1920s but has expanded in recent years to become one of the largest litigation practices in the country with more than 570 lawyers and support staff and offices in London, Leeds, Birmingham, Bristol, Manchester, Sheffield, Newcastle-upon-Tyne, Cardiff, Edinburgh and Northampton.

main areas of work

Personal Injury 66%; Criminal 13%; Commercial Litigation 12%; Employment 5%; Family/Probate 2%; Commercial and Domestic Conveyancing 2%.

trainee profile

Russell Jones & Walker are looking for candidates who are motivated and hard-working with a sense of humour and the ability and confidence to accept responsibility in fee earning work and client care.

training environment

Each trainee will spend six months in four different departments under the supervision of a partner or senior solicitor. Your supervisor will conduct a three-month assessment and six-month review. IT training and an induction programme are provided and a comprehensive in-house education timetable. Liz Dux, the training partner, supervises all aspects of the training contract. The firm is extremely sociable and trainees are encouraged to participate in social and sporting events.

benefits

Season ticket loan, pension, private healthcare (optional), group life assurance.

vacation placements

No scheme in place.

sponsorship & awards

CPE/LPC Funding: grant to assist with fees available (£1,000).

Partners	47
Assistant Solicitors	78
Total Trainees	15

contact
HR Officer (Recruitment)

method of application
Application form –
available from 1 April 2001

closing date for 2003
27 July 2001

application
Training contracts p.a. **5-8**
Applications p.a. **1000**
% interviewed p.a. **5%**
Required degree grade **2:1**

training
Salary:
1st yea r(2000) £19,500
2nd year (2000) £21,250
Holiday entitlement:
4 weeks
% of trainees with a
non-law degree p.a. **50%**

post-qualification
Salary (2000) £30,000
% of trainees offered job
on qualification (2000): **75%**
% of assistants (as at
1/9/00) who joined as
trainees: **c.25%**
% of partners (as at 1/9/00)
who joined as trainees:
10%

salans hertzfeld & heilbronn hrk

Clements House 14–18 Gresham Street London EC2V 7NN
Tel: (020) 7509 6000 Fax: (020) 7726 6191
Email: london@salans.com

firm profile

Salans Hertzfeld & Heilbronn ('SHH') is a multinational law firm with full-service offices in the City of London, Paris and New York, together with further offices in Moscow, St Petersburg, Warsaw, Kiev, Almaty and Baku. The firm has currently over 400 fee-earners, including 100 partners.

main areas of work

LONDON OFFICE

Banking & Finance/Corporate 50%; Litigation 25%; Employment 15%; Commercial Property 10%.

trainee profile

Candidates need to have high academic qualifications and the ability to approach complex problems in a practical and commercial way. The firm looks to recruit those who demonstrate an ability and a willingness to assume responsibility at an early stage, possess common sense and good judgement. Language skills are also valued.

training environment

The firm operates an in-house training scheme for both trainees and assistant solicitors. In addition, trainees will be offered the opportunity to attend external courses wherever possible. Trainees are at all times supervised by a partner and encouraged to take an active part in the work of their department. The caseload of the trainee will, in each case, depend on the trainee's level of expertise and experience. Where possible the firm seeks to recruit its trainees at the end of the training periods.

Partners	100
Assistant Solicitors	203
Total Trainees	7

contact
Alison Gaines
Partner

method of application
Handwritten Letter and CV

selection procedure
2 interviews with partners

closing date for 2003
31 July 2001

application
Training contracts p.a.
3 or 4
Applications p.a. 500+
% interviewed p.a. 5%
Required degree grade 2:1

training
Salary:
1st year (2000) £22,500
2nd year (2000) £23,500
Holiday entitlement:
20 days
% of trainees with a
non-law degree p.a.
Variable
No. of seats available
abroad p.a. None at
present

post-qualification
Salary (2000) Variable
% of trainees offered job
on qualification (2000):
100%

overseas offices
Almaty, Baku, Kiev,
Moscow, New York, Paris,
St Petersburg, Warsaw.

shadbolt & co

Chatham Court Lesbourne Road Reigate RH2 7LD
Tel: (01737) 226277 Fax: (01737) 226165
Email: sally_thorndale@shadboltlaw.co.uk
Website: www.shadboltlaw.co.uk

firm profile
Established in 1991, Shadbolt & Co is a specialist firm servicing business clients in the UK and internationally. Well known for its strengths in major projects, construction and engineering and more recently for its company commercial practice. All partners have City backgrounds.

main areas of work
Corporate and Commercial Disputes 40%; Projects/non-contentious Construction and engineering 30%; Company and Commercial 30%.

trainee profile
Mature self-starters with a strong academic background and outside interests. They should be able to take responsibility, have good interpersonal skills and be able to play an active role in the future of the firm. Linguists are particularly welcome. Travel is favourably viewed.

training environment
Four six-month seats from: corporate/commercial, commercial property, employment, projects/non contentious construction, and litigation, including seats in London, Hong Kong and Paris. Where possible, individual preference is noted. Work has an international bias. Trainees are seconded to major plc construction/engineering clients. Trainees are rapidly integrated and immediately take active roles and early responsibility. All trainees sit with partners/senior solicitors who monitor progress. One appraisal is held per seat. In certain seats trainees may be given their own files. There is a lunch time lecture programme and trainees participate in publishing a construction law and other updates. The PSC is taught externally. The firm's atmosphere is young and informal, and there are various social and sporting activities.

benefits
Permanent health insurance, pension (qualifying period).

vacation placements
Places for 2001: 6; Duration: 2 weeks; Remuneration: £150 p.w.; Closing Date: 16 March 2001.

sponsorship & awards
LPC fees partly payable when trainee commences work.

Partners	21
Assistant Solicitors	22
Total Trainees	12

contact
Sally Thorndale

method of application
Handwritten letter and CV

selection procedure
Interview(s)

closing date for 2003
31 August 2001

application
Training contracts p.a. **6**
Applications p.a. **200**
% interviewed p.a. **10%**
Required degree grade **2:1**

training
Salary:
1st year (2000) **£20,000**
2nd year (2000) **£24,000**
Holiday entitlement:
20 days
% of trainees with a
non-law degree p.a. **50%**
No. of seats available
abroad p.a. **1/2**

post-qualification
Salary (2000) **£30,000**
% of trainees offered job
on qualification (1999):
100%
% of assistants (as at
1/9/99) who joined as
trainees: **20%**
% of partners (as at 1/9/99)
who joined as trainees: **0%**

other offices
London, Hong Kong, Paris.

sharpe pritchard

Elizabeth House Fulwood Place London WC1V 6HG
Tel: (020) 7405 4600 Fax: (020) 7831 1284
Email: abadcock@sharpepritchard.co.uk
Website: www.sharpepritchard.co.uk

firm profile

Sharpe Pritchard is best known for its work with the public sector. It has strong litigation, public procurement and parliamentary departments. It has expanding commercial, property and planning departments.

main areas of work

Litigation 40%; Commercial/Procurement 20%; Parliamentary 15%; Property and Planning 25%.

trainee profile

Trainees will need to show good intellectual capabilities, effective communication skills, resourcefulness and an ability to work as part of a team.

training environment

The firm's training consists of seats normally between four and six months in length in the following areas: Administrative law and judicial review, general litigation, employment law, contracts and commercial, property work. There is also a prospect of undertaking parliamentary and planning work. You would normally share an office with the solicitor responsible for supervising your work. A review of progress is carried out at the end of each seat. In addition you will have regular meetings throughout your training period with the training partner. The firm has an in-house series of seminars taking the form of both skills training and updates in the law and you are encouraged to attend these.

benefits

Season ticket loan.

sponsorship & awards

Possible financial assistance with LPC.

Partners	11
Assistant Solicitors	12
Total Trainees	8

contact
Ashley Badcock Senior Partner

method of application
Letter and CV

selection procedure
Interview with the Senior Partner

application
Training contracts p.a. 4

training
Salary:
1st year (2000) c.£20,000
2nd year (2001) c.£21,000
Holiday entitlement:
25 days

sheridans

14 Red Lion Square London WC1R 4QL
Tel: (020) 7404 0444 Fax: (020) 7831 1982
Email: general@sheridans.co.uk

firm profile
A Holborn firm specialising in litigation and the entertainment and media industry, and offering private client and commercial services including property and company work.

main areas of work
Commercial and other litigation including Media, Family and Crime 35%; Entertainment and Media 40%; Property and Planning 15%; Company/Commercial 10%.

trainee profile
Candidates should be intelligent, ambitious and self-confident with excellent communication and interpersonal skills.

training environment
Trainees spend six to eight months in each department (litigation, company/commercial, property and planning). Working alongside senior partners or solicitors, you will be involved with a whole variety of work. There are regular trainee and department meetings. In the second year, trainees may be given a limited number of their own files. Early responsibility is encouraged. Trainees are not usually placed in media and entertainment (at least not until their last six months, due to its particularly specialised nature). The training programme is being expanded to include in-house seminars and video assisted learning schemes. Full computer and technology training is provided. Trainees are expected to work hard and think on their feet. The firm is friendly and informal and organises a range of social/sporting activities.

benefits
Life assurance.

sponsorship & awards
LPC funding is variable for those who have accepted training contracts.

Partners	16
Assistant Solicitors	9
Total Trainees	6

contact
Cyril Glasser

method of application
Letter and CV

selection procedure
2 interviews

application date for 2003
1–31 August 2001

application
Training contracts p.a. **2-3**
Applications p.a. **700**
% interviewed p.a. **8%**
Required degree grade **2:1**

training
Salary:
1st year (2000) **£20,000**
2nd year (2000) **£22,000**
Holiday entitlement:
20 days
% of trainees with a
non-law degree p.a. **16%**

post-qualification
Salary (2000) **£32,000**
% of trainees offered job
on qualification (2000): **75%**
% of assistants (as at
1/9/00) who joined as
trainees: **80%**
% of partners (as at 1/9/00)
who joined as trainees:
33%

shoosmiths

The Lakes Bedford Road Northampton NN4 7SH
Tel: (01604) 543000 Fax: (01604) 543543
Email: Northampton@shoosmiths.co.uk
Website: www.shoosmiths.co.uk

firm profile

The firm operates in three principal divisions – commercial, financial institutions and claims compensation, each with its own management structure designed to enable a responsive approach to the markets they serve. The firm has in excess of 1,200 members of staff and 78 partners.

main areas of work

Business Services, Banking, Commercial Property, Personal Injury, Financial Institutions and Private Client.

trainee profile

You will be confident, motivated and articulate with natural intelligence and the drive to succeed, thereby making a real contribution to the firm's commercial success. You will want to be a part of a winning team and will care about the kind of service you give to your clients, both internal and external.

training environment

Shoosmiths recognises that lawyers need more than just legal training to survive in today's challenging commercial environment. That is why every opportunity will be made available to you so that you can develop both personally and professionally. A training contract with Shoosmiths is divided into four seats lasting six months each, with one compulsory seat being in either the Corporate/Commercial Department or the Litigation Department. Trainees can move around the regional offices should they wish with all Shoosmiths staff accessible and happy to give assistance. In addition to the compulsory Professional Skills Course, the firm offers a comprehensive programme that includes managerial, organisational and IT training. Social and sporting activities are organised regularly by local offices and by the Shoosmiths Group as a whole.

benefits

Life assurance, pension after 3 months.

vacation placements

Places for 2001: 25; Duration: 2 weeks; Remuneration: £120 p.w.; Closing Date: 29 February 2001.

sponsorship & awards

Funding £10,000 - split between fees and maintenance.

Partners	78
Assistant Solicitors	104
Total Trainees	26

contact
Claire Lewis

method of application
Application form

selection procedure
Assessment centre - half day

closing date for 2003
31 July 2001

application
Training contracts p.a. **12**
Applications p.a. **2,000**
% interviewed p.a. **10%**
Required degree grade **2:1**

training
Salary:
1st year (2000) **£16,000**
2nd Year (2000) **£17,250**
Holiday entitlement:
23 days

post-qualification
Salary (2000) **£30,000**

offices
Northampton, Nottingham, Reading.

sidley & austin

1 Threadneedle Street London EC2R 8AW
Tel: (020) 7360 3600 Fax: (020) 7626 7937
Email: zzell@sidley.com
Website: www.sidley.com

firm profile

Founded in Chicago in 1866, Sidley & Austin is now one of the largest law firms in the world, with approximately 900 lawyers practising on three continents. The firm has over 60 lawyers in London and is expanding fast.

main areas of work

Banking, Capital Markets, Banking Regulation, Structured Finance and Securitisation, Corporate & Commercial Law, Tax and Commercial Property.

trainee profile

Sidley & Austin is looking for focused, intelligent and enthusiastic individuals with personality and humour who have a real interest in practising law in the commercial world. Trainees should have a 2:1 degree (not necessarily in law) and three A-levels at A and B grades. Trainees would normally be expected to pass the CPE (if required) and the LPC at the first attempt.

training environment

Sidley & Austin are looking to recruit 6-8 trainee solicitors to start in September 2003/March 2004. The firm is not a typical City firm and it is not a 'legal factory' so there is no risk of you being just a number. The team at Sidley & Austin in London is young, dynamic and collegiate. Everyone is encouraged to be proactive and to create their own niche when they are ready to do so. Trainees spend a period of time in our four specialist groups: International Finance, Corporate & Commercial, Tax and Property. Sidley & Austin in London does not have a separate litigation department, although some litigation work is undertaken. In each group you will sit with a partner or senior associate to ensure that you receive individual training that is both effective and based on a real caseload. In addition, there is a structured timetable of training on a cross-section of subjects and an annual training weekend.

benefits

Healthcare, disability cover, life assurance, contribution to gym membership, interest free season ticket loan.

sponsorship & awards

CPE and LPC fees paid and maintenance p.a.

Partners	15
Assistant Solicitors	36
Total Trainees	10

contact
Zoë Zell

method of application
Covering letter and employee application form
- Please call 0800 731 5015

selection procedure
Interview(s)

closing date for 2003
27 July 2001

application
Training contracts p.a. **6-8**
Applications p.a. **500**
% interviewed p.a. **15**
Required degree grade **2:1**

training
Salary:
1st year (2000) £26,250
2nd Year (2000) £29,500
Holiday entitlement:
22 days
% of trainees with a non-law degree p.a. **50%**

post-qualification
Salary (2000) £44,100

overseas offices
Chicago, Dallas, Hong Kong, Los Angeles, New York, Shanghai, Singapore, Tokyo, Washington D.C.

simmons & simmons

21 Wilson Street London EC2M 2TX
Tel: (020) 7628 2020 Fax: (020) 7628 2070
Email: recruitment@simmons-simmons.com
Website: www.simmons-simmons.com

firm profile

Simmons & Simmons is one of the major international law firms. It has developed an increasingly international practice to serve the needs of its clients and has ten offices in different locations across the globe. An extensive network of overseas contacts enables the firm to extend its reach far beyond those countries in which it has offices and offers clients a multi-jurisdictional service of the highest quality.

main areas of work

Corporate/Corporate Finance/M&A 41%; Commercial/ IP/EC 14%; Property 13%; Litigation 12%; Banking and Capital Markets 10%; Tax 6%; Employment 3%; Environment 1%.

trainee profile

While a good academic record and sound commercial judgement are important, strength of character and outside interests are also taken into consideration.

training environment

Trainees are involved in the firm's work from the start of their contract. Simmons & Simmons allocate each trainee a training principal to oversee their training and career development. Each move to a new department is accompanied by a structured series of seminars on relevant areas of law. Simmons & Simmons supports the Battersea Legal Advice Centre and provides advice on a *pro bono* basis to prisoners on 'death row' in Jamaica.

benefits

Season ticket loan, fitness loan, PRP, group travel insurance, group accident insurance, group health insurance.

vacation placements

Places for 2001: 40-50; Duration: to be confirmed; Remuneration: £200 p.w.; Closing Date: 24 February 2001.

sponsorship & awards

In the absence of Local Authority funding the firm will pay LPC fees and, where necessary, CPE fees and offer a maintenance allowance of £4,500 for those at Law School in London or Guildford and £4,000 elsewhere.

Partners	144
Assistant Solicitors	326
Total Trainees	148

contact
Katharyn White

method of application
Application form, CV
and covering letter

selection procedure
Assessment day:
document exercise,
interview and written
exercise

closing date for 2003
24 August 2001

application
Training contracts p.a.
50-60
Applications p.a. **2,700**
% interviewed p.a. **10%**
Required degree grade **2:1**

training
Salary:
1st year (2000) £25,000
2nd year (2000) £28,000
Holiday entitlement:
22 days
% of trainees with a
non-law degree p.a. **50%**
No. of seats available
abroad p.a. **18**

post-qualification
Salary (2000) **£42,000**
% of trainees offered job
on qualification (2000):
91%

overseas offices
Abu Dhabi, Brussels,
Hong Kong, Lisbon,
Madrid, Milan, New York,
Paris, Rome, Shanghai.

sinclair roche & temperley

Royex House 5 Aldermanbury Square London EC2V 7LE
Tel: (020) 7452 4000 Fax: (020) 7452 4001

firm profile

A major international law firm, founded in 1934. Over two thirds of the work handled in the London office is for non-UK clients. Particular expertise is in shipping, aviation, international trade and energy, also emerging markets. Areas of work include shipping and commercial litigation and arbitration, collision, salvage and marine insurance, ship finance, aviation, oil and gas, company commercial and tax, commercial property, project, asset and trade finance and EC law.

main areas of work

Shipping and Commercial; Litigation; Ship and Project Finance; Company/Commercial; Marine Casualty and Insurance; Commercial Property; Aviation; EU; Tax.

trainee profile

An employer offering equal opportunities looking for motivated trainees with a strong personality and good academic record. Commitment and interest in the firm's and their clients' businesses are essential.

training environment

Four six month seats. Trainees sit with a partner or senior assistant. As well as gaining the requisite legal skills, business development and management skills will be covered. Client contact is encouraged. A thorough programme of continuing professional training through lectures, seminars and external courses is provided.

benefits

Private health cover, discretionary bonus, PHI, accident insurance, subsidised sports club membership.

vacation placements

Places for 2001: 10-12; Duration: 2 weeks; Remuneration: £160 p.w.; Closing Date: 28 February 2001, subject to availability.

sponsorship & awards

CPE and LPC fees paid and £4,000 maintenance p.a.

Partners	31
Assistant Solicitors	68
Total Trainees	22

contact
Dawn Morgan

method of application
CV and covering letter

selection procedure
Interview

closing date for 2003
31 October 2001 subject to availability

application
Training contracts p.a. **6-8**
Applications p.a. **1,500**
% interviewed p.a. **2%**
Required degree grade **2:1**

training
Salary:
1st year (2000) £22,500
2nd year (2000) £23,500
Holiday entitlement:
20 days
% of trainees with a
non-law degree p.a. **Varies**
No. of seats available
abroad p.a. **Varies**

post-qualification
Salary (2000):
£37,000-40,000
% of trainees offered job
on qualification (1/9/00):
86%
% of assistants (as at
1/9/00) who joined as
trainees: **31%**

overseas offices
Bucharest, Hong Kong, Shanghai

slaughter and may

35 Basinghall Street London EC2V 5DB
Tel: (020) 7600 1200 Fax: (020) 7600 0289
Website: www.slaughterandmay.com

firm profile
One of the leading law firms in the world, Slaughter and May enjoys a reputation for quality and expertise. The corporate and financial practice is particularly strong and lawyers are known for their business acumen and technical excellence. International work is central to the practice and lawyers travel widely. No London partner has ever left the firm to join a competing practice.

main areas of work
Corporate and Financial 66%; Commercial Litigation 11%; Tax 7%; Property (Commercial) 6%; Pensions and Employment 5%; EC and Competition Law 3%; Intellectual Property 2%.

trainee profile
The work is demanding and the firm looks for intellectual agility and the ability to work with people from different countries and walks of life. Common sense, a mature outlook and the willingness to accept responsibility are all essential. The firm expects to provide training in everything except the fundamental principles of law, so does not expect applicants to know much of commercial life. Trainees are expected to remain with the firm on qualification.

training environment
Four or five seats of three or six months' duration. Two seats will be in the corporate and financial department, a property seat is optional, and one seat in either Litigation, Intellectual Property, Tax or Pensions and Employment. In each seat, a partner is responsible for monitoring your progress and reviewing your work. There is an extensive training programme which includes the PSC. There are also discussion groups covering general and specialised legal topics.

benefits
BUPA, STL, pension scheme, membership of various sports clubs, 24 hour accident cover.

vacation placements - Summer 2001
Places: 60; Duration: 2 weeks; Remuneration: £225 p.w.; Closing Date: Before 9 February 2001 for penultimate year (of first degree) students only.

sponsorship & awards
CPE and LPC fees and maintenance grants are paid; some grants are available for postgraduate work.

Partners	117
Assistant Solicitors	380
Total Trainees	142

contact
Neil Morgan

method of application
Covering letter and CV to include full details of all examination results.

selection procedure
Interview

application
Training contracts p.a. **75+**
Applications p.a. **3,000**
% interviewed p.a. **20%**
Required standard:
Good 2:1 ability

training
Salary:
1st year £25,000
2nd year £28,000
Holiday entitlement:
25 days on qualification
% of trainees with a
non-law degree p.a. **50%**
No. of seats available
abroad p.a. **approx 30**

post-qualification
Salary (2000) **£42,000**
% of trainees offered job
on qualification (2000):
100%

overseas offices
Brussels, Hong Kong,
New York, Paris,
Singapore.

speechly bircham

6 St Andrew Street London EC4A 3LX
Tel: (020) 7427 6400 Fax: (020) 7427 6600
Email: trainingcontracts@speechlys.co.uk
Website: www.speechlybircham.co.uk

firm profile
Speechly Bircham is an independent mid-sized City law firm with an excellent client base including a number of well-known corporate and institutional clients. Speechly Bircham's strong commercial focus is complemented by a highly regarded private capital practice. The firm handles major transactions and commercial disputes, and provides a number of specialist advisory services, notably tax.

main areas of work
Corporate 30%; Property 20%; Litigation 25%; Private Capital 25%.

trainee profile
Both law and non-law graduates who are capable of achieving a 2:1. The firm seeks intellectually dynamic individuals who enjoy a collaborative working environment where they can make an impact.

training environment
Speechly Bircham divides the training contract into four six-month seats. Emphasis is given to early responsibility and supervised client contact providing trainees with a practical learning environment.

benefits
Season ticket loan, private medical insurance, life assurance.

vacation placements
Places for 2001: 8 places. The firm's summer placement scheme for students gives them the chance to experience a City legal practice. In a three-practice placement, students will be asked to research and present on a legal issue at the end of their placement.; Duration: 3 weeks; Remuneration: £200 p.w.; Closing Date: 14 February 2001.

sponsorship & awards
CPE tuition and LPC tuition fees plus a maintenance grant of £4,000.

Partners	37
Assistant Solicitors	39
Total Trainees	10

contact
Nicola Swann
Human Resources Director

method of application
Application form

selection procedure
Interview

closing date for 2003
15 August 2001

application
Training contracts p.a. 5
Applications p.a. 1,000
% interviewed p.a. 5%
Required degree grade 2:1

training
Salary:
1st year (2000)·£23,000-£24,000
2nd Year(2000) £25,000-£26,000
Holiday entitlement:
20 days
% of trainees with a
non-law degree p.a. 50%

post-qualification
Salary (2000) £38,000

steele & co

2 Norwich Business Park Whiting Rd Norwich NR4 6DJ
Tel: (01603) 627107 Fax: (01603) 625890
Email: personnel@steele.co.uk
Website: www.steele.co.uk

firm profile

Steele & Co is an innovative and progressive commercial firm with an increasingly national client base. It is recognised in particular for the strength of its commercial practitioners and for the range and quality of its services to local authorities and the commercial sector.

main areas of work

The firm offers a full range of corporate, property, litigation and public sector services. The firm is dedicated to delivering high quality value for money services to its clients regardless of location.

trainee profile

Candidates will be highly motivated, with a strong academic record and previous legal work experience.

training environment

The aim is to ensure that every trainee will wish to continue their career with the firm. The training programme consists of four six-month seats in the following departments: company commercial, commercial property, civil litigation, commercial disputes, employment, family and public sector. You will have some choice in the order of you seats. Trainees are encouraged to get involved and gain hands on experience early on in their training contract. Bi-monthly meetings provide a forum for discussion of topical issues. The offices are open-plan providing a supportive and learning environment which reflects our accreditation to both ISO 9001 and Investor in People. Trainee Solicitors are appraised at the end of each seat and are part of the firm's mentor scheme. There is an active sports and social life.

benefits

Permanent health insurance, accident insurance, legal services.

vacation placements

Places for 2001: Places offered throughout the Easter and Summer vacation.

Partners	13
Assistant Solicitors	18
Total Trainees	10

contact
Ann Chancellor
Human Resources
Manager

method of application
Handwritten letter and CV

selection procedure
Interview

application
Training contracts p.a. **6**
Applications p.a. **300-400**
Required degree grade **2:1**

post-qualification
% of trainees offered job
on qualification (2000):
100%

stephenson harwood

One, St Paul's Churchyard London EC4M 8SH
Tel: (020) 7329 4422 Fax: (020) 7606 0822
Email: sharon.green@shlegal.com

firm profile

Established in the City of London in 1828, Stephenson Harwood has developed into a large international practice, with a commercial focus and a wide client base.

main areas of work

Corporate; Banking; Litigation; Property; Private Capital; Shipping.

trainee profile

The firm looks for high calibre graduates with excellent academic records and an outgoing personality.

training environment

As the graduate intake is relatively small, the firm gives trainees individual attention, coaching and monitoring. Your structured and challenging programme involves four six-month seats in either corporate or banking, litigation, property and another seat of your choice. These seats include "on the job" training, sharing an office and working with a partner or senior solicitor. In-house lectures complement your training and there is continuous review of your career development. You will have the opportunity to spend six months abroad and have language tuition where appropriate. You will be given your own caseload and as much responsibility as you can shoulder. The firm plays a range of team sports, has its own gym, subsidised membership of health clubs and has privileged seats for concerts at the Royal Albert Hall and the London Coliseum and access to private views at the Tate Gallery.

benefits

Subsidised membership of health clubs, season ticket loan and 25 days paid holiday per year.

vacation placements

Places for 2001: 21; Duration: 2 weeks; Remuneration: £200 p.w.; Closing Date: 16 February 2001.

sponsorship & awards

£6,900 fees paid for CPE and LPC and £4,500 maintenance p.a.

Partners   79*
Assistant Solicitors 115*
Total Trainees   40
* denotes world-wide figures

contact
Graduate Recruitment

method of application
Application form only

selection procedure
Interview with 2 partners

closing date for 2003
27 July 2001

application
Training contracts p.a. 18
% interviewed p.a. 10%
Required degree grade 2:1

training
Salary:
1st year (2000) £23,000
2nd year (2000) £25,000
Holiday entitlement:
25 days
% of trainees with a
non-law degree p.a. 46%
No. of seats available
abroad p.a. 8

post-qualification
Salary: (2000) £40,000
% of trainees offered job
on qualification (2000): 82%
% of assistants (as at
1/9/00) who joined as
trainees: 37%
% of partners (as at 1/9/00)
who joined as trainees:
46%

overseas offices
Brussels, Guangzhou,
Hong Kong, Madrid,
Piraeus, Singapore.

tarlo lyons

Watchmaker Court 33 St. John's Lane London EC1M 4DB
Tel: (020) 7405 2000 Fax: (020) 7814 9421
Email: trainee.recruitment@tarlolyons.com
Website: www.tarlolyons.com

firm profile

Tarlo Lyons was founded in 1927 and undertakes increasingly specialised and highly sophisticated work for commercial clients. The firm has particular expertise in Information Technology and Telecommunications Law (including a significant e-commerce practice), Entertainment Law (specifically live stage, TV and film), Commercial Litigation and Gaming and Licensing Law. It holds Investor in People accreditation.

main areas of work

Information Technology, Telecommunications and E-commerce; Dispute Resolution; Company/Commercial; Property; Entertainment.

trainee profile

Candidates need to demonstrate intellectual capacity combined with common sense, resourcefulness and a sense of humour. Basic IT skills essential; languages valued. A well spent gap year or commercial experience can be an advantage.

training environment

Trainees are introduced to the firm during a two day induction course. Training consists of six month seats in four of the following five departments: property, litigation, IT/telecoms, company/commercial and entertainment. You will be allocated to a Supervisor in each Department, who will monitor your workflow and training. In addition you will meet with the Training Partner every 2-3 months for a formal review. Trainees are encouraged to attend relevant external courses on technical matters. The PSC is taught externally. The firm has a friendly, open door policy and trainees take part in a wide range of marketing, sporting and social events.

benefits

Contribution to private health insurance and season ticket loan.

sponsorship & awards

LPC fees paid.

Partners	23
Assistant Solicitors	30
Total Trainees	6

contact
Trainee Recruitment
Co-ordinator

method of application
Application form available
from website

selection procedure
2 Interviews with partners

closing date for 2003
10 August 2001

application
Training contracts p.a. 3
Applications p.a. 400+
% interviewed p.a. 5%
Required degree grade 2:1

training
Salary:
1st year (2000) £20,000
on average
2nd year (2000) £22,000
on average
Holiday entitlement:
22 days
% of trainees with a
non-law degree p.a. 50%

post-qualification
Salary (2000) £37,000+
(salary levels may
increase subject to
market conditions.)

taylor joynson garrett

Carmelite 50 Victoria Embankment Blackfriars
London EC4Y 0DX
Tel: (020) 7300 7000 Fax: (020) 7300 7100
Website: www.tjg.co.uk

firm profile

Taylor Joynson Garrett is a major City and international law firm, with an impressive UK and international client base. The firm, which has offices in London, Brussels and Bucharest, has recognised expertise in its corporate and intellectual property practices, as well as strength in depth across the full range of commercial disciplines.

main areas of work

Corporate 25%; Litigation 21%; Intellectual Property 19%; Private Client 9%; Commercial Property 13%; Banking 7%; Employment 6%.

trainee profile

Academic achievement is high on the firm's list of priorities, and a 2:1 or better is expected. It wants individuals who have good communication skills and will flourish in a competitive environment. Strength of character, determination and the ability to think laterally are also important.

training environment

Trainees will have six-month seats in four different departments, with the possibility of a placement in Brussels. You will be supervised by a partner or assistant and appraised both two months into, and at the end of, each seat. There will be plenty of opportunity to take early responsibility. The firm works closely with external training providers to meet the needs of the PSC. The course is tailored to suit the firm's needs, and most of the training is conducted in-house. A full sports and social calendar is available.

benefits

Private medical care, permanent health insurance, STL, subsidised staff restaurant, non-contributory pension scheme on qualification.

vacation placements

Places for 2001: 30; Duration: 2 weeks; Remuneration: £200 p.w.; Closing Date: 23 February 2001.

sponsorship & awards

CPE and LPC fees paid and £4,000 maintenance p.a.

Partners	88
Assistant Solicitors	116
Total Trainees	43

contact
Trainee Solicitors'
Recruitment Department

method of application
Firm's application form

selection procedure
2 interviews, 1 with a
partner.

closing date for 2003
11 August 2001

application
Training contracts p.a. 25
Applications p.a. **1,600**
% interviewed p.a. **10%**
Required degree grade **2:1**

training
Salary:
1st year (2000) £24,000
2nd year (2000) £27,000
Holiday entitlement:
25 days
% of trainees with a
non-law degree p.a. **40%**
No. of seats available
abroad p.a. **2**

post-qualification
Salary (2000) **£41,000**
% of trainees offered job
on qualification (2000): **90%**
% of assistants (as at
1/9/00) who joined as
trainees: **51%**
% of partners (as at 1/9/00)
who joined as trainees:
31%

overseas offices
Brussels, Bucharest

taylor vinters

Merlin Place Milton Rd Cambridge CB4 0DP
Tel: (01223) 423444 Fax: (01223) 426523
Email: pt@taylorvinters.com
Website: www.taylorvinters.com

firm profile

One of the largest firms in East Anglia, based in the University City of Cambridge. The largest single office firm in Cambridge.

main areas of work

Company Commercial; Intellectual Property; Commercial Litigation; Commercial Property; Claimant Personal Injury; Private Client.

trainee profile

Candidates should have energy, enthusiasm, intelligence, common sense, a friendly nature and a good sense of humour. Non law degree graduates are welcomed.

training environment

The training contract comprises four seats; commercial/intellectual property, property/planning, claimant personal injury and commercial litigation. Opportunities exist for exchanges with European Network firms. Trainees' progress is reviewed and assessed every three months. There is an extensive in-house training programme within all departments and firmwide. The PSC is also organised in-house.

benefits

The main benefits are a pension, private medical insurance and life insurance. Many social activities are actively encouraged, from a theatre club to karaoke. Cambridge of course now has the largest pub in Europe.

vacation placements

Places for 2001: 14; Duration: 1 week.

Partners	22
Assistant Solicitors	55
Total Trainees	10

contact
Paul Tapner

method of application
Application form

selection procedure
Single interview with two partners

closing date for 2003
31 August 2001

application
Training contracts p.a. 5
Applications p.a. 300
Required degree grade 2(ii)

training
Salary:
1st year (2000) £15,000
2nd year (2000) £16,500
Holiday entitlement:
23 days
% of trainees with a
non-law degree p.a. 40%

post-qualification
Salary (2000) £27,000
plus benefits

taylor walton

36-44 Alma Street Luton LU1 2PL
Tel: (01582) 731161 Fax: (01582) 457900
Email: luton@taylorwalton.co.uk
Website: www.taylorwalton.co.uk

firm profile

Strategically located in Luton, Harpenden, St Albans and Hemel Hempstead, Taylor Walton is a major regional law practice advising both businesses and private clients. Its strengths are in commercial property, corporate work and commercial litigation, whilst maintaining a strong private client side to the practice. It has a progressive outlook both in its partners and staff and in its systems, training and IT.

main areas of work

Company/Commercial 15%; Commercial Property 20%; Commercial Litigation 15%; Employment 5%; Personal Injury 5%; Family 5%; Private Client 10%; Residential Property 20%; Relocation 5%.

trainee profile

Candidates need to show excellent intellectual capabilities, coupled with an engaging personality so as to show that they can engage and interact with the firm's clients as the practice of law involves the practice of the art of communication. Taylor Walton sees its partners and staff as business advisers involved in clients businesses, not merely stand alone legal advisers.

training environment

The training consists of four six month seats. The training partner oversees the structural training along side a supervisor who will be a partner or senior solicitor in each department. The firm does try to take trainees' own wishes in relation to seats into account. In a regional law practice like Taylor Walton you will find client contact and responsibility coupled with supervision, management and training. There is an in-house training programme for all fee earning members of staff. At the end of each seat there is a post seat appraisal conducted by the training partner, the trainee and the supervisor. The PSC is taught externally. The firm is friendly with an open door policy and there are various sporting and social events.

vacation placements

Places for 2001: 2-3; Duration: up to 4 weeks; Remuneration: agreed with trainee; Closing Date: 30 April 2001.

Partners	22
Assistant Solicitors	31
Total Trainees	6

contact
Jim Wrigglesworth

method of application
CV with covering letter

selection procedure
First and second interview with opportunity to meet other partners

closing date for 2003
30 September 2001

application
Required degree grade:
2:1 or above

teacher stern selby

37–41 Bedford Row London WC1R 4JH
Tel: (020) 7242 3191 Fax: (020) 7242 1156
Email: rr@tsslaw.co.uk
Website: www.tsslaw.co.uk

firm profile

A central London-based general commercial firm, with clientele and caseload normally attributable to larger firms. It has a wide range of contacts overseas.

main areas of work

Commercial Litigation 32%; Commercial Property 39%; Company and Commercial 17%; Secured Lending 7%; Residential Conveyancing/Probate 3%; Personal Injury/Education/Judicial Review 2%.

trainee profile

Emphasis falls equally on academic excellence and personality. The firm looks for flexible and motivated individuals, who have outside interests and who have demonstrated responsibility in the past. Languages an advantage.

training environment

Trainees spend six months in three departments (Company Commercial, Litigation and Property) with, where possible, an option to return to a preferred department in the final six months. Most trainees are assigned to actively assist a partner who monitors and supports them. Trainees are expected to fully immerse themselves and take early responsibility. After a short period you will conduct your own files. Trainees are welcome to attend in-house seminars and lectures for continuing education. The atmosphere is relaxed and informal.

vacation placements

Places for 2001: Possibly to those that have accepted or applied for training contracts.

sponsorship & awards

CPE Funding: none; LPC Funding: unlikely.

Partners	16
Assistant Solicitors	18
Total Trainees	6

contact
Russell Raphael

method of application
Letter and application form

selection procedure
2 interviews

closing date for 2003
31 October 2001

application
Training contracts p.a. 3
Applications p.a. 500
% interviewed p.a. 5%
Required degree grade:
2:1 (not absolute)

training
Salary:
1st year (2000) £20,750
Holiday entitlement:
4 weeks
% of trainees with a
non-law degree p.a. 50%

post-qualification
Salary (2000) £31,000
% of trainees offered job
on qualification (2000): 66%
% of assistants (as at
1/9/00) who joined as
trainees: 50%
% of partners (as at 1/9/00)
who joined as trainees:
44%

theodore goddard

150 Aldersgate Street London EC1A 4EJ
Tel: (020) 7606 8855 Fax: (020) 7606 4390
Email: recruitment@theodoregoddard.co.uk
Website: www.theogoddard.com

firm profile

Theodore Goddard is a long-established City firm which supports clients not only in the traditional legal specialisations expected of a City firm but also in the media & communications sector. It is distinctive in that it punches above its weight in the size of the transactions it handles. With a reputation for having a friendly, unstuffy atmosphere, trainees are given early responsibility and are viewed as an integral part of the firm from day one. This is demonstrated by the offer of a permanent contract from the outset.

main areas of work

Corporate, corporate finance and corporate tax; banking; PFI; commercial litigation; commercial property; employment; intellectual property & music; film; audio-visual; e-commerce; advertising; sport.

trainee profile

The firm seeks graduates from all disciplines who can demonstrate academic excellence. In an increasingly global, technology-driven market, the firm is looking for those who think they will enjoy a fast-paced, intellectually demanding working environment.

training environment

Theodore Goddard's training is exceptional; it has won five awards both from within the legal profession and across all sectors of employment. Trainees spend six months in four practice areas with the option of three months in Paris, Brussels, or at a client. All trainees are consulted about seat preferences.

benefits

Pension, profit-related bonus, permanent health insurance, private medical insurance, subsidised health and fitness club membership and firm restaurant.

vacation placements

Places for 2001: 20 in the Summer vacation (70 open day places in the Christmas and Easter vacations); Duration: 2 weeks; Remuneration: £200 p.w.; Closing Date: For summer placements and Easter open days - end of February 2001. For Christmas open days - mid November 2000.

sponsorship & awards

CPE and LPC fees paid in full. £4,200 maintenance paid for London and South East, £3,750 elsewhere.

Partners	59
Assistant Solicitors	190
Total Trainees	33

contact
Recruitment Manager

method of application
Firm's application form

selection procedure
Initial interview followed by second interview

closing date for 2003
31 August 2001

application
Training contracts p.a. 20
Applications p.a. 3000
% interviewed p.a. 5-10%
Required degree grade
2:1+

training
Salary:
1st year (2000) £25,000
2nd Year (2000) £28,000
Holiday entitlement:
25 days
% of trainees with a
non-law degree p.a. 40%
No. of seats available
abroad p.a. 8

post-qualification
Salary (2000) £40,000
% of trainees offered job
on qualification (2000):
100%

overseas offices
Brussels (associated
offices worldwide)

A-Z SOLICITORS

505

tlt solicitors

One Redcliff St Bristol BS99 7JZ
Tel: (0117) 917 7777 Fax: (0117) 917 7778
Email: sstacey@TLTsolicitors.com
Website: www.TLTsolicitors.com

firm profile

Trumps Lawrence Tucketts is the third largest firm in Bristol and one of the top 100 in the country. The combined firm has over 100 lawyers, a total complement of over 250 people and a joint turnover of £10m+.

main areas of work

Commercial and Corporate 34%; Property and Planning 26%; Litigation 11%; Family 7%; Banking and Lender Services 22%.

TLT has very strong corporate/commercial teams which undertake a wide range of work including acquisitions and disposals, joint ventures and OFEX work. The property and planning teams undertake a range of work including planning and advocacy, advice to regulatory authorities, and building and construction claims. TLT has one of the leading dispute resolution practices in the region. Particular emphasis is on insolvency, professional indemnity and negligence, mortgage possession proceedings and general commercial matters. The family team is consistently acknowledged as the best in the region. The private client team handles conveyancing, wills, trusts and probate as well as other less traditional financial services.

trainee profile

A strong academic background is preferred and a resourceful personality is also a consideration.

training environment

Trainees indicate their preference for three or four seats of six months each, which the firm tries to match. All trainees sit with another lawyer, but in every case their work is drawn from all parts of the team or department so that they gain as much experience as possible. Review meetings are held regularly. TLT strives to give you a high level of responsibility and involvement, while ongoing lectures are designed to extend your knowledge. Sports and social activities are available.

benefits

Subsidised health insurance, subsidised sports and health club facility, pension

vacation placements

Places for 2001: A minimum of 8 places each year;

sponsorship & awards

Interest paid on LPC up to £6,000; maintenance grant of £3,500

Partners	27
Assistant Solicitors	33
Total Trainees	13

contact
Human Resources

method of application
Firm's application form

selection procedure
Assessment Day

closing date for 2003
15 August 2001

application
Training contracts p.a. 8
Applications p.a. 1000
% interviewed p.a. 1.5%
Required degree grade: n/a

training
Holiday entitlement:
25 days
% of trainees with a
non-law degree p.a. 50%

post-qualification
Salary (2000) market rate
% of trainees offered job
on qualification (2000): 85%
% of assistants (as at
1/9/00) who joined as
trainees: 25%
% of partners (as at 1/9/00)
who joined as trainees:
25%

travers smith braithwaite

10 Snow Hill London EC1A 2AL
Tel: (020) 7295 3000 Fax: (020) 7295 3500
Email: Graduate.Recruitment@TraversSmith.com
Website: www.traverssmith.com

firm profile

A leading medium-sized corporate, financial and commercial law firm with the capability to advise on a wide range of business activities. The practice offers small, closely-knit teams providing consistent service to clients.

main areas of work

Corporate 38%; Litigation 15%; Property 15%; Banking 14%; Tax 8%; Pensions 5%; Employment 5%.

trainee profile

Candidates should have a strong academic background with at least 28 points at 'A' level (excluding General Studies). They must have ambition, determination and a sense of humour. They must take their careers but not themselves seriously.

training environment

Training consists of four six-month seats taken from the corporate, commercial, banking/corporate recovery, employment, litigation, property, pensions, financial services, and corporate tax departments. There is no crowd to get lost in; trainees quickly get to know each other and everyone else in the firm. They are treated as individuals and given immediate responsibility for handling deals and clients. Formal training includes a comprehensive programme of in-house training and seminars, a weekly technical bulletin to keep staff abreast of changes in the law. Trainees sit with partners. Social and sporting activities are enjoyed by the whole firm.

benefits

Private health insurance, season ticket loans, luncheon vouchers, subsidised sports club membership

vacation placements

Places for 2001: 45; Duration: 3 weeks; Remuneration: £200 p.w.; Closing Date: End March 2001.

sponsorship & awards

LPC and CPE fees paid and between £4,000 and £4,500 maintenance p.a.

Partners	47
Assistant Solicitors	89
Total Trainees	36

contact
Christopher Carroll

method of application
Handwritten letter and CV

selection procedure
Interviews

closing date for 2003
September 2001

application
Training contracts p.a. **20**
Applications p.a. **1,600**
% interviewed p.a. **15%**
Required degree grade **2:1**

training
Salary:
1st year (2000) **£25,000**
2nd Year (2000) **£28,000**
Holiday entitlement:
20 days
% of trainees with a
non-law degree p.a.
Approx 50%

post-qualification
Salary (2000) **£42,000**
% of trainees offered job
on qualification (2000):
100%
% of assistants (as at
1/9/00) who joined as
trainees: **70%**
% of partners (as at 1/9/00)
who joined as trainees:
33%

trowers & hamlins

Sceptre Court 40 Tower Hill London EC3N 4DX
Tel: (020) 7423 8000 Fax: (020) 7423 8001
Email: gradrecruitment@trowers.com
Website: www.trowers.com

firm profile
Trowers & Hamlins is a substantial international firm. A leader in housing and public sector law, the firm also has a strong commercial side. The firm has regional offices in the UK, offices in the Middle East and links with Jordan, Yemen, Singapore, USA and Europe.

main areas of work
Property (Housing, Public Sector, Comm.) 35%; Company and Commercial/Construction 32%; Litigation 27%; Private Client 6%.

trainee profile
Personable, enthusiastic candidates with a good academic record and wide-ranging outside interests. The ability to work under pressure and with others, combined with versatility are essential characteristics.

training environment
Trainees will gain experience in four seats from: company/commercial, construction, property, international, litigation, employment and private client. Trainees are encouraged to learn from direct contact with clients and to assume responsibility. The training programme is flexible and, with reviews held every three months, individual preferences will be considered. A training officer assists partners with the training programme and in-house lectures and seminars are held regularly. There are opportunities to work in Manchester, Exeter and the Middle East. The firm encourages a relaxed atmosphere and blends traditional qualities with contemporary attitudes. Activities are organised outside working hours.

benefits
Season ticket loan, private health care after 6 month's service, Employee Assistance Programme & discretionary bonus, Death in Service.

vacation placements
Places for 2001: 15-20; Duration: 3 weeks; Remuneration: £175 p.w.; Closing Date: 1 March (Summer). Open Day (date TBC).

sponsorship & awards
CPE and LPC fees paid and £4,000 – £4,250 maintenance p.a.

Partners	65
Assistant Solicitors	72
Total Trainees	26

contact
Graduate Recruitment Office

method of application
Letter, application form and CV

selection procedure
Interview(s), essay and practical test

closing date for 2003
1 August 2001

application
Training contracts p.a.
12–15
Applications p.a. **1,600**
% interviewed p.a. **4%**
Required degree grade:
2:1+

training
Salary:
1st year (2000) £23,000
2nd year (2000) £25,000
Holiday entitlement:
20 days (year 1)
22 days (year 2)
% of trainees with a non-law degree p.a. 40%
No. of seats available abroad p.a. Between 4 and 6

post-qualification
Salary (2000) £37,500
% of trainees offered job on qualification (2000): 90%
% of assistants (as at 1/9/00) who joined as trainees: 40%
% of partners (as at 1/9/00) who joined as trainees: 45%

overseas offices
Abu Dhabi, Dubai, Oman, Bahrain, Cairo.

uk branch offices
Manchester, Exeter.

walker morris

Kings Court 12 King Street Leeds LS1 2HL
Tel: (0113) 283 2500 Fax: (0113) 245 9412
Email: nbc@walkermorris.co.uk
Website: www.walkermorris.co.uk

firm profile

Based in Leeds, Walker Morris is one of the largest commercial law firms in the North, providing a full range of legal services to commercial and private clients. It is increasingly gaining an international reputation.

main areas of work

Commercial Litigation 32%; Commercial Property 30%; Company and Commercial 22%; Building Societies 12%; Private Clients 4%.

trainee profile

Bright, articulate, highly motivated individuals who will thrive on early responsibility in a demanding yet friendly environment.

training environment

Trainees commence with an induction programme, before spending four months in each main department (commercial property, corporate and commercial litigation). Trainees can choose in which departments they wish to spend their second year. Formal training will include interactive role plays, interactive video, lectures, workshops and seminars. The PSC covers personal work management, advocacy and professional conduct. Individual IT training is provided. An option exists for a four-month trainee exchange programme with a leading Parisian law firm. Emphasis is placed on teamwork, inside and outside the office. The firm's social and sporting activities are an important part of its culture and are organised by a committee drawn from all levels of the firm. A trainee solicitors committee also organises events and liaises with the Leeds Trainee Solicitors Group.

vacation placements

Places for 2001: 30-40 – over 3 weeks; Duration: 1 week; Remuneration: £100 p.w.; Closing Date: 28 February 2001.

sponsorship & awards

CPE Funding: Fees + £1,000; LPC Funding: Fees + £1,000.

Partners	37
Assistant Solicitors	73
Total Trainees	20

contact
Nick Cannon

method of application
Application form and covering letter

selection procedure
Telephone and face to face interviews

closing date for 2003
31 July 2001

application
Training contracts p.a. **15**
Applications p.a.
approx 600
% interviewed p.a.
Telephone: **16%**
Face to face: **10%**
Required degree grade: **2:1**

training
Salary:
1st year (2000) **£17,250**
2nd year (2000) **£18,500**
Holiday entitlement:
24 days
% of trainees with a non-law degree p.a.
30% on average
No. of seats available abroad p.a. **1**

post-qualification
Salary (2000) **£27,500**
% of trainees offered job on qualification (2000): **90%**
% of assistants (as at 1/9/00) who joined as trainees: **60%**
% of partners (as at 1/9/00) who joined as trainees: **47%**

ward hadaway

Sandgate House 102 Quayside Newcastle upon Tyne NE1 3DX
Tel: (0191) 204 4000 Fax: (0191) 204 4001
Email: personnel@wardhadaway.com
Website: www.wardhadaway.com

firm profile

Ward Hadaway is one of the most progressive commercial law firms in the North of England. The firm is firmly established as one of the North East region's legal heavyweights.

main areas of work

Litigation: 37%; Property: 33%; Company/Commercial: 24%; Private Client: 6%.

trainee profile

The usual academic and professional qualifications are sought. Sound commercial and business awareness are essential as is the need to demonstrate strong communication skills, enthusiasm and flexibility. Candidates will be able to demonstrate excellent interpersonal and analytical skills.

training environment

The training contract is structured around four seats (Property, Company/Commercial, Litigation and Private Client) each of six months duration. At regular intervals, and each time you are due to change seat, you will have the opportunity to discuss the experience you would like to gain during your training contract. The firm will always try to give high priority to your preferences. You will share a room with a partner or associate which will enable you to learn how to deal with different situations. Your practical experience will also be complemented by an extensive programme of seminars and lectures. All trainees are allocated a 'buddy', usually a second year trainee or newly qualified solicitor, who can provide as much practical advice and guidance as possible during your training. The firm has an active Social Committee and offers a full range of sporting and social events.

benefits

23 days holiday. Death in service insurance. Pension (post qualification).

vacation placements

Places for 2001: 12; Duration: 1 week.

sponsorship & awards

LPC fees paid and £2,000 interest free loan.

Partners	41
Assistant Solicitors	50
Total Trainees	15

contact
Carol Todner
Personnel Manager

method of application
Application form and
handwritten letter

selection procedure
Interview

closing date for 2003
31 July 2001

application
Training contracts p.a. 8
Applications p.a. 400
% interviewed p.a. 10%
Required degree grade 2:1

training
Salary:
1st year (2000)
(1st six months) £15,500
(2nd six months) £16,000
2nd Year (2000)
(1st six months) £16,500
(2nd six months) £17,000
Holiday entitlement:
23 days
% of trainees with a
non-law degree p.a. varies

post-qualification
Salary (2000) £25,000
% of trainees offered job
on qualification (2000):
100%

warner cranston

Pickfords Wharf Clink St London SE1 9DG
Tel: (020) 7403 2900 Fax: (020) 7403 4221
Email: Joy-Iley@Warner-Cranston.com
Website: www.warner-cranston.com

firm profile

A London and Coventry based firm formed in 1979 with an international reputation for handling all types of commercial transactions. Its underlying principle is one of big firm expertise, coupled with a personal service.

main areas of work

Company Commercial and Finance 37%; Commercial Litigation 20%; Employment 15%; Construction and Arbitration 7%; Property 14%; Personal Injury 4%; Debt Recovery 3%.

trainee profile

Proactive, commercially-minded graduates with a practical hands-on approach, who welcome responsibility.

training environment

The firm invests heavily in training, with in-house seminars (including advocacy course), drafting programmes and vital business skills courses. The firm aims to provide an informal but fast-paced working environment, where trainees are immediately given demanding work. A fine balance between supervision and responsibility is observed. There are four seats available, in company commercial, litigation, employment and property. Progress is reviewed regularly by a senior partner. An entrepreneurial atmosphere is encouraged, allowing trainees to flourish in what the firm calls the 'Warner Cranston Alternative'. The firm is located in attractive offices near London Bridge, overlooking the Thames.

benefits

BUPA, IFSTL, life assurance, permanent health insurance, pension contributions (after qualifying period).

vacation placements

Places for Summer 2001: 12; Duration: 2 weeks; Remuneration: £400; Closing Date: 31 March 2001.

sponsorship & awards

CPE/LPC fees and maintenance grant plus interest-free loan.

Partners	22
Assistant Solicitors	35
Total Trainees	8

contact
Joy Iley
Human Resources
Manager

method of application
Application form and
covering letter

selection procedure
Assessment Day:
2 interviews, aptitude test
and presentation.

closing date for 2003
31 July 2001

application
Training contracts p.a. 4
Applications p.a. **1000**
% interviewed p.a. **3%**
Required degree grade **2:1**

training
Salary:
1st year (2000) £22,500
2nd year (2000) £25,000
Holiday entitlement:
25 days
% of trainees with
a non-law degree**25%**

post-qualification
Salary (2000) **£39,000**

A-Z

SOLICITORS

511

watson burton

20 Collingwood Street Newcastle upon Tyne NE99 1YQ
Tel: (0191) 244 4444 Fax: (0191) 244 4500
Email: enquiries@watsonburton.co.uk
Website: www.watsonburton.co.uk

firm profile

Watson Burton is a medium sized commercial firm with a practice extending across the country and into Europe from a strong regional base. It has a single office in Newcastle upon Tyne and as a policy recruits trainees to retain as solicitors.

main areas of work

Corporate and Commercial 20%; Commercial Property 20%; Commercial Litigation 30%; Private Client 10%; Personal Injury 20%.

trainee profile

Watson Burton are not the biggest commercial firm in the North of England but the firm regards itself as being consistently one of the best in terms of the services it gives to its clients and the result it delivers on instructions. The firm recruits trainees who enjoy working as part of a successful team and have the ability to enjoy challenging and interesting work. The firm prefers to recruit trainees with Law degrees.

training environment

Training is delivered through three eight month seats in each of the firm's principal departments (Commercial & Corporate; Commercial Property; Commercial Litigation). In this way trainees receive an adequate period of exposure to each of the main commercial disciplines. The firm aims to produce well-rounded and confident commercial lawyers. Actual seating arrangements vary from department to department. The lengthy period in each seat enables us to give trainees early responsibility for their own workload, under expert supervision. Feedback is given regularly. The PSC is taught externally with a consortium of other Newcastle law firms. Watson Burton is a friendly firm with a young partnership. Sporting activities include the rowing team, five-a-side and eleven-a-side football, mixed hockey and a lot of social activities (featuring the Bigg Market and Quayside).

benefits

Competitive salary, good prospects.

vacation placements

Places for 2001: 15; Duration: 1 week; Remuneration: none; Closing Date: 15 June 2001. Apply to Allan Henderson.

Partners	18
Assistant Solicitors	19
Total Trainees	8

contact
Margaret Cay
Graduate Recruitment
Manager

method of application
Handwritten letter and
typed or printed CV

selection procedure
Single interview with
Partners

closing date for 2003
31 August 2001

application
Training contracts p.a. 4-5
Applications p.a. 1,000
% interviewed p.a. 15
Required degree grade 2:1

training
Salary:
1st year (2000) tba
Holiday entitlement:
20 days

post-qualification
% of trainees offered job
on qualification (2000):
100%
% of assistants (as at
1/9/00) who joined as
trainees: 45%
% of partners (as at 1/9/00)
who joined as trainees:
60%

watson, farley & williams

15 Appold Street London EC2A 2HB
Tel: (020) 7814 8000 Fax: (020) 7814 8141/2
Website: www.wfw.com

firm profile

Established in 1982, Watson, Farley & Williams has its strengths in corporate, banking and asset finance, particularly ship and aircraft finance. The firm aims to provide a superior service in specialist areas and to build long-lasting relationships with its clients.

main areas of work

Shipping; Ship Finance; Aviation; Banking; Asset Finance; Corporate; Litigation; e-commerce; Intellectual Property; EC and Competition; Taxation; Property; Insolvency.

trainee profile

Outgoing graduates who exhibit energy, ambition, self-assurance, initiative and intellectual flair.

training environment

Trainees are introduced to the firm with a comprehensive induction course covering legal topics and practical instruction. Seats are available in at least four of the firm's main areas, aiming to provide trainees with a solid commercial grounding. There is also the opportunity to spend time abroad, working on cross-border transactions. Operating in an informal, friendly and energetic atmosphere, trainees will receive support whenever necessary. You will be encouraged to take on early responsibility and play an active role alongside a partner at each stage of your training. The practice encourages continuous learning for all employees and works closely with a number of law lecturers, producing a widely-read 'digest' of legal developments, to which trainees are encouraged to contribute. All modules of the PSC are held in-house. The firm has its own sports teams and organises a variety of social functions.

benefits

Life assurance, PHI, BUPA, STL, pension, subsidised gym membership.

vacation placements

Places for 2001: 30; Duration: 2 weeks; Remuneration: £200 p.w.; Closing Date: 31 March 2001.

sponsorship & awards

CPE and LPC Fees paid and £4,500 maintenance p.a. (£4,000 outside London).

Partners	58
Assistant Solicitors	150
Total Trainees	24

contact
Graduate Recruitment Officer

method of application
Handwritten letter and application form

selection procedure
Interview and assessment

closing date for 2003
31 July 2001

application
Training contracts p.a. **12**
Applications p.a. **1,500**
% interviewed p.a. **5%**
Required degree grade:
2:1 ideally

training
Salary:
1st year (2000) £25,000
2nd year (2000) £28,000
Holiday entitlement:
22 days
% of trainees with a non-law degree p.a.
50%
No. of seats available abroad p.a. **12**

post-qualification
Salary (2000) **£43,500**
% of trainees offered job on qualification (2000):
90%
% of assistants (as at 1/9/00) who joined as trainees: **35%**
% of partners (as at 1/9/00) who joined as trainees: **4%**

overseas offices
Moscow, New York, Paris, Piraeus, Singapore.

A-Z SOLICITORS

wedlake bell

16 Bedford Street Covent Garden London WC2E 9HF
Tel: (020) 7395 3000 Fax: (020) 7836 9966
Email: legal@wedlakebell.co.uk
Website: www.wedlakebell.co.uk

firm profile

Based in Covent Garden, this medium-sized friendly firm has shifted its focus towards corporate finance, e-commerce, media and IP. It has an office in Guernsey, and links with the European Union through TELFA and with the U.S.

main areas of work

Corporate/Commercial 33%; Property 24%; Litigation 23%; Private Client 20%.

trainee profile

In addition to academic excellence, Wedlake Bell looks for flexibility, enthusiasm, a personable nature, confidence, mental agility and computer literacy in their candidates. Languages are not crucial.

training environment

Trainees have four seats of six months. You will be encouraged to meet clients and accept responsibility as soon as possible. WB prides itself on its training programme and aims to retain its trainees post-qualification. Seats available in corporate finance, banking, construction, IP/IT & media, pensions/employment, litigation, property and private clients.

benefits

On qualification: life assurance, medical insurance, PHI, subsidised gym membership and travel loan

vacation placements

Places for 2001: 6; Duration: 3 weeks in July; Remuneration: £150 p.w.; Closing Date: End of February.

Partners	32*
Assistant Solicitors	44*
Total Trainees	12

contact
Natalie King

method of application
CV and covering letter

selection procedure
Interviews in September

closing date for 2003
End August 2001

application
Training contracts p.a. 6
Applications p.a. 800
% interviewed p.a. 3%
Required degree grade 2:1

training
Salary:
1st year (2000) Not known
2nd year (2000) Not known
Holiday entitlement:
20 days (25 on qualifying)
% of trainees with a
non-law degree p.a. 25%

post-qualification
% of trainees offered job
on qualification (2000):
100%
% of assistants (as at
1/9/00) who joined as
trainees: 50%

overseas offices
Guernsey

weightmans

Richmond House 1 Rumford Place Liverpool L3 9QW
Tel: (0151) 227 2601 Fax: (0151) 227 3223
Email: info.liv@weightmans.com
Website: www.weightmans.com

firm profile
Weightmans is one of the country's largest defendant-based insurance practices. It also has a thriving commercial division. With over 400 staff in Liverpool, Manchester, Birmingham and Leicester, Weightmans is renowned as a responsive, consistent, solution-driven firm which offers genuine value for money. Weightmans is committed to the development of its employees and to the highest standards of client care. The firm is committed to harnessing new IT developments to reduce the cost of service delivery. The firm is developing a new on line business which will offer its clients full access to all case information; costs to date and other vital case related information. The on-line service will also offer a number of new value added services. The firm increasingly uses the internet to keep clients up-to-date on the latest case reports, to provide useful statistical and trend information and for 'live' performance status reports for clients on existing case loads.

main areas of work
Insurance litigation, professional indemnity, employment, commercial, commercial property, licensing.

trainee profile
Weightmans looks to recruit individuals who can enhance its high professional standards and contribute to the solution-driven culture of the practice as a whole. Applications from a wide variety of academic backgrounds are considered with a preference to those whose academic record demonstrates an ability to study with discipline and common sense to achieve results.

training environment
Weightmans provides quality training split into four seats, each of six months. There are regular appraisals and opportunities to discuss progress.

Partners	55
Assistant Solicitors	140
Total Trainees	Varies

contact
Jeni Davies - HR Assistant
Bill Radcliffe -
Training Principal

method of application
Application forms and brochures are available from Jeni Davies, HR Assistant in Liverpool

closing date for 2003
31 July 2001

other offices
Birmingham, Leicester and Manchester.

weil, gotshal & manges

One South Place London EC2M 2WG
Tel: (020) 7903 1000 Fax: (020) 7903 0990
Email: weil.london@weil.com
Website: www.weil.com

firm profile

Weil, Gotshal & Manges' London office was established in January 1996 as the European headquarters of its long-established New York parent. The office has since grown rapidly to become the second largest office of the firm. Housing over 200 staff, it is one of the largest US-based international law firms in London.

main areas of work

The firm advises some of the world's leading international corporations and financial institutions on: Acquisition Finance, Banking, Biotech, Capital Markets, Commercial Litigation, Competition, Consumer Finance, Corporate, E-Commerce, Environmental, Mergers & Acquisitions, Pensions,Private Equity, Project Finance, Real Estate, Securitisation, Share Option Schemes, Structured Finance, Taxation, Telecoms.

trainee profile

Notwithstanding its emphasis on academic ability, the firm is looking for trainees with personality, commitment and drive who would feel comfortable in this young, dynamic office.

training environment

Trainees who join the firm in 2003 will complete four six-month seats, one of which may be undertaken in the firm's New York office. In order to ensure its trainees receive adequate support and on-the-job training they each work closely with a senior associate or partner. The practical experience gained through exposure to client work is enhanced by regular internal seminars and attendance at external conferences. Weil, Gotshal & Manges aims to keep all trainees on qualification.

benefits

Pension, Permanent Health Insurance, Private Health Cover, Life Assurance, subsidised gym membership, season ticket loan.

vacation placements

Places for 2001: 12 summer vacation placements. Closing date 31 January 2001.

sponsorship & awards

The firm will pay tuition fees and a maintenance allowance for CPE/LPC.

Partners	20
Assistant Solicitors	80
Total Trainees	9

contact
Graduate Recruitment Dept

method of application
Application Form

closing date for 2003
31 July 2001

application
Training contracts p.a. 10
Required degree grade 2:1

training
Salary:
1st year (2000)
Above market rate
Holiday entitlement:
23 days

overseas offices
Brussels, Budapest, Dallas, Frankfurt, Houston, Menlo Park (Silicon Valley), Miami, New York, Prague, Warsaw, Washington DC

white & case llp

7-11 Moorgate London EC2R 6HH
Tel: (020) 7600 7300 Fax: (020) 7600 7030
Email: efalder@whitecase.com
Website: www.whitecase.com

firm profile

White & Case is a law firm with over 1000 lawyers in 39 offices worldwide. It works with financial institutions, multi-national corporations and governments on major international corporate and financial transactions and complex disputes.

main areas of work

In the London office: Project finance; Corporate finance; Banking; M&A and acquisition finance; Joint ventures; Company/commercial; Capital markets; Construction; Litigation, arbitration and ADR; European and UK competition law; Intellectual property.

trainee profile

Trainees should be enthusiastic, be able to show initiative and have a desire to be involved with innovative and high profile legal matters. You should have an understanding of international commercial issues.

training environment

The firm's English law trainees are important and valued members of the London office and often work on multi-jurisdictional matters requiring close cooperation with lawyers throughout the firm's established overseas network. You will spend six months in each seat, and cover the majority of work dealt with in the London office during the course of the two-year contract. You will be sitting with an associate or partner, and experience gained from working with your supervisor and other lawyers will be backed up with more formal legal knowledge training sessions. You are encouraged to spend six months in one of our overseas offices to gain a fuller understanding of the global network. The Professional Skills Course is run throughout the contract.

benefits

BUPA, gym membership contribution, life insurance, pension scheme, permanent health scheme, season ticket loan.

vacation placements

Places for 2001: 15-20; Duration: 2 weeks; Remuneration: £250; Closing Date: end of February 2001.

sponsorship & awards

CPE and LPC fees paid and £4,500 maintenance p.a. Prizes for commendation and distinction in the LPC.

Partners	24
Assistant Solicitors	45
Total Trainees	13

contact
Ms Emma Falder

method of application
Covering letter and cv

selection procedure
Interview

closing date for 2003
31 July 2001

application
Training contracts p.a. 20
Applications p.a. 1300
% interviewed p.a. 2.5%
Required degree grade 2:1

training
Salary:
1st year (2000) £30,000
Holiday entitlement:
25 days
All trainees are encouraged
to spend a seat abroad

post-qualification
Salary (2000) £55,000

overseas offices
Almaty, Ankara, Bangkok, Berlin, Bratislava, Bombay, Brussels, Budapest, Dresden, Düsseldorf, Frankfurt, Hanoi, Helsinki, Ho Chi Minh City, Hong Kong, Istanbul, Jeddah, Johannesburg, London, Los Angeles, Mexico City, Miami, Moscow, New York, Palo Alto, Paris, Prague, Riyadh, São Paulo, Singapore, Shanghai, Stockholm, Tokyo, Warsaw, Washington DC.

whitehead monckton

72 King St Maidstone ME14 1BL
Tel: (01622) 698000 Fax: (01622) 690050
Email: Enquiries@Whitehead-Monckton.co.uk

firm profile

Whitehead Monckton traces its roots to 1780 and is now one of the largest legal practices in Kent. From these beginnings the firm has developed a modern, progressive practice with a substantial and diverse client base. The firm offers a first-rate legal service and is able to do so by delivering specialist skills to the highest professional standards. Its principal office is at Maidstone and it has a branch office at Tenterden. Within the firm there are four main departments which provide a focus for specialist skills. The four departments are commercial, litigation, private client and property. The work of each department is complex, demanding and varied.

trainee profile

Whitehead Monckton looks to engage new trainee solicitors each year. The firm seeks graduates from any discipline who have an interest in applying their skills to the law. There is no minimum qualification but good academic results are often a guide to ability and it is ability the firm seeks.

training environment

Whitehead Monckton provides a friendly yet demanding working environment and much is expected of those who work with us. If the standard is attained it will be a rewarding experience. It is, however, a two-way relationship and the extent to which any trainee benefits will always depend upon his or her attitude, willingness to learn and initiative. The firm aims to provide trainee solicitors with experience in most areas of its work and in each department during their training period. Sometimes this is modified to suit individual interests or particular needs. The wish is that trainees will become part of the firm and develop his or her own skills. The firm aims to foster those skills through increasing responsibility during the training period. The extent and speed of this process depends upon the individual and the skill he or she demonstrates. The trainee can usually expect to undertake most of the tasks performed in a department. The prospects of any trainee after completion of the training period depend entirely upon their demonstrated ability.

Partners	12
Assistant Solicitors	6
Total Trainees	4

contact
The Training Partner

method of application
Firm's application form accompanied by a handwritten letter and a full CV

selection procedure
Interviews (in December of year of application)

closing date for 2003
1 November 2001

application
Training contracts p.a. 2

wiggin and co

The Quadrangle Imperial Square Cheltenham GL50 1YX
Tel: (01242) 224 114 Fax: (01242) 224223
Email: law@wiggin.co.uk

firm profile

Based in Cheltenham, with offices in London and Los Angeles, Wiggin and Co is a 'city-type' niche practice. It specialises in the tax and company/commercial fields, and in media, communications, technology and entertainment.

main areas of work

Private Client 40%; Media and Entertainment 40%; Litigation 12%; Property 8%.

trainee profile

Candidates will have a strong academic background, be personable and show a willingness to work hard individually or as part of a team.

training environment

The training is divided into four six-month seats. Trainees will spend time in four out of five departments, namely the company/commercial, media, property, litigation and private client departments. In each department you will sit with a partner or a senior solicitor. You will be encouraged to take an active role in transactions, assume responsibility and deal directly with clients. In-house lectures and seminars are held regularly and training reviews are held every three months. The firm offers the attraction of Cheltenham combined with technical ability and experience akin to a large City firm. Its relatively small size encourages a personal approach towards staff and client relations.

benefits

Life assurance, private health cover, pension scheme, permanent health insurance.

sponsorship & awards

CPE and LPC Fees and £3,000 maintenance p.a. Brochure available on request.

Partners	12
Assistant Solicitors	14
Total Trainees	5

contact
Sean James

method of application
Letter and CV

selection procedure
2 interviews

closing date for 2003
21 August 2001

application
Training contracts p.a. **2/3**
Applications p.a. **1,700**
% interviewed p.a. **2%**
Required degree grade **2:1**

training
Salary:
1st year (2000) **£22,000**
2nd year (2000) **£25,700**
Holiday entitlement:
20 days
% of trainees with a
non-law degree p.a. **60%**

post-qualification
Salary (2000) **£32,200**
% of trainees offered job
on qualification (2000):
100%
% of assistants (as at
2000) who joined as
trainees: **17%**
% of partners (as at 2000)
who joined as trainees:
17%

overseas offices
Los Angeles

withers

16 Old Bailey London EC4AM 7EG
Tel: (020) 7597 6000 Fax: (020) 7597 6001
Email: mailto@withers.co.uk
Website: www.withers.co.uk

firm profile

Withers is a thriving, medium-sized practice, with approximately 280 staff and 48 partners. The firm combines a market leading private client and family law practice with a wide range of corporate and commercial work including corporate finance, banking, intellectual property, insolvency, professional negligence, commercial litigation and property. The firm's clients range from large companies and institutions to successful entrepreneurs and individuals.

main areas of work

Private Client and Charities 40%; Litigation 19%; Corporate, Company and Commercial 17%; Property (Agricultural, Commercial and Residential) 13%; Family 11%; International 5%

trainee profile

As well as a keen intellect, trainees should have the confidence and social skills to interact successfully with clients and colleagues, and the determination and ambition to do well. They should show business acumen, entrepreneurial flair and commercial awareness. A genuine international outlook and foreign languages, particularly Italian, would be an advantage.

training environment

Trainees spend six months in four of the firm's five departments sitting with a senior solicitor or partner. This practical training is supplemented by an extensive in-house training programme. You will work as part of a small team and the firm's size ensures responsibility is given at an early stage in your career.

benefits

Interest free season ticket loan, private medical insurance, life assurance, social events, cafe facilities

vacation placements

Places for 2001: 20; Duration: Easter (3 weeks), Summer (3 weeks); Closing Date: 23 Feb 2001.

sponsorship & awards

CPE and/or LPC fees are paid and £4,000 maintenance p.a. A cash prize is awarded for distinction or commendation in CPE and/or LPC.

Partners 48*
Assistant Solicitors 80*
Total Trainees 21

contact
Graduate Recruitment Officer

method of application
Application form and covering letter

selection procedure
2 interviews

closing date for 2003
3 August 2001

application
Training contracts p.a. **10**
Applications p.a. **1,500**
% interviewed p.a. **5-10%**
Required degree grade **2:1**

training
Salary:
1st year (2000) **£23,000**
2nd Year (2000) **£25,000**
Holiday entitlement:
20 days
% of trainees with a non-law degree p.a. **40%**

post-qualification
Salary (2000) **£33,500**
% of trainees offered job on qualification (2000):
90%
% of assistants (as at 1/9/00) who joined as trainees: **8%**
% of partners (as at 1/9/00) who joined as trainees: **36%**

overseas offices
Paris and Associate Italian office

wragge & co

55 Colmore Row Birmingham B3 2AS
Tel: 0800 096 9610 Fax: (0121) 214 1099
Email: gradmail@wragge.com
Website: www.wragge.com

firm profile

Wragge & Co is a leading law firm providing a full range of quality legal services to clients in commerce, finance and industry, including over 165 listed companies. The firm is renowned for its strategy of having successfully and distinctively developed a national firm from its base in the Midlands.

main areas of work

Wragge & Co enjoys a national reputation in areas such as corporate, litigation, property, employment, tax, pensions, intellectual property, information technology, transport and logistics, utilities, project finance, PFI and EC/Competition law. The firm has a substantial number of international connections, regularly represents UK clients doing business overseas and acts as project manager on international transactions. Wragge & Co frequently works with professional advisers in foreign jurisdictions, in addition to acting for overseas clients in the UK and elsewhere. Around 25% of the firm's work is international.

trainee profile

Graduates should be of a 2:1 standard at degree level, with some commercial work experience gained either via holiday jobs or a previous career. Candidates should also have polished communication skills, be practical with a common-sense approach to work and problem solving, and be able to show adaptability, enthusiasm and ambition in their applications.

training environment

Wragge & Co places considerable emphasis on transforming trainees into competent, commercially-minded lawyers. You will spend six months in four areas of the firm's business, usually corporate, property and litigation, with a chance to specialise in a final seat of your choice. The firm offers trainees the opportunity to spend six months in Brussels doing EU/Competition law, London doing intellectual property law, on secondment with one of its clients, or possibly seconded to one of its professional departments such as marketing. From day one, you will work on live files with direct client contact. The more aptitude you show, the greater the responsibility you will be given. As well as the Graduate Recruitment & Training Team, you will be supported by a mentoring partner, a trainee in the in-take above, and on a daily basis your supervisor. Introductory courses are provided at the start of each seat in addition to your Professional Skills Course training. There is also a Trainee Committee which is active in the firm and regularly meets with the Man-

Partners	94
Assistant Solicitors	258
Total Trainees	42

contact
Julie Cox
Graduate Recruitment &
Training Manager

method of application
Application form or on-line

selection procedure
Telephone interview and
Assessment Day

closing date for 2003
10 August 2001

application
Training contracts p.a. **25**
Applications p.a. **1,000**
% interviewed p.a. **10%**
Required degree grade
2:1 (preferred)

training
Salary:
1st year (2000) £17,000
2nd Year (2000) £18,500
Holiday entitlement:
23 days
% of trainees with a
non-law degree p.a. **Varies**

post-qualification
Salary (2000) **£30,000**
% of trainees offered job
on qualification (2000):
100%
% of assistants (as at
1/9/00) who joined as
trainees: **28%**
% of partners (as at 1/9/00)
who joined as trainees:
47%

aging Partner and Graduate Recruitment & Training Manager to discuss topical issues relating to their training.

benefits

Life assurance, permanent health scheme, pension, interest free travel loans.

vacation placements

Places for 2001: Easter 2001: 20 places, Summer 2001: 48 places; Duration: 1 week 2 weeks; Remuneration: £150 p.w. £125 p.w.; Closing Date: Closing date for applications: 16 February 2001 Apply by application form or on-line.

sponsorship & awards

CPE and LPC fees paid. Maintenance grant of £3,500 for LPC, and £3,000 per year for CPE students.

trainee comments

'I wanted to work somewhere offering the same quality of work as a large City law firm without actually having to go to London. Wragge & Co ranks highly in the Legal Directories and I had been to an Open Day which I thoroughly enjoyed – I felt immediately at ease with the buzzing yet relaxed atmosphere. It was the City law firm outside London! Starting work is difficult, but Wragge & Co made it as easy as possible. Right from the beginning I felt extremely involved and valued as a member of the team. Induction training and lots of support helped me settle in quickly. My first seat was in the Construction Litigation Team where I have worked with my supervisor on their larger cases, going to client meetings, speaking to clients on the telephone and attending court. I am currently in Property Development where I am running my own files and enjoying the responsibility of being my own boss to some degree! The social life in Birmingham is thriving. Wragge & Co trainees form a strong community and there is always something going on such as Karaoke, Greek dancing, general drinking sessions and BTSS (Birmingham Trainee Solicitors Society) events. Birmingham itself is often misjudged by those who have never visited the city. Over the last few years, it has been greatly developed and modernised, resulting in a thriving centre of shops, wine bars, pubs and restaurants, especially around the newly renovated canal system. Birmingham caters well for young professionals, and anyone who comes here is pleasantly surprised. So far training with Wragge & Co has been an excellent choice.' (Katie Smart, studied Law at the University of Birmingham).

Wragge&Co

blackstone chambers (P Baxendale QC and C Flint QC)

Blackstone House Temple London EC4Y 9BW DX: 281
Tel: (020) 7583 1770 Fax: (020) 7822 7350
Email: clerks@blackstonechambers.com
Website: www.blackstonechambers.com

chambers profile

Established at its old site 2 Hare Court for many years, Blackstone Chambers recently moved to new purpose built fully networked premises in the Temple.

type of work undertaken

Chambers' formidable strengths lie in three principal areas of practice of commercial, employment and public law. Commercial law includes financial/business law, international trade, conflicts, sport, media and entertainment, intellectual property and professional negligence. All aspects of Employment law, including discrimination, are covered by chambers' extensive employment law practice. Public law incorporates judicial review, acting both for and against central and local government agencies and other regulatory authorities, human rights and other aspects of administrative law.

pupil profile

Chambers looks for articulate and intelligent applicants who are able to work well under pressure and demonstrate high intellectual ability. Successful candidates usually have at least a 2:1 honours degree, although not necessarily in law.

pupillage

Chambers offers 4 12 month pupillages to those wishing to practice full time at the Bar normally commencing in October each year. Pupillage is divided into 3 or 4 sections and every effort is made to ensure that pupils receive a broad training. The environment is a friendly one; pupils attend an induction week introducing them to the chambers working environment. Chambers prefers to recruit new tenants from pupils wherever possible.

mini pupillages

Assessed mini-pupillages are available and are an important part of the application procedure. Applications for mini-pupillages and for pupillages must be made by 30th June; earlier applications are strongly advised and are preferred in the year before pupillage commences. Application forms for pupillages or mini-pupillage are available on request.

funding

Awards of £25,000 per annum are available. The pupillage committee has a discretion to consider applications for up to £5,000 of the pupillage award to be advanced during the BVC year.

No of Silks	23
No of Juniors	36
No of Pupils	4 (current)

contact
Ms Julia Hornor
Practice Manager

method of application
Chambers' own
application form

pupillages (p.a.)
12 months: 4
Required degree grade:
Minimum 2.1
(law or non-law)

income
Award: £25,000
Earnings not included

tenancies
Junior tenancies offered
in last 3 years: 100%
No of tenants of 5 years
call or under: 9

essex court chambers (Gordon Pollock QC)

24 Lincoln's Inn Fields London WC2A 3EG DX: 320
Tel: (020) 7813 8000 Fax: (020) 7813 8080
Email: clerksroom@essexcourt-chambers.co.uk
Website: www.essexcourt-chambers.co.uk

chambers profile

Essex Court Chambers is one of London's leading commercial sets. In Chambers Directory 1999, Essex Court Chambers appeared in eight categories as a "leading set": Arbitration, Commercial Litigation; Insurance & Reinsurance; Shipping; Banking; Energy & Utilities; Media & Entertainment and Aviation, and was "highly regarded" for Employment.

Twelve of its silks were recognised as "leading" in one or more fields with Head of Chambers Gordon Pollock QC leading the "Stars at the Bar". 25 Juniors were recommended; 13 in two or more areas of specialisation.

type of work undertaken

Barristers at Essex Court Chambers advise on a wide range of international and domestic commercial law and appear as Counsel in litigation and commercial arbitration worldwide. In addition to the "leading" areas of specialisation above, Essex Court Chambers has expertise in the following areas of law: Administrative/Judicial Review, Agriculture/Farming; Chinese; Company/Insolvency; Construction; Engineering; Commodities; Computer; Employment; Sports; Environmental; European; Financial Services; Human Rights; Injunctions/Arrests; Fraud; International Trade and Transport; Professional Negligence; Public International; Product Liability and VAT. For further information see the website; a detailed brochure is also available on request.

pupil profile

The best candidates are required for this set's intellectually demanding work. (2:1 or higher preferred)

pupillage

Up to 4 12 month funded pupillages are offered each year for an October start. Applications are welcomed through PACH in 2001 for pupillage in October 2002 and for deferred pupillage in October 2003.

mini pupillages

Application by letter and CV to the Pupillage Secretary for funded places for those already embarked on legal studies.

funding

£25,000 per annum, payable in two instalments. Applications to advance part are considered for the BVC year; interest free loans are also available.

No of Silks 18
No of Juniors 42
No of Pupils 4

contact
Pupillage Secretary

method of application
PACH (pupillage); Letter and CV (mini-pupillage)

pupillages (p.a.)
12 months: **4**
Required degree grade: **2:1**

income
£25,000 p.a.

tenancies
Junior tenancies offered in last 3 years: **7**

4 essex court (Nigel Teare QC)

4 Essex Court Temple London EC4Y 9AJ
DX: 292 London (Chancery Lane)
Tel: (020) 7653 5653 Fax: (020) 7653 5654
Email: clerks@4sx.co.uk

chambers profile

4, Essex Court is one of the foremost and longest-established sets of Chambers specialising in commercial law. Chambers has remained in Essex Court although it moved from No 2 to No 4 some 6 years ago. Chambers has kept abreast of the latest technological advances in Information and Computer Technology. 4, Essex Court offers a first class service at sensible fee rates and has a staff renowned for their openness and fairness.

type of work undertaken

The challenging and rewarding work of Chambers encompasses the broad range of commercial disputes embracing Arbitration, Aviation, Banking, Shipping, International Trade, Insurance and Re-insurance, Professional Negligence, Entertainment and Media, Environmental and Construction Law. Over 70% of Chambers' work involves international clients.

pupil profile

4, Essex Court seeks high calibre pupils with good academic qualifications (at least a 2:1 degree) who exhibit good written and verbal skills.

pupillage

Chambers offers a maximum of 4 funded pupillages of either 6 or 12 months duration. 12 months pupillages are reviewed after 6 months. Pupils are normally moved amongst several members of Chambers and will experience a wide range of high quality commercial work. Outstanding pupils are likely to be offered a tenancy at the end of their pupillage.

mini pupillages

Mini - pupillages are encouraged in order that potential pupils may experience the work of Chambers before committing themselves to an application for full pupillage.

funding

Awards of up to £28,000 p.a. (£14,000 per 6 months) are available for each funded pupillage - part of which may be forwarded during the BVC, at the Pupillage Committee's discretion.

| No of Silks | 8 |
| No of Juniors | 28 |

contact
Ms Michelle Dean
Secretary to Pupillage
Committee

method of application
PACH

pupillages (p.a.)
1st 6 months: 4
2nd 6 months: 4
12 months:
(reviewed at 6 months)
Required degree:
good 2.1+

income
1st 6 months:
up to £14,000
2nd 6 months:
up to £14,000
Earnings not included

tenancies
Current tenants who
served pupillage in
chambers: 19
Junior tenancies offered
in last 3 years: 9
No of tenants of 5 years
call or under: 7
Income (1st year):
c. £40,000

20 essex street (Iain Milligan QC)

20 Essex Street London WC2R 3AL DX: 0009 (Ch.Ln.)
Tel: (020) 7583 9294 Fax: (020) 7583 1341
Email: clerks@20essexst.com
Website: www.20essexst.com

chambers profile

20 Essex Street is a premier set of commercial chambers whose reputation goes back over 60 years and which continues to prosper.

type of work undertaken

The practising members of 20 Essex Street specialise in Commercial and EC Law. Most members of Chambers specialise in Commercial Law, in particular shipping, international sales, carriage by land, sea and air, insurance and reinsurance, and every type of domestic and international commercial agreement, appearing in the High Court (principally the Commercial Court), Court of Appeal and House of Lords as well as in arbitrations. A part of Chambers' work comprises EC Law, with certain members of Chambers appearing before the European Court of Justice.

pupil profile

Chambers look for candidates with a good academic background who seek to practise at the commercial bar. Chambers usually require a First or a strong 2:1 honours degree, though not necessarily in law.

pupillage

Pupillage begins in October and is for twelve months. Usually Chambers take between three and five pupils each October. All applications must be made though PACH, in accordance with the deadlines set by PACH. For the pupillage year 2002/3 chambers will also consider year early offers from those who are eligible. Year early applicants should have a first class degree or a reference indicating the expectation of such.

mini pupillages

Although not essential we strongly encourage those who may wish to apply for a pupillage here to apply for a mini-pupillage first. Write to Michael Coburn enclosing a CV and indicating the dates on which you would like to come. Write before Easter for summer mini-pupillages and before Christmas for Easter mini-pupillages.

funding

Up to five funded pupillages with awards of £25,000 for twelve months of which up to £5,000 can be drawn during the Bar Vocational Course.

No of Silks	15
No of Juniors	26
No of Pupils	up to 5

contact
Write to Andrew Baker about pupillage or Michael Coburn about mini-pupillage.

Other enquiries: write to Neil Palmer, Senior Clerk.

method of application
For pupillage, through PACH

pupillages (p.a.)
12 months: up to 5

income
Five pupillage awards of £25,000 p.a.

3 hare court (Mark Strachan QC)

3 Hare Court Temple
London EC4Y 7BJ DX: 212
Tel: (020) 7415 7800 Fax: (020) 7415 7811

chambers profile

Whilst individual practices within Chambers differ significantly, most members of Chambers specialise in the field of commercial and business law. This includes everything from international arbitration to sale of goods and employment law. Members of Chambers frequently appear in the Privy Council undertaking constitutional, human rights cases and other appellate work. The work of Chambers also includes most areas of non-specialist civil litigation such as personal injury and landlord and tenant work. There is also work in the field of public and administrative law.

pupil profile

Chambers seeks to have 3 or 4 pupils at any time and offer 12 month pupillages. Chambers are well aware that the aim of most pupils is to secure a tenancy and to this end seek to recruit one tenant of sufficient calibre every year. Pupils will be reviewed after 5 months and given an indication of whether they have any prospect of becoming a tenant at the end of the year.

mini pupillages

Mini-pupillages and student visits are available. Application by letter and CV to Michael Oliver.

funding

It is Chambers' policy to offer finance to two pupils for 12 months. There are two awards of up to £25,000, being £12,500 for the first six months and £12,500 from earnings and/or Chambers' funds in the second six months.

No of Silks	4
No of Juniors	19
No of Pupils	3

contact
James Dingemans
Michael Oliver
(Chambers Manager)

method of application
PACH

pupillages (p.a.)
12 months: 3

tenancies
Junior tenancies offered in last 3 years: 3
No of tenants of 5 years call or under: 5

old square chambers (John Hendy QC)

1 Verulam Buildings Gray's Inn London WC1R 5LQ
DX: 1046 Chancery Lane/London
Tel: (020) 7269 0300 Fax: (020) 7405 1387
Email: moor@oldsquarechambers.co.uk
Website: www.oldsquarechambers.co.uk

chambers profile
A highly specialised, forward thinking set committed to expansion.

type of work undertaken
Employment, personal injury, product liability and environmental law. Public law and human rights issues are encompassed within these areas. There is some business and mercantile work and some medical negligence. There is much use of European jurisprudence. In employment law, members of chambers have been involved in many of the ground-breaking cases of the past 20 years. Chambers' profile in personal injury law is excellent, particular strengths are disaster and multi-party litigation. Environmental law work is predominantly on large 'toxic tort' litigation - damage caused by pollution. Fields of practice are organised around Special Interest Groups in chambers enabling the sharing of information and effective marketing.

pupil profile
Chambers look for intelligent candidates who have the potential to be excellent advocates. You must be motivated to come to the bar and wish to practise in at least one of chambers' specialist fields. You must have ability to cope with hard work and deal with many different people. Chambers is committed to equal opportunities. Chambers' recruitment methods are designed to avoid discrimination on the grounds of race, gender, disability, sexuality or religion.

pupillage
Chambers offer high quality training, generously funded. Pupils spend 3 months with each pupil supervisor. Preferences for fields of work will be considered. There is the opportunity to undertake work for silks on complex and sometimes high profile work.

mini pupillages
Mini pupillages are available but in demand. Preference is given to final year students. Send Philip Mead your CV and a letter explaining your interest in chambers.

funding
2002 grant: between £18,000 and £20,000 for 12 months in London, £14,000 in Bristol. 2nd six pupils undertake work on their own account, fees are retained without any deduction.

No of Silks	7
No of Juniors	33
No of Pupils	3

contact
Sarah Moor

method of application
PACH

pupillages (p.a.)
12 months: 3

tenancies
Junior tenancies offered in last 3 years: 4

For more information see our Website or write to Sarah Moor

annexes
Hanover House
47 Corn Street
Bristol BS1 1HT
Tel: (0117) 927 7111
Fax: (0117) 927 3478

5 paper buildings (G. Carey QC & J. Caplan QC)

5 Paper Buildings Temple London EC4Y 7HB DX: 365
Tel: (020) 7583 6117 Fax: (020) 7353 0075
Email: clerks@5-paperbuildings.law.co.uk

chambers profile

5 Paper Buildings are a leading, well established set of Chambers specialising in all areas of criminal law. Members undertake a broad range of work with an emphasis on commercial fraud. Members of Chambers have appeared in some of the largest fraud cases in recent years: Guinness, BCCI, Maxwell etc. Other tenants undertake civil and commercial litigation including contempt, restraint of trade, civil actions against the police.

pupillage

When Chambers recruit pupils they look for candidates who have the abilities to become successful advocates. When interviewing, Chambers are looking at applicants as potential tenants. Chambers offer 12 month pupillages, as well as 2nd and 3rd six pupillages. Pupils can look forward to a variety of work in and around London. Chambers also offer an education programme for all pupils.

mini pupillages

Mini pupillages are available - contact Senior Clerk, Stuart Bryant. Student visits are not available.

funding

Twelve month pupils will receive an award of approximately £6,000 in their first 6 months and with 2nd six pupils are guaranteed earnings of £7,500. On successful completion of Bar Finals, up to £1,000 may be claimed in advance, for guaranteed earnings.

| No of Silks | 8 |
| No of Juniors | 27 |

contact
Emma Deacon
Pupillage Committee

method of application
12 months and 2nd six months via PACH
3rd six months by application form only available from Chambers

pupillages (p.a.)
1. Chambers offer 3 pupillages a year through PACH: a combination of 2nd six and 12 months pupillages.

2. In addition, Chambers offer 3 3rd six pupillages in October

tenancies
Junior tenancies offered in last 3 year: 5
No of tenants of 5 years call or under: 5

18 red lion court (Anthony Arlidge QC)

18 Red Lion Court London EC4A 3EB DX: 478 LDE
Tel: (020) 7520 6000 Fax: (020) 7520 6248/9
Email: chambersofarlidgeclerks@18rlc.co.uk

chambers profile
Chambers operate from a spacious listed building off Fleet Street near the Temple. Comprising 20 silks and 45 juniors, chambers offers one of the most comprehensive cross-sections of expertise in the field of criminal law.

type of work undertaken
18 Red Lion Court covers the whole range of crime, defending and prosecuting at all levels. Particular strengths are commercial fraud, Inland Revenue and VAT offences, money laundering, corruption, drugs and drug trafficking and sex cases, including child abuse and obscene publications. Individual members are involved in international human rights cases from Rwanda to Santa Monica. Others have written well respected practitioners texts on a wide range of topics. Chambers' work is centred primarily on the South Eastern circuit with an emphasis on London and East Anglia. Much of the East Anglian work is serviced by our annexe in Chelmsford.

pupil profile
Chambers look for pupils with potential to develop into first class advocates. Pupils are selected for a combination of marked intellectual ability, together with good judgement and independent personalities.

pupillage
Chambers offer 4 or 5 funded twelve months pupillages. Funded pupils will receive £12,000, made up of half award, half guaranteed earnings. Chambers' pupils receive excellent training. In addition to experiencing a broad range of work, all pupils participate in an in-house advocacy programme. Nearly all chambers' pupils get tenancies with chambers or elsewhere. Chambers do not offer 2nd or 3rd six pupillages. Sponsored pupils are accepted.

pupillage applications
Applications should be made for an application form to Stephen Requena.

mini pupillages
Available subject to numbers all year round. Applications with c.v., should be made to Tom Forster.

No of Silks 20
No of Juniors 45
No of Pupils 4/5

contact
Stephen Requena
Pupillage Secretary

method of application
By application form, supplied on request

pupillages (p.a.)
12 months: 4/5

income
12 months: £12,000 (made up of awards and guaranteed earnings)

tenancies
Junior tenancies offered in last 3 years: 5

annexes
Chelmsford

3 verulam buildings (Christopher Symons QC/John Jarvis QC)

3 Verulam Buildings Gray's Inn London WC1R 5NT
DX: LDE 331
Tel: (020) 7831 8441 Fax: (020) 7831 8479
Email: clerks@3verulam.co.uk
Website: www.3verulam.co.uk

chambers profile

3 Verulam Buildings is a large commercial set with a history of expansion by recruitment of tenants from amongst pupils. Over the past ten years at least two of its pupils have become tenants every year. Chambers occupies recently refurbished, spacious offices overlooking Gray's Inn Walks with all modern IT and library facilities. Chambers prides itself on a pleasant, friendly and relaxed atmosphere.

type of work undertaken

A wide range of commercial work, in particular banking and financial services, insurance and reinsurance, commercial fraud, professional negligence, company law, entertainment, insolvency, public international law, EU law, arbitration/ADR, environmental law, building and construction as well as other general commercial work. Members of Chambers regularly appear in high profile cases and a substantial amount of Chambers' work is international.

pupil profile

Chambers looks for intelligent and ambitious candidates with strong powers of analysis and reasoning, who are self confident and get on well with others. Candidates should normally have at least a 2.1 grade in an honours subject which need not be law.

pupillage

Chambers takes 4 funded twelve months pupils every year through PACH. Each pupil spends three months with four different members of Chambers to gain experience of different types of work. Chambers also offers unfunded pupillages to pupils who do not intend to practise at the Bar of England and Wales.

mini pupillages

Mini pupillages are available for one week at a time for university, CPE or Bar students who are interested in finding out more about Chambers' work. Chambers considers mini-pupillage to be an important part of the recruitment process. Candidates should have, or expect to obtain, the minimum requirements for a funded 12 month pupillage. Applications are accepted throughout the year and should be addressed to Ian Wilson.

funding

In the year 2001-2002 the annual award will be at least £25,000 payable monthly.

No of Silks	12
No of Juniors	37
No of Pupils	6

contact
Ms Natalie Baylis
(Pupillage)
Mr Ian Wilson
(Mini pupillage)
Pupillage Committee

method of application
PACH, or for unfunded pupillage and mini pupillage CV and covering letter stating dates of availability.

pupillages (p.a.)
1st 6 months: 2
12 months: 3-5
Required degree grade: 2.1

income
At least £25,000 per annum.

Earnings not included

tenancies
Current tenants who served pupillage in chambers: 37
Junior tenancies offered in last 3 years: 5
No of tenants of 5 years call or under: 11

index (of law firms, sets and law schools)

notes

notes

notes

notes

notes

notes

notes

notes